THE ENDS OF LIFE

Sir Keith Thomas is a Fellow of All Souls College and former President of Corpus Christi College, Oxford. He is the author of several highly acclaimed books on early modern England, including *Religion and the Decline of Magic and Man and the Natural World*. A former trustee of the National Gallery and the British Museum, he is an Honorary Vice-President of the Royal Historical Society. He has held visiting professorships at Columbia, Louisiana State, Princeton and Stanford Universities; and is a Foreign Honorary Member of the American Academy of Arts and Sciences. He was President of the British Academy between 1993 and 1997.

Praise for *The Ends of Life*

'Dazzling erudition...urbanity...wit...suppleness of language... There cannot have been a more widely read historian or one with his capacity to impose order on so formidable a range of material.'

Blair Worden, *Standpoint*

'The broad humanity of Thomas's approach...creates intimacy between reader and material, as he amuses, puzzles and challenges us....Thomas's style is sharp, wry, amused, the product of a unique intellect that steers away from false generalizations and embraces ambiguity.'

Hilary Mantel, *New York Review of Books*

'A compellingly readable book, richly researched, fascinatingly detailed, delightfully written...Thomas has formidable organisational ability, and an unerring eye for detail. Almost every page offers something to intrigue, amuse, provoke.'

Eamon Duffy, *London Review of Books*

'Endlessly fascinating...elegant, incisive and entertaining.'

Tim Blanning, *Sunday Telegraph*

A new book by the most learned, original and witty historian now living and writing in England – conceivably in English – is a rare treat....Every page, almost every paragraph. yields marvels and surprises.'

Wilfrid Prest, *Australian Book Review*

'An admirable and impressive work, the fruit of colossal reading.'

Bernard Richards, *Oxford Magazine*

'A triumphal demonstration that one of our leading historians is still at the height of his powers. The writing is lucid and elegant, peppered with dry wit and overseen by an infallible eye for anecdotes.'

Peter Marshall, *Literary Review*

'Thomas's connecting prose is graceful and sometimes crisply epigrammatic. *The Ends of Life* is a pleasure to read.'

Michael Dirda, *Washington Post*

'Not a dull page, nor a paragraph without a piquant fact or quotation.'

Ferdinand Mount, *Spectator*

'It takes an exceptional scholar, drawing on years of reading in original sources as well as today's social science, to do the subject justice. Fortunately, Keith Thomas's intimate knowledge of English life in the years between the Reformation and the American Revolution makes *The Ends of Life* the rare historical work that is as absorbing as it is deep.

Edward Tenner, *The Wilson Quarterly*

'The sheer wealth and diversity of material in *The Ends of Life* makes it a fascinating read.'

Lisa Jardine, *Financial Times*

'Captivating. Reading this book in company must be irritating to others because it is so hard to resist reading so much of it out loud. It's just full of wonderful sentences and phrases... *The Ends of Life* deserves to be cherished as a glorious late supplement to Robert Burton's *The Anatomy of Melancholy* and John Aubrey's *Brief Lives*.'

David Sexton, *Evening Standard*

'It takes phenomenal learning and scholarly chutzpah to pull off a book like this, Happily, Thomas has deep reserves of both... a brave and sensitive book.'

Jonathan Wright, *The Independent on Sunday*

'Any new book by Sir Keith Thomas is a major event... He has taken a mighty subject... and he treats it mightily... The result is pure delight... This is peerless scholarship lightly worn'

John Morrill, *BBC History Magazine*

'No one will ever know early modern England again as intimately, as immediately, as exhaustively, as Keith Thomas now does.... A delight to read. Dry, sardonic, pithy, constantly interesting... It is hard, indeed, to imagine a better introduction to the early modern world. It will be immediately and universally recognized as indispensable, not just for historians, but for anyone interested in the past.'

David Wootton, *Times Literary Supplement*

'Full of surprises, packed with information that no one else could have found, and so witty and absorbing that a pang of disappointment came over me when I turned over eagerly for another chapter and found myself in the notes.'

Claire Tomalin, *The Guardian*

THE ENDS OF LIFE

ROADS TO FULFILMENT
IN EARLY MODERN ENGLAND

•

KEITH THOMAS

OXFORD
UNIVERSITY PRESS

OXFORD
UNIVERSITY PRESS

Great Clarendon Street, Oxford OX2 6DP

Oxford University Press is a department of the University of Oxford.
It furthers the University's objective of excellence in research, scholarship,
and education by publishing worldwide in

Oxford New York

Auckland Cape Town Dar es Salaam Hong Kong Karachi
Kuala Lumpur Madrid Melbourne Mexico City Nairobi
New Delhi Shanghai Taipei Toronto

With offices in

Argentina Austria Brazil Chile Czech Republic France Greece
Guatemala Hungary Italy Japan Poland Portugal Singapore
South Korea Switzerland Thailand Turkey Ukraine Vietnam

Oxford is a registered trade mark of Oxford University Press
in the UK and in certain other countries

Published in the United States
by Oxford University Press Inc., New York

British Library Cataloguing in Publication Data
Data available

Library of Congress Cataloging in Publication Data
Data available

Typeset by SPI Publisher Services, Pondicherry, India
Printed in Great Britain
on acid-free paper by
CPI Group (UK) Ltd, Croydon, CR0 4YY

ISBN 978-0-19-924723-3 (Hbk)
978-0-19-958083-5 (Pbk)

3 5 7 9 10 8 6 4 2

To Emily and Edmund

We must enjoin every one that has the power to live according to his own choice to set up for himself some object for the good life to aim at (whether honour or reputation or wealth or culture), with reference to which he will then do all his acts, since not to have one's life organized in view of some end is a mark of much folly.

Aristotle, *Eudemian Ethics*, 1241^b (rev. Oxford translation, ed. Jonathan Barnes, Princeton, 1984)

PREFACE

This book is a revised and expanded version of the Ford Lectures given in the University of Oxford in Hilary Term 2000. I thank the Electors for inviting me to give the Lectures and my faithful audience for coming to the South Schools each week to hear them. For more than a century, the appointment to the Ford Lectureship has been recognized as one of the greatest honours which historians of Britain can receive. It is also one of the most daunting. In 1950 one of Oxford's finest historians, G. N. (later Sir George) Clark, was invited to give the Ford Lectures. He planned to speak on the grand theme of 'War and Peace in History'. When it came to the notice in the lecture list, his subject had shrunk to 'King James I and Dutch "Imperialism" in Asia'; and when the lectures were eventually published, their title was 'The Colonial Conferences between England and the Netherlands in 1613 and 1615'.*

It is easy to lament this triumph of scholarly caution over intellectual ambition, but when I contemplate the scale of the task I rashly set myself fifty years later, I can see just how wise Sir George Clark was. He chose a small, well-defined topic and gave it definitive treatment. I proposed a huge, amorphous theme and discussed it in a very general way. I wanted to encourage historians to give more thought to the problems I outlined. So I used a broad brush, in the expectation that the picture I was painting would be refined by future scholars.

I did not realize quite how soon this expectation would be fulfilled. Since 2000 there has been a huge proliferation of published writing on the social and cultural history of early modern England, much of it of exceptionally high quality. My pleasure in this development has become increasingly wry. With my lectures still unpublished, I have found myself overtaken by younger scholars who have independently investigated virtually every topic I discussed, and often done so with much greater thoroughness. Sometimes their work has led me to modify my arguments. More frequently, it has provided valuable

---

* *Oxford University Gazette*, no. 2647 (14 Dec. 1949), 274; *Bibliotheca Visseriana*, xvii (Leiden, 1951). I learned about Clark's original intention from the late Richard Pares.

supporting evidence. In either case, it has robbed much of my subject matter of the novelty it may have once possessed. But it has also provided welcome reassurance that the problems with which this book is concerned are of wide general interest.

I have listed most of these new publications in my endnotes, and I apologize to anyone whose work I have unwittingly overlooked. The bulk of scholarly publication these days is so great that no one can be sure of having read it all. It is invidious to single out particular authors, but I must particularly acknowledge my indebtedness to the writings of Maxine Berg, the late Alan Bray, Bernard Capp, Richard Cust, Faramerz Dabhoiwala, Barbara Donagan, Frances Harris, Steve Hindle, Ralph Houlbrooke, Martin Ingram, Roger B. Manning, Peter Marshall, Craig Muldrew, Alexandra Shepard, Robert B. Shoemaker, Paul Slack, John Styles, David Turner, Amanda Vickery, and Garthine Walker, all of whom have recently published valuable work on topics closely related to my theme. Neil Davie, Mark Jenner, and Peter Sherlock have kindly allowed me to cite their unpublished doctoral theses. I am also grateful to the many other historians, living and dead, whose findings and insights I have plundered in order to supplement my own reading in the sources of the period. There is a competitive element inherent in most scholarship; and in British universities these days it is disproportionately fostered by the Research Assessment Exercise. But historical inquiry remains an essentially collaborative activity in which we all learn from each other.

I have received much helpful assistance from librarians and archivists. In particular, the staff of the Bodleian, especially the Upper Reading Room and Duke Humfrey's Library, have been endlessly obliging. There cannot be many living readers for whom over the years they have fetched and carried more books. I also thank Norma Aubertin-Potter and Gaye Morgan of the Codrington Library for much good-humoured assistance. For useful references and for help on particular points, I am grateful to the late Gerald Aylmer, George Bernard, Janet Bloom, the late Sir Howard Colvin, Sir John Elliott, James Griffin, Arnold Harvey, Christoph Heyl, Susan Laithwaite, Mandy Marvin, the late Rodney Needham, Charles Philpin, Jim Sharpe, John Simpson, and John Walsh. I also thank lecture and seminar audiences at the universities of Berkeley, Exeter, Kent, Princeton, and Stanford for listening to parts of this book and offering stimulating criticism and suggestions.

In Oxford, Corpus Christi College generously gave me leave from my duties as President to enable me to compose the lectures, while All

Souls College has provided me with a privileged environment in which to prepare them for publication. The Oxford University Press's anonymous readers offered encouragement and sensible advice, more of which I should have taken. The Press's editors, Ruth Parr, Christopher Wheeler, and, especially, Matthew Cotton, have been patient and encouraging. Laurien Berkeley has been a meticulous and sensitive copy-editor. Edmund Thomas read the text of the original lectures and made many searching criticisms. Emily Gowers suggested the jacket illustration. My wife has urged me on, constructively criticized the final text, and sustained me throughout.

All Souls College, Oxford
February 2008   K.T.

Postscript

I have taken advantage of this reprinting to correct a few errors, misprints and infelicities. I am grateful to Sir Brian Harrison, Peter Marshall, Wilfrid Prest, John Simpson, Quentin Skinner and Tom Weil for spotting them.

September 2009   K.T.

CONTENTS

CONTENTS

PLATES

FIGURES

INTRODUCTION

A century hence... by slow degrees the thoughts of our forefathers, their common thoughts about common things, will become thinkable once more.

F. W. Maitland, *Domesday Book and Beyond* (Cambridge, 1897)

In 1818 the poet Samuel Taylor Coleridge advertised a course of lectures, to be delivered at the Crown and Anchor Tavern in the Strand, on the history of philosophy. In the prospectus, he explained that all he required from his auditors was 'a due interest in questions of deepest concern to all, and which every rational creature, who has arrived at the age of reflection, must be presumed, at some period or other, to have put to his own thoughts:—What, and *for* what am I made? What *can* I, and what *ought* I to, make of myself? And in what relations do I stand to the world and my fellow men?'[1]

These are perennial questions, to which, in every age, answers have been given, both explicitly by philosophers and theologians, and implicitly by the rest of us in the conduct of our lives. How should we live? Should we pursue wealth or pleasure or fame? Should we be trying to help our fellows or to advance ourselves? Are our greatest satisfactions to be derived from our work or from personal relationships or from the esteem of others? Should everything be subordinate to the quest for eternal salvation? What is the *summum bonum* of human life? In this book, whose subject, though portentous enough, is at least more modest than Coleridge's, I consider the meaning of such questions for the men and women of early modern England. What did they seek to make of themselves? What goals did they pursue? What were the objectives which, in their eyes, gave life its meaning?

Such questions arise naturally out of any investigation into the past. We cannot hope to understand the behaviour of people long dead, unless we can reconstruct the mental assumptions which led them to act as they did. My aim is to identify some of the central values of the English people between the early sixteenth and late eighteenth centuries and to examine the ways in which those values were accepted, challenged, and reformulated in response to the social and cultural developments of the time. By asking how people made their choices and justified their actions, both to themselves and to others, I hope to advance the project on which I have been intermittently engaged for most of my scholarly life, namely that of constructing a retrospective ethnography of early modern England, approaching the past in the way an anthropologist might approach some exotic society.

Out of the many concerns which contemporaries regarded as central to a life well lived, I have chosen six: military prowess, work, wealth, reputation, personal relationships, and the afterlife. I have given them the rather grandiose title of 'the ends of life'. They are only a selection from a larger range of possible themes; had time and space permitted I would like to have discussed such concerns as intellectual inquiry, aesthetic delight, public service, private charity, and physical pleasure.[2] I have also deliberately chosen to omit any sustained discussion of religion. It was central to the lives of many contemporaries, but is too large a subject to be adequately treated here. As it is, most of the objectives I have included were not so much ends in themselves as means to an end: salvation, perhaps, or self-esteem or happiness. But whether ends or means, it was from them that the men and women of early modern England largely derived such sense of identity, self-respect, and personal fulfilment as came their way. Without them, life was poor indeed.

It would, of course, be misleading to think of people as having pursued lifelong objectives in some systematic fashion. The French philosopher Pierre Charron, whose works were translated into English in the early seventeenth century, declared that a 'fundamental point of wisdom' was 'the fixing to one's self of a particular end, and then chalking out some determinate track, or course of life, which may be proper for leading us to that end'. But he went on to observe that 'the greatest part of mankind' did nothing of the sort.[3] For most people, life was a matter of moving from one short-term expedient to another. For many, the quest for subsistence was so all-absorbing that larger questions about how they should live seldom arose: mere life was a more urgent matter than the quality of life. As a contemporary wrote in 1689 about what he called 'the lower sort of mankind', 'they know no other ends of life than food, raiment, sleeping, and rising up early to take pains; all their care is what they should eat, and wherewithal to be clothed, and how to get money for necessary things. They know no other reason for their coming into the world.'[4] Or, as Daniel Defoe put it twenty years later, they lived 'in a daily circulation of sorrow, living but to work, and working but to live, as if daily bread were the only end of wearisome life, and a wearisome life the only occasion of daily bread'.[5]

In early modern England, most people had to make the best of the circumstances in which they found themselves. Their lives, like ours, were usually unplanned, and the business of daily living got in the way of the formulation of any longer-term strategy. Their paths were shaped by their birth and upbringing and governed by habit and routine, into which conscious choice seldom entered. Their energies went into making a living, maintaining a family, and simply getting by. Their values were implicit, rather than consciously articulated; and they were shaped for them by the social relationships in which they found themselves and the cultural influences to which they were exposed. Their needs, desires, and aspirations were those which their world allowed them to formulate. Even the privileged minority who lived in comfortable circumstances, with the leisure and the self-determination to articulate their aims in life, seldom gave the matter much thought. Those who did were all too easily distracted by what the philosopher Thomas Hobbes (1588–1679) called the 'desire of ease and sensual delight'.[6] Samuel Pepys (1633–1703) was a highly successful Admiralty civil servant. But he confessed that he was very easily diverted: 'music and women I cannot but give way to, whatever my business is'.[7] Sir Dudley North (1641–91) pursued a distinguished career as a merchant, financier, and economic thinker, yet his brother tells us that when 'scraping a stick or turning a piece of wood . . . he was incomparably pleased than in all the stages of his life before'.[8]

As a Welshman, I should emphasize that this book is concerned with England, narrowly defined. It is not an essay in the 'British' history which historians in these post-devolutionary days are so frequently enjoined to practise. For although Wales entered into a political, ecclesiastical, and legal union with England in 1536, and Scotland into a political one in 1707, the cultural, social, and linguistic differences between the three countries in the early modern period remained considerable. Ireland would have been even harder to fit into the story. In each part of the British Isles there were groups who had close affinities with English life: the English-speaking Welsh gentry, the Protestant settlers in Ireland, the Scottish nobility after the Union, and the intellectuals of the Scottish Enlightenment. But the bulk of the population in Scotland, Wales, and Ireland continued to live lives

which differed in important respects from those of their English counterparts. To project our present-day preoccupation with 'Britishness'
backwards into the early modern period would only mislead. Nevertheless, the history of the rest of the British Isles offers many instructive
parallels to developments in England. So does that of Continental
Europe; many of the most influential currents of thought in early
modern England originated across the Channel. At every stage of
this book it was tempting to point to striking similarities and contrasts
between developments in England and the rest of Europe, not to
mention the New World. But, in the interests of space and coherence,
that temptation has, for the most part, had to be resisted.

The period covered is a long one. It is only during the last fifty years
that the term 'early modern' has come into general circulation among
historians.* There is no general agreement as to when the early
modern period began and ended, any more than there is about the
dating of 'medieval' and 'modern'. In recent historical writings, early
modern times are variously said to have started at different dates
between 1300 and 1560 and to have ended at sundry points between
1660 and 1800. My focus in this book is on the period 1530–1780.
Those 250 years, from the Reformation to the American War of
Independence, have a certain unity, but it should not be exaggerated.
None of the topics I discuss can be said to have started or stopped
then. My dates are only approximate and I have frequently strayed
across them.

In stepping back, so as to consider some central preoccupations of
English men and women over so long a period, I have inevitably
sacrificed nuance for the sake of the general outline. I may also have
unintentionally given an impression of underlying continuity in what
was a period of very considerable social and intellectual change. Early
modern England was a complex and diversified society, marked by
great differences of wealth and poverty, considerable regional and
local variation, profound religious divisions, and huge inequalities in
education and intellectual sophistication. It had room both for Sir
Isaac Newton, who erected a cosmological synthesis which would last
for two centuries, and his father, who died unable to sign his name.
A tangled inheritance of incompatible ideas—classical, Christian, and
chivalric—generated a host of competing and sometimes deeply

---

* When in 1976 I gave a lecture to the British Academy entitled 'Age and authority
in early modern England', the President, Sir Isaiah Berlin, introducing me, remarked
that he had never previously encountered the expression.

opposed attitudes to life. The country was a mosaic of separate communities and social groupings, each inhabiting its own mental world and frequently ignorant or disdainful of the values and outlook of others. That is why so much of the best historical research on the period has taken a microscopic form, examining small communities or even single lives. I have not followed that path. But I have tried to emphasize that the values with which I am concerned were very differently regarded at different times, and in different social and intellectual milieux.

In order to establish these values, I have inferred what I can from the way in which people managed their daily lives, for some of their most fundamental beliefs were expressed in deeds rather than words. But my primary source has been the writings and recorded utterances of the period. Intellectually sophisticated works of theology and philosophy can illuminate the desires and dilemmas of ordinary life, no less than letters, diaries, poems, and plays. Speeches, depositions in the law courts, and recorded conversations allow us to hear people talking, even if their words are filtered through a scribe or intermediary. The reasons people give publicly for their actions may tell us little about their real motives, but they are usually a helpful guide to the received values of the time. In this book I have cited contemporaries so liberally that at times my text comes close to being a collage of quotations. *Collector, non auctor, ego sum* ('I am the collector, not the author').[9] I have some sympathy with the German cultural critic Walter Benjamin (1892–1940), whose ideal was a work consisting entirely of quotations, put together so skilfully that it could dispense with any accompanying text.[10]

Yet a relentless diet of quotations is not only bad for the reader's digestion. It also raises some serious methodological issues.[11] First, there is the problem of context. Anyone who seeks to identify people's underlying assumptions must necessarily draw on remarks made in a wide range of different circumstances and expressed in a variety of literary genres. We all know from our daily lives that a remark ripped out of its context cannot necessarily be taken at its face value: sometimes it may even convey a meaning wholly unintended by the speaker. Many of the contemporary opinions I have quoted were intended as reflections on the topics with which I am concerned and can be fairly cited as such. But others were casual observations or short-term responses to immediate problems whose authors might have been surprised to find them treated as representative of a more enduring attitude. Many critics regard such decontextualized use of contemporary utterances as an unacceptable way of proceeding. It is quite wrong, they say, 'to cite writers from different periods and classes, writing within different circumstances, and using a wide variety of genres as if they are commensurable'.[12] To this charge, I can only plead that I am well aware of the perils that beset source-miners and quotation-mongers. Before quoting a text I have always tried to ask myself who said or wrote it, and why. I have, however, usually refrained from inflicting this information upon the reader. To those perfectionists who feel that historians should pause every time they quote a contemporary document in order to give a full account of the circumstances in which it was composed and an assessment of the textual and contextual problems it presents, I can only say that, had I done so, little would have been gained, while this book would have become infinitely long as well as infinitely tedious.[13]

A second problem arises from my habit of illustrating an attitude or practice by bringing together evidence culled from very different social and intellectual milieux and different periods of time, some-times even separated by a century or more. I hope that this approach does not indicate any lack of sensitivity to the distinctive qualities of each particular era or social grouping, or to the changing meaning of language. When citing examples drawn from widely separated dates I do so self-consciously, in the conviction that some problems, values, and assumptions persisted over long periods of time. Most historians these days are, to use the terminology made familiar by the late J. H. Hexter,[14] splitters rather than lumpers. They are trained to look for differences rather than similarities. My approach in this book is that of the lumper, who believes that the relentless urge to draw distinctions often results in some striking resemblances and continuities being overlooked.

Finally, I should remind the reader that the views expressed by contemporaries were inevitably constrained by the linguistic and conceptual resources available at the time. Their sentiments tended to be expressed in terms of a conventional formulation or pattern of argument, what intellectual historians nowadays call a 'discourse'. Modern scholars have shown that much political and religious argu-ment was a matter of competing discourses. Indeed virtually all topics were discussed within some or other discursive tradition. I have not spent much time examining the pedigree of these discourses, but I hope that I have made it clear that when contemporaries pro-nounced upon such subjects as luxury or honour or friendship, they usually did so within a framework of established conventions.

It is not easy to justify assertions about the alleged frequency or infrequency of some particular belief or attitude in the past. How many examples does one need to cite in order to prove the point? Lacking any satisfactory method of quantifying these matters, all I can do is to record my impressions after long immersion in the period. I am well aware that other historians may have formed different impressions. Travellers to a foreign country, even anthropologists, seldom return with exactly the same accounts of the places they have visited.

I

FULFILMENT IN AN AGE OF LIMITED POSSIBILITIES

If Heav'n the Grateful Liberty would give,
That I might chuse my Method how to Live ...

John Pomfret, *The Choice*, 1700

THE IDEA OF FULFILMENT

This book is concerned with some of the different ways in which the inhabitants of early modern England sought to live fulfilling lives. Of course, people at that time did not talk of fulfilment. The word had not come into existence; it does not even appear in Samuel Johnson's great *Dictionary* of 1755. It is only in the last century or so that expressions like 'human fulfilment' or 'self-realization' have entered everyday usage; and it might seem anachronistic to apply them to the early modern period when such terms were unfamiliar. Yet it is helpful to do so if, by looking at the past in the light of such concepts, we are enabled to gain a better sense of what life meant for the men and women of the time.

When we speak of human fulfilment today, we usually have in mind two distinct, though closely associated, notions. One is of fulfilment as the full development of people's distinctive capacities—their musical talent perhaps or their athletic skills. The other is of fulfilment as the gratification of their deepest desires—their wish to be loved, say, or their craving to be famous. Some philosophers have called the first 'capacity-fulfilment' and the second 'aspiration-fulfilment'. Together they constitute what is widely regarded as the sum of human felicity.[1] Of course, all capacities cannot be realized, any more than all desires can be satisfied. There are many different ends whose pursuit might result in a fulfilling

8

life; and no individual can pursue them all. But in the modern liberal West, as well as in many other parts of the world, it is axiomatic that all human beings are entitled to fulfil themselves in the way they choose and that, so far as possible, society should be ordered in such a way as to enable them to do so. When in 1994 Nelson Mandela gave his first State of the Nation address as President of South Africa, he declared that 'the purpose that will drive this government shall be the expansion of the frontiers of human fulfilment'.[2]

A key ingredient in this notion of fulfilment is personal autonomy. Fulfilment is gained by achieving the objectives individuals have set for themselves, rather than by conforming to an inherited role or an externally prescribed code of behaviour. Everybody should be able to choose the goals which are right for him or her. In keeping with this point of view, one modern philosopher declares that human well-being requires the 'control of one's own destiny and the ability to lead a life of one's own choice'. 'Choosing one's own course through life,' writes another, 'making something of it according to one's own lights, is at the heart of what it is to lead a human existence.'[3]

In fact, of course, fulfilment does not necessarily require personal autonomy.[4] A reluctant conscript might discover to his surprise that a military life is the one that suits him best. The bride pushed into an arranged marriage might find in her arbitrarily assigned husband a true soulmate. People are not always the best judges of their own interests. Nevertheless, our normal assumption today is that liberty of choice is an essential precondition of human flourishing.

Human development, accordingly, is widely envisaged as a process of expanding 'capabilities', of enabling people to choose their own identity and to lead free and creative lives. This notion has been employed by the economist Amartya Sen as a way of measuring the degree of hardship suffered by the inhabitants of Third World countries. Rather than assessing deprivation in terms of income and GNP, or of subjective satisfaction and dissatisfaction, he suggests that we should examine the limits to what people can be or do—the constraints upon their ability to act as free agents and to realize their capabilities. Seen this way, underdevelopment means not just scarcity of resources, but 'capacity deprivation', inability to enjoy essential human possibilities. The philosopher Martha Nussbaum has even made a list of the 'central human functional capabilities' which she regards as essential to personal fulfilment: they include 'having certain guarantees of non-interference with certain choices that are especially personal or definitive of selfhood, such as choices regarding marriage, childbearing, sexual expression, speech, and employment'.[5] This approach is recognizably similar to the concept of 'life chances', defined by the sociologist Ralf Dahrendorf as the sum of opportunities offered to individuals by the society in which they live.[6]

These attempts to identify the ingredients of human fulfilment are in direct line of descent from the thinking of classical antiquity. The Greek and Roman philosophers devoted much energy to determining what constituted an objectively desirable life, *eudaimonia*, as they called it, the flourishing, well-being, and happiness which came from the realization of one's *daimon*, or true nature. They did not all agree; indeed one Roman scholar collected no fewer than 288 different opinions from philosophers as to what constituted human felicity.[7] But the most influential views, if not at the time, then certainly for posterity, were those of Plato and Aristotle. Both men located the highest form of life in mental activity and philosophical contemplation, though in Aristotle's case active participation in the political and cultural life of the city state was deemed to be a satisfactory second-best. Aristotle, moreover, was clear that intellectual speculation needed to be backed up by good health, friends, and an adequate share of worldly goods. He believed that the highest form of fulfilment was available only to an elite possessing the necessary leisure and education.[8]

What distinguishes many modern proponents of human fulfilment from those of classical antiquity is that, instead of putting forward a single model of the good life, they accept that there is a host of acceptable ways of living, according to individual choice. Fulfilment is regarded as an individual matter, peculiar to the person concerned. It is seen as self-fulfilment, self-realization, personal authenticity. Central to this conception is the idea of the unique individual, endowed at birth with distinctive qualities and capable of autonomous reflection, self-examination, and self-direction.[9]

This notion was articulated in the Romantic movement of the later eighteenth and early nineteenth centuries.[10] For the German philosopher Immanuel Kant (1724–1804), individual autonomy was a precondition of the moral life,[11] while the Swiss Jean-Jacques Rousseau (1712–78) preached the doctrine of personal authenticity, urging that men should be true only to their own consciences. The French Revolution encouraged, at least among literary intellectuals, a cult of self-expression and a desire for emancipation from the constraints of social convention. In the Napoleonic age, freedom was seen as individualistic self-realization.[12] In Germany, the notion of *Bildung* (self-development) emerged as a guiding principle of education. It was expressed in 1791 by Wilhelm von Humboldt, when he said that 'the true end of man' was 'the highest and most harmonious development of his powers to a complete and consistent whole'.[13] This doctrine was appropriated in mid-nineteenth-century Britain by John Stuart Mill, who maintained that 'the good of the species' could 'in no other way be forwarded but by...each taking for his exclusive aim the development of what is best in himself'. He praised 'experiments of living', 'varieties of character', and 'the free development of individuality'. Among his contemporaries were the poets Alfred Tennyson, who wrote, 'I would but ask you to fulfil yourself,' and Robert Browning, who in one of his poems lamented what he calls a 'life unfulfilled'.[14]

The free development of the individual was a goal on which nineteenth-century thinkers of very different complexions could agree. It was central for Karl Marx, whose indictment of capitalism was that it frustrated the all-round fulfilment of most men and women; his goal was a condition of material abundance that would confer 'on each human being full scope for self-realization, in a society in which the free development of each will be the condition of the free development of all'.[15] The Dane Søren Kierkegaard (1813–55) urged the importance of individual choice as against an externally imposed code of values, while the German Friedrich Nietzsche (1844–1900) sought the actualization of man's highest possibilities with his Delphic injunction 'Become the person you are.'[16] In 1876, under the influence of G. W. F. Hegel, the English philosopher F. H. Bradley adopted the term 'self-realization', which had been coined by his colleague at Merton College, Oxford, William Wallace, two years earlier. The concept became integral to the social thought of late Victorian Idealist philosophers like T. H. Green, for whom the *summum bonum* (highest good) was 'the full realization of human capabilities'.[17] This was the doctrine expressed by Oscar Wilde in his libel action against the Marquess of Queensberry in 1895, when he declared that 'the realization of oneself' was 'the prime aim of life'.[18] Twenty years later, in faraway China, the young Mao Zedong announced that 'the goal of the human race lies in the realization of self...What I mean by the realization of self consists in the development of our physical and mental capacities to the highest degree.'[19]

In the twentieth century, the search for 'authenticity' became a central preoccupation of Existentialist philosophers like Martin Heidegger and Jean-Paul Sartre, though, unlike the Romantics, who saw authenticity as a matter of getting in touch with one's own inner nature, the Existentialists thought of individuals as creating their nature by their own choices.[20] In the 1960s the requirement to be 'true to oneself' and to 'do one's own thing' became the watchword of liberated youth. In the following decade, feminists invoked the notion of human fulfilment in the cause of women's emancipation. In order to realize their untapped potentialities, women were encouraged to break away from exclusive concentration on their traditional role as wives, mothers, and home-makers, to plan their own lives and to embrace a wider range of possibilities.[21]

The dissemination of the contraceptive pill in the 1960s added 'sexual fulfilment' to the list of human potentialities. The pleasures of the body had been championed in the eighteenth century by the philosophers of the Enlightenment, and in the early twentieth by apostles of birth control like Marie Stopes.[22] But only now could they be safely enjoyed. Freudian psychoanalysis encouraged the idea that human beings needed to be freed from unconscious repressions which prevented them from being truly themselves. The Austrian psychoanalyst Wilhelm Reich (1897–1957) asserted that regular orgasms were essential for the mental health of both men and women. In the later twentieth century, as sexual activity ceased necessarily to involve reproduction and as divorce became easier, there emerged an 'overwhelming preoccupation with self-fulfilment, personal freedom of choice, personal development and lifestyle, and emancipation'. By the 1990s, writes a modern historian, in all laws relating to marriage, divorce, parenthood, and sexual partnerships, the 'acknowledgement of an overriding right to individual "self-fulfilment" had largely displaced the earlier priority of safeguarding the performance of vital social obligations and functions'.[23]

Self-realization thus became the orthodoxy of the Western world in the later twentieth century. It could not have done so without the unprecedented prosperity which freed most people from anxiety about their means of subsistence and gave them the resources with which to enhance their personal satisfactions. The idea that individuals should be allowed to choose their own way of living was greatly encouraged by the free movement of labour and the unimpeded reign of consumer choice in a mass market. Only when economic and physical security were assured could men and women concentrate on realizing their personal capabilities and aspirations.[24] For centuries, human fulfilment had been regarded as the privilege of a favoured elite. Now it seemed potentially open to everyone.

In recent decades, both the morality and the logical coherence of the idea of fulfilment have been questioned. On the one hand, a growing number of critics point to the selfishness inherent in the narcissistic notion of 'authenticity' and lament the amoral indifference to the welfare of others which the reckless pursuit of individual realization can engender: 'Within the family,' writes one historian, 'the pursuit of self-fulfilment has been self-defeating.'[25] On the other hand, 'postmodernist' thinkers dispute the very notion of the self as possessing a given identity which is capable of being realized. Rather than thinking of individuals as born with inherent desires, tastes, and capacities waiting to be fulfilled, they regard the self as a malleable entity, created and shaped by social interaction. For them, as for their Existentialist predecessors, human development is a matter of self-creation, not self-realization.[26]

Despite these moral and epistemological doubts, the modern liberal notion of human fulfilment continues to place a high value upon the realization of each person's distinctive capabilities and desires. It also implies that liberty, autonomy, and personal choice are vital ingredients in that realization.

THE CONSTRAINTS OF THE AGE

It need hardly be said that these present-day notions of human fulfilment were largely alien to the thinking of the early modern period. The material circumstances of the time placed huge limits on the scope for individual choice. Many of the 'basic capabilities' which modern Western philosophers regard as prerequisites of a satisfactory life were totally out of the reach of most people. Poverty, ill health, and premature death stunted innumerable lives. The idea that every person was endowed with unique capacities which could be cultivated and developed was only embryonic. So too was the notion that people should be allowed to choose their own goals and direction in life. Social roles and norms of behaviour were strictly prescribed and freedom of human action was often very limited. The very notion of an entitlement to personal fulfilment in this world would have been hotly disputed.

Religious teachers of all persuasions agreed that it was only in the next life that true felicity could be attained. The goods of this world were desirable, but intrinsically imperfect. The great Elizabethan theologian Richard Hooker conceded that riches, friends, children, and honour were 'naturally every man's desire, because they are good'. But he stressed that they were not ends in themselves. The true end of human life was the enjoyment of God, 'which being once attained unto, there can rest nothing further to be desired'. The Shorter Westminster Catechism issued by Parliament in 1647 said the same: the 'chief end of man' was 'to glorify God, and to enjoy him forever'. In an age of Christian orthodoxy it was axiomatic that human fulfilment would be complete only in the life to come. In this world one should seek not personal gratification but the means of making oneself useful to others; for usefulness, as Daniel Defoe put it in 1706, was 'the greatest pleasure, and justly deem'd by all good men the truest and

Figure 1.1 Inculcating the faith. The Jacobean minister, Alexander Strange, holds a packed congregation in rapt attention.

noblest end of life in which men come nearest to the character of our Blessed Saviour, who went about doing good'.[1]

Although the hold of conventional Christian ideas on the population at large was by no means complete, there is no doubt that the lives of most individuals throughout the early modern period were at the very least intermittently influenced by this conviction that their ultimate objective was religious salvation. God, it was believed, had endowed all parts of the creation with ends and purposes which they were obliged to follow. As the Restoration divine Isaac Barrow put it, 'we may easily observe every creature about us incessantly working toward the end for which it was designed, indefatigably exercising the powers with which it is endowed, diligently observing the laws of its creation'.[2] The ultimate human objective was, therefore, not a matter for individual choice, but had been prescribed by the Creator. 'The end of our being', wrote a pious lady in 1645, 'is God's glory, and that same, and no less, should be the end of every action of a Christian's life.' The brilliant political economist Sir William Petty (1623–87) thought that, once the people had become prosperous, 'we should busy ourselves about...ratiocinations upon the works and will of God...This exercise is the natural end of man in this world, and that which best disposeth him for his spiritual happiness in that other which is to come.'[3]

The legacy of the classical world was enlisted to serve this Christian purpose. Most of the ancient schools of moral philosophy had taught that in order to achieve happiness it was necessary to live a virtuous life. This theme was a popular one among early modern moralists. In the humanist Thomas Starkey's *Dialogue between Pole and Lupset* (begun in 1529), Lupset observes that men are ordained by nature to live 'together in virtue and honesty...This is the end of man's life; to this every man ought to look; to this every man ought to refer all his acts, thoughts and deeds.' Similarly, Sir Richard Barckley, writing in 1598, declared that the *summum bonum* of man was 'goodness itself'.[4]

A virtuous life was generally taken to involve performing the duties appropriate to one's place in society. In the sixteenth century, the prevailing social theory was hierarchical and prescriptive. It presupposed an organic society made up of 'sundry estates and degrees', each discharging some necessary function. In the later Middle Ages, it had been common to say there were three estates: those who fought, those who prayed, and those who laboured. In the early modern period, social classifications became much more elaborate. The mid-Tudor scholar and secretary of state Sir Thomas Smith asserted that 'we in England divide our men commonly into four sorts: gentlemen, citizens or burgesses, yeomen artificers, and labourers'. Other Tudor commentators found five, six, or more social grades. In 1549 the clerical writer Robert Crowley reckoned that there were no fewer than twelve social ranks, like the months in the year.[5] What the authors of such classifications had in common was their assumption that each particular status or occupation called for distinctive qualities, virtues, skills, and aspirations. As one seventeenth-century divine put it, "Tis the place, the calling, the offices of a man that speaks a man.'[6] An individual's ends in life were predetermined by his or her position in the overall scheme.

Only occasionally was that position assumed to have been a matter of choice. The opportunities on offer to the poorest sections of the population—labourers, cottagers, and their families—were highly restricted. They had to seek subsistence where they could find it. A formidable combination of guild ordinances, apprenticeship laws, and poor law regulations severely limited the ability of individuals to take up whatever form of employment they fancied; and their inherent aptitudes and interests can seldom have been a determining consideration. In the middling ranks, there was more scope for personal preference, but options were normally restricted by parents' resources and their network of acquaintance. In agriculture, mining, and handicrafts there was a strong, though not invariable, presupposition in favour of occupational continuity between father and son. In his *Utopia* (1516), Sir Thomas More assumed that that would be the norm; and in the mid-seventeenth century, the historian James Howell commended the Chinese for their 'wholesome piece of policy', whereby 'the son is always of the father's trade'.[7] At the upper levels of society, choice was also limited. The heir of a nobleman or gentleman had his role in life predetermined: whatever his personal tastes, he had to take on the management of the family estates and the public responsibilities that went with them. Younger sons had potentially more freedom, but, in the seventeenth century, they were in practice usually assigned by their fathers to the law, the Church, and the business world, often in that order and regardless of aptitude.[8]

When a child's future occupation was not already settled in advance by birth and circumstances, it was widely held that the decision should be made by others on his behalf. 'Let parents choose betimes the vocations and courses they mean their children should take,' advised Francis Bacon. Unless 'the affection or aptness of the children be extraordinary', they should 'not too much apply themselves to the disposition of their children, as thinking they will take best to that which they have most mind to'.[9] All contemporary moralists agreed that parental consent was important in the choice of a career; and most of them assumed that, although the child's aptitudes should be taken into account, it was the parents who would take the lead in deciding.[10] Sir Thomas Elyot, writing in the reign of Henry VIII, attributed English inferiority in the visual arts to the fact that many children with natural aptitudes for painting and carving had been forced by their fathers into mundane work as tailors or cobblers. The brilliant barrister Sir John King (1638–77), a physician's son, had wanted to become a Cambridge don and a clergyman, but he was 'very obedient and pliable' to the commands of his parents, who insisted that he should become a lawyer.[11] In the mid-eighteenth century, there were many complaints that middle-class fathers ignored the views and capacities of their sons when finding them jobs; they were more likely to apprentice them to what they regarded as a secure and respectable employment rather than one suited to their particular abilities: 'the genius, the natural talents, nor so much as the constitution of youth are seldom or never consulted'.[12]

Once established in their occupations, people were expected to stay there. Contemporary moralists were hostile to most forms of social or occupational mobility. The Church of England taught that the social hierarchy was divinely ordained and that it was a religious duty to be content with one's lot. 'God hath appointed every man his degree and office,' declared the official *Homilies*, 'within the limits whereof it behoveth him to keep himself.' The inequalities of this world would be blotted out in the next. Meanwhile, it was un-Christian for a yeoman to desire to be a lord or gentleman. Even the vagrant, dying of starvation in the street, should not grumble at his lot. To be discontented with one's position in life was a breach of the Eighth Commandment.[13] The great Puritan oracle William Perkins (1558–1602) taught that contentment ('contentation') was 'a virtue, whereby a man is well pleased with that estate wherein he is placed'; 'every man must judge that particular calling in which God hath placed him to be the best of all callings for him'. Changing one's occupation was permissible, but only for the weightiest of reasons.[14] In the reign of Charles II, Isaac Barrow told his Cambridge audience that, 'if God had elected to us the calling of rustics, or of artificers, we had been impious in not diligently following it'; and the Presbyterian cleric John Flavel urged his readers to be satisfied with the occupation in life in which they found themselves: 'Providence is wiser than you, and ... hath suited all things better to your eternal good than you could do, had you been left to your own options.'[15] In the mid-eighteenth century, it was still being urged that the secret of felicity was for people to be content with the station in life which God had allotted them.[16]

The distaste for upward social mobility took many forms: hostility to low-born royal counsellors;[17] prejudice against marriages between couples of unequal social position;[18] schemes to limit the amount of land which could be bought by merchants, yeomen, and other plebeians,[19] and to prevent non-gentry from entering the Inns of Court;[20] laws to confine agricultural labourers to the soil and to set property limits on those seeking to be apprenticed;[21] dislike of episcopacy because many bishops were of humble origin.[22] The great vice was 'ambition', a word which, before the seventeenth century, was used in an exclusively pejorative sense.[23] Ambition was 'the unlawful and restless desire in men to be of higher state than God hath given or appointed unto them'.[24] To seek to better one's position was a sign of 'pride' and 'presumption'. It was wrong to change one's calling merely for the sake of advancement. Those who succeeded in doing so were 'upstarts' or 'mushrooms'.[25]

Such attitudes made education a particularly sensitive issue because of its potentialities as a social escalator. Educational opportunities greatly expanded in the post-Reformation era. Elementary schools and teachers multiplied, the grammar schools became more numerous, and the two universities grew larger. Protestant clergy thought it important that all children should be instructed in basic literacy, so that they could read and understand the Bible; and some urged that the children of the poor should be taught for free.[26] But their concern was to save souls, not to increase social mobility. Children were expected to learn only what was requisite for their 'degree and quality'. The sons of traders and craftsmen should receive the training necessary to enable them to practise their vocations, while university education should be reserved for gentry and would-be clergymen. Certain vocations, such as the Church, the law, and medicine, needed constant replenishment with new talent, professionally trained. But the numbers required for this were strictly limited. As the physician John Jones put it in 1579, 'the greatest part of all youth should be brought up in husbandry, and daily labours, and not in toyish devices, needless for our commons; a lesser part [as]...artificers and merchants; and the least number of all [as]...scholars'. Ignorance was no bad thing in 'the vulgar sort, who be subject and obey'.[27]

Throughout the early modern period, social conservatives lamented that there were too many schools, and that educating people above their station made them discontented with their lot. Even the little group of educational reformers gathered around the Polish exile Samuel Hartlib in the 1640s did not want education to promote social mobility. They favoured 'common schools' for the populace; 'mechanical schools' for craftsmen and artificers; and 'noble schools' for the upper classes.[28] John Milton similarly wanted universal free education which would lead people 'to a competence of learning and to an honest trade', but 'without soaring above the means wherein they were born'; nor should they 'gad for preferment out of their own country [i.e. home district]'.[29] The Interregnum saw many proposals for widening access to higher education. But few went as far as the anonymous author of the radical pamphlet *Tyranipocrit* (1649), who wanted 'to educate all men's children alike'. Most rejected such ideas as socially unrealistic, while, for the aristocracy, the idea that education and intelligence might replace birth and wealth as qualifications for high political office was deeply threatening.[30]

After 1660 the prevailing view among the governing classes was that it was acceptable to pick out children of exceptional talent, so that they could be educated for a higher position and instilled with the values of the elite, but that advanced education was inappropriate for the mass of the population because it would make them discontented with their station in life. As the Marquess of Newcastle told Charles II, 'there are very few that can read that will put their hands to the plough or the cart'.[31] In 1690 a pamphleteer proposed that it should be made illegal for any child to stay in school after the age of 15, unless his parents were worth at least £300 a year (the income of a well-to-do gentleman).[32] In the eighteenth century it was common to oppose the education of the poor, on the grounds that it would make them discontented with the drudgery to which they were born. The number of grammar schools founded in the Reformation period had been excessive, thought the future bishop White Kennett in 1706: it 'almost bordered', he said, 'on the former superstition of founding cells and monasteries'.[33] In a celebrated judgement of 1751, Lord Chancellor Hardwicke explained that, 'though at the Reformation greater invitations were made to bring the poor to schools, that is not so proper now, for at present the poor had better be trained up to agriculture'.[34] 'Ignorance', agreed the writer and politician Soame Jenyns in 1757, was a cordial administered to the poor 'by the gracious hand of providence, of which they ought never to be deprived by an ill-judged and improper education'.[35]

Many observers assumed that the inequalities of the social structure reflected the unequal distribution of human abilities. Like Aristotle, they believed that some men were intended by nature to rule, others to obey, and that they had been placed accordingly. The son of a 'clown' usually proved as much a clown as his father, thought the Jacobean MP Thomas Scott, and the gentleman's son as much of a gentleman; only 'extraordinarily' did people transcend their birth and education.[36] William Perkins believed that 'diversity of personal callings' reflected 'diversity of gifts'; and the Norwich doctor Thomas Browne agreed, declaring in 1646 that 'the wisdom of God hath divided the genius of men according to the different offices of the world and varied their inclinations according to the variety of actions to be performed therein; which they who consider not, rudely rushing upon professions and ways of life unequal to their natures, dishonour not only themselves and their functions, but pervert the harmony of the whole world'.[37]

Other commentators accepted that the distribution of human talents did not necessarily correspond with the social hierarchy and that many persons of great natural ability were condemned to pass their lives in humble occupations with their potential unrealized. As one seventeenth-century schoolmaster put it, there were many 'rare sparks of virtue and ingenuity covered over with rubbish of poverty'. Sir William Petty thought that many were 'now holding the plough, which might have been made fit to steer the state'.[38] Yet though it was recognized that so much ability went unrealized, relatively little concern was expressed. Some even thought it a good thing: it made an unequal society more acceptable by proving that there was no damned merit about it. As a Caroline clergyman explained: 'the great overseer of all things judges it convenient that not a few of the strongest parts, and most choice endowments, should be employed in low ranks, lest those orders should seem despicable, and none be thought deserving that were not aloft'.[39] Correspondingly, the upper classes were not encouraged to fulfil themselves by realizing talents which were inappropriate to their social position. A gentleman might be naturally gifted as a poet or a painter, but, according to some authorities, such pursuits should be followed only in his spare time, 'as a secret pastime or recreation'.[40]

Nowhere were social and cultural constraints more obvious than in the differing prescriptions for men and women. Around the physical difference of sex was erected a huge apparatus of distinctions of gender, that is of culturally specific assumptions about the intrinsic qualities and appropriate social roles of men and women. In innumerable spheres of life, what was 'comely' for one sex was thought uncomely for the other.[41] Masculinity and femininity were envisaged as opposing categories; and to the polarity male–female were linked a whole range of associated oppositions: strong and weak; hard and soft; rational and emotional; serious and frivolous; public and private; active and passive.[42] As a result, the lives of women were more circumscribed than those of men. For them, the concept of vocational choice barely existed. Although girls might be taught practical domestic skills and apprenticed to some occupation, most usually as domestic servants, it was generally assumed that their ultimate destiny was marriage, after which their husbands would decide how their time was to be spent. Within marriage it was axiomatic that the husband should rule the wife, even in those embarrassingly inconvenient cases where the wife happened to be 'wiser, more discreet and provident than the husband'.[43]

Women, it was assumed, would find their primary fulfilment as wives, mothers, and home-makers. There was no acknowledged obvious place in contemporary social theory for those who, for whatever reason, remained unmarried. The diarist John Evelyn observed in 1676 that a young woman who chose not to marry would make herself 'singular and fantastic'.[44] Unmarried women were regarded as anomalies. Tudor municipalities forced the younger ones into service, believing it to be unacceptable that they should be allowed to live by themselves.[45] In practice, many adult women never married and some of them managed to pursue effective careers as traders, teachers, rentiers, and moneylenders. Alternatively, they ran households and looked after children for their relatives.[46] Yet the social prejudice against them was so strong that it is doubtful whether many of them can have deliberately chosen their single state.[47]

A generally accepted sexual division of labour gave to men (or, more precisely, to men of the upper and middling classes) grammar school and university education, the learned professions, religious office, warfare, diplomacy, politics, and government. Men also had a monopoly of most forms of skilled work outside the home. To women were assigned the domestic tasks of cooking, cleaning, child-rearing, laundering, and dairying. As one authority put it, the man's calling was to handle things 'abroad'; the woman's calling was to deal with things 'at home': 'he without doors, she within'.[48]

Figure 1.2 The care of young children was women's work. Here women are shown nursing a baby, tending a sick child, and buying medicine.

Of course, facts did not correspond to these prescriptions, particularly among the poorer classes, where all members of the household were expected to contribute to the family budget, and where the sexual division of labour was extremely fluid. A late seventeenth-century observer noticed that among labouring people, 'the condition of the two sexes' was 'more equal than amongst gentlemen, city traders or rich yeomen'.[49] Gender had different implications at different social levels and at different periods. There were women in early modern England who ran businesses and wrote books, and many female wage-earners who did heavy manual labour in fields, mines, and work-shops.[50] Upper-class women often confounded conventional expect-ations by playing an active role in the management of landed estates and their husbands' political affairs.[51] The patriarchal political thinker Sir Robert Filmer (d. 1653), was conservative in his social assumptions, but he conceded that there was no virtue of which the female sex was incapable: 'even sailing and war and government of kingdoms have been oftentimes well handled by women'.[52]

Yet the boundaries kept shifting. During the later Middle Ages, women gradually lost their monopoly of the brewing business. In the eighteenth century they gave up reaping corn, men took over the dairying trade, and midwifery ceased to be an exclusively female occupation.[53] The shape of things to come was foreshadowed by the physician Peter Chamberlen, who remarked in 1649 that, although milking cows was 'a thing ordinarily used by women through the prevalency of custom', it was 'fitter for men, in regard of women's tenderness and danger of going in the wet, beside the labour of bringing it home'.[54] By 1800 gender divisions had shar-pened, particularly among the middling and upper classes, where men and women lived lives which were in some ways more different from each other's than they had been in the past.[55] The sexual division of labour became more rigid; and so did the assumption that men and women embodied complementary human qualities which justified that division and called for different forms of personal fulfilment.

In neither case was that fulfilment meant to include sexual experi-mentation. Fornication and adultery were treated by the ecclesiastical courts as punishable offences. Sodomy was a capital crime. Divorce with the right to remarry was not permitted until near the end of the seventeenth century, and then only for the tiny majority of individuals who could afford to promote a bill in the House of Lords. Many Protestant clergy unsuccessfully supported the idea of altering the law so as to make possible divorce and remarriage in cases of adultery and desertion. But the poet John Milton was virtually alone in pro-posing in the 1640s that the union could also be broken if it proved uncongenial (to the husband); and the idea of divorce for incompati-bility was put forward only very intermittently during the following century.[56] The accepted doctrine was that, once married, people should stay married, regardless of whether they found the marital relationship a satisfactory one, just as they should stick to their occupation whether or not it was congenial. No one explicitly defended the right of married couples to decide not to have children if they so wished; and the legitimacy of non-procreative sex was widely regarded as questionable. There was an undercurrent of hostility to the remarriage of widows, particularly if they were beyond the age of childbearing.[57]

'Generations of women', writes a modern commentator on the Islamic world, 'have assured the survival of our species at the expense of their self-realization as persons.'[58] He might have said the same about women in the West. It is impossible to know how many girls there were in early modern England like Elizabeth Ashbridge, born in 1713, the daughter of a Cheshire surgeon, who confessed that she 'sometimes wept with sorrow that I was not a boy'.[59] In her case, it was because her sex prevented her from becoming a minister of religion. But that was only one of many disabilities to which women were subject.

In recent years, historians have begun to see that these orthodoxies imposed equally formidable constraints upon men. Although the terms 'manly' and 'masculine' were always used in a favourable sense, they implicitly closed off a great range of options. Not only were all males assumed to aspire to the condition of heterosexual marriage (homosexual acts being strictly prohibited and bachelors seen as anomalies*), but the charge of so-called 'effeminacy' was repeatedly raised against those who were so unmasculine as to ride in coaches or enjoy French cooking or spend too much time in female company, including that of their wives, or be addicted to drink or music or poetry. Even religion was suspect: in Bunyan's *Pilgrim's Progress*, Faithful is told that 'it was a pitiful, low, sneaking business for a man to mind religion' and that 'a tender conscience was an unmanly thing'.[60] Ideas about what was or was not appropriate conduct for a man varied enormously according to the social context. They also changed over time. But there was a recurring tendency to equate masculinity with reason and self-control and to regard any form of sensual indulgence as a sign of 'effeminate' weakness.[61]

---

* Like old maids, bachelors were also sometimes said to be doomed to lead apes in hell. See e.g. *London Jests* (1720), 114.

Men were also subject to censure if they flouted the sexual division of labour. A minister lamented in 1642 that 'many foppish husbands do so intermeddle in the...peculiar employments of the women, taking upon them the managing of their cookeries, their dairies and housewifery, as if they must have an oar in each boat'.[62] A contemporary diarist noted that 'in England it is held a shame for a man to do the offices of a woman in housewifery, as washing, milking, making cheese, butter, &c.'* Such a man would be mockingly called a 'Molly cot', a 'Bessy', a 'cotman', or a 'Mary Ann', in the same way that a girl who played with boys or otherwise intruded into the masculine sphere was dismissed as a 'tomboy'.[63] Far from portraying men as the complacent beneficiaries of the patriarchal values of the age, many historians now represent manhood in early modern England as a precarious state, beset by a host of anxieties, from failure to achieve economic independence to deceit by an unfaithful wife. Manhood, we are told, 'had to be continually proved and asserted'.[64]

The prevailing assumption, therefore, was that human beings, according to their sex and social position, would pursue different goals in life. Their duty was to conform to God's will and discharge the duties appropriate to the position in which they found themselves. Taken literally, this doctrine set severe limits to individual aspirations. If all that was required was the performance of one's allotted social role and that role was prescribed in advance, there was little scope for the exercise of self-determination. Moralists implied that a satisfactory performance of these limited expectations would bring contentment in this world and salvation in the next. But the individual's personal fulfilment was never the primary consideration: the emphasis was on the proper functioning of the system as a whole. As Thomas Starkey explained, man's end was to foster the common weal, regardless of 'his own vain pleasures, frail fantasies and singular profit'. Or, as the Puritan minister William Gouge (1578–1653) put it, 'every one is set in his place by God, not so much for himself, as for the good of others'.[65]

Advice literature repeatedly told the young that their duty was not to themselves but to the society in which they lived. 'Private ends' were portrayed as incompatible with the public interest. The error of the acquisitive and the ambitious was that they put their own 'private

---

* He thought this 'a great damage', since men were 'the best cooks, brewers, bakers and midwives'; *Crosby Records: A Cavalier's Note Book*, ed. T. Ellison Gibson (1880), 188.

commodity' before the 'public profit' of the whole.[66] Here the Christian stress on unselfishness blended easily with neoclassical notions of civic responsibility. 'The heathen man Tully', an Elizabethan MP told Parliament, 'saith that man is not born for himself only, but partly for his parents, partly for his children, and partly for his country.' Cicero's maxim was frequently repeated, sometimes with the additional gloss that the interests of posterity should also be borne in mind.[67] Even those who urged that children's natural aptitudes should be respected in the choice of occupations were usually concerned less to ensure the fulfilment of the child than to make the most effective use of all available talents. The great Presbyterian divine Richard Baxter (1615–91) thought that every man should choose the calling which was most agreeable to his mind and body, but that was not the calling which would bring him most ease, wealth, and honour; it was the one 'in which he may be most serviceable to God for the doing of the greatest good in the world... God and the public good must be our chiefest ends in the choice.'[68]

Romantic ideas of authenticity, of being 'true to oneself', could hardly be formulated when there was such strong hostility to the idea of people choosing their own objectives in life, regardless of the general interest. As the Puritan divine Thomas Hooker put it in 1648: 'There must of necessity follow the distraction and desolation of the whole, when each man hath liberty to follow his own imagination and humorous devices and seek his particular.'[69] Most people were caught up in a web of mutual interdependence, obligation, and reciprocity which included not only their family and kin, but also their neighbours and the local community. Their supposed purpose in life was as much to ensure the continuity of those units as to advance their careers or enhance their own individual well-being. The first obligation of a landed aristocrat was not to himself, but to the perpetuation of his lineage and family estate; the continuation and, if possible, the advancement of the line were all-important (pl. 1).[70] At a lower social level, there was a widespread sense of obligation to close kin: even nephews, cousins, and in-laws, and even when kinship ties conflicted with religious and political loyalties.[71] Personal decisions were supposed to be taken with the family's interests in mind; and parental consent was to be sought in all the principal actions of life, regardless of whether or not the child exceeded the father in wisdom and intelligence. Even when children had come of age, thought the Puritan William Ames (1576–1633), parents should retain their authority 'in those things which seem to be of moment for the government of the family'.[72]

Marriage, in particular, was regarded as a business affecting more than just the two individuals involved. For the upper classes, matrimony was primarily a matter of transferring property and forging dynastic alliances; the interests of the lineage came first. At lower social levels, marriage involved the intervention of relatives, friends, intermediaries, and go-betweens. As William Perkins once said to 'a coy virgin', 'Thy virginity is not all thine to dispose of: in part it's thy parents'; father hath a stroke in it, mother another, and kindred a third: fight not against all, but be his whom they would have thee.'[73] Most moralists held that it was the duty of parents to provide suitable marriages for their children, while at the same time recognizing that the child's consent was also necessary. By the standards of most of the world, young people in England (as in north-west Europe more generally) were permitted a remarkable degree of freedom in their choice of marriage partner, particularly among the lower classes, but there was a constant tension between individual preference and familial choice.[74]

The pluralism which underlies modern liberal social theory rests on the assumption that people pursue different goals and that those differences should be respected. In the early modern period, by contrast, disagreement about matters of politics and religion was more likely to be perceived as evidence of error or sinfulness. The expression of heterodox opinions could lead to severe punishment. Save during the Cromwellian Protectorate, it was not until after 1689 that a degree of religious toleration was officially permitted; and not until the nineteenth century that Catholics and Jews lost their civil disabilities. It was also well into the eighteenth century before it was accepted that politicians could pursue opposing objectives without regarding each other as guilty of treason. In an age of violently competing political and religious opinions, the accepted ideal was moral unanimity. Those who failed to adhere to conventional expectations, whether in their religion or their tastes or their personal behaviour, were accused of the great vice of 'singularity', of following their 'private fancy and vanity'. 'Desire not to be singular, nor to differ from others,' warned a Jacobean cleric, 'for it is a sign of a naughty spirit, which hath caused much evil in the world from the beginning.'[75] Even a group of separatists in late Elizabethan Dover strongly denied any intention 'to become singular'.[76]

Idiosyncrasy in dress was widely regarded as morally reprehensible: 'confusedly every man or woman to wear as them liketh' was, in the words of the Protestant cleric Thomas Becon (1512–67), 'greatly discommendable and ought by the highest powers to be restrained'.[77] In Lancashire in the 1620s, there were rigid conventions about the clothes to be worn by women of the different social classes: 'if any had transgressed these bounds,' recalled a contemporary, 'she would have been accounted an ambitious fool'.[78] The Puritan preacher Samuel Torshell (1604–50) relates how he 'once persuaded a good woman to leave off a singular dress' by reminding her that 'we must go dressed like our neighbours'.[79] Margaret Cavendish, the bluestocking Duchess of Newcastle (1623?–1673), was exceptional in her belief that clothes should reflect individual personality; 'I did dislike any should follow my fashions, for I always took delight in a singularity, even in accoutrements of habits.'[80] Nonconformity in dress was easier for an aristocrat than for someone in humbler circumstances, but the Duchess's privileged position did not protect her from ridicule.

Within the often highly integrated village communities, opinion was extremely hostile to those individuals who did not adhere to established norms, particularly in areas where open-field agriculture was still practised and close cooperation between neighbours was essential.[81] Any departure from conventional mores might occasion collective disapproval. In their proceedings against sexual and other offenders, the church courts depended overwhelmingly upon the support of their fellow parishioners, who reported the offences and readily assisted with subsequent inquiries. The way in which misdemeanours were described reveals that it was the rules of the community as much as those of God which were being enforced: visiting a married woman, 'to the offence of the neighbours'; living together, 'to the offence of their neighbours', begetting a bastard, 'to the great offence of the neighbours'; concealing the birth of a child out of wedlock 'from the knowledge of all other neighbours'.[82] They were easily offended, these neighbours. Youths who had no masters, single women who lived on their own, cohabiting couples who could not prove they were married, new arrivals who concealed their place of origin, persons who expressed unconventional opinions on religious or political matters: all might find themselves in trouble. Others conformed for the sake of a quiet life, like the Dorset copyholder who reluctantly signed an enclosure agreement in 1626, in order that 'he might not be singular'.[83]

NEW ASPIRATIONS

The idea that individuals should be permitted to fulfil themselves in whatever way they chose was thus profoundly foreign to the official thinking of early modern England. The prevailing social theory subordinated the claims of personal development to what were thought to be the needs of the social order. But that social theory was a poor guide to the way in which many people of the time actually behaved. Contemporary prescriptions were repeatedly flouted or ignored; and the search by men and women for personal fulfilment is abundantly evident in the decisions and choices they made in their daily lives. Most people may have lacked autonomy, in the sense that they did not choose for themselves their values or their plan of life. But they had agency, that is to say the ability to make the best of the position in which they found themselves. They were able to manoeuvre within the structures which enclosed them and they often succeeded in manipulating them to their individual advantage.

Movement up and down the social scale, for example, was everywhere to be seen, and, despite the protests of the moralists, there were few legal restraints to stop it. The conservative social doctrines which were so extensively preached in Tudor England were wildly out of line with reality; for economic expansion, and with it the appearance of new occupations and new sources of wealth, constantly challenged the notion of a static social order. As an eyewitness asked in 1575, 'do we not daily see men basely born, yet, through God's providence, using the means of their bringing up in schools of learning or profession of law, or giving to them abundance of riches, or prospering them in service to their prince, or such like, do we not see them daily advanced to honour?'[1] Few were contented with their lot, complained another Elizabethan; the remainder were driven by 'fond self-love, impatient ambition or irksome discontent of [their] estate'. Most men, agreed a Caroline preacher, were 'continually complaining, never satisfied, but always desirous to change their condition'.[2] The existence of a widespread desire to get on in life was indisputable. It was only in some ill-defined past golden age that 'each man [had] kept his degree' and been content to stay in his vocation.[3]

In the sixteenth and seventeenth centuries, many lawyers, merchants, and yeomen made fortunes and established themselves as landed gentlemen. Noble families died out through failure of male heirs and were renewed by recruitment from below. Boys from the middling sort worked their way up the educational ladder into the professional classes, sometimes becoming leaders of the Church or great ministers of the Crown. Further down, the picture is more obscure. Smallholders and cottagers may have been less interested, and certainly were less successful, in advancing themselves. It was difficult for the child of a poverty-stricken family to get very far, since, by the seventeenth century, money premiums had usually to be paid on behalf of those who wanted to be apprenticed to all but the very poorest trades.* The pressure of population on limited resources gave market-oriented yeoman farmers the chance to expand at the expense of their poorer neighbours, growing numbers of whom were forced into the ranks of the landless, the servants, and the wage-labourers. Similarly, many of the younger children of the well-to-do were compelled to move downwards in order to subsist. The social order was one of constant mutability. 'Is there any poor now, that some of their ancestors have not been rich?' asked a contemporary in 1696. 'Or any rich now that some of their ancestors have not been poor?'[4]

During the early modern period an ideology legitimizing the quest for personal advancement can be seen taking shape. Like many other tendencies of the age, it had medieval roots. The ideal of sponsored social mobility was implicit in the great legacy of fourteenth- and fifteenth-century educational endowments designed to identify talented boys of humble origins and to educate them in school and university for high positions in Church and State.[5] In the Tudor period these endowments were much enhanced; and academic proficiency was frankly recognized as a route to advancement in public life. The heralds regarded a university degree as bringing with it the status of gentleman; and able students hoped to rise in the world. The majority of Elizabethan bishops had modest social origins.[6] John Robinson, the pastor of the Pilgrim Fathers, declared that there was 'in men an inbred desire, and that inordinate usually, to hoist up their children as high as may be'.[7] Contemporaries commented on the huge sacrifices that parents were prepared to make in order to advantage their children, not least by paying for their schooling or apprenticeships, in the belief that education would 'greatly difference' their offspring 'from others not so well educated'.[8] At Oxford the phenomenally industrious Dr Prideaux, Rector of Exeter College between 1612 and 1642, kept the old leather breeches he had worn as a

---

* An interesting exception was Sir Edmund Saunders (d. 1683), who began life 'no better than a beggar boy' and ended up as Lord Chief Justice.

young man in order to show his pupils the social depths from which his diligence had raised him. It was said that three men in his college lost their lives in vain attempts to emulate his industry.[9]

Sixteenth-century educational thought was strongly meritocratic. It was a cardinal doctrine of humanist educators that the teacher's task was 'to descry capacities' in his pupils and enable them to develop their potential.[10] The Tudor grammar schools, with their competitions, their prizes, and their pupils seated in academic order, fostered the spirit of emulation. The school was a competitive arena where the gentleman's son took 'the place due to his industry, not his birth', and began to 'see somewhat in persons of lower fortunes worthy to be honoured'.[11] In the reign of Henry VIII, Archbishop Cranmer famously resisted an attempt to confine places in King's School, Canterbury, to the sons of gentlemen, claiming that 'poor men's children' were 'many times endowed with more singular gifts of nature...as with eloquence, memory, apt pronunciation, sobriety, with suchlike, and also commonly more given to apply their study than is the gentleman's son delicately educated'. He had known, he said, 'no small number' of well-born children who were 'very dull and without all manner of capacity'. If the gentleman's son was not apt for learning, then the poor man's child should be admitted in his place. Cranmer's Elizabethan successor as archbishop, John Whitgift, had similar views.[12] Many remarked that country schools gave opportunities to poor children of exceptional talent, though the aim, of course, was not to encourage the pupils' talents to develop in different directions, but to bring them all to the same humanist goal of eloquence and erudition.[13]

Rejecting aristocratic complaints about low-born royal counsellors, like Thomas Cromwell, a tradesman's son, whom Henry VIII made his chief minister and raised to the earldom of Essex, humanists like Sir Richard Morison, Sir John Cheke, and Sir Thomas Elyot regarded it as axiomatic that men 'of virtue', that is to say people like themselves, undistinguished by birth but outstanding for their rhetorical and literary skills, should be allowed to rise to high office. The author of *The Institution of a Gentleman* (1555) defended those who rose by their abilities rather than their birth, declaring that the pejorative term 'upstart' was 'lately invented by such as pondered not the grounds of honest men of rising or coming to promotion'. Ambition was not a fault in itself, thought Elizabeth's secretary of state Sir Francis Walsingham, provided that titles and power were sought not for their own sake but as a reward for doing good. Humanists were hostile to the notion that birth alone entitled some men to rule others. Virtue was the true nobility; and the commonwealth should give scope to those of talent whatever their social origins.[14] The aristocracy lived happily enough with the idea that they owed their position to their personal qualities, but this classically inspired doctrine had long-lasting anti-hereditary implications which reached their apotheosis in the temporary abolition of the House of Lords in 1649.[15] The ethos of the ensuing Commonwealth period was expressed by John Milton, who, as a good classical republican, urged what he called 'the civil rights and advancements of every person according to his merit'.[16]

Those moralists who urged people to stay in their places had always accepted that some social movement was unavoidable. Not even Edmund Dudley, Henry VII's minister and a rigid exponent of the three-estates theory, insisted that children should remain in the same station of life as their parents.[17] Socially unequal marriages had their defenders; and when, as sometimes happened, aristocratic ladies married their grooms, or gentlemen wed their housekeepers, the reaction was not invariably unfavourable.[18] Most moralists tacitly legitimized upward mobility for the able by conceding that there were circumstances in which it was perfectly acceptable to change one's calling and improve one's position in life, provided that the aim was to serve the public good. In general, however, social mobility was quietly accepted, rather than strenuously advocated. The humanists approved of upward ascent for the university-educated, but were less sympathetic to those who rose by making money.[19]

Within the trading communities, by contrast, there had long been an ethic favouring active self-advancement. Among the London apprentices, the myth of Dick Whittington, first expounded in 1605, reflected an undisguised ambition for wealth and fame. The authors of literature aimed at the trading classes encouraged such aspirations. The Elizabethan novels of Thomas Deloney purveyed an almost Smilesian ideology of self-help, while in the 1630s Thomas Powell published several versions of his *Plaine Path-Way to Preferment*, which freely celebrated the desire for wealth and success, and gave some cynical advice on how to achieve them. In a pamphlet of 1677 the economic writer John Houghton held out the prospect that children of poor cottagers might become merchants and substantial traders.[20] Economic writers of the sixteenth and seventeenth centuries assumed that most people would naturally seek to improve their conditions of life and that there was little point in trying to prevent them from doing so.[21] The speculative builder Nicholas Barbon declared in 1678 that 'all men by a perpetual industry are struggling to mend their former condition'; and the third Earl of Shaftesbury asserted in 1699 that 'every creature has a private good and interest of his own, which nature has compell'd him to seek'.[22] This view of human motivation would be summed up in 1776 by Adam Smith, when he declared that 'the desire of bettering our condition' ('that great purpose of human life') 'comes with us from the womb, and never leaves us till we go into the grave'.[23]

Implicit in the ideal of self-betterment was the notion that children should not be predestined to careers for which they were unsuited, but that parents should wait to see what form their natural abilities (or 'genius') took. As John Milton put it, 'the nature of each person should be especially observed and not bent in another direction', 'for God does not intend all people for one thing, but each one his own work'.[24] William Gouge considered that, 'as there are divers callings, so there are divers abilities of sundry children: some are fittest for callings of wit and learning; others for callings that require an able and strong body'. In his view, the final choice should depend on the child's abilities and 'his inclination to what calling he is most dis-posed'. (Gouge himself had wanted to be a don. But at the age of 29, when he was a Fellow of King's College, Cambridge, his father, 'much against his mind, took him from the University, upon a marriage which he had prepared for him'.[25])

In practice, it seems that many children were allowed some say in deciding their future occupations, at least when genuine options were available.[26] Well-to-do parents found it easier to take a tolerant attitude. In 1682 Sir William Petty advised his friend Sir Robert Southwell concerning the future of his child: 'Let nature work, and let him follow his own inclinations.'[27] Sir Daniel Fleming wrote in 1693: 'I have usually advised and persuaded my children, as much as I thought was fitting, being not willing to make use of any compulsion or importunity unto any of them, when of the age of discretion.'[28] The future bishop Simon Patrick (1626–1707), the son of a Lincoln-shire merchant, was offered a free apprenticeship by a rich wholesale grocer, but, he tells us, 'my father was so kind as to leave me to my own choice and I persisted in my desire to be a scholar'.[29] In 1747 an author published *A General Description of all the Trades*, 'by which parents, guardians, and trustees may, with greater ease and certainty, make choice of trades agreeable to the capacity, education, inclin-ation, strength and fortune of youth under their care'.

The mobility and independence of young people was a marked feature of pre-industrial England. Far from being determined by their parents, as the theorists would have liked, their life-choices were only too fluid. Many children among the lower ranks of the population left home around the age of 15 to go into service or to be apprenticed; thereafter they usually had to make their own way in the world.[30] Separated from their parents at an early age, these youthful wage-earners enjoyed a high degree of autonomy, frequently changing their employer at the end of the year. William Gouge deplored the custom, 'more usual than lawful', of children binding themselves as apprentices without the consent of their parents. His fellow divine Richard Stock (d. 1626) lamented that 'many children, who sometime without asking consent, [or] if denied, do dispose of themselves at their own pleasure in what calling they like, as if their parents had no power over them'.[31]

Young people tended to be highly mobile. They were prominent among the vagrant population, for their search for employment and desire for betterment meant that many of them were often on the roads, usually to the towns and cities, which were seen as offering new opportunities and greater freedom of expression.[32] Unattached young men between the ages of 15 and 24 were the largest single category of emigrants to America in the seventeenth and eighteenth centuries.[33] When in 1655 Oliver Cromwell sought to encourage emigration to Jamaica, he offered 20 acres of land to any male aged 12 and upwards.[34] In the later seventeenth century there were children of 11, 12, and 13 who put their marks to contracts of indentured servitude in the New World.[35] Many of the several hundred thousand men and women who emigrated to America from England and Wales in the seventeenth and eighteenth centuries were motivated by a desire for personal independence.[36]

For many philosophers of the eighteenth-century Enlightenment, it would become a cardinal principle that all careers should be open to the talents and that every man should be entitled to seek advancement to the limits of his ability. They envisaged a social order based on achievement, not ascription. Their justification was no longer the convenience of society or the duty of citizens to make full use of the talents God had given them. It was the individual's right to self-realization.[37] In 1776 Adam Smith wanted 'a society…where every man was perfectly free both to choose what occupation he thought proper, and to change it as often as he thought proper'.[38] He opposed legal restraints on the free circulation of labour from one employment to another; he thought the apprenticeship laws were encroachments upon liberty; and he regarded the law of settlement, which prohibited a man from seeking work in another parish unless he had a certificate, as 'an evident violation of natural liberty and justice'.[39] He condemned conventions which obliged everyone to continue in their profession and devolve it upon their children, as in India and ancient Egypt, where 'every man was bound by a principle of religion to follow the occupation of his father'. For Smith, the right to choose and change one's occupation was an essential ingredient of freedom. He welcomed the growth of commercial society because it enhanced personal liberty by weakening inherited obligations to ancestry and kin.[40]

Adam Smith seems to have been content with the notion that women should find fulfilment as 'mistresses of a family'.[41] But by his time, many voices had been raised in support of greater personal freedom for females. Renaissance Italy had generated a stream of literary feminism which challenged some of the norms of patriarchal culture, particularly the crippling effect of social convention on women's lives, the subordination of wives to their husbands, and the exclusion of females from educational opportunities on the grounds of their supposed intellectual inferiority. In England echoes of this debate could be heard throughout the sixteenth and seventeenth centuries.[42] In the 1640s some of the sects thrown up by the Civil War claimed that women had the right to teach and preach, a claim to which the Quakers gave some institutional recognition.

More radically, some early modern thinkers disputed the assumption that men and women differed in their innate capacities. Some drew inspiration from the separation of mind and body by the French philosopher René Descartes (1596–1650), using it to argue that men and women were intellectually equal because the human mind had no sex.[43] Others pursued the egalitarian implications of the epistemology of John Locke (1632–1704), who portrayed the human mind at birth as a clean slate (tabula rasa), on which subsequent experience left its mark; from this one could infer that women's inferiority was a result of their education and upbringing. In the later seventeenth and early eighteenth centuries, a little band of mostly well-to-do feminist pamphleteers responded to these two intellectual influences by pleading for women's greater access to education, urging a more equal distribution of power within marriage, and praising the single life and the greater freedom it brought with it. Margaret Cavendish, Duchess of Newcastle, made a character in one of her plays declare that women who could afford to support themselves 'were mad to live with men, who make the female sex their slaves'.[44] Other writers inveighed against the 'tyranny of custom' which relegated women to domesticity and frivolity, and made politics and authority the exclusive business of men. Female inferiority, they maintained, was acquired, not natural, and they cited the example of brute animals as proof that there was no innate difference in sagacity between the sexes.[45]

Some of these authors respected the notion that men and women should occupy separate spheres and therefore confined themselves to arguing only that women should be allowed more education. But others wanted females to enter the professions. In 1739 one proto-feminist claimed that there was 'no science, office, or dignity which women had not an equal right to share in with the men'.[46] In the same spirit, the writer Roger North (1651–1734) argued that it was social pressure, notably the need to find a suitable husband, which led upper-class girls to affect excessive delicacy and to waste their time on needlework and shopping. He contrasted English women with their counterparts in the Netherlands, who were good at accountancy and business, simply because it was expected of them. He also pointed out that when poor women were forced to do heavy labour, as in agriculture or the building trades, they proved themselves capable of greater endurance than the men: charwomen and nurses, for example, survived extremes of hunger and sleeplessness. If men were bred as women and vice versa, he concluded, it would be the male sex which would be regarded as the weaker vessel.[47] By the early eighteenth century, it was not at all unusual to assert that women were of equal intellectual capacity to men. The Scottish philosopher David Hume (1711–76) observed that it 'often' happened that wives possessed a 'superior spirit and genius' to that of their husbands.[48] Yet the impact of these literary declarations upon the actual lives of women was very slight. Women played a prominent part in the cultural life of Hanoverian England as actresses, artists, poets, and novelists. But otherwise, fulfilment for women continued to be thought of in traditional terms.

In the religious sphere, by contrast, the scope for personal autonomy greatly expanded. It had always been accepted that it was every individual's personal responsibility to take appropriate steps to secure his or her salvation. But in the Middle Ages, that responsibility had been subject to the oversight of the Catholic Church. In the sixteenth century, the Reformation ushered in a new age of religious pluralism, with the Church of England confronted by Catholic recusants on the one side, and a variety of Protestant separatist groups on the other. Like the godly Puritans of the early seventeenth century and the Dissenters of the Restoration era, the recusants were striking examples of personal self-direction taking priority over the demands of social convention. Of course, many, perhaps most, were Catholics because that had been the religion of their family or the local squire. Similarly, many Dissenters had been born into a tradition of nonconformity. But for others, whether Catholic or Protestant, the refusal to conform was a deliberate personal choice. Even after Protestant Dissenters had been given freedom of worship in 1689, such a distancing from established ways in faith and manners required courage and independence of mind.

Religious nonconformists believed that they were merely following God's commands, but it is not too fanciful to see in them an anticipation of the later doctrine that people should be true to themselves. This was particularly the case with the Quakers, who emerged in the 1650s as a sect who, in the words of a contemporary, '[made] the light which every man hath within him to be his sufficient rule'.[49] It was also true of sundry other Protestant enthusiasts, like Richard Coppin, a believer in universal salvation, who maintained in 1655 that 'there is no man but hath God in him'.[50] No government could survive, thought a Restoration bishop in an attack upon such sectarians, 'if everyone must follow the dictate of his own conscience, that is, in plain terms, be bound only to obey himself'.[51]

INDIVIDUALITY

The modern idea of human fulfilment presupposes that each human being possesses a distinctive individual identity, independent of his or her social role. The general acceptance of this idea has long been seen as one of the most crucial, and yet most elusive, mental developments of the early modern period.[1] In fact, it may not have been an early modern development at all, for there is plenty of evidence for the existence of a sharp awareness of individuality since the days of classical antiquity.* It is true that medieval moralists thought in terms of ideal patterns and types of behaviour rather than unique personalities. Originality was not prized and personal identity tended to be conceived of in generalized terms. Hence the famous assertion by the Swiss historian Jacob Burckhardt (1818–97) that, in the Middle Ages, 'man was conscious of

---

* The eminent ancient historian Arnaldo Momigliano (1908–87) remarked that 'it is my impression that Greek and Roman historians, and especially biographers, talk about individuals in a manner which is not distinct from our own'; *The Category of the Person*, ed. Michael Carrithers et al. (Cambridge, 1985), 89.

himself only as a member of a race, people, party, family, or corporation—only through some general category'.[2]

Yet, then as now, no two persons were identical in physical appearance; and every human being had some unique bodily characteristics.* From at least the twelfth century, there is clear evidence, at least among the knightly and clerical classes, for a belief in the physical and mental singularity of individuals. It can be seen in a variety of contexts: in the use of personal seals and heraldic indicators of personal identity; in the recognition in the Church's penitential manuals that individuals had private intentions and secret thoughts; in the knowledge that people made choices on matters of public loyalty or personal vocation; in the psychological realism of poetry and romance; and in the emergence from anonymity of authors and artists.[3] In the late medieval countryside the laws of the manor and the by-laws of the community were persistently evaded or broken by individualistically minded opportunists.[4] At the same time, the growing complexity of the occupational structure enhanced diversity and multiplied the differences between people. The great motor behind the sense of individual identity was the growth of a market economy, in which land, goods, and labour were freely bought and sold. New economic opportunities gave rise to personal competition and mobility. They widened the scope for personal choice in such matters as dress and domestic equipment; and they made acquisitive and ego-centred behaviour increasingly common.[5]

In early modern times, this sense of individuality becomes more visible. Since the later thirteenth century, English painters and sculptors had on occasions produced lifelike 'counterfeits' of real people; and by 1500 artists were frequently expected to paint portraits which did not just emphasize office, status, and lineage, but were accurate likenesses of the sitter.[6] Literature showed the same preoccupation. 'Aretine's glory', wrote the Elizabethan poet Gabriel Harvey of the Italian poet and pornographer, was 'to be himself; to speak and write like himself; to imitate none but himself, and ever to maintain his own singularity.'[7] The medical theory of the day, which classified people into types determined by their predominant humours (bodily fluids), allowed for the existence of only four temperaments ('sanguine', 'phlegmatic', 'melancholic', and 'choleric'). But by also

---

* John Evelyn regarded this as a signal instance of God's providence, for 'were it otherwise and men had been made like another, the whole government and polity of the world must long since have run into confusion and sad disorder'; *Numismata* (1697), 335–6.

taking into account differences in diet and way of life, it concluded that everyone was effectively unique. Examine a thousand individuals, said the sixteenth-century German physician Paracelsus, and you will find that each one of them has a different disposition. In a hundred thousand, declared another authority, every one will have 'a health peculiar and proper to himself'.[8] With this physiological determinism went a belief that people had no option but to realize themselves in their own distinctive way. 'Why did you wish me milder?' asks Shakespeare's Coriolanus. 'Would you have me false to my nature? Rather say I play the man I am.'[9]

Not everyone regarded human beings as unique personalities. The 'character' writing of the early Stuart period, by Sir Thomas Overbury, John Earle, and others, typecast people by their occupations and temperaments.[10] Many contemporary autobiographies narrated what their authors did (*res gestae*) or what external occurrences befell them ('accidents', 'providences', 'sufferings', and 'deliverances'), but said nothing about their subjective feelings. Yet, partly in response to the influence of Tacitus and other classical authors, there were some notable seventeenth-century historical writings, like the Earl of Clarendon's *History of the Rebellion* or Bishop Burnet's *History of His Own Time*, which reveal a developed sense of the complexity of individual character and an awareness that personality is the product of a long process of development over time.[11]

The same feeling for personal uniqueness colours the vivid pen portraits by the antiquarian John Aubrey (1626–97) which have come to be known as his 'Brief Lives'; and it animates Roger North's lives of his brothers Francis, Dudley, and John, in which, like a portrait painter, he sought to depict 'the peculiar features whereby the subject is distinguished from all others'.[12] The dramatist William Congreve (1670–1729) thought there was 'a singular and unavoidable manner of doing or saying anything, peculiar and natural to one man only, by which his speech and actions are distinguish'd from those of other men'. 'Every mechanic', wrote the author and politician Richard Steele in 1713, 'has a peculiar cast of head and turn of wit, or some uncommon whim, as a characteristic that distinguishes him from others of his trade, as well as from the multitudes that are upon a level with him.'[13] John Locke similarly believed that 'each man's mind has some peculiarity, as well as his face, that distinguishes him from all others'; while the essayist and diplomat Sir William Temple (1628–99) boasted that the peculiar freedom and variety of English life generated true originals: 'we are ... more unlike one another than any nation I know'.[14]

This sense of personal uniqueness may have been more evident in the case of men than of women, who tended in contemporary memoirs (written by men) to be described almost exclusively in terms of their looks, demeanour, and morals. Individuality in women was rare, thought Congreve, while the poet Alexander Pope could declare that 'most women have no characters at all'.[15] Women were defined primarily by reference to their marital status and were not encouraged to develop idiosyncrasies of personality or behaviour. When James Granger compiled his *Biographical History of England* (1769), he employed ten different categories in which to divide the men according to their rank and profession; the women were bundled together in one. The very poor also tended to be undifferentiated, at least in the eyes of their social superiors. Where the people are poor, thought Sir William Temple, 'their actions and lives are all of a piece'. Karl Marx would say of nineteenth-century French peasants that they had 'no diversity of development, no variety of talent, no wealth of social relationships', but lived like 'potatoes in a sack'.[16]

Yet in early modern England, the idea that everyone had a distinctive 'inner' self, held in check by the demands of living with other people, was widely expressed. It was reflected in the growth of a larger vocabulary for self-description.[17] It was implicit in the widely acknowledged need to conceal one's true religious sentiments at times of persecution. It was latent in the frequent allegations that prevailing codes of civility and good manners generated 'insincerity' and 'feigning', because the individual's real feelings and 'true' self were concealed under a public mask. There were many people, thought Sir Henry Wotton (1568–1639), 'who think it perfection enough to have a good outside.' Samuel Pepys's diary is a revelation of the secret life which could be concealed under a suave public manner. Thomas Hobbes was certain that even 'the most sober men', would not want 'the vanity and extravagance' of their thoughts in idle moments to be known by others.[18] The prevailing literary topos was of life as a stage on which everyone played a part, self-consciously fashioning themselves to fit the role they had chosen. The writer John Hall claimed in 1649 that, in public life, man 'is but a theatrical person, and in a manner but personates himself; but in his retired and hid actions, he pulls off his disguise, and acts openly'.[19]

Individuality could be expressed within the family or the village by persons who lived ordinary lives in the sphere into which they had been born; it did not necessarily require emancipation from the constraints of an inherited position. Just as parents observed the 'nature', 'aptitudes', 'genius', and 'constitution' of their children, so the diaries, memoirs, and letters of the seventeenth and eighteenth centuries abound in descriptions of people at all social levels, not as types but as richly differentiated individuals, notable for their distinctive skills, virtues, vices, and quirks of character. The more literate could create a distinctive self and private identity in their letter-writing to friends and relatives[20] and in diary-keeping and spiritual autobiography they could practise the introspection and self-scrutiny encouraged by the religion of the time. Although the results were often stereotyped, this process could sometimes lead to remarkable essays in self-examination, in which individuals conducted a searching scrutiny of their physical constitution, temperament, abilities, qualifications, emotional inclinations, and spiritual state—what one Derbyshire minister called in 1608 'the inside of my life'.[21] Roger North's highly self-conscious autobiography *Notes of Me* (written in the 1690s) is a striking example: it includes an account of his school-days ('where I began . . . to have a sense of my self') and an analysis of his intellect and temperament entitled 'A few transient observations of my self'.[22] Self-knowledge was generally regarded as the first step to wisdom, and introspection a necessary condition for a moral existence.[23] In 1673 Margaret Blagge, a young maid of honour at the court of Charles II, wrote that 'the more I know myself, the less I like myself, and yet for the treasures of the world, I would not but know myself: and I pray I may do so still more and more, till I come to know even as I am known'.[24]

The autonomous, decision-making, morally responsible individual is often taken to be a specifically modern invention. To those looking for anticipations of this kind of modernity, the early modern period presents a mixed picture. On the one hand are generations of men and women who followed unchosen habits and routines, conforming to the conventional expectations of the time and, so far as we can tell, leading unquestioning lives, even when that meant drudgery and subordination. On the other hand, there is widespread evidence of active agency, mobility, self-help, and independence of spirit. The legal system had always presupposed the existence of individuals responsible for their actions and capable of independent decision-making; and a common-law tradition favourable to private property and personal rights fostered litigiousness and a readiness to defend individual liberties. Subordinate persons, from landless labourers to married women, found scope for negotiation, evasion, and accommodation. Throughout the period, the arbitrary enclosure of common land and the speculative exploitation of food shortages provoked waves of rioting and popular protest. The public events of the time—the Reformation, the Civil War, the Revolution of 1688, and the Hanoverian succession—confronted people at all social levels with agonizing problems of religious and political allegiance which could not be easily evaded. The upheavals of the mid-seventeenth century were particularly notable for what one historian has called 'the attempts of various groups of the common people to impose their own solutions to the problems of their time'.[25] But in all periods men and women were sooner or later forced to make difficult choices, whether on politics, religion, work, or their personal lives, as the dilemmas they brought to contemporary astrologers abundantly demonstrate.[26] Like the financial markets of the twenty-first century, the agriculture of the later Middle Ages afforded plenty of scope for personal decision-making, while the increasingly complex economy of the early modern period required business people to be alert to market conditions, to take risks, and to formulate their strategies.[27] Contemporaries had no doubt about the reality of personal responsibility and the importance of individual choice.

Aristotle had taught that nature endows all parts of the living world with ends and purposes which are meant to be realized; and the idea that men should pursue goals consistent with their true nature was held by many classical philosophers. That was why Thomas Browne could write in the 1630s that 'every man truly lives, so long as he acts his nature, or some way makes good the faculties of himself'.[28] Twenty years later, John Evelyn expressed the wish that every gentleman would take up some virtuous pursuit, in order to achieve what he called 'that incomparable fruition of a man's self'; and, a few decades after that, Roger North, describing his brother Francis's flourishing state as a Member of Parliament and Attorney General, wrote that 'his condition in life was like that of a plant set in a proper soil, growing up from small beginning into expanded employment'.[29] Here, surely, we can see something approaching the modern concept of self-realization. Browne, Evelyn, North, and their contemporaries knew that people had individual talents and qualities which deserved full expression; and they were aware that men and women were capable of filling other roles than those into which they had been born. It was not enough to require them to discharge unchosen obligations; they were also entitled to realize their nature as unique human beings.

Of course, the circumstances of the time set severe limits to the degree of self-realization to which individuals could aspire. The poor, in particular, found it particularly difficult to assert an autonomous identity.[30] Yet even in that unequal and tradition-bound world, there were innumerable individuals who carved out their own destinies, unimpeded by the social and economic barriers in their way. They chose their ends of life for themselves. Others accepted the positions in which they found themselves and elected to pursue the ends which had been allocated to them by life's lottery. Yet even then it was sometimes possible to achieve a kind of fulfilment. The nature of that fulfilment is the subject of the following chapters.

2

MILITARY PROWESS

ARMS AND THE MAN

It is held
That valour is the chiefest virtue and
Most dignifies the haver.

William Shakespeare, *Coriolanus* (1608–9?), II. ii

Since time immemorial, all societies which depend upon force for the acquisition and retention of their means of subsistence have regarded physical courage as the supreme proof of manhood. From Homeric Greece to pre-Tokugawa Japan, prowess in warfare has been seen as the highest form of human achievement. Early modern England had a sophisticated agricultural and commercial economy, but it had not wholly abandoned the values of the heroic age. 'Fortitude, called manliness,' said an Elizabethan writer, was 'the most proper virtue belonging to a man'. The profession of arms, wrote another, was 'the noblest and most profitable occupation that a worthy mind should desire'.[1] In the later Middle Ages, killing the enemy in battle had been widely accepted as the ultimate test of manliness. War was portrayed as an indispensable source of masculine pleasure and an intrinsically ennobling activity.[2] In chivalric literature, as a modern historian has observed, 'the actual physical process of knocking another knight off his horse and, if required, hacking him down to the point of submission or death, appears time and again as something like the ultimate human quality...It gives meaning to life.' In the exhilaration of combat, warriors found their identity.[3]

The underlying assumption was that it was right and necessary that human strength and moral determination should be exercised in demanding feats of martial prowess. War, preferably in a just cause, was an elevating experience, a celebration of assertive masculinity. It was a source of enjoyment, a form of self-affirmation, a way of living more intensely. The Greeks and Romans had their martial heroes, Hector, Alexander, and Caesar, while chivalric tradition bequeathed a similar constellation, headed by Arthur, Charlemagne, and Godfrey of Bouillon. Along with the biblical warriors Joshua, David, and Judas Maccabeus, they made up the Nine Worthies, the role models for ambitious young manhood.[4]* For men, particularly high-ranking men, the supreme end of life was the performance of deeds of military prowess.

In medieval social theory, accordingly, the aristocracy were seen as a military estate, established to protect the clergy and the commons. They owned armour, wore swords, and rode horses. For them, war was not just an exciting and enjoyable activity: it was their essential purpose in life and the justification for their privileged status.[5] The heraldic coats of arms which indicated their superior status had originated as aids to identification in battle; and they owed their honour to 'glory got by courage of manhood'.[6] Archbishop Cranmer was informed in 1539 that 'the most part of the nobility came up by feat of arms and martial acts'. As the Caroline divine Joseph Bentham remarked: 'In such honourable repute was the martial man that all or most of the titles of honour had their original from the field: witness the title of *Dukes*, for their valour in leading; of *Marquess*, from defending some bounds and frontiers; of *Barons*, from being the strength of the war. Witness the title of *Knight*, signifying a soldier; of *Baronet* or *Banneret*, because his father was dubbed in the field under a banner; of *Esquire*, for being an armour-bearer to a knight.'[7] Nearly two hundred years later, another Bentham, Jeremy, the founder of utilitarianism, would put it more brutally: 'So many hundred years ago, a man's supposed ancestor was, it is supposed, numbered among those whose whole life was a life of oppression and depredation, embellished with incidental acts of murder, upon a scale more or less extensive: for this cause it is that, by himself and others, respect is required to be paid to this descendant of that same malefactor.'[8]†

---

* In Richard Lloyd, *A Briefe Discourse of . . . the Nine Worthies* (1584), the legendary English hero Guy of Warwick takes the place of Godfrey of Bouillon. In 1622 the engraver Robert Vaughan included the Black Prince and King Henry V along with Tamerlane, Süleyman the Magnificent, and other famous warriors in a new set of 'modern' worthies.

† His analysis had been anticipated by the clergyman and geographical compiler Samuel Purchas, who commented in his *Purchas his Pilgrim* (1619), 438–9, on the 'public latrocinies, rapes, murders [and] hell upon earth' which lay behind most titles of nobility; and by the sectaries of the New Model Army, who asked: 'What were the lords of England but William the Conqueror's colonels? Or the barons but his majors? Or the knights but his captains?'; *Reliquiae Baxterianae*, ed. Matthew Sylvester (1696), i. 51.

Yet, though the nobility, knights, and esquires of later medieval England were generally believed to occupy their superior position because they, or their ancestors, had excelled in battle, they had never been an exclusively military estate. Since the twelfth century, many of the functions performed by the upper classes had been administrative rather than martial. Their castles were intended as much for comfort, elegance, and display as for defence; and they themselves were deeply involved in the economic exploitation of their landed possessions. Medieval England, it has been said, had the most agriculturally-minded aristocracy in Europe; and their ability to live off their estates made it less necessary for them to pursue the spoils of war. There had been periods which had seen their remilitarization, notably the wars of Edward III in the mid-fourteenth century. But the steady trend was towards the evolution of the aristocracy as a peaceful landowning class. Their heraldic devices were coming to signify social standing rather than military experience.[9] 'How many knights be there now in England that...knoweth his horse and his horse him?' asked William Caxton in 1484.[10] A century later, the ex-soldier Barnaby Rich lamented that 'nobility in these days (for the most part) have laid aside the practice of arms; she endeavoureth not (as she hath done) the deeds of chivalry, whereby she is grown utterly unable to serve her country'.[11]

By early modern times, it had become common for educated humanists all over Europe to assert the claims of the robe against those of the sword. In place of military skills, they declared, knowledge of rhetoric and law was the primary qualification for royal service. In England the diplomat Sir Thomas Elyot urged that the tongue and the pen could be more effective weapons than the sword and the spear; and the scholar–administrator Sir Thomas Smith declared that a kingdom 'is not so much won or kept by the manhood and force of men as it is by wisdom and policy, which is got chiefly by learning'.[12] Sir Francis Bacon told the second Earl of Essex that it was not 'martial greatness' that would advance his career, but being 'bookish and contemplative', while the Jacobean admiral Sir William Monson grumbled that 'for one that is preferred by arms, there are twenty by learning': the soldier was 'but a servant to the learned'.[13] In the courtesy manuals of the sixteenth and early seventeenth centuries, the emphasis was more on the nobleman's civility than his valour.[14] Arms were yielding to the toga.

Yet though the state needed its lawyers, diplomats, and administrators, the claim that military prowess was the most admirable form of human fulfilment continued to be made. Even the most pacific sixteenth-century landowners saw themselves as having an affinity with the bloodthirsty heroes of the classical epics and chivalric legends on which they were reared. They liked to imagine the warlike feats of their ancestors; and when they were buried, their funeral effigies and brasses depicted them in full armour, dressed for battle, even if they had never seen active service.[15] The ability of the peerage and gentry to raise their tenants, servants, and dependants for military service was crucial to the security of the early Tudor kings. In 1513 virtually all fit members of the nobility turned out for Henry VIII's campaign in France, in the same way as their ancestors had done for Henry V at Agincourt.[16]

Just as some late medieval writers had suggested that to win a battle was 'the greatest good and the greatest glory of life',[17] so many Tudor military men regarded the elation of warfare as a uniquely satisfying experience. 'What more excellent spectacle can there be to them that are lords and conquerors?' asked Barnaby Barnes, who had served with the second Earl of Essex in France in 1591, 'than in the open fields to pursue their enemies in flight? To wound, slaughter and captivate them? To see their horses with the riders distressed? To see many of them which have received wounds neither to find surgery nor means of escape, some of them desperately to resist and presently to fall down? Lastly, to see the whole camp covered with weapons, armour, and dead bodies, and the ground dyed into purple with their enemies' blood?'[18] What fun indeed!

During the sixteenth century, the Crown, when raising armies for foreign service, gradually replaced the magnates and their retinues with foreign mercenaries and national levies, conscripted on a county basis. There was no standing army, other than a few garrisons, but, under the medieval Statute of Winchester 1285 and the Militia Act 1558, all citizens were required to keep arms and every able-bodied man of military age was a potential soldier. In practice, from 1573, those eligible for militia service were divided into trained and untrained, with only the trained bands being summoned for annual exercises, and then only for purposes of home defence. The notion that all the male civilian population should have military skills was increasingly out of touch with reality.[19]

The aristocracy were slow to relinquish the belief that military prowess was their particular forte, distinguishing them from the rest of society. Although their household retainers had diminished in number and their tenants were less ready to perform military service, the magnates remained capable of raising troops at times of need and, as Lord Lieutenants, they played their part in organizing

ANTIQVA IN-
SIGNIA FAMI-
LIÆ DES EWES
DYNASTARVM
DE KESSEL.

INSIGNIA
GESTA AB
EO RVM POS-
TERIS.

Figure 2.1 Clad in full armour, with his head on a cushion and a fierce dog at his feet, this military figure looks every inch a medieval knight. He is Geerardt (or Garrat) D'Ewes (d. 1591), a London bookseller and publisher.

the militia.[20] A contemporary described the stocks of weapons still to be found in the houses of the Elizabethan nobility—'the very sight whereof appalled my courage'. Before the Civil War, agreed John Aubrey, the halls of JPs were 'dreadful to behold'.[21] The Tudor gentry were expected to display a 'more manly courage' than the rest of the population. Indeed, the government thought it important that the trained bands should be led by local gentlemen, even if they were personally unskilled in military matters.[22] Many believed that noble or gentle status needed to be revalidated in every generation. A man descended from a noble house, thought Sir Richard Barckley in 1598, 'must take upon him a thousand enterprises in the wars, offer himself to an infinite number of perils, hazard his life, shed his blood to die in the bed of honour; otherwise he shall be accounted a carpet knight,[*] an effeminate man, and had in contempt'.[23] The courtesy writer James Cleland ruled in 1607 that, however learned in arts and sciences a young nobleman might be, and however perfect in all exercises, he was not worthy to be esteemed unless he also possessed the virtue of valour.[24] Urging on the Herefordshire gentry in the reign of Charles I, Viscount Scudamore declared that 'he which is a gentleman, and hath a lusty body, doth degenerate from the virtue of his ancestors and is unworthy of the name of a man' if he declined to undergo regular military training.[25] In 1632 the poet and parson George Herbert took an essentially medieval view when he wrote that 'all gentlemen...are to know the use of their arms: and as the husbandman labours for them, so must they fight for, and defend them, when occasion calls'. He could have been paraphrasing *Piers Plowman*.[26] In the Restoration era, the scholar Isaac Barrow could still identify courage as a virtue without which one could only 'equivocally' be a gentleman.[27]

The Royalist Sir Henry Slingsby tells us that when Charles I took an army to Scotland in 1639, 'the greatest part of the nobility and gentry of this kingdom was personally engaged'; and in the ensuing Civil War, a third of the peerage led armies in the field. The historian Clarendon thought that it would have been impossible for Parliament to have raised an army, had the Earl of Essex not consented to lead it.[28] But, despite the presence of a hard core of professionals who had gained military experience fighting on the Continent in the Thirty Years War for the Dutch, the Swedes, the Spaniards, and other foreign armies, it soon became obvious that eighty years of domestic peace had taken

---

[*] That is, one who was more at home in a lady's boudoir than on the battlefield.

their toll. As one of Charles I's chaplains later recalled, 'the nobility and gentry of England, in the generality of them, had so much degenerated from the martial prowess of their ancestors...that, in the beginning of these unnatural wars, there were very few to be had ... fit to have command in an army or that knew anything belonging to the art of war'.[29] As the war went on, many of the aristocratic commanders on both sides were superseded; and the outcome of Charles I's defeat was the emergence during the Commonwealth and Protectorate of England's first professional standing army.

Until that time, however, military training remained a necessary part of a gentleman's education. An essential qualification was horsemanship, particularly riding the so-called great horse, 'the theatre on whose back heroic men should act out the part of their valour'.[30] The unwillingness of the universities to offer training in riding and fencing led many young gentlemen to go off to the noble academies of France and Italy. It also stimulated a long series of abortive projects for noble academies in England.[31] In 1751 the great-grandchildren of Edward Hyde, Earl of Clarendon, left his papers to Oxford University, so that the proceeds of publishing them could be used to fund a riding academy, which their ancestor had recommended as essential for a gentleman's education. The university chose to accumulate the interest and, to its eternal shame, used it in 1872 to establish the Clarendon Laboratory.[32]

In the early modern period, the military value of the mounted knight steadily diminished. With the use of artillery, the development of siegecraft, and the enhanced role of infantry, warfare became technically more demanding. There were fewer pitched battles and there was less opportunity for hand-to-hand combat or the clash of men on horseback. Military success depended on the collective actions of well-trained armies, not on dazzling feats of individual heroism. Disciplined obedience was what mattered most; sheer animal vigour became less important. As the old hands complained, 'it is nothing nowadays to be a soldier, for they never come to pitched fields, as they were wont in our old English wars'.[33] The Restoration satirist Samuel Butler would sardonically comment that 'a hero was nothing but a fellow of a great stature and strong limbs, who was able to carry a heavier load of arms on his back, and strike harder blows, than those of a lesser size; and, therefore, since the invention of arms came up, there can be no true hero in great fights, for all men's abilities are so levelled by gunshot, that a dwarf may do as heroic feats of arms that way as a giant, and if he be a good marksman, be too hard for the stoutest Hector and Achilles too'. Gunpowder, agreed an eighteenth-century commentator, made warfare 'depend more upon science than personal courage or bodily strength'.[34]

Even so, bravery continued to be the soldier's most essential qualification. It was 'the greatest, the most generous and heroicallest virtue'.[35] The word 'virtue' literally meant manliness and it was often used as a synonym for courage and military prowess.[36] Among the many terms for effectiveness in battle, two of the most frequently employed in the fifteenth and sixteenth centuries were 'manhood' and 'manfulness'. 'So manly a man' was the Lord Montague, says the chronicler, that he spared no one.[37] The Elizabethan hero Sir Richard Grenville, at dinner with Spanish captains, so as to show what he was made of, crushed the wine glasses, chewed, and swallowed them, the blood pouring out of his mouth.[38]

In the upbringing of boys, a high value was set on physical courage. James I's son Prince Henry was praised because, as a child, he wept much less than other boys when he fell over and hurt himself, and, at the age of 7, successfully beat up a boy who was a year older.[39] The endurance of pain was a basic feature of contemporary boys' education, for floggings and the teaching of grammar were inseparable.[40] Grammar school boys were encouraged to engage in mock battles, and informal fighting between schoolboys was common. The pacific divine Richard Baxter claimed never to have struck a man in anger, 'save boys at school when we boxed each other', and never to have harmed anyone, 'save once, when I was a lad: I hurt a man's leg with playful wrestling'.[41] Physical combat, of a more or less ritualized kind, was a part of masculine culture at every social level. Just as the upper classes had their 'roisters', 'hectors', and duellists, so the lower classes had their street bullies, 'ruffians', and 'roaring boys'. These were the braggarts and fighters whom contemporaries called 'swaggering fellows' or 'manly men' and who supposedly regarded murder as 'a manly deed'.[42] There were 'wild Hectorian gentlemen' who killed people in drunken affrays and gangs of disorderly young men who 'jetted' through the streets at night, breaking windows and insulting passers-by.[43] In Elizabethan Shrewsbury, fights among schoolboys and apprentices regularly accompanied the annual election of town bailiffs.[44] In the taverns, drinking and gambling easily led to violent quarrels.[45] Sometimes such violence was a matter not of random assault, but of stylized encounters as rule-regulated as the aristocratic duel.[46] In 1599 the Worcestershire quarter sessions had to deal with the case of three husbandmen from the village of Hagley, who, armed with bills and pikestaffs, went to the top of a nearby hill 'and hooted and shouted and called for the cowardly boys of Old Swinford to come forth' to fight with them. But most brawls and assaults were regarded as private matters and did not reach the law courts.[47] Everywhere, social conditions encouraged physical self-reliance; in the seventeenth century, it was common to go armed when travelling on the roads, especially at night.[48]

Violence and masculinity were closely associated. The Tudor *Homilies* complained that 'the common sort of men' regarded meekness as 'a token of a womanish cowardness; and therefore they think it is a man's part to fume in anger, to fight with fist and staff'.[49] 'If a man be a roister, and knowing how to fight his fight,' lamented the preacher John Northbrooke in 1571, 'then he is called by the name of honesty. If he can kill a man, and dare rob upon the highway, he is called a tall man, and a valiant man of his hands.'[50] Football and other popular sports were extremely violent, often leading to physical injury and sometimes to death. Horse racing at Doncaster had to be suspended in 1615 because it provoked 'suits, quarrels, murders and bloodshed'.[51] Cockfighting was praised as a display of aggressive masculinity, while hunting, archery, and wrestling were obvious simulations of warfare.[52]

'Men of feminine courage', as Thomas Hobbes called them, were widely disdained. The 'blemish of cowardice' stuck to the poet Sir John Suckling after he and two or three others in 1634 attacked Sir John Digby outside a playhouse, only to be put to ignominious flight when Digby and his attendant vigorously fought back.[53] A Gloucestershire conscript who wept openly when called up for service in Ireland in 1609 was mocked by his comrades as 'cotqueen, milksop, dishwash'—all terms with feminine associations.[54] Women were generally believed to be attracted by displays of masculine courage and to despise cowards. It was often they who egged on duellists and fighters, and taunted the hesitant.[55] 'Women will account thee ... a dastard if thou be not venturous,' wrote a Jacobean author; and 'the name of a dastard' was 'a base by-word of great reproach'. Writing in *The Spectator* a century later, Joseph Addison agreed: 'nothing recommends a man more to the female sex than courage'.[56]*

---

* The phallic associations of warfare were made only too apparent in one of the banners carried by Royalist soldiers in the Civil War. It depicted 'a naked man with sword in hand, and something else in readiness', with the motto *In utrumque paratus*, indicating that the bearer was prepared to fight with either weapon; *A Catalogue of Coronet Devises, both in the Kings and the Parliaments side, in the Late Warres*, in Henry Estienne, *The Art of Making Devises*, trans. T. B[lount] (1650), 74.

Physical toughness was regarded as essentially a male quality, for there was little explicit recognition of the courage shown by women who repeatedly underwent the life-threatening agonies of early modern childbirth.[57] Literary compilations celebrated Boadicea-like heroines of biblical and classical times, the female equivalent of the Nine Worthies.[58] These were figures from a mythical past, but they had their early modern counterparts. When the French landed on the Isle of Wight in August 1545, they were repulsed by 'certain women', who 'fought and shot their arrows so swiftly that they did incredible hurt'.[59] During the English Civil War, many females displayed bravery, defending their homes or carrying material in sieges. Some even fought as soldiers.[60] At all periods, there were women who dressed as men and joined the army or the Navy, or who led rioters as female 'captains'.[61] Some women were involved in duels and other violent encounters;[62] and in the early eighteenth century there were even female professional boxers.[63] A substantial minority of serious crimes of violence was committed by women.[64]

Courageous women might be praised for their 'masculine' spirit, or described as 'viragos' (manlike women), a term which had not yet taken on its pejorative meaning.[65] But they were regarded as aberrations from the norm. A few contemporaries conceded that women could be just as brave as men and just as effective in warfare. One feminist tract even made the case for female soldiers and generals, deploring the practice of stigmatizing cowardly men as 'effeminate' and of praising courageous women as 'manly'.[66] Throughout the early modern period, however, women were much less likely than men to carry weapons, to take part in fights, or to commit assaults.[67] Theirs was supposed to be the courage of loyalty, quiet suffering, and stoical endurance; physical courage in battle was not a quality which they were expected to display and they lost no face if they did not do so. The very idea of a martial woman was profoundly incompatible with contemporary assumptions about gender identities, which grew more rigid on this point during the course of the eighteenth century.[68]

For women, therefore, there was no question of achieving fulfilment by military prowess. But, for men, the most honourable death remained death in battle, sanctified in the sixteenth century by nationalist sentiment and religious approbation. 'I had lief be wounded and die for the right and worship of England than be taken alive of England's enemies.' Thus a textbook for schoolboys in 1519.[69] 'Dulce et decorum est pro patria mori' was a 'godly sweet sentence', thought the Edwardian preacher Thomas Becon; while the Homilies taught that those slain in foreign war won 'an honest commendation in this world' for their valour; and, dying with a good conscience in serving God, their prince, and their country, were 'children of eternal salvation'. Arthur Golding wrote of Sir Philip Sidney that he died 'of manly wounds...in the open field, in martial manner, the honourablest death that can be desired, and best beseeming a Christian knight'.[70] The Jacobean minister William Gouge declared that 'for a soldier to die in the field in a good cause, it is as for a preacher to die in a pulpit'.[71] In this way, the prospect of honour in this life and enduring fame thereafter continued to be the primary incentive to perform deeds of physical courage. By inspiring troops with a love of glory, by flattering the dead and the wounded, and by heaping ignominy on the cowards who ran away, rulers and governments persuaded successive generations of soldiers and sailors to do their bidding.

In Elizabethan and Jacobean times quasi-chivalric values of this kind were encouraged by the jousts, tilts, and 'barriers',* which until 1625 were a regular feature of life at the royal court. These colourful pageants provided a stage on which ambitious young courtiers could establish a reputation for dashing heroism.[72] Sixty years later, an onlooker could still recall the magnificent sight of Sir James Scudamore, who, in the 1590s, entered 'the tiltyard in a handsome equipage, all in complete armour, embellished with plumes, his beaver close, mounted upon a very high bounding horse (I have seen the shoes of his horse glitter above the heads of all the people)...Her Majesty Queen Elizabeth, with a train of ladies, like the stars in the firmament, and the whole court looking upon him with a very gracious aspect'.[73] Militarily anachronistic though they were, such occasions kept alive the idealization of equestrian prowess and physical valour (pl. 3).

So did the chivalric romances, which were a conspicuous element in contemporary reading, particularly from the end of the sixteenth century, when translations of the Spanish and Portuguese romances of *Palmerin* and *Amadis de Gaule* reached England, adding to the already considerable volume of chivalric literature in circulation.[74] With their emphasis on 'exploits of wars' and their deliberate intention 'to set on fire the lusty courages of young gentlemen',[75] these works contributed to the chivalric vogue which coloured the aspirations of courtiers and apprentices alike, and in the 1610s and 1620s

---

* Named after the palisades enclosing the ground in which the tournament took place.

gave a romantic flavour to the military exercises of the trained bands of London and the provincial cities.[76] Their popularity encouraged the extensive use in literary panegyric and on funeral monuments of the terms 'heroic' and 'heroical' as a form of obsequious praise. Lord Herbert of Cherbury (d. 1648) believed his fifteenth-century ancestor Sir Richard Herbert of Colebrook to have been an 'incomparable hero... more than is famed of Amadis de Gaul, or the Knight of the Sun'.[77]

Much contemporary historiography was strongly bellicose. In the late fifteenth century, William Caxton's revival of chivalric values had invoked Richard I, Edward I, Edward III, and other military heroes of the medieval past.[78] Henry VIII's French wars had been a self-conscious attempt to emulate the glories of Agincourt, accompanied by translations of Tito Livio's life of Henry V (1513) and of Froissart's chronicles (1523–5). Under Elizabeth, a great deal was made of John of Gaunt's 'conquest' of Castile in the fourteenth century, and of 'brave Talbot', the fifteenth-century Earl of Shrewsbury who was the 'terror of the French'; in the later seventeenth century, it was claimed that French mothers were still quietening their crying children by threatening them that Talbot would come.[79] The English soldier of fortune John Smythe provoked a quarrel at a dinner in Antwerp in 1568 by asserting the superior bravery of the English, citing Poitiers, the Black Prince in Spain, the *condottiere* Sir John Hawkwood in Italy, and the conquest of Cyprus by Richard I.[80] The only book to be officially prescribed by the Elizabethan Privy Council for study in the grammar schools was Christopher Ocland's *Anglorum Praelia* (1580), a xenophobic account of English conquests in France, battles in Scotland, and adventures in Spain.[81] In the almanacs, Henry VIII's capture of Boulogne in 1544 was represented throughout the seventeenth century, along with the defeat of the Armada, as one of the great dates of English history.[82] The French campaigns of Edward III and Henry V were repeatedly invoked: in the 1620s, in the wars against Louis XIV, and again in the Seven Years War.[83]

Throughout the early modern period, 'high courage and manliness' were claimed as defining national qualities. The English, thought Francis Bacon, were 'a choleric and warlike nation'. In 1657 in his guide to would-be young poets, Joshua Poole suggested as suitable epithets for his fellow countrymen: 'stout, courageous, valiant, truehearted, hardy, bold, audacious, adventurous, warlike'. John Milton invoked 'the old English fortitude', while the Puritan lady Lucy

Hutchinson was convinced that the English could 'easily...subdue the world', if they wished to.[84] In the reign of Anne, the victories of Marlborough produced an orgy of self-congratulation, with the superiority of English valour being attributed to the climate, the constitution, and the way in which English children were brought up.[85] 'Our men are the stoutest and best,' claimed Daniel Defoe in 1726, 'because, strip them naked from the waist upwards, and give them no weapons at all but their hands and heels, and turn them into a room or stage, with the like number of other men of any nation, man for man, and they shall beat the best men you shall find in the world.'[86]

For Tudor commanders, Roman valour was as important an inspiration as medieval chivalry. Not that the two traditions were alternatives, for chivalric tradition had been much influenced by classical example.[87] The people of Rome had famously regarded 'no glory so great, no renown so honourable' as that which had been gained by military valour; their martial discipline was exemplary; and they had honoured 'valiantness' above all other virtues. By equating virtue with valour they had laid the foundations of their greatness.[88] When the first Earl of Essex died in 1576, while campaigning in Ireland, the preacher at his funeral declared that he was, 'for prowess, magnanimity and high courage, to be compared to the old Roman captains'. His fellow officer Sir John Norris was later described as 'a new Hector, another Alexander, or rather a second Caesar'.[89]

Medieval warriors had not usually been highly educated, but, in the sixteenth century, under humanist influence and with the growing elaboration of military science, learning came to be regarded as essential for a commander; and the combination of arms and letters was particularly admired. It was well exemplified by such figures as Sir Edward Vere, who commanded a regiment in the Netherlands and was killed in 1629 at the siege of Bois-Le-Duc, leaving behind a thousand-page manuscript translation of Polybius. 'All summer in the field, all winter in his study', commented John Hampden.[90]

This neoclassical stress upon the value of military accomplishment intensified in the mid-seventeenth century, when it acquired quasi-democratic overtones. In civic–republican theory, the preservation of liberty required every citizen to possess weapons, whereas most seventeenth-century rulers wanted their own forces and were increasingly uneasy about the prospect of arming the whole people. Hence the opposition of figures like the Puritan antiquary William Prynne to the idea of a standing army in place of a national militia; and the desire of John Streater, the Cromwellian soldier-cum-pamphleteer, for 'the begetting and increasing of heroicness in the breast of a people'.[91] The political theorist James Harrington believed that 'the glory of a man on earth' could 'go no higher' than fighting in a just cause, while the pamphleteer Richard Hawkins defended Cromwell's campaign in Flanders on the Machiavellian grounds that vigorous participation in a successful war was a sign of national 'virtue' and an essential antidote to ease and indolence.[92] Roman history, it was repeatedly claimed, showed that war was a necessary healing and purging ritual for an 'effeminate' state, given over to softness and luxury. Warfare was invigorating, peace debilitating, and the fall of the Roman empire a warning of what would happen if martial discipline and 'manly exercises' were neglected.[93] This had been the refrain of the group of militant Protestants and unemployed soldiery who in the early years of James I's reign clustered around Henry, Prince of Wales, fretting at the King's peace with Spain and urging the resumption of a more aggressive foreign policy.[94] Throughout the early modern period, there were diatribes against the 'effeminizing' effect of material prosperity: 'dainty diet and womanlike wantonness' were repeatedly blamed by swordsmen, fencing masters, and other interested parties for turning English youth into 'tenderlings' and 'cowardly dastards'.[95]

As well as testifying to the nation's moral health, military prowess was also valued as a means of social ascent for outstanding individuals. Success on the battlefield, or even the tiltyard, earned honours, financial rewards, and titles for many Tudor gentlemen. Occasionally, as in the spectacular cases of Charles Brandon, Henry VIII's military commander, who became first Duke of Suffolk and married the King's sister, or, later on, John Churchill, Queen Anne's captain-general, made first Duke of Marlborough, it could pitchfork successful soldiers into the highest ranks of the peerage. In deference to the realities of social change, heraldic writers conceded that public service and the law were also acceptable routes to honour. But most of them continued to give primacy to military virtue.[96] The Essex gentleman Thomas Lucas refused to buy a title from James I because he thought such distinctions worthless 'unless they were gained by heroic actions'.[97] Conversely, one of the reasons given for rejecting titles of honour by the Quaker apologist Robert Barclay, himself the son of a Scottish mercenary who had served under Gustavus Adolphus of Sweden, was that 'the most frequent' source of such titles, and the one 'accounted among men most honourable', was 'fighting, or some great martial exploit'.[98] In medieval fashion, Elizabethan commanders in the field frequently conferred immediate knighthood upon those who had displayed outstanding valour in battle; and so did Charles I during the Civil War.[99] He also issued medals for bravery and loyal service, as did his Parliamentary opponents, who continued the practice during the Commonwealth and extended it to the Navy.[100]

It was unusual for ordinary troops to receive such public recognition. When Tudor and Stuart armies fought overseas, the rank and file were usually there because they had been pressed by the authorities or driven by hardship to seek this dangerous means of subsistence. Often they were vagrants and masterless men who had been swept up by the authorities. They hoped for spoils and booty, but were not in search of honour and glory. A Jacobean preacher dismissively described them as 'the base and faeculent vulgar, whose muddy brains and dull spirits neither can conceive nor dare attempt so high designs'.[101] It was even alleged that many common soldiers, on their return, would boast in their cups 'how many places they had fled and run away, taking as it were a glory to tell who had fled fastest'.[102] In the eighteenth century, the recruitment of other ranks was closely related to the civilian labour market, with the armed forces usually the employer of last resort.[103]

Not that their leaders always had higher motives; it was not just the hope of glory which led young gentlemen to go on overseas campaigns. As one historian has drily remarked, 'those most deeply influenced by the knightly ideal were nearly always the most in need of money'.[104] Late medieval warfare had been a trade as much as a theatre of honour; and in the early modern period, military adventure abroad continued to offer younger sons and impoverished gentry the prospect of plunder, ransom, and emolument.[105] 'The soldiers say they fight for honour,' remarked the sardonic lawyer John Selden, 'when the truth is they have their honour in their pocket.'[106]

Yet there is no reason why we should not take at face value the endlessly repeated assertions by members of the social elite that war was attractive because it gave them the opportunity to display what they believed to be the highest qualities of manhood. 'Worthy men go to wars with joy, hoping to gain honour,' as Margaret Cavendish put it in 1664.[107] For centuries, wars had been initiated, less for strategic reasons than because aristocrats brought up in a military ethos were culturally predisposed to war. Sir John Harington pointed out in 1605 that 'our captains and men of war' did not want peace; and Thomas Hobbes would remark that 'there is no honour military but by war'.

His contemporary, the future bishop Robert Sanderson, believed it to be 'a constant observation, in all times and places, that the embroiling most commonwealths in wars ... hath grown from the restlessness of some ambitious spirits and their immoderate thirst after honour and glory'.[108] It was the desire for honour which accounted for the vogue of the pitched battle in European warfare at the end of the Middle Ages;[109] and the same incentive helped to make it common in the sixteenth century for young gentlemen to spend a period of military service with volunteers in Europe as part of their education. From the reign of Elizabeth onwards, there was a steady exodus of officers and men to fight on the Continent, first in the Dutch war of independence and then in the larger conflict which engulfed Europe after 1618. Thousands of English mercenaries fought in the Thirty Years War. Some of them emulated the knight-errant tradition by fighting in succession on both sides: the runaway London apprentice Sydenham Poyntz, disgusted with the 'dog's life' he was leading, and resolving that 'to live and die a soldier would be as noble in death as life', enlisted first with the Elector of Saxony and then with his opponent, the Emperor. Sir James Turner, a Scottish mercenary, recalled that the maxim of 'military men' in Germany at that time was: 'So we serve our masters honestly, it is no matter what master we serve.' National loyalties came second to personal fulfilment.[110]

Elizabethan campaigns against Irish rebels had afforded opportunities for swordsmen seeking military action, but the Queen's reluctance, and that of her successor, James I, to engage in European warfare generated a continuous undercurrent of discontent from 'martialists' who wanted the chance to prove themselves.[111] Their opportunities diminished further when Charles I discontinued courtly tournaments and, in the 1630s, pursued a pacific foreign policy in Europe. Those seeking a reputation for military prowess had little option but to enlist with a foreign power. Hence the efflux throughout the early Stuart period of 'lusty young men, desirous, of a gallantness of mind, to adventure themselves and see the wars'. The names of some of these 'brave English chieftains achieving honour by their valour in foreign countries' were duly listed by a contemporary chronicler.[112]

In 1578 Philip Sidney was warned by his friend Hubert Languet against fighting in the Netherlands, 'out of mere love of fame and honour, and to have an opportunity of displaying your courage'. This did not stop him from advising his brother Robert, when he was travelling on the Continent in 1580, that, 'if there were any good wars', he 'should go to them'.[113] War was 'the field where all cases of manhood [were] determined', the stage on which to display those qualities of courage, bravura, high-spiritedness, and self-control which their admirers called 'generosity', 'magnanimity', or 'greatness of heart', and which they believed could be fully exhibited only by 'prowess' (another key word) in battle. 'I love them for their virtue's sake, and for their greatness of mind,' wrote the second Earl of Essex of military men. 'We . . . say of a man that is valiant', agreed the Elizabethan preacher George Gifford, that 'he is a man of a great mind.'[114]

This was not empty verbiage, for contempt for death was thought to indicate greatness of soul; and the display of physical courage in the face of danger showed an ability to master the weaker instincts. Men who could control their passions in this manner could reasonably be expected to show generosity of spirit in other contexts. 'Of all honour,' thought the political writer William Sprigg in 1657, 'that's truest which hath been won by the sword in a purple field of blood'; the 'best gentleman' was the one who made his fortunes by 'hewing them out of his enemies' bowels'. As the Elizabethan military adventurer Sir Roger Williams had put it, the more who died, the greater the honour of the fight.[115]

In an age when the word 'bravery' meant both courage and ostentatious clothing, and when soldiers on active service were exempted from the sumptuary laws relating to dress because 'their bravery was their honour', there was a theatrical quality to warfare.[116] 'Fail never in time of wars', James I advised his son, 'to be galliardest and bravest, both in clothes and countenance.'[117] The Earl of Leicester described Roger Williams, at the taking of Duisburg in 1586, running up and down under enemy fire, clad in a golden helmet with a great plume of feathers.[118]*

In this quasi-chivalric world, personal glory could be more important than the achievement of the military objective. Commanders were more concerned to make a name for boldness than for judgement and they preferred to fight alongside their troops in the front line rather than to conduct operations from the rear. Troops were encouraged to attack the enemy too soon; and it was thought more honourable to take a town by the sword than to starve it out.[119] Officers sometimes

---

* Sir Edward Coke thought that expensive clothes could help to save the soldier's life by making him appear a suitable candidate for ransom; *Commons Debates 1628*, iv, ed. Mary Frear Keeler et al. (New Haven, 1978), 92.

drew lots for the privilege of being the first to engage the enemy, and military discipline was often impeded by the determination of some hot-headed youth to achieve glory by a spectacular, if unhelpful, demonstration of his personal courage, much to the disgust of the professional soldiers, who believed in discipline.[120] At the siege of Guisnes in 1558, the English commander, Lord Grey of Wilton, refused to surrender, although his position had become untenable, and urged his troops to fight to the death for the sake of 'honesty, duty and fame'. But the soldiers mutinied, declaring that 'they for his vain glory would not sell their lives'.[121] On the naval expeditions to Cadiz in 1596 and the Azores in 1597, there was much jostling and rivalry between Sir Walter Ralegh, the Earl of Essex, and the other leaders as to who should get at the enemy first, so as to reap most honour and booty.[122]

When Edward Herbert was serving as a volunteer at the siege of Jülich in 1610, he was challenged to show his mettle by the Frenchman Balagny, 'one of the gallantest men in the world, having killed eight or nine men in single fight'. Announcing, 'Je suis Balagny, allons voir qui faira le mieux,' the Frenchman rushed out of the trenches, into a hail of enemy bullets, defying Herbert to follow him, which he did, both miraculously surviving and thereby winning the bubble reputation in the cannon's mouth.[123] This was not leading from the front, but a bid to secure attention, in accordance with Baldassare Castiglione's cynical advice in his influential work *Il Libro del Cortegiano* (1528) that the courtier in battle should separate himself from 'the multitude' and 'undertake notable and bold feats' on his own, having first taken care to ensure that they would be witnessed by influential persons. There was no point in being brave if nobody was there to see it.[124]

Equally egotistic was the practice of issuing individual challenges as an alternative to full battle between opposing armies. In Elizabethan times, the most famous of these challenges was made by the second Earl of Essex at the siege of Rouen in 1591, when he invited the French governor to single combat, in which he would maintain, not only that the quarrel of the French King (which the English troops were supporting) was more just than that of the Catholic League, but also that 'my mistress is more beautiful than yours'.[125] When Edward de Vere, Earl of Oxford, on his European travels, arrived in Palermo in 1572, he issued a general challenge 'to fight a combat with any whatsoever, in the defence of his prince and country'. To his disgust, no Italian came forward to accept this invitation.[126]

The early years of the English Civil War were marked by a series of such challenges, in which individual commanders invited their opposite numbers to settle the issue by personal combat. At Edgehill, the Earl of Northampton had to decline a challenge from Lord Brooke because 'he was gross and corpulent and therefore unfit for a duel'.[127] In 1643 the Earl of Newcastle sought trial by battle with the Parliamentary commander, Ferdinando, Lord Fairfax, 'conformable to the examples of our heroic ancestors, who used not to spend their time in scratching one another out of holes, but in pitched fields determined their doubts'. Fairfax had the future on his side when he rejected this invitation, saying that he proposed to fight the war 'without following the rules of Amadis de Gaule or the Knight of the Sun'.[128]*

Of course, Newcastle was a dinosaur, like Essex before him. Once it came to be accepted that war was something to be waged systematically, in pursuit of a defined political objective, there was little room for those who took up arms merely to achieve honour and who ranked the winning of personal glory higher than the attainment of strategic goals. Significantly, one of the questions which the young King Edward VI had been invited to ponder by his political instructor, William Thomas, was: 'whether they that fight for their own glory are good and faithful soldiers?'[129] There was a difference between war as a theatre of honour and war as realpolitik.

THE WANING OF THE MILITARY IDEAL

> *No more*
> *Thy force nor fortitude, as heretofore,*
> *Will gain thee glory.*
>
> Homer, *Odyssey* 22, lines 693–5; trans. George Chapman, 1616

The steady trend during the sixteenth and seventeenth centuries was towards the evolution of soldiering as a specialized occupation, rather than an activity in which all gentlemen and many citizens could and would effectively participate. The nucleus of these emerging professionals was the corps of paid troops and professional 'captains' who made their livelihood by manning garrisons and fighting campaigns

---

* Francis Bacon had remarked in 1616 that 'the law of England is not taken out of Amadis de Gaul'; James Spedding, *The Letters and the Life of Francis Bacon* (1861–74), vi. 109.

for the Tudor monarchs in Scotland, Ireland, France, and the Nether-lands.[1] To them should be added the thousands of officers and men who chose to fight for other powers as volunteers or mercenaries in European wars. Some spent their lives abroad. Others returned to assist in selecting and drilling the trained bands. When the Civil War broke out in 1642, it was the veterans, back from the Continent, who provided the nucleus of commanders on either side.[2]

So, even before the great mobilization of the 1640s, there existed a cadre of professional soldiers, constituting a separate military subcul-ture and, in some ways, estranged from the rest of the population. Jealous in honour, sudden and quick in quarrel, they had their own standards and conventions, marked by extreme touchiness at the slightest imputation of cowardice, a penchant for violence, and a distinct contempt for lawyers and courts.[3] The Civil War temporarily interrupted this shift to military specialization by involving a tenth of the adult male population in armed hostilities. But its outcome was the emergence between 1646 and 1660 of a professional standing army. With its disbandment at the Restoration, many swordsmen went abroad again, returning only in the late 1680s.[4] Charles II retained a small permanent establishment of garrisons and household guards. They formed the nucleus of the often drunken and disorderly young men about town who helped to make the capital such a dangerous place. The Restoration rake, it has been rightly said, was an officer with no wars to go to.[5] The abolition in 1660 of tenure by knight service seemed another nail in the coffin of the aristocratic military tradition.[6] But in practice the officers of the new guards regiments were drawn exclusively from noble or gentry families.[7]

Between 1689 and 1713 the wars against Louis XIV led to the formation of a large standing army which was reduced but not wholly disbanded when the conflict ended. Although commissions in it were held by career professionals as well as gentlemen, the tone of the officer class, particularly in the higher ranks, remained socially pre-tentious. The notion that the gentry were a military reserve ready to be called upon for the country's defence died hard.[8] Through the eighteenth century and beyond, the system of purchasing commis-sions retarded the complete professionalization of the army and enabled gentry families to supply generations of army officers. Noble-men could still raise whole regiments; and the tradition of military service by gentlemen continued until the twentieth century. The of-ficers of the Navy, which had since 1677 insisted on lower-deck experience for all those seeking commissions, were, at least until the end of the eighteenth century, socially much more diverse.[9]

Soldiering had become a full-time profession much like any other, but it retained an aristocratic flavour at commissioned level; and many contemporaries continued to regard it as the noblest and most honourable occupation for a man.[10] Within this distinctly aggressive milieu, personal courage, not to say recklessness, continued to be prized. Of Major Richard Creed, who was killed at the battle of Blenheim in 1704, it was said that he was 'never more himself than when he look'd an enemy in the face'.[11] From such men came a large proportion of the duellists of the late seventeenth and eighteenth centuries; while the bastardy cases of eighteenth-century London suggest that military personnel were exceptionally active in the seduction of women.[12]

The professional army officer was a very different figure from the medieval knight; he could not independently seek glory for himself, but had to subordinate his own ambitions to the commands of his superiors. In the world at large, his prowess, though greatly admired, was no longer regarded either as the highest form of endeavour or as a necessary accomplishment for persons of rank or social ambition. In the later seventeenth century, the nobility and gentry became overwhelmingly civilian in style and appearance. Their castles, long in decay, had been 'slighted' after the Civil Wars,[13] their stocks of weapons had diminished or been converted into mere decoration, in patterned displays of 'furniture of arms' or sculpted trophies, and they were ceasing to represent themselves on their funeral monuments as military figures.[14] In the drama of the late seventeenth century, military reputation dwindled in importance as a component of aristocratic honour.[15]

The educational theorists were ceasing to recommend military training for young gentlemen. In 1700 John Wallis, Oxford's professor of geometry, maintained that, for those entering public life, a training in logic and philosophy was more valuable than any amount of equestrian skill. Riding the great horse had lost its military utility, because heavy armour was made useless by firearms; and the Civil War had brought in 'a ruder way of riding'. 'The nature of fighting is now changed,' thought Daniel Defoe in 1697; it needed time and application to master fortification, gunnery, and engineering.[16] In any case, martial exercises did not appeal to the London beaux who gave so much attention to their dress, their periwigs, their perfume and powder, and who travelled by coach or sedan chair, 'riding on horseback being now thought too troublesome'.[17] During the course of the eighteenth century, gentlemen gradually stopped wearing the swords which had once been their indispensable badge of rank. After Beau Nash, the great choreographer of the new civility, had forbidden the carrying of weapons in good society, it was said that 'a sword seen in the streets of Bath would raise as great an alarm as a mad dog'. By 1780 swords were no longer worn anywhere with informal dress.[18]

In the words of the historian Edward Gibbon, the exercise of arms had ceased to be an occasional duty and had become a separate trade. The nation gave itself over to 'the peaceful occupations of trade, manufactures and husbandry', leaving national defence to be the business of a semi-professional army under the control of a civilian parliament.[19] It was a momentous change, made possible by the advanced nature of Britain's economic development and by its reliance on naval strength rather than land forces for its everyday security. As the future bishop Thomas Sprat had pointed out in 1667, it was now 'rightly understood that British greatness will never be supported or increased in this age, by any other wars but those at sea'. Britain was an island, observed the economist Nicholas Barbon in 1690, and 'therefore requires no military force to defend it'.[20]

Among the population at large, the traditional obligation of all adult males to perform military service at time of need had become increasingly attenuated. At the Restoration the militia had been re-established, but within a decade sank into a decay from which it was not resurrected until the coming of the Seven Years War in 1756. Even then, service was by lot and affected only a small proportion of the population.[21] It is true that in 1689 the Bill of Rights had converted the age-old duty of citizens to keep arms into the right of all Protestant subjects to possess them,[22] that the wars against Louis XIV drew some 15 per cent of adult males of military age into the armed forces, and that that figure would be surpassed during the French Revolutionary and Napoleonic Wars. But throughout the eighteenth century, Britain's rate of military participation per head of population was much lower than that of other European powers.[23]

The long-term consequence of this civilianization of the population and professionalization of the military was that valour and military prowess ceased to be moral qualities expected of all men of ambition and tended instead to be regarded as more akin to the technical qualifications of an occupational group. Fortitude was a necessary virtue for soldiers, thought Thomas Hobbes in the 1660s, but 'for other men, the less they dare, the better it is, both for the commonwealth and for themselves'. With the growth of a specialist defence force, observed Adam Smith in 1766, courage diminished among the bulk of the people, and they grew 'effeminate and dastardly'.[24] As Francis Bacon had noticed a century and a half previously, commerce and manufactures did not encourage a fighting spirit: 'the sedentary and within-door arts, and delicate manufactures (that require the finger rather than the arm)' had a natural 'contrariety to a military disposition'.[25]

This was the abiding lament of those who adhered to the civic-humanist tradition. For them, the new reliance on a professional army seemed a potential threat to liberty, which they sought to diminish by championing the idea of an armed nobility and a popular militia, thus distributing the duty of national defence as widely as possible. In the century after the Restoration of Charles II, republicans like Algernon Sidney kept alive the belief in the importance of martial exercises and a warlike nobility as 'the pillars of manlike liberty'.[26] 'Those old hospitable Gothick halls, hung round with the helmets, breast-plates, and swords of our ancestors,' declared a journalist in 1739, were 'the terror of former ministers, and the check of kings.'[27] A standing army was repeatedly denounced as incompatible with the spirit of a free government. When the Seven Years War broke out, many 'patriots' supported the revival of the militia as a means of eliminating national 'effeminacy' and a political counterbalance to the standing army.[28] To delegate military valour to specialists, maintained the Scottish philosopher Adam Ferguson, was to undermine 'the genius and character of man'.[29]

In the population at large, however, there was always a strong current of hostility to military values. The chivalric ethic never had exclusive sway. Distaste for the wastefulness and brutality of war had been widespread among the medieval administrative class and the traders of London. It was strongly expressed in the late four-teenth and early fifteenth centuries by John Gower, Thomas Hoccleve, John Lydgate, and other contemporary writers.[30] The medieval Church's doctrine of the lawfulness of a just war had never adequately resolved the inherent tension between the military life and the pacific impulse of primitive Christianity. Although the Church had permitted or even encouraged certain forms of military activity, it had unequivocally declared that wars conducted for the sake of glory and self-aggrandizement were morally unacceptable.[31] In the late fourteenth and early fifteenth centuries, Wyclif and some of the Lollards rejected military values altogether, lamenting the admiration extended to those 'that be great warriors and fighters and that destroy and win many lands'. Some of them were strongly pacifist, regarding manslaughter in battle as contrary to the New Testament, and condemning knights who went crusading against heathens in order 'to get them a name in slaying of men'.[32]

In the sixteenth century, these arguments reappeared. Several early Tudor humanists, led by John Colet, Dean of St Paul's, rejected the scholastic doctrine of just war in favour of the Stoic view that all war was fratricide. A member of Henry VII's household defended the King's pacific policy in 1502–3, declaring that it was wrong to praise princes for 'effusion of blood, strife and battles'.[33] In the following reign, Sir Thomas More, though not against war as such, was vehemently hostile to fighting for fighting's sake, his Utopians counting 'nothing so much against glory as glory gotten in war'.[34] The Henrician Protestant Simon Fish published a tract which deplored the 'horrible and dangerous' business of war, arguing that the only lawful wars were wars of defence, and then only if the alternative of buying off the enemy had failed.[35] Bishop Stephen Gardiner, Sir William Paget, and other mid-Tudor statesmen shared these peaceful preferences.[36] In 1578 a military writer lamented that there were some people 'whose conscience be so pure (as they say themselves) that they can allow of no wars either to be good or godly, considering what murders, spoils and other outrages are by them committed'. He would have had in mind the clandestine groups of Anabaptists and Familists, many of whom rejected the state's coercive authority, including the right to make war.[37]

Moralists of all complexions had always been ambivalent about the virtue of bravery in battle, for it so easily slid over into unfeeling cruelty. There was something 'brutish' and inhumane about physical violence, however just the cause.[38] And if the cause was unjust, such violence became reprehensible. In the fifteenth century, even Henry V had declared against wars fought for the sake of worldly glory; and, in the Elizabethan age, the militaristic ninth Earl of Northumberland condemned a warlike disposition as 'barbarous, cruel, inhumane, if necessity requires it not'.[39] Plays like George Chapman's *Bussy D'Ambois* (1607) and Shakespeare's *Coriolanus* (c.1608) represented the bloody self-assertiveness of the vainglorious warrior as a dangerous and antisocial anachronism. The Stoic and early Christian distaste for homicidal heroes like Alexander the Great was frequently expressed. Robert Burton, the Jacobean anatomist of melancholy, thought soldiering an honourable and necessary profession, but he regarded Alexander and his ilk as 'bloody butchers, wicked destroyers and troublers of the world, prodigious monsters, hell-hounds, feral plagues, devourers, common executioners of human kind'. Many others shared his aversion for these 'lawless thieves' and 'great butchers of mankind'.[40] A popular anecdote retailed the reply made by a captured pirate brought before Alexander the Great: he was a pirate, he said, because he had only one ship. 'Had I a fleet, I should be a conqueror.'[41] The contrast between the respective fates of the murderer and the military hero was a long-enduring literary topos.

Godly Protestant preachers still felt the need for Christian knights, like Sir Philip Sidney, to fight and die in the cause of religion, but they were extremely hostile to wars fought merely for the sake of glory and to private duels undertaken in the defence of honour. They admired Christian fortitude, but they held no brief for choleric and boastful swordsmen. Like the early Tudor humanists Erasmus, More, and Vives, they repudiated the values of chivalric romance. Simon Fish, who associated men of war with 'thieves, ruffians, common women and bawds', wanted people to be kept from reading 'wild stories of battles, of love, and other fables', while the educational writer Roger Ascham famously attacked books of chivalry for their glorification of 'open manslaughter and bold bawdry', as in Sir Thomas Malory's *Morte d'Arthur*, where 'those be counted the noblest knights that do kill most men without any quarrel'.[42] The clergy were horrified by the foul language, rape, and robbery associated with sixteenth-century soldiers.[43] Far from being saluted as paragons of human achievement, Tudor military men were viewed with contempt and hostility by many of their civilian contemporaries, who detested 'the profession of cutting of throats'. Hence the strongly defensive element which is present in much contemporary writing about the soldier's life.[44] In a frequently echoed piece of advice, William Cecil, Lord Burghley, warned his son against training his children for the wars: 'for he that sets up...to live by that profession can hardly be an honest man or a good Christian'.[45]

Burghley shared the essentially pacific values of the towns, the lawyers, and the trading classes, many of whom despised the profession of arms 'as a vile and damnable occupation' and held that soldiers were not 'worthy to come into the company of civil people'.[46] It was notorious that common soldiers, coming home from the wars, could 'never again endure either order or labour; and so return but to corrupt the commonwealth with their lawless manners'.[47] At the beginning of Elizabeth's reign, the City of London was reluctant to allow apprentices and craftsmen to engage in military training, lest it lead them into 'idleness and insolency'.[48] According to the poet George Gascoigne in 1575, the common people complained that the chief cause of wars was 'princes' pride'.[49] The extreme difficulty which every late Tudor and early Stuart government found in raising troops to fight in foreign wars speaks for itself.

Sir Philip Sidney himself had observed that behind the golden swords, shining armour, and surface glamour of chivalric display lay the hideous reality of blood, broken weapons, and mangled bodies; and in *The Faerie Queene* Edmund Spenser's Red Cross Knight is advised by a holy man to renounce 'earthly conquest' and the 'guilt of bloody field'.[50] In the seventeenth century, there was an increasing disposition to regard war as an uncivilized activity, sometimes a painful necessity, but in no sense a necessary form of human fulfilment, leave alone the highest form. In one of her poems, Margaret Cavendish painted a horrific picture of a battlefield strewn with mutilated body parts: 'Guts did like sausages their bodies entwine.'[51] Some people undoubtedly enjoyed fighting in the Civil War, but very few admitted it. Most contemporaries would have sympathized with Samuel Hartlib's hopes for the time when 'all at last [would] come to live in plenty and peace &c, and all wars cease'.[52]

The decade of the 1650s was notable for the emergence of a religious sect who would in due course make pacifism one of their guiding beliefs. The Quaker Peace Testimony was formally proclaimed in a *Declaration* of January 1661. Whether it sprang from first principles or was forced upon the Friends by the need to protect themselves against persecution is debatable. But the Testimony was unequivocal: 'All bloody principles and practices we...do utterly deny, with all outward wars and strife, and fightings with outward weapons, for any end or under any pretence whatsoever.'[53] This position was not unique to the Quakers. It was held by some of the sectarians of the 1640s, including the Muggletonians, and by the Caroline theologian William Chillingworth, of whom it was said that 'he did really believe all war to be unlawful'.[54] But it remained an extreme viewpoint. Much more general in the seventeenth century was the repudiation of the chivalric ideal of a military life pursued for the sake of glory. William Ames, who had been chaplain to Sir Horace Vere, the commander of English troops in Holland, and knew what he was talking about, declared that it was evil to fight out of 'ambition' or 'desire of honour', and that to delight in war was 'barbarous and cruel'. 'No people whatsoever are more barbarously savage and relentless than soldiers,' observed the radical physician

Humphrey Brooke (1618–93). The Earl of Clarendon thought it 'horrible' 'that men should kill one another for want of somewhat else to do (which is the case of all volunteers in war)'. For Thomas Hobbes, 'a disposition of the mind to war' was an offence against the law of nature; he advised his readers to shun those classical texts which gave 'a strong, and delightful impression of the great exploits of war'. If it came to a battle, he saw no reason why conscripts should not run away.[55]

Even John Milton, who had welcomed the republic created in 1649 by a martial citizenry, developed scruples about the pursuit of honour through warfare. For his choice of epic theme, he turned away from wars ('hitherto the only argument | Heroic deemed').[56]* In *Paradise Lost* (1667) the archangel Michael condemns the bellicose culture which awaits Adam's descendants:

> For in those days might only shall be admired,
> And valour and heroic virtue called;
> To overcome in battle, and subdue
> Nations, and bring home spoils with infinite
> Manslaughter, shall be held the highest pitch
> Of human glory, and for glory done
> Of triumph, to be styled great conquerors,
> Patrons of mankind, gods, and sons of gods,
> Destroyers rightlier called and plagues of men.

In *Paradise Regained* (1671) Jesus rejects Satan's offer of 'fame and glory', of the kind enjoyed by Philip of Macedon or Julius Caesar:

> They err who count it glorious to subdue
> By conquest far and wide, to overrun
> Large countries, and in field great battles win,
> Great cities by assault: what do these worthies,†
> But rob and spoil, burn, slaughter, and enslave
> Peaceable nations, neighbouring, or remote,
> Made captive.[57]

The satirical mockery of the chivalric tradition, commonplace in the wake of *Don Quixote* (1605–15), reached its peak in the

---

* Horace had regarded *res gestae regumque ducumque, et tristia bella* ('the achievements of kings and commanders, and melancholy wars') as the proper subject for heroic verse; *De Arte Poetica*, line 73.
† So much for the Nine Worthies of chivalry.

literature of the later seventeenth century. For Samuel Butler, author
of *Hudibras* (1662–78), knightly daring was

> that noble trade
> That demi-gods and heroes made,
> Slaughter, and knocking on the head;
> The trade to which they all were bred.
> And is, like others, glorious when
> 'Tis great and large, but base if mean.[58]

In similar vein, the Earl of Rochester derided the glory-seeking monarch Louis XIV as

> the French fool who wanders up and down
> Starving his people and hazarding his crown.[59]

John Locke, like Hobbes before him, proscribed classical histories
which portrayed 'slaughter' as 'the laudable business of mankind' and
represented the 'butchery and rapine' committed by Alexander and
Caesar as the 'highest instances of human greatness'. He thought that
children 'should, from the beginning, be bred up in an abhorrence of
killing or tormenting any living creature'.[60]

When the poet John Philips celebrated the Duke of Marlborough's
victory at Blenheim, he included a gruesome account of the horrors of
the fight. Marlborough himself described Malplaquet (1709) as 'a
very murdering battle', declaring that the unprecedented numbers of
killed and wounded 'grieved my heart'.[61] Jonathan Swift in 1710–11
accused him of prolonging the War of the Spanish Succession in order
to gratify his own avarice and ambition; and in *Gulliver's Travels*
(1726), Swift's virtuous Houyhnhnms were startled to learn that in
England the trade of a soldier was held 'the most honourable of all
others; because a soldier is a Yahoo hired to kill in cold blood as many
of his own species, who have never offended him, as possibly he
can'.[62]

By this time, it had come to be accepted that military valour should
not be self-seeking, but was to be displayed only when the state
required it. There was no call for 'a foolhardy madness, better
beseeming such a knight-errant as is described in the romances'.[63]
When men were killed in war it was a tragic sacrifice, not a crowning
glory. If an army was needed, ordinary citizens should pay taxes to
support it; they did not have to fight themselves, but could get on with
the business of making money, safe in the knowledge that victory

would go to the side with the longer purse.[64] In general, however, war was to be regarded as 'one of the greatest calamities to which mankind can be subjected' and peace 'the only natural foundation of happiness'.[65]

This outlook left little room for classical notions of heroism, with what the hymn-writer Isaac Watts described as 'their false and foolish notions of courage, greatness and honour'.[66] True heroism was that displayed by quiet people: what Milton termed 'the better fortitude | Of patience and heroic martyrdom', and what John Bunyan called 'true valour'.[67] For Sir Thomas Browne, the early Christian martyrs were 'the true and almost only examples of fortitude: those that are fetch'd from the field, or drawn from the actions of the camp, are not oft-times so truly precedents of valour as of audacity, and at the best attain but to some bastard piece of fortitude'. John Dryden agreed: the classical poets had wrongly made heroes of 'athletic brutes' and 'ungodly man-killers'—'a race of men who can never enjoy quiet in themselves, till they have taken it from all the world'.[68] For Richard Steele, it was Christ who exemplified true fortitude, not 'Macedonia's madman', as Alexander the Great was now commonly described. His *Christian Hero* (1701) was a panegyric to 'that sublime and heroic virtue, meekness', a quality which ordinary people could display in their daily life.[69] A hermit in a cell could be as heroic as Alexander, thought Mary Evelyn, wife of the diarist.[70] Heroism was thus defined more in terms of endurance than of action; and it was open to women as well as men.[71]

Implicit in this position was an alternative model of masculinity itself, with the emphasis laid not on physical aggression, but on strength of character. Conquering one's own passions was a greater achievement than conquering other men. This was not a new idea, but had a long ancestry in Stoic and Christian tradition. In the Tudor age, the *Homilies* stressed that 'true strength and manliness' meant overcoming one's wrath; while John Foxe described his martyrs as 'the true conquerors of the world by whom we learn true manhood', 'more worthy of honour than an hundred Alexanders, Hectors, Scipios and Juliuses'. Catholics said the same of their martyrs.[72] During the seventeenth and eighteenth centuries, it became a commonplace to contrast the quiet sufferer's Christian fortitude with the reckless and foolhardy bravery of the military hero.

In the sociological theory of the Enlightenment, martial prowess was associated with a cruder, less-developed stage in social evolution: that primitive time of war, 'the infancy of nations', when nothing was in honour but 'virtue military'; when kings were 'little more than generals of their armies'; when their subjects were 'more lavish of their blood than of their sweat'; and when 'the only means of attaining to power and distinction' were 'strength and courage'.[73] 'Among all uncultivated nations,' wrote David Hume, 'courage is the predominant excellence'; and 'bodily strength and dexterity, being of greater use and importance in war,' is 'much more esteemed and valued than at present'.[74] 'In a rude society', agreed Adam Smith, 'nothing is honourable but war' and 'every man is a warrior'. 'Savages' were required to display 'heroic... firmness' and inexpressible courage under torture, qualities which Smith optimistically believed were no longer generally required, now that civilization had progressed and defence was the business of paid specialists. Dr Samuel Johnson similarly thought that competition for riches had replaced competition for martial glory and that a man who placed honour only in successful violence was 'a very troublesome animal in time of peace'; on his visit to the western isles of Scotland, he wondered whether it might not, however, be useful to preserve the military spirit in some 'remote and unprofitable provinces, where it can commonly do little harm, and whence it may be called forth at any sudden exigence'.[75]

Just as Tudor and Stuart commentators had welcomed the disappearance of the old bands of the nobility's armed retainers, so, in the eighteenth century, many contemporaries hailed the passing of militarism as a sign of progress, a necessary part of the transition to a commercial society. In 1756 the Lord Chancellor told the House of Lords that a nation of merchants, manufacturers, artisans, and husbandmen, defended by a professional army, was vastly preferable to a nation of soldiers; as proof, he cited the recent state of Scotland.[76] The historian of the College of Arms complacently reflected that it was 'more pleasing to the mind to honourably enrich one's family with wealth acquired by industry and frugality, than [to conduct] the most successful campaign, because that is obtained at the expense of the lives and fortunes of others, to which a good mind must have a repugnance'.[77] The essentially destructive achievement of the military hero was coming to be seen by many as inferior to that of the 'great man'—the scholar, inventor, or artist, from whose work everyone benefited.[78]

Of course, in a commercial state, warfare remained a crucial instrument of policy; and at times of international conflict the old ideals of military heroism would resurrect themselves. The wars of the mid-eighteenth century helped to rehabilitate military values. They generated pride in Britain's accomplishments as a maritime nation and led contemporaries to see the army in a more positive light.[79] 'Come, cheer up, my boys, 'tis to glory we steer,' sang the eighteenth-century sailor, while the British grenadier was encouraged to regard himself as a hero comparable to Alexander, Hercules, Hector, Lysander, 'and such great names as these'. The eighteenth century saw some spectacular displays of national bellicosity; and in General Wolfe and Admirals Anson, Vernon, Howe, Rodney, and Nelson, there would be new generations of popular military and naval heroes.[80] 'There is nothing more august in the world,' declared one of Marlborough's clerical admirers, 'nothing more dazzling to martial eyes than a victorious general, marching in his greatness at the head of his forces, with the temples of his head wreath'd about with laurels, attended with other ensigns of greatness.'[81]

Although there was a continuing undercurrent of radical and Non-conformist hostility to 'the red coated slaves', pursuing their 'trade of murder',[82] most contemporaries accepted that the country still needed professionals capable of military prowess when it was needed. The emphasis was now upon disciplined patriotism and professional skill, rather than, as in the past, on aggressive self-glorification. But physical courage was still important. Hence the de facto toleration, well into the nineteenth century, of the duel, despite numerous legal prohibitions; for, as the political philosopher Bernard Mandeville remarked in 1732, the passions of pride and courage were 'necessary to society'.[83] David Hume did not share the uncritical admiration for military heroism exhibited by 'the generality of mankind', who, he thought, still regarded it as 'the most sublime kind of merit'. In his opinion, 'men of cool reflection' were too aware of 'the infinite confusions and disorder' which the cult of military prowess brought in its train. But even Hume had to admit that 'when we fix our view on the person himself, who is the author of all this mischief, there is something so dazzling in his character, the mere contemplation of it so elevates the mind, that we cannot refuse it our admiration'.[84]

The prestige of the military life received an enormous boost from the wars of the French Revolutionary and Napoleonic era; and the nineteenth and twentieth centuries would show, only too painfully, that the long-held notion of masculine fulfilment as something best achieved in violent combat was very far from having been extinguished by the progress of commerce and industry. When John Ruskin lectured in 1865 at the Royal Military Academy, Woolwich, he told his audience that he hoped that they loved 'fighting for its own sake'; and he declared that 'the game of war is only that in which the full personal power of the human creature is brought out'.[85] Coming though it did from Britain's leading aesthete, this was an example of what has been called 'martialism', the doctrine that war is the supreme instrument of human endeavour, 'the most essential affirmation of man's nature', a transcendent activity that enables men to feel 'exalted and fulfilled'.[86] It is an ideology which would have many followers in modern times.

In the Victorian era, the notion of physical conflict as the supreme masculine activity was kept alive in games and sports which were transparent surrogates for warfare. 'This is worth living for,' wrote Thomas Hughes, author of *Tom Brown's Schooldays* (1856), of rugby football: 'the whole sum of school-boy existence gathered up into one straining struggling half-hour, a half hour worth a year of common life.' Sir Lawrence Jones (1885–1969), writer and banker, believed that he had had 'more enjoyment, a more vivid sense of the delight of living, with every faculty at full stretch, when pursuing and killing birds and beasts than in any other activity'; while the sometime Oxford don Ernest Bennett could write in 1899 that 'whether killing rats with a terrier, rejoicing in a prize fight, playing a salmon, or potting Dervishes', killing 'is a big factor in the joy of living'.[87] 'You should have seen our men setting out from here for the trenches—absolutely radiant with excitement and joy to be getting back to fight again,' wrote the poet Julian Grenfell to his mother in February 1915. 'I *do* love fighting.' Grenfell and his aristocratic contemporaries still held the romantic view that the soldier was a free agent and warfare a dangerous but deeply seductive game. 'Playing it,' writes a modern scholar, 'they fulfilled themselves and became entirely what they had been raised to become.'[88]

Despite this continuing stress on physical courage, loyalty, sacrifice, and the pleasure of killing, the retreat from martial values went further in Britain than in most other European countries. Soldiers and sailors wore civilian dress when off duty, and their political and social presence was muted. This did not prevent Dr Johnson from declaring that 'every man thinks meanly of himself for not having been a soldier, or not having been at sea...Were Socrates and Charles the Twelfth of Sweden both present in any company, and Socrates to say, "Follow me and hear a lecture in philosophy"; and Charles, laying his hand on his sword, to say, "Follow me and dethrone the Czar," a man would be ashamed to follow Socrates.'[89] Without disrespect to the sage of Lichfield, it can be safely said that, by

Johnson's day, there was no longer near-unanimity that military prowess offered the highest form of human fulfilment. It was the oldest and most basic form of masculine self-realization, and it was still highly admired within the specific context of professional soldiering. But, as a universal aspiration, it had had its day. It was too closely associated with a rudimentary economy and an archaic social structure; it was exclusively masculine; and its moral value was highly contested. In the ensuing chapters, we shall examine other, more peaceful ways in which men, and women, at all social levels, sought to fulfil themselves.

APPENDIX
MONARCHS AND MILITARY PROWESS

There is no art or other knowledge so seemly or necessary for a prince as the art military.

Sir Walter Ralegh (attrib.), *The Cabinet-Council*, ed. John Milton (1658)

The value attached in this period to military prowess is well illustrated by the expectations held of contemporary rulers.[1] In the Middle Ages, it had been an essential requirement of a monarch that he should be able to lead in battle and defeat the enemy. Henry VIII was in this tradition, 'not unmindful', as the historian Polydore Vergil put it, 'that it was his duty to seek fame by military skill'.[2] The young Edward VI was keenly interested in military matters;[3] and the two men who ruled sucessively in his place, Edward Seymour, Duke of Somerset, and John Dudley, Duke of Northumberland, were both serious military figures, with many warlike achievements to their credit. Elizabeth I, like Mary before her, was debarred by her sex from engaging in warfare, but she 'loved martial men' and her oratory embodied the bellicose assumptions of her age. At Tilbury in 1588, she appeared in breastplate and helmet, mounted on a charger.[4] A contemporary wrote of the 'peacemaker', James I, that he 'was the most cowardly man that ever I knew. He could not endure a soldier or to see men drilled, to hear of war was death to him.'[5] In fact, James had taken the field on six occasions before he came to England and he was depicted in armour on the ceiling of the Banqueting House.[6] He urged his son to 'let your countenance smell of courage and magnanimity when you are at the wars'; and in Henry, Prince of Wales, he had an heir of whose outstanding fondness for martial exercises his posthumous admirers made a great deal.[7] Charles I's rule was notable, after the first few years, for its strong commitment to peace at a time when the rest of Europe was locked in bloody conflict. Yet he cultivated a military image; and the Venetian envoy reported in 1637 that the King handled arms like a knight and his courser like a riding master. When the Civil War came, Charles placed himself at the head of his troops and, though no great military leader, conducted himself with bravery.[8] Charles II's military career ended at the battle of Worcester in 1651, but his brother James II was a professional soldier with the French and the Spanish in the 1650s; later, as Lord High Admiral, he commanded the British fleet in two Anglo-Dutch wars; and, as the ex-King, he was present at the battle of the Boyne in 1690. His successor, William III, the military leader of the European coalition against Louis XIV, was a martial prince *par excellence* and regarded war as a ruler's profession; he was at his best on the field of battle.[9] Queen Anne had herself portrayed as a warrior woman, commanding her armies.[10] George I was a man of great personal courage with a considerable military reputation, while George II distinguished himself at Oudenarde in 1708, charging sword in hand at the head of his dragoons until his horse was shot under him. At the age of 60 he appeared at Dettingen, the last British monarch to lead his troops into battle, and returned to be celebrated by Handel as a true hero.[11]

3

WORK AND VOCATION

Go, till the fields, and with inglorious sweat,
An honest, but a painful living get;
Your old neglected callings now renew,
And bid to glorious war a long adieu.

Charles Cotton, 'On the Death of the Most Noble
Thomas Earl of Ossory', 1680

The conquering of idleness is a greater and more acceptable conquest to
God, yea and more profitable and commodious to the realm, than the
winning of castles, cities and forts, yet obtained with less dangers, cares
and troubles.

(anon.), 'A discourse how the poor may be relieved', c.1580;
BL, Lansdowne MS 95 (3), fol. 217

THE PRIMAL CURSE?

In the early modern period, the idea that work might offer a route to human fulfilment had to surmount some formidable obstacles. The two dominant intellectual traditions, Christian and classical, in their different ways both encouraged the notion that work was a tedious, even cruel, necessity, and that, ideally, life would have been better if people did not have to work at all.

From the Greeks was derived the notion that the best life was one of leisure: not idleness, of course, but virtuous activity of mind and body, involving no manual labour and unconstrained by the need to earn a living.* From Christianity came the doctrine that labour was an

---

* This notion can hardly have been representative of the views of ordinary Athenians, who must have been well aware of the indispensability of agricultural and

78

Figure 3.1 'Skill and pains brings fruitful gains' says the caption to this picture of well-dressed gardeners planting a Jacobean orchard.

unpleasant and unavoidable form of expiation for Adam's sin. With the Fall of Man, the earth had been cursed and no longer yielded its produce willingly. It was only by the sweat of their brows that Adam and his posterity could hope to eat bread; though, as early modern commentators hastily explained, in the case of magistrates, ministers, 'men of high degree', or those 'of noble family and extraction', 'sweat of the brow' was not to be taken too literally.[1]

Work, it was assumed, was performed only in response to some constraint, physical or economic. The natural human impulse was to idleness. As the scholar-administrator Sir John Cheke observed in 1549, 'Every man is easily and naturally brought from labour to ease...from diligence to slothfulness.' Or as John Locke would put it more than a century later, 'labour for labour['s] sake is against nature'. Everyone knew that there would be no work in heaven.[2]

Evidence for this supposedly innate human disposition to idleness was everywhere to be found. It could be observed among the native peoples of North America, whose reluctance to labour was notorious

other labour. But it was the one espoused by Plato and Aristotle and therefore transmitted to early modern Europe.

79

and whose way of life seemed to demonstrate 'the proneness of human nature to a life of ease, of freedom from care and labour'. As modern anthropologists have pointed out, hunter–gatherers typically have much leisure for sleep and gossip because they can satisfy their relatively modest needs with comparatively little exertion.[3] When John Wesley went to Georgia as a missionary in the 1730s, he was shocked to see 'a large company of reasonable creatures, called Indians, sitting in a row on the side of a river, looking sometimes at one another, sometimes at the sky, and sometimes at the bubbles on the water. And so they sat (unless in the time of war) for a great part of the year, from morning to night.'[4] Some of the English colonists who ran away to join the Indians or who refused to return from captivity gave as their reason that 'they can live with less labour, and more pleasure and plenty, as Indians, than they can with us'.[5] It was a feature of all 'rude' nations, thought Adam Ferguson in 1767, that their inhabitants were 'still averse to labour, addicted to war, admirers of fortitude, and in the language of Tacitus, more lavish of their blood than of their sweat'.[6]

This apparently innate aversion to labour could also be seen nearer home. Since at least the fourteenth century, observers had complained that journeymen did the minimum amount of work necessary to keep them in food and drink and then devoted themselves to relaxation.[7] In the oft-quoted words of Daniel Defoe, writing in 1704, 'there's nothing more frequent than for an Englishman to work till he has got his pocket full of money, and then go and be idle, or perhaps drunk, till 'tis all gone'.[8] Workers were assumed to have a limited target of earnings and to be ready to stop work as soon as that target had been reached. 'The price of labour', thought Roger North, 'is such as they can make a good living of two or three days' work in a week. "And why more?", say they. "This provides bread, food, and ale; if we are sick and old, &c, the parish must provide for us."'[9] In the words of the great German sociologist Max Weber: 'A man does not "by nature" wish to earn more and more money, but simply to live as he is accustomed to live and to earn as much as is necessary for that purpose. Wherever modern capitalism has begun its work of increasing the productivity of human labour by increasing its intensity, it has encountered the immensely stubborn resistance of this leading trait of pre-capitalistic labour.'[10]

When assessing such accounts, it is important to remember that underemployment was a chronic feature of the early modern economy. Much labour was seasonal, governed by the weather and the harvest.[11] Employees who took days off were not necessarily idling. Moreover, in an economy of makeshifts and expedients, it was usual for working people to have several employments, and to divide their time between them. Working habits were intrinsically irregular.[12] Many employees, especially apprentices and living-in servants, had no control over the hours they laboured. But those who were able to determine the pace at which they worked often chose to alternate bouts of idleness, especially on Mondays, with intense activity later in the week, when they pushed themselves hard, to compensate for slackness earlier on, like modern students writing weekly essays.[13] Francis Place, who in the 1790s worked over sixteen hours a day making breeches, recalled 'the sickening aversion [for labour] which at times steals over the working man . . . I have felt it, resisted it to the utmost of my power; but have been so completely subdued by it, that [in] spite of very pressing circumstances, I have been obliged to submit, and run away from my work. This is the case with every workman I have ever known.'[14]

It is tempting, therefore, to dismiss the supposed popular indifference to the prospect of working longer hours and earning more as an illusion, created by unsympathetic employers, wishing to justify their keeping down wages in order to secure more labour time from their workers. Contemporary observers certainly exaggerated the extent of voluntary idleness; and some modern studies have found little or no direct evidence for this alleged leisure preference.[15] Yet the volume of contemporary testimony to the existence in the early modern period of what modern economists call a backward-sloping labour supply curve is too great to be totally dismissed. The very poor desperately sought employment in order to keep the wolf from the door; and the very ambitious tried to better themselves by earning as much as they could. But even Adam Smith, who favoured high wages because he thought they made 'the greater part' of workmen more industrious, even to the point of ruining their health by overwork, conceded that there were others who preferred to take time off, if their earnings were high enough to permit it.[16]

Many suggestions have been offered as to why some people should have preferred leisure to the chance of working longer and thereby improving their living conditions. Historians have adduced the lack of readily available consumer goods on which to spend extra earnings; the absence of facilities for saving; the high value attached to leisure-time sociability; and the pessimistic awareness that a sudden boost in wages was likely to be a temporary affair which would not last long enough to justify upsetting established patterns of spending. As a contemporary remarked in 1697, ''tis observable that where Englishmen find constant employment (as they have in the fishery), they work harder and cheaper (everything consider'd) than any in Europe: witness the labourers in our mines, also our artificers at Birmingham'.[17]

Common to all these explanations is the underlying assumption that work itself was never done for its own sake, but only out of economic necessity, and that 'few people worked if they could afford to be idle'.[18] It was a widespread assumption in the early modern period that people worked *for* a living, but that work itself was not part of that living. John Donne, Dean of St Paul's between 1621 and 1631, remarked in one of his sermons that 'work' was 'a word that implies difficulty, and pain, and labour, and is accompanied with some loathness, with some colluctation [i.e. struggling]'; while the economic writer Sir Dudley North, who thought that the great incentive to work was the terror of starving, declared that if any task was agreeable to perform, that meant that it was not work at all, but pleasure: 'it is incident to the true notion of work not to delight in it'.[19]

It was in accordance with this, highly negative, view of work that, when Adam Smith came to expound his theory of wages in the later eighteenth century, his basic premiss was that 'in the inferior employments, the sweets of labour, consist[ed] altogether in the recompense of labour'. By agreeing to work, the labourer was surrendering 'his ease, his liberty, and his happiness'.[20] This loss was something for which his employer had to compensate him; hence, indeed, the modern American term 'compensation' as a synonym for remuneration.[21] Samuel Pepys observed that 'most men that do thrive in the world do forget to take pleasure during the time that they are getting their estate, but reserve that till they have got one, and then it is too late for them, to enjoy it with any pleasure'.[22] There was no suggestion here that work might in itself be intrinsically pleasurable.

Many of the well-to-do commentators who assumed that the working population in early modern England was waiting for the slightest opportunity at which to down tools shared the same preference for leisure which they attributed to their inferiors. 'I am ... one ... of the idle sort of people ... nowadays termed gentlemen,' explained Thomas Isham, heir to a Northamptonshire estate, in 1585. He was echoing Sir Thomas Smith's famous description of a gentleman as one who was able to live 'idly and without manual labour'.[23] 'Amongst us,' observed Robert Burton, 'the badge of gentry is idleness: to be of no calling, not to labour, for that's derogatory to their birth.'[24] In 1669 a gentlewoman set out to starve herself to death because she was in poverty, but believed it better to die than to earn money by pursuing some ungenteel occupation.[25] Richard Steele satirized this attitude in his comedy *The Conscious Lovers* (1722), where one of the characters from a gentry family, faced with the prospect of marriage with a merchant's daughter, comments, in a line worthy of Oscar Wilde, that 'We never had one of our family before who descended from persons that did anything.'[26]

Of course, most gentlemen led active and busy lives, whether in public life or in running their estates. Theirs was a seamless way of life, in which the distinction between work and relaxation was far from clear. Concerned to maintain their honour and social standing, the gentry regarded such activities as entertaining, hunting, and even gambling as no less obligatory than supervising their employees or attending quarter sessions. Strongly committed by both duty and self-interest to the ideal of participation in public affairs, they objected not to work as such, but to certain kinds of work, performed under certain social circumstances. Neoclassical ideas taught them to seek their fulfilment as magistrates and legislators in the service of the commonwealth, not as manual labourers toiling in the fields.[27] Renaissance humanists had perpetuated the classical prejudice against that kind of work. To earn one's living 'with hand and sweat of the body', declared an Elizabethan bishop, was 'illiberal and servile'.[28] The ethnographer John Bulwer noted in 1653 that in England, no less than in China, long fingernails were admired as 'the crests of idle gentility', signs that their owner did not work with his hands.[29]* Domestic service, menial employment, and petty trading were all thought incompatible with gentility. In the early seventeenth century, it was asserted that no one could be a gentleman who had 'walked horses barefoot for threepence' or whose mother rode to market on a pair of panniers to sell butter.[30]

The gentry were in no way averse to physical exertion as such. Indeed, their favourite recreations—hunting and tennis—were distinctly strenuous: 'much more toilsome', as a contemporary

---

* Van Dyck's portraits of George Gage (in the National Gallery, London) and Archbishop Laud (in the Fitzwilliam Museum, Cambridge) lend some support to this view.

remarked, than the work of many artisans. The difference was that the artisans worked for money and out of necessity, whereas the gallants played tennis freely and by choice. Even so, tennis was energetic enough to occasion some social anxieties. James I's son Prince Henry incurred some disapproval when he was spotted playing the game 'in his shirt, rather becoming an artisan than a prince'. Margaret Cavendish, Marchioness of Newcastle, claimed in 1664 that, since work was a curse, there could be no recreation in such a sweaty activity.[31]

So long as the social elite thought it desirable to subsist without manual labour, it was hardly surprising that the lower classes were believed to take the same view. In the literature of the time, the reluctant worker is a familiar figure. It would be a fine day, thought the Elizabethan poet George Gascoigne, 'when Davy Diker digs and dallies not'.[32] The Elizabethan Bishop of Durham James Pilkington complained that 'the labouring man will take his rest long in the morning; a good piece of the day is spent afore he come at his work; then must he have his breakfast, though he have not earned it, at his accustomed hour, or else there is grudging and murmuring; when the clock smiteth, he will cast down his burden in the midway, and, whatsoever he is in hand with, he will leave it as it is, though many times it is marred afore he come again; he may not lose his meat, what danger soever the work is in. At noon he must have his sleeping time, then his bever [snack] in the afternoon, which spendeth a great part of the day; and when his hour cometh at night, at the first stroke of the clock he casteth down his tools, leaveth his work, in what need or case soever the work standeth.'[33]

This indictment would have been more impressive if it had not so obviously been an elaboration of the phraseology used in a statute of 1495 regulating wages and hours of work.[34] Even so, it has been calculated that, by modern standards, seventeenth-century brick-layers went about their work in a distinctly leisurely manner.[35] In the early modern period, craftsmen and labourers worked much longer hours than is usual today—seldom fewer than ten a day and frequently more.[36] But they probably worked at a slower pace. In 1696 an observer said of the gangs mending the highway that they 'work when they list, come and go at their pleasure, and spend most of their time in standing still and prating, and looking after their fellows, whom they send out from their work, most shamefully, to stop passengers for a largess'.[37] Then as now, it was a popular pastime to watch other people not working.

On the margins of society were the squatters who set up cottages on the mountains, heaths, and wastes, living simply and 'given to little or no kind of labour'.[38] When the antiquary Thomas Machell toured the Lake District in the 1690s, he discovered that the cottagers of Bowness undertook no employment, save begging, never permitting their children to do a day's work for pay. In the previous forty years, only one man had taken a job; he was 'sore exclaimed against for breaking their custom; and his neighbours told him 'twas never a good world since Bowness people went to work'.[39]

At times of disorder, this latent anti-work ethic could come bubbling to the surface. Bartholomew Steere, a carpenter who was involved in the Oxfordshire rising of 1596 against enclosures, was said to have urged his companions: 'Care not for work, for we shall have a merrier world shortly... and I will work one day and play the other.' In 1678 Henry Geeve, a Biggleswade labourer, confessed to having been lured into stealing corn from a barn by James Blazeden, who told him 'that if he would be ruled by him and keep his counsel, he need never do [a] day's work as long as he lived'.[40] The Somerset JP Edward Hext is famous for his account in 1596 of 'divers wandering, suspicious persons' who preferred to hazard their lives by confessing to capital felonies than be sent to the house of correction, where they would be forced to work.[41]*

It was against such attitudes that generations of preachers and moralists contended. The idea that work was a religious duty, to be pursued regardless of one's own inclinations, was in no way the invention of the Protestant divines of post-Reformation England, leave alone peculiar to so-called Puritans. Since the twelfth century, a number of prominent medieval theologians had maintained that the purpose of mankind was to labour.[42] Late medieval preachers regularly denounced idleness and proclaimed the obligation of all members of society to toil in their particular vocations. Their sermons occasionally reflected the patristic idea of labour as a penance, a form of bodily mortification, but, more frequently, they were positive in spirit: work was a duty owed by man to God, a rewarding activity and a social good from which the whole community benefited.[43] In the century after the Black Death the shortage of labour stimulated a work ethic among employers and wage-earners alike.[44]

The stress upon the high value of work in a secular vocation was reiterated in the early sixteenth century by the teaching of Christian

* For debtors who preferred to stay in gaol than come out to work, see Francis Fuller, *Medicina Gymnastica*, 2nd edn (1725), 152.

humanists like Desiderius Erasmus, Sir Thomas More, and Thomas Starkey, all of whom urged the importance of leading an active life for the good of the common weal.[45] Their doctrines were further developed and extended by the clergy of the Reformation era; and in the ensuing century the message was reiterated by numerous moralists and writers of advice.[46] Much of it was common to Catholics as well as Protestants.† Its main contention was that the clergy were not the only ones who had a special calling or vocation (*vocatio*) from God. Every lay person was also called, both by a 'general' calling to repentance, faith, and the service of God, and by a 'particular' calling to perform some specific occupation. This particular calling was 'a certain kind of life imposed on man by God'; its object was what William Perkins called 'the common good' and Richard Baxter the 'public welfare'.[47]

An individual calling was to be strenuously pursued. As the Puritan divine Samuel Hieron (1572–1617) put it, each man's calling was appointed 'to be as it were the testimony of his religion, and the matter in which he should show himself what is in him'.[48] Women were equally required to work. The Puritan Thomas Gataker (1574–1654) ruled that it was 'no shame or stain therefore for a woman to be housewifely, be she never so well born, be she never so wealthy. For it is the woman's trade so to be: it is the end of her creation; it is that that she was made for.'[49] Daily tasks had a spiritual value; and working could be as much an act of religion as praying in church. 'Be not sorry that thy master doth not suffer thee to go the church to hear mass,' enjoined an early Protestant tract. 'For thou mayst please God as well in doing thy work.' 'The business of our callings,' agreed a Hanoverian divine, 'is an act of religion.' In the historian R. H. Tawney's famous words, 'mundane toil' became 'itself a kind of sacrament'.[50]

The clergy were emphatic that it was a duty to glorify God by following one's particular vocation: 'Every person, of every degree, state, sex or condition without exception, must have some personal and particular calling to walk in.'[51] In a marked departure from previous thinking, the Reformers utterly rejected the contemplative ideal of medieval monasticism. Active employment should be sought in the world, not out of it. 'Hereby', wrote William Perkins, 'is

† One recusant priest even accused Protestants of encouraging idleness by teaching that salvation was obtained by faith rather than works, thus implying that 'idleness is the perfection of a Christian's life'; Matthew Kellison, *A Survey of the New Religion* (Douai, 1605), 321.

overthrown the condition of monks and friars... This monkish kind of living is damnable, for... every man must have a particular and personal calling, that he may be a good and profitable member of some society.'[52] Those who were in a position to work, but chose not to, were thieves, living off the labours of others.[53]

This was not just a condemnation of monks, beggars, vagrants, and the idle poor. It also implied that the gentry were forbidden to lead a life of conspicuous idleness.[54] It was as demeaning for the rich to live by the labours of the poor as for beggars to subsist upon charity. Charles II's courtiers, said a radical pamphleteer in 1663, were 'filthy idle drones, who will not work'.[55] Many sectaries believed that the clergy should also earn their living by some useful trade.[56] After all, God himself was 'the everlasting worker', who had laboured intensively to create the world, resting only on the seventh day.[57]* It was to deflect such charges that the Elizabethan bishop John Jewel was careful to correct the impression that kings, magistrates, and others in authority did not work: 'There is no labour comparable to the labour of the prince,' he assured his hearers. 'These labours are greater than all the labours of the body.'[58] Subsequent economic writers agreed that there was 'a labour of the brain as well as of the body'. When in 1700 failing eyesight denied the elderly Samuel Pepys the use of books and papers and left him with nothing to do but sit and think, he consoled himself with the reflection that 'thinking, I take it, is working'.[59]

The choice of the calling was crucial. It was not so much a matter of personal inclination, though that had to be taken into account, as of ensuring that the talents and gifts with which individuals had been endowed were employed most effectively. A person's talents were indicators of God's intentions for him and there was a duty to ensure that those intentions were realized. Talents were there to be used for the good of others.[60]

Ministers insisted that every legitimate occupation, however lowly, was honourable in the sight of God. Had not Christ been a carpenter

---

* There were some sceptics about this, like William Selby, rector of Elton, Nottinghamshire, who asked in 1708: 'Was God Almighty a drone? If not, what was he doing before he made the earth?'; J. D. Chambers, *Nottinghamshire in the Eighteenth Century*, 2nd edn (1966), 54 n. The usual answer, provided by St Augustine, was that he was busy making a hell for scoffing atheists who asked that question: *The Divine Weeks and Works of Guillaume de Saluste, Sieur du Bartas*, trans. Joshua Sylvester, ed. Susan Snyder (Oxford, 1979), i. 112–13. Augustine also provided an intellectually more sophisticated reply: *Confessions*, xi. 12, 13.

and St Paul a tentmaker? William Tyndale explained in 1527 that washing dishes, cobbling shoes, and preaching the Gospel all pleased God equally.[61] 'God doth consecrate every man's vocation,' agreed the Edwardian bishop Hugh Latimer; 'though he be a poor shepherd or cobbler, that is not the matter.' In the words of the poet George Herbert:

> A servant with this clause
> Makes drudgery divine:
> Who sweeps a room, as for thy laws,
> Makes that and th'action fine.[62]

This attitude contrasted strikingly with the traditional view of ordinary labour as vile and demeaning: a view vigorously expressed in 1616 in a lament by the unreconstructed future bishop Godfrey Goodman: 'How many trades are base and ignoble, not befitting the dignity of man's condition, as cobblers, tinkers, carters, chimney sweepers?'[63] Of course, the clergy regarded a wide range of occupations as unnecessary, sinful, or pernicious. There was no need for sellers of lace, feathers, and wigs, while stage-players, jugglers, dancers, keepers of alehouses and bowling alleys, prostitutes, and thieves were all beyond the pale.[64] The impudent claims made by some beggars that they were working just as hard as anybody else when they travelled from town to town in search of food were indignantly rejected.[65]* But honest trades, however menial, were freed from the contempt latent in the old aristocratic ideology. 'Stoop and work,' said Bishop Pilkington. 'Be not ashamed of it; it is the greatest honour that ever ye shall win.'[66] This stress on the spiritual equality of all forms of labour was a distinctively Protestant theme.

Work was praised as a remedy for that notorious mother of all vices, idleness. The attachment of early modern preachers to this medieval commonplace accorded with their deeply pessimistic conviction that only labour could keep away the foul desires to which the heart of man was subject. As William Gouge succinctly expressed it: 'lust [may] be kept down by man's diligence in his calling'. Hard work was recommended as the most effective preservative against sin, particularly sexual sin.[67] In Jacobean Banbury, the vicar William Whately advised application to business as the best way of avoiding the temptation to commit adultery: 'for pains in a calling will

---

* In fact, begging by locals within the parish was semi-legal and the aged poor did indeed regard it as work; Steve Hindle, *On the Parish?* (Oxford, 2004), 70–1.

88

consume a great part of that superfluous nourishment that yields matter to this sin. It will turn the blood and spirits another way.'[68] In the eyes of the godly, work served much the same purpose as did compulsory games in the eyes of Victorian headmasters. It was also suggested that, for women, continual labour was 'a singular remedy' against their natural tendency to 'rashness, and forwardness of the tongue'.[69]

Preachers and godly laymen alike shared an obsessive conviction that as much time as possible should be devoted to labour. Sleep was to be cut down to the minimum,[70] and time spent on meals strictly rationed.[71] Recreation was permissible, but only so far as was necessary to refresh body and mind to fit oneself for further labour.[72] This applied to children no less than adults, 'there being', in the words of the sectary Thomas Tryon (1634–1703), 'nothing more pernicious, nor promotes idleness and vanity more, than children's play.'[73] Baxter stressed, however, that people should not allow toil to distract them from spiritual concerns: the duties of one's particular calling should not get in the way of the general calling to seek salvation. So little was this warning heeded that, a century later, John Wesley could lament that work had become, for some people, such an obsession as to constitute a rival religion.[74]

The utility of labour as a social discipline was emphasized by many moralists. Employment, they claimed, 'civilized' men and made them 'tractable and obedient to superiors' commands'.[75] A dedicated workforce was preferable to a disorderly and dangerous underclass. Hence the need for laws to make labour compulsory and to punish the deliberately idle. Men without callings were 'exceedingly vicious', thought the Puritan divine Richard Sibbes (1577–1635); he instanced 'some gentlemen and beggars'.[76]

Of course, it was accepted that work had a productive function as well as a disciplinary one. As early as 1535, an anonymous writer declared that 'the whole wealth of the realm riseth out of the labours and works of the common people'. An Elizabethan writer agreed: labouring people nourished the rest of society by supplying them with everything necessary for life.[77] This was one of the reasons why the Statute of Artificers 1563 compelled all men and women under 60 to serve in agriculture if they had no other means of subsistence. Throughout the period, the administration of the poor law was animated by the notion that the best way to prevent poverty was to compel people to work.[78]

By the later seventeenth century, when population growth was slackening off and demand for labour increasing, it was a commonplace among economic writers that national prosperity depended upon the volume and intensity of the work performed by ordinary people.[79] The Quaker John Bellers (1654–1725) declared that 'regularly labouring people are the kingdom's greatest treasure and strength, for without labourers there can be no lords; and if the poor labourers did not raise much more food and manufacture than what did subsist themselves, every gentleman must be a labourer, and every idle man must starve'. Sir William Petty attached so much importance to a well-trained labour force that he propounded a proto-Keynesian scheme of public works: the unemployed should be put to 'build a useless pyramid upon Salisbury Plain, bring the stones at Stonehenge to Tower-Hill, or the like; for... this would keep their minds to discipline and obedience, and their bodies to a patience of more profitable labours when need shall require it'.[80] In the harsh words of two modern historians, 'from medieval England to the wider reaches of the late nineteenth-century British empire, the project of creating "free" labour, disciplining it to often extremely heavy physical work and controlling its wage demands through criminal sanctions was a sustained project, deeply embedded in law and economy and culture.'[81]

This was the secular version of the work ethic. A population habituated to constant labour was commended, not because it was more godly, but because it was more productive. Human labour was believed to have a dynamic potentiality for future growth. As Isaac Barrow observed, it raised people 'above rude and sordid barbarism' and generated 'all those arts whereby human life is civilized, and the world cultivated'. 'In the industry of man,' thought his contemporary the heraldic writer Edward Waterhouse, 'there is such a latent power and life of actuation that it comes near the verge of miraculous.'[82]

Yet for all this talk about the indispensability of labour, whether for production, or social discipline, or salvation, it was only occasionally suggested that work might be a positive and fulfilling experience for the workers themselves. Few of the clergy who preached this work ethic saw it as their task to portray labour as intrinsically pleasurable. Work was commended as a form of dutiful renunciation, a means of holding at bay the turbulent desires of the flesh, a proof of spiritual health, and an indispensable way of driving off poverty and preventing disorder. But many preachers seemed to imply that, for all its social and moral value, labour was, in itself, an inherently joyless activity, justified only by its material compensations in this world and its spiritual rewards in the next. The economic writers said even less about work's intrinsic pleasures, since they regarded its value as wholly instrumental. For Petty, 'labour' was 'the simple motions of men in order to [produce] commodities, for so many hours as he is naturally able to endure the same'.[83] In the later eighteenth century, the working year lengthened and fewer holidays were celebrated. The leisure preference dwindled away.[84] Few attributed this change to the inherent pleasures of work as such; most contemporaries assumed that the driving force was the desire of the workers to increase their earnings.

THE REWARDS OF LABOUR

Yet behind the emphasis upon the social, economic, and moral imperatives of labour, we can discern the rudiments of an altogether more positive view: one which, instead of representing work as a tiresome means to a desirable end, portrayed it as intrinsically satisfying in itself and stressed its potentialities for human happiness and fulfilment.

These potentialities had been visible in the garden of Eden, which Adam had been required to 'dress' and to 'keep', and where, most theologians agreed, the work in which he and Eve had engaged had been intrinsically enjoyable. Of course, it had been light work, with no hard digging and no weeds or pests with which to contend; it was 'a pleasant exercise', which Adam pursued 'more for delight than for the gain'.[1] This was the state of affairs to which Utopian thinkers wished to return, hoping, like one Jacobean bishop, that labour might once again be 'as it were playing, and with pleasure'. For the Fifth Monarchist Mary Cary, the rule of the saints would mean that work would cease to be 'toilsome and burdensome' and instead become 'pleasant, easy' and 'as recreation'.[2]

Even before that happy day, the possibility was recognized that work could be its own reward. Implicit in the religious discourse about labour was the notion that the glorification of God by work in a vocation was man's primary end, an expression of his nature and therefore an essential means of human fulfilment. 'With labour,' said the Marian preacher Roger Edgeworth, 'a man shall be shining and bright afore God and man.'[3] In the sixteenth century, it was a commonplace to assert that man was 'born to labour, as a bird is born to fly'.[4] This was a reference to a much-contested verse in the book of Job (5: 7). In the King James translation man is said to be born 'unto trouble, as the sparks fly upwards' (for in Old Testament Hebrew, as in Greek, labour and pains were expressed by the same word). But the Latin Vulgate and the Geneva Bible had rendered the key word as, respectively, *labor* (labour) and 'travail' (painful labour). The implication was that work was the essence of the human destiny and that it enabled people to realize themselves. In Milton's words,

> other creatures all day long
> Rove idle unemployed, and less need rest;
> Man hath his daily work of body or mind
> Appointed, which declares his dignity.[5]

Because human beings were created to work, it was thought that they would degenerate in mind and body if they gave themselves over to idleness. John White (1575–1648), 'the patriarch of Dorchester', accordingly recommended that pioneer emigrants to North America should deliberately choose to settle in an infertile area, where hard labour would be required to wrest a living from the soil.[6]

It was accepted that those people in occupations which best fitted their capacities were fortunate indeed, 'seeing that everyone, by instinct of nature, delighteth in that wherein he is like to be most excellent'.[7] But there was also a plethora of well-to-do commentators who were ready to assure the poor labourer of his good fortune, whether or not his job suited him, because manual toil was good for his health and a sedentary job would have been physically debilitating.[8]

More remarkable were those moralists who thought that even manual tasks should be regarded as positively enjoyable.[9] Henry VII's minister Edmund Dudley urged labourers and ploughmen to 'delight' in their work; the early Protestant Simon Fish expected everyone to labour 'diligently and joyfully'; and the young Edward VI wanted youth brought up to 'think their travail sweet and honest'.[10] The Marian bishop Thomas Watson remarked that 'all labour seemeth painful, so long as it is weighed only in the consideration of a man's mind. But when we come to the experience of the thing, and begin to go through a little of the labour, then is all the fear of the grief driven clean away. The success of the work bringeth sweetness.'[11] The Jacobean surveyor John

Norden maintained that all men could find 'true delight' in the prosecution of their callings; Edward Waterhouse thought that, 'to a virtuous and well-poised mind that understands itself created for public good, honest labour is a delight, and diligence in it a recreation'; and the Puritan clergyman Richard Rogers (1551–1618) urged Christians to go 'cheerfully' about their callings.[12] Richard Baxter observed that idleness deprived men of 'the great delight of doing good', which he described as 'a pleasure exceeding all voluptuousness'. He wanted all labour, even of the humblest kind, to become a delight; the schoolmaster's profession, 'though usually but poor and painful', was particularly one 'to be chosen and delighted in', because it was so useful and so inherently rewarding.[13]

At the end of the seventeenth century, the merchant John Cary persuaded the corporation of Bristol to establish workhouses, where boys and girls would be brought up 'to delight in labour'.[14] The Nonconformist minister Richard Steele advised tradesmen that they should 'delight' to be in their shops and warehouses, 'as everything doth to be in its place'; if obliged to leave them temporarily, they should be restless until they returned. Daniel Defoe agreed that it was crucial for success in business that the tradesman should enjoy his work: 'to follow a trade, and not to love and delight in it, is a slavery or bondage, not a business'.[15]

In a hymn, specially published in 1641 for the use of labourers, George Wither wrote:

> For, labour yields me true content,
> (Though few the same do see)
> And, when my toiling hours are spent,
> My sleeps the sweeter be.
> Though labour was enjoin'd at first,
> To be a curse for sin,
> Yet man, by being so accurst,
> May screw a blessing in.
> And he that with a patient mind,
> This penance doth sustain,
> Shall by his pains true pleasures find,
> And many comforts gain.[16]

This is not quite Marx's notion of labour as the ultimate form of self-realization.[17] But explicit in Wither's verses is a distinctly positive view of what the labouring process has to offer. It was echoed in 1769 by the weavers of Spitalfields:

> May upright masters still augment their treasure,
> And journeymen pursue their work with pleasure.[18]

The classic statement of the psychological importance of work was provided in the mid-eighteenth century by the philosopher David Hume. In his *Essays*, he asserted that when 'men are kept in perpetual occupation', they 'enjoy as their reward *the occupation itself* [my italics], as well as those pleasures which are the fruit of their labour. The mind acquires new vigour; enlarges its powers and faculties; and, by an assiduity in honest industry... satisfies its natural appetites.' Hume observed that many people became passionately absorbed in their work, and he suggested that underpinning that passion lay an innate human craving for activity and employment. Only when that craving was thwarted did the poor, in frustration, turn to drink, and the rich to hunting and gambling.[19]

Like most classic statements, Hume's observations on the psychological indispensability of employment had a long prehistory. The Elizabethan archbishop Edwin Sandys came near the concept of work as a human imperative when he attributed to 'the wise man' the view that 'work... [is] even as needful for men as meat'.[20] The Jacobean scholar Robert Burton observed that, though the nobility and gentry of his day had everything in abundance, they were disproportionately subject to melancholic gloom because they lived lives of idleness, counting it a disgrace to work: 'their bodies... full of gross humours, wind, crudities, their minds disquieted, dull, heavy, &c, care, jealousy, fear of some diseases, sullen fits, weeping fits, seize too familiarly on them'. By contrast, 'an hired servant, a poor handmaid, though ancient, that is kept hard to her work, and bodily labour' was seldom 'troubled in this kind'.[21] Roger North similarly thought that the attraction of labour, apart from the pleasure of resting after it, was that it 'takes off the tedium of life, which compensates and overpays all the trouble of it'.[22] 'Bored' and 'boredom' are terms which were invented only in the later eighteenth and early nineteenth centuries.[23] But the condition they described was there long before that, as is made clear by the complaints of early modern aristocrats about the 'weariness' and 'dullness' of their 'tedious' lives on their rural estates, and by their endless quest for 'diversion'.[24] The radical theologian Joseph Priestley (1733–1804), who had been librarian to the Earl of

Shelburne, was convinced that the middle ranks of society (those 'above the fear of want' yet with 'a sufficient motive for the constant exertion of the faculties') were more fortunate than the upper classes, who were generally unhappy through want of necessary employment.[25]

Hume's view of work had been anticipated in the previous century by Thomas Hobbes, who declared roundly that work was emphatically good and idleness torture.[26] The scientist Robert Boyle (1627–91) similarly noted that absorption in work was the best way of taking one's mind off other cares: 'to those whose thoughts are very seriously taken up with some business or another, the hours steal by undiscernedly'.[27] 'Up, and at the office all morning,' writes Samuel Pepys in 1668, 'and so to it again after dinner and there busy late, choosing to employ myself rather than go home to trouble with my wife.'[28]

In 1692 Bishop Gilbert Burnet summed up what we may suspect to have been received wisdom among the professional classes when he observed that there was no greater felicity than to be fully occupied by a satisfying and appropriate job. 'All men that are well suited in a profession that is agreeable to their genius and inclination are really the easier and the better pleased the more they are employed in it.'[29]

It is not hard to find examples of those who exemplified this assertion. Pepys, a civil servant, admitted to his diary that he found his work 'a delight'.[30] The Leicestershire schoolmaster John Brinsley claimed in 1612 to have found 'more true delight and pleasure' in teaching children than 'in the pleasantest recreation'.[31] The Worcestershire minister Thomas Hall (1610–65) observed that 'he had this happiness above many other men. . . . [that] he found himself best when he was most strongly employed'.[32] Mrs Constance Pley, a Portsmouth supplier of naval stores, wrote in 1666 that, now that her children were dead, business was 'all the delight' she took in this world.[33] The turner Nehemiah Wallington recalled of his mother (who died in 1603) that, 'when others recreated themselves on holidays and other times, she would take her needlework and say "Here is *my* recreation".'[34] A retired Oxford shoemaker who died in 1721 'used to complain that he was never easy' after he left off his trade, 'and that he was a happy man when he followed his business'.[35] The Hertfordshire farmer William Ellis (d. 1758) put his children to work at the earliest possible age, and boasted of his ploughman son that, 'if he is kept idle but one day in the house, he protests it is more disagreeable to him than labouring all that time'.[36]

The early modern period abounds in examples of that supposedly more recent species the workaholic who cannot be happy unless engaged in his labours. Sir William Temple remarked that some persons, once inured to labour by necessity, could not leave off what had 'grown a custom very necessary to their health, and to their very entertainment'.[37] The hours worked by some of the great intellectual and administrative figures of the period are truly awe-inspiring. When John Locke advised sedentary workers to spend at least three hours a day doing manual labour for their health's sake, he assumed that that would still leave them with nine hours for their ordinary work.[38] Tough, but manageable, we might say. But the orientalist John Gregory (1607–46) worked sixteen hours a day. So did the judge Sir Matthew Hale (1609–76), when he was a law student, though in later life he came to think that six hours of intense work a day was quite enough.[39] Cardinal Wolsey, according to his biographer, could write letters for twelve hours at a sitting, never rising once 'to piss nor yet to eat any meat'.[40] The parliamentarian John Pym started work at 3 a.m. and went on until midnight.[41] Archbishop John Williams also took only three hours' sleep a night, whereas General Monk needed four.[42] William Gouge, spent no time on recreation, 'study and pains' being always 'his chiefest pleasure and delight'.[43] Sir John King, the top Chancery lawyer of his day, died of overwork in 1677 at the age of 39. 'His industry was so great', we are told, 'that he never slept five hours together... and towards the latter end of his time not three hours together, neither had he time to refresh nature by seasonable repasts and rest, his employment in his calling was so great, and over-pressed by [a] multitude of clients.'[44]

Robert Boyle exemplified the restlessness which was so typical of these driven men. 'When I have found myself fit for nothing else,' he tells us, 'I have often times... used a spade in a garden, sawed or cleft wood, grafted trees, and divers such other things, in pursuance of a principle of mine that... to do anything... is better than to do nothing.'[45] Such constant activity did not stem from devotion to the task in hand; it arose from fear of being left alone with oneself.

Most of these obsessive workers came from the professional classes. What about those further down the social scale, who laboured in harsher conditions for much less recognition or reward? Did they enjoy their work? Or was Adam Smith right to claim that, in the inferior employments, the sweets of labour consisted altogether in the recompense of labour, namely the goods which it enabled the labourer to buy?[46]

This is not a question which many historians have thought worth asking. Perhaps the answer is so self-evident. As the historian of the coal industry in this period remarks, 'it cannot be said that there were many who hired themselves out to toil underground with motives beyond the need to earn a living'.[47] In an age of increasing wage-dependence, the poorer classes resorted to innumerable desperate shifts to find the means of subsistence. There is little direct evidence of what they thought about their work, but the suggestion that they valued it for its own sake seems obviously incompatible with all the negative indications: laws enforcing compulsory labour, a high drop-out rate among young servants and apprentices,[48] a rapid turnover in servants hired for the year,[49] strikes and refusals to work unless wages were raised or hours shortened,[50] and the general belief of employers that all workers needed careful supervision; 'too many' hired servants, thought the farmer William Ellis, proved 'untoward, sulky, saucy or idle'.[51] Adam Smith was certain that long apprenticeships created in the young 'an aversion to labour'.[52] Even the godly turner Nehemiah Wallington (1598–1658) once confessed that 'I went into my shop to my employment, more out of conscience to God's commands than of any love I had unto it.' He derived more satisfaction from his daily religious exercises than from his work.[53] Innumerable lives must have resembled that of Edward Shadbolt of Amwell, Hertfordshire, who on his death in 1635 was described by the local vicar as 'a labouring man of above threescore and ten years of age, always a good labourer, no spender, without children, seldom ate good meat or drank good drink or wore good clothes, yet lived and died very poor and miserable'.[54]

The picture, however, was not always so black. In 1411 the poet Thomas Hoccleve, who had been a clerk in the Privy Seal Office, crouched all day over parchment, recalled the cheerful life lived outside his window by the Westminster artisans and tradesmen:

> Thys artificers se I day by day
> In the hootteste of al hyre bysynesse
> Talken and singe and make game and play
> And forth hyr labour passyth with gladnesse.[55]

Singing or whistling at work was very common in the early modern period; and though it was often just an antidote to monotony, it could sometimes express genuine cheerfulness.[56] In 1653 the gentlewoman Dorothy Osborne described her encounter with 'a great many young wenches [who] keep sheep and cows and sit in the shade singing of ballads'. 'I talk to them, and find they want nothing to make them the happiest people in the world, but the knowledge that they are so.'[57] Of course, her perceptions were shaped by the conventions of pastoral literature, which portrayed the lives of rural workers as happy and contented. The same is true of the Marchioness of Newcastle, who observed in 1664 that 'country housewives take more pleasure in milking their cows, making their butter and cheese, and feeding their poultry than great ladies do in painting, curling, and adorning themselves'.[58]

Yet we should not be too quick to dismiss such observations as the product of an artificial literary tradition or of a conspiracy to deceive the poor into thinking that theirs was the best of all possible worlds and to reassure the rich that their comforts did not involve the exploitation of others. The mid-twentieth-century historian W. G. Hoskins believed that, in Elizabethan England, 'for many more than today, there was work that satisfied some at least of their creative instincts, even the labour in the fields'.[59] The small peasant with his own land has always lived for his work: his family holding is the reason for his being. It is the landless labourer who works only because he has to.[60] Yet, even for the agricultural labourer, work had many distinctive satisfactions: the variety of tasks, the pleasures of the natural world, the rhythm of the changing seasons, the sense of visible achievement involved in rearing animals and bringing crops to harvest. 'I very much delighted in holding the plough,' wrote Josiah Langdale (who converted to Quakerism in 1693), 'it being an employment suitable to my mind and no company to disturb my contemplation.'[61]

Not that all agricultural work was solitary. An eighteenth-century French agronomist concluded, after closely watching Suffolk farmworkers, that they did 'their work in a very casual way, taking frequent rests and talking a great deal'.[62] The labourer–poet Stephen Duck (1705–56) evoked the 'throng | Of prattling females' who worked in gangs at haymaking, chattering incessantly. They appear again in the late eighteenth-century poems of the rural clergyman James Hurdis, this time weeding the young wheat, but as voluble as ever:

> Lo! where the gossipping banditti stand
> Amid field idle all, and all alike
> With shrill voice prating, fluent as the pye.[63]

The agricultural expert Arthur Young (1741–1820) thought that English women took part in haymaking 'for pleasure'. Hence the employer's maxim that it was desirable to insert one man in a gang of women, so that his presence would inhibit female gossip.[64]

In modern times, the social relationships of the workplace are among work's chief satisfactions.[65] In the early modern period, work and sociability were tightly intertwined. Women sat or walked together when spinning and sewing; and they chatted at the washing-place and in the market.[66] Many married couples first met as fellow servants.[67] Apprentices and young servants were notoriously liable to gossip and fool around. As the proverb had it, one boy equalled one day's work, two boys equalled half a day's work, and three boys equalled no work at all. Much work was still done within the house-hold, on the farm, or in other little groups who knew each other intimately, shared the same values, and had plenty to talk about. In 1660 Pepys spent an enjoyable evening with the plasterers working on his house; he gave them drink and was 'very merry' with them, 'it being my luck to meet with a sort of drolling workmen upon all occasions'.[68]

When work was carried out in much larger units—workshops, mines, paper mills, breweries, warehouses, shipyards, and govern-ment offices—other forms of sociability emerged. There would be regular breaks for gossipy refreshment—a 'bever' or a 'yo-ho' (so-called from the shouted signal to stop).[69] Much drinking took place, for it was widely believed that strong drink was necessary for the performance of heavy labour, and masters wanted to deter their men from making a visit to the alehouse as an excuse for stopping work.[70] One of the 'judgements' noted by a seventeenth-century Puritan con-cerned the fatal accidents which befell a fiddler and a band of drunken colliers working in the Nottingham coalpits.[71] Intervals of rest were an important feature. 'Look about now into your fields,' urged an Essex clergyman in 1652; 'you shall find the weary workmen sweetly sleeping on the ground; to sleep on the ground is one of the pleasures of the summer.'[72]

The elaborate social world of the workshop, with its male bonding, its initiation rituals and rites of passage, its treats and its forfeits, its banter and repartee, and its heavy practical jokes, so well documented for the nineteenth century, was already in existence in the early modern period. What a picture of life in a Jacobean printing-house is evoked by the information that the boys who ran errands and took the sheets as they were printed off 'commonly black and daub themselves; whence the workmen do jocosely call them "devils", and sometimes "spirits", and sometimes "flies"'![73] When we find Elizabethan shipwrights being forbidden to bring guests into the victualling-houses at mealtimes without leave, or Samuel Pepys telling us that during his afternoons in the Navy Office he found it 'a great pleasure...to talk with persons of quality', we are reminded that there was a great deal more to work than work.[74]

The late medieval and early modern period is often portrayed as a golden age for those craftsmen who owned their own tools and materials, worked on their own premises, and enjoyed autonomy, social recognition, and scope for genuine creativity (pl.5). Many did not achieve this happy position.[75] But individual craftsmanship was widely respected; and the artisan's technical skill always separated him from the common labourer. The dignity of skilled work was enhanced by the craft guilds and companies, with their rituals and hierarchies, their strict control of admissions, and their supervision of production standards.[76] Workers of other kinds could also take pride in their distinctive skills, for even manual labourers might be extremely specialized.[77] In Elizabethan times the Derbyshire lead miners had a strong sense of collective identity, regarding themselves as 'the ancient and skilful miners', 'expert workers', by contrast with 'women, children, and unskilful folk'.[78] The cutlers of Hallamshire were commended in a parliamentary statute of 1624 for 'their industry and labour', by which they had 'gained the reputation of great skill and dexterity'.[79] John Evelyn's experience of English building operations convinced him that there was 'hardly a nation under heaven more conceited of their understandings and abilities and more impatient of direction than our ordinary mechanics. For let one find never so just a fault with a workman, be the same of what mystery soever, immediately he shall reply, "Sir, I do not come hither to be taught my trade. I have served an apprenticeship, and have wrought ere now with gentlemen that have been satisfied with my work." And sometimes not without language of reproach or casting down his tools, and going away in wrath; for such I have frequently met withal.'[80]

Small workshops gave the workers control of their time, their working conditions, and the process of production. So did many of the domestic outputting industries, like weaving, wool-combing, or nailing. Mineworkers were noted for their vigorously independent spirit and retained a good deal of autonomy, whether as free miners owning their own tools and sharing in the proceeds, or as wage-earners with alternative sources of employment to which they could turn.[81] Such occupations, it has been claimed, offered 'an independence, a self-respect, and a control of much of the working environment that was probably much superior to that of the average curate or schoolteacher or clerk'.[82] By contrast, the advent in the eighteenth century of new machinery and larger capitalist enterprises would eventually erode the craft traditions of the past, turn the independent worker into a wage slave, reduce his skills to mechanical operations, impose a new time-dominated discipline, and lead inevitably to discontent and alienation.[83]

The contrast with what had gone before should not be exaggerated, for there had never been a period when all journeymen could expect to become masters, and much work had always been poorly paid and lowly regarded. Even in 1500 the majority of the population were at least partly dependent on wage-earnings.[84] Moreover, the craft guilds had always been hostile to the unskilled and to women, whose work they tended to regard as by definition unskilled. Nevertheless, the decline of the craft tradition undoubtedly lowered the status of the working artisan.

In their own communities, diligent workers did not have to be exceptional craftsmen to win their neighbours' esteem. When Owen ap Morris, a plasterer, was killed by falling off a ladder in Shrewsbury in 1577, he was lamented as 'a true honest, labouring poor man and of good report'.[85] At the end of the sixteenth century, the vicar of Rolleston, Nottinghamshire, recorded with respect the deaths of such humble figures as Christopher Bettinson, 'a painful workman in ditching and mowing'; Richard Walker, 'somewhat tall, slow of speech, a still, quiet and gentle young man, diligent in serving his master... and keeping his sheep'; William Forrest, 'skilful' in 'ditching, mowing, sheep-clipping and such like'; and Nicholas Darwin, 'a painful labourer in ditching, mowing, and other laborious works', who died in 1588 aged at least 90, having never been ill in his life.[86] At Amwell in Hertfordshire the vicar noted the decease in 1634 of John Allen, 'aged above four score years, a labouring man and of good and honest reputation, a pensioner to the New River to cleanse and keep the head, an old servant to the church to guard the chapel door, to control unruly boys and correct intruding dogs, living always poorly but never miserably'.[87] Sir Henry Slingsby's gardener Peter Clark died in 1640: 'he was for no curiosity in gardening, but exceeding laborious in grafting, setting and sowing, which extreme labour shortened his days'.[88]

Richard Gough's history of Myddle in Shropshire (*c*.1700) enumerates similar figures, admired for their industry and, when appropriate, their skill.[89] Most localities had their counterparts, like one Parker, a famous farrier at Rothley, Leicestershire; or Richard Callis, a bonesetter, whose 'useful skill, unwearied industry, and charitable readiness in restoring broken limbs' was lamented on a headstone of 1711 in Waterperry churchyard, Oxfordshire; or Mrs Isabel Denton of Beeston, near Leeds, who in the reign of Charles I, having a feckless husband and many children to support, was said to have invented straw hats and baskets.[90] In early eighteenth-century Oxford, the journals of the antiquarian Thomas Hearne abound in references to the specialized skills of humble folk in the locality: 'an ingenious wheelwright', 'an excellent jockey', 'very famous for curing smoky chimneys'.[91] Later in the century, the Glamorganshire clergyman William Thomas remarks in his diary upon many relatively uneducated members of the community who won admiration for their skilful labour. He mentions John Coles, carpenter, of Cowbridge, 'a great estimator and measurer of all artificers' work'; Jane Jenkin of Whitton, 'a very knowing woman with the sick and wounded'; and Thomas French of Wenvoe, 'a very knowing man in several branches of knowledge, as clock- and watch-work, etc'.[92]

'Sir, I am a true labourer: I earn that I eat, get that I wear, owe no man hate, envy no man's happiness ... and the greatest of my pride is to see my ewes graze and my lambs suck.'[93] We should hesitate before dismissing Shakespeare's old shepherd as a figure of literary fantasy. It is true that Elizabethan shepherds, unlike those of pastoral poetry, tended to be wage-earners rather than owner–proprietors, but many people of the lower classes in early modern England thought of their work and themselves with a genuine sense of satisfaction; and they were encouraged to do by the preachers, who gave them a sense of dignity and purpose, assuring them that hard work was a virtue which deserved to be honoured and that the best Christian life involved getting one's living by one's own labour. Many of the trades which the gentry despised as menial brought self-respect to their practitioners. A regular occupation was a sign of respectability; and the ability to support a family was proof of manhood. Whereas from idleness, in the words of the *Homilies*, flowed 'loss of name, fame, reputation'.[94]

A job well done would always excite admiration. Revealingly, the employer who recommended including a man in a group of women workers to prevent them from gossiping also advised including a woman among a gang of men, so as to give the latter an incentive to show off their strength and skill.[95] Manual work gave the opportunity for the display of muscle, courage, and stamina, while technical competence, even in supposedly 'unskilled' occupations, could then, as now, evoke the admiration of others. 'It is a great pleasure to be in the country this harvest season,' runs a late fifteenth-century school text; 'to see the reapers how they strive who shall go before [the] other.' Conversely, an ill-ploughed furrow could bring as much shame to the ploughman as did cowardice to the soldier.[96] When in 1637 a passenger from New England complained that he would have got home faster if the ship's master had only taken advantage of a favourable wind, his aspersions upon the captain's professional ability led to a fight and a suit in the Admiralty Court.[97]

The hard-working, self-supporting, technically competent individual was always admired; and the existence in local dialects of a large repertoire of derogatory names for lazy people is evidence of what many of their fellow labourers thought about the feckless and the indolent.[98] Industriousness was not just prized for its practical utility. It was a moral quality which gave the individual dignity and social acceptance. Isaac Barrow thought that it showed 'an ingenuous and generous disposition of the soul', and a proud disinclination to live upon the labours of others.[99] Seventeenth-century building workers regarded it as extremely offensive to describe someone as a 'lubbard' or 'an idle fellow'; and the respectable poor made a point of stressing that they wanted work, not charity.[100] If they sought relief, there was no better claim than to have a reputation as 'an honest poor man and a painful labourer'.[101] The words 'laborious' and 'honest' were virtually interchangeable.

Figure 3.2 A despised but necessary occupation: an eighteenth-century nightman advertises his readiness to empty privies and cesspits.

Of course, occupations varied greatly in status and prestige. Some were thought to be unmanly because they could equally well be performed by women: brewers, bakers, and cooks all suffered from this stigma.[102] Some, as we have already seen, were condemned by moralists as disreputable.[103] A few were universally regarded as odious: butchers, night-soil carriers, and, above all, executioners: hanging and whipping were so much against nature, thought Bishop Jeremy Taylor, that 'none but the vilest part of mankind are put to do it unto others'.[104] In every occupation, from domestic service to coal mining, there was a hierarchy of esteem, reflecting differing degrees of skill, responsibility, and remuneration, with each rank possessing a strong sense of its superiority to those below.[105] In the mines, hewers were paid up to twice as much as those who hauled and carried the coal, and in the building trade plumbers might earn four times as much as labourers.[106] Many people escaped easy categorization because they had more than one employment. But everywhere, the independent worker was admired more than the wage-earner or 'hireling'.[107] An Oxfordshire witness in a Jacobean case in the church courts was discredited on the grounds that he was 'accounted a mercenary man that wrought for wages, sometimes in one parish and sometimes in another'.[108] Dependence was usually a greater stigma than the nature of the work performed.

Yet however contemptible the status of the job, satisfaction could be obtained from doing it well. As the poet John Dryden ironically remarked, 'there is...a vast difference betwixt the slovenly butchering of a man, and the fineness of a stroke that separates the head from the body, and leaves it standing in its place. A man may be capable, as Jack Ketch's wife said of his servant, of a plain piece of work, a bare hanging; but to make a malefactor die sweetly was only belonging to her husband.'[109] In modern times, the sweepers of Varanasi, India, are regarded as utterly polluted by other castes, but they themselves have a strong sense of self-esteem, and pride themselves on their toughness.[110]

Early modern women gained respect for being active and industrious. The ladies of the Elizabethan court were said to be constantly occupied in needlework, spinning silk, distilling medicine, and devising dainty dishes; and seventeenth-century cookery books contain many recipes attributed to aristocratic ladies, such as the Countess of Rutland's recipe for Banbury cake and 'the Lady Abergavenny's cheese'. In the eighteenth century, housekeeping could give genteel women status and satisfaction.[111] Well-to-do females were thought much less likely to be bored than their male counterparts, because they always had a variety of occupations with which to 'fill up the void'.[112] Lower down the social scale, many male suitors shared the attitude of the Jacobean Wiltshireman who said that he wanted 'not a fine wife', but 'one that can work'.[113] Among country folk, a good dairymaid enjoyed 'esteem, and reputation', whereas a 'fine or delicate' gentlewoman was 'misliked ... and called a clean-fingered girl, as though that were a great ignominy'.[114] Good housekeeping was universally respected. As a preacher remarked in 1677, 'the well ordering of the house seems to be, more particularly, the woman's office ... and if she perform that part well, good housewifery is her praise'.[115] A colossal amount of labour went into all the scrubbing and washing and cooking and sweeping necessary to keep the seventeenth-century home clean and presentable. Yet, for many women, this was not a chore but a source of deep satisfaction. Mary Ferrar, mother of Nicholas Ferrar (1592–1637) of Little Gidding, even felt it necessary to warn her daughters against the sin of taking too much delight in housework: 'to seek these kind of businesses for pleasure, and to make them your delights, and to pride yourself for your care and curiosity in them, is a great vanity and folly'.[116]

In addition to running their households, women of the middling classes were often involved in their husbands' business affairs, managing them in their absence or after their deaths. At a lower social level, there was scarcely any productive occupation in which women did not play at least some part. They could be blacksmiths, butchers, building labourers, chimney sweeps, colliers, and agricultural workers; they went out in fishing boats; they were heavily involved in the textile industries; and they participated in a wide range of retail trades. In Jacobean Southampton one widow ran a slaughterhouse, where she killed pigs, sheep, and cattle.[117] It is likely that at least some of this work enhanced female status and self-esteem. A London constable deposed in 1593 that he was loath to draw an accused woman into discredit, 'because he saw that [she] always took great pains and laboured hard for her living'; and it was not uncommon in the law courts for women to assert proudly that they lived honestly by their labour of their own hands.[118] But though many female occupations, from midwifery to embroidery, were technically demanding, women were less likely to be applauded by contemporaries for their skills and dexterity than were men. Public and professional life, business success, technical know-how, and hard manual labour were all seen as intrinsically masculine.

The sexual division of labour was intensified by an increasing separation during the early modern period of work from the home.[119] The Curlylocks ideal of female exemption from productive labour became more evident among the upper and middling classes.[120] In 1609 the Earl of Northumberland advised his son that, although among 'the poorer sort' wives might help to manage their husbands' business, it was quite inappropriate for the wives of 'great men' to be involved in such matters. In the later seventeenth century, Richard Baxter expressed concern that girls in gentry families were 'taught no calling, nor exercised in any employment, but only such as is meet for nothing but ornament and recreation...They are betimes engaged in a life of idleness'.[121] The eighteenth century would see a great expansion of leisure and fashion industries designed to meet this new demand.

Of course, the exclusion of the female sex from both external employment and domestic labour was a luxury which only the relatively wealthy could afford. But it would become a common middle-class aspiration; and it was assisted by growing opportunities to buy in the market food, clothes, and other goods which in earlier times would have been made at home. Among the poorer classes, female labour remained crucial to the family economy and there was no question of the man being the sole breadwinner. Some wives of artisans even regarded it as shameful for a woman to be dependent upon her husband's earnings.[122] But, because of their family duties, women moved in and out of the labour market, and their work was usually poorly paid and low in status. For men, work was a primary source of self-esteem. It was less so for women, particularly when, as a consequence of the increasing separation between home and work-place, housework and child-rearing tended increasingly not to be regarded as 'work' at all.

Men, however, usually looked to their work as the source of their sense of identity. Since 1413, when an Act had required original writs to identify an individual's 'estate, degree or mystery', occupation had been a basic principle of social classification; though it was frustrated by the tendency of so many individuals to combine different occupations or to move from one form of employment to another. The huge number of occupational surnames today reminds us of this bygone equation of man and job. In financial accounts and parish records individuals were frequently identified by their work: 'Arnold the carpenter', 'Jones the old cinder picker', 'Margaret the swineherd's daughter'. In the 1690s the churchwardens of All Saints, Newcastle, referred to craftsmen by their trades, as in 'Bricklayer Johnson', 'Joiner Harrison', or 'Plumber Hall'.[123] Many individuals left details of their occupation or symbols of them on their tombstones.[124]

Men were what they did. Women, by contrast, tended to be defined in terms of their husband's or father's occupation rather than their own; if they remarried, they changed their identity and often their job. Only single women were likely to be categorized by their occupation. This was not a universal rule, though, for there certainly were married women who chose to identify themselves in terms of their work, like the Jacobean cheesemaker's wife who described herself as 'a butter-woman by profession'.[125]

Occupation shaped the individual's self-consciousness. As Adam Smith would write, 'the understandings of the greater part of men are necessarily formed by their ordinary employments'.[126] Every trade had its technical vocabulary, so bafflingly arcane to the outsider that Samuel Johnson did not even attempt to include it in his great *Dictionary*.[127] The language of seafaring was said to be 'utterly unintelligible to a land-man', while a schoolmaster remarked in 1654 that anyone who thought he was good at rendering English into Latin should try translating some of the workers' terms for preparing hemp: 'to *ripple* it; to *brake* it; to *swingle* it; to *heckle* it'.[128] Even personal 'character' tended to be seen as an attribute of the individual's employment, since each occupation was thought to generate its own distinctive values, attitudes, and mannerisms. The possibility that individuals pursuing the same trade might differ radically from each other in personality and outlook was seldom articulated.[129]

The body, no less than the mind, was subjected to this occupational deformation. 'We commonly know a baker or a tailor by his legs,' wrote the mid-seventeenth-century physician John Bulwer.[130] Miners could be identified by the pallor of their skin.[131] An early eighteenth-century doctor noted that 'the legs, thighs and feet of chairmen, the arms and hands of watermen, [and] the backs and shoulders of porters, grow thick and strong and brawny'.[132] Samuel Johnson had no doubt that 'it is easy to guess the trade of an artisan by his knees, his fingers or his shoulders'. In his view, 'There is no man who works at any particular trade, but you may know him from his appearance to do so. One part or other of his body being more used than the rest, he is in some degree deformed.'[133] A century and a half later, the sociologist Émile Durkheim would claim that the greater the division of labour, the greater the physical differences between individuals.[134]

In the early modern period, work was expected to fill most of the hours of daylight, the amount of officially available leisure time was small, and the distinction between work and leisure was often unclear. In such circumstances, the closer texture of social life made it almost impossible to throw off an occupational identity outside working hours. There *were* working people who also had reputations as singers, dancers, wrestlers, and storytellers. But, typically, it was during the long hours of labour that individual identity was forged.

Today, when the working week for most people is much shorter than it used to be, the highest prestige attaches not to leisure, as in the past, but to extreme busy-ness. Typically, those in high-status occupations work exceptionally long hours and take relatively few holidays.[135] Symbolic of the change is the fact that what used, perhaps mistakenly, to be thought of as a distinctively Protestant viewpoint has been officially endorsed by the Roman Catholic Church: in his encyclical letter *Laborem exercens* (1981) Pope John Paul II declares that 'through work man not only transforms nature, adapting it to his needs, but he also achieves fulfilment as a human being'. 'In an achievement-oriented society', remarks a modern historian, 'work becomes sacred both as the essential source of social validation and as the locus for self-fulfillment.'[136]

Yet most of the modern British population have a more instrumental attitude to work. Many find their true identity outside work altogether, in sports, recreations, and hobbies. Anonymous in the office or factory, they emerge in their leisure hours as ballroom dancers or bungie-jumpers or builders of Salisbury Cathedral in matchsticks. Work is an area in which they expect little in the way of self-realization. It is in the use of their leisure that they seek to fulfil themselves.[137]

In the sixteenth and seventeenth centuries, by contrast, the accepted view of work as a painful necessity did less than justice to the richness of actual experience. Of course, the meaning of work to those who performed it varied enormously according to the context. The variety of employments, the different relationships to the means of production, and the inequalities of status and reward make generalization impossible. We can only guess what most people thought about their work, for they have left no record of their feelings. In so far as they were capable of conceptualizing their work as something separate from the rest of their lives, it is likely that many of them felt profoundly ambivalent about it. Yet, for some contemporaries at least, work was not a curse but a source of fulfilment: not a means to an end, but an end in itself; not a job, but a vocation. For the professional and business classes, work was as interesting and absorbing as it is today. For scholars and artists it could be an obsession. To craftsmen, it offered opportunities to win esteem for their skill and ingenuity. Least fortunate were the wage-earning, manual workers, who, in one historian's words, 'dug and shovelled in all weathers, repetitiously banged hammers in noisy and sulphurous workshops, or crouched at the coalface in ill-lit and poorly ventilated tunnels'.[138] For them, such work can hardly be said to have been fulfilling; and it is not surprising that it was among them that the preference for freedom and leisure lasted longest. Yet ghastly though their conditions of labour frequently were, they could at least enjoy companionship, the pride of overcoming physical danger, the esteem of their workmates, and the pleasure of rest after heavy exertions. An observer wrote in 1630 of the Devonshire tin miners that 'no labourer whatsoever undergoes greater hazard of peril or danger', yet, he added, 'they sleep soundly in their beds and have a kind of content therein, for that they aim at no better.'[139] Perhaps some of them might even have agreed with the Enlightenment philosopher who said that 'the grand recipe for felicity' was constant employment: 'The idle are the only wretched.'[140]

4

WEALTH AND POSSESSIONS

Is it not a point and chief point (think you) of great policy and wisdom to advance our stock and family? Is it not in the opinion of most men a happy thing to be rich? Do not all men delight in, and therefore desire a fair, large and beautiful house? To be lord of many manors, to receive many revenues, doth it not engender great favour, bring much worship and reverence?

William Blandy, *The Castle; or, Picture of Pollicy,* 1581

men like ants
Toil to prevent imaginary wants;
Yet all in vain, increasing with their store,
Their vast desires, but make their wants the more.

Sir John Denham, *Cooper's Hill,* 1642

GOODS AND THE SOCIAL ORDER

In the early modern period it was often said that wealth was something which everybody desired. 'All men studieth on every side how that they may wax rich,' complained a late medieval writer, 'and every man almost is ashamed to be holden a poor man.'[1] In fact, most people were more concerned to avoid poverty than to become rich. What small husbandmen, cottagers, and day-labourers in Tudor England sought was a reliable supply of the resources necessary to sustain life. They lived from hand to mouth and did not expect to accumulate a surplus; they did not seek to build up savings; and they were more concerned to avoid risk than to maximize profits.[2] This had always been the ethic of peasant societies and it would long survive in the less developed parts of the world.[3]* By comparison with the endless struggle for subsistence and security, the pursuit of wealth was a specialized occupation, indulged in by only a minority of the population. Of course, most landowners were vigorously acquisitive, regarding the enlargement and retention of their family property as an important objective; merchants and lawyers had a desire for gain which was notoriously 'inordinate';[4] and even in the lower reaches of agrarian society, there was plenty of ruthless opportunism. The network of internal markets and the ubiquity of credit had long accustomed people to the notion of profit and financial success. 'Many parents' were said to 'moil and toil,... cark [labour anxiously] and care . . . pinch and spare, to leave their children store of wealth'.[5]

Yet acquisitiveness had yet to find its ideological justification. Many inhabitants of rural communities seem to have been hostile to the maximization of individual gain, preferring a customary allocation of resources and rewards which would ensure the perpetuation of the group as a whole. Theirs was a non-accumulative ethic, in which neighbourly responsibility, obligations to family members, and contributions to parochial causes ranked higher than the unremitting pursuit of self-interest. Accumulation was disapproved of because it was thought, often rightly, to be at the expense of someone else. Anyway, how could a poor husbandman ever hope to grow spectacularly rich, unless by marrying many wives or by discovering buried treasure?[6]

This was the attitude of most sixteenth-century moralists. It was right to seek the worldly goods which were necessary for 'the maintenance of every man's state according to his degree'.[7] But once those needs had been satisfied, the pursuit of additional wealth was undesirable; and it was wrong to covet clothes, diet, and possessions which were inappropriate to one's social position.[8]

In the Christian tradition, riches had always been regarded as an impediment to salvation. They were despised by all truly pious persons. Treasure was to be sought in heaven not earth. The only valid justification for great wealth was that it enabled its holders to do good works, by benefiting religion, the poor, and the common weal.

---

* When the antiquarian John Aubrey visited Ireland in 1661, he 'saw the manner of living of the natives, scorning industry and luxury, contenting themselves only with things necessary'; *Thomas Hobbes: The Correspondence*, ed. Noel Malcolm (Oxford, 1994), ii. 520.

Charity was the essential social duty of the rich.[9] Avarice, by contrast, was a sin, indicating a selfish indifference to the welfare of others. This was the tacit contract between the rich and the rest of society: their good fortune was acceptable only because a share of it went back in the form of largesse: charity, gift-giving, and hospitality.[10] To most theologians in the century after the Reformation the idea of wealth without obligation was unacceptable. Economic inequality was justified by the argument, derived from Aristotle, that it enabled the rich to practise the virtue of liberality, just as it called on the poor to display the virtue of patience. That was why God had decreed that there would always be poor in the land.[11] Large-scale generosity was an expression of superior social status. The very word 'generous' was derived from *generosus*, meaning 'well-born'. Not that aristocratic liberality was disinterested; by the distribution of gifts, hospitality, and patronage, prudently bestowed, the well-to-do could create relationships of dependency which were indispensable for their social and political standing.[12]

For mid-sixteenth century 'Commonweal' publicists like Hugh Latimer or Robert Crowley, it was axiomatic that private gain was antithetical to the public good. Holding that great riches could neither be acquired nor retained without sin, they denied that individuals were entitled to do what they wished with their own and instead urged that the rich should employ their resources for the good of everyone. For John Hales, an active economic reformer in the reign of Edward VI, it was the government's aim to 'take away the inordinate desire of riches, wherewith many be encumbered'.[13] In 1603 Absolon Gethyn, an Oxford don, posed the question 'whether it be lawful in a well-governed commonwealth for every man to heap up as much riches as he may without any stint at all?', predictably answering with a firm negative. To make wealth 'an aim and end' in itself was a wicked mistake.[14]

The aristocratic ethos was equally hostile to unrestrained money-making. Those fortunate enough to have inherited riches were happy to dismiss the search for profit by others as 'sordid' and 'ignoble', unworthy of persons of 'better birth' and 'generous disposition'; some even held it 'the prime and essential part of a lord to be ignorant of what he hath'. Aristocrats were not expected to ration their expenditure to fit their income. Their role was to be prodigal, while manifesting a lordly indifference to money.[15] Moralists in the civic-humanist tradition subscribed to the Aristotelian doctrine that a certain amount of wealth was necessary for a life of virtue. But they regarded private enrichment beyond that point as a serious diversion from civic commitment.[16]

Aristocratic prejudice, Christian teaching, and classical tradition thus all reinforced a deep-rooted suspicion of moneymaking as a prime objective of human life.

Yet the utility of wealth could hardly be denied. An Elizabethan satirist observed that a rich man whose coffers were full of gold could count on having his 'reverence, courtesy, cap and knee', however hideous his personal appearance and manners:

> Yea, let him cough, hawk, spit and fart, and piss,
> If he be wealthy, nothing is amiss.

Conversely:

> let him but want money, and 'tis plain,
> He's th'only brief and abstract of disdain,
> Despised, scorn'd, dejected, and contemn'd.
> And round about with miseries behemmed.[17]

Commentators accused 'the common sort of people' of holding the 'gross error' and 'churlish opinion' that all 'noble birth and gentry' originated in riches.[18] The aristocracy might claim that they owed their position to valiant ancestors and superior virtue, but everyone knew that their authority rested on material resources. As one seventeenth-century lawyer observed, 'the most general way of arriving at the title of gentleman is by wealth'.[19]

Early modern aristocrats needed money to maintain their necessary style of life and to sustain their personal honour. The case had not been forgotten of George Nevill, who, having been created Duke of Bedford in 1470, was, eight years later, degraded from all his titles by Act of Parliament, on the grounds that he had no 'livelihood' to support them.[20] High rank carried with it the obligation to live in an appropriate style and to shoulder the accompanying financial responsibilities. In the words of the Elizabethan Sir Thomas Smith, 'a gentleman...must go like a gentleman'. Or, as the Puritan preacher John Preston (1587–1628) put it: 'men in higher rank and calling need more than men of an inferior degree to maintain their place and dignity'.[21] In 1658 Sir Henry Slingsby advised his sons never to be sparing in their expenditure, 'where reputation invites you to spend'.[22] Gentlemen lost face if they found themselves unable to bear what contemporaries called 'the port, charge and countenance of a gentleman', like Sir Edward Dering, who, in 1673, because of the fall of rents and his loss of office as a commissioner of the Privy Seal, was forced to follow a course of 'general frugality'.[23] Sir John Lowther (1582–1637) warned his sons that, 'without...wealth (the supporter and up-holder of gentry and worldly reputation), nobility or gentility is a vain and contemptible title here in England, and always hath been...Preserve your estate if you will preserve your gentry and nobility of blood, which is nothing else but a descent of riches.'[24]

At lower social levels, it was equally prudent for private men 'justly and moderately to enrich themselves', as Thomas Hobbes put it.[25] For even the humble had to finance an appropriate style of life if they were to retain their credit and esteem. An Elizabethan doctor lamen-ted that, if someone's merits were under discussion, the first question asked was 'what is he worth?'[26] The men of most wealth, an Essex clergyman remarked, were usually called 'the best men of the parish'. It was they who were normally regarded as the 'chief' inhabitants or 'the better sort' (as opposed to 'the poorer sort' or 'meaner sort'); and, it was they who usually took the lead in parochial government.[27] In the law courts, a witness without substance was a witness without credit. When in 1574 the Ecclesiastical Commission for the diocese of Gloucester in 1574 required a defendant to produce six 'honest men' to swear in his defence, it defined 'honest' to mean 'such as have six or eight oxen apiece and keepeth ploughs of their own'. In the church courts the testimony of poor men as compurgators was not admit-ted.[28] 'Men's honesties are now measured by the subsidy book,' lamented Barnaby Rich in 1617. 'He that is rich is honest.' If a poor man wished to be regarded as honest, the onus was on him to prove it.[29] 'Whosoever wanteth money', agreed the writer Henry Peacham in 1641, 'is ever subject to contempt and scorn in the world, let him be furnished with never so good gifts, either of body or mind.'[30] Small wonder that the scholar Isaac Barrow concluded that, of all human objectives, wealth was that which men most desired, 'as the great storehouse of their needs and conveniences, the sure bulwark of their state and dignity, the universal instrument of compassing their designs and pleasures'.[31]

It was, however, expenditure rather than income which demon-strated status; for the social hierarchy was envisaged as a hierarchy of consumption. As a sycophantic Devonshire clergyman told his gentry patrons in 1701, 'there is undoubtedly more of the Hero often seen in a noble expending, than in a niggardly getting or keeping an estate'.[32]

Aristocrats defended their possession of plate, jewellery, and rich clothing on the Aristotelian grounds that those of superior rank needed to display the virtue of magnificence. This was supposedly something different from vulgar ostentation, but the distinction was a fine one. The pursuit of virtue through magnificence could, in principle, justify almost unlimited accumulation. How otherwise could the nobility finance buildings on a heroic scale and furnish them appropriately?[33] In the absence of a banking system, jewels, gold, and silver plate provided a good way of locking up savings, while their conspicuous display on public occasions demonstrated their owners' creditworthiness. According to 'divers of good experience and judgment', the value of the plate in the realm in 1635 far exceeded that of the coinage in circulation.[34]

The forms of consumption favoured by the early modern English aristocracy multiplied in the early modern period and they were nothing if not blatant: huge houses in the country and elegant residences in town, sumptuous feasts, horses, dogs, coaches, servants, and pompous funerals. During the seventeenth century, there was a shift away from old-style rural, open-house hospitality towards a more private and (for half the year) urban form of living. Less was spent on household retainers, more on travel, furniture, private entertaining, gambling, and the London life.[35] The objects of expenditure changed over time, but the essential principle was constant: opulent display was an essential ingredient of aristocratic rule.

Social differences were expressed in the consumption of food. Commenting on the Lord's Prayer, an Elizabethan bishop explained that, when praying for their daily bread, 'some men may pray for more than others may... for great men have need of more than mean men'.[36] In 1541 Archbishop Cranmer and his colleagues accordingly ordered that the tables of archbishops should offer not more than six kinds of flesh at a meal, bishops not above five, deans and archdeacons four, and all other clergy not more than three.[37] The upper classes consumed white bread rather than brown, meat rather than vegetables, wine rather than ale, and (more curiously) white eggs rather than brown.[38] They also enjoyed luxuries like venison, pheasants, small birds, and sugar. Conversely, rye and barley bread, gruels, pottage, fat bacon, root vegetables, beans, cheese, and, in the eighteenth century, bread and butter had plebeian associations. Coarse food was appropriate for coarse bodies.[39] Within a large household, servants and apprentices were unlikely to eat as well as their employer and his family.[40] The belief that those of higher social level were entitled to a superior diet accounts for the practice in some churches of providing two grades of Communion wine: muscatel or malmsey for 'the better sort', claret for the others.[41]

The consumption of other goods was also stratified socially. Dress was the most striking example: a single gown bought by Henry VIII in 1544 cost over £200, more than a plasterer working on Eltham Palace could earn in twenty years.[42] In Tudor times, a sequence of statutes and proclamations set limits to what could be worn by different social groups. Though much flouted in practice, these sumptuary measures expressed the widespread view that people's appearance and expenditure should accord with their social position.[43] Dressing below one's rank was as much an offence as dressing above it. The great seventeenth-century judge Sir Matthew Hale discovered this when, as a young law student, his negligent way of dressing led to his being seized one day by the press-gang. The experience, it was claimed, 'made him return to more decency in his clothes' thereafter.[44]

Housing varied spectacularly with rank and pretension. Contemporary architects usually assumed that, in their scale and decoration, houses should reflect their owners' social position. When Lichfield Cathedral close was rebuilt in the 1660s, following the medieval plan, the bishop's house was allowed a front of 240 feet, the deanery 120 feet, and the canons' houses 60.[45] The later Stuart hearth tax was based on the assumption that the size of people's houses was an index of their wealth. The mansions of the nobility were several hundred times as expensive to build as the cottages of the poor, many of whom lived in flimsy huts which could be easily pulled down and re-erected elsewhere.[46] In the age which saw the erection of great palaces like Wollaton Hall and Hatfield House, there were people dwelling in caves and hollow trees; in London, which was increasingly overcrowded, ten persons were discovered living in a room 12 feet square, containing one bed.[47] More subtle differences of status were reflected in the height of the rooms, and the architectural detail. In the Elizabethan countryside, chimneys and glass windows denoted exceptional prosperity, while in south Gloucestershire, in the late seventeenth century, the windows in gentlemen's houses usually had stone mullions, whereas yeomen had only wooden ones.[48]

A nobleman's house was a showplace, permanently on display. From the seventeenth century onwards, visitors could often obtain admission by tipping the servants and, once admitted, could see not just the public rooms, but the private apartments, even the owner's clothes.[49] Carved chimney pieces, plaster ceilings, panelled wainscot, tapestries, carpets, lacquered cabinets, linen, porcelain, and plate were all indicators of wealth and social distinction.

Every detail of domestic furnishing and decoration had its social overtones, from the kind of floor (earthen, stone flags, tiles, or wooden boards) to the ostentatious firedogs and firebacks which decorated the hearth in a prosperous household.[50] Typically, labourers slept on straw, husbandmen on flock mattresses, yeomen on feathers, and gentlemen on mattresses of down.[51] The fifteenth-century distinction between 'gentlemen's sheets' and 'yeomen's [i.e. servants'] sheets' was maintained into the seventeenth century, when the sheets used by servants were still inferior in quality to those of the master's family and distinguished accordingly in household inventories.[52] Contemporaries enjoyed the story of the beggar boy who said that, if he were king, he would lodge every night up to his ears in dry straw.[53] For lighting, 'sweet' wax candles were socially superior to 'stinking' tallow candles (and four times as expensive).[54] Carpets were a symbol of high status and were not originally placed on the floor. In 1555, when the Protestant martyr Nicholas Ridley was interrogated by his persecutors, there was a carpet on the table. But when the turn came of his colleague Hugh Latimer, it was removed, because Latimer did not hold the degree of doctor. Perceiving no covering on the table, he sardonically placed his old felt hat under his elbows.[55]

Seating was designed as much for the sake of expressing hierarchy as for comfort. In peasants' houses there might be a chair for the head of the household, but benches or stools for the rest. When James I visited Oxford in 1605, a temporary theatre was built in Christ Church hall; the front-row benches, reserved for 'ladies and the King's servants', were 8 inches wide, with 16 inches of knee room; those behind them had 6 and 12 inches, while persons at the rear had to stand.[56]

Equally conspicuous were social differences in modes of transport. The horse gave its rider superiority over the pedestrian; and the person who travelled by coach was superior to the one who rode on horseback. The greater the number of horses pulling the coach, the grander the occupant. In great houses, the stables were important places of display.[57]

Servants and retinues were also important accoutrements of rank. Persons in authority could not decently appear in public without large trains of attendants. Sitting next to the Earl of Clarendon at the Privy Council in 1660, Charles II passed him a note saying that he proposed to visit his sister in Tunbridge Wells, but would take only his night bag. 'You will not go without forty or fifty horse?' replied his minister; to which the Merry Monarch scribbled back, 'I count that part of my night bag.'[58]

In these and innumerable other obvious ways, the consumption of goods gave visual expression to the social hierarchy. Possessions were used to signify power, wealth, ancestry, mental cultivation, and nobility of character. As a result, most commodities acquired a distinctive set of symbolic meanings and associations, full of social resonance. To possess them was inevitably an act of self-definition.

This was the context within which, in the early modern period, there took place a vast expansion in the range and quantity of commodities available for purchase. Merely to list some of the goods which were rare or non-existent in the early sixteenth century but commonplace by the mid-eighteenth is to give some idea of the change: tobacco, sugar, coffee, and tea; books, clocks, looking-glasses, forks, porcelain, pictures, and newspapers; coaches and sedan chairs, wallpaper, curtains, and cushions; glass windows and drinking vessels, mahogany and upholstered furniture. Some of these commodities were luxuries, enjoyed only by the rich. But even husbandmen and craftsmen acquired pottery, pewter, glass, linen, knives, pens, needles, and a range of tools, cooking vessels, and domestic utensils, on a scale which had never been seen before. They and their families bought stockings, caps, gloves, lace, ribbons, and, in the eighteenth century, cottons and lighter textiles.

Nearly all these goods were subject to regular shifts in fashion. In high society, styles of dress and ornament came and went at a bewildering pace. A mid-seventeenth-century witness tells us that, in 1645 and 1646, the fashionable gallant was wearing 'a narrow brimmed hat, a long waist... breeches to his knees, boots and boot-hosetops, and great jingling spurs'. In 1648 and 1649 a broad-brimmed hat, long breeches, 'boots with the tops trailing on the ground, little spurs that must not jingle in the least. In 1652 and this present year 1653 we think it ridiculous to wear boots, but [only] shoes and stockings.'[59] No wonder that a preacher in 1665 could speak of 'these consuming days'.[60]

The many historians who have studied this process like to label it a 'consumer revolution', comparable to the growth of mass consumption in the late nineteenth and twentieth centuries, though they disagree as to whether the 'revolution' occurred in the mid-sixteenth century, the late seventeenth, or the eighteenth; for each of those periods appears to have seen an accelerated spurt in the availability and acquisition of new commodities. Indeed, the late fourteenth and fifteenth centuries had already witnessed a growth in the aristocratic consumption of silks, furs, jewels, bed hangings, and silver plate, rapid changes of fashion in dress and adornment, and a great expansion of expenditure by tradesmen and peasantry on clothes, food and drink, tools, furniture, and household equipment. Between 1450 and 1550 there was a particularly dramatic increase in the quantity and variety of imported ceramic wares.[61] In the late sixteenth and seventeenth centuries, houses became larger and more diversified; and household contents multiplied.[62] In the late seventeenth and eighteenth centuries, the middle classes greatly increased their consumption of imported groceries, glassware, furniture, linen, cottons, chintzes, pictures, clocks, looking-glasses, haberdashery and fine ceramics.

These changes were made possible by the growth of international trade with Europe, Asia, and America, and the manufacture of new products at home, often thanks to the immigration of foreign craftsmen. They were accompanied and facilitated by new marketing and advertising techniques and by improvements in methods of sale and distribution, reflected in the increasing separation of retailing from production, a rise in the number of shops, chapmen, and other outlets, and the emergence of shopping as a leisure activity.[63] As early as 1549, the display in London shops was said to be so glittering as to 'make any temperate man to gaze on them and to buy somewhat, though it serve to no purpose necessary'.[64] Above all, there was a growing acceptance of the notion that the purpose of working was not just to acquire the means of subsistence but to amass a surplus with which to purchase additional goods.

This was not a new idea as such. As early as 1535, Thomas Lupset believed that one could 'on all sides... see men sweating in a continual work, both of body and of mind, to get... worldly goods'.[65] But, allegedly, a section of the population still retained its preference for leisure rather than more spending power.[66] Why was this preference eventually broken down? And why did the acquisition of ever more goods become an overwhelming preoccupation?

POSSESSIONS AND THEIR MEANING

Some of the new commodities, like pots and pans, clocks and mirrors, washable cottons, tools and equipment, had an obvious functional utility; and it is not surprising that people should have wanted them.

Others, like tobacco, tea, and coffee, were physically addictive, even if, initially, they might take some getting used to: in 1657 the inhabitants of the London parish of St Dunstan's in the West prosecuted one James Farr 'for making and selling of a drink called "coffee", whereby in making the same he annoyeth his neighbours by evil smells'.[1] Yet coffee was as important for its sociable connotations as for its inherent drinkability; as with so many other commodities, its attraction to purchasers can only be understood if its social meaning is taken into account. Historians often write as if the desire for, say, comfortable chairs was self-evidently something which everyone would want to satisfy at the first opportunity. But a western European has only to visit a Japanese house to realize that notions of comfort are culturally relative. People unused to upholstered furniture do not have a desire for it. As Sir Walter Scott wrote in 1819 of the household of his fictional creation Cedric the Saxon: 'of comfort there was little and, being unknown, it was unmissed'.[2] The German philosopher Hegel would argue that 'the need for greater comfort does not exactly arise within you directly; it is suggested to you by those who hope to make a profit from its creation'.[3] But the striking fact about the growth in consumption during the early modern period is that it got under way before the appearance of large-scale advertising; and though much energy went into marketing and selling, commercial pressures are not sufficient to explain the apparently limitless demand for new goods.

Nor was the utility of the new commodities always apparent. Some were positively inconvenient, like the coaches which were so awkward to manoeuvre in seventeenth-century London. 'I have seen a great lord, in his coach drawn with six horses, stayed at the turning of a street either by a carman or a collier,' wrote a contemporary in 1656, 'when many a poor man hath slipt by and got safe home.'[4] Sir Thomas Browne thought that physicians kept coaches in London 'more for state than for business', while Lord Fermanagh remarked in 1704 that 'a glass coach is an inconvenient way of travelling in the month of August, but 'tis beauish'.[5] Of course, coaches made it easier for the gentry to come in from the provinces, but if we want to know why Londoners bought them, we should recall Samuel Pepys, who decided in April 1667 that it was not 'too much . . . in degree or cost' for him to keep a coach. His motive was that he was 'ashamed' to be seen in a hackney (a hired cab), and the idea pleased his wife 'mightily'. He and his wife lay together in bed, talking about it; and when at last she saw the coach he had chosen, she was 'out of herself for joy almost'. But when his colleague Thomas Povey was shown the desired object, he found 'most infinite fault with it, both as to being out of fashion and heavy'. Pepys, somewhat chastened, accepted this advice and chose another one, this time with Povey's advice. A new coach was duly ordered, along with a fine pair of black horses, 'the beautifullest almost that ever I saw'. In late November 1668, Pepys was at last able to ride in his own coach: 'it being mighty pleasure to go alone with my poor wife in a coach of our own to a play; and makes us appear mighty great, I think, in the world'. He and his wife were 'mightily pleased with our journey and our condition of doing it in our own coach'. He noticed with satisfaction that other people were also 'mightily pleased with our coach'. He also reassured himself that it was 'a very great convenience', 'carrying me to several places to do little jobs'.

Alas for human vanity! A few months later, all Pepys's pleasure in his coach had disappeared. For his colleague John Creed had told him that he had heard how 'fine' his coach and horses were, and advised him 'to avoid being noted for it'. Pepys was greatly 'vexed to hear notice taken of [it], it being what I feared'.[6]

This poignant episode reveals many of the ingredients which entered into the early modern pursuit of goods: a desire to signify one's ascent in the world; deference to fashion and the judgement of other people; anxiety to please a discontented wife; pleasure in the intrinsic features of the desired object; pride in displaying it to the world, followed by remorse at being thought by others to have exceeded one's station, possibly by corrupt means.

What Pepys's coach demonstrates is that many of the goods purchased in the early modern period were acquired, not for convenience or to satisfy a physical need, but to allay what many commentators were learning to call 'imaginary', 'artificial', or 'phantastic' wants, those desires which the seventeenth-century economist Nicholas Barbon labelled 'the wants of the mind', and which many contemporaries deplored.[7] 'If you can live without want,' Sir Walter Ralegh told his wife, 'care for no more: the rest is but vanity.'[8]

Yet vanity was a powerful force. Adam Smith would conclude that the desire to better one's condition did not arise out of physical needs, for they were strictly limited. It sprang from the desire for esteem. What every one wanted was 'to be observed, to be attended to, to be taken notice of with sympathy, complacency and approbation'.[9] As Aristotle had remarked long ago, riches were not an end in themselves but a means to some other end.[10] Foremost among those other ends was the admiration of others. Smith thought that, for most people, 'the chief enjoyment of riches consists in the parade of riches'. The theologian Archibald Campbell (1691–1756) had said this before him: riches were a means to acquire honour, 'instruments whereby we lift ourselves up to the respect and esteem of other people'. Few goods would be worth having if there was no one else in the world to admire them.[11] 'If we survey the appendages of our persons,' wrote the radical philosopher William Godwin (1756–1836), 'there is scarcely an article that is not in some respect an appeal to the good will of our neighbours, or a refuge against their contempt.'[12] Visible prosperity was valued because it brought admiration and approval, whereas the symbols of poverty were despised as shameful. Honour and social esteem were the real goals of economic man.

Whether as ingredients in the grand style of the nobility, as accessories of middle-class respectability, or as props to lower-class self-respect, houses, clothes, and domestic goods played an indispensable role. Around 1430 a Warwickshire lady, Margaret Walkerne, wrote to her stepfather, asking for a loan, because she was about to give birth and likely to be visited by sundry ladies and gentlemen, but lacked 'honest bedding, without the which mine husband's honesty and mine may not be saved'. Four hundred years later, a London woman begged the poor law overseer to help her, because her 'only decent gown' was pledged to the pawnbrokers and she felt unable to appear out of doors.[13] In the intervening centuries, innumerable individuals experienced the shame of being unable to afford the goods they believed to be essential in order to gain or retain the esteem of others. A corresponding number of people acquired objects they did not need because they seemed socially necessary; like Lady Oglander in the Isle of Wight (d. 1644), who 'never wore a silk gown but for her credit when she went abroad [i.e. out of the house], and never to please herself'.[14]

By the later seventeenth century, even small tradesmen had begun to follow the practice of setting aside half the house to impress visitors, thus making an essential distinction between what have been called 'front-stage' goods, to be seen and admired by others, and 'back-stage' goods, for practical and private use by the family.[15] Though some of them put private comfort above public display, the middling classes tended to spend much less on the kitchen than they did on the best bedroom, in which they entertained.[16] Around 1700 bed hangings, pewter, plate, china (densely stacked on the mantelpiece), clocks, and soft furnishings were all front-stage goods; and it was a common practice to cover up the furniture with paper or cloth, so that it would be preserved fresh and clean for company.[17] When the Parliamentary general Sir William Waller had his goods seized by the state in 1649, he recognized it as a just judgement for 'my vanity in furniture'.[18]

Books were also front-stage objects, often acquired for ostentation rather than use. 'Some covet to have libraries in their houses,' it was said, 'as ladies desire to have cupboards of plate in their chambers, only for show.' People gathered books together, 'well printed, bound and gilded, to serve only for ornaments, which they never look in themselves, nor suffer others [to do so], for fear of fouling them'.[19] John Bunyan commented severely on 'the pride of a library', 'when men secretly please themselves to think 'tis known what a stock of books they have; or when they take more pleasure in the number of, than the matter contained in their books'.[20] A visitor to an Oxford bookshop in 1710 was told that a customer had ordered a yard of books, because that was the size of the empty space in his bookcase at home.[21]

The imitation of others was a powerful driving force. From pewter to tea, the new goods worked themselves down the social scale. Just as Mrs Pepys in 1666 bought a gown at 15 shillings a yard, because she had just seen the King's mistress, Lady Castlemaine, buy the same, so the East India Company attracted attention for its wares by distributing free samples to Charles II and his brother the Duke of York.[22] In the 1770s the brilliant entrepreneur Josiah Wedgwood priced his vases very high, so as to make them 'esteemed ornaments for palaces'. But, once 'the great people ha[d] had their vases in their palaces long enough for them to be seen and admir'd by the middling class of people', he dropped the price in order to secure a larger market. Like other clever salesmen, he realized the importance of associating his goods with the socially eminent.[23]

Unsurprisingly, most of the new goods were more likely to be found in the town than in the country and in rich districts rather than poor ones.[24] It was not necessarily the wealthy who were the most likely to acquire them; country gentlemen, for example, could maintain their local standing without finding it necessary to purchase all the latest commodities. But, usually, social status and the hierarchy of consumption were closely related.[25] The centre of emulative consumption was London, where citizens notoriously had dearer houses, dearer furniture, and richer clothes. 'This is a comely parlour, very neatly and trimly apparelled, London-like,' says a character in an Elizabethan dialogue.[26] When the steward of a Cornish gentry family visited the capital in 1671, he wrote back describing 'the vanities of London, everybody in coach and clothes endeavouring to surpass one the other'.[27] In the same decade Sir William Petty noted that the inhabitants of cities and towns acquired 'more commodities' and made 'greater consumptions' than those who lived in 'wild, thin-peopled countries... out of the sight, observation, and emulation of each other'.[28] Household inventories suggest that, in the early eighteenth century, Londoners exceeded all others in their expend-iture on front-stage goods, having proportionally more clocks, pictures, and decorative objects of every kind. In 1725 in Cumbria only 2 per cent of households could have a cup of tea; in London 57 per cent could.[29] In 1780 in some parts of Somerset, tea was still almost unknown.[30]

'Diminish not your stocks for your wife's pleasure,' warned Edmund Dudley in 1509.[31] Married women were thought parti-cularly responsible for stimulating competitive expenditure: in the mid-sixteenth century, on jewellery, trinkets, and 'dainty meat'; in Jacobean times, on sugary foodstuffs and the London season; in the eighteenth century, on tea-drinking and its accompaniments, elegant tables and porcelain bowls and teapots; and, in all periods, on clothes.[32] As the proverb had it, 'dear bought and far fetched' were 'dainties for ladies'.[33] At the beginning of the eighteenth century, the London physician and philosopher Bernard Mandeville believed that 'the variety of work that is perform'd, and the number of hands employ'd to gratify the fickleness and luxury of women' was 'prodi-gious'.[34] Shops were the mecca of leisured urban women; and it was common to accuse ambitious wives of running up unnecessary shop-ping bills at their husbands' expense. Wives were also said to egg on their husbands to further extravagances. In the mid-seventeenth cen-tury, it was 'thro' the importunity of his wife' that the Hertfordshire gentleman Arthur Poulter began to build 'a very fair house of brick', which he never lived to complete; and in Restoration Oxford, it was allegedly the Warden of Merton's wife who forced him to put the college to 'unnecessary charges and very frivolous expenses', includ-ing a large looking-glass and new furniture for the Lodgings, because the old furniture was 'out of fashion'.[35] For Richard Baxter the concern to beautify rooms was simply 'feminine trifling'.[36]

In the 1690s Roger North wrote that 'the whole employ of the sex [women] is a kind of trade in emulation. They see nothing which another hath, but they have a mind to the same, if not a better of like kind. All these setting[s]-out of rooms, closets, etc., have this secret behind the cabinets and corner shelves: "I am here to *outdo* some-body..." Go with them to china houses and shops, and there all the faculties of the soul are exerted, and intent upon the calculat[ion] of more or less in prettiness: "This is pretty, that more pretty, but another pretty beyond all."... But the truth at bottom is, "This will appear better than what another lady had, *ergo* it is prettier"; and so the comparison is not of the things themselves, but as they are connect [ed] with persons.'[37]

In fact, of course, it was not only the female sex who engaged in this competitive shopping. Well-to-do men spent heavily on horses, carriages, clothes, paintings, watches, plate, wigs, books, and other luxury objects without incurring the same odium.[38] Besides, much female expenditure was of a vicarious kind, designed to bolster the husband's position: as a Jacobean moralist remarked, 'there cometh credit and praise to the man by the comely apparel of his wife'.[39] Nevertheless, women spent more time in shops because they were usually responsible for provisioning the household; and middle-class housewives were coming to think of houses as places in which goods were displayed. The wives of better-off farmers were notoriously house-proud, keeping their floors spotless, and polishing and scouring their pewter dishes until they shone. More goods meant more cooking, more washing up, and more housework. In eighteenth-century London, even modest rented rooms had copper kettles, walnut-framed looking-glasses, curtains, and white cotton counterpanes.[40]

Lower down the social scale, among the working poor, the new goods had little initial impact. In the absence of probate inventories for the poor, it is hard to generalize, but it is clear that furnishings were sparse and over half of the domestic budget went on food.[41] The emphasis was more on immediate consumption than on enduring possessions;[42] though, by the later eighteenth century, cotton and linen, pewter, pottery, tea sets, and decorative household items would reach even labourers' cottages (pl. 8). Carpets and curtains arrived rather later.[43] 'Best' clothes had always been important. An early eighteenth-century observer thought that 'the poorest labourer's wife in the parish' would half-starve herself and her husband in order to buy a second-hand gown and petticoat, rather than 'a strong wholesome frieze', because it was more 'genteel'. Even when under-nourished and poorly housed, the lower classes were prepared to devote some of their limited resources to goods which boosted their self-esteem and helped them to create social relationships with others.[44]*

For the consumption of goods was as much conformist in spirit as competitive. Most people bought commodities out of a desire to keep in line with the accepted standards of their own peer group rather than to emulate those of the one above: similarity in living styles was an important source of social cohesion; and anxiety to do the right thing was more common than the urge to stand out. As Josiah Wedgwood remarked, 'Few ladies, you know, dare venture at anything out of the common style 'till authoris'd by their betters—by the ladies of superior spirit who set the *ton*.'[45]

Of course, goods were cherished for themselves as well as for their social meaning. The very word 'commodity' indicated that the object in question was intrinsically desirable. In the late sixteenth century, it became common for owners to indicate their close relationship to their houses, furniture, pots, and other domestic objects by writing, painting, stamping, or carving their name and initials on them.[46] By the eighteenth century, this practice was largely confined to books, children's samplers, and vernacular pottery. But a mixture of aesthetic and proprietary pleasure continued to generate deep emotional attachment to attractive fabrics, well-made furniture, and decorated china (pl. 7).[47] As the critic Walter Benjamin would observe, ownership is the most intimate relationship one can have to an object.[48] The wills of aristocratic ladies reveal an obvious pleasure in the lovingly detailed elaboration of their clothes, linen, porcelain, and other favourite possessions; and the same emotional attachment to particular goods can be found in the wills of women lower down the social scale. Perhaps domestic chattels were more important to women than to men because that was often all they had to leave.[49]

Strong sentimental value was attached to goods with intimate personal or family associations, like the gifts, keepsakes, and mementoes left by friends and relations as tokens of affection and gratitude and as pleas for remembrance; or the variety of objects, ranging from beds and books to pictures and silver plate, which testators might bequeath as inalienable heirlooms, to be transmitted downwards, along with the family freehold.[50] In 1628 Thomas Bate, a mercer in Retford, Nottinghamshire, bequeathed to his son 'a gold ring which

---

* For those close to destitution in a Lancashire slum of the early twentieth century, 'any new possession helped to stifle fear'; Robert Roberts, *The Classic Slum* (Harmondsworth, 1973), 32.

was my father's'. 'When thy father is dead,' remarked a contemporary preacher, 'his garment or his ring is dear to thee; this thou carriest upon thy finger and wouldst not lose it for anything.'[51] In 1756 Mrs Dewes, an aristocratic lady, wrote a letter prescribing that 'the old china cup with the gilt cover and saucer, that has a setting in gold belonging to it, Mary must have, and give it to her daughter if she has one, if not, to one of her brother's daughters, as it has gone from daughter to daughter these three hundred years!* ...These trifles I give to renew in her mind whenever she sees them, the constant tenderness of her truly affectionate mother.'[52]

In the sixteenth century, when fashions changed more slowly than they did later, it was possible to hand down most clothes and household goods, along with the associations which went with them. Thus a Nottinghamshire yeoman's will of 1550: 'to Richard Fulwood, my brother, my best doublet sleeved with velvet, for [the] term of his life; and after his decease to remain to John Fulwood, his son'. Or a Lincolnshire bequest in 1591: 'I give unto Oswould Browrige my coat that was Mr Welby's.'[53]

Many goods were acquired in order to establish and maintain closer relations with other people. In 1627 a guide for sailors suggested that ships should carry stocks of 'marmalade, suckets, almonds, confits', and other sugar-based concoctions, so as to be able 'to entertain strangers'.[54] In the eighteenth century there was high expenditure on furnishing and decorating rooms in which to receive visitors and the equipment with which to offer them tea; this was the social context for the enormous growth in the import of Chinese porcelain and the manufacture of domestic chinaware.[55] At New Year, and at christenings, weddings, and funerals, goods were exchanged as 'tokens' and 'remembrances'.[56] Courting couples gave each other gloves, rings, and other objects as their relationship progressed.[57] Preparing for childbirth, well-to-do seventeenth-century ladies bought 'fine and costly child-bed linen, swaddling clothes, mantles, and the like, as also fine beds, cradles, baskets, and other furniture for their chambers, as hangings, cabinets, plates, artificial flowers, looking-glasses, screens, and many such like things of great cost and charge, besides their banquets of sweetmeats and other junkets, as cakes, wafers, biscuits, jellies and the like': all so as to be able to entertain their 'gossips' in suitable style when they were lying in.[58]

---

* An exaggeration, for Chinese porcelain is unlikely to have been in Mrs Dewes's family in the fifteenth century.

Their husbands derived comparable pleasure from exchanging goods. In what, in the north of England, were called 'handicaps' and, in Norfolk, 'swaps', the gentry met for long drinking sessions, at which they ritually challenged each other's possessions, betting horses, saddles, pistols, whips, dogs, and watches against each other in a competitive form of exchange.[59] This was in addition to the endless flow of gifts—game, wine, dogs, gloves, rings—which went to and fro between gentry families, their patrons, and clients, or between officials and those with whom they did business. At the Navy Office, Samuel Pepys reflected in 1664 that he was growing in estimation 'and have things given more oftener than I used to have formerly; as to have a case of very pretty knifes with agate hafts by Mrs Russell [a ship's chandler]'.[60]

Goods were employed to create and maintain every kind of social relationship. Whether it was a political alliance or a business association or a tie of kinship or a bond formed by personal affection, the exchange of gifts played an indispensable role in consolidating the link.[61] Goods were the essential vocabulary and small change of social intercourse. That was one of the reasons why people wanted them.

Possessions could also be linked to daydreams and fantasies when they were used to express not what people were, but what they wanted to be. It has been said with some brutality that in modern times 'individuality is attained by assembling a unique collection of commodities'.[62] In his novel *The Portrait of a Lady* (1881), chapter xix, Henry James has one of his characters observe: 'There's no such thing as an isolated man or woman; we're each of us made up of some cluster of appurtenances. What shall we call our "self"? Where does it begin? where does it end? It overflows into everything that belongs to us—and then it flows back again. I know a large part of myself is in the clothes I choose to wear. I've a great respect for *things*! One's self—for other people—is one's expression of one's self; and one's house, one's furniture, one's garments, the books one reads, the company one keeps—these things are all expressive.' More cruelly, another novelist, Kurt Vonnegut, writes of one of his characters that, 'like so many Americans, she was trying to construct a life that made sense from the things she found in gift shops'.[63]

In the early modern period, domestic possessions were already beginning to take on this function of expressing not just their owners' social position, but also their personal interests and sensibilities. The sixteenth-century Italian writer Pietro Aretino believed that one could tell someone's character from his dwelling; and his claim was repeated by Roger North in 1698. 'The centrality of the house and its furnishings to the self-definition of its inhabitants', so conspicuous a feature of modern British middle-class life, was fully evident in eighteenth-century England. The way in which the domestic interior was decorated and the nature of the possessions displayed within it made a powerful statement about their owner.[64] Possessions were symbols of refinement and politeness. They helped to define individual identity. They even shaped their owners' physical deportment and behaviour, for knives and forks, cups and teapots, fragile porcelain and increasingly delicate furniture, imposed a distinctively mannered way of eating, drinking, moving, and sitting. In this way the consumption of goods created social differences as well as expressing them.[65]

The process was assisted by the rise of the idea of taste. 'Taste' is a term which first acquired prominence in England in the later seventeenth century. As goods multiplied, it became a central concept of aesthetic theory and an important form of cultural differentiation. As a contemporary noted in 1633, 'great folks' always had a tendency to 'think nothing of that which is common and ordinary people may easily come by'.[66] Taste involved transcending mere financial criteria when assessing the value of goods and introducing instead a subtler and more elusive yardstick. It implied a capacity for discrimination, of the kind shown in 1606 by the wine connoisseur Captain Dawtrey, who, 'taking the glass in his hand, held it up awhile betwixt him and the window, as to consider the colour; and then putting it to his nose, he seemed to take comfort in the odour of the same'.[67] It required the ability to choose the best out of a wide range of functionally indistinguishable options, like the fifty different patterns of wallpaper which on one occasion in 1752 confronted the poet William Shenstone.[68] The essayist Joseph Addison compared a person who had true taste in literary matters to the man who could identify each of ten different kinds of tea or any combination of them.[69]

The ways in which the later Stuart and Hanoverian elite spent their money and their leisure show just how vital a reputation for taste had become. The replacement of vernacular architecture by classical, the interior decoration of houses, the laying-out of grounds, the appreciation of letters and the fine arts, all bore testimony to the centrality of taste as an ingredient of politeness and a principle of social distinction. For, despite its aesthetic and philosophical overtones, the concept of taste was a profoundly social one. Taste was notoriously a quality which the vulgar lacked, for they were without the necessary

Figure 4.1 In the eighteenth century the choice of one wallpaper rather than another could be an important act of social and aesthetic discrimination.

education and experience, whereas connoisseurs were cultivated, well travelled, and 'conversant with the better sort of people'.[70] 'Those who depend for food on bodily labour', ruled the critic Lord Kames, 'are totally devoid of taste.'[71] The middle-class inhabitants of the London suburbs were scorned by their social superiors for their bad taste, manifested in the embarrassingly derivative style of their houses and gardens.[72] Taste was the prerogative of the 'polite'. It was a faculty which required education, foreign travel, and close conformity to the standard set by an elite minority. In Samuel Johnson's words, 'a few, a very few, commonly constitute the taste of the time'.[73]

In France, the rules of good taste emanated from the royal court, but in England they were disseminated by an aristocratic network. Some gentlemen were leaders of taste, connoisseurs, and amateur architects.[74] But many had to buy advice from others if they were to choose correctly from the artefacts on offer. Great magnates had always needed experts to help them with their legal and financial affairs. Now they needed experts on taste. To furnish their houses, choose their pictures and books, lay out their grounds, and make their other acts of discrimination, they became dependent upon an army of middle-class professionals: architects, gardeners, cooks, artists, literary critics, cabinet-makers, and 'upholders'.* The landscape gardener Lancelot ('Capability') Brown was the son of a small Northumberland yeoman, but he removed mounts, knots, and avenues from aristocratic gardens with the same autocratic finality as that with which Beau Nash (ex-Carmarthen Grammar School) had removed the Duchess of Queensberry's apron in the assembly rooms at Bath, on the grounds that it was a garment fit only for servants.[75]

The competition thus shifted away from the conspicuous display of opulence to a more restrained demonstration of elegance, refinement, and fastidious discrimination. 'One may know a gentlewoman almost as well by seeing her choose a mantua or a ribbon, as by going to Garter or Clarenceux [the heralds].'[76] The ownership of culturally esteemed objects became a symbol of status; and the claim to superior sensibilities, defined as the capacity to feel pain at what causes no pain to others, emerged, in Jeremy Bentham's words, as 'a mark of... belonging to the ruling few'.[77] The purchasing power of the middling and lower classes might rise, but the elite could hold on to its monopoly of cultural capital by asserting that wealth was not enough. 'Nowadays,' ruled an influential French cookery book of 1674, 'it is not the prodigious overflowing of dishes... the extraordinary piles of meat which constitute a good table... It is rather the exquisite choice of meats, the finesse with which they are seasoned, the courtesy and neatness with which they are served.'[78] Similarly, Lord Chesterfield advised his son to shine in his dress, not 'by a clumsy load of gold and silver, but by the taste and fashion of it'.[79] Contemporary paintings suggest that the interiors of aristocratic houses in the mid-eighteenth century were often bare and uncluttered. 'Neat', meaning simple, clean, and sparely elegant, was a key term in the aesthetic lexicon of the period.[80]

In modern times, there is nothing which more exactly defines social differences than personal tastes, whether in food or music or

* In R. Campbell, *The London Tradesman* (1747), 169–70, an upholder is defined as 'the man on whose judgment I rely in the choice of goods... a connoisseur in every article that belongs to a house'.

wallpaper or the choice of children's names. The choices which people make in these areas of life may seem spontaneous and genuine, but, without any apparent pressure or coercion, they usually conform to class lines. The possessions which we place in our living spaces and the way we decorate those spaces instantly reveal our sensibilities, our preoccupations, and our social milieux. That is why they will evoke the admiration of some observers and the disdain of others.* This state of affairs was already in evidence in the early modern period.[81]

FROM HOSTILITY TO ACCEPTANCE

Meanwhile, the consumption of new goods was unleashing a torrent of contemporary criticism. From the sixteenth century onwards, there were denunciations of 'immoderate purchasings', 'unlawful spending and consuming', and what one Protestant divine called 'the inordinate and unsatiable desire of having'.[1] Moralists pointed to the waste of resources which could have been better employed in relieving the poor; to the adverse consequences for the balance of trade of the import of foreign commodities; and to the ruinous effects of self-indulgence upon an individual's health and finances. They attacked 'wasters' and 'spenders' and were contemptuous of what they called 'superfluities', 'needless toys', 'vain trifles', 'fantasies', 'new fangles', and 'trumpery trash'.[2]

Adam Smith was in this tradition when he said that it was the desire of great lords for 'frivolous and useless' objects which brought down the feudal system: they bartered their authority 'for the gratification of the most childish, the meanest and the most sordid of all vanities'. Luxuries were 'contemptible and trifling', 'trinkets and baubles, fitter to be the play-things of children than the serious pursuits of men'.[3]

Distaste for frivolities was reinforced by the classical notion that luxury weakened the state, undermined civic virtue, and led eventually to despotism. The 'civic-humanist' belief was that comfortable living had an enervating effect, sapping the martial spirit and reducing military effectiveness; the very word 'luxury' had connotations of excessive fleshly indulgence. Republican virtue required frugality, whereas abundance produced 'effeminacy'; and the lure of private comforts distracted citizens from a commitment to public

---

* Hence the anthropologist Mary Douglas's description of modern shopping as 'an agonistic struggle to define not what one is but what one is not'; *Thought Styles* (1996), 104.

service.[4] In 1757, when the hapless Admiral John Byng was shot for failing to recover Minorca, the caricaturists chose to represent his ineffectiveness by portraying him surrounded by his collection of porcelain.[5] As late as 1876, at the opening of the chapel of Keble College, Oxford, the Marquess of Salisbury praised the new college's distinctive commitment to a frugal style of living, declaring that 'luxury' was sapping the 'very fibre and manliness' of the nation.[6]

Similar sentiments had been expressed in Tudor times. The schoolmaster William Horman warned in 1519 that 'nice arras' and 'newfangled garments' made men womanly. The Bible translator William Tyndale (d. 1536) thought that eating 'wanton' delicacies had so effeminized them 'that there remaineth no more tokens of a man than their beards'. The Elizabethan archbishop Matthew Parker complained that, in the reign of Henry VIII, Cardinal Wolsey had ruined the clergy by wearing silk and thus introducing them to 'the Asiatic luxury'; while the physician John Caius lamented that people were now so 'nice' at table that 'the old manly hardness, stout courage and painfulness of England' was 'utterly driven away'.[7] In 1549 one of the speakers in A Discourse of the Commonweal noted that 'like excesses, as well in apparel, as in fare, were used in Rome a little before the decline of the Empire, so as wise men have thought it was the occasion of the decay thereof'.[8]

Throughout the early modern period, commentators repeatedly harked back to 'the plainness and hardness of the people of old', contrasting the military vigour of 'our plain forefathers' with the soft and luxurious habits of their descendants. The exact location of this age of primitive simplicity was variously located at any point between the Old Testament patriarchs and the reign of Queen Anne, but its virile austerity remained constant.[9] It was asserted that effeminacy was generated by the new objects of expenditure, from coaches, which robbed men of their riding skills,* to tea, which emasculated them as they sat sipping in female company.[10] This objection to 'foreign, effeminate and superfluous commodities'[11] was not just a classical topos: it reflected the central role of women in the purchase of objects for domestic consumption and the association of the new goods with domesticity and an unmilitary style of life.

* When in 1678 John Thoresby, Yorkshire wool merchant and ex-Parliamentary soldier, had to take a coach in order to transport his sick son, he found it hard 'to endure the effeminacy of that way of travelling'; The Diary of Ralph Thoresby, ed. Joseph Hunter (1830), i. 28 n.

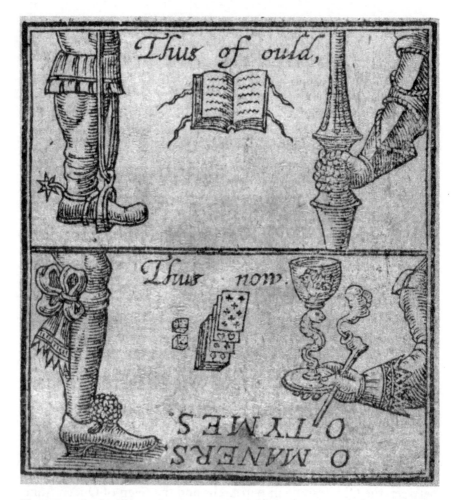

Figure 4.2 In this illustration to a sermon published in 1627 the luxurious self-indulgence of modern times is contrasted with the military virtue of the past.

There was also a Christian ascetic tradition in which new goods appeared as sinful 'vanities', symbols of human pride, and dangerous distractions from the godly life. A polemic against 'vain expense', 'pride in apparel', and 'unlawful spending and consuming' had been conducted by the Lollards and was particularly strident among Puritans and sectarians.[12] As a seventeenth-century economic writer noted, the imitation of court fashions bore 'an ill name amongst many grave and sober people'.[13] The godly condemned 'epicurism in diet', gluttonous 'diversities', and a 'fine dainty tooth'. Food was for preservation not pleasure.[14] In 1644 the Puritan congregation of

Uggleshall, Suffolk, had their rector ejected for, among other things, 'eating custard after a scandalous manner'; he used to pour sack into it and consume it 'with great greediness'.[15] When the Welsh Methodist Howell Harris visited London in 1744, his scruples 'about buying tea for fear of mis-spending God's money' were not overcome until he called on his fellow Methodist George Whitefield, 'where I found the Lord had provided tea things for me'.[16] Richard Baxter had expressed similar puritanical hostility to the genteel enjoyment of possessions in 1673, when he condemned 'needless curiosity about rooms and furniture, and accommodations', along with 'superfluous recreations, buildings, ornaments … equipage, attendants, entertainments, visitations, braveries and a world of need-nots (called by the names of handsomeness, cleanliness, neatness, conveniencies, delights, usefulness, honour, civilities, comeliness, etc)'.[17]

In their early days, the Quakers refused altogether to engage in most forms of conspicuous consumption, rejecting banquets, lace, ribbons, curtains, tea-tables, porcelain, and fine furniture. The Irishman Joseph Pike, who joined the Friends in the 1660s, records the consequences: 'Our fine veneered and garnished cases of drawers, tables, stands, cabinets, scrutoires, &c., we put away, or exchanged for decent plain ones of solid wood, without superfluous garnishing, or ornamental work; our wainscots or woodwork we had painted of one plain colour; our large mouldings or finishings of panelling, &c., our swelling chimney-pieces, curiously twisted banisters, we took down, and replaced with useful plain woodwork, &c.; our curtains, with valances, drapery, and fringes that we thought too fine, we put away or cut off; our large looking-glasses with decorated frames, we sold, or made them into smaller ones; and our closets, that were laid out with many little curious or nice things, were done away.'[18] In time, however, even the Quakers began to succumb to the temptation of luxury goods. In 1770 Elizabeth Fothergill, niece of the great Quaker naturalist John Fothergill, confessed to sharing the notorious feminine weakness 'for feeling so much pleasure at the sight of china, silks, etc.'.[19]

The aristocratic ideal of magnificence encountered hostility among the middle classes, many of whom lauded 'godly parsimony' and disapproved of those who were 'spendthrifts' or 'squandered' their substance, while some economic writers castigated those who were 'mere spenders and consumers'.[20] Extreme hostility was displayed towards the apparent frivolities of fashion change. The Church's canons of 1604 expressed the wistful hope that, 'in time', 'newfangleness of apparel' would 'die of itself'; and in 1621 a Member of

Parliament called for a statute to establish 'a settled fashion'.[21] That great pace-setter Charles II announced in 1666 that he would inaugurate a fashion in clothes that would never alter. But, as John Evelyn commented, the King's resolution was too good to last and his specially designed 'Persian vest' (which was meant to be the answer) went the way of everything else, especially after his arch-rival Louis XIV had put his footmen into it.[22]

More radical figures objected to luxury expenditure, because it intensified social inequalities. A pamphleteer observed in 1649 that coaches were more appropriate for poor cripples than for healthy young aristocrats; while another, in 1698, believed that, if the privileged were to give up their luxuries, there would be enough for everybody; he therefore urged that 'most severe penalties' should be imposed on 'changes of modes in clothes, rich garments and furnitures, and all superfluities and vain and unnecessary expenses'.[23]

Yet other contemporaries objected to the new forms of consumption for the opposite reason, namely that they threatened to undermine the traditional social hierarchy. For a luxury was, by definition, an object of expenditure inappropriate to the purchaser's social position. 'Necessary goods', ruled William Perkins, were 'those goods without which a man's state, condition and dignity wherein he is cannot be preserved,' whereas a luxury, in the words of an eighteenth-century journalist, was an expense 'above the rank' of the buyer.[24] No form of consumption, 'how pompous soever', was a luxury if it was appropriate to the consumer's position in society. Those who attacked the new luxuries were usually careful to emphasize that their strictures did not apply with the same force to 'noblemen and great personages', who were entitled to live in a way that befitted their rank and condition.[25] In the same spirit, the law courts continued to uphold the medieval doctrine that a husband was liable for his wife's debts, provided that what she bought was suitable to his degree. Sir William Petty was unusual in giving a socially neutral definition of 'necessaries' as 'such commodities as without which a man cannot live to the usual period of men's age in that health and strength as a man is naturally capable of'.[26]

Social conservatives were therefore much distressed when persons of lower status acquired goods that had once been reserved for their superiors. A key objection to 'excessive and wanton apparel', voiced since at least the fourteenth century, was that it resulted in 'a confusion of such degrees and callings as God hath ordained, when as men of inferior degree and calling cannot be by their attire discerned from men of higher estate'.[27] The Elizabethan Jesuit Robert Parsons proposed in 1596 that, when Catholicism was restored to England, the 'commonalty' should be reduced 'again to their old simplicity, both in apparel, diet, innocency of life, and plainness of dealing' and that the distinctions between labourers, husbandmen, yeomen, and gentry should be strictly guarded.[28] On the eve of the Restoration the Marquess of Newcastle lamented that 'every citizen's wife will have six horses in her coach, which is most unfitting', while the Marchioness was upset that 'every Turkey merchant's wife' had her floors covered with carpets. In her view, commoners should 'live according to their quality, not according to their wealth'. If they outconsumed the nobility, it would lead to 'alteration in the state'.[29]

It was in reaction to this increased consumer spending by people below the level of the gentry that the myth arose of the supposedly earlier and happier age, when the lower classes had been content with their station in life and had not aspired to better themselves. In those days, as one commentator rather cumbersomely put it, 'there was (not by sumptuary laws, or magistratic sanction, but by common agreement, and general understanding), as it were, a settled way of garb, equipage, diet, household stuff, clothes, [and] education of children; and men of prudence held themselves concerned in discretion and thrift not to exceed the bounds of their degree in any of the forementioned things'.[30]

Yet, despite this nostalgia for an ordered society, in which people consumed only what was appropriate for their station, the Tudor sumptuary laws, prescribing social distinctions in dress, lapsed in 1604 and were never renewed. This did not reflect any slackening in the conviction of the upper classes that the different levels of society should be dressed differently. Throughout the seventeenth century and beyond, there were repeated demands for laws to control the consumption of goods of every kind. Clothes, furniture, coaches, tobacco, feasts, pastry shops were all proposed at one time or another as fit subjects for legislation.[31] Yet to no effect. From time to time, Parliaments legislated against foreign imports, but otherwise there was no more sumptuary legislation at a national level. The eighteenth-century Nonconformist Philip Doddridge concluded that people should voluntarily impose on themselves the restraints which they had been spared by the indulgence of their superiors.[32]

Why was so little action taken? At the time, the reasons given were that sumptuary laws were impossible to enforce, and that, if consumption had to be restrained, it was better to do so by indirect taxation or by the upper classes' setting an example of restraint. There were also constitutional difficulties about such regulation.[33] But the root causes were obvious: producers of new goods had no desire to limit their market, and consumers were hostile to any attempts to impose limits on their freedom. As Henry Peacham pointed out in 1641, prodigality was very good for 'tailors, haberdashers, shoemakers, sempsters, hostelers and the like'.[34] Arguments against state interference with the consumption of goods became more explicit during the course of the seventeenth century. Inevitably, those who put them forward were usually interested parties. It was the pharmacist and dealer in exotic imports John Houghton who argued in 1677 that the import of foreign luxuries was good for the domestic economy, and the speculative builder Nicholas Barbon who maintained in the following year that emulative consumption in London stimulated industry and economic growth.[35] In the ensuing decades, a lobby of economic writers urged that countries with sumptuary laws were 'generally poor';[36] and that the demand of the 'consumer' (a word which was just beginning to lose its former pejorative sense of waster and squanderer[37]) was essential to provide employment and keep the economy buoyant. Labourers who wanted better clothes and furnishings would work harder and swell demand.[38] 'Instead of urging the people to be less consumers,' maintained the timber merchant Jacob Vanderlint, 'things should be made so plentiful that they might be greater consumers.'[39] Human appetites were insatiable and the deliberate creation of 'imaginary wants' through changes in fashion was to be encouraged. For fashion wore out more apparel than the man; and people bought new goods before the old ones were worn out. 'Costly stuffs', lamented a Jacobean preacher, 'within a few days' wearing must be cast off and given to some serving man or maid and soon after become good for nothing.'[40] The Tudor *Book of Homilies* had noticed that 'we are loath to wear such as our fathers hath left us; we think that not sufficient or good enough for us'. By the end of the seventeenth century, it had become pointless for 'every considerable family' to keep a wardrobe to be handed down; for clothes grew out of date.[41] As contemporaries were well aware, the economic implications of the change were enormous.

The debate about 'luxury' dragged on throughout the eighteenth century. But the essential economic case had been made by 1700. Vanity and social emulation were indispensable preconditions for trade and employment. Through their 'luxury', the rich contributed to the maintenance of the poor. Consumption was the object of the economic process.[42] As the political writer Edward Forset had urged as early as 1606, it was the sovereign's duty 'to cherish in the subjects an appetite of acquiring of commodities'.[43] The same view was expressed by the Jacobean supporters of an English silk industry, who pointed to the benefits which would redound 'to all sorts of labouring people as to others'.[44] It was often reiterated. In 1709 Bernard Mandeville jocularly proposed a reverse sumptuary law, compelling everyone to buy new clothes every month, purchase new furniture every year, and eat four meals a day. So little did he think of 'the pernicious tenets of the Catos, the Senecas, and other moral-mongers that extolled content and frugality, and preach'd against gluttony, drunkenness and the rest of the supporters of the common-wealth'.[45]

This attitude eroded the old distinction between desirable 'neces-sities' and reprehensible 'luxuries'. For those whose desires were infinite, luxuries now became necessities; as Lord Halifax sardonic-ally observed, 'we call all "necessary" that we have a mind to'.[46] So-called 'artificial' wants soon came to seem natural. Adam Smith would rule that necessities were not just those goods which were indispensable for the support of life, but 'whatever the custom of the country renders it indecent for creditable people, even of the lowest order, to be without'.[47] By relating the dividing line to prevail-ing conceptions of decency, he accepted that it was a shifting bound-ary. For standards constantly changed; and, as Mandeville had observed, one could not tell what words like 'decency' and 'conve-niency' meant until one knew the quality of the person using them; what the poor saw as intolerable luxury was regarded by the gentry merely as 'decency'.[48] In this way the values of civility, respectability, refinement, and politeness were invoked to legitimize the unceasing acquisition of goods.

Above all, goods were welcomed, because, in Bishop Sprat's words, they were necessary helps to felicity, bringing 'pleasure' and 'greater delight'.[49] At the end of the sixteenth century, William Perkins had allowed that God's temporal blessings could be used 'for our honest delight', and his fellow Puritans John Dod and Robert Cleaver agreed that possessions could be 'ornaments and delights'.[50] In the 1690s economic writers laid increasing stress on the 'delight' which goods could afford;[51] and in the eighteenth century there were many refer-ences to the 'happiness' they generated.[52] The craving for possessions was sanctioned by a hedonistic strain which became increasingly visible in the moral thought of the Hanoverian age.[53]

What we see during the seventeenth and eighteenth centuries is the gradual emergence of a new ideology, accepting the pursuit of consumer goods as a valid object of human endeavour, and recognizing that no limit could, or should, be put to it. Consumption was justified in terms of the opportunities it brought for human fulfilment. The growth of a consumer market, unrestricted by the requirements of social hierarchy, offered increasing possibilities for comfort, enjoyment, and self-realization. Poverty was no longer to be regarded as a holy state; and there was no need to feel guilt about envying the rich; one should try to emulate them. Or so the advocates of laissez-faire commerce would argue. Goods were prized, for themselves, for the esteem they brought with them, for the social relationships they made possible. To interfere with the process of acquisition, by sumptuary laws, was what Adam Smith would call 'the highest impertinence and presumption'; it threatened liberty and personal happiness. The labourer had the right 'to spend his own money himself and lay out the produce of his labour his own way'.[54] The sovereignty of consumer choice triumphed over the notion that consumption should be regulated to fit social status; and the distribution of goods was left to the working of the market. No one yet foresaw that monopolistic capitalism might one day do as much to restrict choice as to enlarge it.

Of course, economic circumstances limited the ability of many to take advantage of the new freedom. In the later seventeenth century, a quarter of the population endured some form of poverty and a seventh were in or near destitution.[55] But even those who could afford to buy more commodities did not necessarily rush to do so. Though consumption was no longer subject to state regulation, it was still constrained by social and moral pressures. The classical, humanist model, with its prescription that individuals should pursue rugged virtue and civic responsibility rather than luxurious self-interest, remained influential. In the countryside many Tudor and Stuart yeomen farmers were hostile to new luxuries, though most of them eventually succumbed to the attraction of larger, lighter, and better-furnished houses.[56] In the towns, there was a good deal of middle-class inhibition about following a luxurious lifestyle. When he was Lord Chief Justice, Sir Matthew Hale chose to live in a very small house at Acton, inferior to the dwellings of many neighbouring farmers, and his habit was 'to be short and sparing at meals', that he might be 'the fitter for business'; 'in his furniture and the service of table and way of living, he liked the old plainness'.[57] The Dissenting clergyman Philip Henry (1631–96) 'steered by the principle that a man's life consisteth not in the abundance of things that he posses-seth'.[58] The great Turkey merchant Sir William Jolliffe claimed in 1746 that he had never bought a book or a picture in his life.[59] Such independent spirits asserted their individuality by perversely *not* con-suming, rather like a modern middle-class family extolling the virtues of 'good plain cooking' or boasting that it does not possess a televi-sion set. Social competition can take many different forms.

To the mystic Thomas Traherne, writing in the 1660s, the desire for new goods was a form of corruption, a loss of childish innocence. It was a sad day when the growing child began to prize 'a drum, a fine coat, a penny, a gilded book'. Adam in paradise had no gorgeous apparel, palaces, or coaches.[60] The happiest state was to need noth-ing, to limit wants, to resist the blandishments of those who purveyed new luxuries. One should curb one's desires to an absolute minimum of authentic needs and despise those goods which required the opin-ion of others for their full enjoyment.

This had been the view of many ancient philosophers—Cynics, Stoics, and Epicureans: wants should be limited because happiness came from self-sufficiency; and dependence on the vagaries of fortune was to be avoided. The refinements of taste were false and unnatural: "'Tis not for us to say, "This is not handsome"; "That's common"; "T'other offends my eye".'[61] In the early modern period, this attitude was shared by utopian writers from Thomas More onwards;[62] and in the eighteenth century, it would be given wide currency by Jean-Jacques Rousseau, who argued that civilized man had enslaved him-self to his own supposed needs.* Whereas hunter–gatherers could satisfy all their material wants, the inhabitants of advanced societies could never hope to possess all that they desired. Captain James Cook found that the aboriginal Australians were 'far more happier than we Europeans; being wholly unacquainted not only with the superfluous but the necessary conveniences so much sought after in Europe, they are happy in not knowing the use of them'.[63]

The more conventional position, however, was that of Jonathan Swift, who said that 'the Stoical scheme' of supplying our wants by restricting our desires was like cutting off our feet when we needed shoes.[64] As one economic writer put it, 'that sort of Reformers who would have nothing made, us'd or consumed, but what nature

---

* In the reign of James I the historical writer Thomas Gainsford had declared that money made men 'slaves to their own proper goods'; *The Rich Cabinet Furnished with Varieties* (1616), fol. 95.

absolutely requires, are but short-sighted and narrow thinkers as well in politics as religion; and though they may adorn their opinions and arguments with the names of Lycurgus, Cato and other sour-reasoners, yet all their discourses tend to no more but to reduce mankind back to be sheep-skin wearers, acorn-eaters and water-drinkers again'.[65]

By the later eighteenth century, complaints about the supposed leisure preference of the labouring classes had largely faded away. The availability of uninterrupted work, the regularity of factory routine, the decline of bye-employments, and the erosion of customary rights were all powerful incentives for workers to continue working, even after the basic needs of subsistence had been met. Fewer holidays, whether official or unofficial ('St Monday'), were taken. Labouring people developed new wants and worked more hours in the week so as to satisfy them, as well as making greater use of the labour of their wives and children. Economic writers stressed the importance of consumer goods in motivating the lower classes to work harder. This process, visible between the mid-seventeenth and late eighteenth centuries, has been called 'the industrious revolution'.[66] At the beginning of the nineteenth century, the political economist T. R. Malthus believed that there was 'a very large class of people' who had 'a decided taste for the conveniences and comforts of life [and] a strong desire of bettering their condition'.[67]

WEALTH AS FULFILMENT?

What a contrast between this new acceptance of limitless desire and the sixteenth-century doctrine that needs were fixed and that superfluities should be given away! How did the belief in the desirability of ever more wealth and possessions come to supersede the older notion that riches were a spiritual danger and their pursuit an unworthy preoccupation? How was it that religious leaders eventually 'acquiesced in the popular assumption that the acquisition of riches was the main end of man'?[1]

Those questions were first posed by the great German sociologist Max Weber, and asked again over eighty years ago by R. H. Tawney, in his *Religion and the Rise of Capitalism* (1926). It may seem ungrateful to say of this remarkable work (which, more than any other book, kindled my own interest in history) that its author never convincingly demonstrated his claim that it was Puritanism which 'transformed the acquisition of wealth from a drudgery or a temptation into a moral duty'.[2] Nor did he adequately support his suggestion that Puritan preachers encouraged 'the attainment of riches as the supreme felicity'.[3] What he did show was that Puritan clergy (along with others) legitimized a business career as an acceptable calling for a godly person to follow. But they never regarded it as more than one of many such acceptable callings;[4] and they continued to believe that the pursuit of wealth for its own sake was reprehensible. Riches were to be employed for the good of all, not for private advantage.[5]

To explain how moneymaking came to be thought a desirable human objective, we have to look beyond Puritanism. Some weight should be given to the influence of a legal tradition which upheld private property and the individual right to lawful acquisition. As a Jacobean recorder of London remarked, the law allowed every man to go his own way and accumulate wealth.[6] Hence the belief of a Tudor rack-renting landlord

> That with his own he might
> always do as he list.[7]

A similar retort was made by a recalcitrant offender before the Court of Star Chamber in 1599: 'My goods are mine own...I will do what I list with them.'[8] Legal individualism of this kind, reflecting a strong sense of personal property, had been visible in late medieval rural society.[9] Ubiquitous in the early modern period, it was forcefully expressed in 1656 by the Leicestershire minister Joseph Lee, who, in defence of enclosing landlords, defiantly asked: 'may not every man lawfully put his commodity to the best advantage, provided he do it without prejudice to others?'[10]

Also important was the influence of classical notions about the indispensability of worldly goods for the pursuit of the good life. Just as, in late medieval Italy, scholastics, mendicant friars, and humanist scholars justified moneymaking and agreed in extolling the moral potentialities of material wealth, so, in fifteenth-century England, Bishop Reginald Pecock followed Aristotle and Aquinas in describing riches as 'the instruments of virtue'.[11] Sixteenth-century writers, from the Henrician humanist Thomas Starkey to the Elizabethan divine George Gifford, argued that worldly prosperity, though undoubtedly a temptation, could, when properly used, positively assist men to do good in this world and to achieve the life to come. Provided it was put to good purposes, the acquisition of wealth was morally acceptable, even desirable, for poverty could have degrading effects. Xenophon's praise of the industrious householder was invoked to prove that men had a duty to provide for themselves and their children. Only if it became a single, overriding aim, was the pursuit of riches unacceptable.[12]

Seventeenth-century religious writers continued this theme, arguing that riches were good in themselves, whereas poverty, far from being a holy state, enfeebled the mind and made it unfitted for any generous enterprises.[13] It was, however, in secular economic literature that the justification of moneymaking was most fully formulated. Between the mid-sixteenth and the late seventeenth centuries, a succession of economic writers developed the model of what we now think of as economic man, buying in the cheapest market, selling in the dearest, relentlessly pursuing his limitless desires. From the *Discourse of the Commonweal* (written in 1549) to Dudley North's *Discourses on Trade* (1691), two guiding propositions were uppermost: first, that people would always seek to maximize their own self-interest, regardless of what legislators or moralists might wish; second, that the pursuit of selfish interests might conduce to the good of the whole, because those interests could, more or less, be made to harmonize, to everyone's benefit. These doctrines were particularly prominent at certain periods: they were tentatively articulated in the reign of Edward VI;[14] they emerged again in the economic debates of the 1620s;[15] they were vigorously advanced by radical defenders of the Commonwealth in the 1640s and 1650s;[16] and they were extensively propagated by John Houghton, Nicholas Barbon, and other late seventeenth-century lobbyists.[17] In the eighteenth century, they would reach their apotheosis in the writings of Adam Smith.

Writers in this liberal economic mode represented trading as a natural human disposition. John Wheeler in 1601 cited the example of schoolchildren, who delighted in buying, selling, and swapping their toys.[18] Merchants, once widely criticized for their selfish pursuit of enrichment, came to be celebrated for their valuable services to society: Bishop Burnet thought that 'the men of trade and business' were 'generally speaking, the best body in the nation, generous, sober, charitable', while David Hume commended them as 'one of the most useful races of men'.[19] Fastidious objections to the pursuit of wealth were swept aside, whether they came from some godly preachers, who still saw it as a threat to religion, or from classical republicans, who continued to regard it as incompatible with civic virtue. It was a great mistake, thought John Evelyn, to think that 'the honour we derive from blood or rapine be preferable to what is gotten by honest industry'.[20] Appropriate linguistic adjustments were urged. Instead of 'filthy lucre', people were encouraged to speak of 'honest advantage'; in place of 'covetousness', they invoked 'prudence', 'good husbandry', 'wise foresight'.[21] Moneymaking activities were made morally neutral by being dignified as legitimate 'interests', which politicians had to respect; indeed, the primary role of the state became that of creating and sustaining the conditions in which individuals could accumulate wealth.[22] In the marketplace, altruism was inappropriate.

The pursuit of personal gain was thus legitimized as a form of endeavour, as morally valid as any other. Preaching in London around 1660 the future Archbishop of Canterbury John Tillotson told his hearers that, when selling goods, the price to be asked was the common market price; 'and if any ask why I make the market the rule, seeing this seems to be as if I should say, let every man get as much as he can, for so men in the market do, I answer, the market is usually more reasonable than the particular appetites of men'.[23] The new ideology carried the assurance that it was possible to be wholly absorbed in one's private affairs and still be indirectly serving the public interest. Self-enrichment could be both socially advantageous as well as personally enhancing. Riches could do good to others, even if their owner had no intention of giving them away.[24]

Liberal economic thought of this kind did not have the field to itself. It was repeatedly challenged by classical humanism, with its hostility to commerce and its emphasis on civic virtue, and by old-style Christian morality, with its stress on charity and unselfishness; significantly, many of the businessmen's defenders found it preferable to lay more emphasis on their charitable activities than their commercial ones. In the eighteenth century, there was a long and complex debate between adherents of these conflicting traditions.

The ultimate triumph of the new economic thought was to represent the quest for profit as a civilizing mission. From late Elizabethan times onwards, it became increasingly common for defenders of trade to praise its eirenic influence, claiming that commerce brought 'the whole world almost' into 'a communion and fellowship'. For Thomas Hobbes, the 'desire of such things as are necessary to commodious living' was one of the passions inclining men to peace.[25] After the Restoration, Thomas Sprat, John Evelyn, and others expatiated on the manner in which business and industry spread politeness and refinement, bringing men from barbarism to civility.[26] The virtues of self-denial were dismissed as those of 'rude and barbarous nations';

and civilization itself came to be seen as a process by which new wants were endlessly multiplied.[27] 'Did men content themselves with bare necessities', wrote Sir Dudley North, 'we should have a poor world.'[28] In 1696 the former press-licenser Edmund Bohun declared that 'the great design of God Almighty' was 'to civilize the whole race of mankind, to spread trade, commerce, arts, manufactures, and by them Christianity, from people to people round the whole globe of the earth'.[29] Here, in embryo, was that belief in the evolution of mankind from barbarism to politeness, by means of trade and industry, which, in the eighteenth century, would be the core of the Scottish historical school's justification of commercial society.[30] The essentials of this narrative were all in place by 1700.

So it was that the quest for wealth and possessions came to be represented as an acceptable goal, increasingly free from guilt and moral censure, and a legitimate route to human fulfilment. When Daniel Defoe visited Norfolk around 1720, he found every man 'busy on the main affair of life, that is to say getting money'.[31] Commerce, noted the Scottish philosopher Adam Ferguson in 1767, was now 'considered as the great object of nations, and the principal study of mankind'.[32] 'Getting of money,' agreed the cotton manufacturer Jedediah Strutt, 'whatever some divines would teach us to the contrary... is the main business of the life of man.'[33]

Yet a nagging doubt remained. Could money and goods really bring happiness? Adam Smith himself concluded that the pleasures of wealth were a deception. They produced 'a few trifling conveniencies to the body', but they left their owner just as exposed 'to anxiety, to fear, and to sorrow; to diseases, to danger, and to death'. 'In what constitutes the real happiness of human life,' he wrote, 'in ease of body and peace of mind, all the different ranks of life are nearly upon a level, and the beggar who suns himself by the side of the highway, possesses that security which kings are fighting for.'[34]

Of course, this was too bland a view. It discounted the wretchedness of the poor, their lower expectation of life, and the human deterioration which accompanied poverty and rejection. Yet Adam Smith's salutary warning that money and possessions did not guarantee felicity interestingly anticipates the view of those modern economists who suggest that, to the comfortably placed inhabitants of developed societies, additional riches can bring, at most, only a trivial amount of extra happiness.[35] It was a warning which few of Smith's contemporaries would bother to heed.

5

HONOUR AND REPUTATION

Though there is not any thing in the world that hath been always more valued and desired than honour, yet there is nothing that has been so little understood and explicated.

Nathaniel Vincent, *The Right Notion of Honour*, 1685

The savage lives within himself, while social man lives constantly outside himself, and only knows how to live in the opinion of others, so that he seems to receive the consciousness of his own existence merely from the judgment of others concerning him.

Jean-Jacques Rousseau, *Discours sur l'origine et les fondements de l'inégalité parmi les hommes*, 1755; Eng. trans., Everyman's Library, 1913

It appears that everyone has the power of obtaining true honour, by promoting the happiness of mankind in his proper station.

John Brown, *Honour: A Poem*, 1743

PRECEDENCE AND SUPERIORITY

In early modern England, the desire to secure the favourable opinion of other people was a primary determinant of human behaviour. Soldiers performed feats of bravery in order to win honour; craftsmen and labourers gained respect by diligent and skilful application to their work; and a major concern of those who pursued riches, spent money, and acquired possessions was to make a favourable impression upon others. For John Locke, 'the principal spring' from which the actions of men took their rise was 'credit and reputation', while, for Adam Smith, 'perhaps the strongest of all our desires' was that of deserving and obtaining the respect of our equals.[1]

Among the nobility and gentry, honour was the supreme value. It was to be ranked 'above all other good things': 'the greatest gift belonging to this life', the 'darling of human affection', the thing 'of highest price among all the objects of desire'.[2] When James Stanley, seventh Earl of Derby, went to his death on the scaffold in October 1651 for supporting Charles II in his unsuccessful attempt to regain the crown, he declared in his dying speech that 'I was born in honour, have lived in honour, and hope I shall die with honour.'[3]

The idea that honour was the supreme earthly goal had classical roots. Aristotle, in his *Ethics*, had ranked it as the greatest of external goods; and the elites of ancient Greece and Rome had made its pursuit their constant objective.[4] Following these precedents, Renaissance humanists urged that virtuous persons should seek honour above everything else. They represented the desire for it as a superior sentiment, 'an intellectual pleasure' which distinguished humans from animals.[5] A man's 'good name', it was asserted, was worth far more than riches. The Elizabethan statesman Lord Burghley thought honour 'the greatest possession that any man can have', while in the view of his contemporary, the theologian Richard Hooker, the 'chiefest' of all earthly blessings was 'reputation'.[6]

Yet 'reputation' and 'honour' are elusive concepts. In 1995 at a conference of the Royal Historical Society, many excellent papers were given on honour and reputation in sixteenth- and seventeenth-century England. But when it came to the summing up, grave doubts were expressed as to whether the term 'honour' had any practical utility as a historical category. For the contributors found that the early modern use of the concept was fluid and contradictory. How could 'honour' have any real meaning when it could on some occasions lead gentlemen to risk their lives in defence of the King against Parliament and on others justify them in fighting duels in defiance of the Crown's edicts? How could honour be the guiding star both of Restoration rakes, intent on a life of wenching and gambling, and of pious virgins, guarding their chastity? Honour, it seemed, was not a single value, but a multiplicity of conflicting values.[7] 'What a pity is it', says Henry Fielding's Jonathan Wild, 'that a word of such sovereign use and virtue should have so uncertain and various an application that scarce two people mean the same thing by it.'[8]

If we are to establish why honour was valued so highly in this period, and by whom, we have to disentangle the concept. Only then can we understand why contemporaries gave it so central place among the ends of life.

In its original sense, honour was the special respect and esteem which was extended to persons of merit. *Honor* was the Latin word for what in the later Middle Ages was called 'worship', the publicly acknowledged superiority of those of high status or virtue. As Sir Edward Dering noted around 1631, 'in all ages and nations...there hath been a constant practice to distinguish between man and man by a different valuation made, arising from some observable worth or want discerned betwixt them, whereby the able and worthy have always been raised in estimation [and], as it were, severed from the unworthy'.[9] This external recognition of superior worth was called honour. In the words of Chaucer's Parson, 'men clepen [call] honour the reverence that man doth to man'. More brutally, Thomas Hobbes defined honour as the recognition of someone else's superior power.[10]

The most obvious forms of external recognition were titles of distinction, that is to say honours as in today's Honours Lists. These were distributed by the monarch. An Act of Parliament declared in 1539 that it was the king's prerogative to give appropriate 'honour, reputation, and placing' to his councillors and other subjects.[11] When James I's favourite, George Villiers, was moved up in 1618 from earl to marquess, a friend congratulated him on the 'augmentation of honour, which His Majesty hath newly conferred on your lordship'.[12] Charles I attached great importance to 'his power to confer honour on any man he pleased'.[13] After the abolition of the monarchy in 1649, the Rump Parliament received a proposal that it should take on the function of granting knighthoods, because 'honour is a principal reward of virtue and hath been in all times in this nation of great encouragement to generous spirits'.[14]

The highest honorific status was enjoyed by the nobility and gentry, who were entitled to external deference from others at public encounters and to be accorded such privileges as 'to sit when others stand, to be covered when others are bare-headed and to ride when others walk'. Rising up, giving way, and standing back were the conventional gestures of respect owed to superiors in daily intercourse.[15] Elaborate rituals at meals and public occasions constantly reminded observers of the hierarchy of honour. The Elizabethan gentleman Sir Francis Willoughby went to the extent of prescribing that when the food was brought into his hall at Wollaton, Nottinghamshire, an usher should walk before it, carrying a rod and 'saying with a loud voice, "Give place, my masters!", albeit no man be in the way'.[16] Magistrates, parents, and other superiors were conventionally saluted with hat-doffing, bowing, curtseying, and similar forms of obeisance, 'for honour['s] sake'.[17] In the universities, juniors were required to show reverence to their seniors.[18] In the municipalities, the mayor was given a special seat to symbolize his superior status.[19] In public life, carefully ranked orders of precedence were composed by the heralds and observed on ceremonial occasions. Degrees of honour were observed even in death, for the treatment of the body, the scale of the funeral, and the place of burial all varied according to the status of the deceased. To dismember the corpse or cast it ignominiously into the ground without ceremony was to do it posthumous dishonour.[20]

Such physical signs of deference were reinforced by appropriate modes of address, descending hierarchically from the 'right honourable' ranks of the peerage, down through the 'right worshipful' and 'worshipful' gentry and merchants, to the 'masters' and 'goodmen' below them. 'In our English style,' explained a commentator in 1639, 'the title "worshipful" is more common than the title "honourable", and inferior thereunto.'[21] An Elizabethan manual on letter-writing prescribed that, when speaking or writing to superiors, 'we must do it with all honour, humility and reverence, using to their personages superlative and comparative terms, as "most high", "most mighty", "right honourable", "most redoubted", "most loyal", "most worthy", "most renowned", altogether according to the quality of their personages'. There were similar rules about socially appropriate forms of layout, spacing, and quality and size of writing paper.[22]

Nowadays, the persistence of these archaic orders of precedence causes us faint amusement, with their pedantic insistence that, say, the son of a life peer comes before a baronet,* but they were once matters of deadly seriousness. In 1625 Roger Williams of Brecon assaulted John Games, declaring that, since he was the fourth son of Sir David Williams, Games ought to have offered to go out of the room before him. Games retorted that he was the second son of Sir John Games and appealed to the Earl Marshal.[23] In 1673 Lord Cholmondeley killed a carter for his 'insolence' in not allowing his coach precedence on the highway.[24] In 1699 Lord Wharton and Lord Cheyne fought a duel after a dispute as to which of them should sit on the right hand of the chairman of the Buckinghamshire quarter sessions.[25]

---

* In 2005, in a circular letter drawing attention to the guidance offered by Debrett's *People of Today Review* on such matters as 'the correct seating of a Lady of the Garter at a formal dinner, or how to address the widow of a Scottish Lord of Parliament's son', its editor correctly observed that 'no other comparable publication contains this sort of thing'.

Within the towns and villages, the order in a procession or in seating at a feast or in the pews of the parish church had a deep symbolic importance, for it involved an explicit, and highly visible, public ranking of an individual's worth and standing. In rural parishes it was common for the congregation to rise when the local gentleman and his family entered the church and for communion to be taken in order of social precedence. (In 1645 the *Directory for Public Worship* explicitly prohibited 'salutations, or doing reverence to any persons present, or coming in' after the service had begun.[26]) In 1634 George Spurstowe, esquire, even brought a case against the local vicar because at Communion he served 'rich and poor, poor and rich, one with another without respect, the beggar with the gentleman and all together'.[27] Relics of this once ubiquitous display of hierarchy and subordination survive in the modern University of Oxford: in the high tables in college halls, the carefully ordered procession at Encaenia, and the Council of the University's practice (only recently abandoned) of rising when the Vice-Chancellor enters the room.

Honour in this sense was a hierarchical concept; there were degrees of honour and some people had more of it than others. As Hobbes observed, honour consisted 'in comparison and precellence': 'if all men have it, no man hath it'.[28] In modern language, it was a zero sum game. A system which required the constant acknowledgement of superiority was bound to generate competition, particularly among equals. In the early modern period, when social mobility was upsetting traditional hierarchies, the need to assert one's superiority was felt intensely, by the old-established and the parvenu alike. Just as fifteenth-century gentlemen vigorously engaged in 'mutual emulation and the pursuit of worship',[29] so honour was a crucial motivating force in the struggle of the Tudor and early Stuart gentry for unpaid local office on the county lieutenancy and the commission of the peace. Although numerous gentlemen felt a strong sense of obligation to perform public service for the common good, and although office could bring power and material reward, the strongest incentive for seeking advancement was the prestige and pleasure which came from discomfiting local rivals. Conversely, the damage which could be done to a gentleman's reputation by demotion was deeply felt. When the Earl of Worcester was dismissed from the lieutenancy by Charles I in 1631, it was said that 'many of the county do put daily affronts upon him and his, he being now, as they term him, Jack out of Office'.[30] The gentry feuds which plagued many counties for generations—Talbot versus Stanhope in Nottinghamshire, Poulett versus Phelips in Somerset, Gawdy versus

Lovell in Norfolk, Beaumont versus Hastings in Leicestershire—were contests between rival lineages for power, patronage, religion, and money, but the chief prize was precedence for its own sake.[31] Until 1640 the selection of the knights of the shire for Parliament was essentially a process of social recognition, the acknowledgement of status. Failure to be elected could mean humiliation.[32]

The competitiveness of the Tudor and Stuart gentry found many other outlets: gambling, where the debts incurred were 'debts of honour', to be paid immediately because they could not be enforced by law, by contrast with debts to tradesmen, which, though legally enforceable, were often slow to be discharged; cockfighting, where the owner's courage was embodied in that of his bird; horse racing, an acknowledged 'theatre of honour';[33] litigation, where prestige was often as much at issue as property;[34] and drinking bouts, notoriously animated by 'mere glory'.[35] At the royal court, at assizes and quarter sessions, on military campaigns, and when passing on the road, there were endless disputes about precedence.[36] At dinners, wrote a Jacobean satirist, 'the meat will be half cold, ere the guests can agree on their places'.[37] Honour, it has been well said, 'was a competitive language which kept the ruling elite in an almost permanent state of agitation'.[38] This was the world that Thomas Hobbes had in mind when he said that men were 'continually in competition for honour and dignity' and that there was 'no other goal, nor other garland, but being foremost'.[39]

The tussle for precedence by the gentry was replicated lower down the social scale in the jostling for place and priority which seems to have characterized every form of public assembly in the early modern period. In the later Middle Ages, there had been innumerable quarrels, sometimes ending in bloodshed, about the order in which parishioners walked in procession or received holy bread.[40] In 1547 the weekly parish processions before mass were abandoned, allegedly because of the 'contention and strife' which had arisen 'by reason of fond courtesy, and challenging of places'.[41] In post-Reformation times, numerous parishes were rent by squabbles about the order of seating in church, as in the acrimonious episode at St Ebbe's, Oxford, on a January evening in 1585, when Margery Hopkins said to Barbara Nicholls, 'If you will not let me come into my own seat, I will sit upon your lap.'[42] When the English settled in Bermuda in the early seventeenth century, they found themselves confronted by the same 'heart-burning and contention' about church seating.[43] Some contemporaries suggested that many went to church 'to seek precedence' rather than to worship God.[44]

Women, whose status usually derived from that of their husbands, were particularly prominent in these disputes: in Sir Edward Coke's opinion, 'the contention about precedency between persons of that sex is ever fiery, furious, and sometimes fatal'.[45] 'I have . . . beheld farmers', nay poor tenants', nay labourers' wives swell, till they almost burst with envy at their neighbours' stepping before or sitting above 'em,' recalled a later Stuart clergyman.[46] Churchwardens struggled to dispose parishioners according to their several ranks and qualities, but there were too many incompatible criteria (age, sex, marital status, place of residence, contribution to the parish rates) and too much change in people's fortunes for stability to be achieved. No wonder that Archbishop Laud would like to have taken the seats away from the churches altogether.[47] Similarly, there were few municipalities which did not witness quarrels like that in Exeter in 1539 between the mayor's wife and one mistress Blackeall 'for superiority and who should go first in procession'.[48] It was sometimes alleged that the social aspirations of traders were really those of their wives and that they accepted municipal office so that their spouses could enjoy the accompanying precedence.[49] As Chaucer had written long before:

> It is full fair to be ycleped 'madame'
> And go to vigils all before
> And have a mantle royally ybore.

Within the towns the precise ranking of clergy and laity was a delicate matter. After Robert Jenison, lecturer at All Saints, Newcastle, had taken his Cambridge doctorate, he enquired in 1630 of his old tutor whether a doctor of divinity ranked as equivalent to a JP, and whether the same precedence extended to the doctor's wife. His only concern, he explained, was to silence those who wished 'to debase our calling and degree'.[50] 'Place, that great object which divides the wives of aldermen,' Adam Smith would remark, 'is the end of half the labours of human life.'[51]

So long as public rituals sought to give visible expression to the social order, and daily social interaction was governed by an acute awareness of differences in rank, the issue of precedence was bound to remain contentious. For the social structure was too complex to be fitted into one single hierarchy, while unceasing social mobility meant that no ordering could retain its credibility for very long.

Similar issues of precedence arose in the international sphere. Since classical times it had been accepted that a state was entitled to undertake war in defence of its honour.[52] In an age of personal monarchy, the enhancement of the ruler's international standing was a recurrent objective. Wars, as the Quaker William Penn sagely remarked, were the duels of princes.[53] Just as Henry VIII staked his honour and that of the realm on his invasion of France in 1513, so Mary I's loss of Calais in 1558 was regarded as an abiding 'disgrace'.[54] When the Earl of Essex sacked Cadiz in 1596, Sir Walter Ralegh reported gleefully that the King of Spain had been 'never so much dishonoured'.[55] Seventy-one years later, when the Dutch fleet sailed up the Medway, attacked the fleet at Chatham, and blockaded London, John Evelyn regarded it as 'a dishonour never to be wiped off'.[56] It was to avoid 'loss of honour and reputation' that the Earl of Strafford had urged Charles I into active warfare against the rebel Scots in 1640.[57]

Early modern diplomatic history is punctuated by endless disputes about precedence between rival ambassadors.[58]* At sea there were recurring arguments over whose ships should do honour to whom by lowering their topsails and striking their flag.[59] These exactly mirrored the 'contending about place and precedency' at home between gentle-men, whose refusal to give way to each other when they met in the street was a common cause of brawling and duels.[60] Any activity involving comparison with other countries could be represented as a matter of national honour, from architecture to scholarship. In 1618 the writer Thomas Gainsford declared that nothing added more honour to a nation than 'regardable edifices', while in 1658 Sir Kenelm Digby assured the mathematician John Wallis that his achievements would 'redound to the honour of our nation'.[61] The Tudor noblemen Henry Fitzalan, twelfth Earl of Arundel, when travelling in Italy, and Lord William Howard, when governing Calais, though both good linguists, made a point of addressing foreigners in English, 'for the honour of our native tongue'.[62]

ARISTOCRATIC HONOUR

Honour was thus the public recognition of superiority. But 'honour' also referred to the exceptional moral qualities on which that super-iority was supposedly based. As Aristotle had taught, honour was 'a

---

* In his visionary proposal in 1693 for a European Parliament, the Quaker William Penn ingeniously suggested that quarrels over precedence could be avoided if representatives of the assembled states met in a round room with a number of doors, making possible simultaneous entrances and exits; *The Peace of Europe* (Everyman's Lib., n.d.), 11.

reverence given to another, for a testimony of his virtue'. It consisted 'not in the admiration of common people, but in the virtue of him that therewith is imbued'.[1] It was 'a kind of history or fame following actions of virtue, actions accompanied with difficulty or danger, and undertaken for the public good'.[2] Honour thus became a synonym for the distinctive values which governed the conduct of the most honourable persons.

Those who lived in accordance with such values commanded the respect of their social equals, their peer group. That respect has been called 'horizontal' honour, as opposed to the 'vertical' honour extended by inferiors to superiors.[3] To retain it, the rules of the group had to be followed. If those rules were internalized and observed for their own sake, rather than merely obeyed in response to external pressure, the person concerned was said to be governed by his own sense of honour. In that case, he drew his self-respect, not from the deference of others, but from his own deliberate adherence to a demanding standard of behaviour. An internal sense of honour was something different from a concern with outward reputation, but the two were not always distinguished from each other, for an honourable man was likely to gain the esteem of his peers. It was this ambiguous combination of inner virtue and outward reputation which gave honour its distinctive quality.

The code of honour espoused by the nobility and gentry of the early modern period has left its mark upon the dramatic literature of the Elizabethan and Restoration periods; and, as a result, has been much studied.[4] Essentially, it was an amalgam of chivalric ideals of loyalty, generosity, and physical courage with classically derived notions about the duty to seek praise and fame in virtuous public service. Thus defined, honour had a precedence which overrode all other considerations: financial gain, erotic love—even life itself, for it was a commonplace that a life without honour was not worth having. A chronicler relates that in 1493 Sir John Savage, captured by the French at the siege of Boulogne, 'of his high courage disdained to be taken of such villains, defended his life to the uttermost and was manfully (I will not say wilfully) slain'. In the same spirit, the second Earl of Northampton was killed in 1643 at the battle of Hopton Heath, when, grievously wounded, and surrounded by Parliamentary troopers, he refused their call to surrender, retorting that 'he scorned to take quarter off such base rogues and rebels as they'.[5] In 1645, after his defeat at Naseby, Charles I commanded his son Charles 'never to yield to any conditions that are dishonourable...though it were for the saving of my life'. A recent biographer convincingly suggests that the maintenance of his honour was the King's central preoccupation.[6]

Keeping one's word, whatever the cost, was a vital ingredient of aristocratic honour, since not to do so could be interpreted as cowardice; and, in Sir Walter Ralegh's words, it was better to die than to live a coward. Honour lost through cowardice was difficult, if not impossible, to retrieve.[7] Men of honour bridled at the suggestion that they should give evidence on oath or sign a written contract: their word was sufficient.[8] In the duelling code, imported from Italy in the later sixteenth century, giving the lie was regarded as the ultimate insult, to be followed inexorably by a challenge to combat, which could be declined only at the risk of ignominy in the eyes of one's equals. The fear of the terrible dishonour which might follow a refusal to fight ensured the survival of the duel among the upper classes and the military until the 1840s, in the teeth of legal prohibitions and religious opinion.[9] Army and naval officers were particularly prickly about wounded honour because courage was the essential virtue of their profession and no imputation of cowardice could be endured.[10] There were attempts to provide legal remedies for damaged honour: the High Court of Chivalry under the Earl Marshal catered for gentlemen who had been insulted by their inferiors or slandered by their equals in a manner likely to provoke a duel;* and for a time there was a special remedy, the action for *scandalum magnatum*, against those who had the temerity to defame a peer of the realm.[11] If the machinery of justice provided no remedy for insult, it was urged, then the man of honour was entitled to take the law into his own hands. Did not Aristotle teach that to put up with insults was slavish? And would not the gentleman's readiness to protect his reputation with his sword encourage others to be civil?[12]

The underlying assumption was that those at the apex of society had a distinctive set of moral standards: their loyalty, bravery, generosity, and veracity were supposedly greater than those of ordinary people. In no other rank of society, it was claimed, would one find such contempt for death, such magnanimity, such concern to keep one's word. The duelling code was socially exclusive: an insult from someone below the rank of gentleman was not to be rebutted with a

---

* It functioned between 1622 and 1640, and again in 1687–1731, but after a judicial ruling of 1703 ceased to hear actions for words; G. D. Squibb, *The High Court of Chivalry* (Oxford, 1959).

challenge to the field, but by some coarser method of retaliation. A challenge from a plebeian was under no circumstances to be accepted. In this way, the nobility and gentry laid claim to a monopoly of personal valour at a time when, as we have seen, their military prowess was conspicuously evaporating.[13]

This kind of honour could not just be inherited and enjoyed. It had constantly to be reasserted. Aristocratic reputation needed to be guarded and any affront speedily avenged. The good name of the individual, his wife, family, and lineage was to be preserved at all costs. This concern frequently generated extreme touchiness, and hypersensitivity to any form of slight. As a result, honour was invoked as justification for almost any kind of self-aggrandizement.

Historians have abundantly described the intemperate language of many early modern aristocrats, the use of hired bullies in the prosecution of feuds, and the total disregard for what might have been thought honourable behaviour by many of those who claimed to be acting in its name.[14] The Tudor musician Thomas Whythorne recalled that he had 'at sundry times...been in the companies of those who be "worshipful", "right worshipful", and also "honourable" ' and had seen 'that the meaner sort...were driven to put up quietly [with] some injuries at their hands; also such things, which the inferior sort either said or did in the presence of their greaters or betters was but to be allowed of as it pleased their superiors to take it'.[15] The insistence on status, when unaccompanied by any concern with high-principled conduct, made aggressive talk of 'honour' potentially menacing to peaceful passers-by. Sir Richard Barckley lamented in 1598 that, 'nowadays', those who were 'furious and passionate and quarrellous' were called 'stout and valiant men that stand upon their honour'. In his attack on the licentiousness of the Restoration stage, the clergyman Jeremy Collier concluded that the dramatists' idea of a fine gentleman was 'a fine whoring, swearing, smutty, atheistical man. These qualities, it seems, complete the idea of honour.' When the novelist and magistrate Henry Fielding compiled his 'modern glossary' in 1752, he defined 'gallantry' as 'fornication and adultery', and 'honour' as 'duelling'.[16]

The duplicity of Charles I in his dealings with Parliament during the last months of his life reminds us that aristocratic honour was a flexible code. But it should not be dismissed as empty rhetoric. The lives and deaths of many Elizabethans—Essex, Grenville, Ralegh— provide abundant proof that men were capable of putting reputation before personal safety.[17] In the English Civil War, the 'punctilio of honour', requiring courage, loyalty, civility, and magnanimity, was a real, though not infallible, constraint upon the behaviour of officers and men on both sides, conducing to the safety of messengers, the granting of quarter, the decent treatment of prisoners, and the standing by promises made. There was nothing quixotic or romantic about this kind of military honour. It was in the interest of all combatants.[18]

Offended honour and the demand for its vindication were important ingredients in the New Model Army's quarrel with Parliament in 1647.[19] In May 1648 Lord Fairfax asked the House of Lords to confirm the articles granted at the King's surrender of Oxford because of his 'deep sense' of the damage which would be done to the honour of Parliament and the Army if such engagements were violated. Anger at the MPs' reluctance to abide by the promises given by the military leaders to defeated Royalists helped to create the sense of alienation which led in 1653 to the Army's forcible dissolution of the Rump Parliament.[20] Of course, there were many occasions when combatants reneged on their promises or broke the accepted conventions of honourable warfare.[21] But dishonourable behaviour did not go unnoticed and was frequently repaid in kind. At the siege of Colchester in 1648, Fairfax refused to treat with the Royalist defender Sir Charles Lucas on the grounds that 'he ... being his prisoner upon his parole of honour, and having appear'd in arms contrary to the rules of war, had forfeited his honour and faith, and was not capable of command or trust in martial affairs'. After the garrison had surrendered, Lucas was executed.[22]

Yet aristocratic honour was not a unified code. Its ingredients changed over time and were incessantly disputed. There was never unanimity about the steps a gentleman was entitled to take in defence of his reputation. Some thought it crucial to avenge every insult, or at least to devise some legal machinery for doing so. Yet other gentlemen held that the superior course was to ignore such slights, on the grounds that honour, being based on virtue rather than the opinion of others, should be unaffected by such trivialities. They dismissed the ethic of the duelling code as 'false' honour; a man of 'true' honour would turn the other cheek. As the Jacobean travel writer Samuel Purchas put it, the irascible gallant who could not swallow the lie was 'effeminately squeamish': how could one mistake for a real man 'this quaking, huffing, puffing, snuffing, snarling, stamping, staring creature, evaporating and fuming away in choler?'[23] The Church had always taught that 'true strength and manliness' was 'to overcome wrath, and to despise injury and other men's foolishness'.[24] 'What one esteems as honour,' wrote an eighteenth-century philosopher, 'another looks upon as a folly or disgrace; one values himself . . . upon his patience in enduring wrongs, another upon his quickness in resenting them.'[25] In practice, it seems not to have been too difficult to avoid combat without losing one's honour.[26]

Early modern nobles and gentlemen thus regarded very different qualities as honourable, according to their particular circumstances and outlook. In the later Middle Ages, honour had come from military prowess, noble lineage, fidelity to one's feudal lord, and the provision of help and protection to one's own dependants. During the sixteenth and early seventeenth centuries, when it came to be generally accepted that the primary fount of honour was the Crown, it was virtuous and skilful service to the monarch which mattered.[27] Yet the duelling classes continued to flout royal commands if they considered that their personal honour was at stake. Even Thomas Hobbes, that great defender of the state's authority, conceded that a son, commanded by the sovereign to execute his father, could refuse to do so, rather than live 'infamous, and hated of all the world'.[28]

The upper classes agreed that their honour required the maintenance of an appropriately dignified style of life, including generosity to the poor, and (until at least the mid-seventeenth century) the provision of open-house hospitality: on his funeral monument, John Digby, Earl of Bristol (d. 1698), was praised for not making his retirement from public affairs an excuse to 'shun such expense as charity, hospitality and his honour called for'.[29] In addition, the gentry variously emphasized, according to personal interest and changing social conditions, the antiquity of their lineage, their holding of public office, their education and learning, their military prowess, their skill in the hunting field, and their piety and godliness. Changing notions about the components of honour were a response to parallel changes in the upper classes' way of life.

The extent to which honour could pull men in different directions became painfully apparent at the outbreak of civil war in 1642. The Cavalier gentry claimed that honour required them to show fidelity to the Crown, however much they disapproved of Charles I's policies, while the aristocrats who led the forces of his opponents believed that their honour demanded the punctilious discharge of the offices which Parliament had entrusted to them.[30] Sir Edmund Verney, the King's standard-bearer, who was killed at Edgehill, is famous for fighting in a cause of which he disapproved; though an opponent of episcopacy, he reluctantly defended it (according to Clarendon) because he had served the King for thirty years and 'could not do so base a thing as to forsake him'.[31] Similarly, Ralph, Lord Hopton, when commanded in January 1646 by the young Prince of Wales to take charge of the discredited Royalist army, 'very generously told the Prince that it was a custom now, when men were not willing to submit to what they were enjoined, to say that it was against their honour; and that their honour would not suffer them to do this or that; for his part, he could not obey his highness at this time without resolving to lose his honour, which he knew he must, but since his highness thought it necessary to command him, he was ready to obey him with the loss of his honour'.[32] On the other side, the third Earl of Essex became a Parliamentary general because he felt that his honour had been impugned by the King's lack of confidence in him.[33]

To aristocrats, it was axiomatic that their code of honour was the only one. They claimed that those below the nobility and gentry did not know what honour was (army and naval officers were ex officio gentlemen). As a contemporary theorist explained, 'Men of great minds are much moved with honour, but . . . the abject and baser sort be nothing affected therewith.'[34] In a battle, a 'mean-bred man' was thought more likely to run away, because he was 'not so apprehensive of the shame'.[35] Traders, who were notoriously ready to tell lies for the sake of their business, were alleged to be less concerned with honour than with financial gain.[36] As for the poor, they were thought to be too preoccupied with the struggle for subsistence to have any time for such rarefied considerations. 'All men naturally strive for honour, and preferment,' wrote Hobbes, 'but chiefly they who are least troubled with caring for necessary things.'[37] 'Leave honour to nobility that can support it,' says the lady's maid in George Farquhar's play The Constant Couple (1699): 'we poor folks . . . have no pretence to't.'[38]

The upper classes thus succeeded in persuading many others that the only true honour consisted of the distinctive values which their special social position required them to adopt. In fact, their claim to sole occupancy of the moral high ground rested upon a gross misrepresentation of the outlook of their inferiors.

THE HONOUR OF THE PEOPLE

It was not only aristocrats and army officers who regarded life as a perpetual struggle to assert honour and standing. A good reputation was valued at every level of society; and individual self-esteem almost always depended on securing the approval of others.

Ordinary soldiers usually had less exalted notions of personal honour than those held by their officers, but they too were governed by the pressure to social conformity. Then as now, it was not the threat of punishment that motivated soldiers to risk their lives in armed combat, but the fear of losing the good opinion of their fellows. In the words of an eighteenth-century military manual, 'They dread having reason to blush at their conduct before a comrade, and in some measure it is this salutary dread that constitutes what we term the spirit of corps, which preserves and cherishes the courage of a soldier.'[1]

In the schools and universities, humanist influence made competition an integral part of the educational system. Every grammar school boy was 'raised to a kind of emulation to exceed his fellows'.[2] In the 1630s the future divine Richard Baxter nearly left Wroxeter Free School out of pique, when he was dislodged from the top place in the form by the future canon of Christ Church Richard Allestree.[3] Just as schoolboys were ranked in order of attainment, so, in the universities, dons were notoriously willing to risk killing themselves with study, rather than be surpassed by others.[4] The learned controversies of the early modern period were singularly crotchety and abusive because the honour of the participants was so deeply involved. As Adam Smith would later remark, a large part of the reward for those who engaged in the learned professions was public admiration.[5]

Honour was also a preoccupation of the inhabitants of corporate towns, concerned as they were to establish their independence of the neighbouring gentry and to assert the legitimacy of commerce as an honourable way of life. They had their coats of arms, their civic officials, and their own forms of ceremonial. They sought to ensure that the community was not disgraced by the misbehaviour of any of its members,* and they insisted that appropriate respect should be extended to their public representatives. The honour of the town was at stake in the frequent battles to enforce the claims by mayors to take precedence over local gentlemen or visiting justices.[6] In cathedral cities there was endless jockeying for ceremonial precedence between

---

* When Elizabeth I visited Lichfield in 1575, the city paid 5 shillings to one William Hillcroft 'for keeping mad Richard [presumably out of sight] when Her Majesty was here'; John Nichols, *The Progresses and Public Processions of Queen Elizabeth* (1823), i. 529.

the civic corporation and the dean and chapter; and in the university towns, between the mayor and the vice-chancellor.[7] Collective activities, from feasts and processions to the compilation of town chronicles and histories, were designed to create civic pride and enhance the community's 'honour'.[8] When the four burgess JPs of Tewkesbury wore their gowns on Sundays, they did so 'for the reputation of the town'.[9]

Guilds and companies showed the same concern for their 'honour and worship', as individual crafts competed with each other for status and recognition. At the future Philip II of Spain's ceremonial entry into Antwerp in 1549, thirty members of the English company of Merchant Adventurers appeared on horseback, magnificently dressed in velvet and satin, wearing gold chains, and with feathers on their horses' heads; 'in which [we are told] they showed themselves for the honour of their prince and country nothing inferior to the merchants of other nations... and surmounting some of them in costly apparel, furniture of themselves and their horses... whereby they won great honour and commendation to themselves and the whole English name'.[10] Such forms of self-assertion implied that commercial wealth constituted as good a claim to honour as the ancient lineage and military prowess of which the gentry boasted. In Elizabethan and Jacobean London, pageants and Lord Mayor's Shows proclaimed the honour of merchants and apprentices; and civic pride was expressed in a host of ballads and popular pamphlets.[11] A London pamphleteer declared in 1678 that 'a man that is born in a great city hath more credit by it among foreigners than to be born of an ancient family; for the former is more known to them than the latter'.[12] 'We merchants...are as honourable...as you landed folks,' says a character in Richard Steele's play *The Conscious Lovers* (1722).[13]

Most small associations and communities, from universities to country parishes, displayed a similar concern with their collective reputation.[14] They had their officers: vice-chancellors and masters of colleges, churchwardens and constables, ale-tasters and overseers of the poor. Most of these posts brought honour and status to their holders. In one Shropshire village, William Parker, who 'affected to be accounted somebody in the parish', rose, with the aid of some well-directed gifts of bacon, to the office of churchwarden; and ever afterwards in conversation would date events by saying that they had occurred so many years 'before or after *I* was churchwarden'.[15]

Even at the most modest social level there was a concern to be well regarded. For honour, as the courtier Fulke Greville (1554–1628) remarked, was something to which 'even the silly artisans aspire [d]'.[16] Ordinary people seldom called it that, but they had other terms of equivalent meaning: 'credit', 'good name', 'reputation', or 'honesty' (in the sixteenth century, the primary meaning of 'honest' was 'deserving of honour'; its association with truth-telling was only just beginning to emerge).[17] Most Tudor villages had their oligarchy of 'chief inhabitants', what Archbishop Parker in 1560 described as 'the honesty of the parish'.[18] 'Honesty' was a less all-embracing term than 'honour', but it served many of the same functions. What it implied was 'respectability', that is to say living in accordance with the best expectations of the community. The word 'respectable' did not come into common usage until the later eighteenth century; until then, it was usual to say that people were 'of good name' or 'of good report', or 'of honest reputation'.[19]

The ingredients of this proto-respectability are clear enough.[20] Masculine 'honesty' was closely associated with marriage (an 'honourable estate', as the Prayer Book had it), and with being master of one's own family and household (a faint stigma attached to childlessness).[21] Physical bravery was important, particularly for young men, who were expected to show strength and toughness, and to be capable of defending themselves. Even for the pacific Joseph Addison, 'the great point of honour in men' was 'courage'.[22] Above all, 'honesty' implied industriousness, integrity in business affairs, and the ability to provide for one's family.[23] These were the qualities which enabled men to be described by their contemporaries as 'of honest report' or 'of good worth and estimation'.

Small farmers, tradesmen, and craftsmen guarded their 'honesty' as zealously as the gentry maintained their 'honour'. Aspersions on their family origins or the reputation of their close relatives were indignantly repudiated.[24] Suggestions that they were not to be trusted could provoke a furious response. 'Take away my good name and take away my life' was 'a proverb among the vulgar', noted John Ray at the end of the seventeenth century; and, sure enough, a Yorkshire country girl in 1696, who had heard some people gossiping that another woman was pregnant, was reported to have reproached them by saying that 'they might as well take her life as her good name from her'.[25]

It was not only the upper classes who vindicated their honour by physical combat. Among the middling and lower ranks, it was equally insulting to give someone the lie; and a scuffle, or, more likely, a fight with bare fists or weapons conducted according to strict rules of fair play, often followed.[26] In seventeenth-century printing-houses, a worker who called one of his workmates a liar had to pay a fine, or 'solace'.[27] Wounded honour was the root cause of much brawling. As a contemporary philosopher noted, 'the meanest of mankind' were 'as apt to take fire upon opprobrious language or defamation, when they understand it, as the most refined'.[28]

Although lumped together as 'the vulgar' by socially superior observers, the working population was highly stratified and its members acutely sensitive to differences in status. In the later Middle Ages, membership of a guild or fraternity had been an important way in which an individual could establish his respectability.[29] In late eighteenth-century London, particular occupations were regarded as 'honourable' or 'dishonourable' according to the degree of independence and self-reliance which they involved. Journeymen tailors, for example, were divided into the 'flints', unionized bespoke tailors, who could set their own rates of remuneration, and the 'dungs' in the ready-made trade, who had no option but to comply with the rates set by magistrates and masters.[30] Occupations were more likely to be regarded as 'honourable' if they had a system of apprenticeship, and if they enjoyed a form of collective organization which gave them some clout in collective bargaining. The 'dishonourable' were unorganized and worked for the mass market. The involvement of women also made some occupations dishonourable, for artisan honour was essentially masculine. Yet women workers also had their standards to maintain. Midwives depended upon certificates and testimonials vouching that they were 'of honest life and conversation'. The female friendly societies of the 1780s and 1790s excluded barrow women, fishwomen, and all who got their living on the streets.[31]

In artisan communities, status and self-respect derived primarily from economic solvency and technical skill. But the widespread concern to gain and maintain respectability also showed itself in other ways. It could be seen in the eagerness of servants and labourers to find the 'best' clothes with which to put on a good show on Sundays and holidays;[32] in the efforts of many people to save enough, or, in the eighteenth century, to join a friendly society, to ensure that they and their families would be buried 'honestly' and 'decently';[33] in the growing use of tablecloths, cutlery, teacups, and similar accoutrements of civility;[34] and in the enduring desire of working people to distance themselves from the marginal, the disabled, and the

disreputable. Women's friendly societies, for example, were concerned about the moral reputation of their members; they fined
drunks and quarrellers and excluded persons with criminal records.
They aimed to promote 'good manners and civil conversation'.[35] All
this foreshadowed the nineteenth-century division of the working
classes into 'respectable' and 'rough'.

The eagerness of people at every social level to defend their reputation was reflected in the lawsuits for defamation which grew in
number in the later sixteenth century. In the later Middle Ages, these
cases had been brought to the church and manorial courts, and, from
about 1500, they were heard by the common law courts as well.[36]
Several decades ago, some pioneering historians showed that defamation cases are invaluable sources for reconstructing what the middling and lower middling classes meant by 'honesty' and 'credit'.[37]
The insulting allegations to which litigants objected reveal, by implication, the values which they cherished, while assertions about the
credibility of individual witnesses reflect contemporary assumptions
about what it was which made some people more reputable than
others.

In recent years, a cohort of scholars has combed through court
records with these insights in mind. Not all of them have heeded the
warning that defamation cases were often just one more stage in a
long-standing quarrel and do not necessarily prove the existence of a
deep desire to defend reputation as such.[38] Neither have they always
remembered that the nature of the jurisdiction determined the type of
insult which was alleged and for which the plaintiff sought redress.
Because adultery and fornication were ecclesiastical crimes, the defamation cases heard by the church courts after the Reformation
mostly concerned sexual insults. False accusations of theft, say, or
perjury, had become the business of the common law. So one must be
careful before proceeding from an analysis of the offensive remarks
alleged under these selective jurisdictions to firm conclusions about
the ingredients of 'plebeian honour' as a whole.

Even so, these legal cases are highly instructive.[39] They show, for
example, that men were quick to defend themselves against accusations of being thieves, rogues, or perjurers; in the later Middle Ages,
allegations of theft were the most common type of defamation case
brought to the York consistory court.[40] A reputation for financial
probity and honest dealing was essential to an individual's economic
standing: as a judge ruled in 1575, it was a great damage to say that
someone was false in all his doings, because no one would have

anything to do with him as a result.[41] Credit was essentially the ability to pay one's debts when called upon to do so. The Tudor businessman John Isham used to say 'to a man careless of his debts, that he learned in Flanders of a Fleming that, if goods were lost, much were lost, if time were lost, more were lost, but if credit were lost, all were lost'.[42] Daniel Defoe, who thought that 'the credit of a trades-man' was 'the same thing in its nature as the virtue of a lady', warned how easily it could be endangered by malicious rumours.[43] When the Norwich cloth manufacturer Philip Stannard was rumoured in 1754 to have 'stopped payments', he dispatched furious letters to his trad-ucers, demanding the 'satisfaction' to which 'every tradesman and man of honour' was entitled.[44] Bankruptcy was a shattering blow to male honour, the worst form of disgrace which a trader could incur.[45]

Defamation cases also show that a man could lose honour if his wife rejected his authority or was sexually unfaithful. Cuckoldry was the staple of early modern comic literature—'the basis of most of our modern plays', thought Joseph Addison in 1712.[46] It was a humiliat-ing accusation, for it implied that the husband was incapable of both ruling his wife and satisfying her sexually. In the eyes of 'the vulgar', a cuckold was 'a fool, a coward and all they can think to be bad in a man'.[47] According to one Elizabethan, 'he that is known to be a notorious cuckold cannot be taken upon [in]quests, and is barred of divers functions and callings of estimation in the commonwealth as a man defamed'.[48] More litigation was provoked by allegations of cuckoldry than might at first sight appear, for some of the women who sued those who called them 'whore' were as much concerned to defend their husbands' honour as their own.[49]

Yet the relationship between cuckoldry and dishonour was complex. The husband who did not condone his wife's adultery or seek to profit from it was a less shameful figure than the 'wittol', or contented cuck-old, who connived in his wife's infidelity.* Some contemporaries even followed the French essayist Michel de Montaigne in denying that a man's honour was diminished by his wife's misconduct. In a play by Thomas Randolph, printed in 1638, one of the characters retorts:

> 'Tis my wife's fault, not mine. I have no reason
> Then to be angry for another's sin.[50]

---

* And could be punished for doing so; Richard Brownlow and John Goldesbor-ough, *Reports of Divers Choice Cases in Law* (1651–2), ii. 37.

At the Restoration court, it was fashionable to say that only fools thought their honour depended on their wives' behaviour; after all, a duke could marry a royal mistress without incurring dishonour.[51]

In the late seventeenth century, the law courts began to treat a wife's adultery as an invasion of property rather than an offence against honour; in an action for 'criminal conversation', damages could be awarded against the wife's seducer, on a sliding scale corresponding to the husband's rank. Such actions were extremely expensive and only a few hundred husbands ever took advantage of this remedy. Nevertheless, the idea that money could compensate for loss of reputation and that litigation was an acceptable alternative to challenging or assaulting a rival represented a distinct change in attitude.[52] Even at a humble social level, it was not unknown for lovers to be forced to pay financial compensation to injured husbands.[53]

In the 1690s John Dunton's popular journal of advice, *The Athenian Gazette*, pronounced that a betrayed husband should incur no shame, unless his wife's infidelity had been caused by his ill treatment. Cuckoldry, he maintained, was a personal misfortune, not a subject for public derision. By 1700 this viewpoint was becoming increasingly common among moralists and literary critics.[54] In the countryside, attitudes could also be tolerant. A Devonshire clergyman said in 1658 that a 'ninnyhammer' (or simpleton) was nine times worse than a cuckold, while an Oxfordshire witness explained in 1679 that, 'in the parish of Charlbury and thereabouts', 'they commonly use the word "cuckold" in a jesting way... to denote greater familiarity and intimacy one with another'.[55] The term was beginning to lose its bite.

Cuckoldry jokes continued throughout the eighteenth century and beyond. But they were too crude for polite society, where a broken marriage was increasingly regarded as a tragedy rather than a joke.[56] As a critic observed in 1777, 'the comic writers of the last age treated this matter as of more importance, and made more bustle about it, than the temper of the present times will well bear'.[57]

Nevertheless, the defamation cases reveal that sexual respectability was an important ingredient in masculine honour. It is true that fornication was widely dismissed as 'a trick of youth'[58] and male unchastity was less widely condemned than its female equivalent. 'Until every one hath two or three bastards apiece,' lamented the Elizabethan Puritan Philip Stubbes, 'they esteem him no man (for that they call a man's deed); insomuch as every scurvy boy of twelve, sixteen or twenty years of age will make no conscience of it to have two or three, peradventure half a dozen several women with child at once.'[59] Many men bragged about the size and potency of their sexual organs and crowed over their conquests.[60] They subscribed to a double standard well exemplified by the married Samuel Pepys, when he wrote in his diary of an encounter with the heavily pregnant Betty Martin that 'I did *ce que je voudrais avec* her most freely', and then 'away, sick of her impudence'—*her* impudence.[61] The aristocratic rakes of the later seventeenth and early eighteenth centuries, in real life no less than on the stage, regarded adultery and sexual promiscuity as a means of enhancing honour, 'a piece of gallantry'. Many Hanoverian gentry boasted of their priapic capacity and thought male chastity positively comic.[62]

The clergy, however, had always condemned sexual infidelity by either sex. So had many lay moralists, some of whom even regarded adultery as a greater sin in men.[63] King James I knew that fornication was 'thought but a light and a venial sin by the most part of the world'. He nevertheless advised his son to keep his body 'clean and unpolluted till you give it to your wife, whom-to only it belongeth'.[64] Many local authorities took a harsh view of male fornicators and adulterers.[65] The frequency with which such terms as 'whoremaster', 'whoremonger', 'roger', or 'poxy knave' were employed as insults, and the equal regularity with which they were indignantly repudiated, shows that, among the population at large, sexual promiscuity could bring dishonour to men as well as to women. Small farmers and craftsmen considered allegations that they had caught the French pox or fathered illegitimate children to be seriously damaging. As respectable married men, or as bachelors seeking that status, they valued a reputation for sexual honesty. Involvement in a bastardy case featuring allegations of deceit and broken promises did no man any good. The Buckinghamshire gentleman John Verney paid £12 to silence those who accused him of having fathered a child by a servant before his marriage, 'being tender of his reputation and unwilling such a thing should come against him in public'. The physician Dr John Raven (d. 1636) was less fortunate; 'attempting to creep to bed to Mistress Bennett', it was said, he 'lost his credit and his purchase'.[66]

It was not difficult for unscrupulous extortionists to blackmail respectable citizens by luring them into compromising situations. The Elizabethan archbishop Edwin Sandys, the poet Michael Drayton, and the antiquary Sir Robert Cotton were all entrapped in this way. So was the virtuous Richard Hooker.[67] Extracting money from putative fathers of illegitimate children became a common crime (pl. 9).[68] Of course, it was the expense, as well as the shame, which led men to deny responsibility for fathering bastard children. But that shame *was* involved, at least for men of the middling sort, seems indisputable. As a Somerset woman said in 1664, when resisting the sexual advances of her lover: if she were to have a child, it would be 'a great disgrace' to both of them.[69] It is possible that in the eighteenth century male promiscuity may have become more acceptable in some sections of society.[70] But there is little evidence to suggest that the Hanoverian middle classes took a more sympathetic view of masculine sexual misconduct than their predecessors had done.

Chastity to women was what courage was to men, the primary constituent of their honour.[71] Once lost, it could supposedly never be recovered. 'Our reputations not easily shaken, and many ways repaired,' noted Fulke Greville, 'theirs, like glass, by and by broken, and impossible to be healed.' A whoremaster's shame, agreed the popular writer John Taylor (1578–1653), was a nine day's wonder, whereas a blemish on a woman's reputation lasted a lifetime.[72] Revealingly, the common lawyers held that it was not actionable to accuse a man of having had the French pox, because, if he had fully recovered, there was no scandal. For a woman, by contrast, it was 'a discredit' ever to have had the disease, because 'thereby others will shun her company'.[73]

The shame which followed the discovery that a woman had had sexual relations outside marriage was potentially very damaging; if she were single, it could make it impossible for her to marry; if she were married, her husband would be entitled to a separation. Even those contemporaries who regarded fornication and adultery as equally sinful in either sex agreed that the practical consequences were much greater for females. Single motherhood was particularly shaming: in 1686 it was asserted that half of the newborn infants left in the streets of London to be brought up by the parish had been abandoned, not because of their mothers' poverty, but to save their reputations.[74] Suicide by an unmarried mother was commonly attributed to her overwhelming feeling of disgrace; and so were infanticide and abortion: 'Thou whom guilty honour kills to hide its shame', begins a poetic *Epitaph on a Child Killed by Procured Abortion* (1740). Sir John Reresby, who had visited the Innocenti hospital for foundlings in Florence in 1657, thought that such institutions prevented 'the barbarous murder of one's own children, too often here committed...for want of some such salve for reputation'.[75]

In practice, of course, a woman of modest origins who became the mistress of some great man could even enhance her honour through her unchastity;[76] like Thomas Hardy's ruined maid ('"Some polish is gained with one's ruin", said she'). It was also possible, in the eighteenth century, for unmarried mothers to deposit their children in a foundling hospital and, picking up where they had left off, return to normal life and, eventually, marriage. Among the poorer classes, where sexual intercourse was common between betrothed couples, and where women were valued as much for their labour as their sexual services, such peccadilloes could be more readily overlooked.[77]

Nevertheless, at all levels of society, accusations of 'whoredom', that is to say of fornication or adultery, were a serious matter for women. When around 1590 a man was prosecuted for saying that there were only three 'honest' women in Swinbrook, Oxfordshire, witnesses were called to explain that, in Swinbrook, 'to say that a woman was not an "honest" woman meant that she was light of her body'.[78] There were many other expressions with the same meaning: 'quean', 'jade', 'harlot', flirt', 'trull', 'baggage', 'bawdy breech', 'strumpet', hackney', 'common as the highway'.[79] Of course, many of these insults, though overtly aimed at women, were really directed at their menfolk. But their effectiveness depended upon the assumption that masculine honour required female chastity.

Yet, though a woman's good reputation began with chastity, it did not end there. The evidence of the church courts is so luridly compelling that it has led many historians to focus unduly on the sexual components of female honour and to give far too little weight to the other qualities and actions which gained or lost women the respect of their neighbours. Although 'whore' was the most common insult, women, like men, might also be reproached for being dirty, dishonest, lazy, drunks, cheats, liars, thieves, witches, and troublemakers.[80] All these forms of behaviour brought dishonour, while their opposites were a source of respect.

Female honour, in fact, had many constituents. Aristocratic women, set apart by birth and breeding, shared in the honour of their class, and were expected to display many of their husbands' virtues, such as hospitality, charity, and, on occasions, even valour. Women at all social levels gained honour from being married and for bearing children. They earned respect for prudent household management, successful child-rearing, hard work and cleanliness, piety, truthfulness, economic standing, and general 'credit'.[81] Skill in 'physic and surgery', thought Sir Robert Filmer, brought 'nobility to women, as arms and learning do to men'.[82] Conversely, the absence of these qualities brought them reproach. To be called a 'dirty slut, stinking drab and idle housewife' was a serious insult.[83] In Thomas Heywood's play *The English Traveller* (1633) a character is deterred from entering a house on the excuse that he is not expected:

> The house is full of women; no man knows
> How on the instant they may be employed;
> The rooms may lie unhandsome, and maids stand
> Much on their cleanliness and housewifery;
> To take them unprovided were disgrace;
> 'Twere fit they had some warning.[84]

Even small children were sensitive to honour and disgrace, being visibly competitive in their games, 'making pre-eminence or honour their end', as they sought to be cock of the dunghill or king of the castle, swearing on their honour, and declaring that they would rather die than tell a fib.[85] The inculcation of shame was regarded as an essential element in children's education. Roger North tells the reveal-ing anecdote of Arthur, the 5-year-old son (b. 1671) of the first Duke of Beaufort, who was very angry with Sir Matthew Hale LCJ for hanging men: 'The judge told him that, if they were not hanged, they would kill and steal. "No," said the little boy, "you should make them promise upon their honour they will not do so, and then they will not".'[86]

The truth was that all individuals, whatever their rank in society, regarded themselves as entitled to honour and respect if they lived in accordance with the standards appropriate to their particular social role. Like actors in a play, they had to perform the part they had been assigned: if it was that of a king, then they should act the king; and if it was that of the porter, they should act the porter; 'for a man may get as much credit by playing the one well as by well acting the other; and like discredit redoundeth unto him if neither be done well'.[87] As the political theorist John Hall of Richmond explained in 1654, 'true honour' consisted in 'the full discharge of the beneficial duties belong-ing to each man's rank and place'.[88] Two hundred and fifty years later, the French sociologist Émile Durkheim examined a doctoral thesis which expounded this very same insight, arguing that the essence of the idea of honour was encapsulated in the phrase 'Act in a way worthy of your role'.[89]

Of course, there was a hierarchy of esteem. As a writer explained in 1641, honour was due to all persons who performed their Christian and public duty in their respective occupation, whatever they happened to be; but the greatest honour went to those who held the positions of authority in Church and Commonwealth. High honour also extended to the professions of divinity, law, and medicine.[90] In the endless debate as to which honourable qualities should be ranked highest, rival social groups pressed self-interested claims for the all-importance of lineage, or military prowess, or wealth, or learning, or public service, or professional knowledge, or godliness, or skill, or hard work, or politeness, or conspicuous display. Some merchants claimed that they were just as honourable as gentlemen, while some gentlemen retorted by deriding trade as a base activity and asserting that apprenticeship extinguished gentility.[91] The learned physician Sir Thomas Browne advised his son in 1667 that it was much more honourable to become 'a great scholar' than 'a noble navigator', while the pious lady Dorothy Moore defended herself in 1645 against the charge of marrying beneath her by declaring that, although her new husband, the clergyman John Dury, was neither rich nor a gentleman, he was one of God's ministers and thus invested with 'the highest degree of honour'.[92] Competing definitions of honour reflected the social and ideological conflicts of the age.

At the bottom of the hierarchy were the outcasts, the beggars and vagrants, who in the eyes of everyone else enjoyed no honour at all. A poor man, said a contemporary wit, was 'in two extremes: first, if he ask, he dies with shame; secondly, if he ask not, he dies with hunger'.[93] There were also those whom the Dean of Worcester had in mind in 1684 when he observed that, in all societies, 'there must be members of dishonour, as well as honour'.[94] Just as the human body had its necessary but shameful features and functions, to be concealed from public view, so there were disreputable but necessary tasks to be performed. When Thomas Noneley, a Shropshire freeholder, was in gaol for debt, he was hired to act as hangman at the execution of a murderer: 'this was a disgrace to Noneley and [h]is family ever after'.[95] Yet, as we have seen, those who did such despised work usually had their own standards and sources of self-respect. As John Robinson, pastor to the Pilgrim Fathers, put it, 'It is an honour to a man to be excellent in his faculty, yea even though it be mean in itself. And so men excelling in mean trades or callings are more regarded than those who are mean in more excellent faculties.'[96]

Even the poor had their pride. Under an Act of 1697 those in receipt of poor relief were, along with their families, required to wear a conspicuous badge on their sleeve. Such badges had originally been devised as an honourable symbol of the deserving poor's entitlement to charity, but by the time they were made compulsory, they had come to be widely regarded as symbols of shame. Some of the poor refused to wear them, even though they had to forgo relief as a consequence.[97]

Thieves notoriously knew what honour was: pirates, highwaymen, and professional criminals had their conventions about what brought glory or disgrace, taking oaths on their honour, refusing to save their lives by betraying their accomplices, and displaying courage ('dying game') on the scaffold.[98] Those outside the law could disregard the opinion of society at large, but they were seldom indifferent to that of their peers. As John Locke wrote, not one man in ten thousand could be 'stiff and insensible enough to bear up under the constant dislike and condemnation of his own club'.[99] The youthful roisterers who engaged in collective drinking, broke windows, assaulted passers-by, and caused disorder on the streets at night had their own unwritten rules and hierarchies of prestige. The machismo of violence, drinking prowess, and sexual bravado brought them honour in the eyes of their comrades, however much it earned the opprobrium of law-abiding citizens.[100]

In short, it is impossible to find any social group which was utterly shameless or for whom considerations of reputation were totally irrelevant. People in even the humblest positions believed that they were entitled to an appropriate degree of respect.[101] The situation was cogently analysed by the now forgotten eighteenth-century philosopher Abraham Tucker (1705–74): 'The professions and situations of men in life rendering different things serviceable to them creates a proportionable variety in their sentiments of honour: the merchant places it in punctuality of payment, the soldier in bravery, the artificer in the completeness of his works, the scholar in acquisitions of learning, the fine gentleman in politeness and elegancy of taste, the lady in her beauty or neatness of dress or skill in family economy. There is no man utterly destitute of honour... But men's notions of it are widely different and discordant.'[102]

Because the upper classes made a greater parade of their 'honour', it is easy to overlook the essential similarity between their commitment to upholding the standards of their group and that of the lower social classes to maintaining theirs. Similarly, because the early modern nobility and gentry defined their honour in terms of such qualities as loyalty, truth-keeping, and courage, we are slow to appreciate that, in other social milieux and at other times, the ingredients of honour could take a different form. In the early modern period, the aristocracy was unique in managing to pass off its particular ethic as synonymous with honour itself. But every sector of society had its own values; and its members gained reputation by conforming to them.

Isaac Barrow concluded that it was honour which made the world go round: for its sake, 'the soldier undergoes hardship, toil and hazard; the scholar plods and beats his brains; the merchant runs about so busily and adventures so far; yea, that for its sake the meanest labourer and artificer doth spend his sweat and stretch his sinews... The great reason of all this scuffling for power, this searching for knowledge, this scraping and scrambling for wealth, doth seem to be that men would live in some credit, would raise themselves above contempt.'[103]

CREDIT AND SHAME

Barrow would have been more accurate if he had noted that, for most people, the conformist desire to avoid shame was a stronger constraint than the egotistic urge to achieve honour. The efforts of attention-seeking gentlemen to maximize their honour were very different in spirit from middle-class notions of 'honesty' and respectability; they also jarred with plebeian ideals of craft and community solidarity. The dread of shame, by contrast, was shared at every social level. If honour was the best thing in life, wrote the early seventeenth-century translator and bibliophile Robert Ashley, then shame was the worst. A man would choose to abandon life itself, agreed an eighteenth-century theologian, rather than forfeit the esteem of his fellows and live an object of universal contempt and derision. 'Compared with the contempt of mankind,' thought Adam Smith, 'all other external evils are easily supported.'[1]

Of course, people were frequently forced by the demands of self-interest or self-preservation to risk social ignominy by breaking the codes to which they were expected to adhere. Like Falstaff on the battlefield at Shrewsbury, they allowed the urge to survive to override the claims of honour. Confronted by a choice between reputation and money, the early seventeenth-century financier Sir Arthur Ingram had no hesitation in choosing money. Similarly, the well-to-do London widow Katherine Austen in 1665, when contemplating the possibility of marriage with a titled gentleman, declared that worldly honour

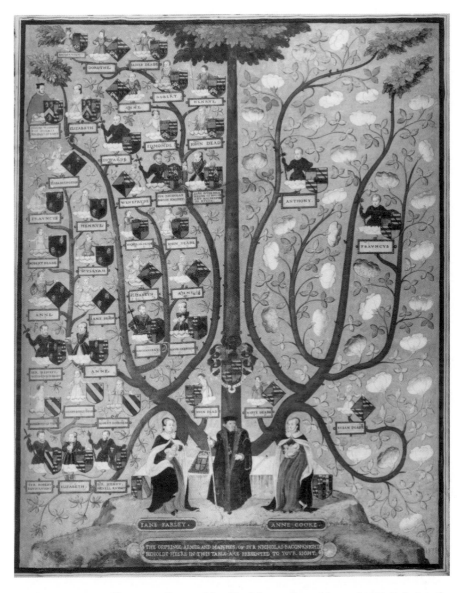

1. The importance of lineage is illustrated by this elaborate Tree of Jesse of 1578. It depicts the dynasty fathered by Sir Nicholas Bacon, a yeoman's son who rose through the law to become Elizabeth I's Lord Keeper. His son Francis, the future philosopher and Lord Chancellor, can be seen on the right.

2. An unknown military commander, traditionally known as Vaughan of Tretower. The frame carries a reproachful inscription of 1560 suggesting that his services to the realm had been insufficiently rewarded.

His three *single Combats Chap*·7·
His *Encounter with* TVRBASHAW *Chap*·7·

His *Combat with* GRVALGO·*Cap*ᵗ *of threehundred horsmen*·
Chap·7

How he slew BONNY:MVLGRO·*Chap*·7·

3. Captain John Smith (1580–1631), the future governor of Virginia, fought with the Austrians against the Turks in Transylvania. In 1602, in response to a challenge issued by the Turkish commander ('to delight the ladies, who did long to see some court-like pastime'), he killed three Turkish officers in single combat with lance, pistol, and sword.

4. A busy diplomat at work with his secretary leaning over his shoulder. As Charles I's envoy in Madrid, Sir Arthur Hopton spent many hours at his desk, composing dispatches on Spanish affairs.

5. The dignity of skilled craftsmanship. John Cuff, Master of the Worshipful Company of Spectacle Makers in 1748, at work with an elderly assistant.

6. Piety and respectability, but only a very modest degree of material comfort, are suggested by this image of a middling-class family meal in the 1720s.

7. An advertisement of 1791, showing how the pride taken by middle-class women in their domestic possessions could be exploited commercially.

8. By the end of the eighteenth century, even a poor cottager might possess a side-table, a china tea-set, books and a clock.

9. Masculine honour was vulnerable to malicious paternity suits. In William Hogarth's painting (1729) a pregnant girl is being coached by her lover into swearing before a magistrate that a respectable elderly citizen (apparently a Dissenting clergyman) is the father of her child.

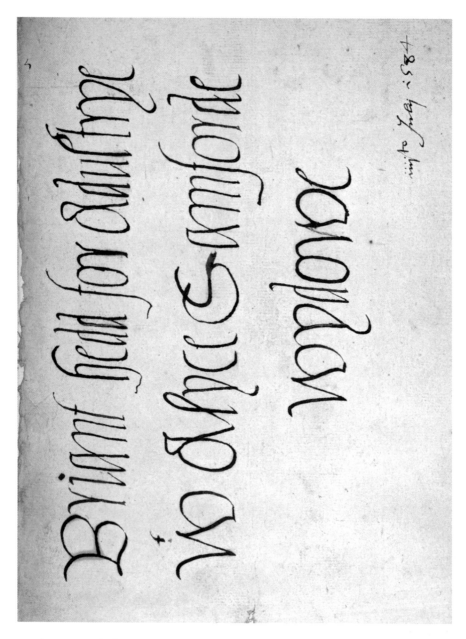

10. A rare survival of the placards which sexual offenders in Elizabethan times were required to wear when doing public penance.

11. The monument in the chapel of Christ's College, Cambridge, commemorating the lifelong friendship of Sir John Finch and Sir Thomas Baines. The inscription observes that, just as their souls had been mingled in life, so their ashes would be mingled in death.

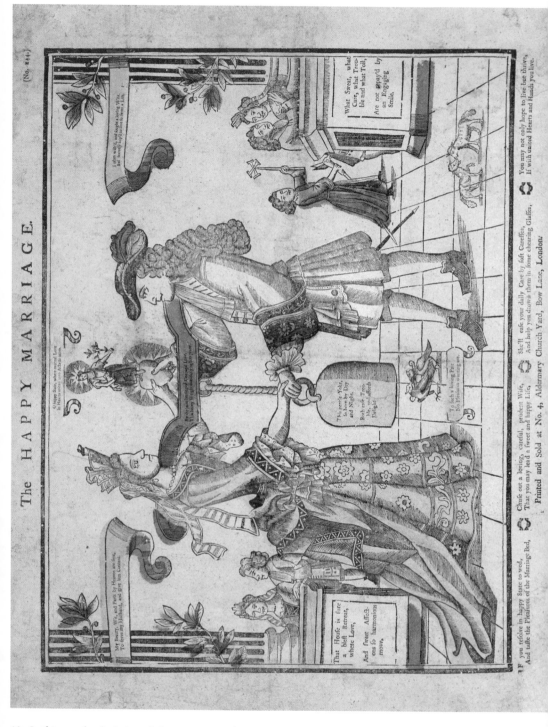

12. In this popular depiction of a happy marriage (c.1701, and often reissued) the emphasis is on the couple's mutual love and affection, but the wife's duty to serve her husband is not forgotten.

13. Male sociability. A convivial evening at an eighteenth-century club.

14. Female sociability. A group of mid-eighteenth-century ladies enjoys a lively tea party.

15. In this unusual portrayal of a deathbed scene, Thomas Braithwaite, an Essex gentleman who died in 1607, aged 31, begins his will with a pious preamble.

16. The plaque erected in 1646 in the church of St Peter Mancroft, Norwich, by a descendant to commemorate the benefactions made by Sir Peter Reade (d. 1568).

was 'not worth anything, unless it be well guarded with wealth'.[2] Robert Burton lamented that 'many base, impudent, brazen-faced rogues...will be...moved with nothing, take no infamy or disgrace to heart, laugh at all; let them be prov'd perjured, stigmatized, convict rogues, thieves, traitors, lose their ears, be whipped, branded, carted, pointed at, reviled, & derided...they rejoice at it...What care they?'[3]

It is likely, however, that some of Burton's outcasts were defiantly adhering to their own, distinctively brazen, code of honour rather than having no honour at all. The same was probably true of the Royalist colonel John Middleton, who was a prisoner at Newcastle in 1649, but broke his parole, ran away to Scotland, and, when required to return, retorted that his life was dearer to him than his honour. The real purpose of his escape was to engage in the fight for what he saw as the honourable cause of Charles II.[4]

Normally, it was a dreadful blow to self-esteem to forfeit the good opinion of one's peers. As Thomas Hobbes remarked, men took it 'heinously to be laughed at or derided' and there was 'no greater vexation of mind than scorn or contempt'.[5] We are told that when in 1591 the second Earl of Essex received the news of Elizabeth I's contempt for his conduct of the campaign in France, it 'put his honour in such an extreme agony and passion that he sounded [swooned] often and did so swell that, casting himself upon his bed, all his buttons of his doublet broke away as that they had been cut with a knife'.[6] After his defeat at Marston Moor in 1644, the Royalist general the Marquess of Newcastle left for the Continent because he 'could not endure the laughter of the court', while the Earl of Sandwich, who had been accused of cowardice during the Second Dutch War, told John Evelyn in 1672 that 'I must do I know not what, to save my reputation'; he died at the battle of Sole Bay a few days later.[7] In 1668 Samuel Pepys read an arousing work of French pornography and then burned it, 'that it might not be among my books to my shame'. Richard Baxter thought that 'most of the lies that are told in the world are to avoid some disgrace or shame, or to get men to think highly of them'.[8]

Loss of honour could drive people to distraction. From the 19-year-old son of the Bishop of Bristol, who killed himself in 1612, to avoid the disgrace of a flogging for losing his money at tennis, to Thomas Gun, a Baptist leader in the Interregnum period, who shot himself after the discovery of his adulterous affair with his landlady, there were many individuals who took their own lives rather than endure public humiliation.[9] Self-murder of this kind, observed a contemporary, was caused by 'shame and confusion, either for what a man hath ignominiously done or suffered, or is certainly likely to do or suffer; whereby he falls under contempt, scorn and importable [unbearable] disgrace with those whose respect he overvalues... So intolerable a thing is shame to some, specially of the noblest natures, that they think the same worse than death.'[10]

Disgrace was not just devastating to the ego. In daily life, a good name was a practical necessity. Persons of 'ill fame' (that is to say, badly thought of by the majority of the parish or, according to some authorities, by its more respected members) could be bound over by a JP or required by a church court to produce compurgators to swear that their bad reputation was undeserved. They might even voluntarily request such compurgation, so as to clear their name from rumour and gossip. 'Ill fame' affected the way in which people were treated by neighbours, employers, business associates, and shopkeepers. It had particularly serious consequences in the law courts, where criminal trial juries were entitled to take into account their own personal knowledge of the accused's reputation. This meant, as one seventeenth-century gentleman remarked, that 'a good name amongst one's neighbours' was of more consequence in England than in other countries.[11] Witnesses and defendants alike lost credibility if they had a bad reputation. It was virtually impossible, for example, for a woman of ill fame to convince a court that she had been raped; and the treatment of offenders could vary considerably according to their degree of respectability.[12] That was why robbing other people of their good fame by de-faming them was so reprehensible.

When most buying and selling was by haggling, when trading agreements were seldom written down, when there were no banking facilities, and when the money supply was hugely inadequate, the economy rested on trust; and the keystone of trust was a reputation for honesty and reliability. It is doubtful whether more than one in ten of all the commercial transactions in seventeenth-century England and Wales involved the exchange of cash: most of the others involved a promise to pay at some specified later date. By the later seventeenth century, it has been estimated, there were over 427 million transactions a year. Every household in the land was enmeshed in a web of credit dealing, most of it based on personal trust.[13] In these circumstances, a good name was vital: for traders building a business, for young people wanting marriage partners, for servants and craftsmen looking for work, for housewives buying goods, for the poor seeking relief;[14] in short, for everyone. Without a good reputation, normal social existence became impossible.

It was because insult did not just wound individual *amour-propre*, but caused measurable material damage, that common-law jurisdiction over defamation grew so rapidly from the sixteenth century onwards. It was also one of the reasons why some early modern political theorists and legal writers believed that personal honour, like life and property, was a good which it was the state's duty to protect.[15]* They knew intuitively that human self-esteem depended upon a sense of being respected by others. A good reputation had an emotional value which greatly exceeded that of any of the material benefits it enabled its holders to obtain.

Honour thus functioned as a social discipline, encouraging all members of society to perform their allotted social role by holding out the incentive of collective approbation and the deterrent of disgrace. The prospect of forfeiting the good opinion of their own community encouraged people to behave in the way expected of them, even when there was no law requiring them to do so. Indeed, it was precisely in those areas where the law was silent or ineffective that a sense of honour was of the greatest importance. The law courts prosecuted theft and manslaughter, but it was honour which outlawed cowardice, idleness, incompetence, insulting words, and behaviour inappropriate to one's sex or social status.

In most towns and villages, constant invigilation by the community was a conservative force, holding people to accepted standards and subjecting them to gossip and ridicule if they departed from them. It was rarely suggested that people's private lives were their own business and there was no inhibition about being what would nowadays be called 'judgemental'.[16] A range of humiliating rituals, from skimmington rides ('rough music') to mocking rhymes, nicknames, and verbal insults,[17] brought informal censure to bear upon forms of personal behaviour which transgressed the standards of the group. Cuckolds and henpecked husbands were subjected to a balladry of verse libels, a heraldry of horns and antlers on doors and windows, and a pantomime of derision performed upon the fingers of the hand. As an Oxfordshire witness explained in 1629: 'for one man to put out two fingers to another man that hath a wife living, in scoffing and disgraceful

---

* In 1948 the right to legal protection against attacks on a person's honour and reputation was included as Article 12 of the United Nations' Declaration of Human Rights.

manner...importeth as much as if he should call the man cuckold and his wife whore'.[18] It was even worse for the adulterers if gossip and ridicule led to prosecution in the church courts, followed by a humiliating public penance (pl. 10). Court officials were inundated with petitions from convicted parties, seeking the commutation of their penance because the 'reproach' and 'disgrace' would be to the 'utter discredit and undoing' of themselves and their families; some were said to be 'almost crazed', 'lunatic', driven out of their minds by the prospect.[19]

The idea that codes of honour have a social utility is not the invention of modern sociologists. It was Cicero who said that it was their sense of shame which deterred men from evil and St Augustine who observed that civic virtue was stimulated by 'the love of praise'.[20] In the early modern period many contemporaries believed that honour and shame were greater spurs to virtue than any innate moral sense. Bernard Mandeville cynically observed in 1732 that an appeal to honour, which boosted the ego and fed the human appetite for self-love, was far more effective than a moral appeal for renunciation and self-denial.[21] Thomas More prescribed penal slavery as the punishment for major offences in his *Utopia* (1516), but his scheme relied essentially on an 'intense communal pressure of honour and blame'. The Interregnum law reformer William Sheppard thought that the best way of deterring a woman from wearing 'whorish' dress was to have 'something of note...written upon the door of her house to her disgrace, there to continue till she wear sober attire'.[22] Shame punishments were integral to the English penal system of the period: convicted persons might be branded, whipped, mutilated, 'carted' through the streets to the sound of bells and basins, stripped half-naked or dressed in ludicrous clothes, labelled with placards, made to ride backwards on an ass, exposed in the cucking stool, the pillory, and the stocks, or compelled to confess their crimes in the marketplace.[23] Criminals were executed in public, not private, 'for their greater shame'; hanging was more shameful than beheading; and hanging in chains was an even greater disgrace.[24] 'Men punish with shame', wrote the Tudor poet Sir Thomas Wyatt, 'as [the] greatest punishment on earth, yea, greater than death.'[25]

Over sixty years ago, the American anthropologist Ruth Benedict popularized the distinction between a shame culture, in which the main sanction for good conduct is the fear of forfeiting the good opinion of others, with resultant exposure to contempt and ridicule, and a guilt culture, where the sanction is an inner conviction of sinfulness and the private torment of an agonized conscience. In the one what matters is what others think of you; in the other what is important is what you think of yourself.[26] In fact, most cultures contain elements of both shame and guilt; and early modern England was no exception. Official religious teaching inculcated a highly developed sense of guilt among believers; and the pains of an afflicted conscience were a staple of Protestant discourse. Yet without a widely diffused sensitivity to shame, there would have been no public penances, no stocks, no branding of foreheads, no cutting off of ears, no hanging in chains, no digging up of regicides' corpses.

THE DECLINE OF HONOUR?

There had always been critics who held that reputation in itself had no moral value. With the Stoics, they maintained that popular esteem was not proof of virtue, that it was absurd to make one's own happiness depend upon the opinion of others, and that it was better to be good than merely to be thought so.[1] They also pointed out that, although honour was conventionally described as the respect paid to virtue, only too many of those in receipt of worldly honour were patently not virtuous at all, but owed their elevation to wealth, luck, and royal favour. King Henry VIII himself was well aware that the 'fame, glory, reputation, honour and strength of princes' depended not on their real merits, but on 'outward appearances'.[2] In the later seventeenth century, the Marquess of Halifax cynically observed that there was something slightly disreputable about having a good reputation, for it meant that the person concerned had spent time cultivating his image: 'the good opinion of mankind requireth so much pains to gain it, that it is no small blemish to the character of those that have it'.[3]

In response to such criticisms, its defenders maintained that honour derived, not from the respect of all men, but from the discriminating commendation of good men—'the better sort'.[4] Many moralists, however, thought this insufficient; they could not accept a system which relied upon the esteem of men, however virtuous, rather than of God. They held that it was wrong to pursue reputation as an end in itself: to behave properly, merely for the sake of being well thought of by others, was not enough.[5] The biblical translator William Tyndale noted that the Roman matron Lucretia killed herself after being raped by Tarquin. But because she did so out of a sense of shame, he denounced her for her pride, which 'God more abhorreth than the whoredom of any whore'.[6] Reputation was only valuable when it came unsolicited, as a reward for virtuous acts. Not honour, but virtue, was the true object of life, 'our primary pursuit or ultimate end'.[7]

According to the Tudor humanist Thomas Lupset, the good Christian 'setteth at naught both honour and dishonour: shame, slander, and worship in the world be nothing in his reputation'; the New Testament taught that it was wrong to love the praise of men more than the praise of God.[8] The Puritan John Downame (1571–1652) thought it wicked to care more about securing a high place among men than a place among the saints in heaven. Precedence on earth was a contemptible issue by comparison with that of the fate of the soul after death.[9] For the same reason, his fellow minister Richard Bernard (1568–1641) condemned the desire for 'vain titles' like 'worshipful' and 'right worshipful'.[10] In the 1650s the Quakers took this view to its logical conclusion by rejecting all titles of honour and refusing to offer any deferential words or gestures to their social superiors. Their leader, George Fox, quoted Christ: 'how can you believe, that seek honour one from another, and not the honour which comes from God only?'[11] The Puritan divine Thomas Brooks declared that there was only one form of honour which mattered. 'That honour which attends holiness is the truest honour, the highest honour, the greatest honour, the happiest honour, the surest honour, the purest honour and the most lasting and abiding honour.'[12]

During the course of the seventeenth and eighteenth centuries, there were some signs that honour was becoming a less explicit preoccupation of public life. In 1651 the Earl of Ormonde lamented that the Dutch were 'entirely governed' not by 'honour or gratitude, which are now wholly lost in nations', but by 'the notion of reason of state'; honour, as the Dutch proverb had it, would buy no butter. Reason of state, or 'the national interest', as it was coming to be called, was superseding the ruler's honour as the dominant consideration in the conduct of foreign policy.[13] The belief that national honour might be at stake continued to influence the conduct of international relations until the twentieth century. But after 1688 the chief concern of those involved in foreign affairs was the balance of power in Europe, not monarchical *amour-propre*. At home, with the rise of party in the later seventeenth century, parliamentary elections were becoming an arena for conflict between rival interests and ideologies, rather than the theatre of honour they once had been. Success or failure in the struggle for office became less a

Figure 5.1 Trading insults in public became less common in the later eighteenth century, but it was far from unknown.

measure of personal prestige, more a test of political and religious opinion.[14]

In the Hanoverian era, increasingly influential codes of civility and politeness repudiated the swaggering gallant as vainglorious and impolite. Good manners now required peaceful accommodation to the feelings of others. Inferiors were to be treated with genial condescension, not arrogance; and rank was not to be rigidly insisted upon. In matters of precedence it was better to give way courteously than inflexibly to stand on one's rights.[15] In the same way, the middling and lower ranks of the population were coming to regard it as unseemly to quarrel about seating arrangements in church, to hurl ribald insults at each other in the street, or to conduct public slanging matches about the sex lives of their neighbours.[16] Everywhere, there was less insistence on hierarchical order, less ceremony when greeting and parting, and less attention to such deferential rituals as the practice of children kneeling daily to receive their parents' blessing.[17] All this was part of a larger process by which social and political authority was increasingly exercised without an elaborate supporting apparatus of visual symbolism.

Meanwhile, some large-scale social and institutional changes were helping to diminish the practical importance of personal reputation. The personal credit of those involved in business transactions continued to be important, particularly in the financial world, where trust in gentlemanly honour remained crucial.[18] But the spread of banks and insurance companies brought greater impersonality into economic life and more bureaucratic methods of ensuring trust and diminishing risk.[19] In the law courts, personal reputation became less important. Judgments in criminal cases were increasingly based on the facts adduced during the hearing, rather than on the accused persons' prior standing in their own community; by the end of the seventeenth century, prosecuting counsel was usually forbidden to adduce evidence of the accused's bad character before the verdict had been reached.[20] The early eighteenth century saw the end of the medieval conception of a trial jury as a body of neighbour-witnesses with personal knowledge of the parties involved in the case. Jurors were now expected to disregard gossip about the accused's bad reputation and to base their verdict exclusively on the evidence produced (though, if the accused's reputation was good, they often continued tacitly to allow it to count in favour of leniency). The local community was ceasing to be directly involved in the judging of criminal cases.[21]

There was also a diminishing concern to make the infliction of public shame part of judicial punishment. From the later seventeenth century, the number of brandings and mutilations dwindled; public penances became infrequent; and the pillory and the cucking stool were used less often. In London, where few members of the crowd were likely to know the criminal concerned, the link between public punishment and personal reputation became more tenuous.[22] The increasing privacy of judicial punishment in late eighteenth-century England was a response by the authorities to the extreme disorder which tended to accompany the public infliction of whippings and other penalties. But it also reflected an embryonic concern for human rights, resting on the conviction that a decent society is 'a society which does not humiliate'.[23]

In London and other large cities, the growing anonymity of daily life set people free from the constant invigilation and moral surveillance which was such a feature of smaller communities. In the metropolis, neighbours took less interest in each other's affairs than they did in country villages, and people passed each other in the street as strangers. 'London is a bad place,' writes Fielding's Joseph Andrews, 'and there is so little good fellowship that next-door neighbours don't know one another.'[24] From the 1730s onward, the responsibility for maintaining public order began to shift from the householder to a semi-professional constabulary.[25] Of course, many districts in big cities were essentially little villages, where anonymity was impossible; and the numerous institutions which continued to set a high value on collective life, whether schools, churches, regiments, or commercial businesses, remained intolerant of any attempt by individuals to escape their surveillance.* Nevertheless, some of the pressures to social conformity were slackening, communal supervision of personal morality was becoming harder to achieve, and the overall trend was towards greater personal freedom.

The legal concession of freedom of worship in 1689 diminished the ability of church officials to monitor the behaviour of the laity; and prosecutions in the church courts for fornication and adultery became less frequent. This decline had begun at the Restoration and in some dioceses seems to have been complete by 1700; elsewhere it was not until after the mid-eighteenth century that such prosecutions dwindled away.[26] Once that happened, people had less incentive to take legal action when they were wrongly accused of sexual offences by their neighbours. Women continued to bring defamation suits to the church courts until their jurisdiction was abolished in 1855. But the number of such cases seems to have declined during the course of the eighteenth century; and suits brought by men became uncommon.[27] The action for *scandalum magnatum* fell into abeyance after 1688. The unauthorized charivaris and skimmington rides, in which villagers expressed their disapproval of other people's private behaviour, lingered on, but a series of judicial pronouncements in the later seventeenth century had established their illegality.[28] The parents of bastard children remained liable to secular punishment, but only if the child's maintenance fell upon the parish. The informal monitoring of personal morals did not cease; indeed in parts of Victorian England it may have intensified. But public prosecutions of fornication and adultery dwindled away. In the eyes of the law, at least, people's sex lives were slowly coming to be regarded as their own affair.[29]

The notion that individuals were entitled to a private life which was not the business of the wider community was vigorously expressed

---

* Having had in 1961 to ask the Governing Body of my Oxford college for permission to retain my tutorial fellowship after getting married, I am well aware that the separation of personal from professional life has been a protracted process.

by several aggrieved offenders against the collective code: from a Devonshire delinquent, charged in 1602 before the Exeter consistory court with having got a woman with child, who retorted that the matter was 'to his own conscience' and he would 'not be sworn for it', to the young Londoner accused of buggery in 1726, who replied that 'I think there is no crime in making what use I please of my own body.'[30] The libertarian politician John Wilkes was in this tradition when he asserted in 1767 that 'no man has the right to inquire into my private amusements if they are not prejudicial to society'. In the 1780s Jeremy Bentham followed him by arguing (though not publicly) for the complete decriminalization of all consensual sexual acts between adults.[31]

The right of the community to invigilate personal behaviour was also challenged by religious Dissenters, who increasingly proclaimed themselves to be independent, recusant, and nonconforming. Their personal fulfilment involved rejecting the standards of the group. As the Puritan Jeremiah Burroughes had asked defiantly in 1639: 'Why...should any account it to be a dishonour to be singular from the world? Singularity is cast upon God's servants as their disgrace, but certainly it is their glory; they *are* singular and their ways are singular, it is true, and they avouch it, they rejoice in it, and bless God for it.' Or, in the words of his fellow preacher Thomas Wilson in 1641: 'till a man seems odd to the world he is never right in religion and righteousness.'[32] Of course, the godly also set store by 'the good opinion and estimation of the wise, virtuous and religious';[33] and the sects quickly became their own little communities of honour, closely regulating the behaviour of their members and encouraging them to secure the esteem of their co-religionists. But the assertion of principled nonconformity was a crucial step. After the Revolution of 1688, religious toleration and a free press helped further to break down the uniformity of opinion on which communal censure had rested.

Early modern England had more than its fair share of free spirits, ready to challenge the social conventions which the codes of honour underpinned. Not just fiery Quakers who walked naked for a sign. But quieter figures like the writer Roger North, who urged indigent gentlemen to show 'a perfect contempt of fame' by avoiding the ostentatious expenditure deemed 'honourable' for their rank, and ignoring taunts about 'how penuriously they live'; and deliberate eccentrics, like Edward Mayer of Wivenhoe, Essex, who in 1641 was denounced as 'an obstinate and refractory fellow, who will not live in rank and order among his neighbours in a house, but will live in a boat drawn up upon dry land'.[34] This interesting predecessor of

Mr Peggotty was a precursor of that range of so-called 'characters', or persons of highly developed individuality, with which it became commonplace in the eighteenth century to boast that England was uniquely endowed.[35] To such persons, codes of behaviour dependent on community sanction were largely irrelevant.

Instead there would emerge the idea that personal fulfilment might require deliberate indifference to what other people felt. Rather than realizing oneself by the exemplary performance of a social role, and thus securing the approval of the group, one should develop one's intrinsic capacities as a human being. Personal self-esteem should not be allowed to depend upon the approval of others. In the early modern period, it was generally believed that it was important to seek and preserve a good name: 'Neglect of our fame is a sin,' thought one minister.[36] In modern times, by contrast, it is more usual to suggest that the desire for approval by others, far from being an admirable instinct, is morally debilitating.[37]

Ultimately, it was the doctrine of human equality which did most to erode traditional notions of honour. For they had always been closely bound up with the maintenance of status in a hierarchical society. In his *Democracy in America* (1835–40), still the most penetrating treatment of this complex subject, Alexis de Tocqueville observed that 'the dissimilarities and inequalities of men gave rise to the notion of honour; that notion is weakened in proportion as these differences are obliterated'.[38] The twentieth-century sociologist Pierre Bourdieu echoed him: 'The ethos of honour is fundamentally opposed to a universal and formal morality which affirms the equality in dignity of all men and consequently the equality of their rights and duties.'[39] Three hundred years previously, John Hall of Richmond had made the same point more succinctly: 'If all were equal, as in nature, outward honour or shame could not be.'[40] Some anticipations of this egalitarian spirit can be detected in the 1790s, when the French Revolution encouraged British radicals to attack hereditary titles and repudiate the old conception of honour as a system of differential esteem.[41] But only in the later twentieth century, as society grew less hierarchical and less patriarchal, did it come to seem inappropriate to expect people to have different ethical standards according to their sex and social position.

Today, if people behave with integrity, decency, and consistency and do what seems to be right, even at some cost to themselves, and even though there is no external pressure forcing them to do so, we say that they have acted honourably. In the early modern period, the upper classes claimed that they were uniquely capable of behaving in that way, but in modern times the notion has been democratized. Honour is now classless; it has become 'common honesty', personal integrity of a kind which transcends the code of any single group. It is a virtue capable of being practised by anyone.[42]

The early modern period, therefore, did not witness a 'decline of honour'. For honour as such did not cease to matter. The late Victorian writer Samuel Butler thought that in his day loss of reputation was unimportant by comparison with loss of money and health. In his view, a man who kept the latter could thrive in great peace of mind without any reputation at all.[43] But the truth was that most of his contemporaries remained highly dependent for their self-esteem upon the opinion of others—not all others perhaps, but certainly their peers, those within their circle, their honour community. In modern times, the law courts continue to provide remedies for slander and libel. Codes of conduct are still policed by gossip and collective scrutiny, and broken only at the cost of external shame and internal anguish. Reputation remains an essential sanction for good behaviour. In business and politics, it is as crucial as ever. That is why governments employ spin doctors, and business schools have lecturers in Reputation Management. Even gangs of delinquent youths claim that what they are seeking is 'respect'.

It is very likely that the desire to be valued by others is a human universal, to be found at all times and in all places. But that desire can take many different cultural forms. During the early modern period, those cultural forms underwent several mutations as the meaning of honour was repeatedly redefined. There were different standards for men, for women, and for members of the different social and occupational layers of society. But, in one way or another, reputation remained an essential precondition of everyone's fulfilment, for on it hinged personal identity and self-esteem. For most people, it was a crucial objective throughout their lives to secure and maximize the respect of others.

6

FRIENDSHIP AND SOCIABILITY

The virtues of a private life
Exceed the glorious noise and strife
Of battles won; in those we find
The solid interest of mankind.

Edmund Waller, 'Epitaph on Sir George Speke',
in *Poems*, ed. G. Thorn Drury, n.d. (1683)

To have a friend whom we know to be frank and loving, neither false nor spiteful, is to have one who will help us to correct our judgment when it is mistaken. This is the whole end of man, through which he can enjoy his existence.

Immanuel Kant, *Lectures on Ethics*, [*c.* 1780–1], trans. Louis Infield, 1930

THE IDEA OF FRIENDSHIP

It is a feature of modern Western society that the private realm of home, family, and personal relationships is often largely detached from the public sphere of work, politics, and professional activities. At the same time, it is to this domestic sphere that many people look for their deepest satisfactions. Social psychologists claim that friendship, love, marriage, and lasting partnerships are a major source of what they call SWB (Subjective Well-Being). Married or unmarried, heterosexual or homosexual, it is in close personal relationships with others that we hope to find fulfilment.[1]

In the early modern period, however, it was common in elite circles to profess indifference to such private concerns, either because they were thought to be selfish preoccupations which conflicted with the common good, or because they were regarded as intrinsically unimportant. In classical antiquity, privacy, as the Latin derivation of the

word reminds us, had been a negative state, a condition of deprivation. The private sphere of household, work, women, and children
was inferior to the public world of army and forum. Early modern
writers in the neoclassical tradition duly gave priority to the active
public virtues, expressing contempt for those who, as one of them put
it, 'mew themselves up at home, and never see the face of a public
assembly, but live as it were in a well or a bottle'.[2] The historians of
the time, like their classical predecessors, reflected this prejudice,
regarding their subject matter as public affairs, not private life.

Yet the idea that it was in the domestic and personal sphere that
people were most truly themselves was everywhere incipient: in the
multiplication of diaries and other personal documents; in the
huge growth of intimate correspondence;[3] and in the expression of
individual tastes in furniture, decoration, food, and clothes. The well-
to-do sought privacy in special places: gardens, studies, closets, and
cabinets. They guarded their secrets in lockets and caskets; and they
preserved symbolic reminders of their intimate relationships in mini-
atures, posies, rings, and locks of hair. If they could afford it, they
increased the number of rooms in their houses, each with its own
specialized function, and some more private than others.[4] 'What,
do you come into my very closet without knocking?' says a character
in Richard Steele's play The Tender Husband (1705), deploring
what she calls 'this intrusion to my privacy'.[5] After the Fire of 1666,
London was rebuilt in anonymous terraces which, being carefully shut
off from the life of the street, enabled their inhabitants to impose strict
control on access to the interior. Within the house, locked doors,
cupboards, and boxes guarded private actions and personal secrets.[6]

In this private sphere people felt able to cast off the mask of
strict self-control required by civility and good manners and reveal
their 'true' selves. It was said of Archbishop Cranmer that he never
allowed his face to reflect his emotions in public, but that 'privately,
with his secret and special friends, he would shed forth many bitter
tears, lamenting the miseries and calamities of the world'.[7] Tradesmen, who had to be careful to maintain a good public manner,
regardless of their personal feelings, needed private space in which
to vent their frustrations. Defoe tells of a shopkeeper who, 'when he
was provok'd by the impertinence of the customers, beyond what his
temper could bear... would go up stairs and beat his wife, kick his
children about like dogs, and be as furious for two or three minutes
as a man chain'd down in Bedlam; and again, when that heat was
over... would sit down and cry faster than the children he had

abused; and after the fit he would go down into his shop again, and be as humble, as courteous and as calm as any man whatever; so absolute a government of the passions had he in the shop, and so little out of it'.[8]

Outside the domestic sphere, a much wider sociability, in the senses of affable relations with other people, was portrayed as one of life's primary satisfactions. Thomas Wilson, scholar and future secretary of state, wrote in 1560 that 'every society or companying together is delightful ... forasmuch as nature hath ordained us to be sociable, friendly, and loving together'.[9] Aristotle had taught that friendship between citizens was society's most cohesive bond. Where friendship ruled, laws were unnecessary.[10] When the young Edward VI listed the pressing tasks of government which faced him, he included 'engendering friendship in all the parts of the commonwealth'; and when Francis Bacon depicted his ideal city in New Atlantis (published 1627), he portrayed it as a place of 'faithful and inviolate friendship'.[11] In some country parishes, the parishioners, after receiving the sacrament (which the Book of Common Prayer required them to do 'in love and charity with [their] neighbours'), would repair directly to the alehouse 'and there drink together as a testimony of charity and friendship'.[12] In Tudor towns, feasts and similar gatherings were seen as important for 'continuing and renewing of amity and neighbourly love, one with another'.[13] The summer bonfires in Elizabethan London, like the church wakes in rural parishes, had the same purpose.[14] Harmony was prized, whereas lawsuits which set neighbour against neighbour were (following 1 Corinthians 6: 7) widely deplored as un-Christian breaches of charity. Many believed that those involved in litigation should not present themselves for Holy Communion, a ritual which, like the mass before it, presupposed the reconciliation of all disputes within the congregation.[15] It was thought important to end all quarrels between neighbours and 'make them friends'.[16] Friendship in this general sense was defined negatively; it meant the absence of enmity, rivalry, or resentment.

Of course, at a time of growing social differentiation, and a drift to oligarchic government in local affairs, such an ideal of universal amity was impossible to achieve. 'Ah, neighbourhood, neighbourhood,' sighed the writer Thomas Nashe in 1592, 'dead and buried art thou with Robin Hood.'[17] The friendship which had united Aristotle's ideal citizens was based on fundamental agreement about the nature of the common good. But in early modern England there was no such agreement: political and religious principles were a matter of bitter dispute; and rural society was riven by feuds and petty hostilities. The harmony of the local community was always precarious and often non-existent. In such circumstances, it was unrealistic to expect to be friends with everyone.

So what, in these circumstances, did contemporaries mean when they spoke of a 'friend'? The term was flexible and capacious; and it was used to characterize many different sorts of relationship. As an eighteenth-century philosopher remarked: 'if we observe the common discourse of mankind, we shall find a friend to be one we frequently visit, who is our boon companion, or joins with us in our pleasures and diversions, or encourages us in our business, or unites in the same scheme, or votes the same way at an election, or is our patron, or dependant, who we hope will help us in rising to preferment or increasing our interest'.[18] These were all 'friends', but of very different kinds.

In the first place, 'friends' were widely equated with kinsfolk: relatives by blood or marriage, who were informal providers of aid and advice and could be relied on to assist in marriage negotiations, to keep an eye on children when they left home, and turn up at moments of family crisis. Throughout the early modern period, so-called 'friends' were most commonly relations.[19] In drinking circles, it was regarded as 'incivility for anyone to suffer the health of a near kinsman to be begun without a ceremonial protestation of endeared amity and affection'.[20] There was nothing new about this, for in virtually all societies it is to their kinsfolk that people look first for support, so much so that many languages have no concept of a friend who is not also a kinsman. Writing about early medieval Europe, the historian Marc Bloch observed that 'the general assumption was that there was no real friendship save between persons united in blood'.[21]

In the second place, 'friends' were allies, backers, associates: persons on whose support one could rely in times of need. They might be clients and inferiors, like the 'King's friends' of Hanoverian politics. Or they might be superiors, that is to say patrons or protectors, who in early modern times provided the equivalent of the 'good lordship' so much sought after in the later Middle Ages. In either case, they were parties to a relationship of what has been called 'lopsided friendship'.[22] 'Be sure to keep some great man thy friend,' William Cecil told his son, in a much-repeated piece of advice.[23] 'A man is advanced as he is befriended,' noted the Jacobean naval commander Sir William Monson.[24] It was in this spirit that John Aubrey in 1680 lamented the death of his 'dear, useful and faithful friend' George Johnson, who had the reversion of the office of Master of the Rolls, and who, 'generously, for friendship and neighbourhood['s] sake (we were born the same week and educated together), gave me the grant to be one of his secretaries—which place is worth 500*li* per annum'. In the late eighteenth century, 'friendship' was still cherished as 'often the means of advancing a man's fortune in the world'.[25]

Third, there was the more general social friendship which arose out of propinquity. This, too, was usually of a practical kind. Both in the country and in the town, neighbours were ideally expected to provide each other with mutual help and support, lending goods, labour, or money.[26] The assumption that they would participate in each other's rites of passage was reflected in the Prayer Book's prescription that persons to be married should come into the body of the church 'with their friends *and neighbours*', and by the enforcement by some local authorities of the duty to attend a neighbour's funeral.[27] In the counties, the gentry were involved in elaborate social networks, sustained by hospitality, the exchange of gifts, and periodic meetings on the hunting field or at quarter sessions.[28]

In all these cases, friends were valued because they were useful. One did not necessarily have to *like* them. 'Are you sure they were all your friends?' asks a character in an Elizabethan dialogue; to which his companion replies, 'Yea, surely, I so think, though some of them I had never seen before that day.'[29] 'I will marry for myself, and not for my friends,' declared a young Elizabethan woman, 'for I know that they care not if I were dead, so that they might have my goods.'[30]

Friendship was thus regarded as one of the many forms of alliance into which individuals might voluntarily enter for the sake of mutual self-interest: lord and retainer, landlord and tenant, patron and client, master and apprentice, employer and servant. These were all instrumental relationships; that is to say they were not ends in themselves, but means to a further end: security, subsistence, education, protection, or advancement. Such alliances were also made between families. Marriage was a recognized way of establishing friendship between two groups of kin; godparenthood was intended to strengthen the bonds between the co-parents, as much as between godparent and child; and the practice among the Tudor upper classes of boarding out children created new ties of amity.[31] In 1576 the first Earl of Essex bequeathed his young son Robert to the Master of the Wards, Lord Burghley, 'to bind him with perpetual friendship to you and your house'. In the early eighteenth century, Roger

North thought that 'allied friends' had a duty to act as trustees for each other's widows and children.[32] Links of this kind could often generate amicable, even affectionate, relationships, but that was incidental to their main purpose. Essentially, they were all ways of artificially enlarging the unit of kindred for the sake of mutual advantage.

Throughout the early modern period, advancement in most walks of life depended primarily on family and friends, patronage and connection. This was the case in government and public office, in the Church, in business, and in the professions; as a seventeenth-century doctor lamented, the best preferments were due not to ability but to 'good fortune and great friends'.[33] Everywhere it was vital to be part of some mutually supporting network. Even schoolboys entered into 'friendships, combinations, factions and a world of intrigues', which were, it was said, 'in quality and instruction, the same as among men'.[34] The private correspondence of the early modern period is preoccupied with the creation and maintenance of such alliances, and the exchange of gifts and preferment; the language employed was that of benefits bestowed and gratitude returned.[35]

The underlying presupposition was that of a hostile world, in which an individual would flounder without a network of supporters; a faithful friend was a strong defence. So long as the state was too weak to guarantee security and support, individuals had to find their own allies. Those who were not friends could be assumed to be enemies, for there was no neutrality: 'He that is not with me is against me.' Friends championed each other's causes, so having many friends meant also having many enemies. The historian Clarendon wrote of James I's favourite, the Duke of Buckingham, that 'his kindness and affection to his friends was so vehement that it was so many leagues offensive and defensive; as if he thought of himself obliged to love all his friends, and to make war upon all they were angry with, let the cause be what it would'.[36]

Nearly all societies have mechanisms which enable individuals to create surrogate kin by making formal alliances with others.[37] In medieval England, one such type of artificial alliance had been the sworn brotherhood between two warriors, a binding relationship, sometimes created by a religious ceremony or a formal document. Such pacts, whose frequency it is impossible to know, created alliances between families, as well as individuals, and the union, which might involve kisses and physical embraces, could be affectionate as well as self-interested.[38] Chivalric literature abounded in tales of the close relationships forged by Roland and Oliver, Amis and Amiloun, and similar brothers-in-arms. When Sir William Neville and Sir John Clanvowe died outside Constantinople in 1391, they were buried in a single tomb, with their helmets kissing each other and their arms impaled, a practice normally reserved for married couples. Neville was reported to have died of grief a few days after Clanvowe's death.[39] Yet brotherhood in arms, like other forms of adoptive kinship, had a distinctly instrumental character, with the two partners swearing to assist each other in emergencies, to secure each other's ransom should that be necessary, and to share equally in the profits of war.[40]

The novelty of the early modern period is that it witnessed the emergence into public view of a type of relationship which differed from these older kinds of alliance in purporting to be based wholly on mutual sympathy, and cherished for its own sake rather than for its practical advantages. In this relationship, the parties were friends in the modern sense, that is intimate companions, freely chosen, without regard to an ulterior end. In Francis Bacon's words, 'It is friendship, when a man can say to himself, I love this man without respect of utility.'[41]

Of course, the conception of non-instrumental friendship was not in itself new. Personal relationships, based on affection rather than on reciprocity, can be found as far back as ancient Greece.[42] But there was no precedent for the volume of extravagant claims made in the early modern period for the life-enhancing value of intimate friendship. There was a torrent of printed literature—sermons, essays, poems, plays, and novels—celebrating the value of 'perfect' friendship, elaborating on the duties of friends to each other and (a constant preoccupation) discussing the problem of how true friends could be distinguished from false ones. A modern bibliography of Elizabethan verse reveals that, of all moral topics, friendship was the one most frequently treated, and that over three hundred poems were devoted to the subject.[43]

In the late fifteenth century, the boys at Magdalen College School, Oxford, were copying out the proposition that, 'amongst all [a man's] other pleasures', the greatest was 'to have a faithful friend to speak all things to as he would to himself'.[44] During the ensuing two centuries, that sentiment was echoed by innumerable philosophers and moralists, who claimed, as a contemporary put it, that friendship was simply 'the best thing in the world'.[45] Bacon declared that friendship

FRIENDSHIP AND SOCIABILITY

multiplied joys and halved griefs: without friends, the world was a wilderness.[46] The Jacobean Recorder of Exeter William Martyn advised his son that 'in the...love of [a faithful friend] will consist a great part of your contentedness in this life'; and the Williamite bishop Gilbert Burnet agreed: 'the chief pleasures of life arise from friendship'.[47] Charles I's chaplain, the celibate Henry Hammond, regarded the union of minds created by friendship as 'the utmost point of human happiness...so that with compassion he reflected on their ignorance who were strangers to it, saying that such must needs lead a pitiful, insipid Herb-John-like life'.[48]* The painter Mary Beale believed that friendship was 'the nearest union which distinct souls are capable of...Next to glorifying our Creator, man seems to be made for nothing more'.[49] From this source, thought the eighteenth-century Scottish philosopher Adam Ferguson, human life derived its 'principal felicity'.[50] As an essayist noted wearily in 1780, 'the praises of friendship, and descriptions of the happiness arising from it, I remember to have met with in almost every book and poem since first I could read'.[51]

The ultimate source for these ambitious claims was a corpus of classical texts, particularly Aristotle's *Nicomachean Ethics* (books 8 and 9) and Cicero's *Laelius de Amicitia*.[52] Aristotle had taught that relationships based on mutual liking were essential for happiness, and that a friend could be a second self, a mirror into which one might look so as to enhance one's own self-knowledge. Cicero had said that, without a friend, life was not worth living. Most classical moralists gave friendship a serious purpose: friends helped each other to achieve a morally superior life. There were lower kinds of friendship, whose aim was merely utility or erotic pleasure, but, in its highest form, the object of friendship was virtue, truth, and the public good. Friendship made it possible for men to live fully as human beings.

This was rather different from the older conception (prominent in the Old Testament) of a friend as someone whose main attraction was that he could be relied upon to hate one's enemies. But it had a close affinity to the friendship of David and Jonathan, whose souls, according to the first book of Samuel (18: 1), were 'knit together', an ideal shared by the author of Deuteronomy, who alludes (13: 6) to 'thy friend, which is as thy own soul'.

The moral dimension to classical theories of friendship had given them a considerable vogue in the Christian world of the Middle Ages.

---

* Herb John (St John's wort) was proverbially inert and tasteless.

194

They were taken up in the cathedral schools, at royal courts, and, particularly, in the monasteries.[53] Monks were persons who had set aside the inherited ties of family and kinship in order to achieve closer union with God; and in that quest friends could assist each other with spiritual advice, admonition, and prayer. In the twelfth century, some vehement claims were made for friendship as a route to divine under-standing and as one of the highest human satisfactions.[54] Ailred of Rievaulx, one of the most influential monastic writers on the subject, cited Cicero over seventy times in his highly influential *De Spiritali Amicitia* (*c.* 1160). (Aristotle's *Ethics*, which lay behind Cicero's thoughts on the subject, was not available until the mid-thirteenth century.) But when we find that St Anselm was capable of writing in passionate, not to say erotic, terms to persons he had never met, we realize that the monastic conception of friendship was something quite different from our modern notion of it as a relationship based on close personal acquaintance. What spiritual friendship reflected was identity of purpose. It did not require bodily proximity or even personal acquaintance. As Cicero had observed, one loved a friend's virtue, not his person.[55]

In post-Reformation England, spiritual friendship would reappear in Protestant guise, but there is little evidence that medieval monas-tic writings played any part in this. Rather, it was a case of back to what Richard Baxter called 'Cicero and the old doctors of friend-ship'.[56] As Clarendon noted, the greatest philosopher (Aristotle) and the best orator (Cicero) had agreed in commending friendship as above all things in the world.[57] From classical mythology and literature were derived famous examples of perfect friendship— Damon and Pythias, Orestes and Pylades—to be set alongside those to be found in the Bible, where, in the poet George Herbert's words, 'David had his Jonathan, Christ his John.'[58] Sixteenth-century writers invented many such idealized pairs of friends, like Musidorus and Pyrocles in Sir Philip Sidney's *Arcadia* or Philamis and Philamour in Thomas Lodge's *Euphues Shadow* or Shakespeare's Hamlet and Horatio.[59] In France, Michel de Montaigne's essay on *amitié* (1580), celebrating the loving union of souls which had linked him to his deceased friend the magistrate Étienne de La Boétie, brought the Renaissance theory of friendship to its peak. For Montaigne, friendship was less a matter of ration-ally choosing a virtuous confidant, as it had been for the classical theorists, than of spontaneously responding to the inexplicable promptings of the heart which drew two unique individuals together: 'par ce que c'estoit luy, par ce que c'estoit moy'. This was friendship, not as reciprocity, but as fusion.[60]

There was general agreement on the necessary conditions for perfect friendship: similarity of character, virtuous inclinations, disinterested affection, and, particularly important, equality in social status, age, and intellect. The bond was horizontal, not vertical. This emphasis on the social and intellectual parity of the two partners distinguished 'perfect' friendship from the fidelity, mutual, but unequal, of king and favourite, lord and vassal, patron and client. It also meant that affectionate relations between maid and mistress, servant and master, even child and parent, could not count as friendship in the true sense of the word.

Even less was perfect friendship to be confused with 'common familiarity and good fellowship'. The 'sharing of talk, news, drink, mixed together' was mere acquaintance. A friend was different from 'a companion [or] countryman, from a schoolfellow or gossip, from a sweet-heart or fellow-traveller'.[61] True friendship was not mere amiability. Such 'common friendship', thought the Marquess of Halifax, echoing the cynical French moralist the Duc de La Rochefoucauld, was 'no more than a kind of barter, an expectation of having need of one another, without the true ground of merit or esteem'.[62] Neither was true friendship to be confused with sexual attraction, common though it was in the seventeenth century to refer to a lover or sexual partner as a 'friend'. Nor was it to be found in cheerful camaraderie or in amicable relations between men of business, what Thomas Hobbes called 'market-friendship'.[63] For in such relationships the participants sought either pleasure or profit, both of them objectives which Aristotle had dismissed as irrelevant to the highest form of friendship, whose aim was virtue.

As portrayed in sixteenth- and seventeenth-century literature, perfect friendship was a spiritual union of two persons: 'one soul in bodies twain'. It was not a physical relationship, but 'love refin'd and purg'd from all its dross'.[64] For love was an irrational passion which sought personal pleasure regardless of the general good; it was a sign of weakness or 'effeminacy',[65] whereas friendship was 'the combination of virtuous minds' and its object was mutual moral improvement and enhanced self-knowledge. An Elizabethan writer defined it as 'a natural goodwill of well-disposed persons, caused through likeness of manners and motions of the mind, fancying each other for nothing else but only for the increase of virtue, not for any pleasure or profit'.[66] Mary Beale thought that, as friendship grew more perfect, 'the love of myself is swallowed up in the love of my friend'.[67]

So close a relationship was not to be rushed. There were innumerable warnings about the perils of false and counterfeit friendship (an obsession of contemporary dramatists) and the importance of not exchanging secrets too early on, a cautionary piece of advice offered in Ecclesiasticus, and much repeated by anxious parents, well aware that youthful friendships seldom lasted.[68] But once the relationship had developed, it became a sacred bond. Friendship was 'holy', 'the most noble of virtues'. Its 'laws' and 'rules' were 'inviolable'; and it should last for ever. As the Henrician propagandist Richard Morison told Thomas Cromwell in 1538, 'Friendship should be like a marriage: for better for worse, for richer for poorer, till death depart.'[69]

Friends could express to each other their most intimate thoughts and anxieties, in what Bacon called 'a kind of civil shrift or confession'. Such confidences were never to be betrayed, unless they involved felony or treason, in which case the bond of friendship ceased to oblige. (There was no question of preferring, like the novelist E. M. Forster, to betray one's country rather than one's friend, for, unlike Bloomsbury friends, early modern friends were supposed to pursue only what was good and to know that public duties always took precedence over private obligation.[70]) Friends were allowed close familiarities: 'My friend may spit upon my curious floor,' sang George Herbert.[71] (This was before the days of floor carpets, when such an act might have tested friendship severely.) Friends exchanged frank, non-flattering advice and, when necessary, criticism, for a crucial requirement was that they should assist their mutual moral growth by pointing out each other's faults. Bishop Sprat thought that because absolute candour was essential, letters between friends, 'if written as they ought to be, can scarce ever be fit to see the light', for 'in such letters the souls of men should appear undressed'.[72] The ability to accept candid advice was a vital test of the relationship. Clarendon cited the royal favourite Buckingham as an example of someone who had gone astray, for want of 'one faithful friend' to warn him 'against the current, or rather the torrent, of his impetuous passions'. Archbishop Laud was another who lacked 'a true friend, who would seasonably have told him of his infirmities, and what people spake of him'.[73] In the last resort, a good man would be willing to lay down his life for the sake of his friend, though, as Sir Thomas Browne remarked, such a notion seemed 'strange to vulgar affections'.[74]

MALE AND FEMALE FRIENDS

What resemblance did this elevated, and essentially literary, conception of friendship bear to reality? Not much, in the opinion of most contemporaries. Friendship was so rare, wrote one Elizabethan, that 'scarce four couple of faithful friends have been since the world began'.[1] Everyone agreed that most friends turned out to be unreliable: 'There are thousands false for one that's true.' Only too often, today's friend proved tomorrow's enemy. A perfect union of souls was rarely met. Some thought it unattainable. Only in heaven would there be 'friendship without design'.[2] Francis Bacon noted that there was 'little friendship in the world', least of all, the much-vaunted friendship between equals. What did exist was the age-old alliance between superior and inferior for mutual material benefit.[3] There was accordingly a nostalgic quality to most writing about perfect friendship: the great friendships were in the past.[4] The Jacobite sympathizer William King (1685–1763) declared that 'in our country, which is governed by money, and where every man is in pursuit of his own interest, it would be in vain to look for a real friendship'.[5]

Machiavellian realists, accordingly, were sceptical about the whole idea of non-instrumental friendship; and the advice given those about to enter the world tended to be brutally unsentimental. For all their chorus of ' "Glad to see you well", "How have you done?", etc', thought the writer Henry Peacham, most people's daily acquaintances were only 'false and seeming friends'. The Restoration cleric Richard Lingard cautioned young gentlemen that, when choosing friends, 'you must not expect them to be such as are described in books and talked of by philosophers; that's a romantic thing, only to be found in *Utopia* or the *New Atlantis*'.[6]

Nevertheless, some young people spent years vainly looking for the perfect friend whom literature had taught them to expect. Sarah Fielding's novel *David Simple* (1744) told the story of the hero's travels through London and Westminster 'in the search of a real friend'.[7] 'I never yet found such a friend! Although I have long time sought for one,' wrote James Keene, an eighteenth-century coal merchant, in the margin of his copy of a book extolling the virtues of friendship.[8] 'Oft have I friendship sought, but sought in vain,' lamented the essayist Hester Chapone (1727–1801). The heroes of William Godwin's novels in the 1790s had the same experience.[9]

High-flown notions of perfect amity did not drive out the older and cruder conception of friendship as a practical alliance for mutual advantage. 'The common and ordinary friendship of the world', explained Henry Peacham in 1638, 'is measured by the benefit one man reaps by another', and 'its utmost bound and extent is, in the country, entertainment for you and your horse a night or two'. Thomas Hobbes declared flatly that friendship was valuable because it conferred mutual protection upon both parties. Even then, the relationship could be precarious, bitter experience teaching that the recipients of benefits did not always reciprocate.[10]

In practice, the two kinds of friendship, affectionate and instrumental, overlapped. Since most people's close friends were neighbours, business colleagues, or near relations, friendship merely strengthened a bond which would have existed anyway. Conversely, there were few affectionate relationships which served no practical purpose. However sentimental in inspiration, friendship could not help being instrumental in its effects: 'our very friendships are but a barter of services and civilities'.[11] The Tudor merchant John Isham said that it was wrong to neglect any of one's friends, for experience had taught him that he was a very mean man who couldn't prove useful once in his lifetime.[12] The Caroline bishop Joseph Hall described 'the true friend' as one who looked for virtue in his partner, but who also 'lift[ed] up his friend to advancement with a willing hand'.[13] In 1704 John Locke wrote to Anthony Collins to say what a treasure it was to have him as a friend: someone who could enlighten him on any matter, large or small, from the principles of knowledge and the foundations of government to advice on where to get a new pair of shoe-buckles.[14] The expectation of reciprocity was always there, even though the literary idealization of perfect friendship tended to overlook its practical dimension.

Nevertheless, the early modern theory of friendship effected something of a transformation in human expectations. It taught that a high-minded, personal relationship could be one of life's greatest pleasures, offering what Roger North called 'inexpressible enjoyments'.[15] Widely disseminated in popular literature, and a favourite theme with the writers of songs and ballads, the literary cult of perfect friendship came to influence notions among the people at large about what they might hope to gain from an ideal personal relationship.[16]

Among men, the most intense friendships were formed in youth, especially when those involved were away from home for the first time, whether as servants, apprentices, schoolfellows, or room-mates at university—'chums', as they were called (from 'chamber fellows'). 'Thou and I were chums together at Brasenose College,' recalled a writer in 1691.[17] 'Such friendships', thought Roger North, 'often happen between persons who live almost at bed and board together, and communicate to each other their most recondite thoughts and designs, and profit each other by mutual counsel.'[18] Youth was the time when the urge to supplement the emotional support afforded by kinship was at its most intense; it was also a time when lack of experience made their judgement of other people highly unreliable. 'Our younger years are not capable of the seriousness and solidities of friendship,' thought one authority.[19] Many parents were understandably nervous about their offspring's choice of intimates, urging a 'sober, moderate friendship', rather than one of passionate intensity, and advising them to keep their secrets to themselves, lest their chosen friend prove false.[20]

There were many close and much-advertised male relationships of the idealized kind, particularly among those whose education had brought them into touch with classical notions of *amicitia*. The early Tudor humanist Richard Pace claimed that, when studying in Italy, he formed with his fellow student John Clark 'a friendship so close, so loyal and constant, that none of the friendships celebrated in literature ever surpassed it'.[21] The future Marian cardinal Reginald Pole, when studying at Padua, met the Venetian gentleman Alvise Priuli; they began an intense personal relationship and became lifelong companions.[22] The poets Philip Sidney, Fulke Greville, and Edward Dyer formed a famous Elizabethan trio.[23] Another comprised three members of Corpus Christi College, Oxford: Edwin Sandys, George Cranmer, and their tutor Richard Hooker; their 'sacred friendship', 'made up of religious principles' and based on 'a similitude of inclinations to the same recreations and studies', was commemorated by Izaak Walton.[24] In 1587 the physician Thomas Newton dedicated his translation of Lambert Daneau's book on friendship to 'my very good friends, Master William Bromley, and Master Reginald Skreven [Scriven]', secretaries to the Lord Chancellor, 'because...I am not ignorant in what a sweet league of mutual love, and Christian sympathy, you twain be linked together'.[25]

In the seventeenth century, Sir Tobie Matthew, the Jacobean courtier, later a Catholic priest, had his inseparable 'comrade' and *fidus Achates* George Gage; Francis Bacon enlarged his essay on friendship at Matthew's request.[26] Edward Hyde maintained 'a most entire friendship without reserve' with Sir Lucius Cary, later Viscount Falkland, until Cary's death in the Civil War, which robbed Hyde of 'the joy and comfort of his life'. The only surviving letter from Cary to Hyde begins 'Dear Sweetheart'. Before that, Cary had been linked with Sir Henry Morison, thus forming a 'noble pair', whose friendship Ben Jonson celebrated in a Pindaric ode.[27] The great lawyer John Selden dedicated his *Titles of Honour* (1614) to Edward Heyward, 'my most beloved friend and chamber fellow'. The physicians Sir John Finch and Sir Thomas Baines met as students at Christ's College, Cambridge, travelled and lived together for thirty-six years, and were buried next to each other in the college chapel, with an inscription which implied that their relationship was a marriage of souls (pl. 11). Finch had had a love affair with a woman, but Baines never loved anyone save Finch.[28] In Westminster Abbey an epitaph commemorated Sir Charles Harbord and Clement Cotterell, 'two faithful friends who lost their lives together' in the battle of Sole Bay in 1672. Twenty years earlier, Cotterell's father, Sir Charles, had been the translator of La Calprenède's novel *Cassandre* (1642–5), notable for its depiction of 'heroic friendship' and passionate embraces between male friends.[29]

The public celebration of these and many other such 'conjunct friendships', as John Aubrey called them,[30] was itself a kind of political statement, the formal announcement of an alliance as binding as that of marriage. The Yorkshire gentleman Sir Henry Slingsby set up the heraldic crests of his 'especial friends' on the posts of the staircase in his house.[31] In the sixteenth and seventeenth centuries, men spoke of 'my *privado*; that is my special and peculiar friend'.[32] But there was nothing private about most of these relationships, which were frequently signalled by ostentatious gestures of physical intimacy. Sometimes, when one friend died, the other celebrated their friendship on his funeral monument.* Occasionally, they were buried together.

It has recently been argued that such friendships should be seen as in direct line of descent from the sworn brotherhoods of the Middle Ages; and that they were consummated liturgically by the joint celebration of the Eucharist.[33] It is true that friendship was often described as 'holy' or 'sacred', and that the Communion service was an

---

* Inigo Jones designed and paid for a monument in the church of St Giles in the Fields, London, in 1634 to the poet George Chapman, 'for ancient friendship'.

Figure 6.1 The caption to this panel from the frontispiece to Richard Braithwaite's *The English Gentleman* (1630) explains that the two friends are expressing their affection by 'hugging one another'.

acknowledged rite of reconciliation, but it is very doubtful whether more than a tiny minority of these close friendships had any such sacramental overtones. There is, however, no doubting their public character or their social and emotional importance. John Donne said that friendship was his 'second religion'.[34]

Imprisoned during the Civil War, the Royalist James Howell pointedly reminded a negligent correspondent that the 'religion of friendship' required its adherents to perform 'certain due rites and decent ceremonies, as visits, messages and missives'.[35] By contrast, when his fellow Royalist Sir Henry Slingsby was in prison, his religious meditations were interrupted by 'assiduate offices of professed amity, visits of friends, with other obliging ties of relation, [which] were daily contriving new, but affectionate ways, how to call me from myself'.[36] When separated, friends sustained their relationship by the exchange of 'familiar letters' ('pictures of the soul') and of painted portraits ('pictures of the body'). 'Many men desire to have the images of their dear friends painted in tables and hung up in their chambers,' wrote a cleric in 1554, 'because they would not forget them, either when they be absent, or... when they be dead.'[37] At dinners they drank pledges to their absent friends.[38] In poems and dedications to books, they proclaimed their relationships without embarrassment.

Among the godly, friends fostered each other's spiritual progress. In Europe, humanist scholars, like Desiderius Erasmus or Justus Lipsius, were the centre of self-conscious circles of like-minded friends, linked by correspondence and the exchange of gifts, though sometimes never meeting face to face.[39] Thomas Fuller thought that making 'a dictionary of their friends' names' in an *album amicorum* was 'but a dull Dutch fashion', but he agreed that it was useful to have 'a selected familiar in every country' with whom to exchange letters.[40] At home, educated clergy, with the letters of Cicero and Seneca as their models, offered each other counsel, advice, and encouragement.[41] Puritan clergy and godly laymen converted their college friendships into lifelong networks.[42] The Elizabethan Family of Love was the first of many religious sects to make intimate friendships and domestic sociability central to their devotional life.[43] The pious London turner Nehemiah Wallington was the 'familiar lover and unfeigned friend' of his fellow tradesman James Cole of Whitechapel; he claimed that their hearts were knit together 'like David and Jonathan'. The Quaker Joseph Pike said the same of his friend Samuel Randall: 'our hearts became knit and united together in a degree like that of Jonathan and David'.[44]

The language of friendship could be extravagant. 'I wish to God it could be my fate to live a monk with you hereafter,' wrote John Aubrey to his friend the antiquarian Anthony Wood in 1671. 'How happy should we two be.' He longed to see him 'with the longing of a woman'.[45] It was not unusual for men, without any sexual intention in mind, to proclaim their friendship with each other in letters awash with erotic imagery. Back in the 1630s, John Winthrop wrote to his friend Sir William Spring: 'I must needs tell you that my soul is knit to you as the soul of Jonathan to David.' He envied Spring's wife for having the felicity of his company and demanded a letter: 'let us hear that sweet voice of thine, my love, my dove'. The sexual innocence of such language is all the more remarkable when we recall that, as governor of Massachusetts, Winthrop oversaw the execution in 1646 of a sodomite, whom he denounced as 'a monster in human shape'.[46]

For the ideal of close masculine friendship coexisted with an equally intense detestation of sodomy as a heinous, 'filthy', and capital offence.[47] In the sixteenth and early seventeenth centuries, male friends could dance with each other, kiss each other, and share a bed without arousing suspicion. Aubrey describes the playwrights Francis Beaumont and John Fletcher living in the same house, wearing the same clothes, sleeping in the same bed, and enjoying 'a wonderful consimility of fancy', without implying any sexual dimension to their relationship.[48] Equally innocent is Shakespeare's description of the extraordinary 'love-death' of York and Suffolk at Agincourt: over Suffolk's neck

> He threw his wounded arm, and kiss'd his lips,
> And so espous'd to death, with blood he seal'd
> A testament of noble-ending love.[49]

Intense personal friendships were publicly celebrated without any hint of scandal, for they were seen as a union of souls not bodies. Fifteenth-century Italian humanists had purged platonic love of its pederastic character.[50] The heterosexual version of Plato's notion had become familiar to an English audience through Sir Thomas Hoby's widely read translation (1561) of Castiglione's *Il Cortegiano*, which culminates in a speech by Pietro Bembo on the spiritual nature of love. It became very fashionable in the time of Queen Henrietta Maria; in 1634 a letter-writer reported of her court that 'there is a love call'd Platonic love which much sways there of late; it is a love abstracted from all corporeal gross impressions and sensual appetite, but consists in contemplations and ideas of the mind, not in any carnal fruition'.[51] 'I love my friend before myself,' wrote Sir Thomas Browne. 'When I am from him, I am dead till I be with him, when I am with him, I am not satisfied, but would still be nearer him; united souls are not satisfied with embraces, but desire to be truly each other, which being impossible, their desires are infinite, and must proceed without possibility of satisfaction.'[52]

Only when there was a marked inequality, in age or class, were contemporaries likely to give male friendship a homosexual interpretation. King James I chose to place his affection for George Villiers in the tradition of heroic friendship and Christian amity: 'Christ had his John and he had his George.' But the difference in rank, compounded by an age gap of twenty-six years, gave rise to a different view, vigorously expressed in 1681 by the 'Protestant joiner' Stephen College when he asserted that Charles II 'came of the race of buggerers, for his grandfather King James buggered the old Duke of Buckingham'.[53]

Tutor and pupil sharing a bedroom; master and secretary closeted together: such conjunctions could excite suspicion and innuendo. In Cambridge in 1627, Joseph Mede, Fellow of Christ's, suspected his colleague William Power of trying to seduce Mede's pupil Justinian Isham into 'some wickedness', though he himself confessed to loving Isham 'with some degree more than a tutor's affection'. At nearby Emmanuel in the 1630s, the young Arthur Bownest found his father strongly resistant to the suggestion that he should go to stay in Suffolk with his passionate friend and room-mate the future archbishop William Sancroft, who was two years older and regarded Bownest as 'my only friend, the better part of my soul'.[54] Seventeenth-century prosecutions for sodomy, though infrequent, typically involved an adult and an adolescent, for homosexual desire was usually conceived of as pederasty, the lust of men for boys.[55] Though condemned as 'abominable', such lust was regarded as a temptation to which many males were subject, but particularly actors, sailors, dons, and schoolmasters. In Renaissance Florence, it was accepted as a normal phase in the transition to adulthood.[56] In England, pederasty was not necessarily thought psychologically inconsistent with subsequent heterosexual marriage; and it certainly did not imply that either party to the relationship was exclusively 'homosexual'. Sodomy was a practice, but not an automatic determinant of sexual identity. The most usual reaction to persons guilty of 'unnatural' vice was to regard them as having surrendered to disreputable impulses which might be felt by anyone.

Nevertheless, the idea of a distinct homosexual identity did exist. It was expressed in the widespread belief that some foreigners, notably Italians and Turks, were especially addicted to homosexual love, and that, even in England, there were men who were 'sodomitically given', that is to say sexually interested only in men or boys: Francis Bacon, for example, whom Aubrey tersely describes as *paiderastes* ('pederast'); or Sir Anthony Ashley (d. 1628), who, though twice married, allegedly 'never loved any but boys'.[57] The sodomite was a recognized type in Elizabethan satirical literature, and the London theatre was notorious for its homoeroticism; around the boy actors there hovered an aura not unlike that surrounding male ballet dancers today. The idea that some persons are innately homosexual by temperament is not an invention of nineteenth-century psychologists, as some have argued, but can be traced back to classical times.[58]

So long as the vocabulary of friendship was virtually indistinguishable from that of erotic love, and so long as the term 'friend' could also mean 'lover', there was potential ambiguity about the nature of any close relationship between two men. What robbed such close relationships of their innocence was a growing anxiety in the later seventeenth and early eighteenth centuries about the dangers of homosexual desire between adult males. During this period it seems to have become more widely accepted that homosexuality was not a universal temptation, but an attribute which distinguished some men from others. As one authority puts it, 'a Renaissance world of polymorphous sexuality... gave way to the eighteenth century world of homosexual self-definition'.[59] A revealing pointer to changing opinion was the replacement, from the 1650s onwards, of boy actors on the stage by women. Previously, it had been acceptable for boys to play female parts because there was, on balance, more anxiety about safeguarding female chastity than about protecting boys from sodomy.[60]

With the emergence of a new and distinctively homosexual subculture, and a greater sense of the male homosexual as a personality type, the older ideal of intense male friendship was seriously threatened. In the eighteenth century, the physical intimacies between male friends which had been readily accepted in Jacobean England were tacitly abandoned; the display of mutual affection became more restrained; and the kiss and the embrace gave way to the handshake. The unspoken fear of homosexuality was robbing intense male friendships of their innocence.[61]

Female friendships, by contrast, attracted less suspicion and lesbianism was not a criminal offence. This was not because it was thought impossible. Classical literature suggested that women could feel physical desire for each other and the notion reappeared in the romances of the early modern period. Pornographic works featured tribades ('rubsters' and 'fricatrices' or 'a she upon a she'); Thomas Blount's *Glossographia* (1661) included 'woman with woman' in his definitions of buggery.[62] But the issue was rarely discussed by moralists, perhaps because there was only one hostile reference to it in the Bible (Romans 1: 26).

In the 1650s the poet Katherine Philips (the 'matchless Orinda'), who at the age of 16 had been married to a Welsh gentleman of 54, formed a much-imitated Society of Friendship. Animated by doctrines of platonic love introduced from France, strongly Royalist in sympathy, and linked by correspondence rather than personal encounters, this group was virtual rather than actual.[63] Its members followed the *précieuse* affectation of giving each other names from contemporary romances: 'Orinda's' friends included 'Ardelia', 'Palaemon', 'Lucasia', and 'Silvander'. Although her society initially included men as well as women, what mattered most to Philips was female friendship, which she celebrated in numerous poems as

> Nobler than kindred or than marriage band,
> Because more free.[64]

Like many other seventeenth- and eighteenth-century literary women, 'Orinda' believed that relationships between females were preferable to the inequalities of marriage and did more for female development. As the poet Mary Chandler would write in 1755:

> Friendship's the sweetest joy of human life:
> 'Tis that I wish—and not to be a wife.[65]

Close friendships between women had a long literary pedigree. Did not Chaucer's Wife of Bath say of her 'gossip', Alisoun, that 'She knew my heart and eke my privity | Bet[ter] than our parish priest'?[66] In Thomas Lodge's *Rosalynde* (1590), Alinda says that 'the world [shall] canonize our friendship, and speak of Rosalynd and Alinda as they did of Pylades and Orestes'.[67] Following Lodge, Shakespeare makes Celia and Rosalind 'coupled and inseparable', while his

Hermia and Helena are 'two seeming bodies but one heart', at least until they fall out over Demetrius and Lysander. The seventeenth century yields non-literary evidence for the intensity of such relationships, often between men's sisters and their sisters-in-law. In 1639 Constance Fowler, a married gentlewoman, wrote of her sister-in-law Catherine Thimelby that 'you never knew two creatures more truly and deadly in love with one another than we are'.[68] In the 1630s Van Dyck painted at least seven double friendship portraits of English aristocratic women, most of them close relatives.[69] James II's daughter, the future Mary II, claimed to love Frances Apsley, who had been her friend since childhood, 'as a wife should do a husband, nay more than is able to be exprest'.[70]

At a less intense level, many women at all social levels, both married and single, had their little groups of friends, linked by kinship, neighbourhood, work, or religion. They spent time in each other's company, exchanged letters and gifts, and provided each other with mutual support. 'Most women' had friends, thought the pious diarist Mary Roberts in 1661.[71] During the later Stuart and early Hanoverian periods, poems and essays by women in celebration of friendship circulated extensively.[72] It was asserted that women were 'more hearty and sincere' in their friendships than men, whose relationships were usually 'clogg'd with so many considerations of interest and punctilios of honour'.[73] The eighteenth century saw many friendships between well-to-do women, frequently conducted in epistolary form. Letter-writing gave women the incentive to reflect on what they had done, seen, and thought. The act of communication with an intimate added meaning 'to every mundane occupation and feeling' and gave new 'opportunities for self-awareness and self-expression'.[74]

Unmarried women tended to have close relationships with their mothers, sisters, and nieces. If they lacked any female relatives, it was not uncommon for them to live with another unrelated woman, usually single or widowed.[75] Westminster Abbey had monuments to Mary Kendall (1677–1710), who lived in 'close union and friendship' with Lady Catharine Jones, who had asked to be buried with her, so that in death they should not be divided; and Katharina Bovey (d. 1727), who had lived 'in perfect friendship' with Mary Pope for nearly forty years. A century earlier, Anne Chitting (d. 1607; three children) and Mary Barber (d. 1600; twelve children) had been buried together in St James's Church, Bury St Edmunds.[76]

In recent years, feminist scholars have taken a keen interest in these networks of female friends, rightly seeing in them an attempt by educated women to establish for themselves a space free from male intervention, and, more speculatively, probing them for evidence of homoeroticism of a physical kind.[77] From the later seventeenth century onwards, close female relationships could give rise to charges of sexual impropriety, though very much less frequently than their male equivalents. By 1795 Mrs Hester Thrale could assert that ''tis now grown common to suspect Impossibilities—(such I think 'em)—whenever two ladies live too much together'.[78] But the general attitude to female friendship was tolerant. In the words of one historian, it was seen as 'nurturing, redemptive, edifying, and, with its pure, unwavering flame, a means of transcending mortal limitations'. The philosopher Mary Astell thought it 'a blessing, the purchase of which were richly worth all the world besides'.[79]

Friendship between a man and a woman was a trickier matter. Persons of different sexes might be 'helpful to each other as Christians', ruled Richard Baxter, but only 'in a state of distant friendship': 'bosom intimacy' between the sexes was 'utterly unfit... because of unsuitableness, temptation and scandal'. Margaret Cavendish agreed that, for women, 'masculine acquaintance most commonly causes suspicion, and a masculine friendship never fails of an aspersion'.[80] Not only might physical attraction get in the way of the union of souls, thereby reducing the relationship to one of pleasure or utility and diminishing its moral purity, but true friendship required equality; and the sexes were not equal. Most early modern authorities took the classical view that women were morally and intellectually incapable of friendship in its more elevated form. It thus became common to assert that male friendship was superior to sexual love between men and women. As a character in one of George Chapman's Jacobean plays remarked, 'what excite[d] the bed's desire' was inferior to 'friendship chaste and masculine'.[81]

Yet spiritual friendships between persons of the opposite sex had been regarded as possible in early Christian times and in medieval monastic circles;[82] and the idea retained some currency in early modern times. Friendship was a relationship of souls, not bodies, and souls were neither male nor female. Hence the possibility of platonic or 'seraphic' love between men and women, even when the two parties were married to other people.[83] John Donne rejected 'this forward heresy | that women can no parts of friendship be'. Baxter thought that women seldom had the understanding and virtue necessary for true friendship, but that it was wrong to dismiss them all as unfitted for it.[84] Even Montaigne, the high priest of male friendship, had discovered a young woman in his old age whom he regarded as capable of that perfect friendship which her sex had hitherto been unable to achieve.[85]

In seventeenth-century England, brothers and sisters sometimes had close relationships. John Finch, the friend of Thomas Baines, wrote affectionate letters almost weekly to his half-sister Anne (Conway), addressing her as 'dearest soul' and 'dearest dear'. The godly minister Samuel Rogers lamented the death in 1638 of his sister Mary ('our beloved Jonathan'): 'very pleasant has thou been unto me, oh, my darling, thy love to me was wonderful, passing the love of women'.[86] There were also some notable examples of intimate friendships between men and women who were unrelated to each other, the best-documented being the married John Evelyn's spiritual friendship with the much younger woman Margaret Blagge (later the wife of Sidney Godolphin), which he sealed in a formal pact in 1672.[87]

The ideal of intense friendship always had a somewhat rarefied quality about it, nourished, as it was, by classical learning and literary affectation. Pure, disinterested friendship was a luxury, available only to those exempt from the pressures of active life and well supported by friends and allies of a more practical kind. Its precondition was leisure and affluence. For those engaged in the battle for subsistence, friendship could not help but remain predominantly instrumental. Aristocrats despised 'stupid common friendship' and contrasted the 'mercenary friendships of the vulgar' with the 'sublime heroic friendship of noble souls'. The 'common people' were incapable of true friendship, they said. All they had were alliances animated by the desire for profit or pleasure; hence their application of the term 'friend' indiscriminately to any neighbour or acquaintance who was not an enemy.[88]

In the eighteenth century, David Hume and Adam Smith would argue that it was only with the arrival of commercial society that truly disinterested friendship had become possible, for it was only then that personal relationships could be entirely separated from business and public affairs. Previously, when society was dominated by patronage and connection, the personal and the instrumental had been hopelessly intertangled. It was the development of a stronger state, an efficient bureaucracy, monetarized exchange, and an impersonal market in labour, commodities, and services which diminished the need for clientage and made individuals less dependent on the good will of others. It was no longer 'from the benevolence of the butcher, the brewer, or the baker that we expect our dinner, but from their regard to their own interest'; and it was the law, not their family and 'friends', who now guaranteed the citizen's safety. Once individuals could satisfy their practical needs without being dependent on personal favour, it became easier to 'purify' human relationships of instrumental considerations. The nearer society came to being an undifferentiated marketplace, instead of a maelstrom of competing factions, the less necessary was it to have sworn allies. Instrumental friendship ceased to be an essential need. Instead, disinterested relationships could at last be founded on mutual esteem and personal affinity.[89]

Yet long before the eighteenth century, affectionate friendship had been sought and found at every social level. Its existence is hinted at by many surnames of medieval origin—Copyner (lover), Bonamy (good friend), Bellamy (fair friend), Companion, Comper (comrade), Coppin and Compain (chum) and, of course, Friend.[90] In the later Middle Ages, people left money for votive masses for the souls of their 'good friends'.[91] In the early modern period, persons of modest means left bequests to their 'especial good friends', or 'very faithful friends', or 'singular good friends', out of 'amity and friendship'.[92] Sometimes they asked to be buried next to their friends.[93] At funerals, rings and tokens were distributed to remind recipients of their friendship with the deceased. In 1652 the mathematician John Greaves bequeathed 'one of my best gold rings' to the great orientalist Richard Pococke in memory of his and of his father's friendship.[94] In 1689 Ann Hulton, a tradesman's wife, mourned the death of Mrs Bradbury, her 'dear friend whom I loved as my own soul'.[95] Seventeenth-century merchants had friends who shared their social life and were mentioned in their wills.[96] Nearly all the diarists and autobiographers of the period seem to have had a circle of close friends whom they saw regularly. When Mr Fitzherbert, a Derbyshire gentleman, hanged himself in 1772, Dr Johnson commented that 'everybody liked him, but he had no friend, as I understand the word, nobody with whom he exchanged intimate thoughts'.[97]

Then, as now, friendship was largely determined by proximity. Women had their 'gossips', neighbours who lent each other household utensils and helped out during pregnancy and childbirth.[98] Men had their schoolfellows, fellow servants, workmates, 'bullies', and 'boon companions', with whom they sometimes forged close bonds, though more often in the shared comradeship of the group ('mateship') than in the closer reciprocity of personal friendship.[99] Such relationships were seldom wholly disinterested, but they were often described as 'intimate' or 'familiar', and we may surmise that the support people offered each other was emotional as well as practical. Friendship helped people to define themselves, to enhance their sense of self. John Aubrey listed people's friends (including his own) in his 'Brief Lives', because they revealed his subjects' social and intellectual affinities and were part of their identity.[100] On tombstones and funeral monuments, and in personal recollections, it was common to celebrate friendship as one of the deceased persons' virtues and to characterize that friendship with such epithets as 'faithful', 'true', 'steadfast', 'sincere', 'constant', 'steady', 'lasting', 'warm', 'reliable', 'helpful', 'disinterested', 'inviolable', and even 'noble'.[101]

Yet close friendship, even between persons of the same sex, was not free from tensions. Most obviously, it conflicted with heterosexual love and matrimony. Typically, youthful friendships ended when one of the pair married. The best friends were unmarried men, thought Francis Bacon; and in Shakespeare's plays the conflict between male bonds and marriage is a recurring theme. Falling in love with a woman cancelled the bonds of male friendship; and the same was true in reverse: 'We may generally conclude the marriage of a friend to be the funeral of a friendship,' remarked Katherine Philips in 1662.[102] Tensions between spouses and each other's friends before marriage resembled those generated by in-laws. It was essential, stressed William Gouge, that husband and wife should 'each of them . . . esteem of the other's friends as of their own'.[103]

Friendship could also conflict with obligations to kinsfolk, for the two categories often failed to overlap. The Earl of Northampton told the House of Lords in 1610 that it was 'very seldom in this age for kindred and friendship to concur in one man'. Francis Finch, who wrote an essay on friendship for Katherine Philips and her friend Anne Owen, also thought it very rare for a true friendship to be contracted between blood relations.[104] Many theorists held that friendship should take precedence over kin relationships: 'I hope I do not break the fifth commandment', wrote Sir Thomas Browne, 'if I conceive I may love my friend before the nearest of my blood, even those to whom I owe the principles of life.'[105] Others thought it wrong that relationships created by personal choice should be given priority over familial ties.[106] There may have been social differences here, for in modern times the working classes are less likely than the middle classes to place obligations to friends above those to relatives.[107]

Friendship could create other difficulties. If the friends were socially unequal, as with a nobleman and his secretary, or, even more, a king and his favourite, the relationship could become subversive of accepted hierarchies.[108] If the friends were members of a larger unit, whether a college, a workshop, or a ship's crew, their close relationship could threaten the smooth working of the whole.

The exclusive nature of friendship also posed an acute religious problem which had bothered churchmen since patristic times. Christian charity enjoined amity to all mankind, not just to a few selected individuals. As the eighteenth-century moralist Soame Jenyns observed, friendship 'is too narrow and confined, and appropriates that benevolence to a single object which is...commanded to be extended over all'.[109] In his *Discourse* on friendship (1657), the future bishop Jeremy Taylor devoted much effort to proving that special friendships were compatible with Christianity; and in 1778 the Quaker lady Mrs Knowles famously defeated Samuel Johnson in a discussion as to whether friendship was a Christian virtue by citing Christ's special love for John.[110] Nevertheless, the Quakers resolutely addressed everyone they met as 'friend', while many godly preachers condemned intense personal relationships as idolatrous (hence Shakespeare's Sonnet 105: 'Let not my love be called idolatry'). Richard Baxter thought it unfit 'for a rational creature to love anyone farther than reason will allow'; he believed that the desire to be loved by others was 'a sin of a deeper malignity than is commonly observed'. 'Intimate special friendship', he wrote, 'hath been so much pleaded for by all sorts of men, and so much of the felicity of man's life hath been placed in it,' that it was hard to speak against it. Nevertheless, it offered perils of which Cicero had been unaware.[111] The only perfect friend was Christ himself.[112] 'He that hath a friend hath two to please,' reflected the poet Thomas Traherne in the 1660s, 'two judgments to satisfy and two wills, his own and another, which here upon earth is inconvenient. It is better only to have an infinite benevolence toward all the world, a moderate friendship with the good and excellent, an entire illimited friendship with God alone.'[113]

In the eighteenth century, it became common to laugh at the 'sublime Platonic notions' about love and friendship which had once had such a vogue. The prevailing ideal of male friendship was low-key and convivial.[114] Adam Smith thought that a prudent man would reject the 'hasty, fond and foolish intimacies of young persons', which, though ardent, were 'transitory', and, instead, prefer 'a sedate, but steady and faithful attachment to a few well-tried and well-chosen companions'. He believed that this 'wise security of friendship' was best extended to several people; if confined to one, it would not be friendship but love.[115]

Of course, intense friendships did not disappear. Romantic friendships between young men, especially students, seem to have revived in the later eighteenth century and would become highly characteristic of Victorian undergraduate life. Nevertheless, there had been a reduction in the temperature since the publicly proclaimed friendships of the Renaissance era. This was partly because same-sex relationships were now more likely to be perceived as homosexual. It was also because changing social conditions had generated a new attitude to private leagues and alliances. In Tudor times, it had been a popular saying that a friend to all was a friend to none. But in the age of the Enlightenment, universal benevolence and fraternity were seen as preferable to exclusive pacts of private amity. Public declarations of friendship now appeared disagreeably factious in their implications. When such alliances were no longer necessary for personal security, the combative ethic of medieval blood brothers, pledged to hate each other's enemies, seemed mischievous and disruptive.[116] Instrumental friendships remained important, but their existence was less likely to be publicly acknowledged.

MARRIAGE AND CHILDREN

A further challenge to intense friendships between persons of the same sex came from the ideal of companionate marriage. As the novelist Samuel Richardson's heroine Clarissa Harlowe put it, marriage was 'the highest state of friendship'.[1] This was a relatively new viewpoint, for which most classical theories of friendship had not prepared the way. Though not ruling out the possibility that husband and wife might attain a friendship involving the cultivation of virtue, Aristotle had thought marriage more likely to be a lower form of amity based on utility and pleasure.[2] In the medieval *chansons de geste*, the ideal friendships were between males—martial comrades, whose love was passing the love of women. The men might also be married, but that was simply for the coarser purposes of reproduction. In the early modern period, most intellectual men thought that the presence of women lowered the tone. The educational gulf between the sexes led sophisticated young males to look to each other for their ideal friendships.

The personal relationship between the married couple had never been seen as the primary purpose of marriage. Aristocratic marriages were political unions, involving the consolidation of dynastic alliances, the transfer of estates, and the perpetuation of the line. Lower down the social scale, marriage was a practical necessity, essential for the conduct of business, the procreation and upbringing of children, and the support of the elderly. Such unions were contracted for social and material reasons as much as for personal ones. In his discourse on friendship, Francis Finch explained that 'there be many that can adore one as a mistress, affect her for a wife, and yet believe her not so proper for all the relations of friendship'.[3] Richard Baxter saw nothing odd about advising married men to keep secrets from their wives, while entrusting them to a friend. Neither did Clarendon, to whom friendship was 'so much more a sacrament than marriage is'. Sir William Monson, who believed that 'the unsecret man never lives in safety', was emphatic that women should never be trusted with a confidence, 'for the weakness of their sex makes them unsecret'. William Scott in his *Essay on Drapery* (1635) gave the same advice to businessmen.[4] Marriage was widely thought of as a physical and practical relationship rather than a moral or intellectual one, and therefore on a lower plane than male companionship.

Yet just as the cult of perfect male friendship was a way of refining the personal alliances which seemed essential to survival in a society governed by patronage and connection, so the ideal of companionate marriage gave a more elevated character to the social and biological imperatives of sex and reproduction. The notion of marriage as a superior form of friendship had long been in circulation; the medieval world, it has been well said, was 'full of married friends'.[5] Although medieval clerics regarded celibacy as a morally superior state to marriage, there was also a strong current of thought which idealized matrimony as an end in itself, rather than just a necessary means of procreation. In late medieval Italy, humanist writers, stimulated perhaps by the need to renew the population after the Black Death, condemned celibacy as unnatural, linked marriage to rediscovered classical ideals of *amicitia*, and claimed that women could assist their husbands to attain virtue and wisdom.[6]

In the early sixteenth century, the notion of companionate marriage was endorsed by many English humanists, who cited the view of the first-century Greek philosopher Plutarch that marriage was the most pleasurable form of love and the most beneficial form of friendship.[7]

Their influence was reinforced by the Protestant rejection of virginity as a holy state. The marriage service in the 1549 Prayer Book departed from pre-Reformation practice by listing 'mutual society, help and comfort' as one of the objects of marriage; and the official *Homily on Matrimony* (1562) declared that marriage was instituted, not just to produce children and to avoid fornication, but also 'to the intent that man and woman should live lawfully in a perpetual friendly fellowship'.[8] Thereafter the language developed to describe perfect friendship was readily applied to marital relationships. The Elizabethan preacher Henry Smith called the husband and the wife 'a pair of friends', while in the mid-seventeenth century Jeremy Taylor described marriage as 'the queen of friendships'. Matrimony was widely celebrated as a union which was both physical and emotional. The future bishop Simon Patrick declared in 1659 that when a man and his wife were both one flesh and one soul, theirs was the highest love of all.[9]

The courtier and natural philosopher Sir Kenelm Digby (1603–65) thought that the primary motive for the marriage of two people should be 'not sordid wealth or other conveniencies, but a divine affection, which may make their souls one'. He believed the female sex was very seldom capable of 'so divine a thing as an assured friendship', but in the beautiful Venetia Stanley, his boyhood sweetheart and later his wife, he claimed to have found 'a masculine and heroic soul', uniquely capable of the most perfect form of amity.[10] The Parliamentary general Sir William Waller recalled how he and his wife, Anne, were 'but as one soul in two bodies'. The Quaker William Penn regarded a wife as 'a second self', capable of being a perfect friend despite her sex, for souls had no sex. God gave Eve to Adam 'for a friend as well as for a woman', agreed Mary Beale.[11] When Mary Clarke wrote in 1675 to her husband, Edward, friend of John Locke, she signed herself 'your affectionate wife and faithful friend'.[12] For Daniel Defoe, marriage was what earlier writers had claimed for friendship: a union of souls; but one which was also a union of bodies. 'In wedlock when the sexes meet,' sang the eighteenth-century poet Nathaniel Cotton, 'Friendship is only then complete.'[13]

James I remarked, rather ambiguously, that marriage was 'the greatest earthly felicity, or misery, that can come to a man'.[14] The early modern period abounds in more confident assertions about the indispensability of matrimony for human happiness. The Puritan Thomas Gataker called it 'a kind of heaven upon earth'; and when Thomas Hobbes, though a bachelor himself, listed the goods which most men valued most, he put, next after life and limb, 'conjugal affection'.[15] Ironically, it was the increasingly high expectations of matrimony that would eventually generate a demand for legal divorce. The essence of John Milton's case in the 1640s for a change in the law was that there was no point in a marriage which had ceased to be personally fulfilling, at least for the husband; a wife should be 'another self, a second self, a very self itself'. That others thought like him is revealed by an interesting case in 1622 of two Wiltshire sectaries, Henry Cheevers and Mary Banfield, who abandoned their legal spouses as unregenerate and elected to live together, like 'David and Jonathan'.[16]

Of course, hopes were often disappointed. There were happy marriages—'My life is but half a life in your absence,' wrote Elizabeth Cromwell to her husband, Oliver—and there were unhappy ones, many couples proceeding, as a preacher put it, to a lifetime of mutual sorrow, 'she to sorrow in her subjection to him, and he to sorrow, yea a great deal of sorrow, in passing his time with her'.[17]

Yet though individual experience, then as now, was diverse, marriage was increasingly regarded as potentially the highest form of friendship. Couples asked to be buried together; and funeral monuments testified to their 'conjugal affection', evoking the vocabulary of classical and biblical friendship. 'They were lovely and pleasant in their lives and in their deaths they were not divided,' says the epitaph to an eighteenth-century dancing master and his wife.[18] Of women, it was claimed that their 'principal happiness' was the affection of their husbands and children. Loving husbands and wives, devoted parents, faithful offspring: by the later seventeenth century, these were increasingly the terms in which people chose to be remembered.[19] Implicit in such epitaphs was a rejection of the common sixteenth-century attitude that it was 'effeminizing' for a man to be too dependent on a woman's company. Marital love was now widely accepted as a principal source of human fulfilment.

Today's feminists tend to be unsympathetic to the early modern ideology of companionate marriage. They see it as another form of patriarchal oppression, in which women, prevented from following a fulfilling career outside the household, were denied self-realization and reduced to serving the practical and emotional needs of men. That, they claim, was the true meaning of the cult of domesticity and the representation of marriage as a haven, where, as Roger North put it, 'the world with all its fetters and chains is far off'.[20] When the Puritan William Ames declared that a wife 'ought in all things so to behave herself, that her husband may content himself in her as in another himself', he came close to making their point (pl. 12).[21]

It was predictable that the death of a beloved wife could be devastating for the husband. Oliver Heywood, the soon-to-be-ejected minister, was beside himself when his wife died in May 1661. 'I want her at every turn, everywhere, and in every work. Methinks I am but half my self without her.'[22] What is more surprising to some modern sensibilities is that the death of these patriarchal husbands could cause equal distress to their wives. Lady Russell wrote of her husband, after his execution in 1683, that 'I want him to talk with, to walk with, to eat and sleep with; all these things are irksome to me now.' In the words of a contemporary verse:

> He first deceas'd. She for a little tried
> To live without him: lik'd it not and died.[23]

With marriage went children, at least in most cases.[24] They were usually regarded as a blessing, and, in the view of some contemporaries, 'the chiefest earthly blessing'. Valued by the rich as a means of perpetuating the lineage and by the poor as a practical investment for their old age, children were also seen as sources of delight and appropriate objects for deep emotional investment.[25] The godly Sarah Savage, who had nine of them around the end of the seventeenth century, felt that her sin was 'too much love of, and too many cares for, my children'.[26] Of course, all children were not equally valuable. As a divine explained in 1596, it was a greater blessing to be the mother of a son than of a daughter. This was particularly true in noble and gentry families, where boys were needed to ensure the continuation of the line. When his tenth daughter arrived in 1659, the Cheshire gentleman William Blundell entered in his journal, 'the thing is called Bridget'.[27] Once a few sons had been born, a girl was perfectly welcome; and in the eighteenth century there are signs, even among the upper classes, of an appreciation of daughters for their own sake.[28] The average life expectancy of infants was short, however: most children died before their parents, thought a contemporary in 1664. Parental grief for the death of children was widely, and often pathetically, expressed.[29]

For many women, motherhood was life's most rewarding human experience.[30] Yet not everybody wanted offspring. 'A strange consideration', noted the childless Samuel Pepys, 'how others do rejoice to have a child born.'[31] Just as some medieval peasants had attempted to limit the size of their families or to avoid offspring altogether, so, according to Sir Walter Ralegh, those lacking the means to nourish children tended to 'think it a blessing, which in nature is a curse, to have their wives barren'. Children were notoriously a burden to the poor.[32] The Jacobean minister Richard Rogers reproached some of his contemporaries for marrying 'where they may be sure they can have no children', or complaining about being encumbered with 'such a company of brats, as they term them'. His colleague William Gouge lamented that some people would not marry because they did not want children; 'others...marry such as are past child-bearing. Others will have two beds, to forbear lying with their wives. Others fret at their wives, because they bring forth many children. Others, having many children, wish them dead; [and others] unnaturally make away their children after they are born, yea, some in the very womb.' Another writer, Thomas Hilder, in 1653 admonished the 'many men and women that are afraid of marriage lest they should have children', along with 'divers who are married that use all means possible to prevent great increase of children': an 'exceeding vile sin' which had 'grown to be an epidemical disease, overspreading the face of the Christian world'.[33] The early eighteenth-century glover and deistical writer Thomas Chubb never married, 'judging it greatly improper to introduce a family into the world without a prospect of maintaining them'.[34] The childless Margaret Cavendish, Marchioness of Newcastle, remarked that, although an aristocratic woman might want children, so as to keep alive her husband's name and family, she had no reason to desire them for her own sake, since her name would be lost anyway.[35] Few women welcomed the prospect of incessant childbearing: 'I was brought abed with a son, which is my tenth child,' wrote Frances Clerke, daughter of Sir John Oglander, in 1651, 'and I pray God, if it be his blessed will, it may be my last.'[36] In 1727 Daniel Defoe commented adversely on 'these modern-witted ladies that desire to marry, but would have no children'.[37]

Against them must be set the increasing number of individuals who freely acknowledged that child-rearing provided them with one of their greatest satisfactions. Two early eighteenth-century epitaphs typify the trend. One is for a Yorkshire gentleman, Thomas Fountayne (d. 1709), of whom it was recorded that 'he loved the company of his friends, but never more enjoyed himself than in the society of his family, knowing how to be easy and pleasant with his children, without losing the respect that was due to him'. The other commemorates a Wiltshire lady, Mary Baskerville of Winterbourne Basset (d. 1724), describing her as 'the very best of grandmothers'. Then, as now, grandmothers were notorious for being more indulgent to their children's children than they had been to their own.[38]

SOCIABILITY

An adequate account of the fulfilment which came from sociability in this period would range far beyond friendship, marriage, and parenthood to embrace many other forms of human interaction, less intimate but no less valued: not just the banquets and other festivities enjoyed by the trade guilds and municipalities,[1] nor the weddings, christenings, churchings, and funerals which enlivened parochial life; not just the camaraderie of the alehouse, the mixed dancing in the villages,[2] the ribald bonding of young men,[3] or the conviviality of the 'ales' and 'drinkings' which seem to have occurred on every conceivable pretext;[4] but also the simpler pleasures of casual encounters; the gossip of women on the doorstep or at the washing place, spinning and knitting together, or working in the fields,[5] of old men on the village bench,[6] and of the congregation loitering in the churchyard after, or even during, the service.[7]

Stern moralists disapproved of this casual chat, which they dismissed as 'idle twit-twat discourse',[8] just as they opposed the church ales, wakes, and other convivial activities, justified in the name of 'good fellowship' and 'good neighbourhood', but, in their view, time-wasting forms of idleness. Like the medieval preachers before them, the godly repudiated the 'common opinion' of 'poor' and 'ignorant' people that 'drinking and bezzling [guzzling] in the alehouse' was 'good fellowship, and shows a good, kind nature and maintains neighbourhood'.[9] Richard Baxter was scathing about the conversation of women: 'they will sit ... many hours to tell you, first, how the affairs go between them and their husbands or children or servants; and then talk of their cattle, house or land; and then tell you of news, and enter into a long discourse of other men's matters ... and next they talk of the weather; and then of the market, what's cheap and what's dear, and then they tell you what this body said to them, and what the other body said, and then they tell you a story of the old times, and how the world is changed and how much better the former times were than these; then they tell you what wrong such a one did them, and what he said of them, and how bad this or that man is, and what they said or did amiss; and what the report of the country is of such and such; then they tell you what clothes such a one wears...and who keepeth a good house and who is niggardly and sparing.'[10]

Educated women were equally contemptuous of the typical conversation of their sex. Margaret Cavendish was bored by the chatter of ladies at a christening, which 'was most[ly] of labours and child-beds, children and nurses, and household servants, and of preserving, and such-like discourses as married women and mistresses of families usually have; at last, they fell into a discourse of husbands, complaining of ill husbands, and so, from husbands in general to their own particular husbands'. Lady Chudleigh (d. 1710) felt the same: 'after they have talk'd of their clothes, of the affairs of their kitchen, of the faults of their servants, and all their other domestic trifles, what can the poor dull creatures say next, if they are not permitted to abuse and ridicule their neighbours, to make reflections on their conduct, to enquire into their concerns, [and] the minutest circumstances of their families?'[11]

Gossip was perceived by most male commentators as a peculiarly female activity, but there is no reason to think that the conversation of most men was very different. Country gentry notoriously talked about dogs, hawks, and horses, the weather, and the price of corn: 'nothing but subsidies, the provision of petty penal statutes for the punishing of rogues, feeding of oxen or sheep, manuring of land or the changes of the seasons, that things are dear or cheap'.[12] The elderly and the sick regaled others with detailed histories of their aches and pains ('many will concern the company in their very stools, and consistency of them'); servants gossiped about their masters; Restoration rakes talked of 'nothing but fighting and fucking'; and most people enjoyed sexual banter and witty repartee.[13] In 1641 the 'principal discourse' of young men among their tippling companions was said to be 'of women and their appurtenances, of cuckolds and cuckold-makers, what men wear horns, what women britches, what willing ones there be in the town or parish, how such pieces are to be handled', and much other 'ribaldry, obscene discourses, songs, tales and jests'; for 'young men...usually at their pot-meetings pervert all occasions of talk into bawdry'.[14] By contrast, the Oxford academic Obadiah Walker thought that 'the frequentest table-talk in England' was 'discourse about divinity'.[15]

Whether theological or bawdy, idle chat was irritating to godly ministers like Richard Baxter, who, like most studious people, hated casual visitors and wanted to be left alone to get on with his work. He was highly critical of the habit of spending whole days in 'complemental visitations' and 'civilities', that is to say the genteel practice of paying courtesy calls on friends, relatives, and neighbours, under 'pretences of decency or seemliness, and civility and good manners, and avoiding offence'. He did not urge 'cynical morosity or unsociableness', but he regarded social calls as 'needless compliments'.[16] He also thought that a meal should not normally last more than a quarter of an hour. Half an hour was quite long enough for entertaining strangers; to spend an hour on it was ridiculous.[17]

The scientist Robert Boyle was similarly hostile to the tyranny of custom, which, in the name of 'civility', required him to waste his time receiving visits from 'every coxcomb' who had nothing better to do, and, even worse, to be obliged to return them. He deplored fruitless chatter about the weather: 'almanac-discourse', as he called it. Swapping dreams and illnesses, he thought, was an equally sinful waste of time.[18]*

Boyle and Baxter were driven men: they had better things to do than spend their days in idle chatter. They would have agreed with the godly Joseph Alleine, who, as tutor at Corpus Christi College, Oxford, in the 1650s, refused to receive visitors who called when he was studying, justifying this apparent discourtesy in terms which must strike a chord with many modern scholars: 'Better it is that they should wonder at thy rudeness than [that] thou shouldst lose thy time; for only one or two will take notice of that, but all posterity would be sensible of this.'[19]

For most people, however, this casual conversation, of which moralists and scholars were so scornful, was of the greatest practical and emotional importance, particularly in an age when most depended for their knowledge of current affairs on oral transmission, and when the first question on meeting was usually 'What news?' It was as much for the sake of the personal encounters and accompanying gossip as for devotional or business reasons that country people made their weekly journeys to church or to market.[20] The attraction of the ale bench was gossip and debate as much as drink;[21] and it was the pleasure of sociability, as well as administrative necessity, that brought the gentry

---

* In France, the virtuoso Nicolas-Claude Fabri de Peiresc also complained of hours wasted in agreeing 'that it was cold weather, or very hot; that the sky was clear, or cloudy, the air healthy or unhealthy; and other such-like things'; *The Mirrour of True Nobility and Gentility... by Petrus Gassendus*, trans. W. Rand (1657), 176–7.

together at assizes and quarter sessions, race meetings and elections. Even the Puritan fast days were social occasions.[22]

Conversation was an indispensable form of human intercourse, whether the polite conversation modelled on the habits of the French salons, which the theorists of civility regarded as the highest form of social refinement, or the 'ingenious conversation' of the clubs, common rooms, and coffee houses, or the everyday chat of ordinary people. Henry Fielding rightly called conversation 'this grand business of our lives, the foundation of every thing'.[23] Daniel Defoe thought Lichfield was the best place of 'conversation and good company' in the Midlands, but for 'the best conversation in England' he chose Greenwich, primarily it seems because of the large number of senior army officers who retired there and regaled the company with Uncle Toby-like memories of their exploits.[24]

Gossip was not a trivial matter. It afforded pleasure to connoisseurs of narrative detail and human idiosyncrasy, not to mention those who enjoyed hearing about the misfortunes of others.[25] It was an important check on unconventional behaviour. It bonded people together and, as with letter-writing, its social and human significance far transcended what was actually said. Its language was 'phatic', that is lacking in meaning but a necessary ingredient of social intercourse. 'Love of converse' was one of humanity's defining characteristics. Like play, conversation was an end in itself.[26]

In the early modern period, public and communal sociability were increasingly supplemented by private and domestic entertaining, of the kind implied in Ben Jonson's poem 'Inviting a friend to supper', or in William Gouge's injunction that husbands and wives should do their entertaining together.[27] The surviving evidence affords only occasional glimpses, but entertaining at home seems to have been very widespread from the sixteenth century if not earlier. In the countryside the gentry had long kept open house for their peer group and extended kin on a scale which is unimaginable today. During the early modern period, they cut down on this older style of hospitality but took up the practice, first developed in London, of paying formal visits on each other by coach.[28] At the same time, the middle classes increasingly separated themselves from the collective celebrations of the local community and moved towards the selected company of family and friends at Friday night suppers or Sunday dinners. For them, the important venues were not the village green or the alehouse, but the private room, the dinner party and, in the eighteenth century, the tea party (pl. 14).[29] Their houses, once so ill-equipped for domestic entertaining, were now designed with differentiated room space, and equipped with all the necessary apparatus, in the form of dining tables, linen, glasses, cutlery, and tea sets.[30] In London, much eating and drinking took place outside the home at cookshops and taverns.[31] 'It is a frequent solemnity, still used with us when friends meet,' noted Robert Burton, 'to go to the alehouse or tavern; they are not sociable otherwise, or if they visit one another's houses, they must both eat and drink.' In the year 1666 Samuel Pepys ate 264 dinners at home, 48 in the homes of others, and 31 with friends in taverns.[32] Just as it became increasingly important for people to choose their spouses for themselves, so it seemed preferable to select one's own friends and associates, rather than to be part of the compulsory conviviality of the neighbourhood. Growing dislike for communal holidays and festivities is reflected in the revealing remark of the Elizabethan Puritan Philip Stubbes that there was no harm in people visiting their friends, but no reason why they should all do so on the same day.[33]

Late medieval England had abounded in guilds and fraternities which pursued a mixture of religious, charitable, and sociable objectives. Guilds, civic corporations, and trading companies continued to be important agents of sociability after the Reformation, though, mostly, only for men. From the seventeenth century onwards, they were supplemented by a host of clubs, societies, and voluntary associations. Their members were like-minded people (again usually men) who gathered to advance a cause or to promote a charity, and, above all, to eat and drink together.[34] In London, literary and convivial 'orders', 'fraternities', and 'societies', alias male drinking clubs, had been ubiquitous since Jacobean times.[35] By the Hanoverian period, regular tavern gatherings over the punchbowl were a boisterous reminder that not all men preferred the pleasures of domesticity. The company of casual friends could be more relaxing than the intensity of family relationships (pl. 13).[36] A drinking song by Henry Purcell (1659–95) echoed the Renaissance ideal of friendship:

> Would ye know how we meet o'er our jolly full bowls?
> As we mingle our liquors, we mingle our souls;
> The sweet melts the sharp, the kind soothes the strong
> And nothing but Friendship grows all the night long.[37]

The semi-formalized company-keeping of clubs and associations was additional to the (largely, but not exclusively masculine) sociability of the tavern, the workplace, and, from the 1650s, the coffee house.[38] In the Restoration period, even the formerly austere Oxford colleges began to build themselves senior common rooms.[39] By the eighteenth century, most substantial English towns had become theatres of sociability, with walks, pleasure gardens, theatres, concert halls, and assembly rooms. Arenas for social competition they may have been, but they also pleased those who delighted in human intercourse for its own sake. No wonder that Joseph Addison proclaimed that man was an animal who delighted in society, or that David Hume declared that, the more the arts advanced, 'the more sociable men become'.[40]

It is apparent, therefore, that in early modern England the pleasures of human intercourse were ranked very high among the roads to human fulfilment. The growth of the market and the consolidation of an impersonal national state had the effect of creating more private space which individuals were free to shape for themselves. In the choice of the friends they made and the company they kept, they were able to show a measure of autonomy and spontaneous self-expression. In interaction with others they developed their own individuality; and in expressing their affection for their friends and their families, they learned that self-fulfilment need not imply selfishness.[41] The negative conception of privacy inherited from classical times gradually gave way to a new, more positive view. To many people, friendship, marriage, domesticity, and casual socializing were coming to seem infinitely more important than the public and political values championed by the civic humanists. It is only recently that historians have emancipated themselves from the classical preoccupation with public affairs and begun to take these human concerns into account.

7

FAME AND THE AFTERLIFE

For naught but fame man after death inherits.

(John Weever), *The Mirror of Martyrs*, 1601, sig. F2

And some there be, which have no memorial; who are perished, as though they had never been; and are become as though they had never been born; and their children after them.

Ecclesiasticus 44: 9

HEAVEN AND HELL

Looking back on his life in 1709, Bishop Gilbert Burnet affirmed that it was only religion which could afford 'true or complete happiness'; in his experience, the pleasures of sense soon became nauseating; public life merely revealed the crookedness of human nature; learning was always imperfect; even friendship 'of the best and noblest sort' had yielded him 'vanity and vexation of spirit'. True religion, however, was an unfailing 'joy and delight'.[1]

In the late seventeenth and early eighteenth centuries, much was said by Anglican divines about the 'pleasantness' of religion and the daily happiness it could bring to those who practised it.[2] It sustained their morale, gave meaning to their existence, and provided consolation against misfortune. Nevertheless, the Church's teaching was that human fulfilment was unattainable in this life. The Church's primary purpose was to prepare its members for the world to come. Only then would the true end of life be attained. The culmination of human existence lay in the four Last Things: Death, when body and soul were separated; Judgement, when the fate of the resurrected body, reunited with the soul, was determined;

Heaven, a place of indescribable felicity, to which the saved would be admitted; and Hell, a location of unspeakable torment, to which the damned would be consigned.

What happened to the soul during the intermediary period between death and resurrection was a matter of debate. Some of the early Protestant reformers believed that the souls of the blessed rested until the Resurrection in a celestial waiting room, 'Abraham's bosom' (Luke 16: 22), while the souls of the damned were held in a condition of misery.[3] But this notion was uncomfortably close to the old Catholic doctrine of purgatory. It was accordingly rejected by most later Anglican divines, who took Christ's remark to the thief crucified with him—'Today shalt thou be with me in paradise' (Luke 23: 43)—to mean that the souls of the righteous went immediately to heaven, for which 'Abraham's bosom' was merely a synonym.[4] In the 1630s the future sectary Laurence Clarkson was brought up to believe that 'the soul at the hour of death...was either by an angel or a devil fetcht immediately to heaven or hell'.[5] The oddity of this orthodox doctrine was that it presupposed that the saved and the damned were identified in advance of Christ's Last Judgement, which thus became a formality. As a consequence, the idea of an intermediary state between death and resurrection lingered on, to be embraced by a number of theologians in the late seventeenth and early eighteenth centuries.[6] Dissatisfaction with the apparent downgrading of the significance of the Last Judgement also sustained a long-continuing succession of so-called 'mortalists', persons who held that the body and soul could not be separated and that the dead slept until the Resurrection.[7]

Nearly everyone agreed, however, that the saved would eventually, in the words of the Church of England's Thirty-Nine Articles, 'attain to everlasting felicity'; and most also agreed that the damned would be condemned to eternal perdition. This was what the Presbyterian minister Richard Baxter called 'the Chief Good', the 'ultimate end'.[8] As the vicar of Chilvers Coton, Cambridgeshire, told his congregation in 1626, 'our life is a journey, either to Heaven or to Hell'.[9]

Since early Christian times, this simple proposition had generated a huge volume of theological debate. In the early modern period, argument and controversy intensified. How many people would be saved? Everybody? One in a hundred? One in a thousand?* Or, as the

* John Bunyan thought that only one in a thousand men, and one in ten thousand women, showed genuine signs of repentance; *Miscellaneous Works*, ix, ed. Richard L. Greaves (Oxford, 1981), 282.

ex-Camden professor of history at Oxford maintained in 1680, probably not one in a million?[10] When was the final destination of particular individuals determined? Before their birth? During their lives? At their death? Or during the intermediary state after death? How far could people influence their own destiny? Did all depend on God's unknown intentions? Or could men save themselves by faith or good deeds? Such issues were the stuff of theological dispute, the central intellectual activity of the age.

The exact nature of human fulfilment in heaven was also a matter of speculation. Few heeded John Donne's warning that nothing certain could be said on the subject. Heaven's joys might be impossible to describe, but that did not prevent innumerable writers and preachers from attempting to do so.[11] Theologians taught that the chief pleasure of the future life was that it enabled the blessed to see God and be united with him in perpetual worship. When Sir Edwin Sandys made his will in 1629, he expressed the hope that he would be allowed access to the heavenly kingdom, 'there with angels and saints to enjoy the happy vision of the most glorious deity'.[12] This beatific vision was something too ineffable for human comprehension, but with the aid of chapters 21 and 22 of Revelation and other scattered Scriptural clues, commentators built up a picture of what life in heaven might be like. Their speculations reveal that many people hoped to find there not just the beatific vision, but also a continuation of the pleasures of this life, though without the accompanying pains and inconveniences. In heaven they would discover the satisfactions which had eluded them on earth: total omniscience, for example: 'God shall create us all doctors in a minute,' thought Donne.[13] Perfect health, also: the resurrected body would be free of all imperfections. There would be no cripples in heaven, no blind persons, no sufferers from chronic disease.[14] It would be 'a glorious body', agreed John Evelyn, 'endued with all spiritual qualities of illumination, agility and aptitude to ascend and pass regions of infinite distance and variety; and that as well women as men'.[15] When Mary Graves, 'a crooked godly maid' of Bishop's Stortford, died in 1635, the local minister reflected that it was 'best for her, who shall be a glorious saint and have a perfect body'.[16] Some even believed that women would be reborn as men,[17]* that black

* The ultimate source for this view may have been the apocryphal Gospel of Thomas (trans. Stevan Davies, 2003), saying no. 114 ('for every female who makes herself male will enter heaven's kingdom'), a pronouncement which has caused much heart-searching among modern commentators. Another key text was Ecclesiastes 7: 14 ('one man among a thousand have I found; but a woman among all those have I not found').

people would become white,[18] and that everyone would be in their early thirties (Christ's age at the time of his death).[19] Many centuries of Christian commentary underpinned these expectations.

The original paradise of Eden had been a garden, but it was usual to imagine heaven as a walled city of magnificent buildings, surrounded by fields of flowers. For the Marian martyr John Bradford, it meant 'mirth without measure, all liberty, all light, all joy, rejoicing, pleasure, health, wealth, riches, glory, power, treasure, honour, triumph, comfort, solace, love, unity, peace, concord, wisdom, virtue, melody, meekness, felicity, beatitude and all that ever can be wished or desired'. He envisaged himself, clad in a white stole, with a palm in his hand, standing before the throne of God.[20] The presence on his list of such goods as wealth, riches, power, and honour suggests that his vision was not exclusively spiritual. The French Jesuit Nicolas Caussin, in a work whose English translation was dedicated to Queen Henrietta Maria, claimed that paradise would bring pleasures comparable, but infinitely superior, to those generated in this life by 'goodly palaces', 'rich hangings', 'exquisite pictures', 'hedges and knots curiously cut', 'alleys and mazes', 'grots and fountains'.[21] John Bunyan imagined a city built of pearls and precious stones, paved with gold, and adorned by orchards, vineyards, and delightful gardens.[22] Richard Baxter stressed the musical joys of heavenly worship: the nearest approximation to it on earth, he thought, was congregational singing.[23]

Each according to his fancy thus portrayed heaven as a place of infinite happiness greatly exceeding the pleasures of this world and more than compensating for its miseries. Fortified by this conviction, people found it possible to welcome death as the gateway to felicity, like Madam Susan Heigham (d. 1695), who, according to her funeral monument, 'departed this life in great transports of joy'.[24]

Yet not everyone was convinced. One eighteenth-century gamekeeper, living in Fernditch Lodge on Cranborne Chase, Dorset, said that he had heard the parson talk about 'a place called Paradise'. 'By the account he gave of it, it seemed to be a desperate pleasant place . . . But when I had considered everything, I made up my mind to believe, and I do now believe, notwithstanding what the parson said, that if there was but a good trout-stream running down Chicken Grove Bottom, Fernditch Lodge would beat it out and out.'[25] Others found the prospect of future bliss intimidating. An Elizabethan preacher promised the inhabitants of Wilton, near Salisbury, that 'to live in heaven together is better than to live in Wilton together'. But an old lady on her sickbed, near Lewes, Sussex, was not so sure; when a well-intentioned neighbour informed her that she would shortly go to heaven and be with God, Jesus Christ, angels, and saints, she answered that 'she had no acquaintance there, she knew nobody there, and therefore she had rather live with her and her other neigh-bours here than to go thither to live amongst strangers'.[26]

Early modern theologians, accordingly, laid increasing emphasis on the idea of heaven as a sociable place where one could catch up with old friends, as well as possibly—for the point was disputed—making new ones.[27] The Puritan Samuel Rogers (echoing Matthew 8: 11 and Luke 13: 28) looked forward to sitting down 'in company with Abraham, Paul, my grandfather [Richard Rogers, the famous Elizabethan preacher] and all other blessed saints'.[28] Richard Baxter envisaged living for ever in the company of Old Testament worthies such as Noah and Moses, and Reformation heroes like Luther and Calvin.[29] The learned Catherine Talbot, in contrast, assumed that the circle of heavenly friendships would be confined to those one had already known on earth: 'the more connections we make here', she wrote in 1749, 'the more friends we shall have to rejoice with here-after in a permanent state of felicity'.[30]

Although some preachers felt that the company of Abraham, Isaac, et al. would more than make up for the absence of wives, children, and 'familiar acquaintance',[31] there was an increasing tendency to hold out to bereaved families the prospect of being reunited in the next world, though with the caution that there would be no marital sex in heaven.[32] The bookseller John Dunton, who had just lost his wife, published in 1698 *An Essay proving we shall know our friends in Heaven*, in which he promised a reunion with loved ones, but warned that, even in heaven, the male soul was grave and taciturn, whereas the female soul 'talks much and cannot forbear twatling upon every thing'.[33] In the eighteenth century, when domesticity was increasingly prized, a great deal of the happiness of heaven was believed to derive from the prospect of reunion with dead spouses, parents, children, and friends. Mary Astell wrote of heaven in 1689:

> For all are Jonathans and Davids here.
> Were there no other happiness than this,
> Vast were the joy, and infinite the bliss.[34]

Elizabeth Rowe's *Friendship in Death* (1728) went into nearly sixty editions.[35] The notion that friendship would continue into the next life was an ancient one, but it seems that it was only in the early modern period that stress was laid on the reunion of the nuclear family. As earthly values changed, so did conceptions of heavenly felicity.

A traditional heavenly pleasure was that of contemplating the agonies of the damned. The miseries of hell were generally agreed to be twofold: first, and worst, eternal separation from the sight of God; second, the pain of the senses. Hell was a place of extreme heat and cold, of stench, howling, and cacophony, of the 'lake which burneth with fire and brimstone' (Revelation 21: 8), of excruciating and unimaginable torment, of 'perfect, absolute and complete misery'. There would be 'screeching and screaming, weeping, wailing, and gnashing of teeth for evermore'.[36] 'All the cruelties in the world', a Dissenting minister told his London congregation in the reign of Charles II, 'cannot possibly make up any horror comparable to the horrors of hell.' On this point he was at one with the Elizabethan Jesuit missionary Robert Parsons, who had devoted a section of his *Christian Directory* to a lurid exploration of this theme, and the Catholic poet Richard Crashaw, who did the same in his *Steps to the Temple* (1646).[37] It is not surprising that, as a boy in the 1660s, John Dunton should have thought of hell as 'a place full of the blackest and the most frightful terrors; as a fiery dungeon, where impenitent sinners should be punished with endless and extreme pain'.[38] The prospect was made worse by the ability of the damned to witness the simultaneous bliss of their friends and relations in heaven;[39] rather like economy-class passengers, huddled in the back of the aeroplane, catching an occasional glimpse behind the curtain of business-class travellers cosseted with hot towels and champagne. Using all means to avoid ending up in hell should be 'our chief employment in this life', thought the Shropshire clergyman and political writer George Lawson.[40]

During the early modern period, this horrific vision of hell was softened by theologians who were increasingly reluctant to accept that God would devise hideous tortures for the beings he had himself created. 'With the despising of purgatory', thought Thomas Starkey in 1536, the people 'began little to regard hell, heaven, or any other felicity hereafter to be had in another life.'[41] In the early years of the Reformation, the 'doom' paintings on the chancel arches of parish churches, depicting the agonies of the damned, were painted over; and there were few visual representations of hell in Protestant England. From the mid-sixteenth century onwards, many sceptics—Anabaptists, Familists,

Antinomians, and other unorthodox religious groups or individuals—rejected the concept of heaven and hell as physical locations, preferring to interpret them allegorically as states of mind, experienced in this world, not the next. 'They say that hell itself is but mere poetry,' lamented Sir John Harington in 1604.[42] There was a long tradition behind Thomas Hobbes's bold assertion in 1651 that what was said in the Bible concerning hellfire was 'spoken metaphorically'.[43]

In the reign of Elizabeth I, Bishop Thomas Bilson had grimly refuted such heresies: 'the fire of hell they will say is metaphorical; they that go thither shall find it no metaphor'.[44] But, from Luther and Calvin onwards, many leading Protestants had inclined to this way of thinking. Even the Puritan authority William Perkins believed that hell's torments were spiritual, not physical.[45] This view was widely expressed by sectarians during the Civil War and Interregnum. Though sternly repudiated by the orthodox, it became widespread in the later seventeenth century among latitudinarian divines and an increasingly deistical aristocracy, some of whom were known to hold that 'men perish entirely at death . . . without any future restoration or renovation of things'. An Independent minister lamented in 1675 that 'many erroneous and deluded persons . . . stoutly and daily assert that there is no hell but what men feel in their own consciences'.[46]

Some religious writers envisaged the ultimate salvation of all mankind, holding the view attributed to the third-century theologian Origen, that the damned would eventually join the others after they had served their time.[47] Others believed that they would endure torment for a finite period and then be eliminated.[48] Yet others maintained, with Hobbes and the Socinians, that the souls of the damned would sleep until the day of judgement, when they would be annihilated. In one way or another, hell was beginning to lose its terrors.[49] When James Boswell visited the great jurist Lord Kames in 1782, he remarked that the doctrine of the eternity of hell's torments did harm. 'No,' said Kames, 'nobody believes it.'[50]

Yet many Protestants were cast into deep despair at the thought that they were damned. In the early seventeenth century, the astrological doctor Richard Napier, practising in north Buckinghamshire, had over ninety patients who came to him because they doubted their prospects of salvation.[51] The last wills of the early modern period, however, do not give the impression of men and women terrified by the prospect of hellfire. Typically, they died, bequeathing their souls to Almighty God, trusting that, through the death and passion of Christ, they would have free pardon and remission of their sins, and leaving their bodies to be buried, as the funeral service had it, 'in sure and certain hope of the resurrection to eternal life'. Formulaic though these preambles were, their tone was optimistic, sometimes cautiously so, sometimes confidently; though few perhaps as confidently as Thomas Merbury, a student at Christ's College, Cambridge, who boldly declared in his will of 1571 that 'I feel inwardly in myself and in my conscience that...I am predestinate to eternal life' (pl. 15).[52] Inscriptions on funeral monuments struck a similar note, citing the virtues of the deceased as implicit proof of their likely salvation.[53] Strict Protestant doctrine denied the efficacy of good works, but, as the preachers frequently lamented, it was a widespread view among ordinary people that those who led decent, honest lives could count on being saved. 'Our common people', thought William Perkins, 'bolster themselves in their blind ways by a presumption that God is all of mercy, and that if they do their true intent, serve God, say their prayers, deal justly, and do as they would be done unto, they shall certainly be saved.' The 'vulgar religion', or 'country divinity', was one of works, not faith. 'Rustic Pelagianism' it has been memorably called.[54]

Near-impossible though it is to generalize about such matters, the impression yielded by the surviving evidence is that intense fear of hellfire was never more than a minority sentiment, found particularly among those who came under Puritan or Dissenting influence, and not always even there.[55] On the other hand, scepticism, implicit or explicit, about the literal reality of a future life, whether in heaven or in hell, was more widely dispersed than the clergy would have liked.[56] The resurrection of the body had never been an easy doctrine to justify to an agricultural population who knew only too well what happened to corpses, whether of men or animals; while, at a high intellectual level, the doctrine of the immortality of the soul had been challenged by philosophers from Aristotle onwards, and was frequently disputed in Renaissance Europe.[57] Preachers regularly denounced the 'atheists' who denied the resurrection of the body and mocked the notion of hell as a bugbear devised to frighten children.[58] A persistent theme in Elizabethan and Jacobean drama was the dread of personal annihilation after death, the fear that life might indeed be a tale told by an idiot, signifying nothing.[59] 'We die like beasts, and when we are gone there is no more remembrance of us.' This sentiment, attributed to Sir Walter Ralegh and his intellectual friends in 1594, was also articulated by some lower-class sceptics. In the later seventeenth century, it became commonplace among libertine freethinkers. The fourth Lord North (who died in 1677) declared that the number of his contemporaries who believed in life after death was very small, 'especially among the vulgar'.[60] Thomas Gostelow, an Oxfordshire gentleman who died in 1702, was a regular churchgoer, but privately expressed his disbelief in a future state; asked why he was so outwardly religious, he explained that 'he did it merely in compliance with custom and to look well in the eyes of the world'.[61]

Such scepticism might have been more audibly expressed had it not been for the belief of the upper classes that it was politically essential to uphold the doctrine of eternal rewards and punishments, as the only way of keeping the common people in good order and obedience. For if there was anything on which clergy and freethinkers agreed, it was that the prospect of punishment in the next world was a more effective sanction for law-abiding behaviour than anything the law could offer. Belief in heaven and hell, they felt, was a political necessity; and any doubts, however well founded, should be kept well away from the ears of the vulgar. When, in 1567, Archbishop Parker refused to dispense Merton College, Oxford, from its statutory obligation to have at least three chaplains, he gave as his reason that, without preachers to maintain religion, subjects would not obey the Queen, nor tenants pay their rents.[62] Neither the Duke of Newcastle, nor his bluestocking wife, Margaret, seems to have believed in an afterlife, but that did not stop the Duke from warning the future Charles II that, 'were there no heaven or hell, you shall see the disadvantage for your government'.[63] Witnesses giving evidence in the courts were frequently reminded of the punishment in the next world for perjury; and the testimony of those deemed to be lacking a 'due sense of religion and a future state' was thought unacceptable.[64] When in the later seventeenth century, the clergyman Thomas Burnet published a book denying the eternal punishment of the wicked, he prudently wrote it in Latin and concluded with a warning to his clerical readers to continue to preach the orthodox view because of its social utility.[65]

It is impossible to say how deeply embedded in early modern England was faith in the reality of an afterlife. Sir Thomas Browne wryly remarked that 'were the happiness of the next world as closely apprehended as the felicity of this, it were a martyrdom to live'; and one of the reasons given by Hobbes for the general lack of concern about the fate of those who were supposedly suffering in hell was that the teachers of such doctrines did not themselves live as if they believed them.[66] Had there been no underlying doubts about the existence of an afterlife, much less would have been said by contemporaries about the importance of being remembered in this world. For posthumous remembrance was an alternative to heaven as a way of overcoming mortality. The body might decay, but reputation was the immortal part.

POSTHUMOUS FAME

Long ago, the great historian Jacob Burckhardt described the obsessive preoccupation of the political and intellectual elite of Renaissance Italy with the idea of posthumous fame. In panegyrics and biographies, in statues and memorials, in pilgrimages to the birthplaces and tombs of famous men, contemporaries accepted and encouraged the overwhelming desire of the ambitious to be favourably remembered by posterity.[1] This was a self-conscious imitation of the conventions of classical antiquity. Lacking a developed conception of the afterlife, the Greeks, and even more the Romans, had laid heavy stress on the importance of posthumous fame as the essential reward and ultimate fulfilment of an honourable and successful life. From Homer to Cicero, 'imperishable fame' was regarded as a proper human aspiration and an indispensable incentive for deeds of heroism or the composition of great works of literature. As the eighteenth-century hymn-writer Isaac Watts wrote of the ancients, 'they were animated with the expectation of fame after death: immortal memory and renown were the rewards of what they called heroic actions'.[2] This classical ideal was expressed by Petrarch in the fourteenth century and became a conspicuous feature of European Renaissance culture. For rulers, warriors, artists, writers, and scholars, the search for fame, both in their own lifetime and after their death, became the supreme objective.

Of course, Burckhardt exaggerated the novelty of this obsession with posthumous renown. It had been shared by Anglo-Norman writers in the twelfth century, and it was integral to the ethos of medieval chivalry, which encouraged the military classes to perform dashing exploits on the battlefield in the hope of posthumous glory. As Sir John Clanvowe wrote around 1390, men made books and songs about the deeds of great conquerors: for it was 'a thing that worldly men desire greatly that their fame might last long after them here upon earth'. 'The thirst for honour and glory proper to the men of the Renaissance', thought the great Dutch historian Johan Huizinga, was 'essentially the same as the chivalrous ambition of earlier times.'[3]

Yet Burckhardt was certainly right to suggest that this chivalric desire for fame was intensified by the late medieval adoption of classical values. Among the upper classes of sixteenth-century England, the preoccupation with posthumous fame was ubiquitous. In *The Governour* (1531), the diplomat Sir Thomas Elyot stressed the importance of gaining 'honour and perpetual memory' for one's deeds.[4] Petrarch's *Trionfi*, which included the triumph of Fame over Death, was translated into English in 1555.[5] The playwright John Pikering wrote in 1567:

> Above each thing, keep well thy fame, what ever that thou lose,
> For fame, once gone, thy memory with fame away it goes;
> And it once lost, thou shalt in sooth accounted like to be
> A drop of rain that falleth in the bosom of the sea.[6]

It was a source of happiness, thought the seventeenth-century antiquarian Sir William Dugdale, to be able to leave behind 'an honourable fame' which would live in the memory of men when our bodies had turned to dust. For the Caroline dramatist John Ford, 'an immortality of a virtuous and everlasting name' was life's greatest reward.[7]

Underlying this search for fame was what a contemporary called 'a secret desire of immortality', a deep-seated wish to avoid that 'bestial oblivion' which was the fate of all animals. To die and be forgotten was 'the most abhorred thing of nature', whereas posthumous fame was 'immortalizing', 'enduring', 'deathless', and 'eternal'.[8] As the lawyer Richard Crompton put it in 1599, fame was everlasting, 'which since our lives are short and momentary, we must by this means make perpetual'. For

> such as not regard to leave some deed of fame
> When they are dead, shall lie, without regard or name
> And soon shall be forgot, as they had never been.[9]

Those who achieved military glory or literary distinction could laugh at death, because their name would be immortal. Those with riches could build monuments to propagate their posthumous fame. 'For that is the secret end at which all mortals aim, however they dissemble the matter.'[10]

In the literary culture of early modern England it was commonplace to regard posthumous remembrance as the ultimate fulfilment of human life. No individual's felicity was complete unless he left a good name to be cherished by posterity. The fact that one would not be there to hear one's praises sung by posterity did not make the prospect any less enticing. For, as Thomas Hobbes observed, 'men have a present delight therein, from the foresight of it, and of the benefit that may redound thereby to their posterity: which though they now see not, yet they imagine'.[11] Moreover, it was important to preserve the fame of outstanding men in order to 'stir up the spirits of the younger sort to the imitation of their virtue'.[12] The example of the dead was an indispensable model to the living.

Wherever we look among the social elite of early modern England, we find that fame was the spur, the acknowledged incentive to perform deeds of merit. Who, but for such a reward, would ever scorn delights and live laborious days?

As Fulke Greville asked,

> what governor would spend his days,
> In envious travail, for the public good?
> Who would in books, search after dead men's ways?
> Or in the war, what soldier lose his blood?
> Liv'd not this fame in clouds, kept as a crown;
> Both for the sword, the sceptre, and the gown.[13]

Urging Queen Elizabeth to found an academy for nobles, Sir Humphrey Gilbert declared that such an action would so spread her fame 'that Your Majesty, being dead, shall make your sepulchre for ever in the mouths of the living'. (A century later Charles II would similarly be told that his support for the Royal Society would render his fame immortal.*)[14] Gilbert himself, like Sir Francis Drake, Sir Richard Grenville, and so many other Elizabethan adventurers, deliberately risked his life for the sake of posthumous glory, the primary motive for courage on the battlefield.[15] The second Earl of Essex thought a contemporary 'did affect nothing in the world so much as fame'.[16] 'Our ambition after death', agreed John Smith, the colonizer of Virginia, was 'to have an honourable memory of our life.'[17]

The importance of leaving behind a good name was repeatedly stressed in the advice literature of the time.[18] It was the desire of 'every generous mind', thought the herald Randle Holme, 'to eternize the memory of his own virtues'. The lust for posthumous renown was the symptom of a 'generous' spirit, betokening indifference to inferior concerns like riches and sensual comfort.[19] 'Without the love of

---

* The frontispiece to Thomas Sprat, *The History of the Royal-Society of London* (1667), depicts Fame crowning Charles II as a reward for his patronage.

ABEL REDEVIVUS
or
The dead yet speaking
By T. Fuller *and other*
Eminent Divines.

Mors vltima linea rerum eſt

Nunc levior cippus non imprimit oſsa!
laudat poſteritas, nunc non é manibus illis
Nunc non é tumulo fortunaque favilla
Naſcuntur viola! Perſ. Sat. 1. 37

Figure 7.1 Those who wrote books could hope to live beyond the grave.

fame,' Sir Joshua Reynolds told his artistic pupils, 'you can never do anything excellent.' His contemporary Dr William Hunter urged the artists of the newly founded Royal Academy to rival those of Greece and Rome. The Olympic race was on, he declared, and the prize nothing less than 'immortality'.[20]

In the world of letters, innumerable writers, from John Skelton in the sixteenth century to Edward Gibbon in the eighteenth, frankly admitted that fame was their primary objective, just as it had been for their classical predecessors.[21] 'Lasting fame and perpetuity of praise', wrote John Milton, was 'the reward of those whose published labours advance the good of mankind.'[22] In the mid-seventeenth century, Sir John Suckling's *Fragmenta Aurea* (1646) was published by a friend 'to perpetuate his memory'. The poems of Herrick, Waller, Carew, and Cartwright were all put out posthumously for similar reasons.[23] 'Some say men write books,' noted Margaret Cavendish, 'not so much to benefit the world, as out of love to fame, thinking to gain them honour of reputation.' Richard Baxter denounced the pride of 'divines and learned men in all professions who make their writings but a means to perpetuate their own names to posterity'.[24] But Milton thought that the desire for immortal fame was 'seated in the breast of every true scholar'.[25] The learned knew that if they did not publish, their learning would perish with them. In the eighteenth century, David Hume confessed that 'love of literary fame' was his ruling passion; while Adam Smith was accused of 'excessive solicitude... about his post-humous reputation'.[26] As a young man, the great oriental scholar Sir William Jones confided to a friend that his supreme objective was 'glory... and I will pursue it through fire and water, by day and night'.[27] Poets came to attach increasing importance to the afterlife of their writings. Oliver Goldsmith satirized the institution of literary reviewing as a 'fame machine'. But the test of time mattered more than a work's immediate reception; for the Romantics, contemporary neglect was almost a sine qua non for proof of genius.[28]

It was not only literary and artistic people who cared what posterity might say about them. Michael Joseph, the blacksmith who led the Cornish rebellion of 1497, admitted that he and his fellow rebel John Flamank had become involved in the rising so as to 'have a name perpetual and a fame permanent and immortal'; 'whereby', commented the chronicler,

ye may perceive vain glory doth inflame
As well the meaner sort as men of greater name.[29]

When Nicholas Udall was hired by the government in 1549 to reply to the West Country rebels who had risen in protest against the imposition of the new Prayer Book, he rather touchingly urged the insurgents to ask themselves whether they really wanted the chroniclers in a hundred years' time to say that 'a certain portion of the English people called Devonshire men and Cornishmen [had] died for Popery', which, by that time, would be 'throughout the Christian world abhorred and detested'.[30] Richard Haydock, a Jacobean physician and Fellow of New College, Oxford, pretended to be able to preach sermons in his sleep, because 'he apprehended himself as a buried man in the University, being of low condition, and if something eminent and remarkable did not spring from him to give life to his reputation, he should never appear anybody, which made him attempt this novelty to be taken notice of'.[31] In 1606 a gang of law students attacked a London brothel and broke all its windows, after resolving 'to do something that they may be spoken of when they were dead'.[32] In Twickenham, Middlesex, in the early seventeenth century, a group of women rioters met in an alehouse, a year to the day after their protest, boasting of their 'valiant' deed, worthy to be remembered 'in the chronicles', and agreeing to hold an annual feast for 'remembrance' sake.[33]

Many of the central social practices of the early modern period, from publishing books to commissioning portraits, become more intelligible when they are seen as the product of this concern with posthumous reputation. Since time immemorial, conspicuous building had been a particularly favoured method of securing the attention of posterity. In the seventeenth century, a great aristocratic house was not just the expression of a distinctive style of life; it was a monument to the achievement of those who had ordered and paid for it.[34] Sir Balthazar Gerbier, author of *Counsel and Advice to all Builders* (1663), pointed out that well-built structures 'like a stock of children continue the name and memory of the owner'.[35] 'When great men erect a stately building,' wrote a divine in 1675, 'they cause their own picture to be hung upon it, that spectators may know who was the chief founder of it.'[36] Hence the practice of decorating great houses with initials, mottoes, and heraldic devices. In the seventeenth century, architects as well as owners were bidding for posthumous fame. Sir Christopher Wren was determined to create enduring monuments; building, he thought, 'ought to have the attribute of eternal'.[37]

Among the social elite, the horror of oblivion was an obsessive preoccupation; so much so as to make one doubt whether the Christian doctrine of the afterlife can have been a living reality for those to whom posthumous fame was so overriding an objective. A modern historian has well remarked that 'the true religion of the man of honour lay in the immortality which honourable deeds conferred, their memory being preserved and celebrated in the community to which he belonged';[38] and it is hard not to feel that the highest value of these seekers after posthumous fame was essentially pagan. Confident believers in the reality of heaven and hell might have been expected to regard their posthumous reputation on earth as a matter of little importance, for the Christian Church had always taught that it was vainglorious to prefer worldly renown to the rewards of heaven. To Sir Thomas Browne, it was 'a contradiction to our beliefs' for men to pray earnestly for the coming of Christ, while simultaneously attempting to prolong their earthly memory by monuments: 'the sufficiency of Christian immortality frustrates all earthly glory, and the quality of either state after death makes a folly of posthumous memory'.[39] In 1655 Margaret Cavendish explicitly attributed the lust for fame to 'doubt of an after being': for her, hell was oblivion, whereas 'after-memory, which is fame' was 'the heaven wherein worthy and honourable men and actions are glorified and live to all eternity'.[40] In the eighteenth century, it was unbelievers, like the philosopher David Hume and the historian Edward Gibbon, who were most concerned with literary fame. There was a close association between religious scepticism and the attempts of the Hanoverian aristocracy to preserve their memory by constructing great mausoleums, set in parks or on hillsides, deliberately detached from any religious context.[41]

Yet just as in the Middle Ages chivalric heroes had sought both honour in this world and joy in paradise, so in post-Reformation England a keen interest in lasting earthly renown could be perfectly compatible with the hope of salvation. 'Thou both here and there immortal art,' wrote Edmund Spenser, addressing the spirit of the dead Sir Philip Sidney.[42] Contemporaries reconciled faith in the Christian afterlife with the classical desire for earthly reputation by suggesting that the virtuous deserved a double reward: in this world and the next. As the herald William Wyrley explained in 1592, 'their souls shall be rewarded with the mercies of God, [and] . . . their doings shall be had in a reverent remembrance with the reports of all good men that shall speak of them'.[43] A Jacobean funeral monument in Witney church declared that Edward Bowman bequeathed his soul to heaven, his body to the earth, and his good name to his posterity.[44]

There was biblical authority for the view that it was a duty to cherish the memory of the righteous and that their names should live for ever.[45] The young John Milton even suggested that one of the pleasures of heaven would be that its residents could look down on the earth and see how famous they had become.[46]

In the later Middle Ages, the memory of the deceased had been preserved through the huge ecclesiastical apparatus of intercession for dead souls. Monasteries, chantries, colleges, almshouses, guilds, fraternities, and parish congregations were all involved in maintaining votive lights, prayers, and masses for the dead. The rich endowed chantry priests to celebrate masses for themselves and their close relatives, either for a term of years or, more optimistically, in perpetuity. They might also provide for almsmen whose primary function was to remember their benefactor in their prayers. The good widow safeguarded her husband's memory by ensuring that a mass was celebrated for him thirty days after his death (his 'month's mind') and annually on his anniversary (his 'year's mind' or 'obit'). 'Trentals' (a set of thirty requiem masses) were a common form of intercession.[47]

The overt purpose of this ceaseless prayer was to speed the dead person's passage through the pains of purgatory, but an equally important function was to perpetuate his memory on earth. Testators left money and other gifts to churches, religious orders, and guilds, in return for which their names were written down in bead rolls and obituary books, recited a month after their death and 'remembered for ever'; in Durham Cathedral the benefactors' book was kept on the high altar and names were read out during services.[48] In 1616 John Moore, a Gloucestershire octogenarian, remembered how, when he was a boy, he and his schoolfellows used to help their schoolmaster, who was also the chantry priest, to say his masses, 'and when they came to the *Memento* then they... did take to their master a libel or paper wherein was the names of such dead persons set down as their friends or kindred desired there should be prayed for and remembered in the said masses, for every [one] of which named they gave a penny'. He remembered it because occasionally the penny was passed on to the boys themselves.[49] This solemn, liturgical naming of the dead was a crucial means of preserving their memory. The confraternity, of which there were some thirty thousand in late medieval England, has been justly described as 'a lay community that endeavoured to provide means of assurance to the individual that his memory would not be obliterated as his body decayed'.[50]

The impact of Protestantism upon this elaborate system of remembrance was wholly destructive. For by rejecting the very notion of Purgatory, the Reformers denied that the intercessions of the living could have any influence on the welfare of the deceased. Prayers for the dead lingered on and were condoned, or even encouraged, by some Anglican churchmen who maintained that their utility did not depend upon a belief in the existence of purgatory.[51] At All Souls College, Oxford, founded in 1437 to pray for the souls of the faithful departed, these prayers continued after the Reformation to be required by the college statutes, a fact which gave the Catholic James II some wry pleasure when he visited Oxford in 1687.[52]* In parochial churches after 1598, the week's entries in the parish register (including burials) were supposed to be read out aloud each Sunday.[53] In its essentials, however, the whole edifice of intercessionary prayer, with its bead rolls, obits, and intercessory masses, was completely dismantled in the mid-sixteenth century, with the dissolution, first of the monasteries, then of the remaining chantries.

Papists deplored this cataclysmic breach with the past. In his *The Supplycacyon of Soulys* (1529), Sir Thomas More depicted the dead souls calling piteously on their friends and relations for remembrance; while Cardinal William Allen lamented in 1565 that there was 'now no blessing of man's memory at all'.[54] Writing at the beginning of the nineteenth century, the philosopher William Godwin looked back on the Reformation era as 'a period, in which a plot was laid to abolish the memory of things that had been, and to begin the affairs of the human species afresh'. A modern Catholic historian has called the change 'an act of oblivion, a casting out of the dead from the community of the living into a collective anonymity'.[55]

But Protestants had other ways of remembering the dead. The first was to give them an appropriate funeral. Since the fate of the deceased was now believed to be beyond human reach, funeral rites might have been thought redundant. That was the view taken by some sixteenth- and seventeenth-century separatists; and the Presbyterian Directory for Public Worship in 1645 prescribed that the dead should be buried 'without any ceremony' (though permitting 'civil respects or differences at the burial, suitable to the rank and condition of the party deceased').[56] But even if the ritual could do nothing for the spiritual fate of the dead, it was important for their earthly reputation. Funerals had a strong memorial element, with their convivial

---

* The provision was removed in 1857.

'drinkings', their distribution of gloves, scarves, and mourning rings to be worn in remembrance, and their doles to the poor, even though the recipients were no longer asked to pray for the soul of the deceased.[57] Churches were decorated with rosemary, bays, and other evergreens, 'that the remembrance of the present solemnity might not die presently, but be kept in mind for many years'.[58] Every detail of the ceremony, from the number of mourners to the place and method of burial, proclaimed the status of the deceased and of the surviving family. Burial inside the church was more honourable than burial outside; and burial in the chancel more honourable than in the aisles or nave: in 1675 it was cited as proof of the minister Thomas Hall's 'deep humility' that he had ordered that his body should be buried 'in the churchyard among the meanest of his neighbours'.[59] Some individuals sought to perpetuate their memory by asking to be buried in the church at the place where they had customarily sat.[60]

The funeral was the first stage in the manufacture of a posthumous reputation. It set a seal on a life and summed it up for posterity. Even those contemporaries who disliked the 'pomp and excess' of ostentatious burials respected the universal wish to be remembered. Lord Herbert of Cherbury died in 1648, prescribing that he should be buried at midnight, 'without pomp or... shew of mourning', but 'desiring my friends nevertheless to love my memory'.[61]

Funeral sermons, the Reformers complained, were 'put in place of trentals'; and it is true that their commemorative function was very similar to that of the masses they superseded. Their origin can be traced back to the funeral *laudationes* of classical times.[62] Many Protestants objected that these sermons were preached only for those who could afford to pay, and that they were particularly inappropriate when the deceased had not been virtuous.[63] Some testators explicitly asked not to have one; and in Scotland in 1561 the Reformers attempted to ban them altogether.[64]*

Nevertheless, it was widely felt that it was right to commemorate the dead and to celebrate their memory. In the seventeenth century, elegies in praise of the deceased were sometimes attached to the hearse during the procession to the grave and subsequently published in a memorial volume.[65] The sermon or 'speech' at the grave was a standard accompaniment of the burial of the well-to-do. Typically, it

---

* In the Westminster Assembly, set up in 1643 to reform the Church, the Scots and English representatives differed on the matter; *The Whole Works of the Rev. John Lightfoot*, ed. John Rogers Pitman (1822–5), xiii. 340.

addressed a general religious theme and touched only briefly upon the life and character of the dead person, whose virtues were expounded for their exemplary value. To that extent, the sermon was about types rather than individuals; and the strictly memorial element was not conspicuous. By the later seventeenth century, however, it had become customary to introduce more personal details. The obituary, in the modern sense of a brief biographical assessment, published in a newspaper immediately after a person's death, made its first appearance in the later seventeenth and early eighteenth centuries. The antiquary John Le Neve published several annual volumes of the lives and characters of eminent persons who died in the last years of Queen Anne. But only with the appearance of the *Gentleman's Magazine* in 1731 did the obituary establish itself as a regular feature.[66] Thereafter it gradually came to be accepted as an indispensable institution.

Funerals were soon over and obituaries quickly forgotten. A 'fair monument', however, was a more enduring way of making the deceased 'memorable to posterities'.[67] All sublunary things were transitory, remarked a Jacobean antiquary, but a man could 'perpetuate the reverend memory of his honourable parents, ancestors, and much beloved friends departed, by erecting unto them ... lively counterfeiting resemblances, effigies, pyramids, epitaphs, and monuments'.[68] Early modern England, accordingly, witnessed the proliferation of funeral monuments, first in the church, then in the churchyard.[69] In the later Middle Ages, such monuments had functioned as a memento mori, proclaiming the Christian triumph over death and reminding spectators of the fate that awaited them. They were essentially prospective, looking forward to purgatory and heaven for their ultimate meaning. They identified the deceased and invited onlookers to pray for his soul. Yet in western Europe since the twelfth century, tombs had also begun to perform a retrospective function by recalling details of individuals' lives so that their memory might be preserved and their virtues imitated. This was a reversion to the practice of classical antiquity.[70] In fourteenth- and fifteenth-century England, the gentry, clergy, and merchant classes made increasing use of monumental brasses, sculpted effigies, incised slabs, and stained-glass windows. Inscriptions became longer and the element of personal commemoration was increasingly marked. Typical of this trend was the London grocer who in 1460 specified the details of the stone to be placed over his grave 'to have me in special memory'.[71]

After the Reformation, funeral monuments no longer sought prayers for the soul of the deceased. Their purpose now was not intercession but commemoration, mixed with moral instruction.

Tombs, wall monuments, and kneeling or recumbent effigies evoked the virtues of the dead person and held them out as an example to the living. They usually preached a religious message, proclaiming the eventual prospect of a joyful resurrection, but they also sought to confer on the deceased a form of secular immortality. They looked to earth as much as to heaven for their rationale. By such images, wrote Bishop Stephen Gardiner, the nobility 'set forth and spread abroad, to be read of all people, their lineage and parentage, with remembrance of their state and acts'.[72]

The desire for posthumous fame was thus a dominant influence on the funerary art of the early modern period.[73] The guiding hope was embodied in the motto inscribed on the tomb of Dr John Caius in the chapel of his Cambridge college chapel, and much used thereafter: *Vivit post funera virtus* ('virtue survives the grave'). In 1560 a royal proclamation declared that church monuments were there 'to show a memory to the posterity of the persons there buried'; their destruction by iconoclasts was reprehensible because it led to 'the extinguishing of the honourable and good memory of sundry virtuous and noble persons deceased'.[74]

Like the chantries before them, such memorials were usually erected only for the aristocracy and gentry. They were a form of social assertion, testifying to the importance both of the dead and also of their surviving descendants. They reflected intensifying social mobility and social competition. With their sometimes extensive load of genealogical and biographical information, and their bold claims (not always justified) to titles, property, and status, church monuments could become important documentary evidence, to be cited in disputes about inheritance and descent. In an early fifteenth-century suit before the Court of Chivalry, the commissioners journeyed to inspect a tomb in a Norfolk village church in order to resolve the matter; and in 1653 one Sussex gentleman specifically provided for a monument as a 'memorial to be left to my posterity for the better deciding of any controversies that in time hereafter may happen amongst them'.[75]*

---

* This preoccupation could lead to some fine pieces of genealogical pedantry. A monument erected in Astwood church, Buckinghamshire, to Samuel Cranmer declared that: 'The antiquity of this family is to be found in Parker *De Antiq. Eccles. Britan:* and in Goodmans [*recte* Godwins] *De Praesul. Angl. &c.* And altho' Saunders *De Schism: Angl.* does out of his malice endeavour to blemish the family, yet Parsons himself in his *Three Conventions* [*recte Conversions*] does not deny the antiquity thereof'; John Le Neve, *Monumenta Anglicana...since the year 1600, to the end of the year 1649* (1719), 193–4.

With the collapse of the old Catholic system of intercession, the primary responsibility for ensuring that people would be remembered was transferred to funeral monuments; and they multiplied accordingly. During the Elizabethan and Jacobean period, aristocratic expenditure on these memorials reached its peak.[76] Intrusive effigies of the dead crowded the churches and joined the living in worship in chancel and aisle.[77] It has been estimated that, between 1530 and 1660, about five thousand carved stone monuments, often carrying sculpted images of individuals, couples, or whole families, were set up in churches; in addition, there were innumerable cheaper panels of engraved stone, brass, or painted wood.[78] In the later seventeenth and eighteenth centuries, funeral sculpture grew ever more ambitious, with portrait medallions, pictorial reliefs, and dramatic figural groupings. A huge volume of human energy and material resources was devoted to this task of commemoration.

It is tempting to regard this trend as indicative of a weakening confidence in the Christian promise of life after death.[79] The angel with a trumpet who figures so frequently on these monuments may possibly have been blowing the bugle of the Resurrection, but is more likely to have been sounding the trumpet of earthly Fame triumphing over Death. Certainly, the prospect of being posthumously remembered was central to the whole project. 'Every man ... desires a perpetuity after death, by these monuments,' wrote the antiquary John Weever. Robert Burton, the anatomist of melancholy, agreed: 'Tombs and monuments ... epitaphs, elegies, inscriptions, pyramids, obelisks, statues, images, pictures, histories, poems, annals, feasts, anniversaries ... they will ... omit no good office that may tend to the preservation of their names, honours, and eternal memory.'[80]

So important were these memorials that many individuals took steps during their lifetime to ensure that they would be adequately commemorated. Just as the Roman emperors erected their own tombs, so, in the later Middle Ages, the well-to-do founded chantries in their own lifetime and specified the sort of memorial they wanted. Their early modern successors displayed no false modesty about designing their own tombs, composing their epitaphs, and leaving money for the periodic repainting of their monuments. They knew that their heirs and executors were not to be relied on; and they believed that to prepare for their own decease was a pious activity, showing a proper sense of human transience.[81] It was in this spirit that Robert Holt, a Suffolk minister, noted in his will of 1613 that his tombstone was in his 'little barn', where he had kept it to 'put me in mind of my mortality'.[82]

Sometimes, people felt it necessary to apologize for erecting their own monument, explaining that they wished to save their descendants trouble and expense or, alternatively, that they wanted to be certain that their memorials would not be unduly pretentious. Archbishop Matthew Parker prepared his own tomb of black marble, so that, while he lived, it would remind him of his mortal condition, and, when he died, inform his posterity of the high place he had occupied; he professed that he did not deserve the eulogistic epitaph composed for it, but regarded it as an incentive to aspire to the virtues it attributed to him.[83] This practice was amiably satirized by the poet Matthew Prior in 1714:

> As doctors give physic by way of prevention,
>   Matt alive and in health of his tomb-stone took care;
> For delays are unsafe, and his pious intention
>   May haply be never fulfill'd by his heir.
>
> Then take Matt's word for it, the sculptor is paid,
>   That the figure is fine pray believe your own eye,
> Yet credit but lightly what more may be said,
>   For we flatter our selves and teach marble to lie.[84]

It has been estimated that, in early modern times, more than 30 per cent of monuments were erected in their subject's lifetime.[85] These essays in self-commemoration were unambiguous bids to be remembered, deliberate attempts to shape and control a posthumous image; though not everyone went so far as Reynold Peckham, a Kentish gentleman and apparently a lifelong bachelor, who in 1523 instructed his executors to mark his grave with a brass depicting a man, a woman, and children.[86]

It may have been the newly arrived and socially less secure who were most anxious to erect tombs which would establish their family's reputation. Richard Boyle, the parvenu first Earl of Cork, had no fewer than four tombs in different places, whereas half the Elizabethan and Jacobean nobility left no monuments at all.[87] In the eighteenth century, few imposing monuments were erected without some further purpose beyond that of mere commemoration: they were intended to fulfil an obligation perhaps or to acknowledge a debt; to advance the prestige of a family; to raise the status of a profession; or to promote a political cause.[88]

In keeping with the doctrine that only exemplary virtue entitled people to be remembered, the inscriptions on funeral monuments tended to commend individuals for their conformity to the models of behaviour appropriate to their social position and for their 'conscientious discharge of the duties respective incumbent upon them', as a mid-eighteenth-century memorial to a Gloucestershire couple put it.[89] Typically, men were praised for their public service, women for their modesty, piety, and charity. A monument at Buckland, Berkshire, to Sir John Yate and his family declared in 1648 that

In this black marble, that each sex may find
White and fair precedents to guide the mind.
   Men, Women, know, remember.
The Baronet was particularly honoured for moral, economical,
   prudential merit.
The Lady was reverenced for sanctimonious zeal, humble and
   constant patience, abundant charity, and admirable justice.
Their daughter Elizabeth ... [was] admired for devout, chaste,
   modest and discreet demeanour, and fervent charity.
   Reader, depart, imitate.[90]

Such didactic epitaphs ('sepulchral lies', Alexander Pope called them[91]) are more revealing of contemporary moral and social attitudes than they are of the persons commemorated. Thus, of William and Anne Bowyer, who died in 1602 and 1603 respectively, a brass plate in Biddulph, Staffordshire, declared that they left 'a commendable memory of their religious zeal, plenteous hospitality, love and kindness to their friends and neighbours, favourable using of their tenants, charitable to the poor, just and christian dealing with all men, care and providence of their children and posterity; and the advancement and augmentation of their house and patrimony'.[92] A century later, the references to hospitality and the advancement of the lineage would probably have been replaced by allusions to the social virtues of civility and affability.

The individuality of the deceased, as opposed to their social status and exemplary qualities, was slower to be evoked. In the later Middle Ages, it was usually thought sufficient to represent the dead generically, by 'the image of a knight', or 'the image of a lady', or, as in the case of a Bedfordshire testator in 1528, 'with one image of a man, and two images of a woman, [and] three children'.[93] But in the fifteenth century, it became increasingly common for testators to ask that their tombs should carry their arms and their 'picture' or 'portraiture'.[94] Their concern was more with the proper representation of their dress and status rather than their physiognomy. But by the later sixteenth century, purely generic effigies were beginning to give way to something more individual.

In the later Stuart period, monuments were less likely to be erected in their subjects' lifetime (though the practice continued well into the eighteenth century). As the memorial came increasingly to be left to the initiative of the survivors, the expression of loss and bereavement became more marked. The virtues of the dead were still proclaimed: as late as 1791, it was urged that 'the chief design of an epitaph is to record and commend the virtues of the person on whose tombstone it is written, and to excite the reader to imitate them'.[95] But it was, increasingly, as the parents, spouses, and children of the living that the deceased were commemorated. 'He lives in their loves that yet surviving be,' declared the monument to Nathaniel Still, who died in 1627. By the eighteenth century, the display of grief on sculptural monuments had become more common. People had always lamented personal loss, but it was something new to pay more attention to the intimate distress of loved ones than to the spiritual fate of the deceased, and to regard the survivors' grief as the most authentic testimony to the enduring importance of the dead.[96]

Typically, it was only the nobility, gentry, and professional people whose tombs carried elaborate epitaphs. The great bulk of seventeenth- and eighteenth-century memorials, whether in the church or churchyard, confined themselves to stating the deceased's name, age, and date of death, with at most a few details of parentage and marriage. Their meaning was personal to the bereaved. The grave was increasingly thought of as something belonging to the deceased's family, a place for weekend visits and remembrance. Roger Lowe, an apprentice to a Lancashire mercer, recorded a visit to his parents' grave in 1663. Four years later, he was there again, with his sister: 'we ... stayed awhile, and both wept'.[97] This was not the fame sought by the Elizabethan adventurers, but an altogether more personal form of remembrance.

Funeral monuments were not the only way in which the memory of the dead was preserved. The art of painting, as a writer pointed out in 1598, was also 'a kind of preservative against death and mortality: by a perpetual preserving of their shapes, whose substances physic could not prolong'.[98] Even the fiercest Protestant iconoclast allowed representations of the human figure for remembrance's sake.[99] Through painted portraits, the faces of the dead could continue to live. That was why so many likenesses were made in the year of the subject's death or very shortly afterwards.[100] It was good, thought the Elizabethan musician Thomas Whythorne, 'for those that are able, to have their counterfeits or pictures...to leave with their friends, especially with their children...who, when they do come to years of discretion, though their fathers be dead, yet may they see what manner of favour they had; and also put in mind that, if they left a good report of their virtues behind them, they may embrace and follow the same'.[101] Long galleries, libraries, and private studies were decorated with the likenesses of scholars, churchmen, and public figures, whose virtues each generation was urged to remember and to emulate. One authority claimed that the arts of painting and sculpture had been invented 'for no other reason but to record and perpetuate the effigies of famous men'.[102]

Between the sixteenth and late eighteenth centuries, the volume of portrait painting in England expanded enormously, as family pictures became a normal part of the furnishings of any large house. Often they included imaginary representations of ancestors, commissioned in order to buttress the pretensions of the lineage. In addition to the sculpted effigies on grand funeral monuments, likenesses of the dead were made as portrait medals, death masks, and, in the case of royal funerals, as effigies to be carried on the hearse. From the 1720s onwards the demand for portrait busts rose rapidly. In 1743 the unmarried daughter of Sir Thomas Hare of Stow Hall, Norfolk, provided in her will for a lifelike wax model of her head and shoulders to be placed near her tomb in the family chapel.[103] It was left to the Utilitarian philosopher Jeremy Bentham to propose that all dead persons should be embalmed and their bodies preserved as 'auto-icons': 'if a country gentleman had rows of trees leading to his dwelling, the auto-icons of his family might alternate with the trees'.[104]

Just as ancestral portraits were handed down the generations, so other keepsakes were bequeathed to family and friends for memory's sake: pieces of silver, drinking glasses, spoons, clothes, books, coins, rings, swords. Symbols of gratitude and affection, these deathbed gifts were tokens of remembrance, relics of lives which had been lived and relationships which were no more. In 1508 John Chesman, a chandler and barber, left to Agnes ('my wife should have been and [i.e. if] God had willed'), 'a gown cloth that should have been my wedding gown'.[105]

Other objects, of symbolic or monetary value, were passed down through families, with instructions that they should never be sold. In 1506 John Turvill of New Hall, near Leicester, left his son and heir a basin and ewer of silver 'to go as an heirloom as long as the world endureth'.[106] Such bequests were sometimes attempts at virtually freezing the whole domestic environment as it was at the time of the testator's death. In 1527 a Lincolnshire testator, having made a bequest for an obit for himself for the next eighty-four years, also prescribed that 'the painted cloth, the table, the long settle, and the chair with the form, as they stand in the hall, do remain in the house...as heirlooms'. In 1571 an Essex husbandman desired that 'my table in the hall with the form, benchboards, stained cloths and lattices in the hall' should 'remain with my house and not to be taken away'. The universal practice of bequeathing clothes, furniture, and household goods meant that many people were surrounded by objects with strong personal associations. Domestic fittings thus often took on a pronounced memorial character.[107]

The disposal of property by will also gave testators the opportunity to exert a posthumous influence upon the fortunes, relationships, and behaviour of those they left behind. Many bequests embodied the pathetic aspirations of men and women to go on living after their death. Few legacies were as bizarre as that of the travel writer Philip Thicknesse (d. 1792), who announced in his will that 'I leave my right hand, to be cut off after death, to my son, Lord Audley, and desire it may be sent him in hopes that such a sight may remind him of his duty to God, after having so long abandoned the duty he owed his Father, who once affectionately loved him.'[108] Yet, in less spectacular ways, the prevailing freedom of testamentary disposition allowed many dead persons to go on ruling from their graves.

THE QUEST FOR IMMORTALITY

'The only way to win immortality', wrote the translator George Pettie in 1581, 'is either to do things worth the writing, or to write things worthy the reading.'[1] Since classical times it had been a commonplace that portraits, tombstones, and other material forms of remembrance were all ephemeral by comparison with the enduring achievements of literary art. A poem was a more lasting memorial than a marble statue or a gorgeous sepulchre. 'Monuments of wit and learning', observed Francis Bacon, 'are more durable than the monuments of power or of the hands. For have not the verses of Homer continued twenty-five hundred years or more, without the loss of a syllable or letter; during which time infinite palaces, temples, castles, cities, have been decayed and demolished?'² Among Renaissance humanists it was a commonplace that the memory of outstanding writers or philosophers lasted longer than that of military or naval heroes because later generations could share their thoughts. Plato and Aristotle remained alive in a way that Alexander could never be.³ Hence the claim in John Evelyn's epitaph that he had 'perpetuated his fame by far more lasting monuments than those of stone or brass—his learned and useful works'.⁴

Writers could also confer immortality upon others. The dead lived briefly through the memories of those who had known them, but, unless those memories were written down, they were soon lost. Who, but for Homer, would ever have heard of Achilles? What better way, therefore, of ensuring lasting fame than by becoming the patron of a poet? Or so the poets claimed. How many great ones were now forgotten, asked Edmund Spenser menacingly, because they had been too mean to cherish some 'gentle wits' who could have made them immortal?⁵ Playwrights were equally important in resurrecting figures from the past: 'there is no immortality can be given a man on earth like unto plays', thought Thomas Nashe.⁶ The desire to be posthumously remembered was a basic motive for literary patronage. Few books were published without a dedicatory eulogy of their sponsor; and the creation of fame was a primary object of the literary endeavour.

It is in this context that we should place the extraordinary surge of antiquarian and historical activity which characterizes the early modern period. The self-conscious desire to preserve the 'memory and fame' of families and individuals underlay the obsessive recording of inscriptions and heraldic devices, threatened as they were by both Protestant iconoclasm and the inroads of time. The concern to safeguard what might otherwise be forgotten was repeatedly articulated in the prefaces to the histories of counties, towns, and villages, and in the numerous family memoirs, genealogies, and biographies, some published at the time, others surviving abundantly in manuscript.⁷ These works had practical utility when claims to property and jurisdiction arose, but their greatest appeal to their gentry patrons was that they protected them and their lineage from oblivion. Historians, it was said, could take away men's fear of death by offering them a second life; and the county history of this period has been aptly described as 'a retrospective ceremonial substitute for the perpetual chantry'.[8] When his brother Isaac died in 1679, the Gloucestershire gentleman William Lawrence wrote a brief biography of him, so 'that the memory of my dearly beloved Brother may remain in my family and not be extinguish't with his life'.[9] The same impulse underlay the biographical dictionaries which poured out from the late seventeenth century onwards, culminating in the *Biographia Britannica* of 1747–66, the ancestor of today's *Oxford Dictionary of National Biography*.[10] We value such works for their scholarly utility, but their original purpose was to preserve their subjects' fame, as a monument to the virtuous and an incentive to others to emulate their example.

Most early modern history and biography was didactic in purpose, intended to teach moral and practical lessons and to encourage the imitation of exemplary lives. Just as Francis Bacon thought that history should concentrate on persons 'worthy of mention' and actions 'of the nobler sort',[11] so Protestants cherished the memory of the godly, in much the same way that the names of saints and martyrs had been preserved in medieval church calendars. It was 'a great duty', thought Richard Baxter, 'to transmit the examples of holy and worthy persons to posterity'.[12]

The desire for posthumous fame was sometimes said to be distinctively aristocratic, a quality which distinguished rulers and great men from their social inferiors. But many believed it to be a universal feature of human nature, claiming that there was 'an innate desire in every man to transmise himself unto posterity'.[13] In the early eighteenth century, the poet Anne, Lady Irwin, wrote that

> Ambitious thoughts the humblest cottage fill;
> Far as they can they push their little fame,
> And try to leave behind a deathless name.[14]

But when it came to posthumous remembrance the cards were stacked in favour of the rich and powerful. It was they who commissioned the oil paintings and the elaborate funeral monuments; and it was their doings and their estates which formed the principal subject of contemporary antiquarian scholarship. The poor were usually excluded from such commemoration. So were women, for modesty, regarded as a necessary female virtue, implied a deliberate avoidance of fame or public attention. At Glympton, Oxfordshire, a monument was erected by Maud Tesdale (d. 1616), widow of Thomas Tesdale, 'by her own command and charge upon her deathbed to propagate his memory rather than her own'; and when the widow of General James

Oglethorpe died in 1787, the local vicar remarked that 'her fortitude of mind, and extensive charity, deserve to be remembered, though her own modesty would desire them to be forgotten'.[15] For an exceptional woman like Margaret Cavendish, who unashamedly invaded the masculine domain by seeking fame as a writer and thinker, and incurring much mockery in the process, it was a matter of great distress that most of her sex were content to die unremembered. 'Shall only men live by fame, and women die in oblivion?' asks a character in one of her plays.[16]

Within the churches, there were relatively few memorial brasses or sculpted effigies for those below the gentry and professional classes. In the churchyards, stone markers or slabs had occasionally been placed over graves since medieval times.[17] But the great majority of churchyard burials seem to have been unmarked or indicated only by wooden crosses, rails, and boards. Well into the seventeenth century, few will-makers envisaged any kind of permanent monument for themselves.[18] Wooden markers then slowly began to give way to more enduring monuments for those who could afford them, typically headstones or slabs, bearing the name or initials of the deceased and the year of death. In areas where stone was scarce, however, names long continued to be written on pieces of wood.[19] The antiquary Samuel Pegge remarked in 1774 that contemporary churchyards contained no gravestones which were more than 200 years old, while in Gloucestershire, the herald Ralph Bigland's late eighteenth-century survey revealed that very few parishes had headstones dated earlier than 1670.[20] Even allowing for the possibility that the earlier stones had been removed to make room for their successors, it seems clear that it was not until the end of the seventeenth century that it became customary for the middling classes to contemplate the possibility of erecting stone markers. When the Bishop of Carlisle toured his diocese in 1703, he noted that some of 'the richer sort of yeomen' had gravestones, but he also found scores of churches and church-yards with no monuments at all.[21]

Writing around 1688, Randle Holme observed that the graves of yeomen, farmers, and rich country freeholders had 'about the head a stone erected about a foot above the ground, in the form of a semi-circle, at the top on which is cut the letters of the defunct's name and year of his death, sometime the name at length, and place of his abode, with the day and year of his departure'. He went on to list the types of gravestone that he considered appropriate to an individual's social rank, but mentioned none for plebeians. By implication, such monuments were inappropriate for 'base and mechanic fellows'. His predecessor the Elizabethan heraldic writer John Ferne had been more forthright, grandiloquently declaring that 'the ungentle person' was 'not worthy of memorial, but that his name should end with his life, and no man shall see the steps of his way, no more than the furrows of a ship is discerned in the swallowing gulfs of the ocean'.[22] In 1722 the poet Thomas Parnell implied that there were three kinds of graves: 'marble tombs that rise on high' for 'the rich' and 'the great'; 'flat smooth stones that bear a name' for the middling sort; and, for poor toilers, wooden markers—nameless 'graves, with bending osier bound'.[23] Until the twentieth century, the cost of lettered gravestones seems to have put them out of the reach of the majority of the population, who continued to have no permanent marker.[24]

This does not mean that the lower classes were indifferent to memorials as such, for, both inside and outside the church, they had more of them, though of an ephemeral kind, than can be inferred from modern survivals. In 1638 Archbishop Laud was informed by the Bishop of Bristol that, in his diocese, 'monuments, even of obscure and mean persons, are grown very common in those parts, and prejudicial both to the walls and pillars...of churches'. In the same year, Matthew Wren, Bishop of Ely, inquired in his diocesan visitation articles as to whether the church contained withered funeral garlands, flags, or 'any other mean toys and childish gewgaws (such as the foolish sort of people prepare at some burials)'. These would have included the so-called 'maidens' crants'*—garlands of ribbons and paper, which were laid on the coffin or carried before it at the funerals of women (and sometimes men) who had reputedly died virgins, and afterwards hung up in the church (where some of them survive to this day).[25] Wren also asked whether the churchyard was 'pestered and cloyed with frames of wood, piles of brick, or stones laid over the grave'.[26] Jonathan Swift, remarking in 1706 on the reluctance of 'most people' to be forgotten, noted that even 'the vulgar' wanted inscriptions over their graves.[27] Gray's *Elegy Written in a Country Church-Yard* (1750) represents the graves of the poor as marked by 'some frail memorial...With uncouth rhimes and shapeless sculpture deck'd...Their name, their years, spelt by th'unlettered muse'. In 1769 an antiquarian referred contemptuously to 'a great deal of trash' in the form of epitaphs relating to 'butchers, coach-drivers,

---

* From the German *Krantz* (wreath).

&c, of whom nothing more is said than that they lived so many years, and died'. Not even the poor went gladly into oblivion.[28]*

There was another, more vicarious, route to immortality. 'Though the father die,' wrote Thomas Becon, paraphrasing Ecclesiasticus 30: 4, 'yet he is as though he were not dead, for he hath left one behind him that is like him.'[29] By begetting offspring, a man could perpetuate his name and leave descendants to preserve his memory. It was 'a certain kind of immortality for the parents to live in their children'.[30]

> How can man perpetual be,
> But in his own posterity?[31]

Sir Henry Lee assured the new Earl of Shrewsbury in 1590 that his father was not 'dead without memorial'; for he had in him 'a picture of himself... to possess long and increase much the greatness and glory of so noble a house'.[32] Sir William Monson told his son in 1625 that 'the great-grandfather of your grandfather was a knight by title and John by name: which name we desire to retain to our eldest sons'. He added that 'because man cannot himself live for ever, he desires to live in his posterity; and if I had a hundred sons, my greatest hope must depend upon you, as you are my eldest'.[33] In 1657 Dr William Rand expressed the hope that John Evelyn would have many fine children 'that may tread in their parents' steps, and as living and speaking statues, effectually present your names and virtues to succeeding generations'.[34] This was what Jeremy Bentham would call 'that agreeable illusion which paints the successive existence of our descendants as the prolongation of our own'.[35]

Landowners saw in their heirs a means of replicating themselves. Primogeniture, the prevailing system of inheritance, was intended to ensure the material security of the eldest male heir and thereby maintain the standing of the lineage. Partible inheritance, by contrast, threatened to bury names and families in what one Elizabethan writer called 'the bottomless pit of oblivion'.[36] In the seventeenth century, London merchants became increasingly dissatisfied with the partible inheritance customary in the City; they wanted their estates to descend to a single heir. As one of them put it, he desired his land to 'continue in my name and blood, so long as it shall please God to

---

* In the mid-twentieth century, a doctor in the East End of London reported that the rich fought harder for life because they had more to lose, but the poor grieved more for their dead relatives because they had less with which to console themselves; John Gross, *A Double Thread* (2001), 44–5.

permit the same'.[37] At lower social levels, widespread occupational continuity between the generations meant that a man's labours were not necessarily terminated by death: he could draw comfort from the expectation that his wife and children would be able to continue to cultivate his holding or practise his trade.

The Bible tells us that Absalom, having no son to keep his name in remembrance, reared up a pillar which he named after himself.[38] The Oxford college founded by Nicholas and Dorothy Wadham is but one example of Francis Bacon's proposition that the care of posterity rested with those who had no posterity: 'the noblest works and foundations have proceeded from childless men, which have sought to express the images of their minds, where those of their bodies have failed'.[39]* In the early modern period, innumerable charitable foundations owed their existence to the childlessness of their founders. Joyce Frankland (1531–87), who established scholarships at four colleges in Oxford and Cambridge, was a widow whose only son had been killed in a riding accident. The Dean of St Paul's found her 'crying or rather howling continually, "Oh my son! My son!" ' He said to her, 'Comfort yourself, good Mrs Frankland, and I will tell you how you shall have twenty good sons to comfort you.' 'How can that be?' she asked. 'You are a widow,' he replied, 'rich and now childless, and there be in both universities so many poor toward [i.e. promising] youths that lack exhibition, for whom if you would found certain fellowships and scholarships, to be bestowed upon studious young men, who should be called Mrs Frankland's scholars, they would be in love to you as dear children, and will most heartily pray to God for you during your life; and they, and their successors after them, being still Mrs Frankland's scholars, will honour your memory for ever and ever.'[40]

Charity and commemoration were inextricably linked, for what donors sought was immortality; and a well-managed charitable institution could live for ever in a way that families never did. A college, a school, a library, a hospital, or an almshouse was a highly effective way of preserving its founder's name.† In the late Middle Ages, bequests for chapels, images, and church ornaments had been a

---

* The antiquary Thomas Hearne, who believed that heads of Oxford colleges should remain celibate, remarked in 1717, 'I know of no married heads that have been benefactors'; *Remarks and Collections*, ed. C. E. Doble et al. (Oxford Hist. Soc., 1885–1921), vi. 109.

† In the way that the Ford Lectures have preserved the memory of their founder, the Revd James Ford. Sir Ernst Gombrich points out that named lectureships 'developed originally out of the educational foundations exemplified by the colleges of the ancient universities, which, in their turn, arose quite naturally from the medieval bequests for chantries'; *Ideals and Idols* (1979), 59.

recognized means of securing the donors' memory. Nearly every village church contained plate, vestments, altar cloths, bells, windows, lecterns, or other pieces of equipment given by individual parishioners. The names of donors were inscribed on the bead roll, or book of 'good doers', so that their benefactors 'should not be forgotten, but had in remembrance and prayed for of all the parish that be now and all of them that be to come'. Self-interest dictated that this annual celebration should be observed, for if the anniversary was not remembered then the endowment might be forfeited.[41] At Swaffham, Norfolk, the church was rebuilt between the late fifteenth and early sixteenth centuries, thanks to the contributions of some one hundred and twenty-five persons, whose donations, large and small, were entered in a special book and whose souls were annually prayed for at Whitsun. Francis Blomefield, the eighteenth-century historian of Norfolk, thought that it was this prospect of having their memory 'eternalized' that encouraged the inhabitants to contribute. A gift to the parish church, observes a modern historian, 'really did ensure a sort of immortality'.[42]

Substantial benefactors expected to have their patronage commemorated by having their likenesses included in stained-glass windows, their names carved in stone, and their coats of arms employed for decorative ornament. In 1457 Margaret Wetherby, widow of a mayor of Norwich, made a bequest to the Augustinian friars for a new library, on condition that, as well as saying masses for the souls of herself and her husband, they would inscribe the couple's names on the glass windows of the library and in all the books 'for future memory'. When in 1537 a Bedfordshire parson left money for a porch for his church, he included provision for a stone to be set in the wall 'for a memory of my name'.[43] It is claimed that, for nearly six centuries, the bell of Merton College, Oxford, was tolled every Friday at 10.30 a.m., the supposed day and hour of the death of Walter de Merton, the college's founder.[44]

The intimate association between benefaction and remembrance was not broken by the Reformation. Protestant benefactors did not usually ask to be prayed for, but they often requested a special service and sermon on the anniversary of their death, in a reformed version of the obits which had commemorated their predecessors. The wife of the Tudor musician Richard Perrott died on 1 May 1557; and it is likely that the famous May Morning ceremony on the tower of Magdalen College, Oxford, is a Protestantized version of the annual obit for which she left money to the college.[45] In 1568 Lord Wharton's will, establishing a grammar school at Kirkby Stephen, Westmorland, pre-scribed that the master and his scholars should go every morning to the founder's tomb in the parish church and there sing a psalm.[46] In 1685 Sir Thomas Spencer left money to the church and vicars of Yarnton, Oxfordshire, on condition that the vicar should read the Anglican Communion service on his birthday, his day of death, and the day of his wife's death.[47] Alderman Sir John Gayer (d. 1649) endowed an annual sermon at the London church of St Katherine Cree 'to com-memorate his great deliverance from a lion which he met with in his travels in Arabia and which suffer'd him to pass by him unmolested'.[48]

Protestant benefactors were as anxious as their medieval predecessors to ensure that they would be remembered by posterity. Just as John Baret left money in 1463 for an image to be re-erected in St Mary's Church, Bury St Edmunds, 'against the pillar where I was wont to sit', as 'a remembrance of me and my friends', so Florence Caldwell of the Haberdashers' Company made a bequest in 1612 for a weekly distribution of bread to the poor of St Martin Ludgate, specifying that it was to be made 'at the place in the said church where I have lately caused a little monument of me, and my wives and daughter, to be lately erected and set up'.[49] Those who bequeathed money to the poor could require the beneficiaries to be present at their funerals, a practice seen by some as 'a popish imitation of such as were desirous after their deaths to have their souls prayed for'.[50] In 1753 Sir Charles Turner built a vestry at Kirby Cane, Norfolk, 'out of a pious and pure regard for the memory of his second wife'.[51] Three hundred years earlier, he would have founded a chantry.

In the churches there were boards and tablets recording the details of local charitable bequests, partly to prevent the funds from being misappropriated, but also to perpetuate the benefactors' memory (pl. 16). Colleges, schools, and almshouses frequently adopted the name of their founders, while bells, plate, and buildings were regularly inscribed with the arms or names of their donors. In what has been called a 'mania for immortalizing themselves', churchwardens freely attached their names or initials to the work carried out in the church during their term of office.[52] City companies displayed lists and portraits of all their benefactors and read out their names once a year. One very reliable way of ensuring posthumous remembrance was to endow an annual dinner.[53]

The annual commemoration of benefactors, as at Oxford University's Encaenia, was an event in the life of most charitable institutions. Its function was closely akin to that of the medieval reading of the bead roll. Indeed, some municipalities continued to maintain their bead roll after the Reformation for this purpose.[54] Charity remained a reliable route to immortality, even though some munificent benefactors, like Sir Thomas Bodley, were notorious for their vanity. Hence the warning by moralists that those (and they were many) who founded schools and hospitals, not out of a concern to do good but from a desire to perpetuate their name, were on a certain route to hell.[55]

Of course, not all philanthropists were self-interested. John Donne remarked of a donor who had provided for his benefaction to be commemorated by an annual sermon that 'his intention was not so much to be remembered himself, as that his posterity and his neighbours might be yearly reminded to do as he had done'.[56] Nevertheless, the belief that a large benefaction would ensure the donor's posthumous commemoration was an essential impulse behind the charitable activity of the early modern period.[57]

In this and so many other ways, the fear of oblivion shaped the social behaviour of men and women in the early modern period. Without it, there would not have been such huge expenditure on funerals and funeral monuments, on buildings and charitable foundations, or on works of art, literature, and scholarship. Neither would religious belief have been so focused on the afterlife and on ways of achieving survival after death. 'That whereunto man's nature doth most aspire', wrote Bacon, 'is immortality or continuance; for, to this, tendeth generation, and raising of houses and families; to this tend buildings, foundations, and monuments; to this, tendeth the desire of memory, fame, and celebration; and in effect the strength of all other human desires.'[58]

People hoped to be remembered, not just briefly, but 'in perpetuity', 'evermore perpetually', 'in perpetual remembrance'.[59] When they said that someone's fame would endure 'for ever', they meant it literally. Henry VII prescribed that masses should be celebrated for him in his Lady Chapel in Westminster Abbey 'continually and perpetually while the world shall endure'.[60] Thomas Cromwell expressed the hope that Henry VIII's fame would be remembered 'while this world endured'.[61] An early Tudor benefactor of the parish of Cople, Bedfordshire, trusted, so his epitaph claimed, to be remembered as long as the parish of Cople should last.[62] Thomas Headland prescribed in his will in 1639 that the poor of Stratfield Mortimer, Berkshire, should, on St Thomas's day, receive twelve dozen loaves of bread, annually, 'unto the world's end'. In Cumnor, Oxfordshire, a similar bequest by another benefactor was required to last 'until the day of doom'.[63] Of the Worcestershire schoolmaster and ejected minister Thomas Hall it was said in 1675 that

> Posterity Hall's learned name shall boast
> When this our isle and Europe quite is lost.[64]

Alas for these empty claims! Most attempts at achieving immortality in this world proved only too futile. Echoing Montaigne, Robert Burton stressed that even military glory was short-lived: 'a name of valour, honour and applause ... lasts not ... For it is but a mere flash, this fame, and, like a rose ... 'tis gone in an instant. Of fifteen thousand ... slain in a battle, scarce fifteen are recorded in history, or one alone, the general perhaps, and after a while his and their names are likewise blotted out, [and] the whole battle itself is forgotten ... And yet ... desire of immortality by this means ... spurs them on, many times rashly and unadvisedly to make away themselves and multitudes of others.'[65] In 1760 Oliver Goldsmith noted that, according to the newspapers, there had died in the last six months no fewer than 'twenty-five great men, seventeen very great men, and nine very extraordinary men'. 'Let me see—forty-six great men in half a year amounts to just ninety-two in a year—I wonder how posterity will be able to remember them all.'[66]

INEXORABLE OBLIVION?

In the Middle Ages, most attempts at perpetual intercession for the dead had broken down. In the thirteenth century, chantries had begun to be founded because of the inability of the monastic orders to cope with the huge demand for intercessionary masses. In turn, many of the chantries lapsed because of the poverty or indifference of their founders' descendants.[1] Only a minority of testators tried to establish masses in perpetuity, most people concentrating on a heavy investment for the first year or so. In the early modern period, the attitude to newly erected funeral memorials could be remarkably casual. After a few years, the graves might be cleared, the gravestones sold, and the brasses reused to commemorate someone else.[2] In the mid-sixteenth century, innumerable tombs and memorials were defaced or destroyed by iconoclastic reformers; epitaphs were obliterated and brasses sold off.[3] In the following centuries, tombs were frequently

moved around, pulled down, sold, or stolen. Overcrowded gra-
veyards were periodically cleared, the stones removed, and the
graves reused. The Northampton physician James Hart noticed
that graves were often dug for new guests before the bodies of the
previous occupants had decayed.[4] Even the bones of the dead, which
in medieval times were customarily lifted and preserved in charnel
houses, ceased to be the object of special attention.[5] 'Gravestones tell
truth scarce forty years,' thought Sir Thomas Browne. 'Our bones in
consecrated ground never lie quiet,' agreed John Aubrey, 'and in
London once in ten years (or thereabout) the earth is carried to the
dung-wharf.'[6]

Jeremy Taylor summarized the common experience: 'There is a
grave digged, and a solemn mourning, and a great talk in the neighbourhood, and when the days are finished...they shall be remembered no more.'[7] Or, as Samuel Pepys remarked in 1664 after burying
his brother Tom, 'Lord, to see how the world makes nothing of the
memory of a man an hour after he is dead.'[8] Sir Thomas Browne
concluded that oblivion could not be avoided: 'The greater part must
be content to be as though they had not been, to be found in the
register of God, not in the record of man.'[9]

The vanity and delusion which underlay the pursuit of fame was
an ancient theme, articulated by the Roman Stoics, preached by
St Augustine, and common in medieval literature from Boethius to
Lydgate.[10] In the early modern period, their arguments were resurrected. Moralists pointed out that the great mass of humanity perished and were speedily forgotten, while the few who were
remembered were as likely to have been wicked as good. Fame was
capricious and uncertain, a matter of chance rather than merit. It was,
said Bacon, 'like a river that beareth up things light and swollen, and
drowns things weighty and solid'. In *Paradise Regained* Milton
observed that on earth

> glory is false glory, attributed
> To things not glorious, men not worthy of fame.

And anyway, even if it was deserved, what good did posthumous
fame do for the dead person? The proper objective for Christians was
eternal life, not earthly reputation. It was folly and vanity for men to
'account this perpetual fame for their felicity'.[11] The Keeper of
Charles I's Library was said to have urged the King to pay £200 to
have a Greek manuscript printed because 'it would appear glorious in

history after his majesty's death'. 'Pish,' said he, 'I care not what they say of me in history when I am dead.'[12] By the early eighteenth century, the desire for lasting fame, so praised by the Elizabethans, was coming to be seen by many as a regrettable human weakness and the pursuit of an illusion.[13]

John Calvin chose to be buried in an unmarked grave; and in England many Protestants regarded epitaphs as popish, and monuments as a vainglorious waste of money which could have been better employed to help the poor. The more 'precise' held that there should be no memorials at all.[14] Lord Chancellor Ellesmere, who died in 1617, requested that he should have no solemn funeral or monument, but be buried in oblivion.[15] Grief was inappropriate for those who were now in divine hands. 'God would have us forget the dead,' thought the Essex minister Ralph Josselin; it was more important to recall the deceased's virtues than to remember their persons.[16] Even some of those who erected monuments had their doubts. The lines on the tomb of Sir Edward Stanley (d. 1632) at Tong, Shropshire, read:

> Not monumental stone preserves our fame
> Nor sky aspiring pyramids our name.
> The memory of him for whom this stands
> Shall outlive marble and defacers' hands:
> When all to time's consumption shall be given,
> Stanley, for whom this stands, shall stand in heaven.[17]

Predictably, the Quakers were initially opposed to all funeral monuments and grave markers; when they did eventually allow tombstones, they expected them to be strictly identical in shape and size, and devoid of moralizing epitaphs, since, as the Friends tartly observed, there was no evidence that such exhortations led to any improvement in human behaviour.[18]* The Quakers also disliked portraits, which they thought served only to make their subjects proud and conceited; it was better to keep alive the memory of loved ones by edifying conversation about their virtues than by hanging ephemeral canvas images on their walls.[19]

---

* In 1846 the Quaker poet Bernard Barton regretted this: 'I own it would feel pleasant to know the precise spot where those I have loved lay. I never feel quite sure which is my Lucy's [his wife's] grave out of the family row. That I might have no doubt which was my mother Jessup's, I planted a tree at the foot of it, which is now three times my own height'; *Selections from the Poems and Letters of Bernard Barton*, ed. by his daughter (1849), 40.

The hope of posthumous fame thus came to be seen by many as a delusion. Far wiser, thought the Elizabethan poet Samuel Daniel, to submit ourselves to 'the law of time, which in a few years will make all that for which we now contend nothing'.[20] As a historian himself, Daniel might have added that it was the scholars who would function as the gatekeepers to fame, determining who was remembered and who was forgotten. For, as another writer pointed out in 1649, it was their prerogative to 'dispense not only life, but estimation and glory unto whom they please'. Military prowess might qualify men for immortality, but without the learned no one would know about them.[21] Richard Steele, writing in *The Tatler*, said the same: 'true fame lives only in the hands of learned men, by whom it is to be transmitted to futurity, with marks of honour or reproach to the end of time'.[22] Today, newspapers and television manufacture ephemeral celebrity, but enduring fame remains largely the creation of scholars, who, in histories, biographies, and works of reference, preserve selected names from the past and consign others to oblivion. Modern historians can even recover the names and lives of once obscure persons, bestowing on them a delayed and wholly unexpected immortality. Instead of grandiose funeral monuments, we have the Cambridge Group for the History of Population and Social Structure.

The cult of posthumous fame did not disappear in the eighteenth century. Politicians, admirals, generals, literary figures, scholars, and creative artists continued to conduct their lives with one eye on what posterity would say about them. Across the Atlantic, the founders of the American republic were particularly conscious of the posthumous reputation which would accrue to those who followed the path of duty and virtue: the federalist Alexander Hamilton regarded 'the love of fame' as 'the ruling passion of the noblest minds'.[23] In the early nineteenth century, the future historian T. B. Macaulay observed that 'the desire of posthumous fame, and the dread of posthumous reproach and execration, are feelings, from the influence of which scarce any man is perfectly free, and which in many men are powerful and constant motives of action'.[24]

Yet since Hanoverian times the emphasis had begun to shift. More people than ever sought fame, but, typically, they wanted it in their lifetime, a goal which the ever-increasing availability of newspapers, pamphlets, and prints now made it much easier to achieve. From Alexander Pope to Horatio Nelson, individuals deliberately manipulated their public image in order to become better known among their contemporaries, a technique which closely paralleled the advertising of commercial brands by entrepreneurs like Josiah Wedgwood. Here were the beginnings of today's celebrity culture, in which the media make some people famous in their own time simply for being famous, rather than for any particular achievements. Short-term celebrity was beginning to replace the long-term quest for immortality.[25] The search for posthumous glory, once so self-conscious and explicit, gradually receded in prominence as a central human objective.

Among the population at large, the desire to give the dead some physical memorial was becoming much more general. But there was less talk of *perpetual* remembrance. Most methods of preserving the memory of human beings were demonstrably fallible. Monuments decayed, graves were dug up, the dead were quickly forgotten. As uncertainty grew about the prospect of a heavenly reward, most people, without explicitly declaring any religious scepticism, chose in practice to devote their main energies to the business of making this life as fulfilling as possible.

Most commonly, their goal was subjective happiness, something quite different from the objective happiness of the Greek *eudaimonia*. Some contemporaries even accepted that it was pointless to offer prescriptions as to how people should live. That had to be their decision. In the mid-seventeenth century, Thomas Hobbes observed that what pleased one man displeased another and that total satisfaction was unobtainable, life being a matter of desire succeeding desire, ceasing only in death: 'but for an utmost end, in which the ancient philosophers have placed felicity, and have disputed much concerning the way thereto, there is no such thing in the world . . . for while we live we have desires, and desire presupposeth a farther end'.[26] John Locke also denied that there was any one prescription for human flourishing, any single end which everyone should pursue: to ask whether it was best to seek 'riches, or bodily delights, or virtue, or contemplation' was like asking whether apples were better than plums. 'The mind has a different relish as well as the palate; and you will as fruitlessly endeavour to delight all men with riches or glory (which yet some men put their happiness in) as you would to satisfy all men's hunger with cheese or lobsters, which, though very agreeable and delicious fare to some, are to others extremely nauseous and offensive.'[27]

In the seventeenth and eighteenth centuries, the Christian religion, in its various forms, continued to enjoy cultural ascendancy in England. Its message remained the traditional one, namely that it was to the next world, not this one, that human beings should look for their fulfilment. In practice, most of the population implicitly took a more secular view: they cherished life for its own sake, not merely as a preliminary to some future state. Highly aware of the satisfactions which they could hope to find in their work and their possessions, the affection of their friends and families, and the respect of their peers, they increasingly sought fulfilment in their daily existence.[28] Here, all around them, were the ends of life.

It was an attitude well expressed by John Dryden in his bleak but defiant rendering of Horace's twenty-ninth ode (book 3):

> Happy the man, and happy he alone,
> He, who can call today his own:
> He, who secure within, can say
> Tomorrow do thy worst, for I have liv'd today.
> Be fair, or foul, or rain, or shine,
> The joys I have possessed, in spite of fate are mine.
> Not Heav'n itself upon the past has pow'r;
> But what has been, has been, and I have had my hour.[29]

NOTE ON REFERENCES

The endnotes are illustrative rather than exhaustive. Even so, they are so numerous that I have dispensed with a formal bibliography. Had I attempted one, it would have been hard to know where to stop, since it is difficult to think of any surviving evidence from the period which has no relevance to my theme.

I have saved space by giving only the main titles of books and articles (omitting their subtitles) and only the primary place of publication. Details of each source are given on its first citation in the notes to each chapter; thereafter a shortened title has been employed. Greek and Hebrew titles have generally been omitted. Unless otherwise stated, the place of publication is London.

In most quotations from contemporary sources (including modern editions of them) the spelling, punctuation, and capitalization have been modernized.

ABBREVIATIONS

Amer.	American
Archaeol.	Archaeological
Aubrey, *Brief Lives*	*'Brief Lives', chiefly of contemporaries, set down by John Aubrey, between the years 1669 and 1696*, ed. Andrew Clark (Oxford, 1898)
Bacon, *Works*	*The Works of Francis Bacon*, ed. James Spedding, Robert Leslie Ellis, and Douglas Denon Heath (1857–9)
Baxter, *Practical Works*	*The Practical Works of . . . Richard Baxter* (1707)
BL	British Library
Bodl. Lib.	Bodleian Library
Boyle, *Ethics*	*The Early Essays and Ethics of Robert Boyle*, ed. John T. Harwood (Carbondale, IL, 1991)
Bull.	*Bulletin*
Burton, *Anatomy*	Robert Burton, *The Anatomy of Melancholy*, ed. Thomas C. Faulkner, Nicholas K. Kiessling, and Rhonda H. Blair (Oxford, 1989–2000)
Cal. S.P.	*Calendar of State Papers*
Capp, *Gossips*	Bernard Capp, *When Gossips Meet: Women, Family, and Neighbourhood in Early Modern England* (Oxford, 2003)
Clarendon, *History*	Edward Hyde, Earl of Clarendon, *The History of the Rebellion and Civil Wars in England begun in the Year 1641*, ed. W. Dunn Macray (Oxford, 1888)
EcHR	*Economic History Review*
EETS	Early English Text Society
EHR	*English Historical Review*
ELH	*English Literary History*
Eng.	English
Evelyn, *Diary*	*The Diary of John Evelyn*, ed. E. S. de Beer (Oxford, 1955)
Grassby, *Business Community*	Richard Grassby, *The Business Community of Seventeenth-Century England* (Cambridge, 1995)
Heal and Holmes, *Gentry*	Felicity Heal and Clive Holmes, *The Gentry in England and Wales 1500–1700* (Basingstoke, 1994)
Hist.	Historical
HJ	*Historical Journal*
HMC	Historical Manuscripts Commission

Hobbes, *Leviathan*	Thomas Hobbes, *Leviathan*, ed. Richard Tuck (Cambridge, 1991)
Hobbes, *Latin Works*	*Opera Philosophica quae Latine scripsit Thomas Hobbes Malmsburiensis*, ed. Sir William Molesworth (1839–45)
Homilies	*The Two Books of Homilies appointed to be read in Churches*, [ed. John Griffiths] (Oxford, 1859)
Houlbrooke, *Death*	Ralph Houlbrooke, *Death, Religion, and the Family in England, 1480–1750* (Oxford, 1998)
Ingram, *Church Courts*	Martin Ingram, *Church Courts, Sex and Marriage in England, 1570–1640* (Cambridge, 1987)
JBS	*Journal of British Studies*
Journ.	Journal
JSH	*Journal of Social History*
Lib.	Library
Mandeville, *Fable*	Bernard Mandeville, *The Fable of the Bees*, ed. F. B. Kaye (Oxford, 1924)
Marshall, *Beliefs*	Peter Marshall, *Beliefs and the Dead in Reformation England* (Oxford, 2002)
Mendelson and Crawford, *Women*	Sara Mendelson and Patricia Crawford, *Women in Early Modern England 1550–1720* (Oxford, 1998)
Milton, *CPW*	*Complete Prose Works of John Milton*, ed. Don M. Wolfe et al. (New Haven, 1953–82)
Nic. Eth.	Aristotle, *Nicomachean Ethics*
ODNB	*The Oxford Dictionary of National Biography*, ed. H. C. G. Matthew and Brian Harrison (Oxford, 2004)
OED	*The Oxford English Dictionary*, 2nd edn, prepared by J. A. Simpson and E. S. C. Weiner (Oxford, 1989)
P & P	*Past & Present*
PBA	*Proceedings of the British Academy*
Pepys, *Diary*	*The Diary of Samuel Pepys*, ed. Robert Latham and William Matthews (1970–83)
Perkins, *Workes*	*The Workes of that Famous and Worthie Minister of Christ, in the Universitie of Cambridge, M. W. Perkins* (Cambridge, 1608–31)
Procs	*Proceedings*
PS	Parker Society
Qtly	*Quarterly*
Rec.	Record
Rev.	*Review*
RO	Record Office
ser.	series
SH	*Social History*

Smith, *Moral Sentiments*	Adam Smith, *The Theory of Moral Sentiments*, ed. D. D. Raphael and A. L. Macfie (Oxford, 1976)
Smith, *Wealth of Nations*	Adam Smith, *An Inquiry into the Nature and Causes of the Wealth of Nations*, ed. R. H. Campbell and A. S. Skinner (Oxford, 1976)
Soc.	Society
Spectator	*The Spectator*, ed. Donald F. Bond (Oxford, 1965)
Stone, *Crisis*	Lawrence Stone, *The Crisis of the Aristocracy 1558–1641* (repr. Oxford, 1979)
Studs	Studies
Tatler	*The Tatler*, ed. Donald F. Bond (Oxford, 1987)
TLS	*Times Literary Supplement*
Trans.	*Transactions*
TRHS	*Transactions of the Royal Historical Society*
Univ.	University
VCH	*Victoria County History*

NOTES

INTRODUCTION

1. S. T. Coleridge, *The Philosophical Lectures*, ed. Kathleen Coburn (1949), 66.
2. I have said something about the first of these in 'The life of learning', *PBA* 117 (*2001 Lectures*) (2002), and about the second in 'Art and iconoclasm in early modern England', in *Religious Politics in Post-Reformation England*, ed. Kenneth Fincham and Peter Lake (Woodbridge, 2006).
3. Pierre Charron, *Of Wisdom*, trans. George Stanhope (1697), ii. 105 (bk ii, ch. 4), 489 (bk iii, ch. 6).
4. Richard Stafford, *Of Happiness* (1689), 225.
5. Daniel Defoe, *Farther Adventures of Robinson Crusoe* (1719; Oxford, 1927), ii. 117–18.
6. Hobbes, *Leviathan*, iii. 70 (ch. 11).
7. Pepys, *Diary*, vii. 69.
8. Roger North, *The Lives of the Right Hon. Francis North, Baron Guilford; the Hon. Sir Dudley North; and the Hon. and Rev. Dr. John North*, ed. Augustus Jessopp (1890), ii. 245.
9. Joannes Susenbrotus (1484/5–1542/3), cit. Brian Vickers, *In Defence of Rhetoric* (Oxford, 1988), 331.
10. See the introduction by Hannah Arendt to her edition of Walter Benjamin, *Illuminations*, trans. Harry Zohn (1973), 47.
11. For some searching criticisms of my use of this method on previous occasions, see L. J. Jordanova, 'The interpretation of nature', *Comparative Studs in Society and History*, 29 (1987), and J. A. Sharpe, review of David Cressy, *Birth, Marriage, and Death*; http://www.hull.ac.uk/renforum/v2no2/sharpe.htm. The origin of these objections can be traced back to J. H. Hexter's remarks about 'source-mining' in his review of Christopher Hill, *Change and Continuity in Seventeenth-Century England*, TLS, 24 Oct. 1975.
12. Jordanova, 'The interpretation of nature', 197.
13. As Bernard Capp has written in response to criticism of his use of church court records, 'the critical evaluation of sources does not have to be spelled out on every line of every page'; http://www.history.ac.uk/reviews/paper/cappB.html.
14. J. H. Hexter, *On Historians* (1979), 242.

CHAPTER I

1. Alan Gewirth, *Self-Fulfillment* (Princeton, 1998), provides an excellent analysis of the concept.
2. http://www.anc.org.za/ancdocs/history/mandela/1994/sp940524.html.
3. Sir Anthony Kenny, 'Beyond a warm feeling', in *The Discovery of Happiness*, ed. Stuart McCready (2001), 227; James Griffin, *Value Judgment* (Oxford, 1996), 29.

4. As is pointed out by Joseph Raz, *The Morality of Freedom* (Oxford, 1986), 376.

5. *The Quality of Life*, ed. Martha C. Nussbaum and Amartya Sen (Oxford, 1993); Amartya Sen, *Development as Freedom* (Oxford, 1999); *Women, Culture, and Development*, ed. Martha C. Nussbaum and Jonathan Glover (Oxford, 1995), 83–5; Martha C. Nussbaum, *Women and Human Development* (Cambridge, 2000), 5, 78–80 (on which, see the justifiably sceptical comments of Mary Beard in *TLS*, 17 Mar. 2000).

6. Ralf Dahrendorf, *Life Chances* (1979).

7. Varro, cit. Augustine, *City of God*, xix. 3.

8. *Nic. Eth.* 1 and 10. 7; Richard Kraut, *Aristotle on the Human Good* (Princeton, 1989); C. C. W. Taylor, 'Introduction' to Aristotle, *Nicomachean Ethics, Books II–IV* (Oxford, 2006).

9. Marshall Berman, *The Politics of Authenticity* (1971); John Rawls, *A Theory of Justice* (Oxford, 1973), 448; Anthony Giddens, *Modernity and Self-Identity* (Cambridge, 1991), esp. ch. 3; Martin Ryle and Kate Soper, *To Relish the Sublime?* (2002), chs 1 and 2.

10. Colin Campbell, *The Romantic Ethic and the Spirit of Modern Consumerism* (Oxford, 1987), 183–4; Charles Taylor, *Sources of the Self* (Cambridge, 1989), chs 20 and 21, and id., *The Ethics of Authenticity* (Cambridge, MA, 1991), 25–9; Gerald N. Izenberg, *Impossible Individuality* (Princeton, 1992).

11. J. B. Schneewind, *The Invention of Autonomy* (Cambridge, 1998).

12. Sudhir Hazareesingh, *The Legend of Napoleon* (2004), 129.

13. Wilhelm von Humboldt, *The Sphere and Duties of Government*, trans. Joseph Coulthard (1844), 11.

14. *The Earlier Letters of John Stuart Mill 1812–1848*, ed. Francis E. Mineka (Toronto, 1963), 207; Mill, *On Liberty* (Oxford, 1991), 63; Alfred Tennyson, *The Princess* (1847), vii. 131; Robert Browning, 'Youth and Art. xvi', in *Dramatis Personae* (1864).

15. G. A. Cohen, *If You're an Egalitarian, How Come You're So Rich?* (Cambridge, MA, 2000), 2; Karl Marx, *Grundrisse*, trans. Martin Nicolaus (Harmondsworth, 1973), 488, 611.

16. Friedrich Nietzsche, *The Gay Science*, trans. Walter Kaufmann (New York, 1974), 219; id., *Ecce Homo* (1908; written 1888), subtitle.

17. *OED*, s.v. 'self-realization'; *The Logic of Hegel*, trans. William Wallace (Oxford, 1874), p. clx; T. H. Green, *Prolegomena to Ethics*, ed. David O. Brink (Oxford, 2003), 407 and *passim*; Sandra M. Den Otter, *British Idealism and Social Explanation* (Oxford, 1996), 29, 79–80, 110–11, 157.

18. *Oscar Wilde: Three Times Tried* (Paris, n.d. [1928]), i. 52. Also Oscar Wilde, *The Soul of Man under Socialism and Selected Critical Prose*, ed. Linda Dowling (2001), esp. 129, 131, 134, 156, 159–60.

19. Quoted in S. A. Smith, *Revolution and the People in Russia and China* (Cambridge, 2008), 80.

20. Jacob Golomb, *In Search of Authenticity* (1975); Charles B. Guignon, 'Existentialism', in *Routledge Encyclopedia of Philosophy*, ed. Edward Craig (1998), iii.

21. See e.g. Betty Friedan, *The Feminine Mystique* (1963).

22. Peter Gay, *The Enlightenment* (New York, 1969; 1977), 184–207; Ross McKibbin, 'Introduction' to Marie Stopes, *Married Love* (Oxford, 2004).

23. D. J. van de Kaa, 'Anchored narratives', *Population Studs*, 50 (1996), 425; Jose Harris, 'Tradition and transformation', in *The British Isles since 1945*, ed. Kathleen Burk (Oxford, 2003), 118.

24. T. J. Jackson Lears, 'From salvation to self-realization', in *The Culture of Consumption*, ed. Richard Wightman Fox and T. J. Jackson Lears (New York, 1983); Raz, *Morality of Freedom*, 369.

25. Avner Offer, *The Challenge of Affluence* (Oxford, 2006), 334. Also Taylor, *Ethics of Authenticity*, 35, 40, 55; id., *Sources of the Self*, 507–8; Robert N. Bellah et al., *Habits of the Heart* (1988).

26. Mark Evans, 'Self-realization', in *Routledge Encyclopedia of Philosophy*, viii.

The Constraints of the Age

1. *The Works of... Richard Hooker*, ed. John Keble, 6th edn (Oxford, 1874), ii. 445; i. 253–4; Philip Schaff, *The Creeds of the Evangelical Protestant Churches* (1877), 676; [Daniel Defoe], *The Case of the Protestant Dissenters in Carolina* (1706), 9.

2. *The Works of Isaac Barrow* (Edinburgh, 1842), i. 478.

3. *The Letters of Dorothy Moore 1612–64*, ed. Lynette Hunter (Aldershot, 2004), 69; *The Economic Writings of Sir William Petty*, ed. Charles Henry Hull (Cambridge, 1899), i. 119.

4. Thomas Starkey, *A Dialogue between Pole and Lupset*, ed. Thomas F. Mayer, Camden, 4th ser., 37 (1989), 14; Sir Richard Barckley, *A Discourse of the Felicitie of Man* (1598), 569.

5. Sir Thomas Smith, *De Republica Anglorum*, ed. Mary Dewar (Cambridge, 1982), 65; *The Select Works of Robert Crowley*, ed. J. M. Cowper (EETS, 1872), 56. For helpful discussion, see David Cressy, 'Describing the social order of Elizabethan and Stuart England', *Literature and History*, 3 (1976); Keith Wrightson, 'Estates, degrees, and sorts', and Penelope J. Corfield, 'Class by name and number in eighteenth-century Britain', both in *Language, History and Class*, ed. Corfield (Oxford, 1991); Wrightson, ' "Sorts of People" in Tudor and Stuart England', in *The Middling Sort of People*, ed. Jonathan Barry and Christopher Brooks (Basingstoke, 1994).

6. Robert Gell, *Gells Remaines*, ed. R. B[acon] (1676), i. 626.

7. Thomas More, *Utopia*, ed. George M. Logan and Robert M. Adams (Cambridge, 1989), 50; *Epistolae Ho-Elianae*, ed. Joseph Jacobs (1890), 522.

8. Heal and Holmes, *Gentry*, 255; Grassby, *Business Community*, 126.

9. Francis Bacon, *The Essayes or Counsels*, ed. Michael Kiernan (Oxford, 1985), 24.

10. e.g. *The Catechism of Thomas Becon*, ed. John Ayre (PS, Cambridge, 1844), 355; John Dod and Robert Cleaver, *A Plaine and Familiar Exposition of the Ten Commandments*, 18th edn (1632), 182; William Gouge, *Of Domesticall Duties*, 3rd edn (1634), 567–71; William Ames. *Conscience, with the Power and Cases thereof* (n.p., 1639), iii. 158; Edward Elton. *Gods Holy Minde touching Matters Morall* (1648), 132; Baxter, *Practical Works*, i. 358: Gabriel Towerson, *An Explication of the Decalogue* (1676), 247–8; Richard L. Greaves, *Society and Religion in Elizabethan England* (Minneapolis, 1981), 380.

11. Sir Thomas Elyot, *The Boke named The Gouernour*, ed. Herbert Henry Stephen Croft (1883), i. 138–40; *A Memoir of the Life and Death of Sir John King by his Father*, [ed. George Henry Sawtell] (1855), 2, 7–8.

12. R. Campbell, *The London Tradesman* (1747; Newton Abbot, 1969), 2; Lawrence Stone, *The Family, Sex and Marriage in England 1500–1800* (1977), 447; Joan Lane, *Apprenticeship in England, 1660–1914* (1996), 33.

13. *Homilies*, 310; *Select Works of Robert Crowley*, 51, 63, 147.

14. Perkins, *Workes*, i. 64, 733 (echoing 1 Corinthians 7: 20). On the ideology of 'contentment', see Helen C. White, *Social Criticism in Popular Religious Literature of the Sixteenth Century* (1944; New York, 1973), ch. 7; Paul Marshall, *A Kind of Life Imposed upon Man* (Toronto, 1996), ch. 5.

15. *Works of Isaac Barrow*, i. 498; John Flavel, *Divine Conduct* (1678), 84.

16. Resta Patching, *Four Topographical Letters* (Newcastle upon Tyne, 1757), 24–5.

17. W. Gordon Zeeveld, *Foundations of Tudor Policy* (Cambridge, MA, 1948), 196–201.

18. *Letters and Papers, Foreign and Domestic, of the Reign of Henry VIII*, ed. J. S. Brewer et al. (1862–1932), ix. 725 (ii); John Ferne, *The Blazon of Gentrie* (1586), 11–12; Andrew Willet, *Hexapla in Leviticum*, ed. Peter Smith (1631), 53; R[obert] C[rofts], *The Way to Happinesse on Earth* (1641), 180; Daniel Rogers, *Matrimoniall Honour* (1642), 166; William Secker, *A Wedding Ring Fit for the Finger* (1658), 45–6; Greaves, *Society and Religion*, 132.

19. *Tudor Economic Documents*, ed. R. H. Tawney and Eileen Power (1924), i. 326; Barnabe Riche, *Allarme to England* (1578), sig. Gii^v; Grassby, *Business Community*, 41.

20. *Tudor Economic Documents*, i. 326; Matthew Carter, *Honor Redivivus*, 3rd edn (1673), 22; Paul Lucas, 'Blackstone and the reform of the legal profession', *EHR* 77 (1962).

21. *Tudor Economic Documents*, i. 326.

22. Robert, Lord Brooke, *A Discourse opening the Nature of that Episcopacie which is exercised in England* (1642), 3; Thomas Hobbes, *Behemoth*, ed. Ferdinand Tönnies (1969), 29–30.

23. Quentin Skinner, 'Some problems in the analysis of political thought and action', *Political Theory*, 2 (1974), 297.

24. Richard Mulcaster, *Positions*, ed. Robert Henry Quick (1888), 144; *The Mirror for Magistrates*, ed. Lily B. Campbell New York, 1960), dedication by William Baldwin; Thomas Floyd, *The Picture of a Perfit Common Wealth* (1600), 281–8; Anthony Esler, *The Aspiring Mind of the Elizabethan Younger Generation* (Durham, NC, 1966), ch. ii; Ian Atherton, *Ambition and Failure in Stuart England* (Manchester, 1999), 13–14.

25. Joseph Bentham, *The Christian Conflict* (1635), 360–4; John Downame, *The Christian Warfare*, 4th edn (1634), 20; W. H. Greenleaf, *Order, Empiricism and Politics* (1964), 54–6; *OED*, s.v. 'mushroom', 'upstart'.

26. [Henricus Bomelius], *The Summe of the Holy Scripture*, [trans. Simon Fish] (1529), sigs. Bviii^v–Ci^v; *England in the Reign of King Henry the Eighth*, pt 1: *Starkey's Life and Letters* ed. Sidney J. Herrtage (EETS, 1878; 1927), pp. xcii–xciii.

27. John Jones, *The Arte and Science of Preserving Bodie and Soule* (1579), sig. Mii^v; J. K[epers], dedicatory preface to his translation of Annibale Romei, *The Courtiers Academie* (n.d. [1598]), sig. A3.

28. *Samuel Hartlib and the Advancement of Learning*, ed. Charles Webster (Cambridge, 1970), 52.

29. Milton, *CPW* vii. 305–6; Don M. Wolfe, *Milton in the Puritan Revolution* (1941; 1963), app. 1.

30. *British Pamphleteers*, ed. George Orwell and Reginald Reynolds (1948), 86; Mary Thomas Crane, *Framing Authority* (Princeton, 1993), 100–1.

31. *A Catalogue of Letters and Other Historical Documents Exhibited in the Library at Welbeck*, comp. S. Arthur Strong (1903), 188. Similarly, Edward Chamberlayne, *Angliae Notitia*, 3rd edn (1669), ii. 524.

32. *A Discourse of the Necessity of Encouraging Mechanick Industry* (1690), 22–6.

33. White Kennett, *The Charity of Schools for Poor Children Recommended* (1706), 24–5; M. G. Jones, *The Charity School Movement* (Cambridge, 1938), 95–6, 144.

34. Francis Vesey, Sr, *Reports of Cases...in the High Court of Chancery...1746–7 to 1755*, 4th edn, ed. Robert Bett (1818), ii. 330.

35. 'A Free Inquiry into the Nature and Origin of Evil', in *The Works of Soame Jenyns* (1790), iii.

36. *The Works of...Dr Thom. Taylor* (1653), i. 146; G. D. Scull, *Dorothea Scott*, new edn (Oxford, 1883), 186–98.

37. Perkins, *Workes*, i. 732; Browne, *Pseudodoxia Epidemica*, ed. Robin Robbins (Oxford, 1981), i. 31.

38. Zachary Mayne, 'Two letters', *Gentleman's Magazine*, lxiv (1974), 11; [William Petty], *Advice of W.P. to Mr Samuel Hartlib* (1648), 4.

39. James Buck, *A Treatise of the Beatitudes* (1637), 112.

40. Elyot, *Boke named the Gouernour*, i. 48; John Locke, *Some Thoughts concerning Education*, ed. John W. and Jean S. Yolton (Oxford, 1989), 256–7.

41. [Richard Allestree], *The Ladies Calling*, 11th imp. (Oxford, 1720), 4.

42. For the intellectual underpinning of these assumptions, see Ian Maclean, *The Renaissance Notion of Woman* (Cambridge, 1980).

43. Robert Pricke, *The Doctrine of Superioritic, and of Subiection* (1609), sigs li^v–lii; *The Works of John Robinson*, ed. Robert Ashton (1851), 240. Margaret R. Sommerville, *Sex and Subjection* (1995), is a useful survey of contemporary prescriptions.

44. Amy N. Froide, *Never Married* (Oxford, 2005), esp. chs 1 and 6; Frances Harris, *Transformations of Love* (Oxford, 2002), 173.

45. Mendelson and Crawford, *Women*, 97; Paul Griffiths, *Youth and Authority* (Oxford, 1996), 380; Froide, *Never Married*, 20.

46. Froide, *Never Married*, chs 3–5; Pamela Sharpe, 'Dealing with love', *Gender and History*, 11 (1999); Judith Spicksley, 'A dynamic model of social relations', in *Identity and Agency in England, 1500–1800*, ed. Henry French and Jonathan Barry (Basingstoke, 2004); ead., ' "Fly with a duck in thy mouth" ', *SH* 32 (2007).

47. Though see below, p. 207

48. William Whately, *A Bride-Bush* (1623), 84.

49. 'A Lady' [Judith Drake?], *An Essay in Defence of the Female Sex*, 3rd edn (1687), 14–16.

50. Below, p. 105.

51. Alison Wall, 'Elizabethan precept, feminine practice', *History*, 75 (1990); Adrian Tinniswood, *The Verneys* (2007), 478–9; Elaine Chalus, *Elite Women in English Political Life, c.1754–1790* (Oxford, 2005).

52. Margaret J. M. Ezell, *The Patriarch's Wife* (Chapel Hill, NC, 1987), 183.

53. Judith M. Bennett, *Ale, Beer, and Brewsters in England* (New York, 1996); Deborah Valenze, *The First Industrial Woman* (New York, 1995), chs 3 and 4; Nicola Verdon, ' "... subjects deserving of the highest praise" ', *Agricultural History Rev.* 51 (2003); Michael Roberts, 'Sickle and scythe', *History Workshop*, 7 (1979); Marjorie Keniston McIntosh, *Working Women in English Society*

(Cambridge, 2005), 170–81; Adrian Wilson, *The Making of Man-Midwifery* (Cambridge, MA, 1995); Doreen Everdon, *The Midwives of Seventeenth-Century London* (Cambridge, 2000), 170–85; *Women's History: Britain, 1700–1850*, ed. Hannah Barker and Elaine Chalus (2005), Chap. 6.

54. Peter Chamberlen, *The Poore Mans Advocate* (1649), 44.

55. Dror Wahrman, *The Making of the Modern Self* (New Haven, 2004), chs 1 and 2.

56. John Halkett, *Milton and the Idea of Matrimony* (New Haven, 1970); James Grantham Turner, *One Flesh* (Oxford, 1987), ch. 6; Roderick Phillips, *Putting Asunder* (Cambridge, 1988), 105–23; Lawrence Stone, *Road to Divorce* (Oxford, 1990), ch. xi.

57. Stephen Collins, ' "A kind of lawful adultery" ', in *The Changing Face of Death*, ed. Peter C. Jupp and Glennys Howarth (Basingstoke, 1997); Susannah R. Ottaway, *The Decline of Life* (Cambridge, 2004), 133–5.

58. Mohammed Arkoun, *Rethinking Islam*, trans. and ed. Robert D. Lee (Boulder, CO, 1994), 62.

59. *Quaker Grey*, introd. A. C. Curtis (1904), 11.

60. John Bunyan, *The Pilgrim's Progress*, ed. W. R. Owens (Oxford, 2003), 72.

61. [Thomas Heywood], *Philocothonista; or, The Drunkard* (1635), 4; Milton, *CPW* v. 42; Susan C. Shapiro, ' "Yon plumed dandebrat" ', *Rev. of Eng. Studs*, new ser., 39 (1988); Linda Phyllis Austern, ' "Alluring the auditorie to effeminacie" ', *Music and Letters*, 74 (1993); Phyllis Rackin, 'Historical difference/sexual difference', in *Privileging Gender in Early Modern England*, ed. Jean R. Brink (Kirksville, MO, 1993); Alan Bray, 'To be a man in early modern society', *History Workshop Journ.* 41 (1996); Laura L. Runge, *Gender and Language in British Literary Criticism 1660–1790* (Cambridge, 1997), *passim*; Philip Carter, 'An "effeminate" or "efficient" nation?', *Textual Practice*, 11 (1997); Elizabeth A. Foyster, *Manhood in Early Modern England* (Harlow, 1999), 56–7.

62. Rogers, *Matrimoniall Honour*, 198.

63. For these and such similar terms as 'cotqueen', 'meg-harry', 'shamel', and 'polly cot', see *The English Dialect Dictionary*, ed. Joseph Wright (1898; Tokyo, 1981), and the numerous regional dialect dictionaries published in the nineteenth century, many reprinted by the English Dialect Society. For 'tomboys', see *OED*.

64. Foyster, *Manhood*, 55, 139.

65. Starkey, *Dialogue between Pole and Lupset*, 38; Gouge, *Domesticall Duties*, 5–6.

66. *Catechism of Thomas Becon*, 115–16; *Prayers and Other Pieces of Thomas Becon*, ed. John Ayre (PS, Cambridge, 1844), 59; William Baldwin, Preface to *Mirror for Magistrates* (1559), ed. Lily B. Campbell (Cambridge, 1938), 64; Floyd, *Picture of a Perfit Commonwealth*, 78, 81; J. A. W. Gunn, *Politics and the Public Interest in the Seventeenth Century* (1969), 17–18, 206–7; Stephen L. Collins, *From Divine Cosmos to Sovereign State* (New York, 1989), 79; Richard Cust, *Charles I* (Harlow, 2005), 185–8.

67. *Proceedings in the Parliaments of Elizabeth I*, ed. T. E. Hartley (Leicester, 1981–95), i. 128 (referring to Cicero, *De Officiis* 1. 23); T[homas] R[ogers], *A Philosophicall Discourse* (1576), fol. 84; John Ford, *Honour Triumphant* (Shakespeare Soc., 1843), 7; Thomas Taylor, *A Commentarie upon the Epistle of S. Paul Written to Titus* (1612), 255; Cecil Aspinall-Oglander, *Nunwell Symphony* (1945), 51; *The Works of . . . Henry late L. Delamer, and Earl of Warrington* (1694), 4; Tim[othy] Nourse, *Campania Felix* (1700), 110.

68. *The Practical Works of the Rev. Richard Baxter*, ed. William Orme (1830), xii. 462. See below, p. 87.

69. Thomas Hooker, *A Survey of the Summe of Church-Discipline* (1648), i. 188.
70. Heal and Holmes, *Gentry*, 356, 372; John Habakkuk, *Marriage, Debt, and the Estates System* (Oxford, 1994), 51–9.
71. David Cressy, 'Kinship and kinship interaction in early modern England', *P & P* 113 (1986); Michael Mascuch, 'Social mobility and middling self-identity', *SH* 20 (1995), 55–8; Naomi Tadmor, *Family and Friends in Eighteenth-Century England* (Cambridge, 2001), 103–12, 140–1, 165, 274–5; David Farr, 'Kin, cash, Catholics and Cavaliers', *Hist. Research*, 74 (2001); Keith Hindle, *On the Parish?* (Oxford, 2004), 48–58.
72. John Stockwood, *A Bartholmew Fairing* (1589), 82–3; Towerson, *Explication of the Decalogue*, 242; Ames, *Conscience*, ii. 158.
73. Rogers, *Matrimoniall Honour*, 303.
74. For helpful discussion, see Ingram, *Church Courts*, 128–42; Ralph Houlbrooke, 'The making of marriage in mid-Tudor England', *Journ. of Family History*, 10 (1985); Alan Macfarlane, *Marriage and Love in England 1300–1840* (Oxford, 1986), 13–47; articles by John R. Gillis, Richard Wall, and Steven King in *International Rev. of Social History*, 44 (1999); Diana O'Hara, *Courtship and Constraint* (Manchester, 2000); Loreen L. Giese, *Courtship, Marriage Customs and Shakespeare's Comedies* (Basingstoke, 2006), ch. 1.
75. OED, s.v. 'singularity'; *The Diary of Sir Henry Slingsby*, ed. Daniel Parsons (1836), 203–4; Helen Berry, 'Sense and singularity', in *Identity and Agency*, ed. French and Barry, 179, 194; Richard Kilby, *The Burthen of a Loaded Conscience*, 6th imp. (Cambridge, 1616), 89.
76. Patrick Collinson, *From Crammer to Sancroft* (2006), 161.
77. *Catechism of Thomas Becon*, 440.
78. *The Life of Adam Martindale*, ed. Richard Parkinson (Chetham Soc., 1845), 6–7.
79. Samuel Torshell, *The Hypocrite Discovered and Cured* (1644), 15.
80. Margaret, Duchess of Newcastle, *The Life of William Cavendish, Duke of Newcastle*, ed. C. H. Firth, 2nd edn (n.d.), 175.
81. Joan Thirsk, 'Enclosing and engrossing', in *The Agrarian History of England and Wales*, iv: *1500–1640*, ed. Thirsk (Cambridge, 1967), 255; David Underdown, *Revel, Riot and Rebellion* (Oxford, 1985), 11–17.
82. Southwell Minister Act Books (transcript by W. A. James in Reading Univ. Lib.), xxi. 42–3; Keith Thomas, *Religion and the Decline of Magic* (Harmondsworth, 1978), 629; Ingram, *Church Courts*, index, s.v. 'gossip'; Ian W. Archer, *The Pursuit of Stability* (Cambridge, 1991), 77–8; David Underdown, *Fire from Heaven* (1992), 100; Griffiths, *Youth and Authority*, 265; Capp, *Gossips*, 271 and *passim*.
83. J. H. Bettey, 'The revolts over the enclosure of the royal forest at Gillingham 1626–30', *Procs Dorset Natural History and Archaeol. Soc.* 97 (1976), 22.

New Aspirations

1. *The Papers of Nathaniel Bacon of Stiffkey*, ed. A. Hassell Smith et al. (Norfolk Rec. Soc., 1979), i. 150.
2. Aegremont Ratcliffe, 'Epistle dedicatorie' to his trans. of *Politique Discourses* (1578), sig. Aiiiᵛ; Bentham, *The Christian Conflict*, 363.
3. *The Minor Poems of John Lydgate*, ed. Henry Noble MacCracken (EETS, 1911–34), ii. 845; Thomas Dorman, *A Proufe of Certayne Articles in Religion* (Antwerp, 1564),

fol. 138; *The Works of James Pilkington*, ed. James Scholefield (PS, Cambridge, 1842), 485; J. H. Hexter, *Reappraisals in History*, 2nd edn (Chicago, 1979), 82.

4. *John Bellers 1654–1724*, ed. A. Ruth Fry (1935), 37. On social mobility: Lawrence Stone, 'Social mobility in England, 1500–1700', *P & P* 33 (1966); id., *Crisis*, 38–9; id. with Jeanne C. Fawtier Stone, *An Open Elite?* (Oxford, 1984), on which, see J. V. Beckett, 'Social mobility and English landed society', *Social History Soc. Newsletter*, 12 (1987); K. B. McFarlane, *The Nobility in Later Medieval England* (Oxford, 1973), 9, 11, and ch. 2; Christine Carpenter, *Locality and Polity* (Cambridge, 1992), 134–8, 151–2; Heal and Holmes, *Gentry*, 8–9, 11–12, 245; Richard Grassby, 'Social mobility and business enterprise in seventeenth-century England', in *Puritans and Revolutionaries*, ed. Donald Pennington and Keith Thomas (Oxford, 1978); Steve Rappaport, *Worlds within Worlds* Cambridge, 1989), ch. 8; E. A. Wasson, 'The penetration of new wealth into the English governing classes from the Middle Ages to the First World War', *EcHR* li (1998); Craig Muldrew, *The Economy of Obligation* (Basingstoke, 1998), ch. 9; id., 'Class and credit', in *Identity and Agency*, ed. French and Barry, 149–55; Keith Wrightson, *Earthly Necessities* (New Haven, 2001), 142–4, 192–3, 200–1, 303; Gregory Clark, *A Farewell to Alms* (Princeton, 2007), 130–1, 160–2.

5. Michael J. Bennett, 'Education and advancement', in *Fifteenth-Century Attitudes*, ed. Rosemary Horrox (Cambridge, 1994).

6. Felicity Heal, *Of Prelates and Princes* (Cambridge, 1980), 245.

7. *Works of John Robinson*, i. 248.

8. Thomas Cobbet, *A Fruitfull and Usefull Discourse* (1656), 230; Dorothy Leigh, *The Mothers Blessing* (1616), 1–3.

9. William Turner, *A Compleat History of Remarkable Providences* (1697), i. 138; John Prince, *Danmonii Orientales Illustres* (1701), 515.

10. Sir Henry Wotton, *A Philosophical Survey of Education*, ed. H. S. Kermode (Liverpool, 1938), 15; Elyot, *Boke named the Gouernour*, i. 38; *The Autobiography of Thomas Whythorne*, ed. James M. Osborn (1962), 2–3 (following Cicero, *De Officiis* 1. 31).

11. [Christopher Wase], *Considerations concerning Free-Schools* (1678), 72–3.

12. *Narratives of the Days of the Reformation*, ed. John Gough Nichols (Camden Soc., 1859), 273–5; John Strype, *The Life and Acts of John Whitgift* (Oxford, 1822), ii. 375.

13. Richard Bernard, *The Ready Way to Good Works* (1635), 341–2; Mulcaster, *Positions*, chs 36 and 37; Anthony Grafton and Lisa Jardine, *From Humanism to the Humanities* (1986), 156.

14. *OED*, s.v. 'upstart'; *Cottoni Posthuma*, ed. J.H. (1672), 336; Zeeveld, *Foundations of Tudor Policy*, ch. 8; W. R. D. Jones, *The Tudor Commonwealth 1529–1559* (1970), 100–6; Quentin Skinner, *Foundations of Modern Political Thought* (Cambridge, 1978), i. 45–6, 81–2, 236–41, 257–9; J. P. Cooper, 'Ideas of gentility in early-modern England', in *Land, Men and Beliefs*, ed. G. E. Aylmer and J. S. Morrill (1983).

15. Margo Todd, *Christian Humanism and the Puritan Social Order* (Cambridge, 1987), 182–200; Markku Peltonen, *Classical Humanism and Republicanism in English Political Thought 1570–1640* (Cambridge, 1995); Alex Davis, *Chivalry and Romance in the English Renaissance* (Woodbridge, 2003), 48–9, 61.

16. Milton, *CPW* vii, rev. edn, 458 (though for the limits to his faith in meritocracy, see above, p. 19); G. E. Aylmer, *The State's Servants* (1973), 61–2.

17. As was pointed out by Sylvia L. Thrupp, *The Merchant Class of Medieval London* [*1300–1500*] (Ann Arbor, 1948; pb 1962), 300.
18. Lewis Einstein, *Tudor Ideals* (1921), 248; *Papers of Nathaniel Bacon*, i. 148–50; Charles Gibbon, *A Work Worth the Reading* (1591), 1–2; H[umphrey] B[rooke], *The Durable Legacy* (1681), 166; *Boswell's Life of Johnson*, ed. R. W. Chapman and L. F. Powell (Oxford, 1934–50), iv. 308.
19. Grafton and Jardine, *From Humanism to the Humanities*, 156; *The Jesuit's Memorial*, ed. Edward Gee (1690), 257.
20. Louis B. Wright, *Middle-Class Culture in Elizabethan England* (Chapel Hill, NC, 1935), chs v and vi; Charles W. Camp, *The Artisan in Elizabethan Literature* (New York, 1924), 25–30, 38–40, 113–14; Margaret Spufford, *Small Books and Pleasant Histories* (1981), 244–50; Laura C. Stevenson, *Praise and Paradox* (Cambridge, 1984), chs 6 and 7; [John Houghton], *Englands Great Happiness* (1677), 19.
21. See below, p. 144.
22. Paul Slack, 'The politics of consumption and England's happiness in the later seventeenth century', *EHR* cxxi (2007), 615; Anthony Ashley Cooper, *Characteristicks of Men, Manners, Opinions, Times*, ed. Philip Ayres (Oxford, 1999), i. 196.
23. Smith, *Wealth of Nations*, i. 341, 343, 345 (II. iii), 540 (IV. v. b); ii. 674 (IV. ix).
24. Milton, *CPW* i. 405.
25. Gouge, *Domesticall Duties*, 542; 'Life of Gouge', in id., *A Learned and Very Useful Commentary on the Whole Epistle to the Hebrews*, [ed. Thomas Gouge] (1655), sig. a2.
26. Ilana Krausman Ben-Amos, *Adolescence and Youth in Early Modern England* (New Haven, 1994), 63–7; Wrightson, *Earthly Necessities*, 66.
27. *The Petty–Southwell Correspondence 1676–1687*, ed. Marquis of Lansdowne (1928; repr. New York, 1967), 105.
28. *The Flemings in Oxford*, ed. John Richard Magrath (Oxford Hist. Soc., 1904–24), iii. 102.
29. *The Works of Symon Patrick*, ed. Alexander Taylor (Oxford, 1858), ix. 412.
30. Ann Kussmaul, *Servants in Husbandry in Early Modern England* (Cambridge, 1981), 3.
31. Gouge, *Domesticall Duties*, 452; Richard Stock, *A Learned and Very Useful Commentary upon the Whole Prophesie of Malachy* (1641), i. 67; Kussmaul, *Servants*, ch. 4; Capp, *Gossips*, 154.
32. Ben-Amos, *Adolescence and Youth*, chs 3 and 4; Griffiths, *Youth and Authority*, ch. 7.
33. Bernard Bailyn, *Voyagers to the West* (1986), 127–9; *The Origins of Empire*, ed. Nicholas Canny (Oxford, 1968), 127–9; Alison Games, *Migration and the Origins of the English Atlantic World* (Cambridge, MA, 1999), 24–5, 27, 47–51; Larry Gregg, *Englishmen Transplanted* (Oxford, 2003), 143.
34. *Cal. S.P. Colonial, America and West Indies 1675–6, and Addenda 1574–1674*, 98.
35. David W. Galenson, *White Servitude in Colonial America* (Cambridge, 1981), 76.
36. Jack P. Greene, *Pursuits of Happiness* (Chapel Hill, NC, 1988), 195–6; James Horn, 'British diaspora', in *The Eighteenth Century*, ed. P. J. Marshall, *Oxford History of the British Empire*, ii (Oxford, 1998), 30–2.
37. See e.g. Anthony J. La Vopa, *Grace, Talent, and Merit* (Cambridge, 1988), 329, 365–6.

38. *Wealth of Nations*, i. 116 (I. x. a).
39. Ibid. i. 152, 138, 157 (I. x. c).
40. Ibid. i. 80 (I. vii) (following Montesquieu, *L'Esprit des lois* (1749), xx. xxii); id., *Moral Sentiments*, 223 (VI. ii. 1).
41. Smith, *Wealth of Nations*, ii. 781 (v. i. f).
42. Constance Jordan, *Renaissance Feminism* (Ithaca, NY, 1990); Simon Shepherd, *Amazons and Warrior Women* (Brighton, 1981); *First Feminists*, ed. Moira Ferguson (Bloomington, IN, 1985).
43. The influential text was Francois Poulain de La Barre, *De l'égalité des deux sexes* (1673), trans. A.L. as *The Woman as Good as the Man; or, The Equality of Both Sexes* (1677).
44. Margaret Cavendish, Duchess of Newcastle, *The Convent of Pleasure and Other Plays*, ed. Anne Shaver (Baltimore, 199), 50.
45. For a striking statement by a High Churchman to this effect, see Adam Littleton, *A Sermon at the Funeral of... the Lady Jane... Wife to the Honourable Charles Cheyne* (1669), 19-20. See, more generally, Alice Browne, *The Eighteenth-Century Feminist Mind* (Detroit, 1987); Hilda Smith, *Reason's Disciples* (Urbana, IL, 1987); Melissa Butler, 'Early liberal roots of feminism', in *Feminist Interpretations and Political Theory*, ed. Mary Lyndon Shanley and Carole Pateman (Cambridge, 1991); Mendelson and Crawford, *Women*, 251-4.
46. 'Sophia, a Person of Quality', *Woman not Inferior to Man* (1739; 1975), 55 (much of this work is lifted from Poulain de La Barre).
47. F. J. M. Korsten, *Roger North (1651-1734)* (Amsterdam, 1981), 137-42.
48. David Hume, *A Treatise of Human Nature*, ed. David Fate Norton and Mary J. Norton (Oxford, 2000), 201.
49. *Reliquiae Baxterianae*, ed. Matthew Sylvester (1696), i. 77.
50. Richard Coppin, *Truths Testimony* (1655), 37.
51. [Benjamin Laney], *Five sermons by the Lord Bishop of Ely* (1668), 97.

Individuality

1. For recent writing on this subject, see *Through a Glass Darkly*, ed. Ronald Hoffman, Mechal Sobel, and Fredrika J. Teute (Chapel Hill, NC, 1997), 200-2; Roy Porter, 'Introduction' to *Rewriting the Self*, ed. Porter (1997).
2. *The Civilisation of the Renaissance*, trans. S. G. C. Middlemore, 2nd edn (Oxford, 1945), 81.
3. On this large subject, see Colin Morris, *The Discovery of the Individual 1050-1200* (1972), and id., 'Individualism in twelfth-century religion', *Journ. of Ecclesiastical History*, 31 (1980); Caroline Walker Bynum, 'Did the twelfth century discover the individual?', ibid. 31 (1980); Natalie Zemon Davis, 'Boundaries and the sense of self in sixteenth-century France', in *Reconstructing Individualism*, ed. Thomas C. Heller et al. (Stanford, CA, 1986); Aaron Gurevich, *The Origins of European Individualism*, trans. Katherine Judelson (Oxford, 1995); Brigitte Miriam Bedos-Rezak, 'Medieval identity', *Amer. Hist. Rev.* 105 (2000); John F. Benton, 'Consciousness of self and perceptions of individuality', in *Renaissance and Renewal in the Twelfth Century*, ed. Robert L. Benson and Giles Constable (Oxford, 1982); D. L. D'Avray, *Death and the Prince* (Oxford, 1994), ch. 2; J. Paul Rylands, 'Merchants' marks and other mediaeval personal marks', *Trans. Historic Soc. of Lancs. and Cheshire*, 62 (1911); Lee Patterson, 'On the margin', *Speculum*, 65 (1990).

4. J. Ambrose Raftis, *Tenure and Mobility* (Toronto, 1964), 210–11.
5. David Aers, *Community, Gender, and Individual Identity* (1988), 77; Alan Macfarlane, *The Origins of English Individualism* (Oxford, 1978); Jane Whittle, 'Individualism and the family–land bond', *P & P* 160 (1998).
6. Andrew Martindale, *Heroes, Ancestors, Relations and the Birth of the Portrait* (The Hague, 1988); Selby Whittingham, *A Thirteenth-Century Portrait Gallery at Salisbury Cathedral*, 2nd edn (Salisbury, 1979); id., *Medieval Portrait Busts at New College, Oxford* (1973); Paul Binski, *Medieval Death* (1996), 102–3; Lorne Campbell, *Renaissance Portraits* (New Haven, 1990), 159, 166, 197; Robert Tittler, *The Face of the City* (Manchester, 2007), 117.
7. *Gabriel Harvey's Marginalia*, ed. G. C. Moore Smith (Stratford upon Avon, 1913), 156.
8. Michael C. Schoenfeldt, *Bodies and Selves in Early Modern England* (Cambridge, 1999), 21–2.
9. *Coriolanus*, III. ii.
10. Benjamin Boyce, *The Theophrastan Character in England to 1642* (Cambridge, MA, 1947); J. W. Smeed, *The Theophrastan 'Character'* (Oxford, 1985).
11. David Nichol Smith, 'Essay on the Character', in his edition of *Characters from the Histories and Memoirs of the Seventeenth Century* (Oxford, 1918).
12. Roger North, *The Lives of the Right Hon. Francis North, Baron Guilford; the Hon. Sir Dudley North; and the Hon. and Rev. Dr. John North*, ed. Augustus Jessopp (1890), i. 100; Richard Wendorf, *The Elements of Life* (Oxford, 1990), 150–69.
13. *The Guardian*, 144 (26 Aug. 1713).
14. *Critical Essays of the Seventeenth Century*, ed. J. E. Spingarn (Oxford, 1908–9), iii. 248; Locke, *Some Thoughts concerning Education*, 265; William Temple, *Miscellanea*, ii, 4th edn (1696), 357–8.
15. *Critical Essays of the Seventeenth Century*, iii. 248, 250; Pope, 'Epistles to Several Persons, ii: To a Lady'.
16. Temple, *Miscellanea*, ii. 358; 'The eighteenth Brumaire of Louis Bonaparte', in Karl Marx and Frederick Engels, *Selected Works* (1950), i. 303.
17. David Wootton, 'Unhappy Voltaire, or "I shall never get over it as long as I live" ', *History Workshop Journ.* 50 (2000), app.: 'The language of self: the birth of self-consciousness'.
18. Wotton, *Philosophical Survey of Education*, 25; Hobbes, *Leviathan*, 55 (ch. 8).
19. John Hall, *An Humble Motion* (1649), 37; Stephen Greenblatt, *Renaissance Self-Fashioning* (Chicago, 1980).
20. James Daybell, *Women Letter-Writers in Tudor England* (Oxford, 2006), 165–74.
21. [Richard Kilby], *Hallelu-iah: Praise Yee the Lord* (Cambridge, 1618), 28; Michael Mascuch, *Origins of the Individualist Self* (Cambridge, 1997), ch. 4.
22. *Notes of Me*, ed. Peter Millard (Toronto, 2000), 89, 94–9.
23. Mordechai Feingold, 'The Humanities', in *The History of the University of Oxford*, iv, ed. Nicholas Tyacke (Oxford, 1997), 319–21.
24. Harris, *Transformations of Love*, 9.
25. Christopher Hill, *The World Turned Upside Down* (1972), 11.
26. Thomas, *Religion and the Decline of Magic*, 362–82.
27. David Stone, *Decision-Making in Medieval Agriculture* (Oxford, 2005); *The Salt of Common Life*, ed. Edwin Brezette DeWindt (Kalamazoo, MI, 1995), p. xvii.

28. Sir Thomas Browne, *Religio Medici and Other Works*, ed. L. C. Martin (Oxford, 1964), 71. See Christopher Gill, 'Panaetius on the virtue of being yourself', in *Images and Ideologies*, ed. Anthony Bulloch et al. (Berkeley, 1993).
29. Michael Hunter, *Science and the Shape of Orthodoxy* (Woodbridge, 1995), 83; North, *Lives of the Norths*, i. 121.
30. Alexandra Shepard, 'Poverty, labour and the language of social description in early modern England', *P & P* 201 (2008).

CHAPTER 2

Arms and the Man

1. John Bossewell, *Workes of Armorie* (1597), fol. 6ᵛ; Geffrey Gates, *The Defence of Militarie Profession* (1579), 12.
2. *The Book of Chivalry of Geoffroi de Charny*, ed. Richard W. Kaeuper and Elspeth Kennedy (Philadelphia, 1996), 103–5; Malcolm Vale, *War and Chivalry* (1981), 30–1; Maurice Keen, *Chivalry* (New Haven, 1984), 152–3.
3. Richard W. Kaeuper, *Chivalry and Violence in Medieval Europe* (Oxford, 1999), 143.
4. *The Prologues and Epilogues of William Caxton*, ed. W. J. B. Crotch (EETS, 1928), 92–5; K. J. Höltgen, 'Die "Nine Worthies" ', *Anglia*, 77 (1959); Keen, *Chivalry*, 119–24; Tessa Watt, *Cheap Print and Popular Piety 1550–1640* (Cambridge, 1991), 212–14; Anthony Wells-Cole, *Art and Decoration in Elizabethan and Jacobean England* (New Haven, 1997), 25, 93, 115, 118–19, 149, 153, 154, 238, 295, 298–9.
5. Marc Bloch, *Feudal Society*, trans. L. A. Manyon (1962), ii. 292; Ruth Mohl, *The Three Estates in Medieval and Renaissance Literature* (New York, 1933), 29, 100, 116, 119–20, 127, 151–2, 205, 317–18; *The Boke of Noblesse . . . 1475*, ed. John Gough Nichols (Roxburghe Club, 1860), 76–7.
6. Maurice Keen, *Origins of the English Gentleman* (Stroud, 2002); Gerard Legh, *The Accedens of Armory* (1562), fol. 23.
7. *Miscellaneous Writings and Letters of Thomas Cranmer*, ed. John Edmund Cox (PS, Cambridge, 1846), 399; Joseph Bentham, *The Christian Conflict* (1635), 2.
8. *The Works of Jeremy Bentham*, ed. John Bowring (Edinburgh, 1838–43), ix. 82 (*Constitutional Code*, I. xiii).
9. Christopher Dyer, *Making a Living in the Middle Ages* (New Haven, 2002), 128; Charles Coulson, *Castles in Medieval Society* (Oxford, 2003); Christine Carpenter, *Locality and Polity* (Cambridge, 1992), 60–5, 92; Maurice Keen, 'Heraldry and hierarchy', in *Orders and Hierarchies in Late Medieval and Renaissance Europe*, ed. Jeffrey Denton (Basingstoke, 1999), 106–8; Pamela Nightingale, 'Knights and merchants', *P & P* 169 (2000); Michael Prestwich, *Plantagenet England* (Oxford, 2005), 389–90; G. L. Harriss, *Shaping the Nation* (Oxford, 2005), 111, 136–7, 175.
10. *The Book of the Ordre of Chyvalry*, trans. William Caxton, ed. Alfred T. P. Byles (EETS, 1926), 123.
11. Barnaby Rich, *A Souldiers Wishe to Britons Welfare* (1604), 13.
12. [Sir Thomas Elyot], *A Preservative agaynste Deth* (1545), sigs A2ᵛ–3; *A Discourse of the Commonweal*, ed. Mary Dewar (Charlottesville, VA, 1969), 24.

13. James Spedding, *The Letters and the Life of Francis Bacon* (1861–74), ii. 43–4 (1596); *The Naval Tracts of Sir William Monson*, ed. M. Oppenheim (Navy Recs Soc., 1902–14), i. 104–5.

14. Ruth Kelso, 'The doctrine of the English gentleman in the sixteenth century', *Univ. of Illinois Studs in Language and Literature*, xiv (1929), 48–9; Anna Bryson, *From Courtesy to Civility* (Oxford, 1998), 273.

15. Carpenter, *Locality and Polity*, 227; Lawrence James, 'The image of an armed man', *Trans. Monumental Brass Soc.* xii (1976, for 1975); Nigel Saul, 'Brasses and history', *The Historian* (Winter 1996), 13; Rachel Dressler, 'Steel corpse', in *Conflicted Identities and Multiple Masculinities*, ed. Jacqueline Murray (New York, 1999).

16. Helen Miller, *Henry VIII and the English Nobility* (Oxford, 1986), 137–42, 159–60; *Henry V*, ed. G. L. Harriss (Oxford, 1985), 40–1; Stone, *Crisis*, 203–4; J. P. Cooper, *Land, Men and Beliefs*, ed. G. E. Aylmer and J. S. Morrill (1983), 51 and ch. 4; C. S. L. Davies, 'The English people and war in the early sixteenth century', in *Britain and the Netherlands*, vi, ed. A. C. Duke and C. A. Tamse (The Hague, 1977), 5–6, 10–12; Penry Williams, *The Tudor Regime* (Oxford, 1979), 111–13, 134; G. W. Bernard, *The Power of the Early Tudor Nobility* (Brighton, 1985), 107, 206–7; id., 'Introduction' to *The Tudor Nobility*, ed. Bernard (Manchester, 1992), 9–10.

17. *Medieval Warfare*, ed. Maurice Keen (Oxford, 1999), 242.

18. Barnabe Barnes, *Foure Bookes of Offices* (1606), 183.

19. Jeremy Goring, 'Social change and military decline in mid-Tudor England', *History*, 60 (1975); Lindsay Boynton, *The Elizabethan Militia* (1967); A. Hassell Smith, 'Militia rates and militia statutes 1558–1663', in *The English Commonwealth 1547–1640*, ed. Peter Clark et al. (Leicester, 1979); Mark Charles Fissel, *English Warfare 1511–1642* (2001), 9, 82–5.

20. Goring, 'Social change and military decline', 188–91; Stone, *Crisis*, 204–6, 215–16; Gladys Scott Thomson, *Lords Lieutenants in the Sixteenth Century* (1923); Victor L. Stater, *Noble Government* (Athens, GA, 1994), 22–5, 38–46. On the military role of the nobility before 1559, see Steven Gunn, David Grummitt, and Hans Cools, *War, Culture, and Society in England and the Netherlands* (Oxford, 2007), pt iii.

21. William Harrison, *The Description of England*, ed. Georges Edelen (Ithaca, NY, 1968), 237; John Aubrey, *Miscellanies upon Various Subjects*, 4th edn (1857), 214.

22. Sir Thomas Smith, *De Republica Anglorum*, ed. Mary Dewar (Cambridge, 1982), 73; *The Institucion of a Gentleman* (1555), sig. Bvii; James McDermott, *England and the Spanish Armada* (New Haven, 2005), 183, 358 n. 56.

23. Roger B. Manning, *Swordsmen* (Oxford, 2003), 16, 34, 61; Sir Richard Barckley, *A Discourse of the Felicitie of Man* (1598), 366.

24. James Cleland, *The Institution of a Young Noble Man* (Oxford, 1607), 230.

25. Ian Atherton, *Ambition and Failure in Stuart England* (Manchester, 1999), 37.

26. *The Works of George Herbert*, ed. F. E. Hutchinson (Oxford, 1941), 277.

27. *The Works of Isaac Barrow* (Edinburgh, 1842), i. 491.

28. *The Diary of Sir Henry Slingsby*, ed. Daniel Parsons (1836), 31; J. S. A. Adamson, 'The baronial context of the English Civil War', *TRHS*, 5th ser., 40 (1990), 101; Clarendon, *History*, ii. 16, 61 n.

29. *The Works of Robert Sanderson*, ed. William Jacobson (Oxford, 1854), v. 115; Stone, *Crisis*, 266. Such comments suggest that what Roger B. Manning

describes in *Swordsmen* as the 'remilitarization' of English aristocratic culture may have been only superficial.

30. [John Streater], *Observations Historical, Political and Philosophical*, 5 (2–9 May 1654), 34.

31. T. W. Jackson, 'Dr Wallis's letter against Mr Maidwell, 1700', in *Collectanea, 1st Ser.*, ed. C. R. L. Fletcher (Oxford Hist. Soc., 1885), 272–83; John William Adamson, *Pioneers of Modern Education 1600–1700* (Cambridge, 1905), 178–9, 182, 189; G. H. Turnbull, *Hartlib, Dury and Comenius* (Liverpool, 1947), 57–64; W. A. L. Vincent, *The Grammar Schools...1660–1714* (1969), 198–201; Roger Lockyer, *Buckingham* (1981), 97; Manning, *Swordsmen*, 273, 442.

32. Harry Carter, *A History of the Oxford University Press*, i (Oxford, 1975), 362, 365; *The Miscellaneous Works of...Edward Earl of Clarendon*, 2nd edn (1751), 325–6.

33. O.B., *Questions of Profitable and Pleasant Concernings* (1594), fol. 11.

34. Samuel Butler, *Prose Observations*, ed. Hugh de Quehen (Oxford, 1979), 214; Abraham Tucker, *The Light of Nature Pursued* (1768–77), v/iii. 47.

35. Edward Cooke, *The Character of Warre* (1626), sig. D2^v; *The Souldiers Catechisme* (1644), 22.

36. Thomas Cooper, *Thesaurus Linguae Romanae & Britannicae* (1578), s.v. 'virtus'; *OED*, s.v. 'virtue'.

37. *The Historical Collections of a Citizen of London in the Fifteenth Century*, ed. James Gairdner (Camden Soc., 1876), 224; *OED*, s.v. 'manhood'.

38. *The Last Fight of the Revenge*, ed. Edward Arber (1871), 92. For a similar feat, Christopher Marlowe, *Tamburlaine the Great* (published 1590), II. iii. 1.

39. Thomas Birch, *The Life of Henry Prince of Wales* (1760), 384.

40. Keith Thomas, *Rule and Misrule in the Schools of Early Modern England*, Stenton Lecture (Reading, 1976), 9–12.

41. N. H. Keeble and Geoffrey Nuttall, *Calendar of the Correspondence of Richard Baxter* (Oxford, 1991), ii. 210. On schoolboy fights and battles: *A History of Shrewsbury School from the Blakeway MSS* (Shrewsbury, 1889), 62–3, 77; *The Diary of Bulstrode Whitelocke*, ed. Ruth Spalding (British Academy, 1990), 46; A. B. Gourlay, *A History of Sherborne School* (Sherborne, 1971), 68; Bernard Capp, *Cromwell's Navy* (Oxford, 1989), 246; Anthony Fletcher, *Gender, Sex and Subordination in England 1500–1800* (New Haven, 1995), 308–9; *The Memoirs of James Stephen*, ed. Merle M. Bevington (1954), 68–9, 113–14.

42. G. R. Owst, *Literature and Pulpit in Medieval England*, 2nd edn (Oxford, 1961), 45; *The Sixth Book of Virgil's 'Aeneid'*, trans. Sir John Harington (1604), ed. Simon Cauchi (Oxford, 1991), 45; Henry Peacham, *The Garden of Eloquence* (1577), sig. Niiij^v; T. S. Graves, 'Some pre-Mohock clansmen', *Studs in Philology*, 20 (1923); Keith M. Brown, 'Gentlemen and thugs in 17th-century Britain', *History Today*, 40 (1990); Daniel Statt, 'The case of the Mohocks', *SH* 20 (1995); Neil Guthrie, ' "No truth or very little in the whole story"?', *Eighteenth Century Life*, 20 (1996); Bryson, *From Courtesy to Civility*, 248–50; *OED*, s.v. 'boy', 'roaring boy', 'roister', and 'ruffian'.

43. Lincoln B. Faller, *Turned to Account* (Cambridge, 1987), 234 n. 6; Frances Harris, *Transformations of Love* (Oxford, 2002), 139; Alexandra Shepard, *Meanings of Manhood in Early Modern England* (Oxford, 2003), chs 4 and 5; Robert B. Shoemaker, *The London Mob* (2004), 164–6; Manning, *Swordsmen*, 142–67.

44. *Early Chronicles of Shrewsbury*, ed. W. A. Leighton (n.p., 1880), 57.

45. Garthine Walker, *Crime, Gender and Social Order in Early Modern England* (Cambridge, 2003), 47–8.

46. Charles Phythian-Adams, 'Rituals of Personal Confrontation in Late Medieval England', *Bull. John Rylands Univ. Lib.* 73 (1991); and see below, pp. 163–4.

47. *Worcester County Records: The Quarter Sessions Rolls, Part I*, comp. J. W. Willis Bund (Worcester, 1899), 23; Manning, *Swordsmen*, 144.

48. *Nottinghamshire Miscellany*, 4 (Thoroton Soc., 1967), 103; Hobbes, *Leviathan*, 89 (ch. 13); Pepys, *Diary*, iii. 201.

49. *Homilies*, 503.

50. John Northbrooke, *Spiritus est Vicarius Christi in Terra* (Shakespeare Soc., 1843), 8.

51. *A Calendar to the Records of the Borough of Doncaster*, iv (Doncaster, 1902), 76.

52. Keith Thomas, *Man and the Natural World* (1983), 183.

53. Hobbes, *Leviathan*, 151 (ch. 21); Aubrey, *Brief Lives*, ii. 241.

54. John Smyth, *The Lives of the Berkeleys*, in *The Berkeley Manuscripts*, ed. Sir John Maclean (Gloucester, 1883–5), ii. 372.

55. *Cottoni Posthuma*, ed. J[ames] H[owell] (1672), 323–5; *Crosby Records: A Cavalier's Notebook*, ed. T. Ellison Gibson (1880), 219.

56. [Joseph Swetnam], *The Araignment of Lewde, Idle, Froward, and Unconstant Women* (1615; 1807), 28; *A Spiritual Chaine and Armour of Choice for Sion Souldiers* (1622), 9; *Spectator*, 99 (23 June 1711), i. 416–17.

57. Though for some exceptions to this rule: Margaret Cavendish, 'A child-bed woman's funeral oration', in *Political Writings*, ed. Susan James (Cambridge, 2003), 226; Linda Pollock, 'Childbearing and female bonding in early modern England', *SH* 22 (1997), 291; Houlbrooke, *Death*, 359.

58. Eugene M. Waith, 'Heywood's women worthies', in *Concepts of the Hero in the Middle Ages and the Renaissance*, ed. Norman T. Burns and Christopher Reagan (1976); Simon Shepherd, *Amazons and Warrior Women* (Brighton, 1981); Marina Warner, *Joan of Arc* (1981), ch. 10; Hero Chalmers, *Royalist Women Writers 1650–1689* (Oxford, 2004), 40–55.

59. *Letters and Papers, Foreign and Domestic, of the Reign of Henry VIII*, ed. J. S. Brewer et al. (1862–1932), xx (2), 114 (no. 20).

60. J. R. Phillips, *Memoirs of the Civil War in Wales and the Marches 1642–1649* (1874), i. 177, 195; C. H. Firth, *Cromwell's Army* (new issue, 1905), 300–1; Antonia Fraser, *The Weaker Vessel* (1984), ch. 9; Charles Carlton, *Going to the Wars* (1992), 56, 165–7; Barbara Donagan, 'The web of honour', *HJ* 44 (2001), 368–9.

61. Dianne Dugaw, *Warrior Women and Popular Balladry, 1650–1850* (Cambridge, 1989); John Walter, 'Grain riots and popular attitudes to the law', in *An Ungovernable People*, ed. John Brewer and John Styles (1980), 72; Fraser Easton, 'Gender's two bodies', *P & P* 180 (2003), 142–9; Guyonne Leduc, 'Women in the army in eighteenth-century Britain', in *The Invisible Woman*, ed. Isabelle Baudino et al. (Aldershot, 2005); Stephen Conway, *War, State, and Society in Mid-Eighteenth Century Britain and Ireland* (2006), 119; Capp, *Gossips*, 316–17.

62. *Women's Worlds in Seventeenth-Century England*, ed. Patricia Crawford and Laura Gowing (2000), 223–5; *The Pepys Ballads*, ed. Hyder Edward Rollins (Cambridge, MA, 1929–32), v. 311–13; Mark Noble, *Memoirs of the Protectoral-House of Cromwell* (3rd edn, 1787), ii. 336–7; HMC, *10th Report*, app. iv, 475–6; Capp, *Gossips*, 218–23.

63. Dugaw, *Warrior Women*, 125; Henry Fielding, *Miscellanies*, ed. Henry Knight Miller (Oxford, 1972–7), i. 111.
64. Walker, *Crime, Gender and Social Order*, chs 3 and 4.
65. *OED*, s.v. 'virago'.
66. Sir Clement Edmondes, *Observations upon Caesars Commentaries* (1600; 1655 edn), 3rd pagination, 138–9; 'Sophia, a Person of Quality', *Woman not Inferior to Man* (1739), 51–2, 55, 60.
67. J. M. Beattie, *Crime and the Courts in England 1660–1800* (Oxford, 1986), 97; J. A. Sharpe, *Crime in Early Modern England 1550–1750* (Harlow, 1984), 109; Robert B. Shoemaker, *Prosecution and Punishment* (Cambridge, 1991), 213; id., *Gender in English Society* (Harlow, 1998), 298–9; id., *London Mob*, 168–70; Walker, *Crime, Gender and Social Order*, 23.
68. John Case, *Sphaera Civitatis* (Frankfurt, 1616), 105–6; Droh Wahrman, *The Making of the Modern Self* (New Haven, 2004), ch. 1; Conway, *War, State, and Society*, 120–1.
69. William Horman, *Vulgaria* (1519), fol. 272.
70. *The Early Works of Thomas Becon*, ed. John Ayre (PS, Cambridge, 1843), 233; *Homilies*, 574; Arthur Golding, 'Epistle Dedicatorie', to Philip of Mornay, *A Woorke concerning the Trewnesse of the Christian Religion*, trans. Philip Sidney and Arthur Golding (1587), sig. *3ᵛ.
71. William Gouge, *Gods Three Arrowes* (1631), 217.
72. Sydney Anglo, *Spectacle, Pageantry and Early Tudor Policy*, 2nd edn (Oxford, 1997), 16–17, 98–100, 108–16, 152–6, 184–5, 295, 299–300; Alan Young, *Tudor and Jacobean Tournaments* (1987); Richard C. McCoy, *The Rites of Knighthood* (Berkeley and Los Angeles, 1989); Steven Gunn, 'Chivalry and the politics of the early Tudor court', in *Chivalry in the Renaissance*, ed. Sydney Anglo (Woodbridge, 1990).
73. William Higford, *Institutions; or, Advice to His Grandson* (1658), 69–70.
74. R. S. Crane, *The Vogue of Medieval Chivalric Romance during the English Renaissance* (Menasha, WI, 1919); Henry Thomas, *Spanish and Portuguese Romances of Chivalry* (Cambridge, 1920), 242–62; Margaret Spufford, *Small Books and Pleasant Histories* (1981), 224–37; *Amadis de Gaule*, trans. Anthony Munday, ed. Helen Moore (Aldershot, 2004).
75. [Diego Ortuñez de Calahorra], *The First Part of the Mirrour of Princely Deedes and Knighthood*, trans. M[argaret] T[yler] (1578), sig. Aiii.
76. Charles W. Camp, *The Artisan in Elizabethan Literature* (New York, 1924), ch. 1; William Hunt, 'Civic chivalry and the English Civil War', in *The Transmission of Culture in Early Modern Europe*, ed. Anthony Grafton and Ann Blair (Philadelphia, 1990); J. S. A. Adamson, 'Chivalry and political culture in Caroline England', in *Culture and Politics in Early Stuart England*, ed. Kevin Sharpe and Peter Lake (Basingstoke, 1994); Tristan Marshall, '"That's the misery of peace"', *Seventeenth Century*, xiii (1998).
77. *The Autobiography of Edward, Lord Herbert of Cherbury*, ed. Sidney Lee, 2nd edn (n.d.), 6.
78. *Prologues and Epilogues of William Caxton*, 83.
79. J. J. Scarisbrick, *Henry VIII* (1968; Harmondsworth, 1971), 42–4; George Whetstone, *The Honourable Reputation of a Souldier* (1585), sigs Ciiᵛ, F1; William Shakespeare, *Henry VI, Part III* (1595), III. iii; Thomas Kyd, *The Spanish Tragedy* (1592), I. iv; *The Works of Thomas Nashe*, ed. Ronald B. McKerrow (1904–10; repr., ed. F. P. Wilson, Oxford, 1966), i. 212; Richard Crompton, *The Mansion of Magnanimitie* (1599), sig. E3; William Sampson,

Virtus Post Funera Vivit (1636), 13; Samuel Clarke, *The Lives of Sundry Eminent Persons* (1683), ii. 192; A. J. Pollard, *John Talbot and the War in France 1427–1453* (1983), 2–5.

80. *Cal. S.P. Foreign, 1569–1571*, 591–2.
81. C[hristopher] O[cland], *The Valiant Actes and Victorious Battailes of the English Nation*, trans. John Sharrock (1585); *Acts of the Privy Council*, new ser., xiii (1581–2), ed. John Roche Dasent (1896), 389–90.
82. Bernard Capp, *Astrology and the Popular Press* (1979), 218.
83. D. A. L. Morgan, 'The political after-life of Edward III', *EHR* cxii (1997); Richard Cust, *Charles I* (Harlow, 2005), 43; R[ichard] H[awkins], *A Discourse of the National Excellencies of England* (1658), 49–54; D.J. (rev. R.C.), *The Wars and Causes of Them, betwixt England and France* (1697); Robert D. Horn, *Marlborough* (Folkestone, 1975), 44, 134, 302, 488; *The Works of the English Poets*, ed. Alexander Chalmers (1810), ix. 339, xvi. 219; *The Diary of Thomas Turner 1754–1765*, ed. David Vaisey (Oxford, 1984), 137; Hannah Smith, *Georgian Monarchy* (Cambridge, 2006), 25–7.
84. Spedding, *Letters and Life of Francis Bacon*, iv. 404; Joshua Poole, *The English Parnassus* (1657; Menston, 1972), 89; Milton, *CPW* iii. 344; Lucy Hutchinson, *Memoirs of the Life of Colonel Hutchinson* (Everyman's Lib., n.d.), 4.
85. John Mackqueen, *British Valour Triumphing over French Courage* (1715), 250–65.
86. Daniel Defoe, *The Complete English Tradesman* (1745 edn; Oxford, 1841), i. 242.
87. Keen, *Chivalry*, index, s.v. 'Romans, chivalry of'; *The Boke of Noblesse*, 20–1, 26–7, 63–8, 78, 83–5.
88. Barnaby Rich, *Allarme to England* (1578), sigs Bi^v–ii; Thomas Churchyard, *A Generall Rehearsall of Warres* (1579), sig. Mi; William Blandy, *The Castle, or, Picture of Pollicy* (1581), fols 10^v–11; Thomas Digges and Dudley Digges, *Foure Paradoxes* (1604), 40–73; *Naval Tracts of Sir William Monson*, iii. 10–11.
89. Walter Bourchier Devereux, *Lives and Letters of the Devereux, Earls of Essex* (1853), i. 149; E[manuel van] M[eteren], *A True Discourse Historicall, of the Succeeding Governours in the Netherlands*, trans. T[homas] C[hurchyard] and R[ichard] R[obinson] (1602), 32.
90. Clements R. Markham, *The Fighting Veres* (1888), 437–8; Lord Nugent, *Memorials of John Hampden*, 5th edn (1899), 77.
91. William Prynne, *Eight Military Aphorismes* (1658), 20; Streater, *Observations*, 30; Markku Peltonen, *Classical Humanism in English Political Thought* (Cambridge, 1995), 113, 209–13, 217, 222–6, 253, 310.
92. *The Political Works of James Harrington*, ed. J. G. A. Pocock (Cambridge, 1977), 312–13; Hawkins, *Discourse of the National Excellencies*, passim.
93. *Discourse of the Commonweal*, ed. Dewar, 83; Blandy, *The Castle*, fol. 18^v; G. R. Waggoner, 'An Elizabethan attitude toward peace and war', *Philological Qtly*, xxxiii (1954); Paul A. Jorgensen, *Shakespeare's Military World* (Berkeley and Los Angeles, 1956), 185–96; John Downame, *Lectures upon the Foure First Chapters of Hosea* (1608), ii. 341; Edmondes, *Observations upon Caesars Commentaries*, i. 144; Mackqueen, *British Valour Triumphing*, 251–2. Modern discussions of this theme include J. G. A. Pocock, *The Machiavellian Moment* (Princeton, 1975), ch. vii; Quentin Skinner, *The Foundations of Modern Political Thought* (Cambridge, 1978), i. 162–6; Peltonen, *Classical Humanism in English Political Thought*, 42–3, 210–12, 216–17, 248–53, 262. See also below, pp. 132–4.

94. Malcolm Smuts, 'Cultural diversity and cultural change at the court of James I', in *The Mental World of the Jacobean Court*, ed. Linda Levy Peck (Cambridge, 1991), 110–11; Robin Headlam Wells, '"Manhood and chevalrie"', *Rev. of Eng. Studs*, new ser., 51 (2000).

95. e.g. J. R. Hale, *On a Tudor Parade Ground* (Soc. for Renaissance Studs, 1978), 3; Blandy, *The Castle*, fol. 18ᵛ; *An Apologie of the Earle of Essex* (1603), sig. F3; Ian Frederick Moulton, *Before Pornography* (Oxford, 2000), 20, 70; Alastair Bellany, '"The brightnes of the noble leiutenant's action"', *EHR* cxviii (2003), 1249–50; James Hart, *The Diet of the Diseased* (1633), 135–6; Conway, *War, State, and Society*, 120; and below, pp. 133–4.

96. John Ferne, *The Blazon of Gentrie* (1586), 37–8; Digges and Digges, *Foure Paradoxes*, 101; Captain John Smith, *Works*, ed. Edward Arber (Birmingham, 1884), 962–3; Matt[hew] Carter, *Honor Redivivus*, 3rd edn (1673), 9; *A Collection of Miscellaneous Grants...of Arms*, ed. Willoughby A. Littledale (Harleian Soc., 1925–6), lxxvi–lxxvii; Manning, *Swordsmen*, 93.

97. Margaret, Duchess of Newcastle, *The Life of William Cavendish, Duke of Newcastle*, ed. C. H. Firth (2nd edn., n.d.), 155.

98. Robert Barclay, *An Apology for the True Christian Divinity* (1676; 5th edn, 1703), 523–4.

99. Markham, *The Fighting Veres*, 233–4, 439; Stone, *Crisis*, 72–4; 'Journal of the siege of Rouen, 1591, by Sir Thomas Coningsby', ed. John Gough Nichols, *Camden Miscellany*, i (Camden Soc., 1847), i. 27; Carlton, *Going to the Wars*, 81.

100. Edward Hawkins, *Medallic Illustrations of the History of Great Britain and Ireland*, ed. Augustus W. Franks and Herbert A. Grueber (1885), i. xiv, 298–332; John Hursley Mayo, *Medals and Decorations of the British Army and Navy* (1897), i. xxviii–xxxi, 9–38; Firth, *Cromwell's Army*, 191; *Encyclopedia Britannica*, 11th edn (1910–11), s.v. 'medal'; Capp, *Cromwell's Navy*, 58, 111.

101. Samuel Buggs, *Miles Mediterraneus* (1622), sig. A3ᵛ; Roger B. Manning, *An Apprenticeship in Arms* (Oxford, 2006), 7, 41, 43–9.

102. Digges and Digges, *Foure Paradoxes*, 50.

103. Roderick Floud et al., *Height, Health and History* (Cambridge, 1990), ch. 2.

104. K. R. Andrews, *Elizabethan Privateering* (Cambridge, 1964), 61.

105. As Malcolm Vale remarks (*War and Chivalry*, 161), more needs to be found out about ransoms in the post-medieval era. For suggestive indications, see Markham, *The Fighting Veres*, 234; Firth, *Cromwell's Army*, 192–6; Viscount Dillon, 'Ransom', *Archaeological Journ.* lxi (1904); Fritz Redlich, *De Praeda Militari* (Wiesbaden, 1956), 30–7; C. G. Cruickshank, *Army Royal* (Oxford, 1969), ch. ix; Geoffrey Parker, *The Military Revolution*, 2nd edn (Cambridge, 1996), 58–9.

106. *Table Talk of John Selden*, ed. Sir Frederick Pollock (1927), 137–8.

107. Margaret Cavendish, Duchess of Newcastle, *CCXI. Sociable Letters* (1664), 386–7.

108. Sir John Harington, *A Short View of the State of Ireland*, ed. W. Dunn Macray (Oxford, 1879), 6; Hobbes, *Leviathan*, 71 (ch. 11); *Works of Robert Sanderson*, v. 112–13.

109. Steven Gunn, 'The French wars of Henry VIII', in *The Origins of War in Early Modern Europe*, ed. Jeremy Black (Edinburgh, 1987), 36.

110. *The Relation of Sydnam Poyntz*, ed. A. T. S. Goodrick, Camden Soc., 3rd ser. (1908), 45; Sir James Turner, *Memoirs of his Own Life and Times* (Edinburgh,

Bannatyne Club, 1829), 14. On this subject, see Manning, *An Apprenticeship in Arms*, pt i; Barbara Donagan, *War in England, 1641–1649* (Oxford, 2008), 40–54.

111. William Camden, *The Historie of...Princesse Elizabeth* (1630), iv. 83; Thomas Smith, *Catalogue of the Manuscripts in the Cottonian Library 1696*, ed. C. G. C. Tite (Woodbridge, 1984), 32.

112. Sir John Smythe, *Certain Discourses Military*, ed. J. R. Hale (Ithaca, NY, 1964), 26; John Stow, *The Annales*, augmented by Edmund Howes (1615), 806.

113. *The Correspondence of Sir Philip Sidney and Hubert Languet*, trans. Steuart A. Pears (1845), 154; *Letters and Memorials of State*, ed. Arthur Collins (1746), i/2. 286.

114. Thomas Middleton, *A Fair Quarrel* (1617), III. i; *The Political Works of Fulke Greville, Lord Brooke*, ed. John Gouws (Oxford, 1986), 79; *Apologie of the Earle of Essex*, sig. C1; George Gifford, *A Treatise of True Fortitude* (1594), sig. A2; *OED*, s.v. 'magnanimity'; Kaeuper, *Chivalry and Violence*, ch. 7.

115. [William Sprigg], *Philosophicall Essayes* (1657), 78–9; Sir Roger Williams, *The Actions of the Low Countries*, ed. D. W. Davies (Ithaca, NY, 1964), 75.

116. *OED*, s.v. 'brave', 'bravery'; Whetstone, *Honourable Reputation of a Souldier*, sig. Biiij^v; *Statutes of the Realm*, 1 Hen. VIII (1509–10), c. 14.

117. *The Political Works of James I*, ed. Charles Howard McIlwain (Cambridge, MA, 1918), 46.

118. *Correspondence of Robert Dudley, Earl of Leycester*, ed. John Bruce (Camden Soc., 1844), 407.

119. *Correspondence of Sidney and Languet*, 137; Fissel, *English Warfare*, 160; Henry Hexham, *A Iournall of the Taking in of Venlo, Roermont, Strale* (The Hague, 1633), sig. *** 2^v.

120. [Sir John Norreys], *The True Reporte of the Service in Britanie* (1591), sigs A4^v–B1; John S. Nolan, *Sir John Norreys and the Elizabethan Military World* (Exeter, 1997), 14, 99; George Whetstone, *A Mirrour of Treue Honour and Christian Nobilitie* (1585), sig. Diii^v.

121. *A Commentary of the Services and Charges of William Lord Grey of Wilton*, ed. Sir Philip de Malpas Grey Egerton (Camden Soc., 1847), 35–6.

122. Julian S. Corbett, *The Successors of Drake* (1900), 74–6, 78, 198; R. B. Wernham, *The Return of the Armadas* (Oxford, 1994), 174–6; R. Davies, 'News from the fleet', in *War: Identities in Conflict 1300–2000*, ed. Bertrand Taithe and Tim Thornton (Stroud, 1998).

123. *Autobiography of Edward, Lord Herbert of Cherbury*, 61–2.

124. Baldassare Castiglione, *The Book of the Courtier*, trans. Sir Thomas Hoby (Everyman's Lib., 1928), 95–6.

125. Devereux, *Lives and Letters of the Devereux*, i. 273. For similar challenges, Fissel, *English Warfare*, 165–6.

126. Edward Webbe, *His Travailes 1590*, ed. Edward Arber (1868), 32.

127. [Thomas Spencer], 'The genealogie, life and death of...Lord Brooke', ed. Philip Styles, in *Miscellany*, i, ed. Robert Bearman (Dugdale Soc., 1977), 178.

128. Adamson, 'Chivalry and political culture in Caroline England', 183; John Rushworth, *Historical Collections* (1721–2), v. 141.

129. John Strype, *Ecclesiastical Memorials* (Oxford, 1822), II. i, 159.

THE WANING OF THE MILITARY IDEAL

1. Manning, *Apprenticeship in Arms*, chs 1–3.
2. Donagan, *War in England*, 51–4; Manning, *Swordsmen*, pt i, and *Apprenticeship in Arms*, chs 1–7.
3. John Norden, *The Mirror of Honor* (1597), 22; Bertrand de Loque, *Discourses of Warre, and Single Combat*, trans. I(ohn) Eliot (1591), sig. A3^v; Sprigg, *Philosophicall Essays*, 78; Manning, *Swordsmen*, ch. 2.
4. Manning, *Apprenticeship in Arms*, ch. 13.
5. Peter Hughes, 'Wars within doors', in *The English Hero, 1660–1800*, ed. Robert Folkenflik (Newark, NJ, 1982), 179.
6. Fabian Philipps, *Ligeancia Lugens; or; Loyaltie Lamenting* (1661), 8.
7. John Childs, *The Army of Charles II* (1976), ch. ii.
8. Richard Baker, 'Honour discoursed of, in the theory of it and the practice' [1675–1713], BL, Sloane MS 881, fol. 123.
9. John Childs, *The British Army of William III* (Manchester, 1987), ch. ii; Geoffrey Holmes, *Augustan England* (1982), ch. 9; John Cannon, *Aristocratic Century* (Cambridge, 1984), 118–20; Ian Roy, 'The profession of arms', in *The Professions in Early Modern England*, ed. Wilfrid Prest (Beckenham 1987), 210–12; Anthony Bruce, *The Purchase System in the British Army* (1980), 13, 66–9; J. A. Houlding, *Fit for Service* (Oxford, 1981), 99–107; John Brewer, *The Sinews of Power* (1989), 56; Edward M. Spiers, *The Army and Society 1815–1914* (1980), ch. 1; Daniel A. Baugh, *British Naval Administration in the Age of Walpole* (Princeton, 1965), ch. 3; N. A. M. Rodger, *The Command of the Ocean* (2004), 112–18, 383–7, 508.
10. e.g. Humphrey Bland, *A Treatise of Military Discipline* (1727), 114–15.
11. John Le Neve, *Monumenta Anglicana...since the year 1700, to the end of the year 1715* (1717), 83.
12. Paul Langford, *A Polite and Commercial People* (Oxford, 1989), 588–9; Randolph Trumbach, *Sex and the Gender Revolution*, i (Chicago, 1998), 250–1, 253–5.
13. H. M. Colvin, 'Castles and government in Tudor England', *EHR* lxxxiii (1968); M. W. Thompson, *The Decline of the Castle* (Cambridge, 1987), ch. 8.
14. Evelyn, *Diary*, iii. 560; Herbert W. Macklin, *The Brasses of England* (1907; repr. Wakefield, 1975), 270, 276–7, 296, 302; Katharine A. Esdaile, *English Church Monuments 1510 to 1840* (1946), 101; Heal and Holmes, *Gentry*, 39; Paul M. Hunneyball, *Architecture and Image-Building in Seventeenth-Century Hertfordshire* (Oxford, 2004), 172.
15. C. L. Barber, *The Idea of Honour in the English Drama 1591–1700* (Göteborg, 1957), 200, 269, 331.
16. Daniel Defoe, *Some reflections on a Pamphlet lately Published* (1697), 21.
17. Jackson, 'Dr Wallis's letter', 315, 319; Richard Berenger, *The History and Art of Horsemanship* (1771), i. 211.
18. 'The life of Richard Nash, Esq.', in *Goldsmith: Selected Works*, ed. Richard Garnett (1950), 495–6; Richard Brinsley Sheridan, *The Rivals* (1775), v. i, in *The Dramatic Works* (1930), 81; Sir John Barnard, *A Present for Apprentices* (1741), 33; *Kalm's Account of His Visit to England...in 1748*, trans. Joseph Lucas (1892), 53; *Johnson's England*, ed. A. S. Turberville (Oxford, 1933), i. 392; Anne Buck, *Dress in Eighteenth-Century England* (1979), 55, 88; A. V. B. Norman, *The Rapier and Small-Sword, 1460–1820* (1980), 30–1.

19. Edward Gibbon, *Memoirs of my Life*, ed. Georges A. Bonnard (1966), 107–8; and comments of J. G. A. Pocock, *Barbarism and Religion*, i (Cambridge, 1999), 95–8.
20. Thomas Sprat, *The History of the Royal-Society of London*, ed. Jackson I. Cope and Harold Whitmore Jones (St Louis, 1959), 404; N[icholas] B[arbon], *A Discourse of Trade* (1690), 60.
21. Boynton, *Elizabethan Militia*; J. R. Western, *The English Militia in the Eighteenth Century* (1965).
22. Joyce Lee Malcolm, *To Keep and Bear Arms* (Cambridge, MA, 1996).
23. Julian Hoppit, *A Land of Liberty?* (Oxford, 2000), 129; André Corvisier, *Armées et sociétés en Europe de 1494 à 1789* (Paris, 1976), 126; Brewer, *Sinews of Power*, 31–2; Conway, *War, State, and Society*, ch. 3.
24. Thomas Hobbes, *Behemoth*, ed. Ferdinand Tönnies, 2nd edn (1969), 45; Adam Smith, *Lectures on Jurisprudence*, ed. R. L. Meek, D. D. Raphael, and P. G. Stein (Oxford, 1978), 540; also id., *Wealth of Nations*, ii. 786– 7 (v. i. f).
25. Francis Bacon, *The Essayes or Counsels*, ed. Michael Kiernan (Oxford, 1985), 95.
26. *Miscellaneous Prose of Sir Philip Sidney*, ed. Katherine Duncan-Jones and Jan van Dorsten (Oxford, 1973), 101–2; Alan Craig Houston, *Algernon Sidney and the Republican Heritage in England and America* (1991), 147, 157–9; Lois G. Schwoerer, *'No Standing Armies!'* (Baltimore, MD, 1974), *passim*; Blair Worden, 'Republicanism and the Restoration, 1660–1683', in *Republicanism, Liberty and Commercial Society 1649–1776*, ed. David Wootton (Stanford, CA, 1994), 165–74.
27. *Gentleman's Magazine*, ix (1739), 641.
28. Edward Wortley Montagu, *Reflections on the Rise and Fall of the Ancient Republicks* (1759; 4th edn, 1778), 382–92; Western, *English Militia*, chs iv and v; John Robertson, *The Scottish Enlightenment and the Militia Issue* (Edinburgh, 1985), chs 3 and 4.
29. Cit. Fania Oz-Salzberger, *Translating the Enlightenment* (Oxford, 1995), 119.
30. George Cary, *The Medieval Alexander*, ed. D. J. A. Ross (Cambridge, 1956), 254–7; John Barnie, *War in Medieval Society* (1974), ch. 5; *Henry V*, ed. Harriss, 4–5, 21; Peter Heath, 'War and peace in the works of Erasmus', in *The Medieval Military Revolution*, ed. Andrew Ayton and J. L. Price (1995), ch. 6; Nigel Saul, 'A farewell to arms?', in *Fourteenth-Century England*, ed. Chris Given-Wilson (Woodbridge, 2002); Caroline M. Barron, *London in the Later Middle Ages* (Oxford, 2004), 17–18, 21; Andrew Lynch, '"Manly cowardyse"', *Medium Aevum*, lxxiii (2004).
31. Frederick H. Russell, *The Just War in the Middle Ages* (Cambridge, 1975), 60–1, 217, 263, 269.
32. *The Works of Sir John Clanvowe*, ed. V. J. Scattergood (Cambridge, 1975), 69 (though, as Dr J. I. Catto points out, Clanvowe's words and deeds were at variance, for he died near Constantinople, possibly on crusade; 'Sir Willliam Beauchamp between chivalry and Lollardy', in *The Ideals of Medieval Knighthood*, iii, ed. Christopher Harper-Bill and Ruth Harvey (Woodbridge, 1990), 47–8); H. S. Cronin, 'The twelve conclusions of the Lollards', *EHR* xxii (1907), 302–3; Anne Hudson, *The Premature Reformation* (Oxford, 1988), 37, 91, 141, 367–70; Ben Lowe, *Imagining Peace* (University Park, PA, 1997), 113–23.
33. *The Receyt of the Ladie Kateryne*, ed. Gordon Kipling (EETS, 1990), 2–3.
34. More, *Utopia* (1516), trans. Ralph Robinson (1551; 1556), ed. Susan Bruce (World's Classics, Oxford, 1999), 97.

35. [Henricus Bomelius], *The Summe of the Holy Scripture*, trans. Simon Fish (1529; Menston, 1973), sigs Pviii^v–Qi.

36. Lowe, *Imagining Peace*, 273–84.

37. Rich, *Allarme to England*, sig. Biii^v; Albert Peel, 'A conscientious objector of 1575', *Trans. Baptist Hist. Soc.* vii (1920); F. G. Emmison, *Elizabethan Life: Disorder* (Chelmsford, 1970), 49–50; Geoffrey Nuttall, *Christian Pacifism in History* (Oxford, 1958), ch. iii; Peter Brock, *Pacifism in Europe to 1914* (Princeton, 1972), 171–3, and id., *The Quaker Peace Testimony, 1660 to 1914* (York, 1990), 3–6.

38. On this theme, see Eugene M. Waith, 'Manhood and valour in two Shakespearean tragedies', *ELH* 17 (1950), and Paul J. Alpers, *The Poetry of the Faerie Queene* (Princeton, 1967), ch. 10.

39. Theodor Meron, *Henry V's Wars and Shakespeare's Laws* (Oxford, 1993), 34 n.; Nina Taunton, *1590s Drama and Militarism* (Aldershot, 2001), 46.

40. Burton, *Anatomy*, i. 45–7; *Certain Queries* (1649), ed. Norah Carlin (1992), 15; John Locke, *Some Thoughts concerning Education*, ed. John W. and Jean S. Yolton (Oxford, 1989), 181 (para. 116); Richard Mulcaster, *Positions*, ed. Robert Herbert Quick (1887), 218; *The Works of Sir Walter Ralegh* (Oxford, 1829), v. 380–2; Ephraim Udall, *The Good of Peace and Ill of Warre* (1642), 33; Scott Mandelbrote, 'Représentations bibliques et édéniques du jardin à l'âge classique', *XVIIe Siècle*, 52 (2000), 648 n. 15; *Dalgarno on Universal Language*, ed. David Cram and Jaap Maat (Oxford, 2001), 123; Baxter, *Practical Works*, i. 798, iii. 413, iv. 560; Thomas Tryon, *The Way to Health, Long Life and Happiness*, 2nd edn (1691), 389, 393; Smith, *Catalogue of the Manuscripts in the Cottonian Library*, 32; [Lady Mary Chudleigh], *The Ladies Defence* (1701), 20; [John Trenchard and Thomas Gordon], *Cato's Letters* (1723–4), iii. 17–18, 196–205; Robert P. Adams, *The Better Part of Valor* (Seattle, 1962), 6–7, 69, 170, 193–4, 264; James Wilson Johnson, 'England, 1660–1800', in *The English Hero*, ed. Folkenflik; Samuel Johnson, in *The Adventurer*, 99 (16 Oct. 1753).

41. Robert Baker, *Witticisms and Strokes of Humour* (*c*.1766), 35.

42. Bomelius, *Summe of Holy Scripture*, sigs Mvi^v, Mi^v; Roger Ascham, *English Works*, ed. William Aldis Wright (Cambridge, 1904), 231; Ronald S. Crane, 'The vogue of *Guy of Warwick* from the close of the Middle Ages to the Romantic revival', *PMLA* xxx (1915), 136–41; G. R. Elton, *Policy and Police* (Cambridge, 1972), 196; William Tyndale, *Doctrinal Treatises*, ed. Henry Walter (PS, Cambridge, 1848), 161; *Markets of Bawdrie*, ed. Arthur F. Kinney (Salzburg, 1974), 169; *Works of Thomas Nashe*, i. 11; Irving A. Leonard, *Books of the Brave* (Cambridge, MA, 1949), 68–9, 88; Adams, *Better Part of Valor*, ch. 13.

43. *The Sermons of Edwin Sandys*, ed. John Ayre (PS, Cambridge, 1841), 257; *Early Works of Thomas Becon*, 251.

44. Edmondes, *Observations upon Caesars Commentaries*, 156–7; Churchyard, *Generall Rehearsall*, passim; Gates, *Defence of Militarie Profession*, 35, 43; *Apologie of the Earle of Essex*, sig. C1^v; *The Works of Thomas Adams* (Edinburgh, 1861–2), i. 43–4; Jorgensen, *Shakespeare's Military World*, 220–3; Schwoerer, 'No *Standing Army!*', 9, 19; Manning, *Apprenticeship in Arms*, 3.

45. Francis Peck, *Desiderata Curiosa* (1779), i. 48.

46. Gates, *Defence of Militarie Profession*, 43; Sir Henry Knyvett, *The Defence of the Realme*, ed. Charles Hughes (Oxford, 1906), 32.

47. Sir Robert Cotton, *An Answer to such Motives as were offer'd by Certain Military Men to Prince Henry*, 2nd edn, ed. Sir John Cotton (1675), 23.

48. Hubert Hall, *Society in the Elizabethan Age*, 3rd edn (1892), 45–6; Camp, *Artisan in Elizabethan Literature*, 125–6.

49. George Gascoigne, *The Posies*, ed. John W. Cunliffe (Cambridge, 1907), 142.

50. Sir Philip Sidney, *The Countess of Pembroke's Arcadia (The New Arcadia)*, ed. Victor Skretkowicz (Oxford, 1987), 344–5; Edmund Spenser, *The Faerie Queene* (1596), I. x. 60.

51. Margaret Cavendish, Duchess of Newcastle, *Poems and Phancies* (1664), 240–5.

52. Paul Slack, *From Reformation to Improvement* (Oxford, 1999), 83.

53. *A Declaration from the Harmles & Innocent People of God, called Quakers* (1660 [1661]), 2.

54. Thomas Edwards, *Gangraena* (1646; repr. Exeter, 1977), i. 34, iii. 9; William Lamont, *Last Witnesses* (2006), 25, 160–1; *The Life of Edward Earl of Clarendon... written by himself* (Oxford, 1857), i. 54.

55. William Ames, *Conscience with the Power and Cases thereof*, Eng. trans. (n.p., 1639), iii. 189, 184; H[umphrey] B[rooke], *The Durable Legacy* (1681), 19; Clarendon, *Miscellaneous Works*, 206; Thomas Hobbes, *The Elements of Law*, ed. Ferdinand Tönnies (1889; 1969), 100; id., *Leviathan*, 225–6 (ch. 29), 151–2 (ch. 21).

56. *Paradise Lost* (1667), ix. 28–9.

57. Ibid. xi. 689–97; *Paradise Regained* (1671), iii. 71–7.

58. Samuel Butler, *Hudibras*, ed. John Wilders (Oxford, 1967), 38.

59. *The Works of John Wilmot Earl of Rochester*, ed. Harold Love (Oxford, 1999), 89.

60. Locke, *Some Thoughts concerning Education*, 180; *The Educational Writings of John Locke*, ed. James Axtell (Cambridge, 1968), 410.

61. *The Poems of John Philips*, ed. M. G. Lloyd Thomas (Oxford, 1927), 15–16; *The Marlborough–Godolphin Correspondence*, ed. Henry L. Snyder (Oxford, 1975), iii. 1360, 1363–4.

62. *Swift vs. Mainwaring: 'The Examiner' and 'The Medley'*, ed. Frank H. Ellis (Oxford, 1985), *passim*; Jonathan Swift, *Gulliver's Travels*, 2nd edn (1727), pt iv, ch. v.

63. Robert Sanderson, *Twenty Sermons* (1656), 326.

64. [Daniel Defoe], *An Argument shewing that a Standing Army, with Consent of Parliament, is not inconsistent with a Free Government* (1698); *The Female Tatler*, 84 (16–18 Jan. 1710); E. J. Hundert, *The Enlightenment's Fable* (Cambridge, 1994), 204.

65. Jacob Vanderlint, *Money Answers All Things* (1734), 65, 24.

66. Isaac Watts, *A Defense against the Temptation to Self-Murther* (1726), 23.

67. *Paradise Lost*, ix. 31–2; N. H. Keeble, *The Literary Culture of Nonconformity in Later Seventeenth-Century England* (Leicester, 1987), 229–35.

68. Sir Thomas Browne, *Religio Medici and Other Works*, ed. L. C. Martin (Oxford, 1964), 26; *Essays of John Dryden*, ed. W. P. Ker (Oxford, 1926), ii. 30–1, 13; *The Poems of John Dryden*, ed. James Kinsley (Oxford, 1958), iv. 1442.

69. *Tracts and Pamphlets of Richard Steele*, ed. Rae Blanchard (Baltimore, 1944), 36. For 'Macedonia's madman', Mandeville, *Fable*, i. 55; Alexander Pope, *An Essay on Man* (1732–4), iv. 220; [John Brown], *Honour: A Poem* (1743), 12.

70. Harris, *Transformations of Love*, 67.

71. Mary Beth Rose, *Gender and Heroism in Early Modern English Literature* (Chicago, 2002), 113.

72. *Homilies*, 139; *The Acts and Monuments of John Foxe*, ed. George Townsend and Stephen Reed Cattley (1837–41), i. 522; *Crosby Records*, 220; Robert

Southwell, *An Epistle of Comfort* (n.d. [1587?]), fol. 137ᵛ; Richard Cust, 'Catholicism, antiquarianism and gentry honour', *Midland History*, xxiii (1998), 57–8.

73. Bernard Mandeville, *Enquiry into the Origin of Honour* (1732), p. iii; Hobbes, *Leviathan*, 68 (ch. 10); John Locke, *Two Treatises of Government*, ed. Peter Laslett (Cambridge, 1960), 357–9 (II, §§108–9); Adam Ferguson, *An Essay on the History of Civil Society 1767*, ed. Duncan Forbes (Edinburgh, 1966), 98, 147; William Alexander, *The History of Women* (1779), i. 102.

74. David Hume, *An Enquiry concerning the Principles of Morals*, ed. Tom L. Beauchamp (Oxford, 1998), 62 (sect. 7), 55 (sect. 6.2); Ernest Campbell Mossner, 'David Hume's "An historical essay on chivalry and modern honour"', *Modern Philology*, 45 (1947), 58.

75. Smith, *Lectures on Jurisprudence*, 527; id., *Wealth of Nations*, ii. 689–90 (v. i. a), 783 (v. i. f); id., *Moral Sentiments*, 206–7 (v. 2. 9); *Boswell's Life of Johnson*, ed. George Birkbeck Hill, rev. L. F. Powell (Oxford, 1934–64), ii. 218 (13 Apr. 1773); Samuel Johnson, *A Journey to the Western Islands of Scotland*, ed. J. D. Fleeman (Oxford, 1985), 76.

76. Western, *English Militia in the Eighteenth Century*, 108–9.

77. Mark Noble, *A History of the College of Arms* (1805), 317.

78. Daniel Fabre, 'L'Atelier des héros', in *La Fabrique des héros*, ed. Pierre Centlivres et al. (Paris, 1998), 238–41.

79. Margarette Lincoln, *Representing the Royal Navy* (Aldershot, 2002), 102–4; Conway, *War, State, and Society*, 141.

80. Linda Colley, *Britons* (New Haven, 1992), 177–83, 257–8; Nicholas Rogers, *Whigs and Cities* (Oxford, 1989), 235–40, 375–6; id., 'Brave Wolfe', in *A New Imperial History*, ed. Kathleen Wilson (Cambridge, 2004); Gerald Jordan and Nicholas Rogers, 'Admirals as heroes', *JBS* 28 (1989); Kathleen Wilson, *The Sense of the People* (Cambridge, 1995), ch. 3 and 255–8; ead., 'How Nelson became a hero', *The Historian*, 87 (Autumn 2005); Alan McNairn, *Behold the Hero* (Liverpool, 1997); Holger Hoock, 'The British military pantheon in St Paul's Cathedral', in *Pantheons*, ed. Richard Wrigley and Matthew Craske (Aldershot, 2004).

81. Mackqueen, *British Valour Triumphing*, 56–7.

82. John Smail, 'Credit, risk, and honor in eighteenth-century commerce', *JBS* 44 (2005), 456; *New Letters from Robert Southey*, ed. Kenneth Curry (New York, 1965), i. 28; E. P. Thompson, *The Making of the English Working Class* (Harmondsworth, 1968), 88; Stephen Brumwell, *Redcoats* (Cambridge, 2002), 54–7; Lincoln, *Representing the Royal Navy*, 32; Geraint H. Jenkins, *A Rattleskull Genius* (Cardiff, 2005), 295.

83. Mandeville, *Enquiry into the Origin of Honour*, 83. Similarly, *Works of Jeremy Bentham*, i. 380.

84. David Hume, *A Treatise of Human Nature* (1739–40), ed. David Fate Norton and Mary J. Norton (Oxford, 2000), 383 (3. 3. 2).

85. *The Crown of Wild Olive* (1866), in *The Works of John Ruskin*, ed. E. T. Cook and John Wedderburn (1909–12), xviii. 460, 470.

86. Karma Nabulsi, *Traditions of War* (Oxford, 1999), ch. 4.

87. All cited in Michael C. C. Adams, *The Great Adventure* (Bloomington, IN, 1990), 10, 44.

88. *Julian Grenfell, Soldier and Poet*, ed. Kate Thompson (Herts. Rec. Soc., 2004), 259; Samuel Hynes, *The Soldiers' Tale* (1997), 41–2.

89. *Boswell's Life of Johnson*, iii. 265–6 (10 Apr. 1778).

Appendix: Monarchs and Military Prowess

1. A little (but not much) more on this subject can be found in Charles Carlton, *Royal Warriors* (Harlow, 2003), chs 4 and 5.
2. *The 'Anglica Historica' of Polydore Vergil*, ed. Denys Hay, Camden ser. (1950), 161.
3. Jennifer Loach, *Edward VI*, ed. George Bernard and Penry Williams (New Haven, 1999; 2001), 153–8.
4. Sir Robert Naunton, *Fragmenta Regalia*, ed. Edward Arber (1870), 62 (and 32); George P. Rice, *The Public Speaking of Queen Elizabeth* (New York, 1951), 96–7; Mary Hill Cole, *The Portable Queen* (Amherst, MA, 1999), 155–63.
5. *A Royalist's Notebook*, ed. Francis Bamford (1936), 193; also Sir Anthony Weldon, *The Court and Character of King James* (1651), in *Secret History of the Court of James the First* (Edinburgh, 1811), ii. 6.
6. Keith M. Brown, 'From Scottish lords to British officers', in *Scotland and War A.D. 79–1918*, ed. Norman Macdougall (Edinburgh, 1991), 134–5; Per Palme, *Triumph of Peace* (1957), pl. vii.
7. *Political Works of James I*, 47; Sir Charles Cornwallis, 'A Discourse of the Most Illustrious Prince Henry, late Prince of Wales' (1641), in *The Harleian Miscellany* (1808–11), iii. 523–4; Birch, *Life of Henry Prince of Wales*, 88, 100, 182–7, 384–6; Roy Strong, *Henry, Prince of Wales and England's Lost Renaissance* (1986), 63–70.
8. Cust, *Charles I*, 160, 365–6, 414–15; *Cal. S.P. Venetian, 1636–9*, 297; Carlton, *Going to the Wars*, 186–7.
9. Manuel Schonhorn, *Defoe's Politics* (Cambridge, 1991), 4, 17, 54–5, 88, 92–7, 137; Abigail Williams, *Poetry and the Creation of a Whig Literary Culture 1681–1714* (Oxford, 2005), 105–21.
10. Carol Barash, *English Women's Poetry, 1649–1714* (Oxford, 1996), figs 16 and 18.
11. Ragnhild Hatton, *George I, Elector and King* (1978), 34–5, 43, 49, 82, 88–9, 100–1, 173; Philip Dormer Stanhope, fourth Earl of Chesterfield, *Characters* (Augustan Reprint Soc., Los Angeles, 1990), 4, 2; James Hayes, 'The royal house of Hanover and the British army, 1714–60', *Bull. John Rylands Lib.* 40 (1957–8); Smith, *Georgian Monarchy*, 21–4, 104–16.

CHAPTER 3

The Primal Curse?

1. *Homilies*, 517; *The Works of John Jewel*, ed. John Ayre (PS, Cambridge, 1845–8), ii. 941; Andrew Willet, *Hexapla in Genesin*, 3rd edn (1632), 1st pagination, 43; *The Works of...Gervase Babington* (1637), iii. 72–3; Gabriel Towerson, *An Explication of the Decalogue* (1676), 452; Robert South, *Sermons Preached upon Several Occasions* (1737), iv. 422.
2. Sir John Cheke, *The Hurt of Sedicion* (1549; facs., Menston, 1971), sig. Eiiii^v; John Locke, 'Of the conduct of the understanding', in *Posthumous Works* (1706), 53; *Dives and Pauper*, ed. Priscilla Heath Barnum (EETS, 1976–2004), i (2), 319–20.

3. *The Papers of Benjamin Franklin*, ed. Leonard W. Labaree et al. (New Haven, 1959–), iv. 481; *The Works of the Late William Robertson* (1826), v. 365–7; Marshall Sahlins, *Stone Age Economics* (1974), ch. 1.

4. John Wesley, *An Earnest Appeal to Men of Reason and Religion*, 5th edn (Dublin, 1750), 19.

5. James Axtell, *The Invasion Within* (New York, 1985), 149.

6. Adam Ferguson, *An Essay on the History of Civil Society 1767*, ed. Duncan Forbes (Edinburgh, 1966), 98.

7. *Tudor Economic Documents*, ed. R. H. Tawney and Eileen Power (1924; 1953), i. 97, 360; Ian Blanchard, 'Labour productivity and work psychology in the English mining industry, 1400–1600', *EcHR*, 2nd ser., xxxi (1978); Christopher Dyer, *Standards of Living in the Later Middle Ages* (Cambridge, 1989), 224–5; Mark Bailey, 'Rural society', in *Fifteenth-Century Attitudes*, ed. Rosemary Horrox (Cambridge, 1994), 162–3, 166–8.

8. [Daniel Defoe], *Giving Alms No Charity* (1704), 27.

9. Roger North, *A Discourse of the Poor* (1753), 60. There is a pioneering account of this phenomenon in Edgar S. Furniss, *The Position of the Laborer in a System of Nationalism* (Boston, 1920). Valuable subsequent discussions include Blanchard, 'Labour productivity and work psychology in the English mining industry, 1400–1600'; Peter Mathias, *The Transformation of England* (1979), ch. 8; id., 'Time for work, time for play', *Vierteljahrschrift für Sozial-und Wirtschaftgeschichte*, 81 (1994); *Labour and Leisure in Historical Perspective*, ed. Ian Blanchard, VSWG Beihefte, 116 (Stuttgart, 1994); John Hatcher, 'Labour, leisure and economic thought before the nineteenth century', *P & P* 160 (1998); Hans-Joachim Voth, *Time and Work in England 1750–1830* (Oxford, 2000), 179–81; Christopher Dyer, 'Work ethics in the fourteenth century', in *The Problem of Labour in Fourteenth-Century England*, ed. James Bothwell, P. J. P. Goldberg, and W. M. Ormrod (York, 2000); Keith Wrightson, *Earthly Necessities* (2000), 321–2.

10. Max Weber, *The Protestant Ethic and the Spirit of Capitalism*, trans. Talcott Parsons (1930), 60. Also Sahlins, *Stone Age Economics*, 69.

11. D. C. Coleman, 'Labour in the English economy of the seventeenth century', *EcHR*, 2nd ser., viii (1955–6); John Rule, *The Experience of Labour in Eighteenth-Century English Industry* (New York, 1981), ch. 2.

12. A. Hassell Smith, 'Labourers in late sixteenth-century England', *Continuity and Change*, 4 (1989), 380; Robert W. Malcolmson, *Life and Labour in England 1700–1780* (1981), 38–41, 45; Donald Woodward, *Men at Work* (Cambridge, 1995), 237–43; Gervase Rosser, 'Crafts, guilds and the negotiation of work in the medieval town', *P & P* 154 (1997), 8–9, 15; Douglas Hay and Nicholas Rogers, *Eighteenth-Century English Society* (Oxford, 1997), 116.

13. Smith, *Wealth of Nations*, i. 100 (1. viii). On 'St Monday', see E. P. Thompson, *Customs in Common* (1991), 372–8; Voth, *Time and Work*, 91–2, 100–2, 119.

14. *Autobiography of Francis Place (1771–1854)*, ed. Mary Thale (Cambridge 1972), 123 n.

15. David Levine and Keith Wrightson, *The Making of an Industrial Society* (Oxford, 1991), 260–1; Christopher Dyer, *An Age of Transition?* (Oxford, 2005), 232–4; Mavis E. Mate, 'Work and leisure', in *A Social History of England, 1200–1500*, ed. Rosemary Horrox and W. Mark Ormrod (Cambridge, 2006).

16. Smith, *Wealth of Nations*, i. 99–100 (1. viii).

17. [James Puckle], *A New Dialogue between a Burgermaster and an English Gentleman* (1697), 20–1.

18. Peter Earle, *A City Full of People* (1994), 99, 101.
19. *The Sermons of John Donne*, ed. Evelyn M. Simpson and George R. Potter (Berkeley and Los Angeles, 1953–62), x. 94; Richard Grassby, *The English Gentleman in Trade* (Oxford, 1994), 332; Roger North, *The Lives of the Right Hon. Francis North, Baron Guilford; the Hon. Sir Dudley North; and the Hon. and Rev. Dr. John North*, ed. Augustus Jessopp (1890), ii. 46.
20. Smith, *Wealth of Nations*, i. 139 (I. x. c), 50 (I. v) (and ii. 709 (v. i. b) on the poor's 'hatred of labour').
21. For its occasional use in Britain, see George Crabbe, *The Borough* (1810), letter xxiv, line 240, in *The Complete Poetical Works*, ed. Norma Dalrymple-Champneys and Arthur Pollard (Oxford, 1988), i. 592; and *OED*, s.v. 'compensation'.
22. Pepys, *Diary*, vii. 70. Pepys resolved not to make the same mistake himself; ibid. 57.
23. W. J. Sheils, *The Puritans in the Diocese of Peterborough 1558–1610* (Northants. Rec. Soc., 1979), 101; Sir Thomas Smith, *De Republica Anglorum*, ed. Mary Dewar (Cambridge, 1982), 72.
24. Burton, *Anatomy*, ii. 68.
25. *The Correspondence of Henry Oldenburg*, ed. A. Rupert Hall and Marie Boas Hall (Madison, WI, 1965–86), vi. 68–70.
26. *The Plays of Richard Steele*, ed. Shirley Strum Kenny (Oxford, 1971), 366.
27. Richard Cust, 'The "public man" in late Tudor and early Stuart England', in *The Politics of the Public Sphere in Early Modern England*, ed. Peter Lake and Steven Pincus (Manchester, 2007).
28. [William Alley], *The Poore Mans Librarie* (1571), i, fol. 23ᵛ.
29. John Bulwer, *Anthropometamorphosis* (1653), 297–8.
30. Richard Cust, 'Honour, rhetoric and political culture', in *Political Culture and Cultural Politics in Early Modern England*, ed. Susan D. Amussen and Mark A. Kishlansky (Manchester, 1995), 98; G. D. Squibb, *The High Court of Chivalry* (Oxford, 1959), 175; *Conversations at Little Gidding*, ed. A. M. Williams (Cambridge, 1970), 135–56.
31. Boyle, *Ethics*, 116; Sir Charles Cornwallis, 'A Discourse of the Most Illustrious Prince Henry, late Prince of Wales' (1641), in *The Harleian Miscellany* (1808–11), iii. 525; Margaret Cavendish, Marchioness of Newcastle, *CCXI. Sociable Letters* (1664), 202.
32. George Gascoigne, 'The Steele Glas' (1576), in *The Glasse of Governement... and Other... Works*, ed. John W. Cunliffe (Cambridge, 1910), 171.
33. *The Works of James Pilkington*, ed. James Scholefield (PS, Cambridge, 1842), 446.
34. 11 Hen. VII (1495), c. 22.
35. Woodward, *Men at Work*, 129–30.
36. *The Economic Writings of Sir William Petty*, ed. Charles Henry Hull (Cambridge, 1899), i. 110; Paul S. Seaver, 'Work, discipline, and the apprentice in early modern London', in *Wellsprings of Achievement*, ed. Penelope Gouk (Aldershot, 1995), 164; Rule, *Experience of Labour*, 57–61; Voth, *Time and Work*, 72–6, 98, 121–3, 245 (an impressive attempt to bring precision to this much-discussed topic).
37. William Mather, *Of Repairing and Mending the Highways* (1696), 29.
38. John Norden, *The Surveyors Dialogue* (1607), 107.
39. *Antiquary on Horseback*, ed. Jane M. Ewbank (Cumberland and Westmorland Archaeol. and Antiquarian Soc., 1963), 118.
40. *Cal. S.P. Domestic, 1595–7*, 344; Beds. and Luton Archives and Records Service, HSA 1679 W 56 (depositions).

41. *Tudor Economic Documents*, ii. 339–40.
42. Jacques Le Goff, *Time, Work and Culture in the Middle Ages*, trans. Arthur Goldhammer (Chicaco, 1980) 68–70, 114–115; Steven A. Epstein, *Wage Labor and Guilds in Medieval Europe* (Chapel Hill, NC, 1991), 174–7; Patricia Ranft, *The Theology of Work* (New York, 2006); Kellie Robertson, *The Laborer's Two Bodies* (New York, 2006), 1–2.
43. G. R. Owst, *Literature and Pulpit in Medieval England*, 2nd edn (Oxford, 1961), 551, 554–7, 568–70; *Wimbledon's Sermon Redde Rationem Villicationis Tue*, ed. Ione Kemp Knight (Pittsburgh, 1967), 60; *Two Wycliffite Texts*, ed. Anne Hudson (EETS, 1993), 3–23.
44. Dyer, *An Age of Transition?*, 235–41.
45. Richard M. Douglas, 'Talent and vocation in humanist and Protestant thought', in *Action and Conviction in Early Modern Europe*, ed. Theodore K. Rabb and Jerrold E. Seigel (Princeton, 1969); Margo Todd, *Christian Humanism and the Puritan Social Order* (Cambridge, 1987), 34–6, 122–7.
46. Max Weber, *The Protestant Ethic and the Spirit of Capitalism* (1904–5; trans. Talcott Parsons, 1930), and R. H. Tawney, *Religion and the Rise of Capitalism* (1926; West Drayton, 1938), have inspired many subsequent studies of this subject, including Robert S. Michaelsen, 'Changes in the Puritan concept of calling or vocation', *New England Qtly*, xxvi (1953); Charles H. and Katherine George, *The Protestant Mind of the English Reformation 1570–1640* (Princeton, 1961), esp. ch. 3; Christopher Hill, *Society and Puritanism in Pre-Revolutionary England* (1964), ch. 4; id., *Change and Continuity in Seventeenth-Century England* (rev. edn, 1991), ch. 3; Timothy Hall Breen, 'The non-existent controversy', *Church History*, 35 (1966); Douglas, 'Talent and vocation in humanist and Protestant thought'; Paul Seaver, 'The Puritan work ethic revisited', *JBS* 19 (1979–80); C. John Sommerville, 'The anti-Puritan work ethic', *JBS* 20 (1980–1); Richard L. Greaves, *Society and Religion in Elizabethan England* (Minneapolis, 1981), ch. 9; Charles L. Cohen, 'The saints zealous in love and labor', *Harvard Theological Rev.* 76 (1983); Todd, *Christian Humanism and the Puritan Social Order*, ch. 5; Edward Terrar, 'A seventeenth-century theology of liberation', *Journ. of Religious History*, 17 (1993); Paul Marshall, *A Kind of Life Imposed on Man* (1996); Claire Walker, 'Gender and work in seventeenth-century English cloisters', *Sixteenth-Century Journ.* 30 (1999); Harvey Goldman, 'Good work from Homer to the present', *Daedalus* (Summer 2005).
47. Perkins, *Workes*, i. 728; Baxter, *Practical Works*, i. 356.
48. *All the Sermons of . . . Samuel Hieron* (1614), 245.
49. Thomas Gataker, *A Mariage Praier* (1624), 18–19.
50. [Henricus Bomelius], *The Summe of the Holy Scripture*, trans. Simon Fish ([Antwerp], 1529), sigs Qii^v–iii; Lewis Atterbury, *Sermons on Select Subjects* (1743), ii. 411; Tawney, *Religion and the Rise of Capitalism*, 199.
51. Perkins, *Workes*, i. 732.
52. Ibid. 732–3; Greaves, *Society and Religion*, 384–6; Tawney, *Religion and the Rise of Capitalism*, 239.
53. *The Catechism of Thomas Becon*, ed. John Ayre (PS, Cambridge, 1844), 106–7; T[homas] W[ilson], *Aenigmatica Sacra*, in *Theologicall Rules* (1615), 2nd pagination, 161; [John Dod and Robert Cleaver], *A Plaine and Familiar Exposition of the Ten Commandements* (1618), 307–8; *Works of Gervase Babington*, iii. 72.
54. William Turner, *A New Booke of Spirituall Physik* (1555), fol. 5; Norden, *Surveyors Dialogue*, sigs A4^v–5, pp. 230–1; John Downame, *A Guide to God-*

lynesse (1622), 258–9; James Hart, *The Diet of the Diseased* (1633), 215; Robert Gell, *Gells Remaines*, ed. R. B[acon] (1676), i. 626; H[umphrey] B[rooke], *The Durable Legacy* (1681), 146; *The Theological Works of the Right Reverend John Sharp* (Oxford, 1929), iv. 105–6; Hill, *Society and Puritanism*, 138–43; Greaves, *Society and Religion*, 390–1.

55. 'Laophilus Tyrannus' [Roger Jones?], *Mene Tekel* (1663), 58.
56. e.g. Thomas Edwards, *Gangraena* (1646; facs., Exeter, 1977), i. 30; Susan Dwyer Amussen, 'The part of a Christian man', in *Political Culture and Cultural Politics*, ed. Amussen and Kishlansky, 224.
57. John Jones, *The Arte and Science of Preserving Bodie and Soule* (1579), 34.
58. *The Works of John Jewel*, ii, ed. John Ayre (PS, Cambridge, 1847), 864.
59. Hart, *Diet of the Diseased*, 21; John Milton, *Samson Agonistes*, lines 1297–9; [John Pollexfen], *Discourse of Trade, Coyn, and Paper Credit* (1697), 44; George Berkeley, Lord Bishop of Cloyne, *The Querist* (1750), 36; *Particular Friends: The Correspondence of Samuel Pepys and John Evelyn*, ed. Guy de la Bédoyère (Woodbridge, 1997), 274.
60. John Brinsley, *Ludus Literarius; or, The Grammar Schoole*, ed. E. T. Campagnac (Liverpool, 1917), 4; John Turner, *The Usurers Plea Answered* (1634), 1–4; 'A Priest to the Temple', in *The Works of George Herbert*, ed. F. E. Hutchinson (Oxford, 1941), 274; John Preston, *Sinnes Overthrow*, 4th edn (1641), 254–5; John Warren, *The Unprofitable Servant* (1655), 10–11; Towerson, *Explication*, 456; *Theological Works of John Sharp*, iv. 90–1, 102–4; Abraham Markland, *Sermons preach'd at... Winchester* (1729), i. 29, 33–5; OED, s.v. 'talent', 5; Marshall, *A Kind of Life Imposed on Man*, 25.
61. William Tyndale, *Doctrinal Treatises*, ed. Henry Walter (PS, Cambridge, 1848), 102; repeated by Perkins, *Workes*, i. 391.
62. *Sermons and Remains of Hugh Latimer*, ed. George Elwes Corrie (PS, Cambridge, 1845), 122; 'The elixir', in *Works of George Herbert*, 185.
63. Godfrey Goodman, *The Fall of Man* (1616), 61.
64. Richard Rogers, *Seven Treatises* (1603), 180; *Works of Gervase Babington*, 73; Joseph Bentham, *The Christian Conflict* (1635), 362; Daniel Rogers, *Matrimoniall Honour* (1642), 222; *The Works of Robert Sanderson*, ed. William Jacobson (1854), 118–19; Baxter, *Practical Works*, i. 357; Towerson, *Explication*, 454. Cf. Le Goff, 'Licit and illicit trades in the medieval West', in *Time, Work, and Culture in the Middle Ages*.
65. *Sermons by Hugh Latimer*, ed. George Elwes Corrie (PS, Cambridge, 1844), 376; Perkins, *Workes*, i. 732.
66. *Works of Pilkington*, 387.
67. William Gouge, *A Learned and Very Useful Commentary on the Whole Epistle to the Hebrewes* (1655), 4th pagination, 37.
68. William Whately, *A Bride-Bush* (1619), 9.
69. *Bathshebaes Instructions to Her Sonne Lemuell*, ed. John Dod and William Hinde (1614), 60.
70. John Archer Gee, *The Life and Works of Thomas Lupset* (1928), 246; Greaves, *Society and Religion*, 387; William Whately, *The Redemption of Time* (1634), 18–23; Samuel Clarke, *The Lives of Sundry Eminent Persons* (1683), i. 4, 34, 138, 143; Baxter, *Practical Works*, i. 321–3; Gerald R. Cragg, *Puritanism in the Period of the Stuart Persecution* (Cambridge, 1957), 134–5; Boyle, *Ethics*, 239.
71. Baxter, *Practical Works*, i. 300.

72. Dudley Fenner, *A Short and Profitable Treatise of Lawfull and Usefull Recreations* (Middleburg, 1590), sigs A5ᵛ–6; Henry Crosse, *Vertues Common-wealth* (1603), sigs Q3ᵛ–4; Robert Bolton, *Some Generall Directions for a Comfortable Walking with God*, 5th edn (1638), 157; Henry Scudder, *The Christians Daily Walke*, 8th edn (1642), 59–60; *The Correspondence of John Locke*, ed. E. S. de Beer (Oxford, 1976–), i. 473–5.

73. *Tho[mas] Tryon's Letters upon Several Occasions* (1700), 115.

74. Baxter, *Practical Works*, i. 357; John Walsh, ' "The bane of industry"?', *Studs in Church History*, 37 (2002).

75. Peter Chamberlen, *The Poor Mans Advocate* (1650), 9.

76. *The Complete Works of Richard Sibbes* (Edinburgh, 1863), vi. 52.

77. *Tudor Economic Documents*, iii. 115; 'The Institucion & Dyssepline of a Souldier', BL, Harleian MS 519, fol. 18.

78. Ann Kussmaul, *Servants in Husbandry in Early Modern England* (Cambridge, 1981), app. 6; Steve Hindle, *On the Parish?* (Oxford, 2004), ch. 3.

79. Furniss, *Position of the Laborer*, ch. ii; Joyce Oldham Appleby, *Economic Thought and Ideology in Seventeenth-Century England* (Princeton, 1978), ch. 6; Steven Pincus, 'The making of a great power?', *European Legacy*, 5 (2000), 536, 539.

80. A. Ruth Fry, *John Bellers 1654–1725* (1935), 124; *Economic Writings of Sir William Petty*, i. 31.

81. *Masters, Servants, and Magistrates in Britain and the Empire, 1562–1955*, ed. Douglas Hay and Paul Craven (Chapel Hill, NC, 2004), 42.

82. *The Works of Isaac Barrow* (Edinburgh, 1842), i. 477; Edward Waterhouse, *Fortescutus Illustratus* (1663), 372.

83. *The Petty Papers*, ed. Marquis of Lansdowne (1927), i. 211.

84. See below, p. 142.

The Rewards of Labour

1. *The Divine Weeks and Works of Guillaume de Saluste Sieur du Bartas*, trans. Joshua Sylvester, ed. Susan Snyder (Oxford, 1979), i. 325; George Walker, *God made Visible in his Workes* (1641), 249; Benjamin Needler, *Expository Notes, with Practical Observations* (1655), 39; John Milton, *Paradise Lost* (1667), iv. 327–31, 616–19; Keith Thomas, 'Work and leisure in pre-industrial society', *P & P* 29 (1964), 56–7.

2. Francis Godwin, *The Man in the Moon* (1638; Hereford, 1959), 39; M[ary] Cary, *The Little Horns Doom & Downfall* (1651), 307–8, 310.

3. *Sermons very fruitfull, godly and learned by Roger Edgeworth*, ed. Janet Wilson (Cambridge, 1993), 253.

4. [Henry Bradshaw], *The Holy Lyfe and History of Saynt Werburge*, ed. Edward Hawkins (Chetham Soc., 1848), 3; Thomas Starkey, *A Dialogue between Pole and Lupset*, ed. T. F. Mayer, Camden, 4th ser. (1989), 53; *The Book of Husbandry by Master Fitzherbert*, ed. Walter W. Skeat (Eng. Dialect Soc., 1882), 1; *Prayers and Other Pieces of Thomas Becon*, ed. John Ayre (PS, Cambridge, 1844), 25; *The Sermons of Edwin Sandys*, ed. John Ayre (PS, Cambridge, 1841), 182; Matthew Kellison, *A Survey of the New Religion* (Douai, 1605), 319.

5. *Paradise Lost*, iv. 616–19.

6. John White, *The Planters Plea* (1630), cit. Axtell, *The Invasion Within*, 150.

7. Thomas Powell, *Tom of All Trades* (1631), ed. F. J. Furnivall (New Shakspere Soc., 1876), 144.
8. In addition to authors quoted in *The Oxford Book of Work*, ed. Keith Thomas (Oxford, 1999), 123–8, see John Caius, *A Booke or Counseill against the Disease called the Sweate* (1552), ed. Archibald Malloch (New York, 1937), fol. 19ᵛ; *Homilies*, 518–19; William Bullein, *Bulleins Bulwarke of Defence against all Sicknesse* (1579), 5th pagination, fol. 18; Thomas Cogan, *The Haven of Health* (1589), 1–2; Everard Maynwaring, *The History and Mystery of the Venereal Lues* (1673), 111.
9. C. H. and Katherine George were virtually alone among historians in detecting in early English Protestant writers an emphasis on 'the positive, creative and even enjoyable aspects of work' (*Protestant Mind of the English Reformation*, 132, 139, 142), but they adduced few texts in support of their view.
10. Edmund Dudley, *The Tree of Commonwealth*, ed. D. M. Brodie (Cambridge, 1948), 48; Bomelius, *Summe of Holy Scripture*, sigs Mviii, Qii; *The Chronicle and Political Papers of Edward VI*, ed. W. K. Jordan (1966), 166.
11. Thomas Watson, *Holsome and Catholyke Doctryne concerninge the Seven Sacramentes* (1558), fol. xciiᵛ.
12. Norden, *Surveyor's Dialogue*, 230; Edward Waterhouse, *The Gentlemans Monitor* (1665), 67; Rogers, *Seven Treatises*, 357.
13. Baxter, *Practical Works*, iii. 642, i. 357 (and 754).
14. John Cary, *An Account of the Proceedings of the Corporation of Bristol* (1700), 19.
15. Richard Steele, *The Trades-man's Calling* (1684), 83; Daniel Defoe, *The Complete English Tradesman* (1745; Oxford, 1841), i. 35.
16. George Wither, *Haleluiah; or, Britans Second Remembrancer* (1641), pt i (Spenser Soc., 1879), 14.
17. Karl Marx, *Grundrisse*, trans. Martin Nicolaus (Harmondsworth, 1973), 611.
18. Alfred Plummer, *The London Weavers' Company 1600–1970* (1972), 327.
19. David Hume, 'Of Refinement in the Arts' and 'Of Interest', in *Essays, Moral, Political, and Literary*, ed. T. H. Green and T. H. Grose (1908 edn), i. 301, 325; id., *A Treatise of Human Nature*, ed. David Fate Norton and Mary J. Norton (Oxford, 2000), 228.
20. *Sermons of Edwin Sandys*, 117.
21. Burton, *Anatomy*, i. 240, 416. Also ibid. ii. 68, and Baxter, *Practical Works*, i. 253 (on constant employment as a cure for melancholy).
22. *Notes of Me: The Autobiography of Roger North*, ed. Peter Millard (Toronto, 2000), 206.
23. Patricia Meyer Spacks, *Boredom* (1995).
24. Stone, *Crisis*, 382–3, 387–92.
25. *Memoirs of Dr Joseph Priestley, to the year 1795, written by himself* (1806–7), i. 82.
26. Hobbes, *Latin Works*, ii. 100.
27. Boyle, *Ethics*, 246–7.
28. Pepys, *Diary*, ix. 354.
29. Gilbert Burnet, *A Discourse of the Pastoral Care*, 3rd edn (1713), 184.
30. Pepys, *Diary*, iii. 125.
31. Brinsley, *Ludus Literarius*, 3.
32. Richard Moore, *A Pearl in an Oyster-Shel* (1675), 47.
33. The National Archives, SP 29/145/47 (letter to Samuel Pepys, 16 Jan. 1665/6). On her, see G. E. Aylmer, *The Crown's Servants* (Oxford, 2002), 228.

34. Nehemiah Wallington, *Historical Notices of Events*, [ed. R. Webb] (1869), vol. i, p. xi.

35. *Remarks and Collections of Thomas Hearne*, ed. C. E. Doble et al. (Oxford Hist. Soc., 1885–1921), vii. 263.

36. William Ellis, *The Modern Husbandman* (1750), ii. 49.

37. Sir William Temple, *Observations upon the United Provinces of the Netherlands*, ed. G. N. Clark (Cambridge, 1932), 130.

38. *Locke on Money*, ed. Patrick Hyde Kelly (Oxford, 1991), ii. 494.

39. *Gregorii Posthuma*, ed. J[ohn] G[urgany] (1650), sig. A4; J. B. Williams, *Memoirs of . . . Sir Matthew Hale* (1835), 375.

40. George Cavendish, *The Life and Death of Cardinal Wolsey*, ed. Richard S. Sylvester (EETS, 1959), 58.

41. Stephen Marshall, *The Churches Lamentation for the Good Man his Losse* (1644), 29.

42. John Hacket, *Scrinia Reserata* (1693), i. 7; Thomas Gumble, *The Life of General Monck* (1671), 469.

43. Thomas Gouge, 'A Narrative of the Life and Death of Doctor Gouge', in Gouge, *Learned Commentary on Hebrewes*, sig. C2.

44. [John King], *A Memoir of the Life and Death of Sir John King* (written 1677), [ed. George Henry Sawtell] (1855), 15–16.

45. Boyle, *Ethics*, 245.

46. Above, p. 82.

47. John Hatcher, *The History of the British Coal Industry*, i (Oxford, 1993), 322.

48. Paul Griffiths, *Youth and Authority* (Oxford, 1996), 327–34; Earle, *A City Full of People*, 64–5; Polly Seleski, 'Women, work and cultural change in eighteenth- and early nineteenth-century London', in *Popular Culture in England, c.1500–1850*, ed. Tim Harris (Basingstoke, 1995), 149–50; Bridget Hill, *Servants* (Oxford, 1996), 132; Tim Meldrum, *Domestic Service and Gender 1660–1750* (2000), 121–3; Wrightson, *Earthly Necessities*, 59; Capp, *Gossips*, 147, 178–81.

49. Kussmaul, *Servants in Husbandry*, 51–6.

50. See e.g. *The Lisle Letters*, ed. Muriel St Clare Byrne (1981), ii. 562–3; George Unwin, *Industrial Organization in the Sixteenth and Seventeenth Centuries* (Oxford, 1904), 220–4, 248–52; HMC, *Various Collections*, i. 155; Christabel M. Hoare, *The History of an East Anglian Soke* (Bedford, 1918), 350; Roger Howell, *Newcastle upon Tyne and the Puritan Revolution* (Oxford, 1967), 292–3; Daniel Baugh, *British Naval Administration in the Age of Walpole* (Princeton, 1965), 323–8; A. P. Wadsworth and Julia de Lacy Mann, *The Cotton Trade and Industrial Lancashire 1660–1780* (Manchester, 1931), 342 and ch. xix; Robert W. Malcolmson, 'Workers' combinations in eighteenth-century England', in *The Origins of Anglo-American Radicalism*, ed. Margaret Jacob and John Jacob (1984); Wrightson, *Earthly Necessities*, 152, 328–9; Alastair J. Reid, *United We Stand* (2004), 11–14.

51. Donald Woodward, 'Early modern servants in husbandry revisited', *Agricultural Hist. Rev.* 48 (2000), 142–3; Ellis, *Modern Husbandman*, iv (i). 150.

52. Smith, *Wealth of Nations*, i. 139 (1. x. c).

53. Paul S. Seaver, *Wallington's World* (1985), 113, 125.

54. *The Parish Register and Tithing Book of Thomas Hassall of Amwell*, ed. Stephen G. Doree (Herts. Rec. Soc., 1989), 126.

55. *Selections from Hoccleve*, ed. M. C. Seymour (Oxford, 1981), 35.

56. OED, s.v. 'whistle'; Cogan, *Haven of Health*, 21; Shakespeare, *Twelfth Night* (c.1600), II. iv; 'On the ploughman', in *The Complete Works . . . of Francis Quarles*,

ed. Alexander B. Grosart (1880), ii. 210; R[obert] C[rofts], *The Way to Happinessse on Earth* (1641), 39; John Cotgrave, *The English Treasury of Wit and Language* (1655), 55; Adam Fox, *Oral and Literate Culture in England 1500–1700* (Oxford, 2000), 27–30, 41; Emma Robertson et al., ' "And spinning so with voices meet, like nightingales they sung full sweet" ', *Cultural & Social History*, 5 (2008).

57. *The Letters of Dorothy Osborne to William Temple*, ed. G. C. Moore Smith (Oxford, 1928), 50–1. On milkmaids, see also Pepys, *Diary*, iii. 221.

58. (Margaret Cavendish), Marchioness of Newcastle, *CCXI. Sociable Letters* (1664), 112.

59. W. G. Hoskins, 'Provincial life', in *Shakespeare in his Own Age*, ed. Allardyce Nicoll, *Shakespeare Survey*, 17 (Cambridge, 1964), 20.

60. David Landes, *The Wealth and Poverty of Nations* (1998), 383.

61. 'Some account of the birth, education, religious exercises and visitations of God to that faithful servant and minister of Jesus Christ, Josiah Langdale', Friends House, London, MS Box 10/10. Howard Newby, *The Deferential Worker* (1977), 289–94, writes of the high intrinsic job satisfaction of modern agricultural work by comparison with other forms of manual labour.

62. *A Frenchman in England 1784. Being the 'Mélanges sur l'Angleterre' of François de la Rochefoucauld*, ed. Jean Marchand, trans. S. C. Roberts (Cambridge, 1933), 77.

63. Stephen Duck, 'The thresher's labour', in *Poems on Several Occasions* (1736), 18–19; James Hurdis, 'The favourite village' (1800), in *Poems* (Oxford, 1808), iii. 168.

64. Arthur Young, *Travels in France and Italy during the Years 1787, 1788 and 1789* (Everyman's Lib., 1915), 10; Kussmaul, *Servants in Husbandry*, 47.

65. Ross McKibbin, *Classes and Cultures* (Oxford, 1998), 129–31, 162.

66. HMC, *Portland*, ii. 266; Capp, *Gossips*, 52–4; and below, pp. 220–1.

67. Vivien Brodsky, 'Single women in the London marriage market', in *Marriage and Society*, ed. R. B. Outhwaite (1981), 95–6; Mendelson and Crawford, *Women*, 111.

68. Pepys, *Diary*, i. 255.

69. Robert Tatersal, *The Bricklayer's Miscellany*, 2nd edn (1734), 28; OED, s.v. 'yoho'.

70. Keith Thomas, *Religion and the Decline of Magic* (1971), 17–19; Henry Stevens, *The Dawn of British Trade to the East Indies* (1886), 40; Rule, *Experience of Labour*, 201; Edwin Chadwick, *Report on the Sanitary Condition of the Labouring Population* (1842), ed. M. W. Flinn (Edinburgh, 1965), 314.

71. Nehemiah Wallington's collection of judgments, BL, Sloane MS 1457, fol. 20^v.

72. R(alph) J(osselin), *The State of Saints Departed* (1652), 14.

73. Joseph Moxon, *Mechanick Exercises on the Whole Art of Printing* (1683–4), ed. Herbert Davis and Harry Carter (New York, 1878; 2nd edn, 1962), 338. On the customs of the printing-house, see ibid. 323–54; Ellic Howe and Harold E. Waite, *The London Society of Compositors* (1948), 30–41; Adrian Johns, *The Nature of the Book* (Chicago, 1998), 74–108. On workshop customs, see 'A Journeyman Engineer' [Thomas Wright], *Some Habits and Customs of the Working Classes* (1867), 83–107; Rule, *Experience of Labour*, 198–201; Joan Lane, *Apprenticeship in England, 1660–1914* (1996), 112–14.

74. 'Orders to be observed by the shippwrights and workmen in the tymes of theire workinge', BL, Harleian MS 253, fol. 14^v; Pepys, *Diary*, ii. 140.

75. Geoffrey Crossick, 'Past masters', in *The Artisan and the European Town*, ed. Crossick (Aldershot, 1997).

76. Malcolm Chase, *Early English Trade Unionism* (Aldershot, 2000), 23–5; Michael Berlin, ' "Broken all in pieces" ', in *The Artisan and the European*

Town, ed. Crossick; Joseph P. Ward, *Metropolitan Communities* (Stanford, CA, 1997), ch. 3.

77. On 'the several sorts of labouring men', see Randle Holme, *The Academy of Armory* (Chester, 1688), iii. 71–2; Smith, 'Labourers in late sixteenth-century England'; and, for a revealing list of the different specialisms of building labourers, Heather Swanson, *Building Craftsmen in Late Medieval York*, Borthwick Papers, 63 (York, 1983), 15.

78. Andy Wood, *The Politics of Social Conflict* (Cambridge, 1999), 24, 174.

79. Clyde Binfield and David Hey, *Mesters to Masters* (Oxford, 1997), 19.

80. John Evelyn, *An Account of Architects and Architecture* (1706), 5, in Roland Fréart, *A Parallel of the Antient Architecture with the Modern*, trans. John Evelyn, 2nd edn (1707).

81. Roger Bury, 'The international diffusion of technology in the early modern period', *EcHR* xliv (1991), 266–7; Levine and Wrightson, *Making of an Industrial Society*, 377, 390–1; Wood, *Politics of Social Conflict*, 103–4, 123, and *passim*.

82. Hay and Rogers, *Eighteenth-Century English Society*, 123.

83. On this large subject, Hay and Rogers, ibid. 122–32, give an admirably succinct summary of what might be called the (E. P.) Thompsonian view of eighteenth-century labour history, expressed in Thompson's *The Making of the English Working Class* (1963) and 'Time, work-discipline and industrial capitalism', *P & P* 38 (1967); and followed (*int. al.*) by Rule, *Experience of Labour*; Malcolmson, *Life and Labour in England*, and Adrian Randall, *Before the Luddites* (Cambridge, 1991).

84. Dyer, *An Age of Transition?*, 211–14.

85. *Early Chronicles of Shrewsbury, 1372–1603*, ed. W. A. Leighton (n.p., 1880), 40.

86. *A Second Miscellany of Nottinghamshire Records*, ed. K. S. S. Train (Thoroton Rec. Soc., 1951), 9, 3, 10, 5.

87. *Parish Register and Tithing Book of Thomas Hassall*, 125.

88. *The Diary of Sir Henry Slingsby*, ed. Daniel Parsons (1836), 64.

89. Richard Gough, *The History of Myddle*, ed. David Hey (Harmondsworth, 1981), 210, 222, 239, 272.

90. William Burton, *The Description of Leicester Shire* (1622), 236; *Parochial Collections made by Anthony Wood and Richard Rawlinson*, transcribed by F. N. Davis (Oxon. Rec. Soc., 1920–9), iii. 320; Ralph Thoresby, *Ducatus Leodiensis* (1715), 21–2.

91. *Remarks and Collections of Thomas Hearne*, viii. 279; ix. 171, 221.

92. *The Diary of William Thomas ... 1762–1795*, trans. J. B. Davies and G. H. Rhys, ed. R. T. W. Denning (South Wales Rec. Soc., 1995), 378, 299, 420.

93. Shakespeare, *As You Like It* (1599–1600?), III. ii.

94. Alexandra Shepard, 'Manhood, credit and patriarchy in early modern England c.1580–1640', *P & P* 167 (2000); *Homilies*, 520.

95. Above, p. 99; Kussmaul, *Servants in Husbandry*, 47.

96. *A Fifteenth Century School Book*, ed. William Nelson (Oxford, 1956), 5; Edmund Spenser, *The Faerie Queene* (1596), VI. ix. 1 (on which, see Anthony Low, *The Georgic Revolution* (Princeton, 1985), 37–8).

97. *High Court of Admiralty Examinations (MS. Volume 53), 1637–1638*, ed. Dorothy O. Shilton and Richard Holworthy (1932), 168–9.

98. e.g. John Ray, *A Collection of English Words not generally used*, 2nd edn (1691), 115; Thomas Sternberg, *The Dialect and Folk-Lore of Northamptonshire* (1851; East Ardsley, 1971), 6; *Regional Glossaries*, ser. B, ed. Walter

W. Skeat (English Dialect Soc., 1873), 6, 11; *The English Dialect Dictionary*, ed. Joseph Wright (1905; 1970), s.v. 'never-sweat', 'shackle-bag', 'shaffle', 'soss'.

99. *Works of Isaac Barrow*, i. 479.

100. Woodward, *Men at Work*, 80; John Walter, *Understanding Popular Violence in the English Revolution* (Cambridge, 1999), 267–8; Wrightson, *Earthly Necessities*, 197.

101. Hindle, *On the Parish?*, 161–2, 224, 383.

102. Powell, *Tom of All Trades*, 164.

103. Above, p. 88.

104. *The Whole Works of Jeremy Taylor*, ed. Reginald Heber, rev. Charles Page Eden (1847–54), x. 78. On the hangman, see also *Damon and Pythias*, [ed. Arthur Brown and F. P. Wilson] (Malone Soc., 1957), sig. Giv; *The Portledge Papers*, ed. Russell J. Kerr and Ida Coffin Duncan (1928), 84; J. H. Lefroy, *Memorials of the Discovery and Early Settlement of the Bermudas or Somers Islands* (1877), i. 510–11 (and ii. 25, 35, 218, 219, 245); Henry Fielding, *Enquiry into the Causes of the Late Increase of Robbers*, 153–4; Smith, *Wealth of Nations*, i. 117 (I. x. b); Samuel Pegge, *Curialia Miscellanea* (1818), 332–3; and below, p. 172. For butchers, Keith Thomas, *Man and the Natural World* (1983), 294–5.

105. David Underdown, *Revel, Riot and Rebellion* (Oxford, 1985), 29; Malcolmson, *Life and Labour in England*, 54; Smith, 'Labourers in late sixteenth-century England', 19; Penelope J. Corfield, 'Defining urban work', in *Work in Towns*, ed. Corfield and Derek Keene (Leicester, 1990), 218; Hill, *Servants*, 151; Wrightson, *Earthly Necessities*, 309.

106. Hatcher, *History of the British Coal Industry*, i. 378–83, 397–402; Woodward, *Men at Work*, 41–2.

107. Hill, *Change and Continuity*, ch. 10; Wood, *Politics of Social Conflict*, 103–5, and *The Experience of Authority in Early Modern England*, ed. Paul Griffiths, Adam Fox, and Steve Hindle (1996), 262–3; Shepard, 'Manhood, credit and patriarchy', 100–1.

108. Oxon. RO, Oxford Diocesan Papers, c 22, fol. 155.

109. *Essays of John Dryden*, ed. W. P. Ker, 2nd imp. (Oxford, 1926), ii. 93.

110. Mary Searle-Chatterjee, 'The polluted identity of work', in *Social Anthropology of Work*, ed. Sandra Wallman, ASA monograph 19 (1979).

111. William Harrison, *The Description of England*, ed. Georges Edelen (Ithaca, NY, 1968), 228–9; W.M., *The Complete Cook*, 42, 109, in *The Queens Closet Opened*, 4th edn (1658); Amanda Vickery, *The Gentleman's Daughter* (New Haven, 1998), 130–1.

112. *Correspondence of Thomas Gray*, ed. Paget Toynbee and Leonard Whibley, with additions by H. W. Starr (Oxford, 1971), ii. 666.

113. Ingram, *Church Courts*, 204.

114. Hannah Woolley (1675), cit. *Women's Worlds in Seventeenth-Century England*, ed. Patricia Crawford and Laura Gowing (2000), 73; *Cyuile and Uncyuile Life* (1579), sig. K1.

115. Edward [Rainbow], *A Sermon preached at the Funeral of the Right Honorable Anne Countess of Pembroke, Dorset and Montgomery* (1677), 12; below, pp. 170–1.

116. Nicholas Ferrar, *The Story Books of Little Gidding*, ed. E. Cruwys Sharland (1899), p. liii.

117. *Court Leet Records*, trans. and ed. F. J. C. Hearnshaw and D. M. Hearnshaw (Southampton Rec. Soc., 1905–8), i/iii. 510. Historians have written much

about women's work in recent years, but the essential starting points remain Alice Clark, *Working Life of Women in the Seventeenth Century* (1919), and Ivy Pinchbeck, *Women Workers and the Industrial Revolution 1758–1850* (1930).

118. Laura Gowing, *Domestic Dangers* (Oxford, 1996), 129–30; Cornelia Beattie, 'The problem of women's work identities in post Black Death England', in *The Problem of Labour*, ed. Bothwell et al., 13; Shepard, 'Manhood, credit and patriarchy', 92; ead., 'Honesty, worth and gender in early modern England', in *Identity and Agency in England, 1500–1800*, ed. Henry French and Jonathan Barry (Basingstoke, 2004).

119. For some pointers, see Karl E. Westhauser, 'Friendship and family in early modern England', *JSH* 27 (1994), 529; John Smail, *The Origins of Middle-Class Culture* (1994), 177–8; Woodward, *Men at Work*, 118–19; Carl B. Estabrook, *Urbane and Rustic England* (Manchester, 1998), 131; Paula McDowell, *The Women of Grub Street* (Oxford, 1998), 295–6; *English Sexualities 1660–1800*, ed. Tim Hitchcock and Michèle Cohen (1999), 41–2.

120. Defoe, *Complete English Tradesman*, vol. i, ch. xxiii; *The Autobiography of William Stout of Lancaster 1665–1752*, ed. J. D. Marshall (Manchester, 1967), 75; Catherine Hall, 'The early formation of Victorian domestic ideology', in *Fit Work for Women*, ed. Sandra Burman (1979); Peter Earle, 'The female labour market in London in the late seventeenth and early eighteenth centuries', *ECHR*, 2nd ser., xlii (1989), 337; K. D. M. Snell, *Annals of the Labouring Poor* (Cambridge, 1985), 27, 66, and ch. 6; Bridget Hill, *Women, Work and Sexual Politics in Eighteenth-Century England* (Oxford, 1989), 49–52; Jeanne Boydston, *Home and Work* (New York, 1990), 8–10, 47, 55; Smail, *Origins of Middle-Class Culture*, 171–4; Anna Clark, *The Struggle for the Breeches* (1995), ch. 2 and pp. 199, 248; Margaret R. Hunt, *The Middling Sort* (1996), 201; Robert B. Shoemaker, *Gender in English Society, 1650–1850* (1998), 114–15, 190, 204.

121. Henry Percy, ninth Earl of Northumberland, *Advice to his Son*, ed. G. B. Harrison (1930), 88; Baxter, *Practical Works*, i. 430.

122. Capp, *Gossips*, 45.

123. David A. Postles, *Social Proprieties* (Washington, 2006), 19–20; Woodward, *Men at Work*, 15.

124. Paul Binski, *Medieval Death* (1996), 102; Kenneth Lindley, *Of Graves and Epitaphs* (1965), 113–27; Hilary Lees, *Hallowed Ground* ([Cheltenham], 1993), 32, 66–7.

125. *Women's Worlds*, ed. Crawford and Gowing, 72. Another instance is cited by Bernard Capp, 'Separate Domains?', in *The Experience of Authority*, ed. Griffiths et al., 127.

126. Smith, *Wealth of Nations*, ii. 781–2 (v. i. f). Also Hume, *Essays, Moral, Political, and Literary*, ii. 245.

127. For example, Captain John Smith, *A Sea Grammar* (1627); Holme, *Academy of Armory*, iii. 162–7; Sir John Pettus, *Fodinae Regales... with a Clavis explaining some Difficult Words relating to Mines* (1670); William A. Craigie, *Pure English of the Soil*, S. P. E Tract xiv (Oxford, 1945); Fox, *Oral and Literate Culture*, 89–95.

128. *Samuel Pepys's Naval Minutes*, ed. J. R. Tanner (Navy Recs Soc., 1926), 260; *Gratii Falisci Cynegeticon*, trans. Christopher Wase (1654), preface.

129. John Barrell, *The Idea of Landscape and the Sense of Place 1730–1840* (Cambridge, 1972), 172–3; J. W. Smeed, *The Theophrastan 'Character'* (Oxford, 1985), 139–50, 169–78.
130. Bulwer, *Anthropometamorphosis*, 432.
131. Wood, *Politics of Social Conflict*, 106.
132. George Cheyne, *An Essay of Health and Long Life*, 6th edn (1725), 49–50. On the peculiar shape of Thames watermen, William Hogarth, 'Analysis of beauty', in *Anecdotes of Mr Hogarth*, ed. Thomas Cook (1803), 168.
133. *Rambler*, 173 (12 Nov. 1751); *Boswell's Life of Johnson*, ed. George Birkbeck Hill, rev. L. F. Powell (Oxford, 1934–64), ii. 218 (13 Apr. 1773).
134. Émile Durkheim, *The Division of Labor in Society*, trans. George Simpson (1932; 1964), 133–4.
135. Jonathan Gershuny, *Changing Times* (Oxford, 2000), 69–72; id., 'Busyness as the badge of honour for the new superordinate working class', *Social Research*, 72 (2005).
136. Ioannes Paulus PP. II, *Laborem exercens*, I. 9 (available at http://www.vatican.va/holy_father/john_paul_ii/encyclicals/documents/hf_jp-ii_enc_14091981_laborem-exercens_en.html); Anthony J. La Vopa, *Grace, Talent, and Merit* (Cambridge, 1988), 397.
137. Robert Blauner, *Alienation and Freedom* (Chicago, 1964), 183; John H. Goldthorpe et al., *The Affluent Worker: Industrial Attitudes and Behaviour* (Cambridge, 1968), 143; Joffre Dumazedier, *Sociology of Leisure*, trans. Marea McKenzie (Amsterdam, 1974), 157, 207; Ross McKibbin, *The Ideologies of Class* (Oxford, 1990), ch. 5.
138. Hatcher, 'Labour, leisure and economic thought', 115. Cf. Edmund Burke's eloquent evocation of the conditions endured by the 'unhappy wretches' employed in lead, tin, iron, copper, and coal mines; *A Vindication of Natural Society* (1756), in *Works* (Bohn edn, 1886), i. 42.
139. Thomas Westcote, *A View of Devonshire in MDCXXX*, ed. George Oliver and Pitman Jones (Exeter, 1845), 33.
140. Thomas Jefferson, *Writings* (Library of America, New York, 1984), 896 (to his daughter, 21 May 1787).

CHAPTER 4

Goods and the Social Order

1. *The Praier and Complaynte of the Ploweman unto Christe* (1531), sig. E5^v.
2. Cf. the comments of Hans Medick, 'The proto-industrial family economy', in Peter Kriedte et al., *Industrialization before Industrialization*, trans. Beate Schempp (Cambridge, 1981), 41, 72, 254; and Michael Mascuch, 'Social mobility and middling self-identity', *SH* 20 (1995), 60–1.
3. George M. Foster, 'Peasant society and the image of the limited good', *Amer. Anthropologist*, lxvii (1965); Samuel L. Popkin, *The Rational Peasant* (Berkeley and Los Angeles, CA, 1979), 8.
4. J. H. Hexter, *Reappraisals in History*, 2nd edn (Chicago, 1979), 100; Geffrey Gates, *The Defence of Militarie Profession* (1579), 35.
5. William Gouge, *Of Domesticall Duties*, 3rd edn (1634), 149.
6. Godfrey Goodman, *The Fall of Man* (1616), 140.

7. Thomas Starkey, *A Dialogue between Pole and Lupset*, ed. T. F. Mayer, Camden, 4th ser. (1989), 24.

8. Edmund Dudley, *The Tree of Commonwealth*, ed. D. M. Brodie (Cambridge, 1948), 45–6; and above, p. 17.

9. Starkey, *Dialogue*, 25–6; George Gifford, *Eight Sermons, upon...Ecclesiastes* (1589), fol. 19; *The Works of George Herbert*, ed. F. E. Hutchinson (Oxford, 1941), 274–5; W. K. Jordan, *Philanthropy in England* (1959), ch. vi; Laura Caroline Stevenson, *Praise and Paradox* (Cambridge, 1984), 137–9.

10. Stone, *Crisis*, 42–3; Felicity Heal, *Hospitality in Early Modern England* (Oxford, 1990).

11. Aristotle, *Politics* 1263b; Deuteronomy 15: 11; *The Diary of John Manningham of the Middle Temple 1602–1603*, ed. Robert Parker Sorlien (Hanover, NH, 1976), 200; George Webbe, *Agurs Prayer* (1621), 261; Francis Herring, *Certaine Rules, Directions, or Advertisements* (1636), sig. C1; John Wilkins, *Sermons Preached upon Several Occasions* (1682), 309.

12. Felicity Heal, 'Concepts of generosity in early modern England', in *Luxury and Austerity*, ed. Jacqueline R. Hill and Colm Lennon, Historical Studies, 21 (Dublin, 1999).

13. *Sermons by Hugh Latimer*, ed. George Elwes Corrie (PS, Cambridge, 1844), i. 477–8; *The Select Works of Robert Crowley*, ed. J. M. Cowper (EETS, 1872), 47, 92, 157; Richard L. Greaves, *Society and Puritanism in Elizabethan England* (Minneapolis, 1081), 551–2; Ethan H. Shagan, *Popular Politics and the English Reformation* (Cambridge, 2003), 278; Alec Ryrie, *The Gospel and Henry VIII* (Cambridge, 2003), 147.

14. Bodl. Lib., MS Ashmole 749, fols 5v–6v; John Preston, *Foure Godly and Learned Treatises*, 3rd edn (1633), 44; Sir Thomas Browne, *Religio Medici and Other Works*, ed. L. C. Martin (Oxford, 1964), 56; Paul S. Seaver, *Wallington's World* (1985), 133–4.

15. William Segar, *Honor Military, and Civill* (1602), 'T.B. to the reader'; Anthony Stafford, *The Guide of Honour* (1634), 44; Norbert Elias, *The Court Society*, trans. Edmund Jephcott, ed. Stephen Mennell (Dublin, 2006), 64–5, 79–80.

16. *Nic. Eth.* 1119b–1123a and *Politics* 1256b; Anthony Grafton, 'Humanism and political theory', in *The Cambridge History of Political Thought 1450–1700*, ed. J. H. Burns (Cambridge, 1991); Christopher J. Berry, *The Idea of Luxury* (Cambridge, 1994), pt ii; Quentin Skinner, *Visions of Politics* (Cambridge, 2002), ii. 225–7, iii. 205; and see nn. 11 and 12 on p. 322 below.

17. [Nicholas Breton], *Pasquils Mad-Cap, and His Message* (1600), sig. A4v; *All the Works of John Taylor the Water Poet* (1630; facs., Menston, 1973), i. 73.

18. [Haly Heron], *A Newe Discourse of Morall Philosophie, entituled, the Kayes of Counsaile* (1579), 26.

19. Bulstrode Whitelocke's 'Annales of his life', BL, Add. MS 53726, fol. 27v.

20. William Burton, *The Description of Leicester Shire* (1622), 265; G. E. C[okayne], *The Complete Peerage*, new edn, ed. Vicary Gibbs et al. (1910–59), ii. 72.

21. Sir Thomas Smith, *De Republica Anglorum*, ed. Mary Dewar (Cambridge, 1982), 73; John Preston, *Sinnes Overthrow*, 4th edn (1641), 251.

22. *The Diary of Sir Henry Slingsby*, ed. Daniel Parsons (1836), 230.

23. Smith, *De Republica Anglorum*, 72; Neil Davie, 'Custom and conflict in a Wealden village: Pluckley 1550–1700', Oxford Univ. D.Phil. thesis (1987),

175–7; Basil Duke Henning, *The House of Commons 1660–1690*, History of Parliament (1983), ii. 210.

24. *The Correspondence of Sir John Lowther of Whitehaven 1693–1698*, ed. D. R. Hainsworth (British Academy, 1983), xiv (echoing William Cecil's famous advice to his son Robert; *Desiderata Curiosa*, ed. Francis Peck (1779), i. 48).

25. *Behemoth; or, The Long Parliament*, ed. Ferdinand Tönnies, 2nd edn (1969), 44.

26. John Jones, *The Arte and Science of Preserving Bodie and Soule* (1579), 77.

27. John Beadle, *The Journal or Diary of a Thankful Christian* (1656), 96; D. M. Palliser, *Tudor York* (Oxford, 1979), 92–3; Keith Wrightson and David Levine, *Poverty and Piety in an English Village* (Oxford, 1995), 103–6; H. R. French, *The Middle Sort of People in Provincial England 1600–1750* (Oxford, 2007), 22–3, 26, 100, 105, 200–1.

28. Tim Stretton, *Women Waging Law in Elizabethan England* (Cambridge, 1998), 213; *The Commission for Ecclesiastical Causes within the Dioceses of Bristol and Gloucester, 1574*, ed. F. D. Price (Bristol and Glos. Archaeol. Soc., 1972), 48; H[enry] C[onset], *The Practice of the Spiritual or Ecclesiastical Courts*, 3rd edn (1708), 394.

29. Barnabe Rich, *The Irish Hubbub* (1617), 29; Ian W. Archer, *The Pursuit of Stability* (Cambridge, 1991), 80; Alexandra Shepard, 'Honesty, worth and gender in early modern England', in *Identity and Agency in England*, ed. Henry French and Jonathan Barry (Basingstoke, 2004).

30. Henry Peacham, *The Worth of a Peny* (1641), 15; similarly, *The Works of Sir Walter Ralegh* (Oxford, 1829), viii. 565.

31. *The Works of Isaac Barrow* (Edinburgh, 1842), i. 467.

32. John Prince, *Danmonii Orientales Illustres; or, The Worthies of Devon* (Exeter, 1701), 246.

33. *Nic. Eth.* 1122^a–1123^a; William Vaughan, *The Golden-Grove*, 2nd edn (1608), sig. I3; Heal, *Hospitality*, 24–9, 188–91; Luke Syson and Dora Thornton, *Objects of Virtue* (2001), ch. 1.

34. HMC, *Finch*, ii. 113; Craig Muldrew, 'Hard food for Midas', *P & P* 170 (2001), 109–12; [Thomas Heywood], *Philocothonista* (1635), 47. On the plate holdings of the nobility, see Philippa Glanville, *Silver in Tudor and Early Stuart England* (1990), 40–5.

35. Christine Carpenter, *Locality and Polity* (Cambridge, 1992), 196–211; Stone, *Crisis*, esp. ch. x; Heal, *Hospitality*, esp. ch. 4; John Habakkuk, *Marriage, Debt, and the Estates System* (Oxford, 1994), 277–91.

36. *The Works of . . . Gervase Babington* (1637), 3rd pagination, 165.

37. *Concilia Magnae Britanniae et Hiberniae*, ed. David Wilkins (1737), iii. 862.

38. *The Owles Almanacke* (1618), ed. Don Cameron Allen (Baltimore, 1943), 90 (bread); *The Englishmans Docter*, trans. Sir J(ohn) Harington (1607), sig. A7; [Jonathan Dove], *Speculum Anni à Partu Virginis M.DC.LXX; or, An Almanacke for the Year of Our Lord 1670* (Cambridge, 1670), sig. A4 (eggs). For social differences in diet, Christopher Dyer, *Standards of Living in the Later Middle Ages* (Cambridge, 1989), 55–71, 134–5, 151–60, 196–9; *Food in Medieval England*, ed. C. M. Woolgar et al. (Oxford, 2006); Alan Everitt, 'Farm labourers', in *The Agrarian History of England and Wales*, iv: *1500–1640*, ed. Joan Thirsk (Cambridge, 1967), 450–3; Andrew B. Appleby, 'Diet in sixteenth century England', in *Health, Medicine and Mortality in the Sixteenth Century*, ed. Charles Webster (Cambridge, 1979); Greaves, *Society and Religion*, 474–5; Pepys, *Diary*, x: *Companion*, 143–7.

39. For contemporary medical theories about socially appropriate diets, see Sheila McTighe, 'Foods and the body in Italian genre paintings about 1580', *Art Bull.* lxxxvi (2004).

40. Amanda Flather, *Gender and Space in Early Modern England* (Woodbridge, 2007), 66–7.

41. Sedley Lynch Ware, *The Elizabethan Parish in its Ecclesiastical and Financial Aspects* (Baltimore, 1908), 79; J. S. Craig, 'Co-operation and initiatives', *SH* 18 (1993), 376; Arnold Hunt, 'The Lord's Supper in early modern England', *P & P* 161 (1998), 49.

42. Elspeth M. Veale, *The English Fur Trade in the Later Middle Ages*, 2nd edn (London Rec. Soc., 2003), 144.

43. N. B. Harte, 'State control of dress and social change in pre-industrial England', in *Trade, Government and Economy in Pre-Industrial England*, ed. D. C. Coleman and A. H. John (1976), esp. 139–43.

44. Gilbert Burnet, *The Life and Death of Sir Matthew Hale* (1682), 20. In fact, he continued to dress in relatively homely fashion; Richard Baxter, *Additional Notes on the Life and Death of Sir Matthew Hale* (1682), sig. A3ᵛ.

45. *VCH Staffs.* xiv. 57.

46. Nicholas Cooper, *Houses of the Gentry 1480–1680* (New Haven, 1999), 16–18; M. W. Barley, 'Rural housing in England', in *Agrarian History of England and Wales*, iv, ch. x; id., 'Rural building in England', ibid. v/2, ed. Joan Thirsk (Cambridge, 1985), ch. 20, esp. 677; J. T. Smith, 'Short-lived and mobile houses in late seventeenth-century England', *Vernacular Architecture*, 16 (1985).

47. Gloucestershire Archives, GDR 20, p. 31; William Vaughan, *The Golden Fleece* (1626), iii. 73; Richard Gough, *The History of Myddle*, ed. David Hey (Harmondsworth, 1981), 32, 56.

48. James Ayres, *Domestic Interiors* (New Haven, 2003), 9, 73; Linda Hall, 'Yeoman or gentleman?', *Vernacular Architecture*, 22 (1991); Antony Buxton, 'Domestic culture in early seventeenth-century Thame', *Oxoniensia*, lxvii (2002); Nicholas Cooper, 'Display, status and the vernacular tradition', *Vernacular Architecture*, 33 (2002).

49. For the ease of access, at least to well-to-do visitors, see e.g. *Passages from the Diaries of Mrs Philip Lybbe Powys*, ed. Emily J. Climenson (1899); 'Horace Walpole's journals of visits to country seats, &c', ed. Paget Toynbee, *Walpole Soc.* 16 (1928); H. J. Louw, 'Some royal and other great houses in England', *Architectural History*, 29: *Design and Practice in British Architecture* (1984) Adrian Tinniswood, *The Polite Tourist* (1998); J. F. Merritt, *The Social World of Early Modern Westminster* (Manchester, 2005), 162–3.

50. Ayres, *Domestic Interiors*, chs 2 and 6.

51. Rachel P. Garrard, 'English probate inventories and their use in studying the significance of the domestic interior, 1570–1700', in *Probate Inventories*, ed. Ad van der Woude and Anton Schuurman, *AAGB Bijdragen*, 23 (1980), 58; William Harrison, *The Description of England*, ed. Georges Edelen (Ithaca, NY, 1968), 201; William Smith and William Webb, *The Vale-Royall of England*, ed. Daniel King (1656), iv. 5.

52. *The Register of Henry Chichele, Archbishop of Canterbury, 1414–1443*, ed. E. F. Jacob (Oxford, 1937–47), ii. 46; *The Papers of Nathaniel Bacon of Stiffkey*, i (1556–1577), ed. A. Hassell Smith et al. (Norfolk Rec. Soc., 1979), 79; *Farmers and Fishermen*, ed. R. W. Ambler and B. and L. Watkinson (Hull, 1987), 95; J. T. Cliffe, *The World of the Country House in Seventeenth-Century England* (New Haven, 1999), 105.

53. Carl Bridenbaugh, *The Beginnings of the American People* (Oxford, 1968), 52.
54. Vivienne Larminie, *The Godly Magistrate* (Dugdale Soc., 1982), 17–18; John Fowler and John Cornforth, *English Decoration in the 18th Century* (1974), 220–4; Ayres, *Domestic Interiors*, 41.
55. *The Acts and Monuments of John Foxe*, ed. George Townsend and Stephen Reed Cattley (1837–41), vii. 540.
56. John H. Astington, *English Court Theatre 1558–1642* (Cambridge, 1999), 84–5.
57. Giles Worsley, *The British Stable* (New Haven, 2004).
58. *Notes which passed at Meetings of the Privy Council between Charles II and the Earl of Clarendon*, ed. W. D. Macray (Roxburghe Club, 1896), 21.
59. William Ramesey, *Astrologia Restaurata* (1653), 18.
60. John Hacket, *A Century of Sermons* (1675), 857. For representative contemporary comment, see Harrison, *Description of England*, ch. xii, and John Stow, *The Annales*, continued by Edmund Howes (1615), 948. Since the pioneering work of A. Elizabeth Levett, *The Consumer in History* (1929), there has been a huge amount of historical writing on this subject. Much of it is listed in *Consumption and the World of Goods*, ed. John Brewer and Roy Porter (1993). Subsequent works include Lorna Weatherill, *Consumer Behaviour and Material Culture in Britain 1660–1760*, 2nd edn (1996); Craig Muldrew, *The Economy of Obligation* (Basingstoke, 1998), chs 1 and 2; Mark Overton et al., *Production and Consumption in English Households, 1600–1750* (2004); Maxine Berg, 'Consumption in eighteenth- and early nineteenth-century Britain', in *The Cambridge Economic History of Modern Britain*, i, ed. Roderick Floud and Paul Johnson (Cambridge, 2004); ead., *Luxury and Pleasure in Eighteenth-Century Britain* (Oxford, 2005); Linda Levy Peck, *Consuming Splendor* (Cambridge, 2005); *Gender, Taste, and Material Culture*, ed. John Styles and Amanda Vickery (New Haven, 2006); French, *Middle Sort of People*, ch. 3; John Styles, *The Dress of the People* (New Haven, 2007). For stimulating studies of similar trends in other countries, see: on Italy, Richard A. Goldthwaite, *Wealth and the Demand for Art in Italy 1300–1600* (Baltimore, 1993); on Ireland, Toby Barnard, *Making the Grand Figure* (New Haven, 2004); on colonial America, T. H. Breen, *The Marketplace of Revolution* (New York, 2004); and on France, the works of Daniel Roche: *The People of Paris*, trans. Marie Evans and Gwynne Lewis (Leamington Spa, 1987); *The Culture of Clothing*, trans. Jean Birrell (Cambridge, 1994); and *History of Everyday Things*, trans. Brian Pearce (Cambridge, 2000).
61. K. B. McFarlane, *The Nobility of Later Medieval England* (Oxford, 1973), 96–101; David Gaimster and Beverley Nenk, 'English households in transition c.1450–1550', in *The Age of Transition*, ed. Gaimster and Paul Stamper (Oxford, 1997); and, especially, Christopher Dyer, 'The consumer and the market in the later Middle Ages', *EcHR*, 2nd ser., xlii (1989); id., *Standards of Living*, esp. chs 3, 6, and 7; id., 'Work ethics in the fourteenth century', in *The Problem of Labour in Fourteenth-Century England*, ed. James Bothwell, P. J. P. Goldberg, and W. M. Ormrod (York, 2000), 36–8; and id., *An Age of Transition?* (Oxford, 2005), ch. 4.
62. N. W. Alcock, *People at Home* (Chichester, 1993), is an exemplary study of this process, as it affected Stoneleigh, Warwickshire, between 1500 and 1800.
63. Margaret Spufford, *The Great Reclothing of Rural England* (1984); Hoh-Cheung Mui and Lorna H. Mui, *Shops and Shopkeeping in Eighteenth-Century England* (1989); Carole Shammas, *The Pre-Industrial Consumer in England and America* (Oxford, 1990), ch. 8; Nancy Cox, *The Complete Tradesman* (Alder-

shot, 2000); Helen Berry, 'Polite consumption', *TRHS*, 6th ser., xii (2002); Claire Walsh, 'Social meaning and social space in the shopping galleries of early modern London', in *A Nation of Shopkeepers*, ed. John Benson and Laura Ugolini (2003); Merritt, *Social World of Early Modern Westminster*, 154–9; Andrew Hann and Jon Stobart, 'Sites of consumption', *Cultural and Social History*, 2 (2005); Berg, *Luxury and Pleasure*, 257–70.

64. Sir Thomas Smith, *A Discourse of the Commonweal of this Realm of England*, ed. Mary Dewar (Charlottesville, VA, 1969), 64.

65. John Archer Gee, *The Life and Works of Thomas Lupset* (1928), 242.

66. Above, pp. 80–2.

Possessions and their Meaning

1. Mark Stephen Rowe Jenner, 'Early modern conceptions of "cleanliness" and "dirt" as reflected in the environmental regulation of London, c.1530–c.1700', Oxford Univ. D.Phil. thesis (1991), 37.

2. *Ivanhoe* (1819), ch. vi. On the novelty of the eighteenth-century concern with physical comfort, see John E. Crowley, *The Invention of Comfort* (Baltimore, 2001).

3. *Hegel's Philosophy of Right*, trans. T. M. Knox (Oxford, 1942), 269.

4. Beadle, *Journal*, 96.

5. Sir Thomas Browne, *Letters*, ed. Geoffrey Keynes (1946), 161; *Verney Letters of the Eighteenth Century*, ed. Margaret, Lady Verney (1930), i. 218.

6. Pepys, *Diary*, viii. 173–4, 209, 246, 399, 455; ix. 260, 333, 342, 379–80, 381, 383, 399–400, 434, 542, 545, 551.

7. N[icholas] B[arbon], *A Discourse of Trade* (1690), 14–15, 72–3; Peter Paxton, *Civil Polity* (1703), 109, 220; Samuel [Bradford], *The Honest and Dishonest Ways of Getting Wealth* (1720), 6–7; William Warburton, *The Alliance between Church and State* (1736), in *The Reception of Locke's Politics*, ed. Mark Goldie (1999), v. 189; Josiah Tucker, *Reflections on the Expediency of a Law for the Naturalization of Foreign Protestants* (1751–2), ii. 10; Richard Cumberland, *The Observer*, iii (Dublin, 1791), 47.

8. *The Letters of Sir Walter Ralegh*, ed. Agnes Latham and Joyce Youings (Exeter, 1999), 264.

9. Smith, *Moral Sentiments*, 50 (I. iii. 2)(and 212–13 (VI. i. 4)).

10. *Nic. Eth.* 1096^a.

11. Smith, *Wealth of Nations*, i. 190 (I. xi. c) (and *Moral Sentiments*, 182 (IV. i. 8)); Archibald Campbell, *An Enquiry into the Original of Moral Virtue* (Edinburgh, 1733), 37, 42–3; *The Political Writings of Jean Jacques Rousseau*, ed. C. E. Vaughan (Oxford, 1962), i. 293.

12. William Godwin, *Enquiry concerning Political Justice*, 3rd edn (1798), ed. Isaac Kramnick (Harmondsworth, 1976), 705.

13. *The Armburgh Papers*, ed. Christine Carpenter (Woodbridge, 1998), 126–7; *Essex Pauper Letters 1731–1837*, ed. Thomas Sokoll (British Academy, Oxford, 2001), 580.

14. *A Royalist's Notebook*, ed. Francis Bamford (1936), 241.

15. Weatherill, *Consumer Behaviour and Material Culture*, 9.

16. Overton et al., *Production and Consumption*, 136; Peter Earle, *The Making of the English Middle Class* (1989), 291–2.

17. *The Connoisseur*, 103 (15 Jan. 1756).

18. Sir William Waller, 'Recollections', in *The Poetry of Anna Matilda* (1838), 131.

19. Sir William Waller, *Divine Meditations upon Several Occasions* (1839), 33; Louis Le Roy, *Of the Interchangeable Course, or Variety of Things*, trans. R. A[shley] (1594), fol. 129.

20. *The Miscellaneous Works of John Bunyan*, ix, ed. Richard L. Greaves (Oxford, 1981), 324.

21. *Oxford in 1710 from the Travels of Zacharias Conrad von Uffenbach*, ed. W. H. Quarrell and W. J. C. Quarrell (Oxford, 1928), 40.

22. Pepys, *Diary*, vii. 298 (and cf. iv. 181); Audrey W. Douglas, 'Cotton textiles in England', *JBS* 8 (1969), 29.

23. *Letters of Josiah Wedgwood 1771 to 1780*, [ed. Katherine Eufemia, Lady Farrer] (1903; repr. Manchester, n.d. [1973]), ii. 91; Neil McKendrick, 'Josiah Wedgwood and the commercialization of the Potteries', in McKendrick et al., *The Birth of a Consumer Society* (1982), 108–12.

24. Lorna Scammell, 'Town versus country', in *Urban Fortunes*, ed. John Stobart and Alastair Owens (Aldershot, 2000); Overton et al., *Production and Consumption* (comparing Kent with Cornwall).

25. Overton et al., *Production and Consumption*, 165–6, 177.

26. Foulke Robartes, *The Revenue of the Gospel is Tythes* (Cambridge, 1613), 123–4; William Bullein, *A Dialogue against the Feuer Pestilence*, ed. Mark W. Bullen and A. H. Bullen (EETS, 1888), 80. On consumption in Elizabethan London, see *Material London*, ed. Lena Cowen Orlin (Philadelphia, 2000).

27. Frances Harris, *Transformations of Love* (Oxford, 2002), 129. The Cornish at this period were getting poorer and consuming less; Overton et al., *Production and Consumption*, 116, 171, 176.

28. *The Economic Writings of Sir William Petty*, ed. Charles Henry Hull (Cambridge, 1899), i. 290.

29. Weatherill, *Consumer Behaviour*, 50, 62.

30. *The Diary and Memoirs of John Allen Giles*, ed. David Bromwich (Somerset Rec. Soc., 2000), 8.

31. Dudley, *Tree of Commonwealth*, 47.

32. John Strype, *Historical Collections of the Life and Acts of . . . John Aylmer*, new edn (Oxford, 1821), 180–1; C. Pyrrye, *The Praise and Dispraise of Women* (1569), sig. Avi; *The Political Works of James I*, ed. Charles Howard McIlwain (Cambridge, MA, 1918), 343; *Epicoene; or; The Silent Woman* (first performed 1609), II. ii, in *The Complete Plays of Ben Jonson*, ed. G. A. Wilkes (Oxford, 1981), iii. 144; [Robert Wilkinson], *The Merchant Royall* (1615), sig. E2; Lorna Weatherill, 'A possession of one's own', *JBS* 15 (1986); G. J. Barker-Benfield, *The Culture of Sensibility* (Chicago, 1992), ch. 4; Stana Nenadic, 'Middle-rank consumers and domestic culture in Edinburgh and Glasgow, 1720–1840', *P & P* 145 (1994), 150–3; Elizabeth Kowaleski-Wallace, *Consuming Subjects* (New York, 1997); Amanda Vickery, *The Gentleman's Daughter* (New Haven, 1998), 162–94, 250–2; Hilary Young, *English Porcelain 1745–95* (1999), 189–92; Capp, *Gossips*, 347–8; Peck, *Consuming Splendor*, 355.

33. Morris Palmer Tilley, *A Dictionary of the Proverbs in England in the Sixteenth and Seventeenth Centuries* (Ann Arbor, 1950), 138.

34. Mandeville, *Fable*, i. 226.

35. Berry, 'Polite consumption'; Sir Henry Chauncy, *The Historical Antiquities of Hertfordshire* (1826), i. 145; *The Life and Times of Anthony Wood*, ed. Andrew Clark (Oxford. Hist. Soc., 1891–1900), i. 395, 398.

36. *Practical Works*, i. 231.

37. F. J. M. Korsten, *Roger North (1651–1734)* (Amsterdam, 1981), 139–41.

38. As is pointed out by Amanda Vickery, 'His and hers', in *The Art of Survival*, ed. Ruth Harris and Lyndal Roper, *P & P* suppl. (2006).

39. *Bathshebaes Instructions to her Son Lemuel*, ed. John Dod and William Hinde (1614), 57.

40. *Kalm's Account of his Visit to England ... in 1748*, trans. Joseph Lucas (1892), 12–13; Barker-Benfield, *Culture of Sensibility*, 158; Overton et al., *Production and Consumption*, 108; John Styles, 'Lodging at the Old Bailey', in *Gender, Taste, and Material Culture*, ed. Styles and Vickery.

41. William Petty's estimate (*The Petty Papers*, ed. Marquis of Lansdowne (1927), ii. 236) accords closely with modern research, e.g. Shammas, *Pre-Industrial Consumer*, 145.

42. J. V. Beckett, 'Elizabeth Montagu', *Huntington Lib. Qtly*, 49 (1986), 157.

43. Peter King, 'Pauper inventories and the material lives of the poor', in *Chronicling Poverty*, ed. Tim Hitchcock, Peter King, and Pamela Sharpe (Basingstoke, 1997); Joan Thirsk, *Economic Policy and Projects* (Oxford, 1978), 175–6; Shammas, *Pre-Industrial Consumer*, 299; Ayres, *Domestic Interiors*, 124.

44. Mandeville, *Fable*, i. 129; Styles, *Dress of the People, passim*.

45. *Letters of Josiah Wedgwood 1771 to 1780*, 363–4.

46. Cary Carson, 'The consumer revolution in colonial British America', in *Of Consuming Interests*, ed. Cary Carson and Ronald Hoffman (Charlottesville, VA, 1994), 553–4.

47. Vickery, *Gentleman's Daughter*, 183–94.

48. Walter Benjamin, *Illuminations*, ed. Hannah Arendt, trans. Harry Zohn (1973), 43.

49. Vickery, *Gentleman's Daughter*, 190, 194, 331; Marcia Pointon, *Strategies for Showing* (Oxford, 1997), 38–43; Maxine Berg, 'Women's property and the industrial revolution', *Journ. of Interdisciplinary History*, xxiv (1993), 246–7; ead., 'Women's consumption and the industrial classes of eighteenth-century England', *JSH* 30 (1996); Katherine J. Lewis, 'Women, testamentary discourse and life-writing in later medieval England', in *Medieval Women and the Law*, ed. Noël James Menuge (Woodbridge, 2000); J. S. W. Helt, 'Women, memory and will-making in Elizabethan England', in *The Place of the Dead*, ed. Bruce Gordon and Peter Marshall (Cambridge, 2000).

50. See below, p. 252.

51. David Marcombe, *English Small Town Life* (Nottingham, 1993), 147; Richard Stock, *A Learned and Very Usefull Commentary upon the Whole Prophesie of Malachy*, ed. Samuel Torshell (1641), i. 73 ('37').

52. *The Autobiography and Correspondence of Mary Granville, Mrs Delany*, ed. Lady Llanover (1861–2), iii. 634, quoted by Jo Dahn, 'Mrs Delany and ceramics in the objectscape', *Interpreting Ceramics*, 1 (2000).

53. *Testamenta Eboracensia*, vi, ed. J. W. Clay (Surtees Soc., 1902), 294–5; Lady Elizabeth Cust, *The Records of the Cust Family* (1898), 301.

54. Captain John Smith, *A Sea Grammar* (1627), 85.

55. Helen Clifford, 'A commerce with things', in *Consumers and Luxury*, ed. Maxine Berg and Helen Clifford (Manchester, 1999); Sarah Richards, *Eighteenth-Century Ceramics* (Manchester, 1999); Young, *English Porcelain*.

56. David Cressy, *Birth, Marriage, and Death* (Oxford, 1997), 165–6, 169, 365–7, 442–8, 453; Marcia Pointon, 'Jewellery in eighteenth-century England', in *Consumers and Luxury*, ed. Berg and Clifford, 126–33.

57. Diana O'Hara, 'The language of tokens and the making of marriage', *Rural History*, 3 (1992); Laura Gowing, *Domestic Dangers* (Oxford, 1996), 159–64; Cressy, *Birth, Marriage, and Death*, 263–6.

58. Margaret Cavendish, Marchioness of Newcastle, *CCXI. Sociable Letters* (1664), 95–6, 186.

59. Korsten, *Roger North*, 158; *OED*, s.v. 'handicap'.

60. *Diary*, v. 62.

61. There is as yet no equivalent study for England to Natalie Zemon Davis, *The Gift in Sixteenth-Century France* (Oxford, 2000), though Ilana Krausman Ben-Amos, *The Culture of Giving* (Cambridge, 2008, but not published at the time of writing) may prove to be it. See also the articles by Felicity Heal: 'Concepts of generosity in early modern England'; Giving and receiving on royal progress', in *The Progresses, Pageants and Entertainments of Queen Elizabeth I*, ed. Jayne Elisabeth Archer et al. (Oxford, 2007); 'Food gifts, the household and the politics of exchange in early modern England', *P & P* 199 (2008). For other suggestive indications, see *Jewels and Plate of Queen Elizabeth I*, ed. A. Jefferies Collins (1955), 100–13; Glanville, *Silver in Tudor and Early Stuart England*, 23–4, 26–36, 40–1, and index; Linda Levy Peck, 'Benefits, brokers and beneficiaries', in *Court, Country and Culture*, ed. Bonnelyn Young Kunze and Dwight D. Brautigan (Rochester, NY, 1992); Vickery, *Gentleman's Daughter*, 188, 192, 205; Catherine F. Patterson, *Urban Patronage in Early Modern England* (Stanford, CA, 1999), 16–24, 163, 176–7, 197–8, 210; Jason Scott-Warren, *Sir John Harington and the Book as Gift* (Oxford, 2001); *Elizabeth*, ed. Susan Doran (2003), 104–10.

62. William Leiss, *The Limits to Satisfaction* (1978), 67.

63. Kurt Vonnegut, Jr, *Slaughterhouse-Five; or, The Children's Crusade* (New York, 1969), 33.

64. Peter Thornton, *The Italian Renaissance Interior 1400–1600* (1991), 18; [Roger North], *Of Building*, ed. Howard Colvin and John Newman (Oxford, 1981), 7; Ross McKibbin, *Classes and Cultures in England 1918–1931* (Oxford, 1998), 85; Charles Saumarez Smith, *The Rise of Design* (2000), 58.

65. Mimi Hellman, 'Furniture, sociability, and the work of leisure in eighteenth-century France', *Eighteenth-Century Studies*, 32 (1999); Robert Bocock, *Consumption* (1993), 64.

66. James Hart, *The Diet of the Diseased* (1633), 73.

67. Lodowick Bryskett, *A Discourse of Civill Life* (1606), ed. J. H. P. Pafford (n.p., 1977), 94 (a passage inspired by Stefano Guazzo, *The Civile Conversation*, trans. George Pettie and Bartholomew Young (1581–6; 1925 edn), ii. 145–8).

68. *The Letters of William Shenstone*, ed. Marjorie Williams (Oxford, 1939), 336; and see Amanda Vickery, 'Neat and not too showey', in *Gender, Taste, and Material Culture*, ed. Styles and Vickery.

69. *Spectator*, 409 (19 June 1712), iii. 527–8.

70. Jonathan Richardson, *Two Discourses* (1719), ii. 65–6; William Shenstone, *Essays on Men and Manners* (1794), 3–5; Henry Home, Lord Kames, *Elements of Criticism*, 6th edn (Edinburgh, 1785), ii. 501–2; Archibald Alison, *Essays on the Nature and Principles of Taste* (Edinburgh, 1815), i. 89–90, 344–5.

71. Kames, *Elements of Criticism*, ii. 499.

72. North, *Of Building*, 9; *The Guardian*, 173 (29 Sept. 1713), ed. Alexander Chalmers (1822), ii. 42; *The Connoisseur*, 33 (12 Sept. 1754); *The Genius of the Place*, ed. John Dixon Hunt and Peter Willis (1975), i. 293–4.

73. Samuel Johnson, *The Adventurer*, 138 (2 Mar. 1754).

74. As was well illustrated by the exhibition in 2007 at the Sir John Soane Museum, London: *A Passion for Building: The Amateur Architect in England 1650–1850*. For earlier gentleman architects, see Cooper, *Houses of the Gentry*, 28–51, 119–23, 217.
75. Dorothy Stroud, *Capability Brown* (1975); Oliver Goldsmith, 'The life of Richard Nash', in *The Works of Oliver Goldsmith*, ed. J. W. M. Gibbs (1885–6), iv. 69.
76. Jeremy Collier, *Essays upon Several Moral Subjects*, 6th edn (1722), i/1. 107.
77. Jeremy Bentham, *Deontology*, ed. Amnon Goldsworth (Oxford, 1983), 358.
78. Stephen Mennell, *All Manners of Food* (1985), 73–4.
79. *The Letters of the Earl of Chesterfield to his Son*, ed. Charles Strachey (1901), i. 391.
80. Vickery, 'Neat and not too showey', 216–17.
81. There is no British equivalent of Pierre Bourdieu's fine study of class differences in taste in twentieth-century France; *Distinction*, trans. Richard Nice (Cambridge, MA, 1984).

From Hostility to Acceptance

1. Francis Trigge, *An Apologie* (1589), 37; Heinrich Bullinger, *The Olde Fayth*, trans. Miles Coverdale (1541; 1547 edn), sig. Avi; *Prayers and Other Pieces of Thomas Becon*, ed. John Ayre (PS, Cambridge, 1844), 59.
2. Thomas Gataker, *Marriage duties briefely couched togither* (1620), 20; Milton, *CPW* vii. 387; Thomas Fuller, *The Holy State and the Profane State* (1840), 89; Barnabe Rich, *Allarme to England* (1578), sig. Cii^v; William Blandy, *The Castle* (1581), fol. 28^v; 'The Institution & Dyssepline of a Souldier', BL, Harleian MS 519, fol. 17^v; John Deacon, *Tobacco Tortured* (1616), 147.
3. Smith, *Wealth of Nations*, i. 418–19, 421 (III. iv); id., *Moral Sentiments*, 180–3 (IV. i. 6–8).
4. John Sekora, *Luxury* (Baltimore, 1977), ch. 1; Berry, *Idea of Luxury*; Alan Hunt, *Governance of the Consuming Passions* (Basingstoke, 1996), ch. 4; and above, p. 24.
5. Bevis Hillier, *Pottery and Porcelain 1700–1914* (1968), pl. viii.
6. *The Standard*, 26 Apr. 1876, quoted in *Keble College: The Record* (Oxford, 1960), 22. Maxine Berg and Elizabeth Eger, 'The rise and fall of the luxury debate', in *Luxury in the Eighteenth Century*, ed. Berg and Eger (Basingstoke, 2003) is a helpful account, but treats its subject as a distinctively eighteenth-century phenomenon, rather than one which pervades the whole of the early modern period.
7. William Horman, *Vulgaria* (1519), fol. 228^v; William Tyndale, *Expositions and Notes on Sundry Parts of the Holy Scriptures*, ed. Henry Walter (PS, Cambridge, 1849), 92–3; John Strype, *The Life and Acts of Matthew Parker* (Oxford, 1821), ii. 445; *A Boke or Counseill against the Disease commonly called the Sweate* (1552), 21, in *The Workes of John Caius*, ed. E. S. Roberts (Cambridge, 1912).
8. Smith, *Discourse of the Commonweal*, 82.
9. e.g. *A Quip for an Upstart Courtier* (1592), in *The Life and Complete Works… of Robert Greene*, ed. Alexander B. Grosart (1881–6), xi. 234–5; Deacon, *Tobacco Tortured*, 144; Hart, *Diet of the Diseased*, 8; Waller, *Divine Meditations*, 85; John Dennis, *An Essay upon Public Spirit* (1711), 8–11; Keith Thomas, *The Perception of the Past in Early Modern England* ([1984]), esp. 14–15.
10. Kowaleski-Wallace, *Consuming Subjects*, 31–3.
11. *Commons Debates 1621*, ed. Wallace Notestein, Frances Helen Relf, and Hartley Simpson (New Haven, 1935), vii. 214.

12. H. S. Cronin, 'The twelve conclusions of the Lollards', *EHR* xxii (1907), 493; G. J. R. Parry, *A Protestant Vision* (Cambridge, 1987), 287; *The Writings of Henry Barrow 1587–1590*, ed. Leland H. Carlson (1962), 493; Roger Crab, *The English Hermite and Dagons Downfall* (1657), [ed. Andrew Hopton] (1990), *passim*.

13. Barbon, *Discourse of Trade*, 65.

14. John Walsall, *A Sermon preached at Pauls Crosse* (1578), sig. Aiiij^v; Vaughan, *Golden-Grove*, sig. H8; Deacon, *Tobacco Tortured*, 150.

15. Collections of John Walker, Bodl. Lib., MS J. Walker c. 1, fol. 271.

16. *Howell Harris's Visits to London*, ed. Tom Beynon (Aberystwyth, 1960), 42–3.

17. Baxter, *Practical Works*, i. 231, 825.

18. *Some Account of the Life of Joseph Pike, written by himself*, in *A Select Series*, ed. John Barclay, v (1837), 66.

19. Marcia Pointon, 'Quakerism and visual culture 1650–1800', *Art History*, 20 (1997), 418–22.

20. Skinner, *Visions of Politics*, i. 152; John Keymer, *A Cleare and Evident Way for Enriching the Natives of England and Ireland* (1650), 17.

21. *Constitutions & Canons Ecclesiastical 1604*, ed. H. A. Wilson (Oxford, 1923), sig. N1^v; *Commons Debates 1621*, v. 497–8.

22. Esmond S. de Beer, 'King Charles II's own fashion', *Journ. of the Warburg Institute*, 2 (1938); Evelyn, *Diary*, iii. 464–5.

23. *Tyranipocrit Discovered* (Rotterdam, 1649), in *British Pamphleteers*, i, ed. George Orwell and Reginald Reynolds (1948), 99; *An Essay concerning Adepts by a Philadept* (1698), 38.

24. Perkins, *Workes*, ii. 125; *New Universal Magazine* (June 1759), 219, cit. Susie I. Tucker, *Protean Shape* (1967), 146–7.

25. Nicholas Bownd, *Sabbathum Veteris et Novi Testamenti* (1606), 211–12; Deacon, *Tobacco Tortured*, 140–1; Jacob Vanderlint, *Money Answers All Things* (1734), 102.

26. Margot Finn, 'Women, consumption and coverture in England, c.1760–1860', *HJ* 39 (1996); *Petty Papers*, i. 210.

27. Perkins, *Workes*, i. 60.

28. Edward Gee, *The Jesuit's Memorial* (1690), 257.

29. *A Catalogue of Letters and Other Historical Documents Exhibited in the Library at Welbeck*, comp. S. Arthur Strong (1903), 211; Cavendish, *CCXI. Sociable Letters*, 136–7. For later protest against the levelling implications of lower-class consumption, see Joyce Appleby, 'Ideology and theory', *Amer. Hist. Rev.* 81 (1976).

30. Edw[ard] Waterhouse, *The Gentlemans Monitor* (1665), 261–2; Thomas, *Perception of the Past*, 14.

31. Greaves, *Religion and Society*, 28; James Spedding, *The Letters and Life of Francis Bacon* (1861–74), vi. 23; Thomas Hobbes, *De Cive: The Latin Version*, ed. Howard Warrender (Oxford, 1983), 202; John Downame, *The Christian Warfare*, 4th edn (1634), 512; *Examen Legum Angliae* (1656), 134–6; *Seventeenth-Century Economic Documents*, ed. Joan Thirsk and J. P. Cooper (Oxford, 1972), 104; *The Vindication of Slingsby Bethel* (1681), 5; John Evelyn, *Numismata* (1697), 235; Daniel Defoe, *The Complete English Tradesman* (1745; Oxford, 1841), ii. 232; Edgar S. Furniss, *The Position of the Laborer in a System of Nationalism* (Boston, 1920), 153.

32. Philip Doddridge, *Reflections on the Conduct of Divine Providence* (1749), 27.

33. *Diary of Sir Henry Slingsby*, 25–6; Joan R. Kent, 'Attitudes of members of the House of Commons to the regulation of "personal conduct" in late Elizabethan and early Stuart England', *Bull. Institute of Hist. Research*, xlvi (1973).
34. Peacham, *Worth of a Peny*, 3.
35. Paul Slack, 'The politics of consumption and England's happiness in the later seventeenth century', *EHR* cxxii (2007); and id., 'Perceptions of the metropolis in seventeenth-century England', in *Civil Histories*, ed. Peter Burke, Brian Harrison, and Paul Slack (Oxford, 2000), 175–8.
36. Richard Grassby, *The English Gentleman in Trade* (Oxford, 1994), 298.
37. *Locke on Money*, ed. Patrick Hyde Kelly (Oxford, 1991), i. 242, is an early example. *OED* gives none before 1745.
38. Barbon, *Discourse of Trade*, 6, 15, 64–70; E. A. J. Johnson, *Predecessors of Adam Smith* (1937), 292, 294; Neil McKendrick, 'The consumer revolution of eighteenth-century England', in McKendrick et al., *Birth of a Consumer Society*, 13–15; Sekora, *Luxury*, ch. 3; Joyce Oldham Appleby, *Economic Thought and Ideology in Seventeenth-Century England* (Princeton, 1978), 168–75; Berry, *Idea of Luxury*, ch. 5; Slack, 'Politics of consumption'.
39. Vanderlint, *Money Answers All Things*, 21.
40. Nehemiah Rogers, *The True Convert* (1620), 272.
41. *Homilies*, 311; John Edwards, *Sermons on Special Occasions* (1698), 276; [Dudley, third Lord North], *Observations and Advices Oeconomical* (1669), 67.
42. Appleby, *Economic Thought and Ideology*, 181; Smith, *Wealth of Nations*, ii. 660 (iv. viii).
43. Edward Forset, *A Comparative Discourse of the Bodies Natural and Politique* (1606), 13–14.
44. Peck, *Consuming Splendor*, 75, 92–8.
45. *The Female Tatler*, 64 (2 Dec. 1709), ed. Fidelis Morgan (1992), 133–4.
46. *The Works of George Savile, Marquis of Halifax*, ed. Mark N. Brown (Oxford, 1989), iii. 193 (cf. iii. 219).
47. [Richard Parrott], *Reflections on Various Subjects relating to Arts and Commerce* (1752), 20; Smith, *Wealth of Nations*, ii. 869–70 (v. ii. k).
48. Mandeville, *Fable*, i. 108; John Walter, *Understanding Popular Violence in the English Revolution* (Cambridge, 1999), 349.
49. Thomas Sprat, *The History of the Royal-Society* (1667), ed. Jackson I. Cope and Harold Whitmore Jones (St Louis, 1959), 380–1, 387.
50. Perkins, *Workes*, iii. 136; John Dod and Robert Cleaver, *A Plaine and Familiar Exposition of the Thirteenth and Fourteenth Chapters of the Proverbs of Salomon* (1608), 21.
51. Barbon, *Discourse of Trade*, 15, 35; [John Gardner?], *Some Reflections on a Pamphlet* (1696), 7; Dalby Thomas, *An Historical Account of the Rise and Growth of the West-India Collonies* (1690), 6; Berry, *Idea of Luxury*, 125.
52. e.g. Henry Fielding, *The Covent Garden Journal and a Plan of the Universal Register-Office*, ed. Bertrand A. Goldgar (Oxford, 1988), 4; [Joseph Harris], *An Essay upon Money and Coins*, i (1757), 31, 32; Oliver Goldsmith, *The Citizen of the World* (1762), letter xi; Berry, *Idea of Luxury*, 144, 148, 152, 163–4; Berg, *Luxury and Pleasure*, 16.
53. Colin Campbell, *The Romantic Ethic and the Spirit of Modern Consumerism* (1987); *Pleasure in the Eighteenth Century*, ed. Roy Porter and Marie Mulvey Roberts (Basingstoke, 1996), chs 1 and 2.

54. Smith, *Wealth of Nations*, i. 346 (II. iii); Parrott, *Reflections on Various Subjects*, 70 (and cf. *The Writings of William Walwyn*, ed. Jack R. McMichael and Barbara Taft (Athens, GA, 1989), 148); Jonas Hanway, *A Journal of Eight Days Journey*, 2nd edn (1757), ii. 263.

55. Tom Arkell, 'The incidence of poverty in England in the later seventeenth century', *SH* 12 (1987).

56. William Lambarde, *A Perambulation of Kent* (1576; Chatham, 1826), 7–8; *Suffolk in the XVIIth Century*, ed. Lord Francis Hervey (1902), 58.

57. Baxter, *Additional Notes on Sir Matthew Hale*, sigs A3^v–4; Burnet, *Life and Death of Sir Matthew Hale*, 60, 167.

58. *Diaries and Letters of Philip Henry*, ed. Matthew Henry Lee (1882), 331.

59. Iain Pears, *The Discovery of Painting* (New Haven, 1988), 14.

60. Thomas Traherne, *Poems, Centuries and Three Thanksgivings*, ed. Anne Ridler (Oxford, 1966), 269, 298, 86–8.

61. Roger L'Estrange, *Seneca's Morals Abstracted in Three Parts* (1679), 323; Arthur O. Lovejoy and George Boas, *Primitivism and Related Ideas in Antiquity* (1935; New York, 1973), chs 4 and 10; Ellis Walker, *Epicteti Enchiridion made English* (1695), 14–15, 77–80, 97, and *passim*.

62. Thomas More, *Utopia*, ed. George M. Logan and Robert M. Adams (Cambridge, 1989), 50, 53–4; [Samuel Gott], *Nova Solyma*, trans. Walter Begley (1902), ii. 133; Joshua Barnes, *Gerania* (1675), 51–2; *Essay concerning Adepts*, 30, 32–3; [Robert Wallace], *Various Prospects of Mankind, Nature and Providence* (1761; facsinite reprint, New York, 1969), 44.

63. *The Journals of Captain James Cook*, ed. J. C. Beaglehole (Hakluyt Soc., 1955–74), i. 399. Cf. Marshall Sahlins, *Stone Age Economics* (1974), 3–4, 14, 37.

64. *A Tale of a Tub and Other Early Works 1696–1707*, ed. Herbert Davis (Oxford, 1939), 244.

65. Thomas, *An Historical Account*, 6.

66. Jan de Vries, 'Between purchasing power and the world of goods', in *Consumption and the World of Goods*, ed. Brewer and Porter, 107–21, 126 n. 63; id., 'The industrial revolution and the industrious revolution', *Journ. of Economic History*, 54 (1994). See also T. S. Ashton, *An Economic History of England: The Eighteenth Century* (1955), 213–17; Martin Daunton, *Progress and Poverty* (Oxford, 1995), 178–80. Evidence for a longer working year after 1750 is provided by Hans-Joachim Voth, *Time and Work in England 1750–1830* (Oxford, 2000), 121–2, 132, and ch. 4, and Chris Evans, 'Work and workloads during industrialization', *International Rev. of Social History*, 44 (1999).

67. *The Works of Thomas Robert Malthus*, ed. E. A. Wrigley and David Souden (1986), iii. 520.

Wealth as Fulfilment?

1. R. H. Tawney, *The Acquisitive Society* (1921), 233.

2. R. H. Tawney, *Religion and the Rise of Capitalism* (1926; West Drayton, 1948), 251.

3. Ibid. 265.

4. I know of no evidence for his assertion that Puritans saw the life of business as '*the* appropriate field for Christian endeavour' (270, my italics).

5. See e.g. Stephen Foster, *Their Solitary Way* (New Haven, 1971), 120; Seaver, *Wallington's World*, 137–8; Steven C. A. Pincus, *Protestantism and Patriotism* (Cambridge, 1996), 97.
6. Cit. Christopher Brooks in *The Middling Sort of People*, ed. Jonathan Barry and Christopher Brooks (1994), 126.
7. *Select Works of Robert Crowley*, 47 (also 92, 157).
8. John Hawarde, *Les Reportes del Cases in Camera Stellata 1593 to 1609*, ed. William Paley Baildon (1894), 104.
9. Christopher Dyer, *An Age of Transition?* (Oxford, 2005), 56; G. R. Owst, *Literature and Pulpit in Medieval England*, 2nd edn (Oxford, 1961), 409.
10. Joseph Lee, *A Vindication of a Regulated Enclosure* (1656), 9. Cf. Dyer, *An Age of Transition?*, 56.
11. Hans Baron, *In Search of Florentine Humanism* (Princeton, 1988), chs 7–9; John F. McGovern, 'The rise of new economic attitudes—economic humanism, economic nationalism—during the later Middle Ages and the Renaissance, A.D. 1200–1550', *Traditio*, xxvi (1970); Gordon Griffiths, 'Leonardo Bruni's justification of the pursuit of wealth', *Journ. of European Economic History*, 32 (2003); Reginald Pecock, *The Repressor of Over Much Blaming of the Clergy*, Rolls Ser. (1860), ii. 308.
12. Starkey, *Dialogue*, 28–9; Gee, *Life and Works of Lupset*, 251; Gifford, *Eight Sermons*, fol. 16; *Works of George Herbert*, 274; Margo Todd, *Christian Humanism and the Puritan Social Order* (Cambridge, 1987), 127–9; Lorna Hutson, *The Usurer's Daughter* (1994), ch. 1; David Harris Sacks, 'The greed of Judas', *Journ. of Medieval and Early Modern Studs*, 28 (1998); and other authors cited in Foster, *Solitary Way*, 110–11.
13. e.g. Downame, *The Christian Warfare*, 442–54; Gabriel Towerson, *An Explication of the Catechism of the Church of England, Part III* (1680), 125–6.
14. Alfred F. Chalk, 'Natural law and the rise of economic individualism in England', *Journ. of Political Economy*, 59 (1951); Arthur B. Ferguson, *The Articulate Citizen and the English Renaissance* (Durham, NC, 1965), 304–11.
15. Johnson, *Predecessors of Adam Smith*, 67, 69; J. A. W. Gunn, *Politics and the Public Interest in the Seventeenth Century* (1969), 230–2; Appleby, *Economic Thought and Ideology*, 49–51.
16. Steve Pincus, 'Neither Machiavellian moment nor possessive individualism', *Amer. Hist. Rev.* 103 (1998).
17. In addition to the references cited on p. 138 above, see Gunn, *Politics and the Public Interest*, 239–53.
18. John Wheeler, *A Treatise of Commerce* (1601; New York, 1931), 6.
19. *Bishop Burnet's History of His Own Time* (Oxford, 1823), vi. 202; David Hume, 'Of interest', in *Essays, Moral, Political, and Literary*, ed. T. H. Green and T. H. Grose (1908 edn), i. 324.
20. Gillian Darley, *John Evelyn* (New Haven, 2006), 2.
21. *Writings of Henry Barrow 1587–1590*, 493; Arthur Dent, *The Plain Mans Pathway to Heaven* (1601), 107; Lee, *Vindication*, 19. Cf. Skinner, *Visions of Politics*, i, ch. 8.
22. [Slingsby Bethel], *The Interest of Princes and States* (1680), 79–85 and *passim*; Albert O. Hirschman, *The Passions and the Interests* (Princeton, 1977), 40–2; id., *Rival Views of Market Society* (New York, 1986), ch. 2; J. P. Sommerville, *Politics and Ideology in England, 1603–1640* (1986), 106; Steve Pincus, 'From holy cause to economic interest', in *A Nation Transformed*, ed. Alan Houston and Steve Pincus (Cambridge, 2001), 286 ff.

23. *The Morning-Exercise at Cripple-Gate*, 4th edn (1677), 195–6.
24. Hirschman, *Rival Views of Market Society*, 39; Roy Porter, *Enlightenment* (2000), ch. 17.
25. Charles Richardson, *A Sermon against Oppression and Fraudulent Dealing* (1615), 17; Hobbes, *Leviathan*, 90 (ch. 14).
26. Sprat, *History of the Royal-Society*, 380–1, 408; J[ohn] Evelyn, *Navigation and Commerce* (1674), 11, and id., *The History of Religion*, ed. R. M. Evanson (1850), ii. 195; John McVeagh, *Tradefull Merchants* (1981), 55.
27. Appleby, *Economic Thought and Ideology*, 174; [Richard Cumberland], *The Observer*, 85 (1785); Smith, *Moral Sentiments*, 204–5 (v. ii. 8); John Stuart Mill, *Principles of Political Economy*, ed. J. M. Robson (1965), 104.
28. Grassby, *English Gentleman in Trade*, 297.
29. *The Diary and Autobiography of Edmund Bohun*, ed. S. Wilton Rix (Beccles, 1853), 134.
30. For brief surveys of this large subject, see J. G. A. Pocock, 'Cambridge paradigms and Scotch philosophers', in *Wealth and Virtue*, ed. Istvan Hont and Michael Ignatieff (Cambridge, 1983), esp. 241–3; and id., *Virtue, Commerce, and History* (Cambridge, 1985), esp. 114–16.
31. Daniel Defoe, *A Tour through England and Wales* (1724–6; 1927), i. 72.
32. Adam Ferguson, *An Essay on the History of Civil Society 1767*, ed. Duncan Forbes (Edinburgh, 1966), 56.
33. R. S. Fitton and A. P. Wadsworth, *The Strutts and the Arkwrights 1758–1830* (Manchester, 1958), 109–10.
34. Smith, *Moral Sentiments*, 182–3, 185 (IV. i. 8–10).
35. Andrew J. Oswald, 'Happiness and economic performance', *Economic Journ.* 107 (1997); Robert H. Frank, *Luxury Fever* (New York, 1999); Richard Layard, *Happiness* (2003).

CHAPTER 5

Precedence and Superiority

1. Lord King, *The Life of John Locke*, new edn (1830), i. 203; Smith, *Moral Sentiments*, 212–13 (VI. i. 3).
2. Robert Ashley, *Of Honour*, ed. Virgil B. Heltzel (San Marino, CA, 1947), 24; Francis Markham, *The Booke of Honour* (1625), 25; *The Works of Isaac Barrow* (Edinburgh, 1842), i. 467, 28.
3. *A Discourse of the Warr in Lancashire*, ed. William Beamont (Chetham Soc., 1864), 82–3. Particularly helpful works on honour include Alexis de Tocqueville, *Democracy in America* (1835–40), trans. Henry Reeve and Francis Bowen, ed. Phillips Bradley (New York, 1954), esp. ii. 161–3, 242–55; *Honour and Shame*, ed. J. G. Peristiany (1965); Arlette Jouanna, 'La Notion d'honneur au XVIe siècle', *Revue d'histoire moderne et contemporaine*, 15 (1968); Hans Speier, *Social Order and the Risks of War* (Cambridge, MA, 1969), ch. 4; Peter Berger, 'On the obsolescence of the concept of honor', *Archives européennes de sociologie*, xi (1970); Bertram Wyatt-Brown, *Southern Honor* (New York, 1982); Julian Pitt-Rivers, 'Honour', in *International Encyclopedia of the Social Sciences*, ed. David L. Sills ([New York], 1986); William Ian Miller, *Humiliation and Other Essays on Honor, Social Discomfort, and Violence* (Ithaca, NY, 1993); Frank Henderson Stewart, *Honor* (Chicago, 1994); J. E. Lendon, *Empire of Honour* (Oxford, 1997); Geoffrey Brennan and

Philip Pettit, *The Economy of Esteem* (Oxford, 2004); John Iliffe, *Honour in African History* (Cambridge, 2005; James Bowman, *Honor: a History* (New York, 2006).

4. *Nic. Eth.* 1095, 1123–4, 1159ᵃ; K. J. Dover, *Greek Popular Morality in the Time of Plato and Aristotle* (Oxford, 1974), 226–9; Douglas L. Cairns, *Aidos* (Oxford, 1993); Lendon, *Empire of Honour*.
5. Quentin Skinner, *The Foundations of Modern Political Thought* (Cambridge, 1978), i. 100–1, 118–19, 121, 132, 178–9, 183, 234–5.
6. *Homilies*, 137; HMC, *Salisbury*, ii. 145; *The Works of... Richard Hooker*, ed. John Keble, 6th edn (Oxford, 1874), ii. 445.
7. *TRHS*, 6th ser., vi (1996), esp. 247–8.
8. *Miscellanies by Henry Fielding*, iii, ed. Bertrand A. Goldgar and Hugh Amory (Oxford, 1997), 43.
9. Neil Davie, 'Custom and Conflict in a Wealden Village: Pluckley 1550–1700', Oxford Univ. D.Phil. thesis (1987), 122.
10. Geoffrey Chaucer, *The Canterbury Tales*, 'The Parson's Tale', line 187; Hobbes, *Leviathan*, ch. 10.
11. G. D. Squibb, *Precedence in England and Wales* (Oxford, 1981), 3.
12. Robert Hill and Roger Lockyer, ' "Carleton and Buckingham: The quest for office" revisited', *History*, 88 (2003), 21.
13. Richard Cust, *Charles I* (2005), 213.
14. Sean Kelsey, *Inventing a Republic* (Manchester, 1997), 123.
15. Markham, *Booke of Honour*, 34; John Ferne, *The Blazon of Gentrie* (1586), 77–9; Sir William Segar, *Honor Military, and Civill* (1602), 211; Perkins, *Workes*, i. 50; ii. 151; Thomas Hobbes, *The Elements of Law*, ed. Ferdinand Tönnies, 2nd edn (1969), 35–6; John Cotgrave, *The English Treasury of Wit and Language* (1655), 197; Anna Bryson, *From Courtesy to Civility* (Oxford, 1998), 88–96.
16. HMC, *Middleton*, 539.
17. Henry Ainsworth, *The Communion of Saints* (1641), 319.
18. *Statutes of the University of Oxford codified in the year 1636*, ed. John Griffiths (Oxford, 1888), 146.
19. Robert Tittler, 'Seats of honor, seats of power', *Albion*, 24 (1992).
20. John Weever, *Ancient Funerall Monuments* (1631), ch. v; Randle Holme, *The Academy of Armory*, ii, ed. I. H. Jeayes (Roxburghe Club, 1905), 482–3; Stone, *Crisis*, 672–81; Michael Neill, *Issues of Death* (Oxford, 1997), 265–81; and pp. 243–4 below.
21. Edmund Gurnay, *Toward the Vindication of the Second Commandment* (Cambridge, 1639), 87; David Postles, 'The politics of address in early-modern England', *Journ. of Hist. Sociology*, 18 (2005); id., *Social Proprieties* (Washington, 2006).
22. William Fulwood, *The Enimie of Idlenesse* (1568), sig. Aiiiᵛ; James Daybell, *Women Letter-Writers in Tudor England* (Oxford, 2006), 47–50.
23. *A Catalogue of the Earl Marshal's Papers at Arundel Castle*, ed. Francis W. Steer (Harleian Soc., 1964), 4.
24. Garthine Walker, *Crime, Gender and Social Order in Early Modern England* (Cambridge, 2003), 125–6.
25. *Letters Illustrative of the Reign of William III*, ed. G. P. R. James (1841), ii. 324.
26. Keith Thomas, *Religion and the Decline of Magic* (Harmondsworth, 1978), 180; Cambridge Univ. Lib., Ely Diocesan Records, B 2/52, fol. 52; B 2/35, fols 21–4; *'Merry Passages and Jeasts'*, ed. H. F. Lippincott (Salzburg, 1974), 126; Robert Shelford, *Five Pious and Learned Discourses* (Cambridge, 1635), 51–2;

Arnold Hunt, 'The Lord's Supper in early modern England', *P & P* 161 (1998), 49; *Acts and Ordinances of the Interregnum*, ed. C. H. Firth and R. S. Rait (1911), i. 585–6.

27. Judith Maltby, *Prayer Book and People in Elizabethan and Early Stuart England* (Cambridge, 1998), 71.
28. Thomas Hobbes, *De Cive: The English Version*, ed. Howard Warrender (Oxford, 1983), 44.
29. Christine Carpenter, *Locality and Polity* (Cambridge, 1992), 624; *The Armburgh Papers*, ed. Christine Carpenter (Woodbridge, 1995), 54; Philippa Maddern, 'Honour among the Pastons', *Journ. of Medieval History*, 14 (1988).
30. The National Archives, SP 16/334/51. See A. J. Fletcher, 'Honour, reputation and local officeholding in Elizabethan and Stuart England', in *Order and Disorder in Early Modern England*, ed. Anthony Fletcher and John Stevenson (Cambridge, 1985); Heal and Holmes, *Gentry*, ch. 5; Richard Cust, 'Honour, rhetoric and political culture', in *Political Culture and Cultural Politics in Early Modern England*, ed. Susan D. Amussen and Mark A. Kishlansky (Manchester, 1995); Michael J. Braddick, *State Formation in Early Modern England c.1550–1700* (Cambridge, 2000), 71, 79, 82, 189; Alison Wall, 'The greatest disgrace', *EHR* cxix (2004); John Adamson, *The Noble Revolt* (2007), 31.
31. W. T. MacCaffrey, 'Talbot and Stanhope', *Bull. Institute of Hist. Research*, 33 (1960); Thomas Garden Barnes, *Somerset 1625–1640* (1961), 36–9, ch. x and *passim*; Stone, *Crisis*, 223; A. Hassell Smith, *County and Court* (Oxford, 1974), ch. ix; Richard Cust, 'Honour and politics in early Stuart England', *P & P* 149 (1995).
32. Mark Kishlansky, *Parliamentary Selection* (Cambridge, 1986).
33. Heal and Holmes, *Gentry*, 309–10.
34. K. B. McFarlane, *The Nobility of Later Medieval England* (Oxford, 1973), 113 n.; Stone, *Crisis*, 241–2; Philippa C. Maddern, *Violence and Social Order* (Oxford, 1992), 65–7, 218–19.
35. Jeremy Collier, *Essays upon Several Moral Subjects*, iii, 3rd edn (1720), 164.
36. e.g. Walter Bourchier Devereux, *Lives and Letters of the Devereux, Earls of Essex* (1853), i. 180–1; Clements R. Markham, 'The Fighting Veres' (Boston, 1888), 424; Fletcher, 'Honour, reputation and local officeholding', 97–9; Heal and Holmes, *Gentry*, 170–1; Thomas Cogswell, *Home Divisions* (Manchester, 1998), 174; Kelsey, *Inventing a Republic*, 124–5; John Childs, *The British Army of William III, 1698–1702* (Manchester, 1987), 52.
37. [Nicholas Breton], *Fantasticks* (1626), sig. F1 (echoing Shakespeare, *Timon of Athens* (1607?), III. vi. 63–4).
38. Kelsey, *Inventing a Republic*, 142 (paraphrasing Richard Cust).
39. Hobbes, *Leviathan*, 119 (ch. 17); id., *Human Nature*, in *The English Works of Thomas Hobbes of Malmesbury*, ed. Sir William Molesworth (1839–45), iv. 53.
40. Mrs J. R. Green, *Town Life in the Fifteenth Century* (1894), i. 154; Eamon Duffy, *The Stripping of the Altars* (New Haven, 1992), 126–7; Caroline Litzenberger, *The English Reformation and the Laity* (Cambridge, 1997), 52–3.
41. *Documentary Annals of the Reformed Church of England*, ed. Edward Cardwell (Oxford, 1839), i. 14, 186–7.
42. *The Archdeacon's Court: Liber Actorum, 1584*, ed. E. R. Brinkworth (Oxon. Rec. Soc., 1942–6), 171. The most detailed study of these quarrels is Kevin B. Dillow, 'The social and ecclesiastical significance of church seating arrangements and pew disputes, 1500–1740', Oxford Univ. D.Phil. thesis (1990). See also Margaret

Aston, 'Segregation in church', in *Women in the Church*, ed. W. J. Sheils and Diana Wood, *Studs in Church History*, 27 (1990), 250–1, 253–4, 265–6; Amanda Flather, *The Politics of Place* (Leicester, 1999); ead., *Gender and Space in Early Modern England* (Woodbridge, 2007), ch. 5.

43. J. H. Lefroy, *Memorials of the Discovery and Early Settlement of the Bermudas or Somers Islands 1515–1685* (1877–9), i. 448.

44. Barnabe Rich, *The Irish Hubbub* (1617), 18.

45. Edward Coke, *The Fourth Part of the Institutes of the Laws of England* (1817), 363 (marginal note).

46. Thomas Bray, *A Course of Lectures upon the Church Catechism*, i (Oxford, 1696), 221.

47. *Reports of Cases in the Courts of Star Chamber and High Commission*, ed. Samuel Rawson Gardiner (Camden Soc., 1886), 143. In articles in *P & P* 171 (2001), *Journ. of Ecclesiastical History*, 53 (2002), and *JBS* 44 (2005), Christopher Marsh suggests that more people accepted these seating arrangements without question than the numerous disputes might indicate.

48. W. J. Harte, *Gleanings from the Common Place Book of John Hooker* (Exeter, n.d. [1926]), 23.

49. Grassby, *Business Community*, 322.

50. Christopher Haigh, 'Anticlericalism and clericalism, 1580–1640', in *Anticlericalism in Britain c.1500–1914*, ed. Nigel Aston and Matthew Cragoe (Stroud, 2000), 28.

51. Smith, *Moral Sentiments*, 57 (1. iii. 2).

52. Richard Tuck, *The Rights of War and Peace* (Oxford, 1999), 22–3; Emmerich de Vattel, *Le Droit des gens; ou, Principes de la loi naturelle* (1758) (Washington, 1916), i. 182.

53. William Penn, *The Peace of Europe* (Everyman's Lib., n.d.), 20.

54. *Tudor Royal Proclamations*, i, ed. Paul L. Hughes and James F. Larkin (New Haven, 1964), 107, 120; Steven Gunn, 'The French wars of Henry VIII', in *The Origins of War in Early Modern Europe*, ed. Jeremy Black (Edinburgh, 1987), 35–6; *John Stubbs's 'Gaping Gulf'*, ed. Lloyd E. Berry (Charlottesville, VA, 1968), 56.

55. *The Letters of Sir Walter Ralegh*, ed. Agnes Latham and Joyce Youings (Exeter, 1999), 152.

56. Evelyn, *Diary*, iii. 486.

57. HMC, *3rd Report*, 3.

58. Garrett Mattingly, *Renaissance Diplomacy* (1955), 252–3, 264, 314 n.–315 n.; *Ceremonies of Charles I*, ed. Albert J. Loomie (New York, 1987), 34–6 and passim.

59. *The Naval Tracts of Sir William Monson*, ed. M. Oppenheim (Navy Recs Soc., 1902–14), iii. 33–6, 41, 45–55, 212–14, 217; T. W. Fulton, *The Sovereignty of the Sea* (1911); *The Tangier Papers of Samuel Pepys*, ed. Edwin Chappell (Navy Recs Soc., 1935), 114, 151, 184, 186, 191, 197, 203; J. D. Davies, *Gentlemen and Tarpaulins* (Oxford, 1991), 63–4.

60. *Crosby Records: A Cavalier's Notebook*, ed. T. Ellison Gibson (1880), 262; HMC, *8th Report*, app., pt i, 122a (no. 168); Alexandra Shepard, *Meanings of Manhood in Early Modern England* (Oxford, 2003), 148, 150.

61. Thomas Gainsford, *The Glory of England* (1618), 246; *Correspondence of John Wallis*, i (1641–59), ed. Philip Beeley and Christopher J. Scriba (Oxford, 2003), 460.

62. William Camden, *Remains concerning Britain*, ed. R. D. Dunn (Toronto, 1984), 30.

Aristocratic Honour

1. William Vaughan, *The Golden-Grove*, 2nd edn (1608), sig. T8ᵛ; *The English Courtier, and the Countrey-Gentleman* (1586), in *Inedited Tracts*, ed. W. C. H [azlitt] (1868), 92.
2. Sir Walter Ralegh, *The History of the World*, new edn (Edinburgh, 1820), v. 471.
3. Stewart, *Honor*, ch. 4.
4. C. L. Barber, *The Idea of Honour in the English Drama 1591–1700* (Göteborg, 1957); id., *The Theme of Honour's Tongue* (Göteborg, 1985); Curtis Brown Watson, *Shakespeare and the Renaissance Concept of Honor* (Princeton, 1960); Jerrilyn Greene Marston, 'Gentry honour and royalism in early Stuart England', *JBS* 13 (1973–4); Mervyn James, *Society, Politics and Culture* (Cambridge, 1986), chs 8 and 9; Anthony Fletcher, *Gender, Sex and Subordination in England 1500–1800* (New Haven, 1995), ch. 7; Cust, 'Honour and politics in early Stuart England', 'Honour, rhetoric and political culture', and 'Catholicism, antiquarianism and gentry honour', *Midland History*, 23 (1998); the contributions by Cynthia Herrup, Felicity Heal, and Nigel Llewellyn to *TRHS*, 6th ser., vi (1996); and Ian Atherton, *Ambition and Failure in Stuart England* (Manchester, 1999), ch. 1.
5. *Hall's Chronicle* (1809), 459; Charles Carlton, *Going to the Wars* (1992), 136–7; Abraham Cowley, *The Civil War*, ed. Allan Pritchard (Toronto, 1973), 91.
6. Clarendon, *History*, iv. 168; Cust, *Charles I*; David L. Smith, *Constitutional Royalism and the Search for Settlement, c.1640–1649* (Cambridge, 1994), 208–10.
7. *The Works of Sir Walter Ralegh* (Oxford, 1829), viii. 563; R. W[ard], *The Character of Warre* (1643), 15; Carlton, *Going to the Wars*, 54–5, 58, 98, 168, 194; Roger B. Manning, *Swordsmen* (Oxford, 2003), 62–4.
8. John Hawarde, *Les Reportes del Cases in Camera Stellata 1593 to 1609*, ed. William Paley Baildon (n.p., 1894), 275; John Locke, *Some Thoughts concerning Education*, ed. John W. and Jean S. Yolton (Oxford, 1989), 193; Davies, *Gentlemen and Tarpaulins*, 63; Steven Shapin, *A Social History of Truth* (Chicago, 1994), ch. 3.
9. Stone, *Crisis*, 252–50; Markku Peltonen, *The Duel in Early Modern England* (Cambridge, 2003); Robert B. Shoemaker, 'The taming of the duel', *HJ* 45 (2002); Donna T. Andrew, 'The code of honour and its critics', *SH* 5 (1980).
10. Arthur N. Gilbert, 'Law and honour among eighteenth-century British army officers', *Hist. Journ.* 19 (1976); N. A. M. Rodger, 'Honour and duty at sea', *Hist. Research*, lxxv (2002).
11. J. C. Lassiter, 'Defamation of peers', *Amer. Journ. of Legal History*, 22 (1978).
12. George Chapman, *Bussy D'Ambois* (1607), II. i; *Nic. Eth.* 1126ᵃ; id., *Rhetoric*, 1367ᵃ; Peltonen, *Duel in Early Modern England*.
13. Above, Ch. 2.
14. Stone, *Crisis*, 223–34.
15. *The Autobiography of Thomas Whythorne*, ed. James M. Osborn (1962), 138.
16. Sir Richard Barckley, *A Discourse of the Felicitie of Man* (1598), 314; Jeremy Collier, *A Short View of the Immorality and Profaneness of the English Stage*

(1698), 143; Henry Fielding, *The Covent Garden Journal and a Plan of the Universal Register-Office*, ed. Bertrand A. Goldgar (Oxford, 1988), 36–7.

17. Watson, *Shakespeare and the Renaissance Concept of Honor*, 121–2; James, *Society, Politics and Culture*, ch. 9.
18. Barbara Donagan, 'Codes and conduct in the English Civil War', *P & P* 118 (1998); ead., 'The web of honour', *HJ* 44 (2001).
19. Austin Woolrych, *Britain in Revolution 1625–1660* (Oxford, 2002), 360.
20. *Journals of the House of Lords*, x. 310–11; Ian Gentles, *The New Model Army* (Oxford, 1992), 42.
21. Carlton, *Going to the Wars*, 172–9; Barbara Donagan, 'Atrocity, war crime, and treason in the English Civil War', *Amer. Hist. Rev.* 99 (1994); *The Civil Wars*, ed. John Kenyon and Jane Ohlmeyer (Oxford, 1998; 2002), 112, 283–5, 292, 295–301.
22. The complex reasons for Fairfax's severity are analysed by Barbara Donagan in *ODNB, s.n.* 'Lucas, Sir Charles'.
23. [Samuel Purchas], *Purchas his Pilgrim* (1619), 210–11; Richard Baker, 'Honour Discoursed of', BL, Sloane MS 881, fols 31, 134, 136 ff.; Keith Thomas, 'The social origins of Hobbes's political thought', in *Hobbes Studies*, ed. Keith C. Brown (Oxford, 1965), 195; Shoemaker, 'The taming of the duel', 541–2; Peltonen, *Duel in Early Modern England*, 114–17, 123–31, 143–4, 252–6.
24. *Homilies*, 139.
25. [Abraham Tucker], *The Light of Nature Pursued by Edward Search, Esq.* (1768–77), i/2. 140.
26. Richard Cust and Andrew Hopper, 'Duelling and the Court of Chivalry in early Stuart England', in *Cultures of Violence*, ed. Stuart Carroll (Basingstoke, 2007), 168; Linda A. Pollock, 'Honor, gender, and reconciliation in elite culture, 1570–1700', *JBS* 46 (2007).
27. This transition is the theme of James, *Society, Politics and Culture*, chs 8 and 9.
28. Hobbes, *De Cive*, 98.
29. John Hutchins, *The History and Antiquities of the County of Dorset*, 3rd edn, ed. W. Shipp and J. W. Hodson (1861–74), iv. 254.
30. Keith Feiling, *A History of the Tory Party 1640–1714* (Oxford, 1924), 55–7; Marston, 'Gentry honor and royalism', 41–3; P. R. Newman, 'The King's servants', in *Public Duty and Private Conscience in Seventeenth-Century England*, ed. John Morrill et al. (Oxford, 1993); Smith, *Constitutional Royalism*, 210–11; Donagan, 'The web of honour', 376; Andrew James Hopper, 'Fitted for despotism', *History*, 86 (2001), 145–6, 148–9, 152–4.
31. *The Life of Edward Earl of Clarendon . . . by himself* (Oxford, 1857), i. 135 (but note G. E. Aylmer's cautionary remarks about this story; *TRHS*, 5th ser., 37 (1987), 2–3).
32. Clarendon, *History*, iv. 131.
33. *ODNB, s.n.* 'Robert Devereux, 3rd Earl of Essex (1591–1646)'.
34. Ashley, *Of Honour*, 40.
35. John Hall of Richmond, *Of Government and Obedience* (1654), 120.
36. Ferne, *Blazon of Gentrie*, sig. Biiij; *Aubrey on Education*, ed. J. E. Stephens (1972), 133; Watson, *Shakespeare and the Renaissance Concept of Honor*, 26.
37. Hobbes, *De Cive*, 153.
38. *The Works of George Farquhar*, ed. Shirley Strum Kenny (Oxford, 1988), i. 166.

The Honour of the People

1. Thomas Simes, *A Military Course for the Government and Conduct of a Battalion* (1777), 210 n. Cf. Avner Offer, 'Going to war in 1914', *Politics and Society*, 23 (1995), 233–4.
2. Bulstrode Whitelocke's 'Annals of His life', BL, Add. MS 57326, fols 5^v–6.
3. *Reliquiae Baxterianae*, ed. Matthew Sylvester (1696), i. 3.
4. Ashley, *Of Honour*, 50; Keith Thomas, 'The life of learning', *PBA* 117 (2002), 221–2, 225–6.
5. Smith, *Wealth of Nations*, i. 117 (1. x. b).
6. Barbara Hanawalt, *'Of Good and Ill Repute'* (New York, 1998), 22–3; *Trans. Historic Soc. of Lancs. and Cheshire*, xl (1888), 154; J. T. Evans, *Seventeenth-Century Norwich* (Oxford, 1979), 69 n.
7. Stanford E. Lehmberg, *Cathedrals under Siege* (Exeter, 1996), 15, 204; Squibb, *Precedence*, 77–8; Robert Tittler, *The Reformation and the Towns in England* (Oxford, 1998), 274; Catherine F. Patterson, 'Corporations, cathedrals and the Crown', *History*, 85 (2000); Carl Estabrook, 'Ritual, space and authority in seventeenth-century English cathedral cities', *Journ. of Interdisciplinary History*, 32 (2002); *The History of the University of Oxford*, iv, ed. Nicholas Tyacke (Oxford, 1997), 120–1.
8. James, *Society, Politics and Culture*, 28, 35; Felicity Heal, *Hospitality in Early Modern England* (Oxford, 1990), ch. 8; Rosemary Sweet, 'Freedom and independence in English borough politics, c.1770–1830', *P & P* 161 (1998), 112–13; ead., *The Writing of Urban Histories in Eighteenth-Century England* (Oxford, 1997); Joyce M. Ellis, 'For the honour of the town', *Urban History*, 30 (2003).
9. Daniel C. Beaver, *Parish Communities and Religious Conflict in the Vale of Gloucester, 1590–1690* (Cambridge, MA, 1998), 77.
10. John Wheeler, *A Treatise of Commerce* (1601; New York, 1931), 109–10.
11. Louis B. Wright, *Middle-Class Culture in Elizabethan England* (Chapel Hill, NC, 1935), ch. 2.
12. [Nicholas Barbon], *A Discourse shewing the Great Advantages that New-Buildings, and the Enlarging of Towns and Cities do bring to a Nation* (1678), 7. For the authorship of this tract, see Paul Slack, 'Perceptions of the metropolis in seventeenth-century England', in *Civil Histories*, ed. Peter Burke et al. (Oxford, 2000), 175–8.
13. *The Plays of Richard Steele*, ed. Shirley Strum Kenny (Oxford, 1971), 359.
14. Capp, *Gossips*, 269–72.
15. Richard Gough, *The History of Myddle*, ed. David Hey (Harmondsworth, 1981), 239.
16. *Poems and Dramas of Fulke Greville First Lord Brooke*, ed. Geoffrey Bullough (Edinburgh, [1939]), i. 192.
17. *OED*, s.v. 'honesty'; William Empson, *The Structure of Complex Words* (1951), chs 9–11; Alexandra Shepard, 'Honesty, worth and gender in early modern England', in *Identity and Agency in England, 1500–1800*, ed. Henry French and Jonathan Barry (Basingstoke, 2004); and see p. 114 above.
18. *Visitation Articles and Injunctions of the Period of the Reformation*, ed. Walter Howard Frere (Alcuin Club, 1910), iii. 85; above, p. 114.
19. *OED*, s.v. 'respectability', 'respectable'. See e.g. *The Parish Register and Tithing Book of Thomas Hassall of Amwell*, ed. Stephen G. Doree (Herts. Rec. Soc., 1989), 78, 86, 96, 116, 123, 125; Gough, *History of Myddle*, 92, 190, 203, 232, 275.
20. Valuable analyses in Shepard, *Meanings of Manhood*; ead., 'Honesty, worth and gender in early modern England'; Capp, *Gossips*, ch. 6.

21. Helen Berry and Elizabeth Foyster, 'Childless men in early modern England', in *The Family in Early Modern England*, ed. Berry and Foyster (Cambridge, 2007).

22. *Spectator*, 99 (23 June 1711), i. 416; above, p. 52.

23. Shannon McSheffrey, 'Jurors, respectable masculinity, and Christian morality', *JBS* 37 (1998), 270; Shepard, *Meanings of Manhood*, ch. 7; ead., 'Honesty, worth and gender', 98, 100–1; Steve Hindle, *On the Parish?* (Oxford, 2004), 161.

24. Elizabeth A. Foyster, *Manhood in Early Modern England* (Harlow, 1999), 33–5.

25. John Ray, *The Wisdom of God Manifested in the Works of the Creation*, 3rd edn (1701), 402; J. A. Sharpe, *Defamation and Sexual Slander in Early Modern England*, Borthwick Papers, 58 (York, [1980]), 3.

26. On the lower-class duel, see J. M. Beattie, *Crime and the Courts in England 1660–1800* (Oxford, 1986), 91–4; Paul Langford, *Englishness Identified* (Oxford, 2000), 149–50; Maximillian E. Novak, *Daniel Defoe* (Oxford, 2001), 210; Robert Shoemaker, 'Male honour and the decline of public violence in eighteenth-century London', *SH* 26 (2001), 193–6, 198–9; id., *The London Mob* (2004), 156, 166–8, 177–8, 194–200; Shepard, *Meanings of Manhood*, ch. 6; Capp, *Gossips*, 188, 262.

27. Randle Holme, *The Academy of Armory* (Chester, 1688), ii. 126.

28. Tucker, *The Light of Nature Pursued*, i/1. 143.

29. Gervase Rosser, 'Crafts, guilds and the negotiation of work in the medieval town', *P & P* 154 (1997), 10–11, 27–8, 30–1; id., 'Solidarités et changement social', *Annales (ESC)*, 48 (1993), 1129.

30. *The Annual Register...for the Year 1764*, 4th edn (1792), i. 66; Peter Linebaugh, *The London Hanged* (Cambridge, 1992), 243–4, 247–8; John Rule, *The Labouring Classes in Early Industrial England* (Harlow, 1986), 35–6.

31. Doreen Everden, *The Midwives of Seventeenth-Century London* (Cambridge, 2000); Anna Clark, *The Struggle for the Breeches* (Berkeley and Los Angeles, 1995), esp. 27, 36–8, 122–6, 201.

32. W.T., *A Godly and Profitable Treatise intituled Absolom his Fall* (1591), fols 27–28^v; John Styles, *The Dress of the People* (New Haven, 2007), 306–14.

33. Gough, *History of Myddle*, 132; A. F. Leach, *English Schools at the Reformation 1546–8* (1896), 230; M. Dorothy George, *London Life in the XVIIIth Century* (1930), 302, 398–9; Tom Laqueur, 'Bodies, death and pauper funerals', *Representations*, i (1983); Clare Gittings, *Death, Burial and the Individual in Early Modern England* (1984), 60–3, 98–9; David Levine and Keith Wrightson, *The Making of an Industrial Society* (Oxford, 1991), 342–3; Peter Clark, *British Clubs and Societies 1580–1800* (Oxford, 2000), ch. 10.

34. Above, pp. 124, 125, 127.

35. Clark, *Struggle for the Breeches*, 37; Joyce M. Ellis, *The Georgian Town 1680–1840* (Basingstoke, 2001), 125.

36. R. H. Helmholz, *The Oxford History of the Laws of England*, i (Oxford, 2004), ch. 11; Sir John Baker, ibid. vi (Oxford, 2003), ch. 44; *Select Cases on Defamation to 1600*, ed. R. H. Helmholz (Selden Soc., 1985), introd.

37. Sharpe, *Defamation and Sexual Slander*; Ingram, *Church Courts*.

38. Sharpe, *Defamation and Sexual Slander*, 22; Ingram, *Church Courts*, 314; Laura Gowing, *Domestic Dangers* (Oxford, 1996), 118; Shepard, *Meanings of Manhood*, 159.

39. For an excellent survey, see Martin Ingram, 'Law, litigants and the construction of "honour" ', in *The Moral World of the Law*, ed. Peter Coss (Cambridge, 2000).

40. Sharpe, *Defamation and Sexual Slander*, 14. Cf. *Lower Ecclesiastical Jurisdiction in Late-Medieval England*, ed. L. R. Poos (British Academy, Oxford, 2001), *passim*.

41. J. H. Baker and S. F. C. Milsom, *Sources of English Legal History: Private Law to 1750* (1986), 638.

42. *John Isham Merchant and Merchant Adventurer*, ed. G. D. Ramsay (Northants. Rec. Soc., 1962), 172.

43. Daniel Defoe, *The Complete English Tradesman* (1745; Oxford, 1841), vol. i, ch. 17.

44. *The Letters of Philip Stannard, Norwich Textile Manufacturer (1751-63)*, ed. Ursula Priestley (Norfolk Rec. Soc., 1994), 87-91.

45. Julian Hoppit, *Risk and Trade in English Business 1700-1800* (Cambridge, 1987), 25-8; Smith, *Wealth of Nations*, i. 342 (11. iii).

46. *Spectator*, 446 (1 Aug. 1712), iv. 68.

47. Margaret Cavendish, Marchioness of Newcastle, *The World's Olio* (1655), 75.

48. *Autobiography of Thomas Whythorne*, 17.

49. Foyster, *Manhood*, 148-64.

50. Montaigne, *Essays*, trans. John Florio (Everyman's Lib., 1910), iii. 96; Thomas Randolph, *The Muses Looking-Glasse*, in *Poems*, 4th edn (1652), 2nd pagination, 46 (the speaker is admittedly a character who irritates by his excessive inability to take offence).

51. [Anthony Hamilton], *Memoirs of the Court of Charles II by Count Grammont*, ed. Sir Walter Scott (1891), 188; Pepys, *Diary*, viii. 120.

52. Sir John Kelyng, *A Report of Divers Cases* (1708), 137; Susan Staves, 'Money for honor', *Studies in Eighteenth-Century Culture*, ed. Harry C. Payne, 11 (Madison, 1982); Lawrence Stone, *Road to Divorce* (Oxford, 1990), ch. ix; David M. Turner, *Fashioning Adultery* (Cambridge, 2002), ch. 6.

53. G. R. Quaife, *Wanton Wenches and Wayward Wives* (1979), 142; Elizabeth Foyster, 'A laughing matter?', *Rural History*, 4 (1993), 8-9.

54. John Dunton, *The Athenian Oracle*, 2nd edn (1704), ii. 359; ibid., 3rd edn (1728), iii. 477-8; *Spectator*, 203 (23 Oct. 1711), ii. 297; Turner, *Fashioning Adultery*, 108-15.

55. *A Strange Metamorphosis in Tavistock* (1658), 7-8; Oxon. RO, Oxford Archdeaconry Papers, c 31, fol. 267 (and c 125, fol. 289).

56. Randolph Trumbach, *Sex and the Gender Revolution*, i (Chicago, 1998), 49, 392-3; Turner, *Fashioning Adultery*, 108-15, 199; S. M. Waddams, *Sexual Slander in Nineteenth-Century England* (Toronto, 2000), 139; Joanne Bailey, *Unquiet Lives* (2003), 163-5.

57. Maurice Morgann, *An Essay on the Dramatic Character of Sir John Falstaff* (1777; new edn, 1825), 185-6.

58. Keith Thomas, 'The Puritans and adultery', in *Puritans and Revolutionaries*, ed. Donald Pennington and Keith Thomas (Oxford, 1978), 260-1; Patrick Collinson, *The Religion of Protestants* (Oxford, 1982), 227-9.

59. *Philip Stubbes's Anatomy of Abuses in England*, ed. Frederick J. Furnivall (New Shakspere Soc., 1877-82), i. 96.

60. Berks. RO, D/A2/ c 168, fols 207, 227, 255; Oxon. RO, Oxford Diocesan Papers, c 25, fol. 62^{r-v}; F. G. Emmison, *Elizabethan Life: Morals and the Church*

Courts (Chelmsford, 1973), 47; Alan Macfarlane, *Reconstructing Historical Communities* (Cambridge, 1977), 145; Tim Meldrum, 'A women's court in London', *London Journ.* 19 (1994), 10–11; Gowing, *Domestic Dangers*, 74; Foyster, *Manhood*, 42–3; Bernard Capp, 'The double standard revisited', *P & P* 162 (1999), 71–2; Shepard, *Meanings of Manhood*, 120–1, 171; Christopher Haigh, *The Plain Man's Pathways to Heaven* (Oxford, 2007), 148, 154.

61. Pepys, *Diary*, vi. 1–2 (she gave birth two months later; vi. 52).
62. Turner, *Fashioning Adultery*, 336–42; Arthur Bedford, *A Serious Remonstrance* (1730), 196, and ch. 13 *passim*; Fletcher, *Gender, Sex and Subordination*, 342–4; Anna Bryson, *From Courtesy to Civility* (Oxford, 1998), ch. 7; Faramerz Dabhoiwala, 'The construction of honour, reputation and status in late seventeenth- and early eighteenth-century England', *TRHS*, 6th ser., vi (1996), 205–7.
63. *Dives and Pauper*, ed. Priscilla Heath Barnum (EETS, 1976–2004), i/2. 67–9; John Case, *Sphaera Civitatis* (Frankfurt, 1616), 517–18; Keith Thomas, 'The double standard', *Journ. of the History of Ideas*, 20 (1959); id., 'Puritans and adultery', 261–2.
64. *The Political Works of James I*, ed. Charles Howard McIlwain (Cambridge, MA, 1918), 34, 36.
65. Thomas, 'Puritans and adultery', 265–7; Ian W. Archer, *The Pursuit of Stability* (Cambridge, 1991), 251.
66. Susan Whyman, *Sociability and Power in Late Stuart England* (Oxford, 1999), 64; *Diary of John Rous*, ed. Mary Anne Everett Green (Camden Soc., 1846), 34; *The Obituary of Richard Smyth*, ed. Sir Henry Ellis (Camden Soc., 1849), 35 (who confuses Dr William Rant with Raven); Garthine Walker, *Crime, Gender and Social Order in Early Modern England* (Cambridge, 2003), 230–7, 275.
67. Capp, 'Double standard revisited', 84–92; id., 'The poet and the bawdy court', *Seventeenth Century*, x (1995); 'The conspiracy of Stephenson Wilcockes his wif and Jones against Sir Robert Cotton to gett money', BL, Add. MS 14049, fols 21–43^v; *ODNB, s.n.* 'Hooker, Richard'.
68. Sidney and Beatrice Webb, *English Local Government: English Poor Law History*, pt i: *The Old Poor Law* (1927), 309–11.
69. *Women's Worlds in Seventeenth-Century England*, ed. Patricia Crawford and Laura Gowing (2000), 155.
70. Dabhoiwala, 'The construction of honour, reputation and status', 212–13. There is, as yet, a lack of supporting evidence for Randolph Trumbach's belief (*Sex and the Gender Revolution*, i. 14–15, 24, 54–5, 194–5) that, after 1730, it was so important for men to demonstrate their heterosexuality that 'it did no harm at all to be known as a whoremonger'.
71. *Spectator*, 99 (23 June 1711), i. 416.
72. *The Prose Works of Fulke Greville, Lord Brooke*, ed. John Gouws (Oxford, 1986), 146; *The Women's Sharp Revenge*, ed. Simon Shepherd (1985), 165.
73. William Noy, *Reports and Cases*, 2nd edn (1669), 151; *The Reports of . . . Thomas Owen* (1656), 34.
74. *An Account of the General Nursery, or Colledg of Infants* (1686), 2nd pagination, 9.
75. *The New Oxford Book of Eighteenth Century Verse*, ed. Roger Lonsdale (Oxford, 1984), no. 223; *Memoirs and Travels of Sir John Reresby*, ed. Albert Ivatt (1904), 93.
76. Dabhoiwala, 'The construction of honour, reputation and status', 210–11.
77. *The Autobiography of Francis Place*, ed. Mary Thale (Cambridge, 1972), 81–2; Thomas, 'Double standard', 206; Anna Clark, 'Whores and gossips', in *Current Issues in Women's History*, ed. Arina Angermen et al. (1989), 51; ead., *Struggle*

for the Breeches, 61; Tim Hitchcock, 'Unlawfully begotten on her body', in *Chronicling Poverty*, ed. Hitchcock et al. (Basingstoke, 1997), 72–7; Tanya Evans, '*Unfortunate Objects*' (Basingstoke, 2005), 176, 202–3, 206.

78. Oxon. RO, Oxford Diocesan Papers, d 16, fols 19, 18^v.

79. Oxon. RO, Oxford Diocesan Papers, c 26, fol. 152; Oxford Archdeaconry Papers, c 33, fol. 70; Leicester City Museum, 1 D41/4/504, 505, 599; *Lower Ecclesiastical Jurisdiction*, ed. Poos, 277, 280, 323–5, 339, 421, 488–9; Gowing, *Domestic Dangers*, ch. 3; Capp, *Gossips*, 189–90.

80. Capp, *Gossips*, 189–97, for an excellent summary.

81. *The Works of Henry Smith* (Edinburgh, 1866), i. 6; Garthine Walker, 'Expanding the boundaries of female honour in early modern England', *TRHS*, 6th ser., vi (1996); Margaret J. M. Ezell, *The Patriarch's Wife* (Chapel Hill, NC, 1987), 101–2; Gowing, *Domestic Dangers*, 66, 129–30; ead., *Common Bodies* (New Haven, 2003), 113–14; Tim Stretton, *Women Waging Law in Elizabethan England* (Cambridge, 1998), 192–3; Bailey, *Unquiet Lives*, 79–80; Shepard, *Meanings of Manhood*, 154, 165–7, 172, 195–202; ead., 'Honesty, worth and gender'; above, p. 104.

82. Ezell, *Patriarch's Wife*, 176.

83. *Catalogue of the Earl Marshal's Papers*, 17; Walker, 'Expanding the boundaries of female honour', 238–9.

84. *Thomas Heywood*, ed. A. Wilson Verity (n.d.), 206 (III. ii).

85. Hall of Richmond, *Of Government and Obedience*, 20; William Barrow, *An Essay on Education*, 2nd edn (1804), ii. 205; Alice B. Gomme, *The Traditional Games of England, Scotland, and Ireland* (1894–8; 1984), 300–1 and *passim*; Ralph A. Houlbrooke, *The English Family 1450–1700* (Harlow, 1984), 148. For a 13-year-old boy obsessed by talk of honour and duelling, see *Crosby Records*, 219–20.

86. Gabriele Stein, *John Palsgrave as Renaissance Linguist* (Oxford, 1997), 413; *The Correspondence of John Locke*, ed. E. S. de Beer (Oxford, 1976–), iii. 175–6; Roger North, *The Lives of the Right Hon. Francis North, Baron Guilford; the Hon. Sir Dudley North; and the Hon. and Rev. John North*, ed. Augustus Jessopp (1890), i. 173.

87. [Guillaume du Vair], *The Moral Philosophie of the Stoicks*, trans. T[homas] I[ames] (1598), 79–80.

88. Hall of Richmond, *Of Government and Obedience*, 21.

89. Steven Lukes, *Émile Durkheim* (1973), 653–4.

90. R[obert] C[rofts], *The Way to Happinesse on Earth* (1641), 86–7, 93, 96.

91. For claims by merchants: Wheeler, *Treatise of Commerce*, 7; *Memoirs of the Life of Mr Ambrose Barnes*, ed. W. H. D. Longstaffe (Surtees Soc., 1867), 36–7; Laura Caroline Stevenson, *Praise and Paradox* (Cambridge, 1984), 128–9; and above, p. 144. For the gentlemanly view of trade as dishonouring: Segar, *Honor Military, and Civill*, 230; Fynes Moryson, *An Itinerary* (Glasgow, 1907–8), iv. 169; Henry Peacham, *The Compleat Gentleman* (1634), ed. Virgil B. Heltzel (Ithaca, NY, 1962), 21–2; James Salter, *Caliope's Cabinet Opened* (1665), 10. For comment on the controversy: Edward Chamberlayne, *Angliae Notitia* (1669), 478–81; G. D. Squibb, *The High Court of Chivalry* (Oxford, 1959), 176–7; Grassby, *Business Community*, ch. 1.

92. *The Letters of Sir Thomas Browne*, ed. Geoffrey Keynes, new edn (1946), 27; *The Letters of Dorothy Moore 1612–64*, ed. Lynette Hunter (Aldershot, 2004), 71.

93. *All the Workes of Iohn Taylor the Water Poet* (1630), ii. 199.

94. George Hickes, *A Sermon preached at the Church of St Bridget* (1684), 7.

95. Gough, *History of Myddle*, 230–1; and above, p. 104.
96. *The Works of John Robinson*, ed. R. Ashton (1851), i. 119; above, p. 104.
97. Steve Hindle, 'Dependency, shame and belonging', *Cultural and Social History*, i (2004).
98. R[ichard] H[awkins], *A Discourse of the Nationall Excellencies of England* (1658), 146; [Edward Stephens], *A Preparation for Death*, appended to *A Plain Relation of the Late Action at Sea* (1690), 6; Richard Steele, *The Christian Hero*, ed. Rae Blanchard (1932), 71; Marcus Rediker, *Between the Devil and the Deep Blue Sea* (Cambridge, 1987), 266, 280–1; Lincoln B. Faller, *Turned to Account* (Cambridge, 1987), 275 n. 19; Andrea McKenzie, 'Martyrs in low life?', *JBS* 42 (2003).
99. John Locke, *An Essay concerning Human Understanding*, ed. Peter H. Nidditch (Oxford, 1975), 357.
100. Shepard, *Meanings of Manhood*, 93–113; and Bernard Capp's review at http://www.history.ac.uk/reviews.
101. On this as a European phenomenon, see Peregrine Horden and Nicholas Purcell, *The Corrupting Sea* (Oxford, 2000), 520–2.
102. Tucker, *The Light of Nature Pursued*, i/2. 140. Similarly Baker, 'Honour Discoursed of', fols 123–5.
103. *Works of Isaac Barrow*, i. 28.

Credit and Shame

1. Ashley, *Of Honour*, 30; Archibald Campbell, *An Enquiry into the Original of Moral Virtue* (Edinburgh, 1733), 46; Smith, *Moral Sentiments*, 61 (1. iii. 2).
2. Anthony F. Upton, *Sir Arthur Ingram* (1961), 103–4; Barbara J. Todd, 'I do no injury by not loving', in *Women and History*, ed. Valerie Frith (Toronto, 1995), 219.
3. Burton, *Anatomy*, i. 262.
4. *The Memoirs of Edmund Ludlow*, ed. C. H. Firth (Oxford, 1894), i. 220.
5. Thomas Hobbes, *Elements of Law*, ed. Ferdinand Tönnies, 2nd edn (1969), 42 (1. ix. 13).
6. Howell A. Lloyd, *The Rouen Campaign 1590–1592* (Oxford, 1973), 114; Paul E. J. Hammer, *The Polarisation of Elizabethan Politics* (Cambridge, 1999), 106.
7. Woolrych, *Britain in Revolution*, 288; Evelyn, *Diary*, iii. 617.
8. Pepys, *Diary*, ix. 58–9; Baxter, *Works*, i. 196.
9. *The Letters of John Chamberlain*, ed. Norman Egbert McClure (Philadelphia, 1929), i. 335; Laurence Clarkson, *The Lost Sheep Found* (1660; Exeter, 1974), 20; Michael MacDonald and Terence R. Murphy, *Sleepless Souls* (Oxford, 1990), 275–84; Grassby, *Business Community*, 199–200.
10. John Sym, *Life's Preservative against Self-Killing*, ed. Michael MacDonald (1988), 221–2.
11. *Autobiography of Thomas Raymond and Memoirs of the Family of Guise*, ed. G. Davies, Camden Soc., 3rd ser. (1917), 102–3.
12. Stretton, *Women Waging Law*, 223; Peter King, *Crime, Justice, and Discretion in England 1740–1820* (Oxford, 2000), 33, 104, 234, 307–10; Faramerz Dabhoiwala, 'Sex, social relations and the law in seventeenth- and eighteenth-century London', in *Negotiating Power in Early Modern Society*, ed. Michael J. Braddick and John Walter (Cambridge, 2001), 88–90; Gowing, *Common Bodies*, 90–2; Shepard, 'Honesty, worth and gender'; J. F. Merritt,

The Social World of Early Modern Westminster (Manchester, 2005), 237; Marjorie Keniston McIntosh, *Working Women in English Society* (Cambridge, 2005), 12.

13. Craig Muldrew, *The Economy of Obligation* (Basingstoke, 1998), 92, 95, 117, and *passim*; id., 'Hard food for Midas', *P & P* 170 (2001), esp. 83, 93.

14. On the practical disadvantages of a damaged reputation, see Ingram, *Church Courts*, 306–19; id., 'Law, litigants and the construction of "honour" ', 143–50; Muldrew, *Economy of Obligation*, ch. 6; Capp, *Gossips*, 208–17.

15. William Sheppard, *The Faithful Councellor*, 2nd edn (1653–4), i. 337–8; *Examen Legum Angliae* (1656), 123; Richard Baxter, *A Holy Commonwealth* (1659), 69; Peltonen, *Duel in Early Modern England*, 136–42, 219–22, 297–8; Adam Smith, *Lectures on Jurisprudence*, ed. R. L. Meek, D. D. Raphael, and P. G. Stein (Oxford, 1978), 8–9.

16. Above, p. 28. On London as 'a surveillant society', see Lena Cowen Orlin, *Locating Privacy in Early Modern London* (Oxford, 2007).

17. E. P. Thompson, 'Rough music', *Annales (ÉSC)*, xxvii (1972); Martin Ingram, 'Ridings, rough music and the "reform of popular culture" in early modern England', *P & P* 105 (1984); id., 'Ridings, rough music and mocking rhymes in early modern England', in *Popular Culture in Seventeenth-Century England*, ed. Barry Reay (1985); id., 'Juridical folklore in England illustrated by rough music', in *Communities and Courts in Britain 1150–1900*, ed. Christopher Brooks and Michael Lobban (1997); Adam Fox, *Oral and Literate Culture in England 1500–1700* (Oxford, 2000), ch. 6; David Postles, *Talking Ballocs* (Leicester, 2003), 64, and *passim*.

18. Oxon. RO, Oxford Diocesan Papers, c 26, fol. 80^{v}.

19. Beds. and Luton Archives and Records Service, ABCP/ fol. 79 (1675); Southwell Act Books (transcript by W. A. James in Reading Univ. Lib.), xxiii. 272, 392, 393 (1579–95); *Speculum Dioceseos Lincolniensis*, ed. R. E.G. Cole (Lincoln Rec. Soc., 1913), 183; *Cal. S.P. Domestic, 1635–6*, 500–1; E. R. C. Brinkworth, 'The Laudian church in Buckinghamshire', *Univ. of Birmingham Hist. Journ.* v (1955–6), 34–5; *Articles of Accusation and Impeachment...against William Pierce* (n.d. [1641]), 6.

20. Cicero, *De Republica*, 5. 4; Augustine, *De Civitate Dei*, v. 13.

21. Bernard Mandeville, *An Enquiry into the Origin of Honour* (1732; 2nd edn, 1971), 42–4 and *passim*. This theme is discussed, with many examples from the seventeenth and eighteenth centuries, in Arthur O. Lovejoy, *Reflections on Human Nature* (Baltimore, 1961), lectures v and vi.

22. Stephen Greenblatt, *Renaissance Self-Fashioning* (Chicago, 1980), 47–53; William Sheppard, *Englands Balme* (1657), 162.

23. For recent discussions, see Shepard, *Meanings of Manhood*, 132–9; Martin Ingram, 'Shame and pain', in *Penal Practice and Culture 1500–1900*, ed. Simon Devereaux and Paul Griffiths (Basingstoke, 2004); Shoemaker, *London Mob*, ch. 4.

24. Robert Horne, *Life and Death* (1613), 288; *A Foreign View of England in 1725–1729*, trans. and ed. Mme van Muyden (1995), 78.

25. Kenneth Muir, *Life and Letters of Sir Thomas Wyatt* (Liverpool, 1963), 39.

26. Ruth Benedict, *The Chrysanthemum and the Sword* (1947), esp. 222–5.

The Decline of Honour?

1. *Moral Philosophie of the Stoicks*, trans. James, 74–5, 79, 98; E. Vernon Arnold, *Roman Stoicism* (1911; 1958), 320.
2. *Cottoni Posthuma*, ed. J[ames] H[owell] (1672), 337; John Rushworth, *Historical Collections* (1721), i. 334; G. D. Scull, *Dorothea Scott* (Oxford, 1883), esp. 151–61; Francis Quarles, *Enchiridion* (1641; 1856), 56, 65, 74, 77, 107; Algernon Sidney, *Discourses concerning Government*, 3rd edn (1751), 202–5; Stone, *Crisis*, ch. iii.
3. Peter R. Roberts, 'Henry VIII, Francis I and the Reformation Parliament', *Parliaments, Estates and Representation*, 27 (2007), 135–6; *The Works of George Savile, Marquis of Halifax*, ed. Mark N. Brown (Oxford, 1989), iii. 401.
4. HMC, *Salisbury*, ii. 234; Henry Crosse, *Vertues Common-Wealth* (1603), sig. D1; Ashley, *Of Honour*, 36; Shepard, 'Honesty, worth and gender', 98.
5. William Ames, *Conscience with the Power and Cases thereof* (1659), iii. 145. Matthew 6: 1 was the key text here.
6. William Tyndale, *Doctrinal Treatises*, ed. Henry Walter (PS, Cambridge, 1848), 183–4; Ian Donaldson, *The Rapes of Lucretia* (Oxford, 1982), esp. ch. 2.
7. Lodowick Bryskett, *Literary Works*, ed. J. H. P. Pafford (n.p., 1972), 76, 231; Ashley, *Of Honour*, 36; David Hartley, *Observations on Man* (1749; facs., Hildesheim, 1967), ii. 259–60.
8. John Archer Gee, *The Life and Works of Thomas Lupset* (New Haven, 1928), 213; John 12: 43.
9. John Downame, *The Christian Warfare*, 4th edn (1634), 482; Robert Porter, *The Life of Mr John Hieron* (1691), 6.
10. Richard Bernard, *Ruths Recompence* (1628), 113.
11. *The Journal of George Fox*, ed. Norman Penney (Cambridge, 1911), i. 213 (quoting John 5: 44); Robert Barclay, *An Apology for the True Christian Divinity*, 5th edn (1703), 519–32; Adrian Davies, *Quakers in English Society 1655–1725* (Oxford, 2000), 46–52, 133–5.
12. *The Complete Works of Thomas Brooks* (Edinburgh, 1866–7), iv. 160.
13. Steven C. A. Pincus, *Protestantism and Patriotism* (Cambridge, 1996), 36; Bulstrode Whitelocke, *A Journal of the Swedish Embassy*, ed. Henry Reeve (1855), i. 117; Tony Claydon, *Europe and the Making of England* (2007), 196.
14. Kishlansky, *Parliamentary Selection*, 106, 134, 226.
15. Penelope J. Corfield, 'Walking the city streets', *Journ. of Urban History*, 16 (1990), 154.
16. Shoemaker, *London Mob*, esp. ch. 3.
17. I hope to discuss this theme in greater detail in the published version of my Menahem Stern lectures (Hanover, NH, forthcoming).
18. P. J. Cain and A. G. Hopkins, 'Gentlemanly capitalism and British expansion overseas, I', *EcHR*, 2nd ser., xxxix (1986), 507–8.
19. Muldrew, *Economy of Obligation*, 4–7, 156, 329.
20. Though it was several more decades before the rule was strictly enforced; John H. Langbein, *The Origins of the Adversary Criminal Trial* (Oxford, 2003), 190–203.
21. Sir William Blackstone, *Commentaries on the Laws of England*, new edn (1813), iii. 343 (III. xxiii); John Marshall Mitnick, 'From neighbor-witness to jury of proofs', *Amer. Journ. of Legal History*, 32 (1988); Dabhoiwala, 'Sex, social relations and the law', 100–1.
22. *Minutes of Proceedings in Quarter Sessions... 1674–1695*, ed. S. A. Peyton (Lincoln Rec. Soc., 1931), vol. i, pp. lxxvii–lxxviii; Beattie, *Crime and the Courts*, 614–15; id., *Policing and Punishment in London 1660–1750* (Oxford,

2001), 307–8, 473–4; Greg T. Smith, 'Civilized people don't want to see that sort of thing', in *Qualities of Mercy*, ed. Carolyn Strange (Vancouver, 1996); Shoemaker, *London Mob*, ch. 4, and id., 'Streets of shame?', in *Penal Policy and Culture*, ed. Devereaux and Griffiths.

23. Avishai Margalit, *The Decent Society*, trans. Naomi Goldblom (Cambridge, MA, 1996), p. x.

24. Shoemaker, *London Mob*, 72–3, 295–7, and *passim*; Henry Fielding, *Joseph Andrews* (1742), ed. Douglas Brooks-Davies, rev. Thomas Keymer (Oxford, 1999), 27 (I. vi).

25. Dabhoiwala, 'Sex, social relations and the law'.

26. Mary Kinnear, 'The correction court in the diocese of Carlisle', *Church History*, 59 (1990); *The Church of England c.1689–c. 1833*, ed. John Walsh et al. (Cambridge, 1993), 5–6; W. M. Jacob, *Lay People and Religion in the Early Eighteenth Century* (Cambridge, 1996), 135–44; Bailey, *Unquiet Lives*, 141; M. F. Snape, *The Church of England in an Industrialising Society* (Woodbridge, 2003), ch. 4; R. B. Outhwaite, *The Rise and Fall of the English Ecclesiastical Courts, 1500–1860* (Cambridge, 2006), 83–4; Andrew Thomson, 'Church discipline', *History*, 91 (2006).

27. Capp, *Gossips*, 378; Meldrum, 'A women's court in London', 2, 6; Trumbach, *Sex and the Gender Revolution*, i. 25–6, 32; Waddams, *Sexual Slander*.

28. J. M. Kaye, 'Libel and slander—two torts or one?', *Law Qtly Rev.* 91 (1975), 530; Ingram, 'Ridings, rough music and the "reform of popular culture" ', 100–1.

29. Blackstone, *Commentaries*, iv. 58–9; Dabhoiwala, 'Sex, social relations and the law'; id., 'Sex and societies for moral reform, 1688–1830', *JBS* 46 (2007).

30. Devon RO, Chanter 902, p. 108; Alan Bray, *Homosexuality in Renaissance England* (1982), 114.

31. P. D. G. Thomas, *John Wilkes* (Oxford, 1996), 66; Bentham, 'Offences against one's self: paederasty' (*c.*1785), available on http://www.columbia.edu/cu/lweb/eresources/exhibitions/sw25/bentham/index.html. For the origins of this new attitude, see the forthcoming book by Faramerz Dabhoiwala, provisionally entitled *Sex and the Enlightenment*.

32. Jeremiah Burroughes, *The Excellency of a Gracious Spirit* (1639), 151; Thomas Wilson, *Davids Zeale for Zion* (1641), 17; and see pp. 27–8 above.

33. Downame, *Christian Warfare*, 434.

34. F. J. M. Korsten, *Roger North (1651–1734)* (Amsterdam, 1981), 135; J. A. Sharpe, *Crime in Seventeenth-Century England* (Cambridge, 1983), 168.

35. Above, p. 39.

36. Downame, *Christian Warfare*, 442.

37. See Berger, 'On the obsolescence of the concept of honour', 343.

38. De Tocqueville, *Democracy in America*, ii. 255.

39. Pierre Bourdieu, 'The sentiment of honour in Kabyle society', in *Honour and Shame*, ed. Peristiany, 228.

40. Hall of Richmond, *Of Government and Obedience*, 16.

41. D. H. Monro, *Godwin's Moral Philosophy* (1953), ch. 4; *A Rattleskull Genius*, ed. Geraint H. Jenkins (Cardiff, 2005), 379; Richard Price, *Political Writings*, ed. D. O. Thomas (Cambridge, 1991), 145–6.

42. Durkheim criticized the author of the doctoral thesis mentioned at p. 171 above for overlooking this more general idea of honour as personal honesty. On it, see Stewart, *Honor*, 47–53.

43. Samuel Butler, *The Way of All Flesh* (World's Classics, 1936), 225.

CHAPTER 6

The Idea of Friendship

1. Michael Argyle, 'Subjective well-being', in *In Pursuit of the Quality of Life*, ed. Avner Offer (Oxford, 1996); Charles Taylor, *Sources of the Self* (Cambridge, 1989), 293.
2. John Hitchcock, *A Sanctuary for Honest Men* (1617), 34–5.
3. See *Early Modern Women's Letter Writing, 1450–1700*, ed. James Daybell (Basingstoke, 2001); and id., *Women Letter-Writers in Early Tudor England* (Oxford, 2006).
4. In *Locating Privacy in Tudor London* (Oxford, 2007), Lena Cowen Orlin argues that the multiplication of rooms in houses was intended less to secure privacy than to accommodate and display more furniture and possessions. But the division of dwellings into more and less private areas was at least as old as Vitruvius; *De Architectura*, v. v. i; and, in the seventeenth century, the desire to achieve greater privacy was explicitly expressed by a number of contemporaries. See John Bold, 'Privacy and the plan', in *English Architecture Public and Private*, ed. John Bold and Edward Chaney (1993).
5. *The Tender Husband* (1705), in *Plays of Richard Steele*, ed. Shirley Strum Kenny (Oxford, 1971), 263; and see Karen Lipsedge, 'Enter into thy closet', in *Gender, Taste and Material Culture in Britain and North America*, ed. John Styles and Amanda Vickery (New Haven, 2006). Orlin, *Locating Privacy*, ch. 8, suggests that the closet began as a locked area used for various purposes and only gradually came to be thought of as private space.
6. Christoph Heyl, 'We are not at home', *London Journ.* 27 (2002), expanded into *A Passion for Privacy: Untersuchungen zur Genese der Bürgerlichen Privat-sphäre in London (1660–1800)* (Munich, 2004); Amanda Vickery, 'An Englishman's home is his castle?", *P & P* 199 (2008).
7. *Narratives of the Days of the Reformation*, ed. John Gough Nichols (Camden Soc., 1859), 244–5.
8. [Daniel Defoe], *The Complete English Tradesman*, 3rd edn (1732), i. 94–5.
9. *Wilson's Arte of Rhetorique 1560*, ed. G. H. Mair (Oxford, 1909), 55.
10. Aristotle, *Nic. Eth.* 1155^a; *Politics* 1262^b, 1280^b; *Folly in Print* (1667), 122; *The Complete Works of William Wycherley*, ed. Montague Summers, iii (1924), 43–5.
11. *The Chronicle and Political Papers of King Edward VI*, ed. W. K. Jordan (1966), 165; Francis Bacon, *The Major Works*, ed. Brian Vickers (Oxford, 2002), 477.
12. *Liturgical Services... set forth in the Reign of Queen Elizabeth*, ed. William Keatinge Clay (PS, Cambridge, 1847), 190; John Aubrey, *Remaines of Gentilisme and Judaisme*, ed. James Britten (Folk-Lore Soc., 1881), 5.
13. *York Civic Records*, ed. Angelo Raine, Yorks. Archaeol. Soc., Rec. Ser. (1939–53), v. 177; Paul Slack, *The Impact of Plague in Tudor and Stuart England* (1985), 295; Gervase Rosser, 'Going to the fraternity feast', *JBS* 33 (1994).
14. John Stow, *A Survey of London*, ed. Charles Lethbridge Kingsford (Oxford, 1908), i. 101; David Underdown, *Revel, Riot and Rebellion* (Oxford, 1985), 63–7.
15. *The Works of Symon Patrick*, ed. Alexander Taylor (Oxford, 1858), ii. 86–7; Richard Moore, *A Pearl in an Oyster-Shel* (1675), 83–4; Richard L. Greaves, *Society and Religion in Elizabethan England* (Minneapolis, 1981), 651–7; John Bossy, *Peace in the Post-Reformation* (Cambridge, 1988), 76–8; Christopher Haigh, *The Plain Man's Pathways to Heaven* (Oxford, 2007), 73; Keith Wrightson, 'The "decline of neighbourliness" revisited', in *Local Identities in Late*

Medieval and Early Modern England ed. Norman L. Jones and Daniel Woolf (Basingstoke, 2007), 29–30.

16. J. A. Sharpe, 'Such disagreement betwyx neighbours', in *Disputes and Settlements*, ed. John Bossy (Cambridge, 1983), 175; Eamon Duffy, *The Stripping of the Altars* (New Haven, 1992), 94–5; Michael Berlin, 'Reordering rituals', in *Londinopolis*, ed. Paul Griffiths and Mark S. R. Jenner (Manchester, 2000).

17. *The Works of Thomas Nashe*, ed. Ronald B. McKerrow (repr. Oxford, 1966), i. 293–4.

18. [Abraham Tucker], *The Light of Nature Pursued by Edward Search, Esq*, iii/2 (1777), 430. Valuable works on friendship in the early modern period include Laurens J. Mills, *One Soul in Bodies Twain* (Bloomington, IN, 1937); Guy Fitch Lytle, 'Friendship and patronage in Renaissance Europe', in *Patronage, Art and Society in Renaissance Italy*, ed. F. W. Kent and Patricia Simons (Canberra, 1987); *The Dialectics of Friendship*, ed. Roy Porter and Sylvana Tomaselli (1989); Lorna Hutson, *The Usurer's Daughter* (1994); Philippa Maddern, 'Best trusted friends', in *England in the Fifteenth Century*, ed. Nicholas Rogers (Stamford, 1994); Ullrich Langer, *Perfect Friendship* (Geneva, 1994); David Wootton, 'Francis Bacon', in *The World of the Favourite*, ed. J. H. Elliott and L. W. B. Brockliss (New Haven, 1999); Naomi Tadmor, *Family and Friends in Eighteenth-Century England* (Cambridge, 2001), ch. 5; Frances Harris, *Transformations of Love* (Oxford, 2002); Alan Bray, *The Friend* (Chicago, 2003); Lynne Johnson, 'Friendship, coercion and interest', *Journ. of Early Modern History*, 8 (2004); Tom MacFaul, *Male Friendship in Shakespeare and his Contemporaries* (Cambridge, 2007); and the articles by Allan Silver cited in n. 90 on p. 347 below.

19. Lawrence Stone, *Family, Sex and Marriage in England 1500–1800* (1977), 5, 97–8; Ingram, *Church Courts*, 139–40, 204–7, 268; Peter Earle, *The Making of the English Middle Class* (1989), 91–2; Laura Gowing, *Domestic Dangers* (Oxford, 1996), 149–59, 167, 253; Diana O'Hara, *Courtship and Constraint* (Manchester, 2000), ch. 1; *Women's Worlds in Seventeenth-Century England*, ed. Patricia Crawford and Laura Gowing (2000), 216; Tadmor, *Family and Friends*, 161, 166, 175–92; David A. Postles, *Social Proprieties* (Washington, 2006), 84–6.

20. *A Pleasing Sinne*, ed. Adam Smyth (Cambridge, 2004), 45.

21. Marc Bloch, *Feudal Society*, trans. L. A. Manyon, 2nd edn (1962), i. 124.

22. Julian A. Pitt-Rivers, *The People of the Sierra*, 2nd edn (Chicago, 1971), 140.

23. *Desiderata Curiosa*, ed. Francis Peck (1779), i. 49.

24. *The Naval Tracts of Sir William Monson*, ed. M. Oppenheim (Navy Recs Soc., 1902–14), i. 103.

25. Aubrey, *Brief Lives*, ii. 9; George Chapman, *A Treatise on Education*, 4th edn (1790), 39; Tadmor, *Family and Friends*, 91–2.

26. *The Poems of Matthew Grove 1587*, ed. Alexander Grosart (Manchester, 1878), 139; Keith Wrightson, *English Society 1580–1680* (1982), 51–4; id. 'The "decline of neighbourliness" revisited', 24–6; Jeremy Boulton, *Neighbourhood and Society* (Cambridge, 1987), 236–47; Ian W. Archer, *The Pursuit of Stability* (Cambridge, 1991), 74–82; Maria Moisa, 'Conviviality and charity in medieval and early modern England', *P & P* 154 (1997), 229–31; Ilana Krausman Ben-Amos, 'Gifts and favors', *Journ. of Modern History*, 72 (2000); Capp, *Gossips*, 55–7, 106–11.

27. George Chandler, *Liverpool under James I* (Liverpool, 1960), 193.

28. Anthony Fletcher, *A County Community in Peace and War* (1975), 44–53; Heal and Holmes, *Gentry*, 307–11; Vivienne Larminie, *Wealth, Kinship and Culture* (Woodbridge, 1995), 129, 140–1; Susan E. Whyman, *Sociability and Power in Late-Stuart England* (Oxford, 1999), 23–33; Katherine W. Swett, 'The account between us', *Albion*, 31 (1999).

29. *Cyuile and Uncyuile Life* (1579), in *Inedited Tracts*, ed. W. C. H[azlitt] (Roxburghe Library, 1868), 33.

30. O'Hara, *Courtship and Constraint*, 33.

31. John Bossy, 'Blood and baptism', *Studs in Church History*, 10, ed. Derek Baker (Oxford, 1973); Stephen Gudeman, 'Spiritual relationships and selecting a godparent', *Man*, 10 (1979); Will Coster, *Baptism and Spiritual Kinship in Early Modern England* (Aldershot, 2002), 157–8; Grant McCracken, 'The exchange of children in Tudor England', *Journ. of Family History*, 8 (1983).

32. *A Collection of State Papers*, ed. William Murdin (1759), 301; *Notes of Me: The Autobiography of Roger North*, ed. Peter Millard (Toronto, 2000), 240.

33. E. Maynwaringe, *The History and Mystery of the Venereal Lues* (1673), 139. Studies of patronage include J. E. Neale, 'The Elizabethan political scene', in his *Essays in Elizabethan History* (1958); Wallace T. MacCaffrey, 'Place and patronage in Elizabethan politics', in *Elizabethan Government and Society*, ed. S. T. Bindoff et al. (1961); Rosemary O'Day, 'Ecclesiastical patronage', in *Church and Society in England*, ed. Felicity Heal and Rosemary O'Day (1975); Linda Levy Peck, *Court Patronage and Corruption in Early Stuart England* (Boston, 1990); Kenneth Fincham, *Prelate as Pastor* (Oxford, 1990), 75–9, 188–98, 255–6, 286–7; G. E. Aylmer, *The King's Servants* (1961), esp. 68–96, and id., *The Crown's Servants* (Oxford, 2002); Norman Sykes, *Church and State in England in the XVIIIth Century* (Cambridge, 1934), esp. ch. iv; Harold Perkin, *The Origins of Modern English Society 1780–1880* (1969), 44–51.

34. North, *Notes of Me*, 90.

35. Linda Levy Peck, 'Benefits, brokers and beneficiaries', in *Court, Country and Culture*, ed. Bonnelyn Young Kunze and Dwight D. Brautigan (Rochester, NY, 1992); John Habakkuk, *Marriage, Debt, and the Estates System 1650–1950* (Oxford, 1994), 281; *John Locke: Selected Correspondence*, ed. Mark Goldie (Oxford, 2002), introd.; Daybell, *Women Letter-Writers*, esp. ch. 9.

36. *John Rainolds's Oxford Lectures on Aristotle's Rhetoric*, ed. and trans. Lawrence D. Green (Newark, NJ, 1986), 341; Clarendon, *History*, i. 39.

37. For an instructive example, see Raymond Firth, 'Bond-Friendship in Tikopia', in *Custom Is King*, ed. L. H. Dudley Buxton (1936).

38. Geoffrey Chaucer, *The Canterbury Tales*, 'The Shipman's Tale', lines 33–42; Maurice Keen, 'Brotherhood in Arms', *History*, xlvii (1962); Yannick Carré, *Le Baiser sur la bouche au Moyen Âge* (Paris, 1992), 127–48; Pierre Chaplais, *Piers Gaveston* (Oxford, 1994), ch. 1; 'Ritual brotherhood in ancient and medieval Europe', *Traditio*, 52 (1997); Bray, *The Friend*, ch. 1.

39. Siegrid Düll et al., 'Faithful unto death', *Antiquaries Journ.* 71 (1991); Bray, *The Friend*, 13–19, 106–8.

40. K. B. McFarlane, 'A business partnership in war and administration, 1421–1445', *EHR* lxxviii (1963); id., *England in the Fifteenth Century* (1981), ch. iii.

41. Francis Bacon, *The Essayes or Counsels*, ed. Michael Kiernan (Oxford, 2000), 80 n.

42. David Konstan, *Friendship in the Classical World* (Cambridge, 1997).

43. Steven W. May and William A. Ringler, Jr, *Elizabethan Poetry* (2004).

44. *A Fifteenth Century School Book*, ed. William Nelson (Oxford, 1956), 44.

45. *Misery's Virtues Whet-Stone: Reliquiae Gethinianae; or, Some Remains of . . . Lady Grace Gethin* (1699), 6.
46. Bacon, *Essayes*, 83, 81.
47. William Martyn, *Youths Instruction* (1612), 43; Gilbert Burnet, *Some Passages in the Life and Death of John Earl of Rochester* (1787), 37.
48. John Fell, *The Life of . . . Dr H. Hammond* (1661), 122.
49. *Women's Worlds*, ed. Crawford and Gowing, 235.
50. Adam Ferguson, *An Essay on the History of Civil Society 1767*, ed. Duncan Forbes (Edinburgh, 1966), 37.
51. *The Mirror*, 8th edn (1790), iii. 24 (5 Feb. 1780).
52. Other sources included Plato, *Lysis*; Aristotle, *Eudemian Ethics* 8 and *Magna Moralia* 2. 11–16; Cicero, *De Inventione* 2. 55; Plutarch, *Moralia* 48e–74, 94a–97b; Seneca, *De Beneficiis* and *Ad Lucilium Epistulae Morales* 3, 9, and 25; and, though he stressed the pleasure of friendship rather than its morality, Epicurus (known from Cicero, *De Finibus Bonorum et Malorum* 1. 20; 2. 24–6).
53. Carolinne White, *Christian Friendship in the Fourth Century* (Cambridge, 1992); Brian Patrick McGuire, *Friendship and Community* (Kalamazoo, MI, 1988); Stephen Jaeger, *The Envy of Angels* (Philadelphia, 1994), 59, 104, 280, 407 n. 105.
54. Colin Morris, *The Discovery of the Individual, 1050–1200* (1972), 97–107; R. W. Southern, *Saint Anselm* (Cambridge, 1990), ch. 7; J. P. Haseldine, 'Love, separation and male friendship', in *Masculinities in Medieval Europe*, ed. D. M. Hadley (1989), and 'Friendship, equality and universal harmony', in *Friendship East and West*, ed. Oliver Leaman (Richmond, 1996).
55. *De Amicitia* 7. 28; Julian Haseldine, 'Understanding the language of *amicitia*', *Journ. of Medieval History*, 20 (1994); Carolinne White, 'Friendship in absence', in *Friendship in Medieval Europe*, ed. Julian Haseldine (Thrupp, 1999).
56. Baxter, *Practical Works*, i. 855. Three separate English translations of Cicero's *De Amicitia* were published between 1530 and 1577.
57. *The Miscellaneous Works of . . . Edward Earl of Clarendon*, 2nd edn (1751), 130.
58. 'The church-porch', in *The Works of George Herbert*, ed. F. E. Hutchinson (Oxford, 1941), 17. John Milton collected biblical texts on friendship; *CPW* vi. 750–1.
59. Mills, *One Soul*, 214–25, 281–2; Curtis Bruce Watson, *Shakespeare and the Renaissance Concept of Honor* (Princeton, 1960), 261–6; Eugene M. Waith, introd. to William Shakespeare and John Fletcher, *The Two Noble Kinsmen* (Oxford, 1989), 49–60.
60. As Natalie Zemon Davis puts it; *The Gift in Sixteenth-Century France* (Oxford, 2000), 184. See Montaigne, *Essais*, ed. Albert Thibaudet (Paris, 1950), I. xxviii; Langer, *Perfect Friendship*, 166–85.
61. Haly Heron, *The Kayes of Counsaile*, ed. Virgil B. Heltzel (Liverpool, 1954), 67; T[homas] R[ogers], *A Philosophicall Discourse* (1576), fols 178ᵛ–179 ('178'); Henry Peacham, *The Complete Gentleman*, ed. Virgil B. Heltzel (Ithaca, NY, 1962), 205; John Earle, *Micro-Cosmographie*, 6th edn (1633), sig. E5; *The Whole Works of the Right Rev. Jeremy Taylor*, ed. Reginald Heber, rev. Charles Page Eden (1847–54), i. 86.
62. *The Works of George Savile, Marquis of Halifax*, ed. Mark N. Brown (Oxford, 1989), iii. 360.
63. Thomas Hobbes, *De Cive: The English Version*, ed. Howard Warrender (Oxford, 1983), 42 (ch. 1).

64. Nicholas Grimald, 'Frendship', in *Tottel's Miscellany* (1557–87), ed. Hyder Edward Rollins, rev. edn (Cambridge, 1966); *The Collected Works of Katherine Philips, the Matchless Orinda*, ed. Patrick Thomas et al. (Stump Cross, 1990–3), i. 165; *The Correspondence of John Locke*, ed. E. S. de Beer (Oxford, 1976–), iii. 672; Mills, *One Soul, passim*.

65. *Essays of John Dryden*, ed. W. P. Ker (Oxford, 1926), i. 228.

66. BL, Sloane MS 881, fol. 15^v; Rogers, *Philosophicall Discourse*, fol. 170^v ('107'^{v}).

67. Beale, 'Thoughts on Friendship', in *Women's Worlds*, ed. Crawford and Gowing, 235.

68. James Cleland, *The Institution of a Young Noble Man* (Oxford, 1607), 193–6; Daniel Tuvill, *Essays Political and Moral and Essays Moral and Theological*, ed. John L. Lievsay (Charlottesville, VA, 1971), 47–5; Simon Daines, *Orthoepia Anglicana* (1640), 85; Robert Heywood, *Observations and Instructions Divine and Morall*, ed. James Crossley (Chetham Soc., 1869), 30; Archibald, Marquess of Argyle, *Instructions to His Son* (written 1660; Glasgow, 1762), 52–3, 57; *Works of Halifax*, ii. 394–6.

69. *The Poems of Nathaniel Wanley*, ed. L. C. Martin (Oxford, 1928), 4; [Charles Johnson], *The Force of Friendship* (1710), 1; Mrs [Hester] Chapone, *Miscellanies in Prose and Verse* (1775), 134–7; *The Poetical Works of Sir John Denham*, ed. Thomas Howard Banks, 2nd edn (Hamden, CT, 1969), 98; HMC, *Salisbury*, xxii. 195; G. R. Elton, *Reform and Renewal* (Cambridge, 1973), 60.

70. Bacon, *Essayes*, 81; A. G. Dickens, 'Estate and household management in Bedfordshire, *c*.1540', *Publications of the Beds. Hist. Rec. Soc.* (1956), 45; *The Works of Sir Walter Ralegh* (Oxford, 1829), viii. 119–20; Samuel Tuke, *The Adventures of Five Hours* (1673), 23; D.A., *The Whole Art of Converse* (1683), 83; Anthony Ashley Cooper, third Earl of Shaftesbury, *Characteristicks of Men, Manners, Opinions, Times*, ed. Philip Ayres (Oxford, 1999), ii. 30.

71. Herbert, 'Unkindnesse', in *Works*, 93.

72. *The Works of Mr Abraham Cowley* (1668), sig. C1.

73. Clarendon, *History*, i. 42; *The Life of Edward Earl of Clarendon . . . written by himself* (Oxford, 1857), i. 57–8.

74. John 15: 13; Sir Thomas Browne, *Religio Medici and Other Works*, ed. L. C. Martin (Oxford, 1964), 62.

Male and Female Friends

1. Richard Edwards, *The Excellent Comedie of Two the Most Faithfullest Freendes, Damon and Pythias* (Malone Soc., 1957), line 2233.

2. Sir Henry Wotton, '[To John Donne]', in *The New Oxford Book of Sixteenth-Century Verse*, ed. Emrys Jones (Oxford, 1991), 508; *The Mirrour of Friendship*, trans. Thomas Breme (1584), preface; *Prayers and Other Pieces of Thomas Becon*, ed. John Ayre (PS, Cambridge, 1844), 151; M.B., *The Triall of True Friendship* (1596), sig. B2; Edward Waterhouse, *The Gentlemans Monitor* (1665), 280–1; Clarendon, *Miscellaneous Works*, 130; Argyle, *Instructions*, 55; *The Works of Thomas Traherne*, i, ed. Jan Ross (Cambridge, 2005), 4; Tim[othy] Nourse, *A Discourse upon the Nature and Faculties of Man* (1686), 245–6; *The Theological Works of . . . Henry More* (1708), 314; [John Dunton], *The Athenian Oracle*, 3rd edn (1728), iv. 466; Sarah Fyge Egerton, *Poems on Several Occasions* (1703), 1–2; *Spectator*, 385 (22 May 1712), iii. 445; Daybell, *Women Letter-Writers*, 120–1.

3. Bacon, *Essayes*, 149.

4. Langer, *Perfect Friendship*, 146–87; *Poems of Matthew Grove*, 120–1; F[rancis] L[enton], *Characterismi* (1631), sig. H2ᵛ; *Miscellanea from the Works of John Sheffield Duke of Buckingham* (n.pl., 1933), 67.

5. William King, *Political and Literary Anecdotes of His Own Times* (1818), 56–7.

6. Langer, *Perfect Friendship*, 218–20; Kevin Sharpe, *Reading Revolutions* (New Haven, 2000), 94–5; Henry Peacham, *The Worth of a Peny* (1641), 34–5; R. Lingard, *A Letter of Advice to a Young Gentleman leaving the University* (1671), 37–8.

7. Sarah Fielding, *David Simple*, ed. Malcolm Kelsall (1969), p. xix.

8. Mary Mollineux, *Fruits of Retirement* (1702), 154, Bodl. Lib., Harding C 2071 (on which he has also written some melancholy verses on his vain search for 'a faithful friend').

9. Chapone, *Miscellanies*, 138; D. H. Monro, *Godwin's Moral Philosophy* (1953), 68.

10. Peacham, *Complete Gentleman*, 204–5; Hobbes, *Latin Works*, ii. 98; *Miscellanea from the Works of John Sheffield*, 66.

11. Sir John Barnard, *A Present for an Apprentice* (Edinburgh, 1761), 40.

12. *John Isham Mercer and Merchant Adventurer*, ed. G. D. Ramsay (Northants. Rec. Soc., 1962), 172–3.

13. *The Works of the Right Reverend Joseph Hall*, new edn, ed. Philip Wynter (Oxford, 1863), vi. 98.

14. *Correspondence of John Locke*, viii. 389 (also 293).

15. F. J. M. Korsten, *Roger North (1651–1734)* (Amsterdam, 1981), 123.

16. Dunton, *Athenian Oracle*, iv. 465–8; Joseph Ritson, *A Select Collection of English Songs*, 2nd edn, ed. Thomas Park (1813), ii. 6, 7, 9, 92, 94; *Old English Ballads 1553–1625*, ed. Hyder E. Rollins (Cambridge, 1920), 223; Natasha Wurzburg, *The Rise of the English Street Ballad, 1550–1650*, trans. Gayna Walls (Cambridge, 1990), 71.

17. *OED*, s.v. 'chum'.

18. Roger North, *General Preface & Life of Dr John North*, ed. Peter Millard (Toronto, 1984), 80.

19. [Francis Finch], *Friendship* (n.p., n.d. [1654]), 19.

20. Argyle, *Instructions*, 56; Martyn, *Youths Instruction*, 52.

21. Richard Pace, *De Fructu qui ex Doctrina Percipitur*, ed. and trans. Frank Manley and Richard S. Sylvester (New York, 1967), 34–5.

22. Pole's most recent biographer believes that theirs was effectively a homosexual marriage; Thomas F. Mayer, *Reginald Pole* (Cambridge, 2000), 442, 444–6.

23. Mills, *One Soul*, 130–1; Ronald A. Rebholz, *The Life of Fulke Greville First Lord Brooke* (Oxford, 1971), 54.

24. Theodore K. Rabb, *Jacobean Gentleman* (Princeton, 1998), 9; Izaak Walton, *The Lives* (World's Classics, 1927), 173.

25. Lambert Daneau, *True and Christian Friendshippe*, trans. T. Newton (1586), sig. A2ᵛ.

26. *Memorials of Affairs of State*, ed. Edmund Sawyer (1725), iii. 384; *Letters of John Chamberlain*, ed. Norman Egbert McClure (Amer. Philos. Soc., Philadelphia, 1939), ii. 306, 339, 452; Bacon, *Essayes*, 226–7.

27. *Life of Clarendon*, i. 35, 174; *State Papers collected by Edward Earl of Clarendon* (Oxford, 1767–86), 141; 'The under-wood', in *Poems of Ben Jonson*, ed. George Burke Johnston (1954), 210–14.

28. Archibald Malloch, *Finch and Baines* (Cambridge, 1917), esp. 34; Jean Wilson, '"Two names of friendship, but one starre"', *Church Monuments*, x (1995); *ODNB*, *s.n.* 'Finch, Sir John', Bray, *The Friend*, 140–6.
29. John Hackett, *Select and Remarkable Epitaphs* (1757), i. 15. Cotterell was 'Poliarchus' in the friendship circle of the 'matchless Orinda' (below, p. 207).
30. *Brief Lives*, i. 10–11, 405; ii. 165.
31. *The Diary of Sir Henry Slingsby*, ed. Daniel Parsons (1836), 6.
32. *Whole Works of Jeremy Taylor*, i. 76.
33. Bray, *The Friend*, *passim*. This eloquent, if occasionally elliptical, work was written to promote a contemporary agenda (the recognition by the Roman Catholic Church of same-sex partnerships). It has a tendency to convert speculation into established fact.
34. *Letters to Severall Persons of Honour* (1651), 85.
35. *Epistolae Ho-Elianae*, ed. Joseph Jacobs (1890), 440.
36. *Diary of Sir Henry Slingsby*, 199.
37. *The Correspondence of Erasmus*, trans. R. A. B. Mynors and D. F. S. Thomson (Toronto, 1974–93), iv. 368; *Translating for King James*, ed. Ward Allen (1970), 151; Alan Stewart, *Philip Sidney* (2000), 124–7; Wilson, '"Two names of friendship, but one starre"'; John Christoferson, *An Exhortation to all Menne* (1554), sig. Uiij.
38. *The Lisle Letters*, ed. Muriel St Clare Byrne (Chicago, 1981), ii. 53, 56.
39. Lisa Jardine, 'Towards reading Albion's classicism', in *Albion's Classicism*, ed. Lucy Gent (New Haven, 1995), 19–21; Peter Burke, 'Humanism and friendship in sixteenth-century Europe', in *Friendship in Medieval Europe*, ed. Haseldine; *Translating for King James*, 151.
40. Thomas Fuller, *The Holy State and the Profane State* (1840), 129.
41. Baxter, *Works*, i. 853, 857; Samuel Clarke, *The Lives of Sundry Eminent Persons* (1683), ii. 199; Langer, *Perfect Friendship*, 25.
42. Rosemary O'Day, *The English Clergy* (Leicester, 1979), 163–5; Alan G. R. Smith, *Servant of the Cecils* (1977), 22, 93; Tom Webster, *Godly Clergy in Early Stuart England* (Cambridge, 1987), *passim*; Francis J. Bremer, *Congregational Communion* (Boston, 1994), 29–31, 37–8, and ch. 2.
43. Christopher W. Marsh, *The Family of Love in English Society, 1550–1630* (Cambridge, 1994), 84, 91, 157, 163, 258.
44. Paul S. Seaver, *Wallington's World* (1985), 95–6; *Some Account of the Life of Joseph Pike Written by Himself* (1837), 41.
45. Bodl. Lib., Wood MS F 39, fol. 135^v; Ballard MS 14, fol. 92.
46. Raymond Stephanson, 'Epicene friendship', *The Eighteenth Century: Theory and Interpretation*, 38 (1997); Michael Warner, 'New English Sodom', in *Queering the Renaissance*, ed. Jonathan Goldberg (Durham, NC, 1994), 343–4.
47. As was pointed out by Alan Bray, whose *Homosexuality in Renaissance England* (1982) has been the essential starting point for much subsequent research.
48. *Brief Lives*, i. 95–6; Bray, *The Friend*, 167–8, 272.
49. *Henry V*, iv. vi. 24–7; discussed by Alan Sinfield, *Faultlines* (Oxford, 1992), 135–7.
50. Jill Kraye, 'The transformation of Platonic love in the Italian Renaissance', in *Platonism and the English Imagination*, ed. Anne Baldwin and Sarah Hutton (Cambridge, 1994).
51. *Epistolae Ho-Elianae*, 317; Erica Veevers, *Images of Love and Religion* (Cambridge, 1989), 16–20, 56–65, 134–5.
52. Browne, *Religio Medici*, 62–3.

53. *ODNB*, *s.n.* 'Villiers, George, 1st Duke of Buckingham'; *The Arraignment, Tryal and Condemnation of Stephen Colledge* (1681), 30; *Secret History of the Court of James the First*, [ed. Walter Scott] (Edinburgh, 1811), i. 274–5; Alastair Bellany, *The Politics of Court Scandal in Early Modern England* (Cambridge, 2002), 254–61.

54. Alan Stewart, *Close Readers* (Princeton, 1997), pp. xv–xvi, 125–7, 175–7, 179; Bodl. Lib., Tanner MS 65, fols 26, 32; Sarah Bendall et al., *History of Emmanuel College, Cambridge* (Woodbridge, 1999), 60–3, 67; Patrick Collinson, *From Cranmer to Sancroft* (2006), 176–7.

55. I owe this observation to Professor Randolph Trumbach. It does not hold in all cases.

56. Michael Rocke, *Forbidden Friendships* (New York, 1996).

57. Aubrey, *Brief Lives*, i. 71; *Secret History of the Court of James the First*, i. 445.

58. R.C., *The Times Whistle*, ed. J. M. Cowper (EETS, 1871), 79; Bruce R. Smith, *Homosexual Desire in Shakespeare's England* (1991), ch. 5; Joseph Cady, '"Masculine love", Renaissance writing, and the "new invention" of homosexuality', in *Homosexuality in Renaissance and Enlightenment England* (New York, n.d. [1992?]); Mary Bly, *Queer Virgins and Virgin Queans on the Early Modern Stage* (Oxford, 2000), 6, 13–14, 70, 113–14, 123–5, 144, 167–8; Rictor Norton, *Mother Clap's Molly House*, 2nd edn (Stroud, 2006), 15–16, 26–7, 107. The case against the interpretation usually associated with Michel Foucault (though first advanced by Mary McIntosh, 'The homosexual role', *Social Problems*, 16 (1968–9)) is summarized by Kenneth Borris, *Same-Sex Desire in the English Renaissance* (New York, 2004), 5–7, 15–17, 25–33, 157, 179, 204.

59. Paul Hammond, *Figuring Sex between Men from Shakespeare to Rochester* (Oxford, 2002), 12.

60. Stephen Orgel, *Impersonations* (Cambridge, 1996), 49.

61. The chronology of this development has yet to be established. But see Alan Bray and Michel Rey, 'The body of the friend', in *English Masculinities*, ed. Tim Hitchcock and Michèle Cohen (1999), 80–2; Bray, *The Friend*, 212; Keith Thomas, 'Afterword', in *The Kiss in History*, ed. Karen Harvey (Manchester, 2005), 192–4.

62. T[homas] B[lount], *Glossographia*, 2nd edn (1661), sig. G5^v; [Edward Howard], *Poems and Essays* (1673), 1st pagination, 10; Emma Donoghue, *Passions between Women* (1993), ch. 6; Bernadette J. Brooten, *Love between Women* (Chicago, 1996), 359–60; Elizabeth Susan Wahl, *Invisible Relations* (Stanford, CA, 1999), 43–72; Harriet Andreadis, *Sappho in Early Modern England* (Chicago, 2001), 3, 59, and *passim*; Valerie Traub, *The Renaissance of Lesbianism in Early Modern England* (Cambridge, 2002); Sarah Toulalan, *Imagining Sex* (Oxford, 2007), ch. 4. Terry Castle, *The Literature of Lesbianism* (New York, 2003), is admirably comprehensive.

63. References to most of the numerous recent writings on Philips can be found in Hero Chalmers, *Royalist Women Writers 1650–1689* (Oxford, 2004), ch. 2.

64. *Collected Works of Katherine Philips*, i. 166.

65. Mary Chandler, *The Description of Bath*, 7th edn (1755), 26. For similar sentiments, Richard Leigh, *Poems*, ed. Hugh Macdonald (Oxford, 1947), 49–50; Elaine Hobby, *Virtue of Necessity* (1985), 139–40, 160; Sylvia Harcstark Myers, *The Bluestocking Circle* (Oxford, 1990), 111; Margaret J. M. Ezell, *The Patriarch's Wife* (Chapel Hill, NC, 1987), 125–6, 162; Donoghue, *Passions between Women*, 121–30; Kathryn King, *Jane Barker, Exile* (Oxford, 2000),

46–7, 63–6, 219, 223–8; Amy M. Froide, *Never Married* (Oxford, 2005), 208–10.

66. Geoffrey Chaucer, *The Canterbury Tales*, 'Wife of Bath's Prologue', lines 531–2.

67. 'Rosalynde: Euphues Golden Legacie', fol. 14, in *The Complete Works of Thomas Lodge* (Hunterian Club, 1883), i.

68. *Tixall Letters*, ed. Arthur Clifford (1815), 109.

69. Zirka Zaremba, 'Reflections on motifs in Van Dyck's portraits', in Arthur K. Wheelock, Jr, et al., *Van Dyck: Paintings* (1991), 63.

70. Benjamin Bathurst, *Letters of Two Queens* (n.d. [1724]), 62; Patricia Crawford, 'Friendship and love between women in early modern England', in *Venus and Mars*, ed. Andrew Lynch and Philippa Maddern (Nedlands, WA, 1995), 50–1.

71. Crawford and Gowing, *Women's Worlds*, 198. On women's friendships, see Lillian Faderman, *Surpassing the Love of Men* (1982), pt i; Irene Q. Brown, 'Domesticity, feminism, and friendship', *Journ. of Family History*, 7 (1982); Ruth Perry, *The Celebrated Mary Astell* (Chicago, 1986), ch. 8; *Maids and Mistresses*, ed. Susan Frye and Karen Robertson (New York, 1999); Mendelson and Crawford, *Women*, 231–42; Donoghue, *Passions between Women*, chs 4 and 5; Sara Mendelson, 'The civility of women in seventeenth-century England', in *Civil Histories*, ed. Peter Burke et al. (Oxford, 2000), 122–3; Barbara J. Harris, *English Aristocratic Women 1450–1550* (Oxford, 2003), ch. 8; Laura Gowing, 'The politics of women's friendship in early modern England', in *Love, Friendship and Faith in Europe, 1300–1800*, ed. Gowing, Michael Hunter, and Miri Rubin (Basingstoke, 2005).

72. Hilda L. Smith, *Reason's Disciples* (Urbana, IL, 1982), ch. 5; Ezell, *Patriarch's Wife*, 124; Harriette Andreadis, 'The erotics of female friendship in early modern England', in *Maids and Mistresses*, ed. Frye and Robertson, 246–55; Richard Greene, *Mary Leapor* (Oxford, 1993), 74–5.

73. 'A Lady' [Judith Drake?], *An Essay in Defence of the Female Sex*, 3rd edn (1697), 132–3.

74. Patricia Meyer Spacks, *Boredom* (Chicago, IL, 1995), 100; Myers, *Bluestocking Circle*, 17.

75. Froide, *Never Married*, 44, 57, 71–2, 85.

76. John Le Neve, *Monumenta Anglicana . . . since the year 1700, to the end of the year 1715* (1717), 173; Wilson, '"Two names of friendship, but one starre"', 78, 83; Bray, *The Friend*, 85, 108–9, 226–9.

77. For a sensible, if occasionally speculative, appraisal, see Margaret R. Hunt, 'The Sapphic strain', in *Singlewomen in the European Past, 1250–1800*, ed. Judith M. Bennett and Amy M. Froide (Philadelphia, 1999).

78. *Thraliana*, ed. Katharine C. Balderston (Oxford, 1942), 949; Randolph Trumbach, 'London's Sapphists', in *Third Sex, Third Gender*, ed. Gilbert Herdt (New York, 1994); Wahl, *Invisible Relations*, 25, 209–11, and *passim*; Rachel Weil, *Political Passions* (Manchester, 1999), 210–11; Andreadis, *Sappho in Early Modern England*, 170–6; Traub, *Renaissance of Lesbianism*, 19–20, 218, and *passim*; Susan S. Lanser, 'Queer to queer', in *Lewd and Notorious*, ed. Katharine Kittredge (Ann Arbor, 2003).

79. Ezell, *Patriarch's Wife*, 123; [Mary Astell], *A Serious Proposal to the Ladies* (1694), 133.

80. Baxter, *Practical Works*, i. 857; Margaret Cavendish, Marchioness of Newcastle, *CCXI. Sociable Letters* (1664), 331.

81. *The Revenge of Bussy d'Ambois* (1613), v. i. 184–5, in *The Works of George Chapman: Plays*, ed. Richard Herne Shepherd (1874), 207; Plato, *Laws* 837b; Montaigne, *Essais*, 220–3 (I. xxviii); Ruth Kelso, *Doctrine for the Lady of the Renaissance* (Urbana, IL, 1956), 140; Tho[mas] B[lount], *The Academie of Eloquence* (1654), 69; Bernard Capp, *The World of John Taylor the Water-Poet* (Oxford, 1994), 114; Clarendon, *Miscellaneous Works*, 133; *Works of Thomas Traherne*, i. 15; Harris, *Transformations of Love*, 77, 248.

82. White, *Christian Friendship*, 10, 88–90, 134–8; McGuire, *Friendship and Community*, 188, 411–12, 422–3.

83. *Whole Works of Jeremy Taylor*, i. 194–5; [John Dunton], *Athenian Oracle*, i, 2nd edn (1704), 26–7, 34–5; Harris, *Transformations of Love*, 81 and *passim*.

84. John Donne, *Elegies*, ed. Helen Gardner (Oxford, 1965), 281; Baxter, *Practical Works*, i. 854–5.

85. *Essais*, 748 (III. xvii).

86. Malloch, *Finch and Baines*, 6; *The Diary of Samuel Rogers 1634–1638*, ed. Tom Webster and Kenneth Shipps (Church of England Rec. Soc., Woodbridge, 2004), 152.

87. The story is told with great learning and sensitivity in Harris, *Transformations of Love*. For other instances, see ibid. 61, 92, 189; Walton, *Lives*, 264–6; Vivienne Larminie, 'Marriage and the family', *Midland History*, ix (1984), 12–15; Anne Laurence, *Women in England 1500–1760* (1994), 89; Brown, 'Domesticity, feminism and friendship'; Diane Willen, 'Communion of the saints', *Albion*, 27 (1995); *ODNB*, *s.n.* 'Masham, Damaris, Lady Masham', 'Pakington, Dorothy, Lady Pakington'; Daybell, *Women Letter-Writers*, 120–1.

88. *Misery's Virtues Whet-Stone*, 3–4; *Epicurus's Morals*, trans. Walter Charleton [1656], ed. Frederic Manning (1926), 115–16; Samuel Masters, *A Discourse of Friendship* (1685), 7, 27; W[alter] D[orke], *A Tipe or Figure of Friendship* (1589), sig. A4.

89. Smith, *Wealth of Nations*, i. 26–7 (I. ii); Allan Silver, 'Friendship in commercial society', *Amer. Journ. of Sociology*, 95 (1990), 'Friendship and trust as moral ideals', *European Journ. of Sociology*, 30 (1989), 277; and 'Two different sorts of commerce', in *Public and Private in Thought and Practice*, ed. Jeff Weintraub and Krishan Kumar (Chicago, 1997); Johnson, 'Friendship, coercion, and interest'.

90. Dave Postles, *Talking Ballocs* (Leicester, 2003), 44–5.

91. *Lincoln Wills*, ed. C. W. Foster (Lincoln Rec. Soc., 1914–30), iii. 30; John Bossy, 'The Mass as a social institution, 1200–1700', *P & P* 100 (1983), 37–43; Joel T. Rosenthal, *The Purchase of Paradise* (1972), 16, 22; Postles, *Social Proprieties*, 88–9.

92. e.g. *Wells Wills*, ed. Frederic William Weaver (1890), 18, 158, 161; Nicolas Harris Nicolas, *Testamenta Vetusta* (1826), ii. 709; Keith Wrightson and David Levine, *Poverty and Piety in an English Village* (Oxford, 1995), 74, 100; Boulton, *Neighbourhood and Society*, 241–2; Daniel C. Beaver, *Parish Communities and Religious Conflict in the Vale of Gloucester 1590–1690* (Cambridge, MA, 1998), 342; *Ashton-on-Mersey and Sale Wills*, ed. Jill Groves (Sale, 1999), 21, 331.

93. *Ashton-on-Mersey and Sale Wills*, 31; *Bedfordshire Wills 1531–1539*, transcr. Patricia L. Bell (Beds. Family Hist. Soc., 2005), 44, 122, 139.

94. G. J. Toomer, *Eastern Wisedome and Learning* (Oxford, 1996), 131 n.; and see above, pp. 126–7.

95. J. B. Williams, *Memoirs ... of Mrs Sarah Savage*, 4th edn (1829), 299.

96. Richard Grassby, *Kinship and Capitalism* (Cambridge, 2001), 241–9.

97. *Boswell's Life of Johnson*, ed. George Birkbeck Hill, rev. L. F. Powell (Oxford, 1934–50), iii. 148–9 (and ii. 228).

98. Capp, *Gossips*, esp. ch. 2 and 327–31; R. A. Houlbrooke, 'Women's social life and common action in England from the fifteenth century to the eve of the Civil War', *Continuity and Change*, 1 (1986), 172; Steve Hindle, 'The shaming of Margaret Knowsley', ibid. 9 (1994), 393, 407; Mendelson and Crawford, *Women*, 237–40.

99. *OED*, s.v. 'bully', 'mate'; Ilana Krausman Ben-Amos, *Adolescence and Youth in Early Modern England* (New Haven, 1994), 179–80.

100. *Brief Lives, passim*; Anthony Powell, *John Aubrey and his Friends* (1948), ch. 8; Michael Hunter, *John Aubrey and the Realm of Learning* (1975), 34–6, 46–7.

101. Numerous examples can be found in such collections as John Le Neve, *Monumenta Anglicana* (1717–19); Ralph Bigland, *Historical, Monumental and Genealogical Collections relating to the County of Gloucester*, ed. Brian Frith (Bristol & Glos. Archaeol. Soc., 1989–95); Sir Thomas Phillips, *Monumental Inscriptions of Wiltshire*, ed. Peter Sherlock (Wilts. Rec. Soc., 2000).

102. Bacon, *Essayes*, 25; Bruce Smith, *Shakespeare and Masculinity* (Oxford, 2000), 62, 67; *Poems of Nathaniel Wanley*, p. xi; *Collected Works of Katherine Philips*, ii. 43.

103. William Gouge, *Of Domesticall Duties*, 3rd edn (1634), 264–6; *Works of Halifax*, ii. 379–80; Elizabeth A. Foyster, *Manhood in Early Modern England* (Harlow, 1999), 128–9.

104. *Proceedings in Parliament 1610*, ed. Elizabeth Read Foster (New Haven, 1966), i. 87; Finch, *Friendship*, 6.

105. Browne, *Religio Medici*, 62; Grimald, 'Frendship', 106; *Mirrour of Friendship*, sig. Bv; Burton, *Anatomy*, iii. 30; Milton, *CPW* vi. 751; *The Dramatic Works of Roger Boyle Earl of Orrery*, ed. William Smith Clark (Cambridge, MA, 1937), i. 235; Dunton, *Athenian Oracle*, ii (1703), 387; Harris, *Transformations of Love*, 252.

106. William Vaughan, *The Golden Grove* (1600), sig. O1; John Downame, *The Plea of the Poore* (1616), 138.

107. Graham Allan, *A Sociology of Friendship and Kinship* (1979), ch. 9.

108. See Curtis Perry, *Literature and Favouritism in Early Modern England* (Cambridge, 2006).

109. Soame Jenyns, *A View of the Internal Evidence for the Christian Religion*, 5th edn (1776), 60–1.

110. *Whole Works of Jeremy Taylor*, i. 71–82; *Boswell's Life of Johnson*, iii. 288–90.

111. Baxter, *Practical Works*, i. 855, 854.

112. Sara Heller Mendelson, *The Mental World of Stuart Women* (Brighton, 1987), 105–7; *The Complete Works of Thomas Brooks* (Edinburgh, 1866–7), i. 263; ii. 185–6; H[umphrey] B[rooke], *The Durable Legacy* (1681), 99.

113. *Works of Thomas Traherne*, i. 14–15.

114. Jonathan Swift, *A Project for Correcting the English Tongue, Polite Conversations, etc*, ed. Herbert Davis with Louis Landa (1964), 95; Samuel Johnson, *The Rambler*, 99 (26 Feb. 1751); John Gregory, *A Comparative View of the State and Faculties of Man* (1765), 61.

115. *Moral Sentiments*, 224–5, 214 (VI. ii. 1; VI. i. 8).

116. Jenyns, *View of the Internal Evidence*, 61; Benjamin N. Nelson, *The Idea of Usury* (Princeton, 1949), 151.

Marriage and Children

1. Samuel Richardson, *Clarissa* (1747–8), iii. 288 (letter 59.)
2. *Nic. Eth.* 1158[b], 1162[a].
3. Finch, *Friendship*, 8.
4. Baxter, *Practical Works*, i. 855; Clarendon, *Miscellaneous Works*, 133; *Naval Tracts of Sir William Monson*, i. 115; William Scott, *An Essay of Drapery 1635* (Boston, 1953), 34.
5. Eileen Power, 'The position of women', in *The Legacy of the Middle Ages*, ed. C. G. Crump and E. F. Jacob (Oxford, 1926), 416. On marital affection in medieval England, see Henry Ansgar Kelly, *Love and Marriage in the Age of Chaucer* (Ithaca, NY, 1975); Alan Macfarlane, *Marriage and Love in England* (Oxford, 1986), 182–4; David d'Avray, *Medieval Marriage* (Oxford, 2005), 2.
6. Reginald Hyatte, 'Complementary humanistic models of marriage and male *amicitia* in fifteenth-century literature', in *Friendship in Medieval Europe*, ed. Haseldine; Anthony F. D'Elia, *The Renaissance of Marriage in Fifteenth-Century Italy* (Cambridge, MA, 2004).
7. As Valerie Wayne puts it in her introduction to Edmund Tilney, *The Flower of Friendship* ([1573]; Ithaca, NY, 1992), 17.
8. *Homilies*, 500; *The Two Liturgies, A.D. 1549, and A.D. 1552*, ed. Joseph Ketley (PS, Cambridge, 1844), 127.
9. Henry Smith, *A Preparative to Marriage* (1591), 33–4; *Whole Works of Jeremy Taylor*, i. 90; *Works of Symon Patrick*, vii. 549. See, in general, William and Malleville Haller, 'The Puritan art of love', *Huntington Lib. Qtly*, 5 (1941–2); Kathleen Davies, 'Continuity and change in literary advice on marriage', in *Marriage and Society*, ed. R. B. Outhwaite (1981); Edmund Leites, *The Puritan Conscience and Modern Sexuality* (New Haven, 1896), ch. 4; Margo Todd, *Christian Humanism and the Puritan Social Order* (Cambridge, 1987), 97–102.
10. *Private Memoirs of Sir Kenelm Digby*, [ed. Sir Nicholas Harris Nicolas] (1827), 6–9, 63.
11. *ODNB*, *s.n.* 'Waller, Sir William'; William Penn, *The Peace of Europe* (Everyman's Lib., n.d.), 37; Crawford and Gowing, *Women's Worlds*, 235.
12. Crawford and Gowing, *Women's Worlds*, 177.
13. [Daniel Defoe], *A Treatise concerning the Use and Abuse of the Marriage Bed* (1727), 27; Nathaniel Cotton, 'Visions in verse' (1751), in *The Works of the English Poets*, ed. Alexander Chalmers (1810), xviii. 40.
14. *The Political Works of James I*, ed. Charles Howard McIlwain (Cambridge, MA, 1918), 34.
15. Thomas Gataker, *A Good Wife Gods Gift* (1623), 62; Hobbes, *Leviathan*, 235–6 (ch. 30).
16. Milton, *CPW* ii. 600; John Halkett, *Milton and the Idea of Matrimony* (New Haven, 1970), 29–30; Ingram, *Church Courts*, 44.
17. *Original Letters and Papers of State addressed to Oliver Cromwell*, ed. John Nickolls (1743), 40; Robert Wilkinson, *A Paire of Sermons* (1614), 31. For studies of individual marriages and varying reflections on the patterns they suggest, see Stone, *Family, Sex and Marriage*; Ralph A. Houlbrooke, *The English Family 1450–1700* (1984), ch. 5; J. A. Sharpe, 'Plebeian marriage in Stuart England', *TRHS*, 5th ser, 36 (1986); Macfarlane, *Marriage and Love*, ch. 9; Wrightson, *English Society*, 90–104; Anthony Fletcher, *Gender, Sex and Subordination in England 1500–1800* (New Haven, 1995), ch. 8; Laurence, *Women in England 1500–1760*, ch. 4; Amanda Vickery, *The Gentle-*

man's Daughter (New Haven, 1998), esp. ch. 2; Mendelson and Crawford, *Women*, 126–48; Grassby, *Kinship and Capitalism*, ch. 2; Harris, *English Aristocratic Women*, ch. 4; Joanne Bailey, *Unquiet Lives* (Cambridge, 2003); Capp, *Gossips*, ch. 3; Daybell, *Women Letter-Writers*, ch. 6.

18. Hackett, *Select and Remarkable Epitaphs*, ii. 120; John Le Neve, *Monumenta Anglicana . . . since the year 1600, to the end of the year 1649* (1719), 202.

19. Joshua Scodel, *The English Poetic Epitaph* (Ithaca, NY, 1991), 214; Houl-brooke, *Death*, 354–9; Sarah Tarlow, *Bereavement and Commemoration* (Oxford, 1989), 131, 133.

20. Korsten, *Roger North*, 108; Michele Bennett and Mary McIntosh, *The Anti-Social Family* (1982), 143; Carole Pateman, *The Sexual Contract* (Cambridge, 1988); Susan Moller Okin, *Justice, Gender, and the Family* (New York, 1989); Ruth Perry, 'Colonizing the breast', *Journ. of the History of Sexuality*, 2 (1991–2), 215–16.

21. William Ames, *Conscience with the Power and Cases thereof*, Eng. trans. (n.p., 1639), iii. 157.

22. *The Rev. Oliver Heywood, B A. 1630–1702; His Autobiography, Diaries, Anecdote and Event Books*, ed. J. Horsfall Turner (Brighouse, 1882–5), i. 177.

23. *Letters of Lady Rachel Russell*, [ed. Thomas Sellwood] (1773), 7; *The Life and Letters of Sir Henry Wotton*, ed. Logan Pearsall Smith (Oxford, 1907), ii. 311.

24. For the number of childless marriages, see T. H. Hollingsworth, *The Demography of the British Peerage*, suppl. to *Population Studies*, xviii/2 (1964), 411; Lawrence Stone and Jeanne Fawtier Stone, *An Open Elite?* (Oxford, 1984), 99–100; E. A. Wrigley et al., *English Population History from Family Reconstitution, 1580–1837* (Cambridge, 1997), 411; Grassby, *Kinship and Capitalism*, 155–7.

25. *Winthrop Papers*, ii, ed. Stewart Mitchell (Mass. Hist. Soc., Boston, 1931), 114; Alan Macfarlane, *The Family Life of Ralph Josselin* (Cambridge, 1970), 111–25, and id., *Marriage and Love*, ch. 4; Linda A. Pollock, *Forgotten Children* (Cambridge, 1983), and ead., *A Lasting Relationship* (1987); Houlbrooke, *English Family*, chs 6 and 7; Crawford and Gowing, *Women's Worlds*, 189; Ilana Krausman Ben-Amos, 'Reciprocal bonding', *Journ. of Family History*, 25 (2000).

26. Williams, *Memoirs of Sarah Savage*, 183.

27. [Edward Topsell], *The Reward of Religion* (1596), 276; *Cavalier*, ed. Margaret Blundell (1933), 79.

28. Judith Schneid Lewis, *In the Family Way* (New Brunswick, NJ, 1986), 65–6; Macfarlane, *Marriage and Love*, 53–4; Mendelson and Crawford, *Women*, 80–2.

29. A[nthony] Walker, *Planctus Unigeniti* (1664), 13; Houlbrooke, *Death*, 234–8; Vickery, *Gentleman's Daughter*, 125, 319 n.; and, especially, Robert Woods, *Children Remembered* (Liverpool, 2006).

30. As is remarked by Patricia Crawford in her pioneering essay 'The construction and experience of maternity in seventeenth-century England', repr. in her *Blood, Bodies and Families in Early Modern England* (Harlow, 2004), 102.

31. Pepys, *Diary*, viii. 598.

32. *Works of Sir Walter Ralegh*, viii. 258–9; *An Ease for Overseers of the Poore* (Cambridge, 1601), 26; Peter Biller, *The Measure of Multitude* (Oxford, 2000), ch. 6.

33. Richard Rogers, *A Commentary upon the Whole Booke of Iudges* (1615; facs., Edinburgh, 1983), 609; William Gouge, *A Very Learned and Very Useful Commentary on the Whole Epistle to the Hebrewes* (1655), iii. 43 (and ii. 77); Thomas Hilder, *Conjugall Counsel* (1653), 18, 22.

34. *The Posthumous Works of Mr Thomas Chubb* (1748), i, p. iv.

35. Cavendish, *CCXI. Sociable Letters*, 183–4.
36. Cecil Aspinall-Oglander, *Nunwell Symphony* (1945), 115.
37. Defoe, *Use and Abuse of the Marriage Bed*, 130.
38. Le Neve, *Monumenta Anglicana, 1700–1715*, 170–1; Phillipps, *Monumental Inscriptions of Wiltshire*, 214. On grandparents: *Works of John Robinson*, i. 246; David Hartley, *Observations on Man* (1749), i. 484.

Sociability

1. See e.g. Rebecca King, 'The sociability of the trade guilds of Newcastle and Durham, 1660–1750', in *Creating and Consuming Culture in North-East England, 1660–1830*, ed. Helen Berry and Jeremy Gregory (Aldershot, 2004).
2. Capp, *Gossips*, 323–4, 339–42.
3. Alexandra Shepard, *Meanings of Manhood in Early Modern England* (Oxford, 2003), ch. 4, and ead., 'Swil-bols and tos-pots', in *Love, Friendship and Faith in Europe*, ed. Gowing et al.; Ben-Amos, *Adolescence and Youth*, 176–80; Paul Griffiths, *Youth and Authority* (Oxford, 1996), chs 3 and 4.
4. Richard Valpy French, *Nineteen Centuries of Drink in England*, 2nd edn (n.d.), chs ix and x; Judith M. Bennett, 'Conviviality and charity in medieval and early modern England', *P & P* 134 (1992).
5. Mendelson and Crawford, *Women*, 209–10; Capp, *Gossips*, 51–5, 330; Amanda Flather, *Gender and Space in Early Modern England* (Royal Hist. Soc., Woodbridge, 2007), 83–4, 121–2; above, pp. 98–9.
6. O'Hara, *Courtship and Constraint*, 48.
7. Christopher Haigh, *Reformation and Resistance in Tudor Lancashire* (Cambridge, 1975), 247; *Miscellanea*, ii, Yorks. Archaeol. Soc., Rec. Ser. (1929), 25; *Works of Symon Patrick*, ix. 238.
8. *Women, Crime and the Courts in Early Modern England*, ed. Jenny Kermode and Garthine Walker (1994), pl. 1; Andrew Yarranton, *England's Improvement by Sea and Land* (1677), 46, 101.
9. Perkins, *Workes*, i, sig. A2; Arthur Dent, *The Plaine Mans Pathway to Heaven* (16th imp., 1617), 166–7; *The Works of Robert Harris* (1635), 518; Henry Church, *Miscellanea Philo-Theologica* (1638), 71; Robert Bolton, *Some Generall Directions for a Comfortable Walking with God*, 5th edn (1638), 161, 192–3; Robert Abbot, *Milk for Babes* (1646), 254; Underdown, *Revel, Riot and Rebellion*, ch. 3.
10. Baxter, *Works*, i. 344.
11. Cavendish, *CCXI. Sociable Letters*, 207–9; *The Poems and Prose of Mary, Lady Chudleigh*, ed. Margaret J. M. Ezell (New York, 1993), 336.
12. Burton, *Anatomy*, i. 321; Thomas Cogswell, *Home Divisions* (Manchester, 1998), 26; Peacham, *Complete Gentleman*, 216–17.
13. *Spectator*, 100 (25 June 1711), i. 420; *Notes of Me: The Autobiography of Roger North*, ed. Peter Millard (Toronto, 2000), 204; Gouge, *Domesticall Duties*, 638; *The Letters of John Wilmot, Earl of Rochester*, ed. Jeremy Treglown (Oxford, 1980), 125; Capp, *Gossips*, 239.
14. R[obert] C[rofts], *The Way to Happinesse on Earth* (1641), 259–60.
15. Obadiah Walker, *Of Education* (Oxford, 1673), 218.
16. Baxter, *Practical Works*, i. 73, 196, 220, 228, 231, 828; iv. 413–14.
17. Ibid. i. 300.
18. Boyle, *Ethics*, 239–40.

19. *The Life and Death of that Excellent Minister of Christ, Mr Joseph Alleine* (1673), 32.

20. Wye Saltonstall, *Picturae Loquentes* ([1631, 1635]) (Luttrell Soc., 1946), 67; Jer [emiah] Dyke, *Divers Select Sermons*, ed. Daniel Dyke (1640), 360; O'Hara, *Courtship and Constraint*, 138–42.

21. *Homilies*, 134; *The Autobiography of William Stout of Lancaster 1665–1752*, ed. J. D. Marshall (Manchester, 1967), 131; O'Hara, *Courtship and Constraint*, 143–4.

22. Patrick Collinson, 'Elizabethan and Jacobean Puritanism as forms of popular religious culture', in *The Culture of English Puritanism, 1560–1700*, ed. Christopher Durston and Jacqueline Eales (Basingstoke, 1996), 50–6.

23. Henry Fielding, *Miscellanies*, i, ed. Henry Knight Miller (Oxford, 1972), 121. See *Spectator*, index, s.v. 'conversation'; Sir Richard Bulstrode, *Miscellaneous Essays* (1715), pp. viii and 1–86; Elizabeth C. Goldsmith, *'Exclusive Conversations'* (Philadelphia, 1988); Marc Fumaroli, *Le Genre des genres littéraires français* (Oxford, 1992); Peter Burke, *The Art of Conversation* (Oxford, 1993), ch. 4; Lawrence E. Klein, 'Gender, conversation and the public sphere in early eighteenth-century England', in *Textuality and Sexuality*, ed. Judith Still and Michael Worton (Manchester, 1993); id., *Shaftesbury and the Culture of Politeness* (Cambridge, 1994), 4–5, 6, 96–100, 118–19.

24. Daniel Defoe, *A Tour thro the Whole Island of Great Britain* (1724–6; 1968), ii. 480, i. 94.

25. *The Civile Conversation of M. Steeven Guazzo*, trans. George Pettie and Barth[olomew] Young (Tudor Translations, 1925), i. 68–9.

26. Henry More, *An Antidote against Atheism*, 2nd edn (1655), 85; Georg Simmel, 'The sociology of sociability', in *Simmel on Culture*, ed. David Frisby and Mike Featherstone (1997), 122–3, 127; Melanie Tebbutt, *Women's Talk?* (Aldershot, 1995).

27. *Poems of Ben Jonson*, 50–1; Gouge, *Domesticall Duties*, 264–5. On the potential conflict between male sociability and family entertaining, see Karl E. Westhauser, 'Friendship and family in early modern England', *JSH* 27 (1993–4).

28. Heal and Holmes, *Gentry*, 286–9; Whyman, *Sociability and Power*, ch. 4; J. F. Merritt, *The Social World of Early Modern Westminster* (Manchester, 2005), 171–2.

29. On Fridays and Sundays: Nicolas Bownd, *Sabbathum Veteris et Novi Testamenti*, 2nd edn (1606), 208; *Stuart Royal Proclamations*, i, ed. James F. Larkin and Paul L. Hughes (Oxford, 1973), 415; John Wells, *The Practical Sabbatarian* (1668), 372; and for domestic entertaining more generally: Thomas Starkey, *A Dialogue between Pole and Lupset*, ed. T. F. Mayer, Camden, 4th ser., 37 (1989), 64; *Letters and Papers, Foreign and Domestic, of Henry VIII*, ed. J. S. Brewer et al. (1862–1932), viii. 595; *Homilies*, 273; Fynes Moryson, *An Itinerary* (Glasgow, 1907–8), iv. 173; Ralph Houlbrooke, *English Family Life, 1576–1716* (Oxford, 1988), 221, 237–8; Heal, *Hospitality*, 106; Capp, *Gossips*, 330; Amanda Flather, *Gender and Space in Early Modern England* (Woodbridge, 2007), 96–109.

30. Carole Shammas, *The Pre-Industrial Consumer in England and America* (Oxford, 1990), 181–8; above, pp. 124, 125, 127.

31. Robert Ashton, 'Popular entertainment and social control in later Elizabethan and early Stuart London', *London Journ.* ix (1983), 9–10; Pepys, *Diary*, x: *Companion*, 416–18; Peter Clark, *The English Alehouse* (1983), 132–3; Sara Pennell, ' "Great quantities of gooseberry pye and baked clod of beef" ', in

Londinopolis, ed. Griffiths and Jenner; Merritt, *Social World of Early Modern Westminster*, 167–8.

32. Burton, *Anatomy*, ii. 26; Ian W. Archer, 'Social networks in Restoration London', in *Communities in Early Modern England*, ed. Alexandra Shepard and Phil Withington (Manchester, 2000), 77–8.

33. Philip Stubbes, *Anatomy of the Abuses in England*, ed. Frederick J. Furnivall (New Shakspere Soc., 1877–9), 153.

34. Capaciously discussed in Peter Clark, *British Clubs and Societies 1580–1800* (Oxford, 2000).

35. Michael Strachan, *The Life and Adventures of Thomas Coryate* (1962), 142–8; Timothy Raylor, *Cavaliers, Clubs, and Literary Culture* (Newark, DE, 1994), pt 2; *Literary Circles and Cultural Communities in Renaissance England*, ed. Claude J. Summers and Ted-Larry Pebworth (Columbia, MO, 2000); Michelle O'Callaghan, *The English Wits* (Cambridge, 2007).

36. Vic Gatrell, *City of Laughter* (2006), 115–27; Robert Sugden, 'Correspondence of sentiments', in *Economics and Happiness*, ed. Luigino Bruni and Pier Luigi Porta (Oxford, 2005).

37. *The Theater of Music* (1685), ii. 19.

38. Steven Pincus, 'Coffee politics does create', *Journ. of Modern History*, 67 (1995); Markman Ellis, *The Coffee House* (2004); Brian Cowan, *The Social Life of Coffee* (2005). On women in drinking establishments, Flather, *Gender and Space*, 110–21, and for some thoughts on 'company', Phil Withington, 'Company and sociability in early modern England', *SH* 32 (2007).

39. *The History of the University of Oxford*, iv, ed. Nicholas Tyacke (Oxford, 1997), 172–3.

40. *Spectator*, 9 (10 Mar. 1711), i. 39; David Hume, *Essays, Moral, Political, and Literary*, ed. T. H. Green and T. H. Grose (1875), i. 301. For urban sociability, see Peter Borsay, *The English Urban Renaissance* (Oxford, 1989); John Brewer, *The Pleasures of the Imagination* (1997); *The Cambridge Urban History of Britain*, ii: *1540–1840*, ed. Peter Clark (Cambridge, 2000), ch. 17.

41. James G. Carrier, 'People who can be friends', in *The Anthropology of Friendship*, ed. Sandra Bell and Simon Coleman (Oxford, 1999); Terry Eagleton, *The Meaning of Life* (Oxford, 20007), 168–70.

CHAPTER 7

Heaven and Hell

1. *Bishop Burnet's History of His Own Time* (Oxford, 1823), vi. 229–30.

2. Sermon I, in *The Works of Isaac Barrow* (Edinburgh, 1842), i; Robert South, Sermon I, in *Sermons preached upon Several Occasions*, new edn (1843), i; Isabel Rivers, *Reason, Grace, and Sentiment*, i (Cambridge, 1991), 23, 37, 251.

3. John Calvin, *Institutes of the Christian Religion*, trans. Henry Beveridge (1957), ii. 267; William Tyndale, *Doctrinal Treatises*, ed. Henry Walter (PS, Cambridge, 1848), lxiii; id., *An Answer to Sir Thomas More's Dialogue*, ed. Henry Walter (PS, Cambridge, 1850), 118, 127, 180; William Fulke, *A Defence of the Sincere and True Translations of the Holy Scriptures*, ed. Charles Henry Hartshorne (PS, Cambridge, 1843), 285–6, 295–6.

4. *The Geneva Bible* (1560; facsimile edn, Madison, WI, 1969), New Testament, fol. 37; Marshall, *Beliefs*, 193–4.

5. Laurence Clarkson, *The Lost Sheep found* (1660; facs. repr., Exeter, 1974), 7.

6. Thomas Burnet, *A Treatise concerning the State of Departed Souls*, trans. [John] Dennis, 3rd edn (1765), chs iii and iv; Philip C. Almond, *Heaven and Hell in Enlightenment England* (Cambridge, 1994), 74–80.

7. William Rounseville Alger, *A Critical History of the Doctrine of a Future Life* (New York, 1867), 430–1; Norman T. Burns, *Christian Mortalism from Tyndale to Milton* (Cambridge, MA, 1972); Christopher Hill, *Milton and the English Revolution* (1977), ch. 25; B. W. Ball, *The English Connection* (Cambridge, 1981), ch. 9; B. W. Young, 'The soul-sleeping system', *Journ. of Ecclesiastical History*, 45 (1994); William Lamont, *Last Witnesses* (Aldershot, 2006), 17, 26, 31, 117–18.

8. Richard Baxter, *The Saints Everlasting Rest* (1650), 7, 10.

9. Darren Oldridge, *Religion and Society in Early Stuart England* (Aldershot, 1998), 127.

10. Lewis Du Moulin, *Moral Reflections upon the Number of the Elect* (1680). For other estimates, see Christopher Hill, *A Turbulent, Seditious and Factious People* (Oxford, 1988), 171 n.

11. *The Sermons of John Donne*, ed. George R. Potter and E. M. Simpson (Berkeley and Los Angeles, 1963–62), viii. 82. For contemporary representations of heaven, see John R. Knott, 'Milton's heaven', *PMLA* 85 (1970); Almond, *Heaven and Hell*, 100–10; Houlbrooke, *Death*, 43–7, 51–2; Colleen McDannell and Bernhard Lang, *Heaven*, 2nd edn (New Haven, 2001); Marshall, *Beliefs*, 188–92, 200–1, 215–20.

12. Theodore K. Rabb, *Jacobean Gentleman* (Princeton, 1998), 389.

13. *Sermons of John Donne*, iv. 128.

14. John Hart, *Christ's Last Sermon* (1666), sig. B7^v.

15. John Evelyn, *The History of Religion*, ed. R. M. Evanson (1850), i. 200.

16. *The Diary of Samuel Rogers 1634–1638*, ed. Tom Webster and Kenneth Shipps (Church of England Rec. Soc., 2004), 56.

17. *Divine Songs of the Muggletonians*, [ed. Joseph and Isaac Frost] (1829), 140; E. P. Thompson, *Witness against the Beast* (Cambridge, 1993), 83–4; Lamont, *Last Witnesses*, 25.

18. [John Dunton], *The Athenian Oracle*, i, 2nd edn (1704), 435–6. Cf. Caroline Walker Bynum, *The Resurrection of the Body in Western Christianity, 200–1336* (New York, 1995), 162, 296, 341 n. 8.

19. [John Dunton], *An Essay proving we shall know our Friends in Heaven* (1698), 2nd pagination, 53.

20. *The Writings of John Bradford*, ed. Aubrey Townsend (PS, Cambridge, 1848–53), i. 340–1.

21. Nicolas Caussin, *The Holy Court*, trans. Sir T[homas] H[awkins] (1650), i. 438.

22. John Bunyan, *The Pilgrim's Progress*, ed. James Blanton Wharey, 2nd edn, rev. Roger Sharrock (Oxford, 1960), 154–5.

23. Baxter, *Saints Everlasting Rest*, 680.

24. John Le Neve, *Monumenta Anglicana . . . since the year 1650, to the end of the year 1718* (1719), 174.

25. William Chafin, *A Second Edition of the Anecdotes and History of Cranborn Chase* (1818), 85–6.

26. *The Workes of... Gervase Babington* (1615), 5th pagination, 64; *The Complete Works of Thomas Brooks*, ed. Alexander Balloch Grosart (Edinburgh, 1866–7), iv. 205.

27. *Old English Ballads 1553–1625*, ed. Hyder E. Rollins (Cambridge, 1920), 156; *Prayers and Other Pieces of Thomas Becon*, ed. John Ayre (PS, Cambridge, 1844), 152; Nicholas Bifield, *The Marrow of the Oracles of God*, 2nd edn (1620), 745; Daniel Featley et al., *The House of Mourning* (1660), 167; Bunyan, *Pilgrim's Progress*, 159–60; Samuel Cradock, *Knowledge and Practice*, 4th edn (1702), i. 245–6; Houlbrooke, *Death*, 45–6; Almond, *Heaven and Hell*, 101–5; Marshall, *Beliefs*, 214–20.

28. *Diary of Samuel Rogers*, 44.

29. Baxter, *Saints Everlasting Rest*, 85.

30. *A Series of Letters between Mrs. Elizabeth Carter and Miss Catherine Talbot*, ed. Montagu Pennington, 3rd edn (1819), i. 263.

31. *Writings of John Bradford*, i. 338; Bifield, *Marrow of the Oracles of God*, 747–8; Marshall, *Beliefs*, 217–18.

32. R[alph] J[osselin], *The State of the Saints Departed* (1652), sig. A4; Sir Thomas Phillipps, *Monumental Inscriptions of Wiltshire*, ed. Peter Sherlock (Wilts. Rec. Soc., 2000), 3, 5. *Women's Worlds in Seventeenth-Century England*, ed. Patricia Crawford and Laura Gowing (2000), 136; Marshall, *Beliefs*, 230; Frederick Parkes Weber, *Aspects of Death and Correlated Aspects of Life*, 4th edn (1922), 410.

33. 2nd pagination, 64.

34. Ruth Perry, *The Celebrated Mary Astell* (Chicago, 1986), 434.

35. *ODNB*, *s.n.* 'Rowe, Elizabeth'.

36. Richard Stafford, *A Discourse of the Misery of Hell and the Happiness of Heaven* (1697), 3; Henry Greenwood, *Tormenting Tophet*, 2nd edn (1615), 10. A useful survey is C. A. Patrides, 'Renaissance and modern views on hell', *Harvard Theological Rev.* 57 (1964).

37. *The Morning Exercises at Cripplegate, St Giles in the Fields, and in Southwark*, 5th edn, ed. James Nichols (1844–5), v. 476; Robert Parsons, *The Christian Directory* (Dublin, 1852), 282–91; *The Poems, English, Latin and Greek, of Richard Crashaw*, ed. L. C. Martin, 2nd edn (Oxford, 1957), 119–21.

38. *The Life and Errors of John Dunton*, ed. J. B. Nichols (1818; New York, 1969), i. 26.

39. N. I. Matar, 'Heavenly joy at the torments of the damned in Restoration writings', *Notes and Queries*, 231 (new ser. 33) (1986); Almond, *Heaven and Hell*, 97–9.

40. George Lawson, *An Examination of the Political Part of Mr. Hobbes his 'Leviathan'* (1657), 186.

41. *England in the Reign of King Henry VIII*, pt i: *Starkey's Life and Letters*, ed. Sidney J. Herrtage (EETS, 1927), p. liii.

42. *The Sixth Book of Virgil's Aeneid*, trans. Sir John Harington (1604), ed. Simon Cauchi (Oxford, 1991), 74; *The Works of Thomas Nashe*, ed. Ronald B. McKerrow (repr. Oxford, 1966), ii. 116; Samuel Richardson, *Of the Torments of Hell* (1658); Burns, *Christian Mortalism*, 59; Pierre Lefranc, *Sir Walter Ralegh, Écrivain* (Paris, 1968), 381; Keith Thomas, *Religion and the Decline of Magic* (Harmondsworth, 1978), 200, 202–3; Christopher W. Marsh, *The Family of Love in English Society* (Cambridge, 1994), 22, 35, 39, 45, 48; Houlbrooke, *Death*, 53–4; David R. Como, *Blown by the Spirit* (Stanford,

CA, 2004), 162–3, 168, 254–5, 265, 329 n., 347 n., 380; Lamont, *Last Witnesses*, 25. For the medieval ancestry of this view, Alan E. Bernstein, 'Ecstatic theology', *Speculum*, 57 (1982); *The Complete Works of St. Thomas More* (New Haven, 1963–), vii. xci.

43. *Leviathan*, 313–14 (ch. 38).
44. Thomas Bilson, *The Effect of Certaine Sermons* (1599), 52.
45. Perkins, *Workes*, iii, 2nd pagination, 258, 532; John Stachniewski, *The Persecutory Imagination* (Oxford, 1991), 23–4; Peter Marshall, 'The map of God's word', in *The Place of the Dead*, ed. Bruce Gordon and Peter Marshall (Cambridge, 2000).
46. Gordon Rupp, *Religion in England 1688–1791* (Oxford, 1986), 260–1; *Complete Works of Thomas Brooks*, v. 114.
47. Sir Thomas Browne, *Religio Medici and Other Works*, ed. L. C. Martin (Oxford, 1964), 8, 290.
48. John Locke, *Writings on Religion*, ed. Victor Nuovo (Oxford, 2002), 232–7.
49. In addition to D. P. Walker, *The Decline of Hell* (1964), see Paul C. Davies, 'The debate on eternal punishment in later seventeenth- and eighteenth-century English literature', *Eighteenth-Century Studies*, 4 (1970–1); Norman Fiering, *Jonathan Edwards's Moral Thought and its British Context* (Chapel Hill, NC, 1981), 225–38; Rivers, *Reason, Grace, and Sentiment*, i. 84; Houlbrooke, *Death*, 50–6.
50. *Private Papers of James Boswell*, ed. Geoffrey Scott and Frederick A. Pottle, xv (n.p., 1932), 299.
51. Michael Macdonald, *Mystical Bedlam* (Cambridge, 1981), 220; and, more generally, Stachniewski, *The Persecutory Imagination*.
52. *When Death Do Us Part*, ed. Tom Arkell et al. (Oxford, 2000), 173.
53. Houlbrooke, *Death*, 352–3; David Hickman, 'Reforming remembrance', *Trans. Thoroton Soc.* 103 (1999), 119–20; Marshall, *Beliefs*, 199–201.
54. Patrick Collinson, *The Elizabethan Puritan Movement* (1967), 37; Perkins, *Workes*, ii. 315; Baxter, *Practical Works*, vol. i, p. xxii; Christopher Haigh, *English Reformations* (Oxford, 1993), 281–4; Ian Green, *Print and Protestantism in Early Modern England* (Oxford, 2000), 502.
55. e.g. Alan Macfarlane, *The Family Life of Ralph Josselin* (Cambridge, 1970), 168.
56. The instances cited in Thomas, *Religion and the Decline of Magic*, 198–205, could easily be multiplied.
57. George T. Buckley, *Atheism in the English Renaissance* (Chicago, 1932), ch. ii; Nicholas Davidson, 'Unbelief and atheism in Italy, 1500–1700', in *Atheism from the Reformation to the Enlightenment*, ed. Michael Hunter and David Wootton (Oxford, 1992), 64–8, 74–81, 84; Stephen Gaukroger, *The Emergence of a Scientific Culture* (Oxford, 2006), 103.
58. Perkins, *Workes*, ii. 389; Francis Cheynell, *The Man of Honour* (1645), 45; William M. Lamont, *Richard Baxter and the Millennium* (1979), 252.
59. Robert N. Watson, *The Rest Is Silence* (Berkeley and Los Angeles, 1994), *passim*.
60. Thomas, *Religion and the Decline of Magic*, 204; Justin Champion, 'May the last king be strangled in the bowels of the last priest', in *Radicalism in British Literary Culture 1650–1830*, ed. Timothy Morton and Nigel Smith (Cambridge, 2002). For medieval anticipations of such disbelief: Susan Reynolds, 'Social mentalities and the case of medieval scepticism', *TRHS*, 6th ser., 1 (1991); Robert Bartlett,

England under the Norman and Angevin Kings (Oxford, 2000), 478–81; John H. Arnold, *Belief and Unbelief in Medieval Europe* (2005), 2, 177, 225–9.

61. Anthony à Wood and Richard Rawlinson, *Parochial Collections*, ed. F. N. Davis (Oxon. Rec. Soc., 1920–9), 123.
62. John Strype, *The Life and Acts of Matthew Parker* (Oxford, 1821), i. 499.
63. Katie Whitaker, *Mad Madge* (2003), 322; *Original Letters Illustrative of English History*, ed. Henry Ellis, 2nd edn (1825), iii. 289. See, more generally, David Wootton, 'The fear of God in early modern political thought', *Historical Papers/ Communications Historiques* (1983) (Ottawa, n.d. [1984?]).
64. Peter Earle, *A City Full of People* (1994), 176; G. I. O. Duncan, *The High Court of Delegates* (Cambridge, 1971), 133 n. 7.
65. Burnet, *Treatise concerning the State of Departed Souls*, 366–7.
66. Browne, *Religio Medici*, 116; Hobbes, *Latin Works*, ii. 110.

Posthumous Fame

1. Jacob Burckhardt, *The Civilization of the Renaissance*, trans. S. C. G. Middlemore, 2nd edn (Oxford, 1945), 87–93.
2. Isaac Watts, *A Defense against the Temptation to Self-Murther* (1726), 22–4; Anton Daniel Leeman, *Gloria* (Rotterdam, n.d. [1949]); Maria Rosa Lida de Malkiel, *L'Idée de la gloire dans la tradition occidentale*, trans. Sylvia Roubaud (Paris, 1968), 3–86; Leo Braudy, *The Frenzy of Renown* (New York, 1986), chs i–iii.
3. Giraldus Cambrensis, *Topographia Hibernica*, in *Opera*, ed. James F. Dimock, v (Rolls Ser., 1867), 3–5; *The Works of Sir John Clanvowe*, ed. V. J. Scattergood (Cambridge, 1975), 69–70; Johan Huizinga, *The Waning of the Middle Ages*, [trans. F. Hopman] (1924; Harmondsworth, 1955), 70; Malcolm Vale, *War and Chivalry* (1981), 78, 174.
4. Sir Thomas Elyot, *The Boke Named the Gouernour*, ed. Henry Herbert Stephen Croft (1883), ii. 265.
5. *Lord Morley's The Tryumphes of Fraunces Petrarcke*, ed. D. D. Carnicalli (Cambridge, MA, 1971).
6. *Horestes*, lines 890–3, in *Three Tudor Classical Interludes*, ed. Marie Axton (Woodbridge, 1982).
7. Sir William Dugdale, *The Antiquities of Warwickshire* (1656), 325; *The Works of John Ford*, ed. William Gifford, with additions by Alexander Dyce (1895), iii. 413–16. For similar sentiments, Louis David Appel, 'The concept of fame in Tudor and Stuart literature', in *Summaries of Doctoral Dissertations*, xvii (Northwestern Univ., Chicago, 1950), 9–13; Curtis Brown Watson, *Shakespeare and the Renaissance Concept of Honor* (Princeton, 1960), 141–5, 388–414.
8. Geoffrey Fenton, *Golden Epistles* (1575), sigs 122ᵛ–3; Robert Ashley, *Of Honour*, ed. Virgil B. Heltzel (San Marino, CA, 1947), 64; William Shakespeare, *Hamlet* (1601), iv. iv; Sir William Cornwallis, *Essayes*, ed. Don Cameron Allen (Baltimore, 1946), 93; Bacon, *Works*, vi. 648; Josua Poole, *The English Parnassus* (1657), 92–3; [Margaret Cavendish], Marchioness of Newcastle, *The Philosophical and Physical Opinions* (1655), sig. B3; ead., *The Worlds Olio* (1655), 2.
9. Richard Crompton, *The Mansion of Magnanimitie* (1599), sigs A4ᵛ, F3.
10. Richard Copley Christie, *Étienne Dolet* (1899), 484–6; Petrus Gassendus, *The Mirrour of True Nobility & Gentility*, trans. W[illiam] Rand (1657), ii. 173.
11. Hobbes, *Leviathan*, 71 (ch. 11).

12. Elias Ashmole, *The Institution, Laws and Ceremonies of the Most Noble Order of the Garter* (1672), 12.

13. John Milton, *Lycidas* (1637); *Poems and Dramas of Fulke Greville First Lord Brooke*, ed. Geoffrey Bullough (Edinburgh, n.d.), i. 193.

14. *Queene Elizabethes Achademy*, ed. F. J. Furnivall (EETS, 1869), 12; Gillian Darley, *John Evelyn* (New Haven, 2006), 171.

15. Richard Hakluyt, *The Principal Navigations, Voyages, Traffiques and Discoveries of the English Nation* (Everyman's Lib., n.d.), v. 119–20; *The Correspondence of Sir Philip Sidney and Hubert Languet*, trans. Steuart A. Pears (1845), 137; Lewis Einstein, *Tudor Ideals* (1921), 260–2; above, Ch. 2.

16. Paul E. J. Hammer, *The Polarisation of Elizabethan Politics* (Cambridge, 1999), 233 n.

17. *The Complete Works of Captain John Smith (1580–1631)*, ed. Philip L. Barbour (Chapel Hill, NC, 1986), iii. 277.

18. e.g. William Martyn, *Youths Instruction* (1612), 101; *The Diary of Sir Henry Slingsby*, ed. Daniel Parsons (1836), 212–13, 228; *The Works of the Right Honourable Henry Late L. Delamer, and Earl of Warrington* (1694), 2.

19. Randle Holme, *Academy of Armory*, ii (Roxburghe Club, 1905), 522; Ben Jonson, *Sejanus his Fall*, Act I, lines 475–501, in *Complete Plays*, ed. G. A. Wilkes (Oxford, 1981–2), ii. 254–5; John Hayward, *The Lives of the Three Normans, Kings of England* (1613), in *The Harleian Miscellany* (1808–11), iii. 116.

20. *Dr William Hunter at the Royal Academy of Art*, ed. Martin Kemp (Glasgow, 1975), 34; *The Discourses of Sir Joshua Reynolds* (World's Classics, 1907), 67.

21. *The Poetical Works of John Skelton*, ed. Alexander Dyce (1843), i. 366; Edward Gibbon, *A Vindication of Some Passages* (1779), 4; *Sir William Davenant's Gondibert*, ed. David F. Gladish (Oxford, 1971), 25–6; O. Elton, 'Literary fame', *Otia Merseiana*, 4 (1904); Braudy, *Frenzy of Renown*, 13–14, 355–6; Richard Terry, *Poetry and the Making of the English Literary Past 1660–1781* (Oxford, 2001), ch. 3.

22. Milton, *CPW* ii. 531.

23. Warren Chernaik, 'Books as memorials', *The Year Book of English Studies*, 21 (1991).

24. Cavendish, *World's Olio*, 3; Baxter, *Practical Works*, iii. 413.

25. Milton, *CPW* i. 319–20.

26. Ernest Campbell Mossner, *The Life of David Hume* (Edinburgh, 1954), 607; Adam Smith, *Essays on Philosophical Subjects*, ed. W. P. D. Wightman and J. C. Bryce (Oxford, 1980), 327.

27. Lord Teignmouth, *Memoirs of the Life, Writings, and Correspondence of Sir William Jones* (1804), 94.

28. Oliver Goldsmith, *The Bee*, 5 (3 Nov. 1759), in *Collected Works*, ed. Arthur Friedman (Oxford, 1966), i. 444; Andrew Bennett, *Romantic Poets and the Culture of Posterity* (Cambridge, 1999).

29. *Hall's Chronicle* (1809), 479–80; *The Mirror for Magistrates*, ed. Lily B. Campbell (Cambridge, 1938), 414, 417.

30. *Troubles Connected with the Prayer Book of 1549*, ed. Nicholas Pocock (Camden Soc., 1884), 147–8.

31. Arthur Wilson, *The History of Great Britain* (1653), 111.

32. John Hawarde, *Les Reportes del Cases in Camera Stellata 1593 to 1609*, ed. William Paley Baildon (n.p., 1894), 315.

33. John Walter, 'Faces in the crowd', in *The Family in Early Modern England*, ed. Helen Berry and Elizabeth Foyster (Cambridge, 2007), 123.

34. H. J. Habakkuk, 'Daniel Finch, 2nd Earl of Nottingham, his house and estate', in *Studies in Social History*, ed. J. H. Plumb (1955), 173; *The Mental World of the Jacobean Court*, ed. Linda Levy Peck (Cambridge, 1991), 15, 167.

35. Cit. Paul M. Hunneyball, *Architecture and Image-Building in Seventeenth-Century Hertfordshire* (Oxford, 2004), 23–4.

36. *Complete Works of Thomas Brooks*, v. 114.

37. Malcolm Airs, *The Making of the English Country House 1500–1640* (1975), 8; Lydia M. Soo, *Wren's 'Tracts' on Architecture and Other Writings* (Cambridge, 1998), 104.

38. Mervyn James, *Society, Politics and Culture* (Cambridge, 1986), 324.

39. Browne, *Religio Medici*, 123.

40. *Worlds Olio*, 1; *Political Writings*, ed. Susan James (Cambridge, 2003), 150.

41. Howard Colvin, *Architecture and the After-Life* (New Haven, 1991), 316–22.

42. 'The ruines of time', line 342, in *Complaints*, in *The Poetical Works of Edmund Spenser*, ed. J. C. Smith and E. de Selincourt, 475.

43. William Wyrley, *The True Use of Armorie* (1592), 21–2.

44. Wood and Rawlinson, *Parochial Collections*, 343.

45. Proverbs 10: 7; Psalms 112: 6; Ecclesiasticus 44: 14; Matthew 26: 13.

46. Milton, *CPW* i. 302.

47. On this large subject, see K. L. Wood-Legh, *Perpetual Chantries in Britain* (Cambridge, 1965); J. T. Rosenthal, *The Purchase of Paradise* (1972); Alan Kreider, *English Chantries* (Cambridge, MA, 1979); Norman P. Tanner, *The Church in Late Medieval Norwich 1370–1532* (Toronto, 1984), 91–110; Eamon Duffy, *The Stripping of the Altars* (New Haven, 1992), 327–37, 368–76; Andrew D. Brown, *Popular Piety in Late Medieval England* (Oxford, 1995), ch. 4; Howard Colvin, 'The origin of the chantries', *Journ. of Medieval History*, 26 (2000); *Death and Memory in Medieval Exeter*, ed. David Lepine and Nicholas Orme (Devon and Cornwall Rec. Soc., Exeter, 2003); *The Bede Roll of the Fraternity of St Nicholas*, ed. N. W. and V. A. James (London Rec. Soc., 2004); the articles by Clive Burgess: ' "For the increase of divine service" ', *Journ. of Ecclesiastical History*, 36 (1985); 'A service for the dead', *Trans. Bristol and Glos. Archaeol. Soc.* 105 (1987); ' "By quick and by dead" ', *EHR* cii (1987); ' "A fond thing vainly invented" ', in *Parish Church and People*, ed. S. J. Wright (1988); 'The benefactions of mortality', in *Studies in Clergy and Ministry in Medieval England*, ed. David M. Smith (York, 1991); ' "Longing to be prayed for" ', in *The Place of the Dead*, ed. Gordon and Marshall; and his edition of *The Pre-Reformation Records of All Saints', Bristol*, i (Bristol Rec. Soc., 1995), esp. pp. xx–xxvi, 4–30.

48. *Liber Vitae Ecclesiae Dunelmensis*, [ed. J. T. Raine] (Surtees Soc., 1841).

49. *VCH Glos.* ii. 401–2.

50. James R. Banker, *Death in the Community* (Athens, GA, 1988), 186.

51. Dr Page of All Souls College, 1635, Bodl. Lib., Barlow MS 54, fols 29–36; *Visitation Articles and Injunctions of the Early Stuart Church*, ed. Kenneth Fincham (Church of England Rec. Soc., 1998), ii. 201; [Edward Stephens], *Of Prayers for the Dead* (1699); *Remarks and Collections of Thomas Hearne*, ed. C. E. Doble et al. (Oxford Hist. Soc., 1885–1921), viii. 168; *Anglicanism*, ed. Paul Elmer More and Frank Leslie Cross (1935), 631–3; *The History of the University of Oxford*, iv, ed. Nicholas Tyacke (Oxford, 1997), 604; Marshall,

Beliefs, 141–8, 180–7; Christopher Haigh, *The Plain Man's Pathways to Heaven* (Oxford, 2007), 205–6.

52. *The Life and Times of Anthony Wood*, ed. Andrew Clark (Oxford Hist. Soc., 1891–1903), iii. 232.

53. D. J. A. Steel, *National Index of Parish Registers*, i (1968), 9.

54. *Complete Works of St. Thomas More*, vii; William Allen, *A Defense and Declaration of the Catholike Churchies* [sic] *Doctrine, touching Purgatory* (Antwerp, 1565), fol. 169ᵛ.

55. William Godwin, *Essay on Sepulchres* (1809), 47–8; Duffy, *Stripping of the Altars*, 494.

56. *The Writings of Henry Barrow 1590–1591*, ed. Leland H. Carlson (1966), 82–3; D. J. Steel, *Sources for Nonconformist Genealogy and Family History* (Chichester, 1973), 672–3; Richard L. Greaves, *Society and Religion in Elizabethan England* (Minneapolis, 1981), 703; *A Directory for the Publique Worship of God* (1645), 73–4; Marshall, *Beliefs*, 152–4.

57. On funeral customs: Clare Gittings, *Death, Burial and the Individual in Early Modern England* (1984); *Memorial Rings...in the Possession of Frederick Arthur Crisp* (n.p., 1908); J. F. R. Day, 'Death be very proud', in *Tudor Political Culture*, ed. Dale Hoak (Cambridge, 1995); David Cressy, *Birth, Marriage, and Death* (Oxford, 1997), chs 18–20; Houlbrooke, *Death*, ch. 9; *Berkshire Probate Accounts*, ed. Ian Mortimer (Berks. Rec. Soc., 1999); Andrea Brady, *English Funerary Elegy in the Seventeenth Century* (Basingstoke, 2006), ch. 3.

58. W[illiam] C[oles], *The Art of Simpling* (1656), 64–5.

59. James Hart, *The Diet of the Diseased* (1633), 142–3; Richard Moore, *A Pearl in an Oyster-Shel* (1675), 83.

60. *Sacred Space in Early Modern Europe*, ed. Will Coster and Andrew Spicer (Cambridge, 2005), 131; Elisabeth Salter, *Cultural Creativity in the English Renaissance* (Basingstoke, 2006), 118.

61. *The Autobiography of Edward, Lord Herbert of Cherbury*, ed. Sidney Lee, 2nd edn (n.d.), 161.

62. *Puritan Manifestoes*, ed. W. H. Frere and C. E. Douglas (1907), 28; Harriet T. Flower, *Ancestor Masks and Aristocratic Power in Roman Culture* (Oxford, 1996), ch. 5; Jessica Martin, *Walton's 'Lives'* (Oxford, 2001), ch. 1.

63. John Canne, *A Necessitie of Separation* (1634), ed. Charles Stovel (Hanserd Knollys Soc., 1849), 112–13; *Cal. S.P. Domestic, 1634–5*, 319; Patrick Collinson, *Godly People* (1983), 519–23; Houlbrooke, *Death*, ch. 10; Marshall, *Beliefs*, 156–61.

64. *The Diary of Sir Richard Hutton*, ed. W. R. Prest (Selden Soc., 1991), p. xvii; David Hickman, 'From Catholic to Protestant', in *England's Long Reformation*, ed. Nicholas Tyacke (1998), 124; Marshall, *Beliefs*, 159. Margo Todd, *The Culture of Protestantism in Early Modern Scotland* (New Haven, 2002), 340–1.

65. *A Century of Broadside Elegies*, ed. John W. Draper (1928); Brady, *English Funerary Elegy*.

66. James Sutherland, *The Restoration Newspaper and its Development* (Cambridge, 1986), 85–9; John Le Neve, *The Lives and Characters of the Most Illustrious Persons who died in the Year 1711* (1713) (continued under a similar title in 1714 for deaths in 1712); Lorna Clymer, 'Poetically figuring the self', *The Center and Clark Newsletter*, 29 (Spring 1997), 5; Stephen Howard, 'A bright pattern to all her sex', in *Gender in Eighteenth-Century England*, ed. Hannah

Barker and Elaine Chalus (1997), 231–2; Houlbrooke, *Death*, 329; Nigel Starck, *Life after Death* (Melbourne, 2006), 1–22.

67. *Trevelyan Papers*, ed. J. Payne Collier et al. (Camden Soc., 1857–72), iii. 127.

68. Robert Reyce, *The Breviary of Suffolk* (1618), ed. Lord Francis Hervey (1902), 2.

69. John Weever, *Ancient Funerall Monuments* (1631); Katherine A. Esdaile, *English Monumental Sculpture since the Renaissance* (1927), and ead., *English Church Monuments 1510 to 1540* (1946); Eric Mercer, *English Art 1553–1625* (Oxford, 1962), 237–51; Brian Kemp, *English Church Monuments* (1980); Richard Rex, 'Monumental brasses and the Reformation', *Trans. Monumental Brass Soc.* xiv/5 (1990); Colvin, *Architecture and the After-Life*; David Bindman and Malcolm Baker, *Roubiliac and the Eighteenth-Century Monument* (New Haven, 1995); Cressy, *Birth, Marriage, and Death*, 469–73; Houlbrooke, *Death*, 343–71; Nigel Llewellyn, *Funeral Monuments in Post-Reformation England* (Cambridge, 2000); Jonathan Finch, *Church Monuments in Norfolk before 1850*, BAR British ser. (Oxford, 2000); Peter Sherlock, 'Piety, honour and memory in early modern England', Oxford Univ. D.Phil. thesis (2000); id., *Monuments and Memory in Early Modern England* (Aldershot, 2008); Vanessa Harding, *The Dead and the Living in Paris and London, 1500–1670* (Cambridge, 2002), ch. 6. The publications of local antiquarian societies abound in descriptions of monuments and there is much valuable material in the journal *Church Monuments*.

70. Erwin Panofsky, *Tomb Sculpture* (1992), 62–3, 69–75; Iiro Kajanto, *Classical and Christian* (Helsinki, 1980); Colvin, *Architecture and the After-Life*, 137–8.

71. Vanessa Harding, 'Burial choice and burial location in later medieval London', in *Death in Towns*, ed. Steven Bassett (Leicester, 1992), 129; Christine Carpenter, *Locality and Polity* (Cambridge, 1992), 227; C. M. Barnett, 'Commemoration in the parish church', *Yorks. Archaeol. Journ.* 72 (2000); Nigel Saul, *Death, Art, and Memory in Medieval England* (Oxford, 2001), and id., 'Bold as brass', in *Heraldry, Pageantry, and Social Display in Medieval Europe*, ed. Peter Coss and Maurice Keen (Woodbridge, 2002).

72. *The Letters of Stephen Gardiner*, ed. James Arthur Muller (Cambridge, 1933), 274.

73. Colvin, *Architecture and the After-Life*, 189, 217–20.

74. *Tudor Royal Proclamations*, ii, ed. Paul L. Hughes and James F. Larkin (New Haven, 1969), 146.

75. Anthony R. Wagner and James G. Mann, 'A fifteenth-century description of the brass of Sir Hugh Hastings at Elsing, Norfolk', *Antiquaries Journ.* 19 (1939); Anthony Fletcher, *A County Community in Peace and War* (1975), 25.

76. Stone, *Crisis*, 579–81.

77. As Heal and Holmes put it; *Gentry*, 338.

78. Llewellyn, *Funeral Monuments*, 6–7.

79. Michael Neill, *Issues of Death* (Oxford, 1997), 40–1, 48, 309–10.

80. Weever, *Ancient Funerall Monuments*, 18; Burton, *Anatomy*, iii. 27.

81. Weever, *Ancient Funerall Monuments*, ch. 5; Thomas Fuller, *The Holy State* (1642; 1840), 151; Shakespeare, *Much Ado about Nothing* (printed 1600), v. iii. 62–6.

82. *Conferences and Combination Lectures in the Elizabethan Church*, ed. Patrick Collinson et al. (Church of England Rec. Soc., Woodbridge, 2003), 217.

83. Symon Gunton, *The History of the Church of Peterburgh*, ed. Symon Patrick (1686), 335; Bindman and Baker, *Roubiliac*, 4; [John Joscelin], *The Life off the 70 Archbishopp off Canterbury*, [trans. John Stubbs] (1574), sigs Cii^v–iii^v.

84. *The Literary Works of Matthew Prior*, ed. H. Bunker Wright and Monroe K. Spears (Oxford, 1959), i. 409.

85. Nigel Llewellyn, 'Honour in life, death and the memory', *TRHS*, 6th ser., vi (1996), 191 (in *Funeral Monuments*, 53, he writes, more vaguely, of 'a large proportion'). Sir Howard Colvin pointed out to me that the only way of securing reliable statistics on the matter is to work through the Prerogative Court of Canterbury's Registers of Wills, noting instructions for burial and provision, if any, for a monument.

86. F. R. H. Du Boulay, *The Lordship of Canterbury* (1966), 156.

87. Amy Louise Harris, 'The Funerary Monuments of Richard Boyle, Earl of Cork', *Church Monuments*, xiii (1998); Sherlock, 'Piety, honour and memory', ch. 9.

88. Bindman and Baker, *Roubiliac*, 2.

89. Ralph Bigland, *Historical, Monumental and Genealogical Collections relative to the County of Gloucester (1791–1899)*, ed. Brian Frith (Bristol and Glos. Archaeol. Soc., 1989–95), ii. 466.

90. Elias Ashmole, *Antiquities of Berkshire* (1719), i. 168–9.

91. *The Poems of Alexander Pope*, ed. John Butt (1963), 353.

92. John Le Neve, *Monumenta Anglicana . . . since the year 1600, to the end of the year 1649* (1719), 4–5.

93. *Bedfordshire Wills 1484–1533*, ed. Patricia L. Bell (Beds. Hist. Rec. Soc., 1997), 52; Saul, 'Bold as brass', 191–3.

94. e.g. *Testamenta Vetusta*, ed. Nicholas Harris Nicolas (1826), i. 156, 175, 235, 339; ii. 420, 443.

95. John Bowden, *The Epitaph Writer* (Chester, 1791), p. xv.

96. Le Neve, *Monumenta Anglicana, 1600–1649*, 104; Kemp, *English Church Monuments*, 105; Joshua Scodel, *The English Poetic Epitaph* (Ithaca, NY, 1991), 9, 312–13; Bindman and Baker, *Roubiliac*, 189.

97. *The Diary of Roger Lowe of Ashton-in-Makersfield, Lancashire, 1663–74*, ed. William L. Sachse (New Haven, 1938), 29, 77.

98. 'R.H. to the reader', in [Giovanni Paolo Lomazzo], *A Tracte containing the Artes of Curious Paintinge Carvinge & Buildinge*, trans. R[ichard] H[aydocke] (1595), sig. iii.

99. Keith Thomas, 'Art and iconoclasm in early modern England', in *Religious Politics in Post-Reformation England*, ed. Kenneth Fincham and Peter Lake (Woodbridge, 2006), 32–3.

100. Mercer, *English Art 1553–1625*, 162–3.

101. *The Autobiography of Thomas Whythorne*, ed. James M. Osborn (1962), 116.

102. John Elsum, *The Art of Painting after the Italian Manner* (1704), 5.

103. A. Pigler, 'Portraying the dead', *Acta Historiae Artium Academiae Scientiarium Hungaricae*, iv (1957), 43–9; Ernst Benkard, *Undying Faces*, trans. Margaret M. Green (1929); *The Funeral Effigies of Westminster Abbey*, ed. Anthony Harvey and Richard Mortimer (Woodbridge, 1999); Malcolm Baker, *Figured in Marble* (2000), 55, 95, 97–8; Andrew Moore, with Charlotte Crawley, *Family and Friends* (1992), 117–18.

104. Jeremy Bentham, *Auto-Icon* (n.d. [1842?]), 3.

105. Heather Swanson, *Medieval Artisans* (Oxford, 1989), 47. For memorial rings and keepsakes: *OED*, s.v. 'remembrance'; *Memorial Rings*; Diana Scarisbrick, *Jewellery in Britain 1066–1837* (Norwich, 1994), 197–9; Houlbrooke, *Death*, 251–2, 254, 269, 274, 276–7, 282–5; Marcia Pointon, 'Jewellery in eighteenth-century England', in *Consumers and Luxury*, ed. Maxine Berg and Helen Clifford (Manchester, 1999), 126–33; and above, pp. 126–7.
106. W. G. Hoskins, *Midland England* (1949), 116.
107. N. J. G. Pounds, *The Culture of the English People* (Cambridge, 1994), 140; J. S. W. Helt, 'Women, memory and will-making in Elizabethan England', in *The Place of the Dead*, ed. Gordon and Marshall; Grant McCracken, *Culture and Consumption* (Bloomington, IN, 1988), ch. 3; Catherine Richardson, 'Household objects and domestic ties', in *The Medieval Household in Christian Europe*, ed. Cordelia Beattie et al. (Turnhout, 2003); above, pp. 126–7.
108. *ODNB*, s.n. 'Thicknesse, Philip'.

The Quest for Immortality

1. 1. *The Civile Conversation of M. Steeven Guazzo*, trans. George Pettie and Barth[olomew] Young (Tudor Translations, 1925), i. 9.
2. Francis Bacon, *The Advancement of Learning*, ed. Michael Kiernan (Oxford, 2000), 52–3. On the classical sources for the idea, Ernst Robert Curtius, *European Literature and the Latin Middle Ages*, trans. Willard R. Trask (New York, 1953), 476–7.
3. Charles Trinkaus, *In Our Image and Likeness* (1970), i. 313; Godwin, *Essay on Sepulchres*, 108–11.
4. Evelyn, *Diary*, v. 622.
5. Burton, *Anatomy*, i. 310; *Poetical Works of Edmund Spenser*, 475.
6. *Works*, i. 212.
7. Some indication of their volume is given in *English County Histories*, ed. C. R. J. Currie and C. P. Lewis (Stroud, 1994), and HMC, *Papers of British Antiquaries and Historians* (2003).
8. George Whetstone, *A Mirror of Treue Honour and Christian Nobilitie* (1585), sig. Aij; Charles Phythian-Adams, 'Leicestershire and Rutland', in *English County Histories*, ed. Currie and Lewis, 230.
9. *The Diary of William Lawrence*, ed. G. E. Aylmer (Beaminster, 1961), 46.
10. Terry, *Poetry and the Making of the English Literary Past*, chs 3 and 5; Keith Thomas, *Changing Conceptions of National Biography* (Cambridge, 2005).
11. Bacon, *Works*, iv. 304.
12. N. H. Keeble and Geoffrey F. Nuttall, *Calendar of the Correspondence of Richard Baxter* (Oxford, 1991), ii. 178.
13. John Hall, *Horae Vacivae; or, Essays* (1646), 53; *The Tatler*, 23 (2 June 1709), ed. Donald F. Bond (Oxford, 1987), i. 183.
14. *Gentleman's Magazine*, vi (1736), 745.
15. Wood and Rawlinson, *Parochial Collections*, 150; Owen Manning and William Bray, *The History and Antiquities of the County of Surrey* (1804–14; repr. 1974), i. 613.
16. Jean Gagen, 'Honor and fame in the works of the Duchess of Newcastle', *Studies in Philology*, lvi (1959); Whitaker, *Mad Madge*, 26, 346.

17. L. A. S. Butler, 'Medieval gravestones of Cambridgeshire, Huntingdonshire, and the Soke of Peterborough', *Procs Cambs. Antiquarian Soc.* l (1957); *Bedfordshire Wills 1480–1519*, ed. Patricia Bell (Beds. Hist. Rec. Soc., 1966), vi; Ben Stocker, 'Medieval grave markers in Kent', *Church Monuments*, i/2 (1986); Houlbrooke, *Death*, 360–1; Judith Middleton-Stewart, *Inward Purity and Outward Splendour* (Woodbridge, 2001), 75; *Death and Memory in Medieval Exeter*, ed. Lepine and Orme, 22; Roberta Gilchrist and Barney Sloane, *Requiem* (2005), 185–7.
18. Marshall, *Beliefs*, 290.
19. HMC, *Portland*, ii. 276.
20. [Samuel Pegge], *Anonymiana* (1809), 325; Houlbrooke, *Death*, 363.
21. William Nicolson, *Miscellany Accounts of the Diocese of Carlile*, ed. R. S. Ferguson (Cumberland and Westmorland Archaeol. and Antiquarian Soc., 1877), 52, and 12, 13, 17, 19, 20, 22, 51, 58, 66, 86, 89, 105, 119.
22. Holme, *Academy of Armory*, ii. 518–22; John Ferne, *The Blazon of Gentrie* (1586), 83.
23. *Collected Poems of Thomas Parnell*, ed. Claude Rawson and F. P. Lock (Newark, DE, 1989), 169.
24. K. D. M. Snell, *Parish and Belonging* (Cambridge, 2006), 460 n. 14. On costs, see Gittings, *Death, Burial and the Individual*, 144–6; Houlbrooke, *Death*, 368–9 n. 91; Llewellyn, *Funeral Monuments*, 163–80; Paul Cockeram, *Memorialisation and the Cornish Funeral Monument Industry, 1497–1660*, BAR British ser. (Oxford, 2006), ch. 4.
25. Rosie Morris, 'The "innocent and touching custom" of maidens' garlands', *Folklore*, 114 (2003).
26. *The Works of... William Laud*, ed. William Scott and James Bliss (Oxford, 1847–60), v. 358; *Visitation Articles and Injunctions*, ed. Fincham, ii. 154.
27. *A Proposal for Correcting the English Tongue, Polite Conversation, Etc.*, ed. Herbert Davis and Louis Landa (Oxford, 1957), 244.
28. John Nichols, *Literary Anecdotes of the Eighteenth Century* (1812–15), ii. 706.
29. *The Catechism of Thomas Becon*, ed. John Ayre (PS, Cambridge, 1844), 354.
30. Joseph Bentham, *The Christian Conflict* (1635), 248.
31. *Campion's Works*, ed. Percival Vivian (Oxford, 1909), 155.
32. E. K. Chambers, *Sir Henry Lee* (Oxford, 1936), 70.
33. *The Naval Tracts of Sir William Monson*, ed. M. Oppenheim (Navy Recs Soc., 1902–14), i. 102, 111.
34. Gassendus, *Mirrour of True Nobility*, sig. A6^v.
35. Jeremy Bentham, *Theory of Legislation*, trans. R. Hildreth (1876), 175.
36. I.M. [Gervase Markham?], *A Health to the Gentlemanly Profession of Serving-Men* (1598; 1931), sig. B4.
37. E[dward] M[isselden], *The Circle of Commerce* (1623), 18; Grassby, *Business Community*, 332, 369–70.
38. 2 Samuel 18: 18.
39. Thomas Fuller, *The History of the Worthies of England*, ed. P. Austin Nuttall (1840) iii. 107; C. S. L. Davies, 'A woman in the public sphere', *EHR* cxviii (2003); Francis Bacon, *The Essayes or Counsels*, ed. Michael Kiernan (Oxford, 1985), 23.
40. John Venn, *Biographical History of Gonville and Caius College* (Cambridge, 1897–1901), iii. 229.
41. *Pre-Reformation Records of All Saints', Bristol*, ed. Burgess, vol. i, pp. xx–xxvi, xl–xli, 4; Burgess, 'The benefactions of mortality'.

42. Francis Blomefield, *An Essay towards a Topographical History of Norfolk* (1805–10), vi. 217–22; Duffy, *Stripping of the Altars*, 335.

43. Tanner, *Church in Late Medieval Norwich*, 120; Blomefield, *Essay towards a Topographical History*, iv. 89; *Bedfordshire Wills 1531–1539*, transcr. Patricia L. Bell (Beds. Family Hist. Soc., 2005), 124.

44. H. J. White, *Merton College* (1906), 12.

45. *ODNB*, *s.n.* 'Perrott, Richard'.

46. Nicolson, *Miscellany Accounts of the Diocese of Carlile*, 227.

47. John Le Neve, *Monumenta Anglicana . . . since the year 1680, to the end of the year 1699* (1718), 63.

48. [John Wilford], *Memorials and Characters* (1741), 450 n.

49. *Wills and Inventories*, ed. Samuel Tymms (Camden Soc., 1850), 38–9; David Hickman, 'Religious belief and pious practice among London's Elizabethan elite', *HJ* 42 (1999), 948.

50. Ian W. Archer, 'The charity of early modern Londoners', *TRHS*, 6th ser., xii (2002), 233.

51. Basil F. L. Clarke, *The Building of the Eighteenth-Century Church* (1963), 71.

52. W. E. Tate, *The Parish Chest*, 3rd edn (Cambridge, 1969), 99–100.

53. J. P. Ward, *Metropolitan Communities* (Stanford, CA, 1997), 113–15; id., 'Godliness, commemoration, and community', in *Protestant Identities*, ed. Muriel C. McClendon et al. (Stanford, CA, 1999); Ian W. Archer, 'The arts and acts of memorialization in early modern London', in *Imagining Early Modern London*, ed. J. F. Merritt (2001); Victor Morgan, 'The Norwich Guildhall portraits', in Moore, *Family and Friends*; Anne F. Sutton, *The Mercery of London* (Aldershot, 2005), 407, 523, 529, 549.

54. Brown, *Popular Piety in Late Medieval England*, 245. The continuity between pre- and post-Reformation practice is cogently emphasized by Ward, 'Godliness, commemoration, and community', 141–4, 157.

55. *The Letters of John Chamberlain*, ed. Norman Egbert McClure (Philadelphia, 1939), i. 413–20; Baxter, *Practical Works*, iii. 411 (and i. 195).

56. *Sermons of John Donne*, x. 190.

57. Overlooked in W. K. Jordan's mammoth studies of early modern philanthropy, where descriptions of individual charitable bequests omit all reference to provisions for the commemoration of the donor.

58. Bacon, *Advancement of Learning*, 52.

59. Robert Thoroton, *The Antiquities of Nottinghamshire* (1677), 47, 60; *Kent Obit and Lamp Records*, ed. Arthur Hussey (Kent Archaeol. Soc., 1936), 3; Nicolson, *Miscellany Accounts of the Diocese of Carlile*, 67; *Testamenta Eboracensia*, ed. James Raine, v (Surtees Soc., 1884), 182–8.

60. Margaret Condon, 'The last will of Henry VII', in *Westminster Abbey: The Lady Chapel of Henry VII*, ed. Tim Tatton-Brown (Woodbridge, 2003), 120.

61. Roger Bigelow Merriman, *Life and Letters of Thomas Cromwell* (Oxford, 1902), i. 30.

62. Houlbrooke, *Death*, 347–8.

63. Ashmole, *Antiquities of Berkshire*, i. 32; Le Neve, *Monumenta Anglicana, 1600–1649*, 36–7.

64. Moore, *Pearl in an Oyster-Shel*, 114.

65. Burton, *Anatomy*, i. 46 (echoing Michel de Montaigne, 'De la gloire', in *Essais*, II. xvi, trans. John Florio (Everyman's Lib., 1910), ii. 351).

66. *Collected Works of Oliver Goldsmith*, ii. 306–7.

Inexorable Oblivion?

1. Colvin, *Architecture and the After-Life*, 152–3 (modified by David Crouch, 'The origin of chantries', *Journ. of Medieval History*, 27 (2001)); id., 'Origin of the chantries', *Journ. of Medieval History*, 27 (2001); Michael Hicks, 'Chantries, obits and almshouses', in *The Church in Pre-Reformation Society*, ed. Caroline M. Barron and Christopher Harper-Bill (Woodbridge, 1985).

2. John Page-Phillips, *Palimpsests* (1980), 17–18; Robert Hutchinson and Bryan Egan, 'History writ in brass', *Trans. Monumental Brass Soc.* xv (1992–6), 148–50, 358–9; Harding, 'Burial choice and burial location', 129–9; Marshall, *Beliefs*, 172–3, 294–5.

3. Margaret Aston, *England's Iconoclasts*, i (Oxford, 1988), 14–15, 270; Marshall, *Beliefs*, 104–8, 168–74; Robert Hutchinson, 'Tombs of brass are spent', in *The Archaeology of Reformation 1480–1580*, ed. David Gaimster and Roberta Gilchrist (Leeds, 2003); Phillip Lindley, ' "Disrespect for the dead"?', *Church Monuments*, xix (2004); Finch, *Church Monuments in Norfolk*, 126–31 Kenneth Fincham and Nicholas Tyacke, *Altars Restored* (Oxford, 2008), 56.

4. Hart, *Diet of the Diseased*, 142.

5. John Le Neve, *Monumenta Anglicana . . . since the year 1650, to the end of the year 1679* (1719), preface; Richard Gough, *Sepulchral Monuments in Great Britain*, ii (n.d.), pp. cccxxii–cccxxiv, cccxxviii–cccxxxiv; Godwin, *Essay on Sepulchres*, 40–1; *The World of Rural Dissenters*, ed. Margaret Spufford (Cambridge, 1995), 227–8; Houlbrooke, *Death*, 332–3; Marshall, *Beliefs*, 294–6.

6. *Religio Medici*, 120; John Aubrey, *Monumenta Britannica*, annot. Rodney Legg, ed. John Fowles (Sherborne, 1980), 710.

7. Jeremy Taylor, *A Funerall Sermon preached at the Obsequies of . . . Frances, Countesse of Carbery* (1650), 8.

8. Pepys, *Diary*, v. 91 (18 Mar. 1664).

9. Browne, *Religio Medici*, 121.

10. Malkiel, *L'Idée de la gloire*, 77–86; John Kerrigan, *Revenge Tragedy* (Oxford, 1996), 189; Braudy, *Frenzy of Renown*, ch. iii.

11. Bacon, *Essayes*, 159; Milton, *Paradise Regained*, iii. 69–70; *Complete Works of St. Thomas More*, iii/2. 174–5; *Vives: On Education*, trans. Foster Watson (Cambridge, 1913), 280–2; *John Rainolds's Oxford Lectures on Aristotle's 'Rhetoric'*, ed. Lawrence D. Green (Newark, DE, 1986), 312–25; *Poems and Dramas of Fulke Greville*, i. 66–7, 199–213; Baxter, *Practical Works*, i. 195, iii. 411–12; Alastair Fowler, *Time's Purple Masquers* (Oxford, 1996), 89, 94, 109–10, 123–4.

12. John Aubrey, *Remaines of Gentilisme and Judaisme*, ed. James Britten (Folk-Lore Soc., 1881), 106.

13. *Spectator*, 255–7 (22–5 Dec. 1711), ii. 490–502.

14. Ferne, *Blazon of Gentrie*, 83; Wyrley, *True Use of Armorie*, 21; *The Writings of Henry Barrow 1587–1590*, ed. Leland H. Carlson (1962), 460–1; Weever, *Ancient Funerall Monuments*, 18; Edmund Gurnay, *Gurnay Redivivus* (1660), 49–52; Joseph Caryl, *An Exposition . . . upon the Three First Chapters of the Booke of Job* (1643), 412–13; Abraham Wright, *A Practical Commentary or Exposition upon the Pentateuch* (1662), 30; Alexander Gordon, 'A Pythagorean of the seventeenth century', *Procs Literary and Philosophical Soc. of Liverpool*, xxv (1870–1), 296; Llewellyn, *Funeral Monuments*, 247.

15. *Letters of John Chamberlain*, ii. 65.

16. Josselin, *State of the Saints Departed*, sigs A2ᵛ–A3.

17. *Antiente Epitaphes*, collected by Thomas F. Ravenshaw (1878), 43.

18. *Minute Book of the Men's Meeting of the Society of Friends in Bristol*, ed. Russell Mortimer (Bristol Rec. Soc., 1971), 36–8; Thomas Clarkson, *A Portraiture of Quakerism*, 3rd edn (1807), ii. 34–9; Kenneth Lindley, *Of Graves and Epitaphs* (1965), 26–8; Steel, *Sources for Nonconformist Genealogy*, 677–8; Gwynne Stock, 'Quaker burial', in *Grave Concerns*, ed. Margaret Cox (York, 1998).

19. Clarkson, *Portraiture of Quakerism*, i. 295–7; Marcia Pointon, 'Quakerism and material culture', *Art History*, 20 (1997), 412–14.

20. *Elizabethan Critical Essays*, ed. Gregory Smith (1904), ii. 384.

21. J[ohn] H[all], *An Humble Motion* (1649), 10; Edward Waterhouse, *An Humble Apologie for Learning and Learned Men* (1653), 193–4; B.B., *The Way to Honour* (1678), 80, 86.

22. *Tatler*, 23 (2 June 1709), i. 182–3.

23. Douglass Adair, *Fame and the Founding Fathers*, ed. Trevor Coulborn (New York, 1974), 274; *The Noblest Minds*, ed. Peter McNamara (Lanham, MD, 1999); Alexander Hamilton et al., *The Federalist*, ed. Max Beloff (Oxford, 1948), 370 (no. lxxii).

24. *Utilitarian Logic and Politics*, ed. Jack Lively and John Rees (Oxford, 1978), 105–6.

25. Stella Tillyard, 'Paths of glory', in *Joshua Reynolds*, ed. Martin Postle (2005); Terry, *Poetry and the Making of the English Literary Past*, 91–2; Dustin Griffin, *Literary Patronage in England, 1650–1800* (Cambridge, 1996), 34; Stefan Collini, *Absent Minds* (Oxford, 2006), ch. 21.

26. Thomas Hobbes, *The Elements of Law*, ed. Ferdinand Tönnies (1889), 23.

27. John Locke, *An Essay concerning Human Understanding*, ed. P. H. Nidditch (Oxford, 1973), 269.

28. Charles Taylor calls this 'the affirmation of ordinary life'. See his *Sources of the Self* (Cambridge, 1989), pt iii.

29. *The Poems of John Dryden*, ed. James Kinsley (Oxford, 1958), i. 436.

INDEX

Books of the Bible are indexed under *Bible*. Crafts, trades and professions are listed under *occupations*.

Bury, St Edmunds: St Mary's church,
    208, 260
Butler, Samuel, author of **Hudibras**,
    50, 71
Butler, Samuel, author of **The Way of
    All Flesh**, 186
Byng, John, admiral, 133

Cadiz, 154
Caesar, Julius, 45, 56, 71, 72
Caius, John, 133, 246
Calais, loss of, 154
Caldwell, Florence, 260
calling: change of, 17–18
    choice of, 16–17, 26, 33, 34, 87
    concept of, 86–9
    purpose of, 25, 87
    see also occupation
Callis, Richard, 102
Calvin, Jean, 232, 264
Cambridge University, 207
    Christ's College, 201, 205
    Emmanuel College, 205
Campbell, Archibald, 122
candles, 117
Canterbury, King's School, 31
'capabilities', 9–10, 11, 13
Capp, Bernard, 273 n. 13
careers, *see* calling; occupations; talents
Carew, Thomas, 239
carpets, 117, 125, 197
Cartwright, William, 239
Cary, John, 93
Cary, Lucius, *see* Falkland
Cary, Mary
Castiglione, Baldassare, 61, 204
Castile, 55
Castlemaine, Barbara Villiers,
    Countess, 123
castles, 46, 64
cathedral cities, 161–2
Catholics, Roman, 27, 36–7, 72
    work ethic, 86, 108
Catholicism, Roman, return of,
    envisaged, 137
Caussin, Nicolas, 227
Cavaliers, *see* Royalists
Cavendish, Margaret, *see* Newcastle
Cavendish, William, *see* Newcastle
Caxton, William, 46, 55

celebrity, 265–6
ceramics, 119; *see also* china;
    porcelain; pottery
challenges to fight, 52, 61–2, 156–7
Chamberlen, Peter, 23
Chandler, Mary, 207
chansons de geste, 214
chantries, 242, 243, 258n, 262
Chapman, George, 67, 198, 201n, 209
Chapone, Hester, 188
'character' writing, 39
'characters', 39, 40–1, 185
charitable bequests, 242, 258–62
charity, 123, 145, 159, 170, 249
Charlbury (Oxon), 167
Charlemagne, 45
Charles I, king, 49, 58, 59, 77, 155–6,
    157, 263–4
Charles II, king, 63, 77, 117–18, 123,
    136, 155, 160, 205
Charles XII, king of Sweden, 75
Charron, Pierre, 2
chastity: male, 167
    female, 148, 167, 169
    see also sexual morality
Chatham (Kent), 154
Chaucer, Geoffrey, 149, 153, 207
Cheevers, Henry, 217
Cheke, Sir John, 31, 79
Chesman, John, 251
Chesterfield, Philip Dormer, 4th Earl,
    131
Cheyne, William, 2nd Viscount
    Newhaven, Lord, 150
childbirth, lying-in, 122, 127
childlessness, 163, 258
children, 21, 190
    abandoned, 159
    boarded out, 191
    bring immortality, 257–8
    death of, 218
    as emigrants, 34
    and honour, 171
    mobility of, 33–4
    and parents, 26–7, 30, 40–1, 111,
        149, 181, 196
    play, 89
    wanted or not, 24, 218–20
    and work, 89
    see also occupation, choice of

Pley, Mrs Constance, 95
Plutarch, 215
Pococke, Richard, bishop, 211
poetry, 24, 252
poets, 253
Poitiers, battle of, 55
Pole, Reginald, cardinal, 200
politeness, 128, 129, 139, 146, 172, 181
political participation, 10
Polybius, 56
Poole, Joshua, 55
poor, the, 30, 112
  children, 218
  goods, 125–6
  graves, 256
  and honour, 160, 172–3
  undifferentiated, 40, 43
  unremembered, 254
poor law, 16, 89–90
Pope, Alexander, 40, 249, 265
Pope, Mary, 208
porcelain, 117, 118, 126, 129
  disapproved of, 133, 135
  for tea-drinking, 124, 127
pornography, 195, 207
portraits, 38
  of benefactors, 260
  disliked, 264
  of friends, 203, 208
  for remembrance, 240, 250–1
possessions: attachment to, 126
  delight in, 139
  hostility towards, 135
  meaning of, 118
  see also goods
posterity, concern for, 26, 258
  desire to be remembered by, 235, 236,
    239, and see posthumous fame
posthumous fame: hope of, 54,
    235–62 passim, 265–6
  a delusion, 262–5
  seen as fulfilment, 235, 236–7
post-modernists, 13
pottery, 118, 119, 126
Poulett family, 151
Poulter, Arthur, 124
poverty: despised, 14, 122
  effects of, 143–4
  extent of, 140
Povey, Thomas, 121

Powell, Thomas, 32
Power, William, 205
Poyntz, Sydenham, 59
prayers, for souls of the dead, 211,
    242–3, 247, 262
preachers, importance of, 234
precedence, 149–51, 180
  disputes over, 150, 152–3, 161–2
Preston, John, 113
Prideaux, John, 30
Priestley, Joseph, 94–5
primogeniture, 257
printing-houses, 99–100, 164
Prior, Matthew, 248
Priuli, Alvise, 300
privacy, 187–8, 338 n.4
  of punishment, 182
  positive view of, 225
private ends, disapproved of, 25–6
private life, entitlement to, 183–4
private sphere, 187
Privy Council, 55
processions, 151, 152, 162
professions, 109, 161, 172, 239
promises, 156, 158
Protestantism: and labour, 86n, 88, 108
  and intercessionary prayer, 243
Prynne, William, 56
public good, 26, 93, 112
public service, 83, 151, 155, 159, 172,
    226
punishment, eternal, 234, see also hell
  shame, 177, 178, 182
Purcell, Henry, 224
Purchas, Samuel, 45n, 158
purgatory, 227, 231, 242, 243
Puritanism, Puritans, 36, 134–5, 143,
    233
Pym, John, 96

Quakers, 35, 37, 135, 180, 184, 213,
    264
  peace testimony, 69
Queensberry, Catherine, Duchess of,
    131

rakes, 63, 148, 168
Ralegh, Sir Walter: actions, 61, 157
  observations, 219
  opinions, 121, 154, 156, 233